Culture, People, Nature

AN INTRODUCTION TO GENERAL ANTHROPOLOGY

Thomas Y. Crowell, New York, Established 1834

MARVIN HARRIS

Culture, People, Nature

AN INTRODUCTION TO GENERAL ANTHROPOLOGY

Second Edition

I- QU- RK

Copyright © 1971, 1975 by Thomas Y. Crowell Company, Inc.

Designed by Hermann Strohbach

Cover photo: Anthro-Photo/DeVore

Title page photo: Anthro-Photo/Lee

Manufactured in the United States of America

Library of Congress Cataloging in Publication Data
Harris, Marvin, 1927-
    Culture, people, nature.

First published in 1971 under title: Culture, man,
and nature.
    Bibliography: p.
    Includes index.
    1. Anthropology. I. Title.
GN24.H23 1975   301.2   74-23093
ISBN 0-690-00708-6

PREFACE

The inspiration for the second edition of this book is the same as for the first. It derives from my belief that anthropology possesses an underlying unity—a unity that must be preserved despite the rapid growth of specialized knowledge. It seems to me that the need for an anthropology with a global and holistic perspective is even greater now than it was a few years ago, since the tendency for college curricula to be atomized remains unchecked.

In preparing this edition I have also remained faithful to the belief that anthropologists routinely deal with facts and theories that are crucial to informed discussions of issues of great and enduring relevance. It is in the attempt to deal with these globally relevant and enduring concerns that I have learned to value the unitary approach. I have never had to hunt for excuses for writing a text that draws upon all four fields. Chapter by chapter the interconnectedness of anthropological knowledge seems to flow as a natural consequence of asking basic questions about the origin and meaning of human existence.

Nonetheless, this edition does differ from its predecessor in a number of respects. I have, of course, tried to update the entire book to make it conform with new research findings and with the on-going development of theory and expert opinion. But I have also tried to be responsive to complaints about the first edition's topical coverage. Extensive new sections on genetics, linguistics, and sex roles have been added and I have written whole new chapters on archaeology, warfare, religion, art, and psychological anthropology. To avoid a substantial increase in the number of pages, cuts had to be made somewhere. I decided that the best place to make the necessary excisions was in the chapters devoted to kinship which many instructors had complained about as being too difficult for beginning students.

One of the criticisms of the first edition that I found most distressing was that I had used too much jargon and too many big words. I am pleased to report that the new edition was placed on a strict diet and seems to have shed several pounds of excess verbiage, hopefully without damage to its brains.

Now I want to explain why I have changed the title of the book. I didn't substitute "People" for "Man" merely for cosmetic reasons or to be popular with my female colleagues and students. The change reflects a thorough-going attempt on my part to rethink, line by line, the implications of the male-centered words and concepts that dominate both anthropological and vernacular discourse. I have found it in the best interest of clarity and accuracy to shun all masculinized nouns and pronouns when referring to roles and activities that are neither naturally nor logically linked exclusively to males. Conventional literary standards obfuscate the extent to which roles and activities are in fact sex-linked. The understanding of basic social and cultural processes has been retarded by adherence to grammatical conventions as a substitute for knowledge and inquiry. With very few exceptions, it is surprisingly easy to use neuter English forms when referring to both males and females and male or female forms when referring respectively to males or females. By adhering to this plan, the small areas of scientific knowledge about sex roles can be distinguished from the vast regions of ignorance about sex roles.

I ask that the changes in question be seen in a larger context. I have tried in general to increase my sensitivity to terms that some readers of the first edition may have found offensive. Adoption of more precise standards is all the more desirable if significant numbers of people are put off by the conventional forms. To my surprise, I discovered that it is easy as well as helpful to get rid of terms such as "Negroid," "Mongoloid," and to stop using "primitive" in relation to human beings who are alive today.

One other series of linguistic changes may be of interest. I have avoided using "we" to denote "I, the writer," or "we, the anthropologists," or "we, the people of the United States," or "you and I, the reader and the writer." In this edition, the writer is known as "I," the reader is "you," and the "we" means "we human beings"—*Homo sapiens sapiens.*

This book has benefitted from massive criticism both friendly and unfriendly which it has been my privilege to receive since the publication of the first edition. So many colleagues and students have played a role in sharpening and reshaping my thoughts and in correcting my errors, that I can no longer conscientiously identify on an individual basis those who have been most helpful. I hope to thank all who have helped if I have written a better and more useful book.

CONTENTS

FIGURES

TABLES AND MAPS

The sciences . . . cannot endure if their practitioners are unable to know more than an ever-smaller portion of what they must know in order to function properly.

Erwin Chargaff

1

INTRODUCTION

What Is Anthropology?

Anthropology is the study of humankind, especially of *Homo sapiens*, the biological species to which we human beings belong. It is the study of how our species evolved from more primitive organisms; it is also the study of how our species developed a mode of communication known as language and a mode of social life known as culture. It is the study of how culture evolved and diversified. And finally, it is the study of how culture, people, and nature interact wherever human beings are found.

This book is an introduction to *general anthropology,* which is an amalgam of four fields of study traditionally found within departments of anthropology at major universities. The four fields are cultural anthropology (sometimes called social anthropology), archaeology, anthropological linguistics, and physical anthropology. The collaborative effort of these four fields is needed in order to study our species in evolutionary perspective and in relation to diverse habitats and cultures.

Cultural anthropology deals with the description and analysis of the forms and styles of social life of past and present ages. Its subdiscipline, *ethnography,* systematically describes contemporary societies and cultures. Comparison of these descriptions provides the basis for hypotheses and theories about the causes of human lifestyles.

Archaeology adds a crucial dimension to this endeavor. By digging

1

up the remains of cultures of past ages, archaeology studies sequences of social and cultural evolution under diverse natural and cultural conditions. In the quest for understanding the present-day characteristics of human existence, for validating or invalidating proposed theories of historical causation, the great temporal depth of the archaeological record is indispensable.

Anthropological linguistics provides another crucial perspective: the study of the totality of languages spoken by human beings. Linguistics attempts to reconstruct the historical changes that have led to the formation of individual languages and families of languages. More fundamentally, anthropological linguistics is concerned with the nature of language and its functions and the way language influences and is influenced by other aspects of cultural life. Anthropological linguistics is concerned with the origin of language and the relationship between the evolution of language and the evolution of *Homo sapiens*. And finally, anthropological linguistics is concerned with the relationship between the evolution of languages and the evolution and differentiation of human cultures.

Physical anthropology grounds the work of the other anthropological fields in our animal origins and our genetically determined nature. Physical anthropology seeks to reconstruct the course of human evolution by studying the fossil remains of ancient human and infrahuman species. Physical anthropology seeks to describe the distribution of hereditary variations among contemporary populations and to sort out and measure the relative contributions made by heredity, environment, and culture to human biology.

Because of its combination of biological, archaeological, and ethnographic perspectives, general anthropology is uniquely suited to the study of many problems of vital importance to the survival and well-being of our species.

To be sure, disciplines other than anthropology are concerned with the study of human beings. Our animal nature is the subject of intense research by biologists, geneticists, and physiologists. In medicine alone, hundreds of additional specialists investigate the human body, and psychiatrists and psychologists, rank upon rank, seek the essence of the human mind and soul. Many other disciplines examine our cultural, intellectual, and aesthetic behavior. These disciplines include sociology, human geography, social psychology, political science, economics, linguistics, theology, philosophy, musicology, art, literature, and architecture. There are also many "area specialists," who study the languages and life-styles of particular peoples, nations, or regions: "Latin Americanists," "Indianists," "Sinologists," and so on. In view of this profusion of disciplines that describe, explain, and interpret aspects of human life, what justification can there be for a

Figure 1-1. ANTHROPOLOGISTS AT WORK (facing page). Archaeologist Ralph Solecki (top left) at Nahr Ibrahim, Lebanon, where excavations have reached Middle Paleolithic, Levalloiso-Mousterian levels (see ch. 9). Linguist Robert Russell (top right) studying Amahuaca Indians of Peru. Physical anthropologists Louis and Mary Leakey (bottom left) inspecting their fossil treasures at Olduvai Gorge, Tanzania (see ch. 4). Ethnographer Elliott Skinner (wearing glasses) (bottom right) conducting an informal interview with a group of Mossi men in Ouagadougou, Upper Volta. (Ralph Skinner—top left; Cornell Capa/Magnum—top right; Robert F. Sisson (c) National Geographic Society—bottom left; Elliott Skinner—bottom right)

single discipline that claims to be the general science of the human species?

The Importance of General Anthropology

Research and publications are accumulating in each of the four fields of anthropology at an exponential rate. Few anthropologists nowadays master more than one field. And anthropologists increasingly find themselves working not with fellow anthropologists of another field but with members of entirely different scientific or humanistic specialties. For example, cultural anthropologists interested in the relationship between cultural practices and the natural environment may be obliged to pay closer attention to agronomy or ecology than to linguistics. Physical anthropologists interested in the relationship between human and protohuman fossils may, because of the importance of teeth in the fossil record, become more familiar with dentistry journals than with journals devoted to ethnography or linguistics. Cultural anthropologists interested in the relationship between culture and individual personality are sometimes more at home professionally with psychiatrists and social psychologists than with the archaeologists in their own university departments. Hence, many more than four fields are represented in the ongoing research of modern anthropology.

The specialized nature of most anthropological research makes it imperative that the general significance of anthropological facts and theories be preserved. This is the task of *general anthropology*. General anthropology does not pretend to survey the entire subject matter of physical, cultural, archaeological, and linguistic anthropology. Much less does it pretend to survey the work of the legions of scholars in other disciplines who also study the biological, linguistic, and cultural aspects of human existence. Rather, it strives to achieve a particular orientation toward all the human sciences, disciplines, and fields. Perhaps the best word for this orientation is ecumenical. General anthropology does not teach all that one must know in order to master the four fields or all that one must know in order to become an anthropologist. Instead, general anthropology teaches how to evaluate facts and theories about human nature and human culture by placing them in a total, universalist perspective. In the words of Frederica De Laguna,

Anthropology is the only discipline that offers a conceptual schema for the whole context of human experience. . . . It is like the carrying frame onto which may be fitted all the several subjects of a liberal education, and by organizing the load, making it more wieldy and capable of being carried.   [1968:475]

I believe that the importance of general anthropology is that it is panhuman, evolutionary, and comparative. The previously mentioned disciplines are concerned with only a particular segment of human experience or a particular time or phase of our cultural or biological development. But general anthropology is systematically and uncompromisingly comparative. Its findings are never based upon the study of a single population, race, "tribe," class, or nation. General anthropology insists first and foremost that conclusions based upon the study of one particular human group or civilization be checked against the evidence of other groups or civilizations under both similar and different conditions. In this way the relevance of general anthropology transcends the interests of any particular "tribe," race, nation, or culture. In anthropological perspective, all peoples and civilizations are fundamentally local and evanescent. Thus general anthropology is implacably opposed to the insularity and mental constriction of those who would have themselves and none other represent humanity, stand at the pinnacle of progress, or be chosen by God or history to fashion the world in their own image.

Therefore general anthropology is "relevant" even when it deals with fragments of fossils, extinct civilizations, remote villages, or exotic customs. The proper study of humankind requires a knowledge of distant as well as near lands and of remote as well as present times. Only in this way can we humans hope to tear off the blinders of our local life-styles to look upon the human condition without prejudice.

Because of its multidisciplinary, comparative, and diachronic perspective, anthropology holds the key to many fundamental questions of recurrent and contemporary relevance. It lies peculiarly within the competence of general anthropology to explicate our species' animal heritage, to define what is distinctively human about human nature, and to differentiate the natural and the cultural conditions responsible for competition, conflict, and war. General anthropology is also strategically equipped to probe the significance of racial factors in the evolution of culture and in the conduct of contemporary human affairs. General anthropology holds the key to an understanding of the origins of social inequality—of racism, exploitation, poverty, and underdevelopment. Overarching all of general anthropology's contributions is the search for the causes of social and cultural differences and similarities. What is the nature of the determinism that operates in human history, and what are the consequences of this determinism for individual freedom of thought and action? To answer these questions is to begin to understand the extent to which we can increase humanity's freedom and well-being by conscious intervention in the processes of cultural evolution.

5

2

EVOLUTION

Like all other forms of life, we human beings are the product of evolution. Evolution is a process of change that affects all aspects of nature. The feature that distinguishes evolutionary change from nonevolutionary change is *transformation:* change of an earlier form or entity into a later form or entity by means of cumulative modifications.

Evolutionary transformations are the object of intense study by scientists in many different fields. Astronomers study the evolution of galaxies; astrophysicists and physical chemists ponder the question of how the heavier elements evolved out of primordial clouds of hydrogen; geologists study the evolution of continents, mountains, drainage systems, and subsurface strata. Biologists study the transformations of organisms. Physical anthropologists study the evolution of humankind; and cultural anthropologists study the evolution of traits, institutions, and whole cultures.

As the Greek philosophers long ago surmised, nothing in the universe remains precisely the same from one moment to the next. Regardless of how brief the interval between two moments of observation, refined measuring procedures will always reveal some differences. Change being unbiquitous and incessant, it becomes necessary to distinguish between evolutionary transformation and two other familiar types of change: variation and growth.

Variation consists of regular alterations that are an inherent property of the form under consideration. Many stellar objects, for example, pulsate rhythmically, growing brighter and dimmer in cycles ranging from seconds to years. Among bioforms, similar cyclical changes take place in many species; for example, rabbits change color with the seasons, and the metabolism of bears alters drastically during hibernation. Among cultural forms, some common examples are the economic cycle of planting and harvesting and the cycle of marriage, child-rearing, family fission, and the establishment of new households. Variations that are inherent in a form are nonevolutionary changes.

Growth is the passage of forms through zygotic, infant, chrysalis, larval, or other immature stages involving regular changes especially characteristic of bioforms. The extent, duration, and type of an organism's growth processes are included among its defining characteristics and do not constitute evolutionary transformation unless there is a significant change in the rate or stages of the maturation process.

Biological Evolution

The mechanisms and processes of evolution differ markedly depending upon the realm of phenomena being studied. Among bioforms, evolution takes place as a result of processes and mechanisms peculiar to the realm of living things. Bioforms possess the power of reproduction. Reproduction is the process by which organisms produce copies of themselves. These copies are never precise. "Errors" in replication occur. Some of these errors are preserved by further reproduction; others are extinguished when the organism dies. The cumulative effect of the preservation of some hereditary variations and the extinction of others results in the modification of the organism's descendants in ways that may ultimately lead to the emergence of new bioforms. In order to understand the evolution of human beings, it is necessary to understand the basic principles that govern animal reproduction, the appearance of hereditary variations, and the preservation of variations through successive generations.

The Genetic Code

All animals possess fundamentally similar systems for producing copies of themselves. In their sex cells they store the information needed to produce copies. The information is stored in the molecules of *deoxyribonucleic acid (DNA),* which is the principal component of the microscopic structures known as *chromosomes.* Chromosomes

7

Figure 2-1. REDUCTION DIVISION. Schematic representation of steps responsible for the random assortment of parental chromosomes in an individual's sex cells.

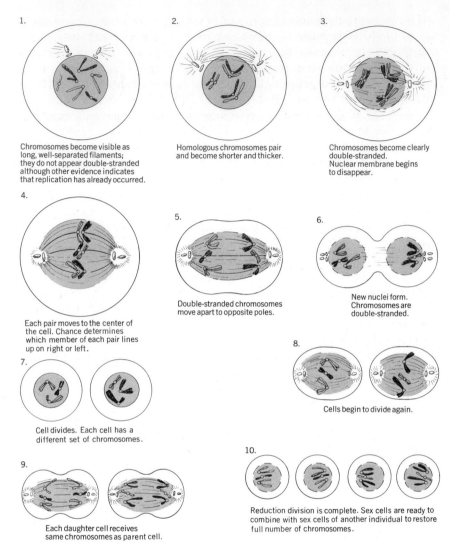

1. Chromosomes become visible as long, well-separated filaments; they do not appear double-stranded although other evidence indicates that replication has already occurred.

2. Homologous chromosomes pair and become shorter and thicker.

3. Chromosomes become clearly double-stranded. Nuclear membrane begins to disappear.

4. Each pair moves to the center of the cell. Chance determines which member of each pair lines up on right or left.

5. Double-stranded chromosomes move apart to opposite poles.

6. New nuclei form. Chromosomes are double-stranded.

7. Cell divides. Each cell has a different set of chromosomes.

8. Cells begin to divide again.

9. Each daughter cell receives same chromosomes as parent cell.

10. Reduction division is complete. Sex cells are ready to combine with sex cells of another individual to restore full number of chromosomes.

are visible in the nucleus of cells shortly before and after they produce a daughter cell by splitting in half. At such times chromosomes look like rods. At other times chromosomes look like long slender filaments.

During the intervals between cell divisions, the chromosomes disappear from view altogether. It is believed that these alterations correspond to the coiling and uncoiling of long chains of deoxyribonucleic acid—rodlike when tightly coiled, filamentary and becoming invisible when uncoiled (Fig. 2-1).

8

Deoxyribonucleic acid consists of three different molecules: a sugar molecule (deoxyribose), a phosphate molecule (phosphoric acid), and four organic bases—adenine, guanine, cytosine, and thymine. A particular combination of deoxyribose, phosphoric acid, and one of the four bases comprises a unit known as a *nucleotide* (Fig. 2-2). A chromosome consists of a double strand of thousands of nucleotides linked together lengthwise by bonds between the sugar and phosphate molecules and crosswise by bonds between the bases (Fig. 2-3). The information necessary for the replication of the organism is determined by the order of appearance of the bases on the DNA chain. If one denotes these bases—adenine, guanine, cystosine, and thymine—by the letters, A, G, C, T, the genetic code can be conceptualized as a kind of alphabet in which different orders of appearance of the "letters" A, G, C, T constitute different "words" or bits of information.

It is believed that these genetic words always consist of "triplets," that is, of only three of the four letters. These triplets are called *codons*. Codons and sequences of codons form *templates*, or models, for the manufacture of ribonucleic acid (RNA), which in turn guides the cellular structures known as ribosomes in the orderly manufacture of amino acids (Fig. 2-5). Amino acids are the building blocks of proteins and enzymes. Long sequences of codons are responsible for

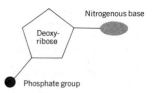

Figure 2-2. A NUCLEOTIDE.

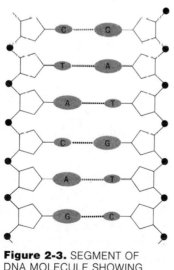

Figure 2-3. SEGMENT OF DNA MOLECULE SHOWING PAIRING OF NUCLEOTIDES IN DOUBLE STRAND. C=Cytosine; T=Thymine; G=Guanine; A=Adenine.

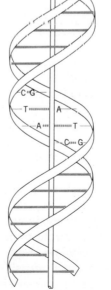

Figure 2-4. DOUBLE HELIX MODEL OF DNA.

9

The Genetic Code

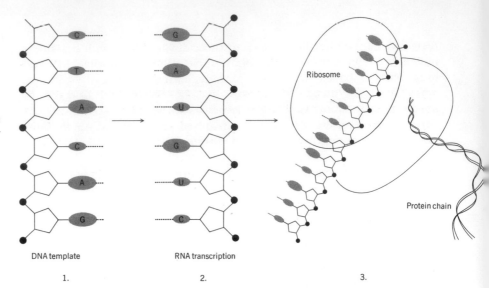

Figure 2-5. SCHEMATIC REPRESENTATION OF THE STEPS IN THE DECODING OF DNA. 1. Sequence of Nitrogenous bases, C,T,A,G, in DNA acts as template for sequence of bases, G,A,U,C, in RNA. 2. RNA carries information to ribosome outside of cell nucleus. 3. Ribosome "reads" RNA message and assembles amino acids to specification. U=Uracil.

DNA template

RNA transcription

Ribosome

Protein chain

1.

2.

3.

the production of these more complex substances, which make possible the reproduction and maintenance of each cell and the growth, maintenance, and reproduction of the whole organism.

Human beings have 23 chromosomes in their sex cells (and 23 *pairs* of chromosomes in their body cells). Fruit flies have only four chromosomes. Many organisms have more than we do; tarsiers, for example, have 80. In all higher organisms, however, the chemical code of the nucleotides is the same; only the message is different.

Heredity

The basic laws of heredity were worked out long before a knowledge of the biochemistry of chromosomes had been achieved. According to the classic formulation of these laws, the information governing the replication of new organisms was contained in hypothetical particles called *genes,* which were strung out along the chromosomes like beads on a string. It is now clear that the genes are not particles but segments of the deoxyribonucleic chains that constitute the chromosomes. Any alteration in the order of bases within a codon triplet, and any alteration in the sequence of codons, may result in a change in the instructions for the manufacture of amino acids, proteins, or enzymes and, hence, in a change in the heredity of the organism. As yet there is no agreement concerning the size of the segment of the deoxyribonucleic chain that corresponds to the classic concept of the gene.

Despite these complications, the concept of the gene as a unit of heredity remains valid. Genes may be thought of as loci (places) on the chromosomes that are associated with the control of an hereditary

10

trait. To understand how traits are inherited, one must understand how the chromosomes and their genes are passed along from parent to offspring.

Within ordinary body cells, chromosomes always occur in pairs. In sexually reproducing organisms one member of a pair represents the contribution of the male parent, and the other member, the contribution of the female parent. Thus we human beings have 46 chromosomes, of which 23 are from our father and 23 from our mother. We receive our complement of hereditary material when a sperm bearing 23 chromosomes unites with an ovum containing 23 chromosomes. Soon after this union, the chromosomes of similar structure pair off and jointly communicate their hereditary instructions to the first cells of the new organism, which is called a *zygote.* The zygote proceeds to divide and differentiate until a whole embryo is constructed and a new human being is ready to be born.

Since it takes 23+23=46 chromosomes to create a new human being, it is clear that only one-half of a father's or mother's 46 chromosomes can be passed on to a particular child. Which 23 of the 46 will be passed on is purely a matter of chance. The halving of the complement of chromosomes takes place during the manufacture of the sex cells in the testes and ovaries. The chromosomes line up at the center of the cell and form homologous pairs. *Homologous* chromosomes are those that have similar genes on them. It is entirely a matter of chance whether the member of the pair that has been contributed by the individual's father or the individual's mother lines up on the right or left. The chromosomes are then pulled to opposite sides of the cell (23, one of each pair, to a side), and the cell then divides in two. Each new sex cell then contains a new assortment of hereditary material created by the shuffling of the homologous chro-

Figure 2-6. DIVISION OF CHROMOSOMES. During the division of cells other than sex cells, each half or daughter cell obtains a copy of each chromosome pair rather than one randomly selected member of each pair. This process is called *mitosis* and is shown taking place in the nucleus of an onion cell. (Struwe from Monkmeyer Press Photo Service)

mosomes—some coming from the mother and the rest from the father in a proportion governed by chance.

The fact that the chromosomes are independently assorted during the *reduction division* of the sex cells (reduction from 46 to 23 chromosomes) is a basic principle of genetics. *Independent assortment* means that hereditary information on one chromosome is passed along independently of the information on all the other chromosomes. It also means that although one-half of our chromosomes come from our father and one-half from our mother, there is no guarantee that one-quarter of our chromosomes come from each of our grandparents, and that it is unlikely that precisely one-eighth of our chromosomes come from each of our great-grandparents. On the sixth ascending generation, where we have 64 great-great-great-great-grandparents, it becomes highly probable that some of these "ancestors" have contributed no chromosomes whatsoever to our 23 pairs. This should have a sobering effect on people who delight in tracing their genealogies more than six generations back to royalty, first settlers, and other dignitaries.

The situation would be even more bleak for such genealogists were it not for the fact that homologous chromosomes exchange segments (genes) with each other. This phenomenon is known as *crossing over,* and it occurs just before reduction division when the 23 pairs of chromosomes are lined up at the center of the cell. Because of crossing over, the chromosomes contributed by any particular ancestor do not remain intact throughout the generations. Thus several different ancestors may contribute genes to each of the 46 chromosomes possessed by one of their descendants, leaving open the possibility that each of as many as 64 ancestors could have contributed some genes to their great-great-great-great-grandchild.

Figure 2-7. CROSSING OVER. Schematic representation of a pair of homologous chromosomes exchanging some of their genes during reduction division.

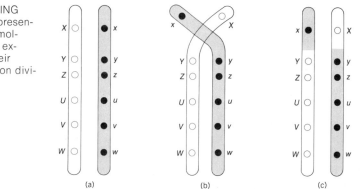

Population Genetics

When the genes at the same locus on a pair of homologous chromosomes contain precisely the same information, the individual is said to be *homozygous* for the trait controlled by that gene. Often, however, the two genes will differ, and the individual is said to be *heterozygous.* Variants of the genes may occupy the same locus on each member of the chromosome pair. The variant genes found at a given locus are called *alleles.*

Because the assortment of chromosomes in the sex cell is governed by chance, it is possible to predict the probable proportions in which two or more alleles will occur in the children of mated pairs whose genetic types are known. For example, suppose that there are two alleles: A and a. This means that three kinds of individuals may occur: AA, Aa, and aa. Each of these combinations is called a *genotype.* The proportion in which genotypes will occur can be calculated from a simple device known as a *Punnett Square.* If ovum and sperm have equal chance of possessing either allele, the zygote has a one-half chance of being heterozygous Aa or aA, a one-quarter chance of being homozygous AA, and a one-quarter chance of being homozygous aa. The following Punnett Square shows that the three genotypes can be expected to occur in the ratio 1 AA : 2 Aa : 1 aa.

	Ova A	a
Sperm A	AA	Aa
a	aA	aa

One of the most important discoveries of modern genetics is that individuals who are heterozygous for a trait cannot always be identified as such by their appearance. Some alleles seem to have no effect on the appearance of a trait if they are in a heterozygous condition. Such alleles are said to be *recessive.* The alleles with which recessives are paired are said to be *dominant.*

In the above example, suppose that A is dominant and that a is recessive. The ratio of the genotypes remains unchanged but the appearances of the individuals AA, Aa, and aA will now all be the same. The appearance of an organism as distinct from its genotype is called its *phenotype.*

This important discovery was first made by Gregor Mendel, the founder of modern genetics. Crossing red-flowered peas with white-

13

flowered peas, Mendel obtained a generation of peas all of which had red flowers:

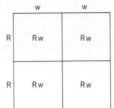

	w	w
R	Rw	Rw
R	Rw	Rw

The reason for this is that all the white-flowered peas were homozygous for the recessive gene w, and all the red-flowered peas were homozygous for the dominant gene R. None of the phenotypes showed the presence of the recessive gene. Then, by crossing the red-flowered heterozygotic peas with each other, Mendel showed that the recessive gene was still present in the genotype:

	R	w
R	RR	Rw
w	wR	ww

Approximately one out of every four pea plants—those homozygous for the recessive w—now bore white flowers.

Although the above Punnett Square indicates three genotypes, which occur in the ratio 1:2:1, there are only two phenotypes, which occur in the ratio 3:1. Many human traits, such as eye color and color blindness as well as hemophilia, sickle cell anemia, and other hereditary diseases, are governed by systems of dominant and recessive genes in which heterozygous individuals are phenotypically indistinguishable from those who are homozygous for a dominant allele. This often makes the heterozygotes "carriers" of undesirable traits. In some instances, however, known as *balanced polymorphisms,* the heterozygotes have an advantage over the homozygote dominants even though the homozygote recessives may be the victims of fatal diseases. The resistance against malaria enjoyed by persons heterozygous for sickle cell anemia is an instance of balanced polymorphism in humans. It should be emphasized that not all recessives are deleterious. If a recessive is not deleterious it will be maintained in a population with the same frequency as a dominant allele.

In the absence of forces leading to evolutionary change, the frequency of two alleles in a breeding population will reach a balance known as the *Hardy-Weinberg equilibrium.* This equilibrium is

14

described in the formula $p^2 + 2pq + q^2 = 1$, where p equals the frequency of allele A and q equals the frequency of allele a.* The two frequencies add up to 100 percent. This formula is essential for measuring the extent to which evolutionary forces are acting upon a given population and preventing it from reaching the expected equilibrium of gene frequencies.

Evolutionary Forces

1. *Drift:* The genetic equilibrium predicted by the Hardy-Weinberg formula pertains to an infinitely large population in which chance alone could not significantly alter the pattern of gene combination. The smaller the population, the greater the likelihood that chance effects will disturb the equilibrium. Such chance effects are called *drift.* For example, in populations with less than 100 breeding members, advantageous alleles can easily be lost from the *gene pool* purely as a result of "accidental" occurrences. (A gene pool is the total inventory of genes and alleles present in a given population.)

2. *Mutations:* These are alterations in the sequence or structure of the nucleotides of the chromosomes that result in new alleles or new genes. Mutations may occur anywhere from once every 50,000 duplications to once every million duplications. Genes subject to the higher rates will tend to decrease in frequency and thus alter the make-up of the gene pool. Regardless of their rate of occurrence, mutations may constitute the raw material for extensive evolutionary change if they are advantageous (see below.)

3. *Migration* and *gene flow:* Gene pools will not achieve Hardy-Weinberg equilibrium if some alleles are carried away by people leaving the population and other alleles are introduced by people entering the population.

4. *Natural selection:* By far the most powerful force preventing the fulfillment of Hardy-Weinberg equilibrium is the failure of genotypes to have a random relationship with reproduction rates. Particular

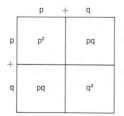

*$p^2+2pq + q^2 = 1$ is merely a way of stating the results of a Punnett Square in which the individual frequencies of alleles are multiplied to obtain their joint probability of occurrence. The probability of occurrence of two events is equal to the product of their probabilities of occurring separately. Hence $(p+q)(p+q)$ equals the probability that p, q, or pq will occur. This probability is equal to 1 (i.e., certainty). Hence $(p+q)(p+q) = 1 = p^2+2pq+q^2$

15

genes and alleles are usually correlated with an organism's selection of a mate, its mating efficiency, frequency of mating, fertility, survivability of offspring, fertility of offspring, and a vast number of additional factors influencing reproductive success. Natural selection denotes any departure from Hardy-Weinberg equilibrium brought about by differential reproductive success. Natural selection may act upon mutations or upon the existing repertory of genes. When acting upon mutations, natural selection can rapidly increase the frequency of a new gene or allele even if the mutation recurs only once in a million duplications. When acting upon genes and alleles already present in the gene pool, natural selection can rapidly raise their frequency. Natural selection can also raise the frequency of genes that were previously rarely combined. An example of the power of natural selection to raise the frequency of a rare combination of genes is the evolution of penicillin-resistant strains of bacteria. The genes conferring resistance are present in normal populations but in only a small percentage of individuals. As a result of the differential reproductive success of such individuals, however, the resistant genotype is soon found in 99 percent of the individuals in populations exposed to penicillin.

"The Struggle for Survival"

The information contained in the genetic code is not sufficient to produce a new organism. For that, the genes need space, energy, and chemical substances. These vital ingredients must be obtained from the environment according to directions contained in the genes.

Unless a parent organism dies immediately after producing a single copy of itself, reproduction tends to increase the size of a population. As a population increases, a point is reached sooner or later at which the space, energy, and chemical substances needed for constructing new organisms become more difficult to obtain. If each organism not only survives its first reproductive episode but goes on to produce more copies of itself, population expansion occurs very rapidly, in fact, exponentially. In a short time there are not sufficient space, energy, and chemical nutrients to permit all the members of the population to reproduce at the same rate. Some genotypes, enjoying greater *reproductive success,* will come to constitute an increasing portion of the population. That is, they will be selected by natural selection.

In general, a genetic innovation will be selected if it increases the reproductive success of an organism relative to the reproductive success of other organisms. In detail, however, the kinds of innovations that produce relative increments in reproductive success are as varied and complex as the astounding multiplicity of life forms that now fill the terrestrial biosphere. The reproductive advantage may derive from a method of gaining and holding space more securely, of obtaining energy in larger or more dependable amounts, of obtaining nutrient materials more rapidly or in greater amounts with more dependability and with less energy cost to the organism, as well as from increased efficiency and dependability of some aspect of the reproductive process itself.

It was Charles Darwin and Alfred Wallace who formulated the basic principles of how biotransformations could result from differential survival and reproduction and who introduced the concept of natural selection. Under the influence of the prevailing philosophy of economic competition, however, both Darwin and Wallace accepted Thomas Malthus's concept of a "struggle for survival" as the main source of selection for reproductive success. Thus in the nineteenth century the process of bioevolution was pictured incorrectly as the direct struggle between individuals for scarce resources and sexual partners, and even more erroneously as the preying upon and destruction of one another by organisms of the same species. Although predation and direct competition do play a role in the evolution of many species, the factors promoting differential reproductive success are in the main not related to an organism's ability to destroy other members of its own population or to prevent them from obtaining nutrients, space, and mates. Natural selection favors cooperation as often as it favors competition. Among the many species of social insects and mammals, individuals who prey upon others and who actively obstruct others from mating and reproducing may lower the average rate of reproduction of all the organisms in their social group relative to the rate achieved by more cooperative populations of the same species.

Adaptation and General Evolution

Because natural selection governs the direction of bioevolution, each transformed organism is fitted to or *adapted to* its habitat. To say that a trait is adaptive is another way of saying that the trait in question has been shaped by its contribution to the organism's reproductive success. That is, an adaptive trait is a trait that has been added to an organism's genetic repertory in conformity with the process of natural selection.

Because of the ubiquitous and unremitting character of natural

17

selection, the continuous appearance of new bioforms, and the continuous alteration in the environment caused by biological and physicochemical processes, traits that were once highly adaptive may become less adaptive, *nonadaptive,* or even *maladaptive* at some later point in time. The evolutionary record consists of better adapted forms replacing forms that under certain definite conditions were less well adapted. It is important to remember that there is no absolute, fixed level of adaptation that guarantees the perpetuation of a species. The essence of bioevolution is its opportunism and pragmatism. A vast range of natural experiments is always being carried out, leading inevitably to the modification and replacement of hitherto marvelously well-adapted species (cf. Alland 1970). In most instances these new species cannot be regarded as either more or less complex, "advanced," or "efficient" than their predecessors. They are simply better adapted under the circumstances. There is no basis for attributing any single or irreversible direction of change to bioevolution.

Nonetheless, despite the purely local, pragmatic, and opportunistic nature of bioevolution, there has been an overall direction to the bioevolutionary process on earth. This direction, which is called *"general evolution"* (cf. Sahlins and Service 1960), has consisted in the gradual filling out and utilization of all the life-sustaining media, starting with the shallow seas and extending to the deep oceans, seashores, the atmosphere, and the continental interiors. Then, as each of these biospaces has been filled with life, more and more complex structures and organic systems have come into existence: first single-celled, then multicelled creatures, then organisms with a few specialized body parts, then forms having hundreds of highly specialized and finely articulated organs. In the series from protozoa to fish to amphibia to mammals to human beings, adaptation has produced steadily increasing amounts of organ specialization and neural, glandular, and sensory coordination. The "higher" or more complex organisms, including our own species, have evolved from "lower" or more simple prototypes by the automatic selection of genetic innovations relatively advantageous for reproductive success. The next three chapters are concerned with the particular sequence of adaptations and evolutionary transformations that led to the emergence of our species, *Homo sapiens.*

3

THE HUMAN PEDIGREE AND HUMAN NATURE

A major objective of modern anthropological inquiry is to provide answers to the questions: What does it mean to say that one is human? Is there a human nature? And, if so, in what does it consist?

Anthropologists, who seldom reach agreement on any subject, are unanimous in their belief that the answers to these questions are to be found in the evolutionary history of our species. The whole of human nature cannot be grasped merely by studying the evolutionary record of our ancestors. But we can never hope to give a proper scientific account of who we are unless we first identify ourselves in relation to the rest of the organic universe. This means that we must examine the selective forces and adaptive responses that have given us our physical shape, our physiological needs, our psychological drives, much of our behavior, and our basic mental capabilities.

From Animal to Primate

Biologists classify organisms by means of a standard set of twenty-one more and more inclusive *categories* ranging upward from species to kingdom. They call the various types of organisms within each category *taxons*. All organisms within a particular taxon have a common ancestor—that is, if the taxonomists have done their job right. So if you are interested in the question: Who am I?—part of the answer lies in finding out to which taxons our ancestors belong at each category level. Ascending from our species, *Homo sapiens,* to

19

Category	Taxon
Kingdom	*Animalia*
Phylum	*Chordata*
Subphylum	*Vertebrata*
Superclass	*Tetrapoda*
Class	*Mammalia*
Subclass	*Theria*
Infraclass	*Eutheria*
Cohort	—
Superorder	—
Order	*Primata*
Suborder	*Anthropoidea*
Infraorder	—
Superfamily	*Hominoidea*
Family	*Hominidae*
Subfamily	—
Tribe	—
Subtribe	—
Genus	*Homo*
Subgenus	—
Species	*Homo sapiens*
Subspecies	*Homo sapiens sapiens*

the animal kingdom, we encounter ever more inclusive groupings of animals to which we owe some aspect of our human nature.

As the table above shows, our species has a pedigree that can be uniquely identified by reference to fourteen taxonomic categories within the animal kingdom. Do not be disturbed by the blanks next to certain categories. They merely indicate that no contrasting taxons in our pedigree are conventionally distinguished at those taxonomic levels (although not all authorities agree).

We humans are *Animalia:* mobile, multicelled organisms that derive energy from ingestion ("eating"). The *Animalia* are now recognized as distinct not only from members of the plant kingdom but from the bacteria, one-celled creatures (*Protista*), and fungi as well.

We are also *Chordata,* the animal phylum all of whose members possess (1) a *notochord,* a rodlike structure that provides internal support for the body; (2) *gill pouches,* lateral slits on the throat; and (3) a hollow nerve chord ending in a brain. (If you don't recognize yourself here, it's because we display the first two of these features only when we are embryos.) The *Chordata* contrast radically with some twenty-four different animal phyla such as the sponges, the stinging jellyfish, the flatworms, the roundworms, the mollusks, and the arthropods (insects, crustaceans, millipedes, spiders).

20

Figure 3-1. EGG-LAYING MAMMALS. The *Echidna,* or spiny anteater (left), and the *Ornithorhyncus,* or duckbill platypus (right), are representatives of the mammalian subclass Prototheria. (Arthur W. Ambler/National Audubon Society—left; Australian News and Information Bureau—right)

Humans are also *Vertebrata,* uniquely distinguished from other subphyla of the *Chordata* by two features: (1) in all adult *Vertebrata* the notochord is surrounded or replaced by a column of cartilaginous or bony discs (the vertebrae); and (2) the brain is encased within a bony covering (the skull or *cranium*).

Among the *Vertebrata* we belong in the superclass *Tetrapoda,* which means literally "four-footed," as distinguished from *Pisces,* the superfamily of the fish. The *Tetrapoda* are divided into four classes: *Amphibia, Reptilia, Aves* (birds), and *Mammalia.* Our class, *Mammalia,* is distinguished from the others by: (1) milk-secreting mammary glands; (2) hair; and (3) incisor, canine, and molar teeth for cutting, tearing, and grinding, respectively. In addition, mammals share with birds the capacity to maintain their internal body environment at a constant temperature; that is, we have built-in thermostats.

The *Mammalia* are usually divided into two subclasses: *Theria,* mammals like us that do not lay eggs; and *Prototheria,* egg-laying mammals, of which the spiny anteater (*Echidna*) and the duckbill (*Ornithorhynchus*) are the best-known and the only surviving representative genera. Both the spiny anteater and the duckbill are found only in Australia, Tasmania, and New Guinea. They have mammary glands but no teats, hair (formed into spines in the case of the *Echidna*), and a rudimentary body thermostat. The duckbill copulates in the water and incubates its eggs inside a burrow for about ten days. The spiny anteater is more land-dwelling and has a pouch into which it places its young after they hatch.

The subclass *Theria,* which does not lay eggs, is divided into two living infraclasses: *Metatheria,* or marsupials, and our own in-

21

fraclass, *Eutheria.* The principal characteristic of *Eutheria* is the presence of the *placenta,* a unique nutrient and waste-exchanging structure that enhances fetal development within the mother's body. *Metatheria* lack part or all of the placental structure. Instead many, though not all, have an external pouch in which the tiny newborn young complete their fetal development. Besides such familiar examples as the kangaroo and the opossum, the metatherians occur in a dazzling variety of forms. Many live an arboreal life feeding on insects and fruits; others are predators; others dig tunnels; others are aquatic; still others are jumpers and gliders. There are marsupials that resemble mice and others that evoke comparisons with foxes, mink, wolves, and squirrels. These resemblances are of great theoretical interest because they are not caused by descent from a common ancestor but by adaptations to similar ecological conditions.

Our infraclass, *Eutheria,* contains sixteen orders, including, for example, insectivores, carnivores, and rodents. The order we belong to is called *Primata,* a taxon that includes monkeys, apes, tarsiers, lemurs, and other close relatives.

The Primate Order

Clawed digits, nonopposable thumb, nonopposable first toe, and wide set eyes are presumed to be primitive mammalian traits. The main direction of primate evolution is characterized by the replacement of clawed digits with flat nails, nonopposable thumbs and toes with opposable digits, and wide-set eyes with eyes set together at the front of the face. These changes were formerly explained as adaptations to

Figure 3-2. AUSTRALIAN MARSUPIALS. Independent adaptations among marsupials resulted in a radiation of forms analogous to wolves, bears, cats, rats, and many other common placental mammals. In this case, the pragmatic and opportunistic processes of natural selection have produced *convergent* rather than *divergent* transformations. The carnivorous marsupial "cat" (top left) stalks small birds and lizards. The koala (top right) lives entirely in trees and eats leaves of the eucalyptus; the baby koala first emerges from its mother's pouch at about six months. "Tasmanian Wolf" (middle), preys on kangaroo, wallaby, and sheep. "Tasmanian Devil" (bottom left) lives in burrows, eats small mammals, birds, and lizards, and resembles a bear. The wallaby baby is nursing within its mother's pouch (bottom right). (R. Van Nostrand/National Audubon Society—top left; Australian News and Information Bureau—top right, middle, bottom left; San Diego Zoo—bottom right)

23

Figure 3-3. GIBBON FOOT. (Gordon S. Smith/National Audubon Society).

a way of life involving extensive climbing and jumping in a forest habitat: clawless opposable digits for grasping branches and for leaping from one tree to another; frontally oriented eyes for stereoscopic vision for running and jumping high above ground. It is now recognized that life in the trees alone is not sufficient to account for the earliest phases of primate evolution. Squirrels, for example, lack all three of the above traits, yet they are accomplished aerial acrobats. It seems likely that the grasping functions of primate hands and feet evolved to facilitate cautious, well-controlled movements in pursuit of small animals and insects amid the lower branches and leaves of forest habitats. The stereoscopic vision of primates resembles that of predator cats and birds which also evolved in relation to predation practiced against small animals and insects (Cartmill 1974). The primate contribution to human nature can be summarized under seven headings, each of which is hypothetically related to the need for feeding or locomoting in an arboreal habitat.

1. *Prehensile hands and feet:* Unlike squirrels and other mammalian arborealists, the primates locomote up and down tree trunks and across tree branches not by means of claws but by means of hands and feet that are adept at grasping and clutching. Their flexible digits, especially the thumb and big toe, are therefore said to be *prehensile.* In many primate species, the big toe, as well as the thumb, is *opposable:* their palmar surfaces can be made to lie against the palmar surfaces of the other digits. Closely associated with prehensility is the absence or reduction of the claws used by several other mammalian orders for climbing, predation, and defense. Instead, most primates have flat nails, which protect and reinforce the tips of their digits without interfering with prehensility.

2. *Specialized functions of the forelimb:* Primates have a highly developed ability to rotate, flex, and extend their forelimbs. These

Figure 3-4. PRIMATE GRIPS.

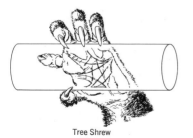

Tree Shrew

Tarsier

Macaque

Human

movements supplement the forelimbs' locomotor and support functions and give rise to the distinction between arms and legs. Arms in conjunction with a prehensile hand are well suited for exploring the space under leaves and between branches and twigs and for clutching and drawing in fruits and berries, as well as for catching small animals and insects.

3. *Visual acuity:* Primate eyes are large proportionate to facial surface and are typically located at or toward the front of the head instead of at the sides. This arrangement helps to produce the stereoscopic vision associated with the arboreally useful capacity to judge distances. In contrast to their well-developed sense of sight, primates have a relatively poor sense of smell. Many other mammals get most of their information by sniffing the environment. Their eyes are located behind their snouts. Dogs, for example, are literally led by their noses. But in an arboreal habitat, seeing is more important than sniffing. Hence the eyes of the primates enjoy an unobstructed front seat in a balcony above the nasal aperture. There is usually no snout. The positioning of primate eyes is also related to prehensility and to the mobility of the forelimbs. Typical primate feeding involves a grasping action that brings objects close to the mouth, where they are examined by the eyes before being ingested. Snouted mammals, on the other hand, monitor their food primarily by the sense of smell.

4. *Small number of offspring per birth:* An active, wide-ranging arboreal mammal would find it difficult to take care of a large litter. Thus primates tend to give birth to no more than two or three infants at a time, and a single offspring per birth is the rule among many primate species.

5. *Prolongation of gestation and infancy:* Most mammalian orders that rely upon large numbers of offspring per birth for reproductive success have short gestation periods followed by rapid onset of sexual

Figure 3-5. TARSIER. A prosimian, the tarsier is a nocturnal, arboreal, insect- and fruit-eating primate. It has binocular, stereoscopic vision; disklike adhesive pads on its digits; elongated hind legs; and a long tail. These characteristics are all suited to hopping along tree limbs. (Arthur W. Ambler/National Audubon Society).

Figure 3-6. RHESUS MOTHER AND CHILD. A typical agile, alert, dexterous, and highly sociable monkey. (L. M. Chace/National Audubon Society)

maturity and adulthood. Having large litters involves a high rate of intrauterine impairment and infant fatalities because of competition for nutrients and for maternal care. In contrast, primates concentrate on one offspring at a time and provide maximum intrauterine and postnatal maternal support and protection per offspring.

6. *Complexity of social behavior:* A further consequence of not having large litters is that patterns of behavior are more social. This arises from the prolonged mother-child relationship and the intense care given to each offspring. Sociality is expressed in mutual grooming (another consequence of manual dexterity), communal feeding, and auditory and visual signal systems for indicating food, danger, and sexual state.

7. *Enlargement of the brain:* Most primates have a high ratio of brain weight to body weight. Each of the aforementioned consequences of life in the trees provides the opportunity or the need for more complicated forms of neural control. The arboreal environment, with its wind-blown, rain-spattered, and light-dappled foliage, requires complex monitoring and interpretation. The exploratory maneuvers of the forelimbs and digits and their capacity for bringing objects close to the eyes for inspection also suggest the need for elaborate neural circuitry. But most important of all is the high level of social interaction. It is no accident that the primates are among the "brainiest" as well as the most social of the mammals. The prolonged

26

dependency of the primate infant, the large amount of auditory, visual, and tactile information passed between mother and offspring, the intense play among juveniles, and the mutual grooming among adults require expanded faculties of information storage, generalization, discrimination, and recall. It is no coincidence that human beings, the brainiest of the primates, are also the most social of the primates. Our brain is above all a consequence of our sociality.

Suborder Anthropoidea versus Suborder Prosimii

The primate order contains two suborders: *Anthropoidea* and *Prosimii*. All monkeys, great apes, and human beings are *Anthropoidea*.

Figure 3-7. PROSIMIANS. Galagos (top left) are African Prosimians. The ancestors of all the primates may have looked like the tree shrew (top right). Below is a ring-tailed lemur. Lemurs locomote in a distinctive manner named "vertical leaping and clinging." (Arthur W. Ambler/National Audubon Society—top left and bottom; San Diego Zoo—top right)

The *Prosimii* consist of lemurs, tarsiers, lorises, and (perhaps) tree shrews. These less familiar cousins of ours are found in Africa, Madagascar, India, and Southeast Asia. From both a biological and behavioral point of view, many of the *Prosimii* appear to stand midway between the *Anthropoidea* and the mammalian order *Insectivora.* The *Anthropoidea,* on the other hand, are sometimes called the "higher primates." They have relatively larger and rounder skull cases, flatter faces, and mobile upper lips detached from the gums. This last is important in the production of facial expressions, which in turn figure in the development of the more advanced forms of primate social life. Lorises and lemurs (but not tarsiers) have their upper lips attached externally to their nose by a moist strip of skin called a *rhinarium,* which can also be seen on the snout of any convenient cat or dog. We humans boast a dry nose and a dry, hairy upper lip. But the two vertical ridges leading toward our nose suggest that someone in our family tree once had a rhinarium.

The Anthropoidean Superfamilies

The suborder *Anthropoidea* is made up of three superfamilies: (1) the *Ceboidea,* or New World monkeys; (2) the *Cercopithecoidea,* or Old World monkeys; and (3) the *Hominoidea,* which include all fossil and contemporary species of both apes and human beings. Old and New World monkeys have different dental patterns that indicate an ancient divergence from a common primate or prosimian ancestor. Old World monkeys have what is known as the cercopithecoid *dental formula:* $\frac{2.1.2.3}{2.1.2.3}$ The figures above the line denote from left to right the number of incisors, canines, premolars, and molars in an upper quadrant of the jaw; the figures below the line, the number in a lower quadrant. (The total number of teeth equals the number in the upper quadrant times two plus the number in the lower quadrant times two.) All ceboidean families have either $\frac{2.1.3.3}{2.1.3.3}$ or $\frac{2.1.3.2}{2.1.3.2}$ patterns. If your wisdom teeth have erupted, you may discover for yourself that we share a $\frac{2.1.2.3}{2.1.2.3}$ pattern with the *Cercopithecoidea.*

Figure 3-8. OLD WORLD MONKEY DENTITION (left); NEW WORLD MONKEY DENTITION (right).

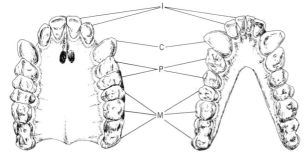

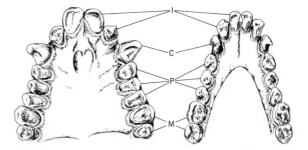

The apes also have this pattern, and on this basis humans, the apes, and the Old World monkeys were formerly lumped together in a single superfamily. Advances in the knowledge of the fossil evidence, however, indicate that hominoids deserve a superfamily of their own.

Characteristics of the Hominoidea

The most significant differences between the *Hominoidea* and the other anthropoids concern modes of locomotion and suspension during feeding. In contrast to the hominoids, monkeys are generally small arboreal animals that make their way on all fours along tree branches and that feed while sitting upright on a narrow limb. Some of the larger monkeys have developed prehensile tails, which help them to cling to small branches as they edge their way out toward fruit and tender leaf-bearing twigs. In a few larger species, the quadrupedal gait is supplemented by a considerable amount of reaching overhead for higher branches and by arm-initiated propulsion across open spaces. This swinging by the arms from branch to branch is called *brachiation*.

Three of the living *Hominoidea*—humans, the gibbon, and siamang—are no longer quadrupedal. The gibbon and siamang are primarily brachiators, swinging from branch to branch with legs tucked up close to their bodies, propelled through graceful trajectories by extraordinarily long and powerful forearms.

Figure 3-9. GIBBONS. These *Hominoidea* are assigned to the family *Hylobatidae*. Their entire anatomy reflects the influence of brachiation. Note especially the huge arms, long fingers, short legs and short thumbs. (Arthur W. Ambler/National Audubon Society)

29

Figure 3-10. ADULT MALE GORILLA. Knuckle-walking involves anatomical modifications in the elbows as well as in the wrists and fingers (above, left). (Claude Schoepf)

Figure 3-11. SUSPENSORY FEEDING. A young orang can eat with its feet as well as its hands (above, right). (Anthro-Photo/DeVore)

Figure 3-12. JUVENILE ORANGUTANS. Note the long forelimbs suitable for brachiation and the prehensile feet with opposable big toes (right). (Claude Schoepf)

Although the chimpanzee, gorilla, and orangutan also have long forelimbs in relation to their hindlimbs, they are too big and heavy as adults to brachiate energetically. The long front limbs, however, are put to good use while they practice *suspensory feeding*—hanging by a combination of arms and prehensile feet and reaching out to pluck off fruity morsels from branches that would not bear their weight. In addition, the larger apes have developed special forms of terrestrial quadrupedalism. This is true of the chimpanzee and gorilla, who spend the majority of their lives foraging on the ground. In this they are similar to ground-dwelling monkeys such as the baboons. But whereas baboons maintain the basic quadrupedal gait by walking on the palms of their hands, gorillas and chimpanzees practice *knuckle-walking*: their long forelimbs are locked at the elbow into a rigid straight line, and their forward weight rests on their knuckles. Orangutans, who are much more arboreal, usually walk on the sides of their fists during their infrequent visits to the ground (Tuttle 1969; Napier 1970). The length of the forelimbs compared to the hindlimbs seems to indicate that the ancestors of all the living pongids (apes) were brachiators and suspensory feeders.

That our own remote ancestors were to some extent arboreal seems highly probable. They may not have been brachiators, however, since the ratio of our forelimbs to hindlimbs is the opposite of what it is in all other living hominoids. At any rate it is now known that our bipedal, terrestrial heritage goes back at least 5 million years (see Chapter 4).

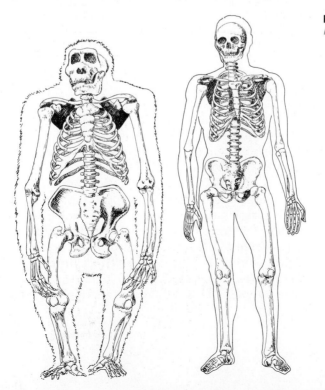

Figure 3-13. GORILLA (left); *HOMO SAPIENS* (right).

Family Hominidae versus Family Pongidae and Family Hylobatidae

The superfamily *Hominoidea* contains three families: (1) the *Hominidae,* all varieties of hominids of which our species is the sole surviving representative; (2) the *Pongidae,* all contemporary and extinct varieties of apes except the gibbon and siamang; and (3) the *Hylobatidae,* the gibbon and siamang and their fossil ancestors.

Anatomically the most striking differences between hominids and pongids all relate to the development of bipedalism in hominids. Obviously there are more profound contrasts between apes and humans than how we stand and walk. But bipedalism has played a crucial role in our evolutionary career and its effects are found in the following areas of our bodies:

1. *The foot:* The bipedal gait was made possible by a restructuring of the prehensile hominoid foot, especially by a rearward extension of the heel bone and a realignment of the big toe. Lifting power from our calf muscles raises the heel bone. Then a forward and upward spring is imparted by leverage against the big toe. Arches extending from front to rear and side to side keep the action springy. The big toe of the human foot, unlike the pongid big toe, is lined up with the rest of the toes and has lost practically all its opposability. Whereas the pongid foot can function as a tactile and grasping organ, the human foot is exclusively an organ of support and locomotion.

2. *Arms and hands:* The great mechanical advantage of hominid bipedalism is that the forelimbs are entirely freed from locomotor functions. The gorilla, the chimpanzee, and the orangutan depend upon their arms either for brachiation or for semierect terrestrial movement. Gorillas and chimpanzees use their knuckles, whereas the orangutan usually walks on its fists or with outspread palms. The gibbon's arms are so long that they would get in the way if used for terrestrial locomotion. Therefore the gibbon in its infrequent excursions to the ground holds its arms high above its head and seems to stagger along like a drunken ballet dancer. And so hominids are the only animals that can comfortably travel long distances on the ground while carrying heavy objects in their hands. Moreover, the dexterity of the hominid hand is unsurpassed; in the gibbon and the orangutan the requirements of climbing and of brachiation have reduced the size and dexterity of their thumb. The chimpanzee and the gorilla are quite dexterous, but our thumb is larger, more heavily muscled, and more supple. The length and strength of the human thumb permit a

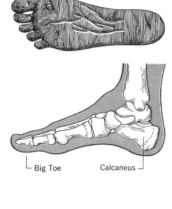

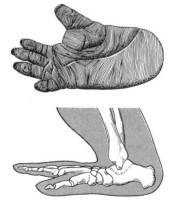

Big Toe   Calcaneus

Figure 3-14. HUMAN FOOT (above); GORILLA FOOT (below).

uniquely precise grip, powerful yet delicate. This grip, almost as much a hallmark of humanity as bipedalism and braininess, has helped to make us the supreme artisans of the animal kingdom.

3. *The lower limbs:* Human legs relative to trunk length are the longest among the *Hominoidea.* The large calf of our lower leg is distinctive; the great ape lower leg is straight, lacking prominent calf muscles. Even more dramatically human is the massive gluteal musculature, which, when we are not sitting on it, provides much of the force for walking up hill, straightening up after bending, and running and jumping.

4. *The pelvic girdle:* In quadrupedal primates the pelvis has the contour of a narrow tube to which the rear legs are attached at close to a right angle. About half of the weight of an animal that moves on all fours is transmitted through the pelvis to the rear legs. Among the *Pongidae* the rear legs bear a higher percentage of the total body weight during terrestrial locomotion. The gorilla pelvis shows some flattening and strengthening as a result of its increased weight-bearing function. But in hominids the center of gravity passes directly through the pelvis, which therefore must support the entire weight of the viscera, trunk, arms, and head. Thus the flattening, broadening, and strengthening of the human pelvis has proceeded much further than in any of the *Pongidae.* The basinlike character of the human pelvis is completed by inward-turning vertebrae and their ligaments at the base of the spine, which close off the bottom portion of the pelvic cavity. A main function of the pelvis is to provide attachments for the powerful muscles that control locomotion and provide support. The greatly enlarged front-to-rear aspect of the human pelvis, especially of the two broad-bladed hip bones, increases the effective force of all the musculature involved in the movement of the upper legs. Muscles attached to these hip bones and to other portions of the pelvis also provide much of the power for moving the lower limbs.

5. *The vertebral column:* To allow upright posture, the human vertebral column has developed a unique curve in the lumbar region.

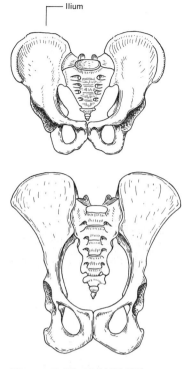

Figure 3-15. HUMAN PELVIS (above); CHIMPANZEE PELVIS (below).

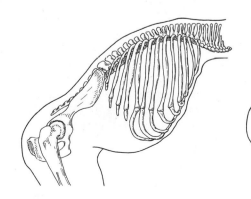

Figure 3-16. GORILLA VERTEBRAL COLUMN (left); HUMAN VERTEBRAL COLUMN (right).

Here the column bends forward over the center of the pelvis and on meeting the pelvis reverses itself to form a sickle with the handle above. Without this curve the body's center of gravity would be altered, and people would have a tendency to topple over backward. Although capable of supporting seven hundred pounds or more, our vertebral column is subject to malfunction. The intense pressures upon the cartilaginous discs between the vertebrae lead to slippage and misalignment and to characteristically human "pains in the back." At its upper end (the cervical region) the human spinal column curves forward, then upward and slightly to the rear, and articulates with our skull at a point close to its center of gravity. The human cervical vertebrae lack the long spiny rearward extensions that anchor the gorilla's large neck muscles (cf. Harrison and Montagna 1969).

6. *The neck:* The head pivots atop the vertebral column on a pair of bony knobs found at the base of our skulls. These knobs are called *occipital condyles.* In pongids the main weight of the head is well forward of the pivot points. The powerful neck muscles needed for stability completely obscure the skeletal contour of the gorilla's cervical region. Hominids are different; our occipital condyles are very close to the head's center of gravity. Our head almost balances by itself at the top of the cervical curve, and the relatively small musculature needed to sustain the "pan-and-tilt" produces our distinctively gracile neck.

7. *The cranium:* The rear portion of the skull to which the neck muscles are attached is called the *nuchal plane.* Among the pongids this area is very large and rises to form an abrupt angle with the rest of the head at the *nuchal crest.* In humans the nuchal crest is absent,

Figure 3-17. BASE OF HUMAN SKULL.

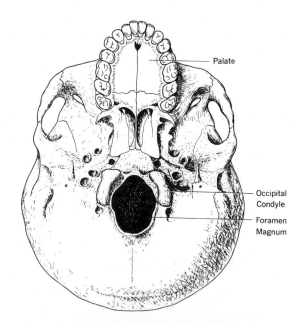

Palate

Occipital Condyle

Foramen Magnum

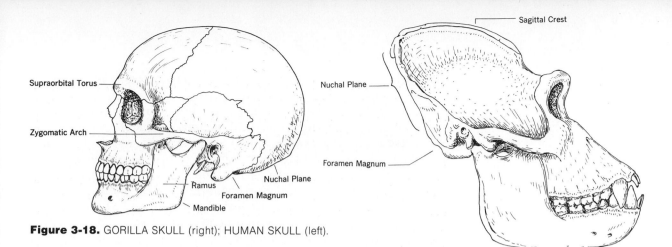

Figure 3-18. GORILLA SKULL (right); HUMAN SKULL (left).

the area of the nuchal plane is greatly reduced, and its position is underneath rather than at the rear of the skull. This repositioning of the nuchal area imparts a smooth, spherical contour to the rear of the human skull, a feature continued into the forehead region and further emphasized by the characteristically hominid reduction in the forward thrust of the face and jaws. The globular shape of the human skull is clearly related to the expansion of its internal cubic dimension to accommodate the largest and heaviest of primate brains. Viewed from the rear, the modern hominid skull is distinguished by its steeply rising side walls and its achievement of maximum width above rather than below the ears. Although a gorilla's skull is more massive than ours, a much smaller space is available inside. Much of the pongid skull is taken up by the thick bones and by the nuchal and sagittal crests, which serve as attachments for muscles and as structural reinforcement.

8. *The face and upper jaw:* The hominid face fulfills an ancient evolutionary trend among most primates toward the reduction of the mammalian snout. Among pongids the face continues to extend well beyond the forehead in the region below the eyes. The forward thrust is continued by the upper jaw, resulting in a relationship known as *prognathism.* In contrast the hominid upper jaw is *orthognathic;* it is aligned vertically with the forehead, directly under the eye sockets. Among gorillas the bony structure of the face is massive and is distinguished by a large bar over the eyes known as the *supraorbital torus.* This structure is thought to be associated with the protection of the upper face from the enormous pressure of the pongid chewing apparatus. During the course of hominid evolution, it became smaller and is virtually absent in most people. The cheek bones and other facial surfaces to which the musculature of the jaw is attached also are less pronounced in hominids than in pongids of comparable body size.

35

Family Hominidae versus Family Pongidae and Family Hylobatidae

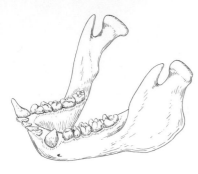

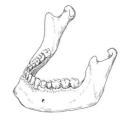

Figure 3-19. GORILLA JAW (above); HUMAN JAW (below).

9. *Jaws and teeth:* Our chewing equipment is one of our most important and distinctive features. Fossilized fragments of jaws and even of single teeth are relied on for tracing hominid phylogeny and for distinguishing between hominid and pongid taxons. Modern pongids have a *dental arcade* in which long parallel rows of molars and premolars are joined by a *u*-shaped curve of canines and incisors. In contrast the hominid arcade is parabolic or v-shaped and greatly compressed to conform to the orthognathism of the hominid face. A pongid's incisors and canines are large by comparison with its molars and massive by comparison with a hominid's incisors and canines; a hominid's incisors and canines are small by comparison with its molars.

These differences imply two fundamentally different feeding adaptations. The massive size of the pongid's front teeth probably relate to the use of incisors and canines to cut and rip the outer covering of woody shoots such as bamboo and wild celery. The dental pattern characteristic of hominids—small incisors and canines relative to large molars—suggests a different diet, one based on substances that are easily processed into bite-size portions by the front teeth but that thereafter must be subjected to a considerable amount of grinding and milling before they can be swallowed. From his studies of grass-eating baboons, Clifford Jolly (1970) has developed the theory that the distinctive features of hominid dentition were adaptations to small, tough morsels such as grass seeds, stems, and gritty roots. Such a diet requires the processing of large quantities of small and/or gritty items; to subsist the animal must feed very often, and the molars must stay in virtually continuous use, milling and grinding the seeds and stems. The importance of milling and grinding in the adaptation of our ancestors is suggested by the flexible way in which our lower jaw is hinged, which produces a side-to-side rotary motion when we chew.

Another feature suggestive of grinding and milling is the delayed eruption of the hominid molars so that as the front molars are worn down they are replaced by fresh molars to the rear. A final aspect of this pattern is that hominid molars are higher than they are either broad or long. This is another feature that would provide a selective advantage in resisting the attrition produced by prolonged milling action (Simons 1968; Simons and Ettel 1970). In fact hominid dentition shows certain analogies with the teeth of the greatest miller and grinder of them all, the elephant. An elephant's molars are massive and have transverse ridges for crushing and grinding roots, grass, branches, and other fibrous and woody substances. Only one of these

36

molars functions at a time in each of the four quadrants of its jaws, but as each wears down it is supplemented from the rear by a new tooth. The analogous adaptation in hominids is the long period—from six to nineteen years of age—during which our first, second, and third molars erupt one after the other.

Another definitive feature of hominid dentition is that our canines project only slightly or not at all above the level of the adjacent teeth. In contrast, the pongid jaw accommodates canines so large that they must protrude into spaces in the opposite arcade in order for the jaws to shut tightly. These canines are especially conspicuous among the male pongids. It is believed that in addition to their value in feeding, they are used for defense against predators and for communicating threats to females and junior males. Reduction in canine size together with generally smaller teeth and jaws leaves us without built-in cutting, piercing, and tearing weapons or tools.

Thus, the basic pattern of hominid dentition weighs heavily against the popular stereotype that our ancestors were bloodthirsty "killer apes." In fact, just the opposite seems to be true (see p. 66). Deprived of canines, and equipped with fingernails and toenails instead of claws, we humans are anatomically curiously harmless creatures. Naked, without weapons or a knowledge of judo or karate, we would find it virtually impossible to kill any large animal, including our own fellow humans.

Hominid Sexuality

The human female is unique among primates in the lack of relationship between the *estrous cycle* and receptivity for coitus. This, too, may be functionally related to hominid bipedalism. Among most mammals the female is sexually receptive during only a few days before and after the mature ovum passes from the ovary to the uterus, the period during which fertilization must take place if the ovum is to become implanted in the uterus wall. The maturation of the ovum puts the primate female into heat. By means of olfactory and visual signals she attracts the male to copulation. Among many primates the estrous climax is signaled by multicolored swellings in the region of the anus and vagina. Estrus in chimpanzees, for example, is signaled by a bright pink swelling in the anal-genital skin, and during estrus as many as twenty male chimpanzees have been observed copulating with a single female (Van Lawick-Goodall 1965).

Although the menstrual cycle of the human female is similar in many respects to that of the pongids and other primates, there are no

Figure 3-20. GELADA BA-BOONS. Female on right is in estrus as indicated by brightly colored "necklace." (Ron Garrison/San Diego Zoo)

external signs indicating the period of maximum fertility. Indeed, women are not normally aware of their own ovulation. If reproduction is to occur, it is necessary for the human female to be receptive throughout the entire estrous cycle and for the male to be continually sexually potent and excitable.

Bipedalism enters this complex as follows: changes in the coloration of the anal-genital region may have become increasingly more difficult to detect in the round-bottomed, sitting and standing hominid female. One conceivable adaptive solution would have depended on increased olfactory cues, but given the general emphasis on sight rather than smell among all the *Hominoidea* this alternative was improbable. (Vaginal scent communication does play a role in the sexual behavior of some monkeys [cf. Michael and Keverne 1968].) Another conceivable solution was the transfer of the estrous signals to the female's upper torso. Interestingly this adaptation is characteristic of the gelada baboons, Jolly's grass-eaters, who forage on their rumps in an upright sitting position. Female geladas have a chest patch of sexual skin that flushes red and develops a necklace of small white protuberances during estrus.

Another alternative solution to the sexual challenge of bipedalism was to abandon the attempt to coordinate female sexual activity with the estrous cycle. This requires a "shotgun" approach in which the level of sexual activity remains high throughout the entire adult life-span regardless of season or estral condition. Under these circumstances selection would favor females who were continually attrac-

38

tive to males. This attractiveness would depend on the elaboration of conspicuous secondary sexual characteristics in visually prominent parts of the female body. Conjecturally the human female's enlarged breasts and curvaceous torso, accompanied by a general absence of body hair except for the pubic region, fulfill this function.

Whatever its origins, the continuous sexual needs and interests characteristic of human nature have much to do with the fact that we display the most intense form of heterosexual sociality in the animal kingdom. Only hominids live in domestic groups in which adult males and females cooperate in the following combination of ways:

1. Both sexes engage in frequent (daily to weekly) heterosexual intercourse unrestricted by estrous cycles or rutting seasons.
2. Both sexes regularly bring different foods to each other and jointly consume the resulting meals.
3. Both sexes jointly provide food and shelter for their infants and juveniles.

Much has been made of the fact that part of this pattern—(2) and (3)—occurs in reduced degree among such social carnivores as wolves and wild dogs (cf. Schaller and Lowther 1969). The intense sexuality of adult human relationships in combination with joint provisioning activities involving different foods renders this comparison rather uninstructive.

And Nature, pandering, be-
stowed
　　On virgin ears erotic lobes
And hung on women hemi-
spheres
　　That imitate their once-
attractive rears:
A social animal disarms
　　With frontal charms.

SOURCE: John Updike, from "The Naked Ape," in *Midpoint and Other Poems* (New York: Fawcett, 1963). Copyright © 1968 by John Updike. Reprinted by permission of Alfred A. Knopf, Inc.

Why We Have Hairless and Sweaty Bodies

Three approaches have been taken toward explaining the possible adaptive significance of the patchy distribution and general reduction in the amount of human body hair. One popular theory, that of the "naked ape" (obviously a misnomer because hominids are *not* apes), has already been mentioned: hairlessness enhances the visual sex cues associated with bipedalism and the loss of anal-vaginal swelling.

An alternative theory, advanced by C. Loring Brace (1967), calls attention to the fact that human beings sweat more than any other creature. This makes it possible for us to get rid of more heat per unit of time than our hairy ape cousins and fur-bearing mammals in general. This in turn may have made the ancestral hominids more efficient as hunters, since a common technique used by modern hunting peoples is to take up the trail of a large herbivore and to keep it moving through the heat of the day until it drops from exhaustion. In arid climates the hunter's lack of hairy covering increases the efficiency with which the evaporation of sweat cools the skin. (Bi-

39

pedalism also helps here because the upright hunter offers a smaller surface for the sun's rays than the back of a running quadruped.) However, no one knows just when the hominids became naked since none of the fossils that have been found tell us anything about the skins of our ancestors. (Never trust a picture or a statue that purports to show either the skin color or the hair of an ancestral hominid.)

Moreover, doubts have been raised (Newman 1970) concerning the advantages of copious sweating under arid sun-drenched conditions. Going "naked" in the sun adds a great heat load to our bodies. Furthermore, sweatier means thirstier. That is why arid-land mammals such as camels and sheep scarcely sweat at all and have thick hair or wool covering their bodies. In order to take advantage of their capacity to run down herbivores in arid habitats, our hominid ancestors would have needed a great deal of cultural equipment and know-how, such as containers for storing water, knowledge of seasonal wells and water-courses, and either clothing or fire to keep them warm at night (dry habitats always get cold after the sun sets).

It is possible therefore that hairlessness did not arise in conjunction with hunting at all but rather with the use of containers, clothing, fire, and other technological and social innovations. All that we really know for sure is that by relying on removable skins and furs, rather than on permanent body hair, hominids were eventually able to adapt to an unprecedented range of climates all the way from torrid deserts to frigid ice fields. As Alexander Alland (1972) put it: "The naked ape has a closet full of clothes." This brings us to what is really the most distinctive evolutionary characteristic of the hominids: the ability to adapt to nature by means of culture.

Hominids and Culture

Anthropologists were formerly of the opinion that only humans were capable of a cultural mode of existence. This opinion can no longer be supported, for socially learned patterns of tool manufacture as well as other varieties of social traditions have been identified among chimpanzees and other living primates (see next chapter). Moreover, archaeologists now have knowledge of a continuous series of stone tools dating back at least 3 million years (to be discussed in Chapter 9). There is no doubt therefore that our ancestral hominids were also culture-bearing animals and to an extent greater than any living apes or monkeys. Able to stand and walk erect, their forelimbs freed entirely from locomotor and support functions, the ancestral hominids manufactured, transported, and made effective use of a substantial repertory of subsistence tools. Pongids survive nicely with only the barest inventory of cultural traits. Hominids, ancient or modern, have always depended on some form of culture for their very existence. Without the manufacture of tools and weapons, the small-canine, clawless ancestral hominids could not have exploited their exposed terrestrial habitat.

The manufacture and use of cultural substitutes for teeth and claws led to an increasingly complex mode of subsistence. This in turn required heightened degrees of social coordination, which in turn required the development of a system of communication capable of exchanging unprecedented amounts of information. The culminating achievement in this chain of cultural and biological innovations was the development—at some as yet unknown period—of the language capacities that are today distinctive of our own species and duplicated nowhere else in the known universe.

So it is part of hominid nature to adapt to nature by means of culture—that is, to depend on socially acquired, learned "traditions" or "repertories" for survival and reproduction. But the capacity for cultural adaptations is not the singular hallmark of human beings. Rather, it is the hominid capacity for cultural adaptation *plus* a distinctive mode of linguistic communication that constitutes a minimal definition of what "human" means in an evolutionary sense. This definition allows for ancient hominids who were neither apes nor humans, but who lived by culture, and yet who, if alive today, would be incapable of learning to speak the present-day languages of the world with the competence that all normal human beings exhibit while still children. It also allows for ancient hominid types who might seem on anatomical grounds to belong to a species other than

Figure 3-21. A YOUNG CHIMPANZEE. We are learning how to communicate with them (see p. 126). (James Welgos/National Audubon Society).

our own but who nonetheless would have to be regarded as human beings if it is demonstrated that they possessed language competence.

Unfortunately assessment of the language capacity of fossil hominids is for the moment based on speculative assumptions (to be discussed in the next chapter). Estimates of when the crucial transition to language use occurred range from 2 million years ago to as recently as 75,000 years ago (Lieberman, Crelin, and Klatt 1972; Hill 1972). But anthropologists are fairly certain of one thing: without the development of terrestrial bipedalism, our human language would not have evolved from the protohuman system of communication. In the beginning there was the foot.

THE PROTOHUMANS

Continuing the story of how human nature evolved, this chapter focuses on the ancestral hominids, the protohumans—those creatures who were just below the status of being human. Here popular curiosity runs high. What kind of creatures were they? Fierce or timid? Carnivores or vegetarians? Hunters or hunted? And how and why did their descendants become human?

But first, some preliminaries. To set the stage, there will be a brief introduction to what is known about the evolutionary background of the *Hominoidea.*

An Evolutionary Clock

Geologists divide the history of the earth into eras, which are subdivided into periods and epochs. Nobody knows exactly when life originated some 3 or 4 billion years ago. The first microorganisms were not fossilized and disappeared without leaving traces that can be found today. About 600 million years ago, by the beginning of the Paleozoic era, the first animals had appeared that were large enough and hard enough to leave abundant fossil remains. In the Cambrian, the first period of the Paleozoic, the *Animalia* were already differentiated into many phyla. The *Chordata,* however, were not yet among them. As shown in Figure 4-1, the phylum *Chordata,* subphylum *Vertebrata,* and superclass *Tetrapoda* were all present by the Devonian period, about 400 million years ago. Thereafter it took about 175

43

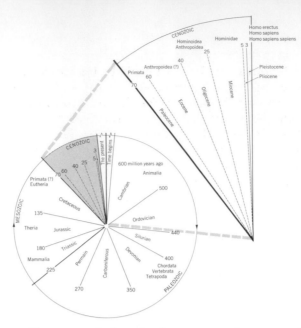

Figure 4-1. EVOLUTIONARY CLOCK.

million years before the first mammals appeared in the Triassic period of the Mesozoic era. The first primates evolved from insectivore prototypes somewhere toward the end of the Mesozoic or the beginning of the Cenozoic era 70 to 60 million years ago. Between 40 and 25 million years ago, during the Oligocene epoch, the *Anthropoidea* were abundant, at least in North Africa, and included both monkeys and apes. In the next epoch, the Miocene, the *Hominoidea* became widespread. Toward the middle of the Miocene, about 13 million years ago, the earliest hominids began to appear. There probably were ground-dwelling, bipedal, tool-using hominids throughout the entire Pliocene epoch. The genus *Homo* appeared sometime during the early Pleistocene, and our own species, *Homo sapiens,* sometime near the end of the Pleistocene.

From Hominoid to Hominid

The ancestral apes already constituted a grouping separate from the ancestral monkeys during the Oligocene, 30 million years ago. Knowledge of these Oligocene monkeys and apes is based mainly on numerous fossils from the Fayum region of Northern Egypt. One group of Oligocene fossil monkeys found in this region was the family *Parapithecidae.* Some of them had the Old World dental formula $\frac{2.1.2.3}{2.1.2.3}$. Another Fayum Oligocene group possibly ancestral to the Old World monkeys is the genus *Oligopithecus,* which also had the Old World pattern. Although *Oligopithecus* is very small, its jaws

44

display certain apelike features, and hence it could be interpreted as the common ancestor of both the *Hominoidea* and the Old World monkeys. But three other kinds of apelike fossils are also present among the Fayum Oligocene materials. The earliest of these is *Aegyptopithecus*, whose four-inch-long skull and jaws and teeth resemble the features of a diminutive gorilla. Similar to *Aegyptopithecus* except for smaller canines is another apelike fossil, *Propliopithecus*. Either of these genera could have been the first of the *Hominoidea*. Both seem to be related to Miocene apes, especially to a group known as the *Dryopithecinae*. The third Oligocene hominoid, *Aeolopithecus*, displays many gibbonlike features and may be discounted as a contender for the ancestry of either the *Pongidae* or the *Hominidae* (Simons 1968).

During the Miocene the *Hominoidea* became very common and

Aegyptopithecus zeuxis

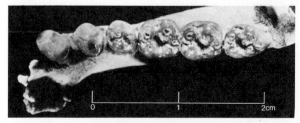

Parapithecus fraasi

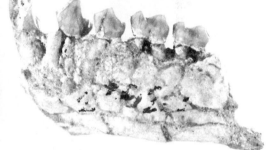

Oligopithecus savagei

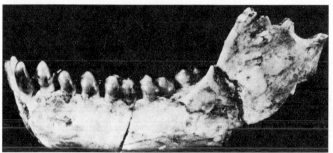

Propliopithecus haeckeli

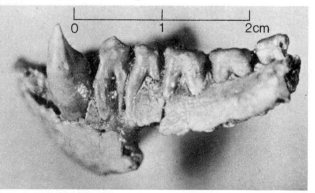

Aeolopithecus chirobates

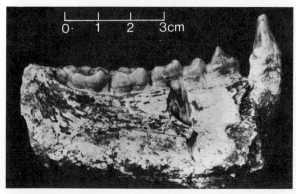

Dryopithecus fontani

Figure 4-2. OLIGOCENE FOSSIL PRIMATES. All but *Dryopithecus* are from the Fayum region of Egypt. (Kälin, 1961—*Parapithecus*; E.L. Simons— *Oligopithecus, Aegyptopithecus, Aeolopithecus*; Eric Delson—*Propliopithecus, Dyropithecus*)

Figure 4-3. RAMAPITHEC-US WICKERI. African Rama-pithecus left and right maxillary (upper jaw) fragments. (Peter Andrews - Alan Walker)

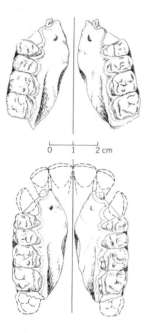

Figure 4-4. TWO RECONSTRUCTIONS OF RAMAPITHECUS. Top, with a parabolic hominid arcade; bottom, with a typical pongid u-shaped arcade. (after Vogel 1973)

46

were widely distributed over the Old World. Specimens of the above-mentioned *Dryopithecinae* have been found in East Africa, Europe, the Middle East, Georgia (U.S.S.R.), India, and China. These apes range in size from that of small gibbons to large gorillas.

Among the Miocene fossils the front-running candidate for the ancestral genus of the *Hominidae* is *Ramapithecus,* fragments of which have been recovered in the Siwalik Hills of northern India; Fort Ternan, Kenya; Yunnan Province, China; southern Germany; Spain; and possibly Greece. This small hominoid lived about 11 to 14 million years ago. According to most authorities, its dentition is strongly hominid. The arcade is parabolic; canines and incisors are small relative to molars and premolars; the canines do not protrude forward as in most apes; the molars are high and heavily enameled, and they erupted in staggered fashion. Other authorities, however, dispute the classification of *Ramapithecus* as a hominid and claim that the fragments of the lower jaw have been erroneously matched (Walker and Andrews 1973; Vogel 1973). Thus, the search for transitional forms linking the hominoids with the first hominids has not yet ended.

The Australopithecines

During the late Pliocene and early Pleistocene epochs protohuman terrestrial hominids became abundant in southern and eastern Africa. Protohumans were probably also present throughout the early Pleistocene in Asia and Indonesia. The first discovery of these creatures was made by Raymond Dart in 1924 at Taung in the Republic of South Africa. Dart gave them the generic name *Australopithecus,* meaning "Southern ape." Since then hundreds of teeth and fragments of skulls, jaws, leg bones, foot bones, pelvises, and other body parts attributed to subspecies, species, genera, and subfamilies of australopithecines (i.e., *Australopithecus*like hominids) have been found. All these supposedly different subspecies, species, genera, and subfamilies share certain basic features that place them in the *Hominidae* and hence distinguish them from "apes." Most importantly, the australopithecines were fully bipedal.

Until recently it was thought that there was something lacking in the australopithecine bipedal stance, and most textbooks stated that they "could run bipedally but were clumsy bipedal walkers." But analyses of the biomechanical properties of the hip joint have shown that the australopithecines may have been better adapted for bipedalism than modern humans. The expansion of the pelvic outlet—the birth canal—in modern human females may have reduced the efficiency of the hip joint. In this regard modern human males who have smaller pelvic openings and narrower hips than modern human females resemble australopithecines more than modern human females do. This in turn may explain why women have not been able to match the track records of male runners (Lovejoy 1974; Lovejoy, Heiple, and Burstein 1973). (See p. 268) Other authorities, however, continue to insist that australopithecine posture differed from human posture (Jenkins 1972). All australopithecines possessed fully hominid jaws and teeth. Their dental arcade was parabolic; their canines projected slightly or not at all; their incisors were relatively small as compared with their premolars and molars. But, all australopithecines had brain-cases whose volume falls below the human range.

A great controversy continues to mark the attempt to identify different australopithecine taxons (Wolpoff 1974b). It quickly became apparent that some of the australopithecines were more "robust"— larger, heavier—whereas others were more "gracile"—smaller, lighter. The robusts had massive jaws and huge molar teeth, heavy brow ridges, and remarkable bony crests and flanges along the top and side of their skulls to which massive chewing muscles were attached; the graciles had smaller jaws and teeth and smaller crests or none at all. Average cranial volume of the graciles was 442 cubic centimeters, whereas the average of the robusts was 517 cubic centimeters (Holloway 1973). The modern gorilla's cranial volume ranges from 420 to 752 cubic centimeters, and the modern human's ranges from 850 to 1700 cubic centimeters. On the basis of a formula relating brain volume to body weight, Holloway (1972) estimates that the graciles weighed on the average about 45 pounds, and the robusts weighed about 53 pounds. Other authorities have estimated the weight of some robust specimens to have been well over 150 pounds (Robinson 1973). According to Henry McHenry (1974), the average height of the South African graciles was 4'9", of the South African robusts 5', and the East African robusts 5'4".

J. T. Robinson advanced the first theory to explain these differences. He proposed that the graciles were primarily meat-eaters and the direct ancestors of modern hominids and that the robusts were primarily herbivores who were hunted to extinction by the graciles. Out of this theory there grew the celebrated popular idea that the ancestral hominids were "bloodthirsty killer apes." But intensive studies of the molar surfaces and patterns of dental wear have failed to demonstrate the existence of dietary specializations associated with the two types. Milford Wolpoff (1971) has shown that relative to body size, the graciles had more molar surface for grinding vegetable materials than the robust forms had; in fact, relative to body weight,

Figure 4-5. TAUNG MANDIBLE. (Photo by Alun R. Hughes, by permission of Professor Phillip V. Tobias)

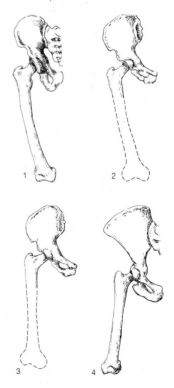

Figure 4-6. ALTERNATIVE INTERPRETATIONS OF FEMORAL ANGLE OF *A. ROBUSTUS*.
1. Chimpanzee femor
2. *A. robustus* femor
3. Alternative angle for same *A. robustus* femor.
4. *H. sapiens* femor

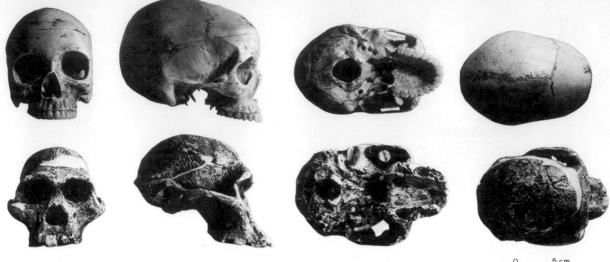

0   5 cm

Figure 4-7. MODERN
HUMAN SKULL (top) COM-
PARED WITH AUS-
TRALOPITHECINE SKULL
(bottom). (From *Physical Anthropology,* 2 ed., by A.J.
Kelso. By permission of the
publisher J.B. Lippincott
Company. Copyright ©
1974. Photos of cast of
australopithecine skull
courtesy of Wenner-Gren
Foundation and with
permission of C. K. Brain,
Transvaal Museum.)

both types of australopithecines had at least as much molar grinding
surface as the purely vegetarian modern gorilla. In addition, detailed
microscopic studies of chipping, abrasion, and dentine exposure
based on the assumption that meat and vegetable diets would show
characteristic differences lead to the conclusion that the graciles and
the robusts had basically similar diets (J. Wallace 1973; 1975).

Another appealingly simple explanation for the difference is that
the graciles and robusts were respectively the females and males of
the same species. But this theory has not been able to contend with
the fact that at two South African sites—Sterkfontein and Makapansgat—only graciles have been found, whereas at two others—
Kromdraai and Swartkrans—only robusts have been found. One can
hardly expect only females to have died in one place and only males at
another. Moreover studies of the differences in the tooth sizes of the
various individuals represented at these places reveal variations
within each population that are best explained by assuming that two
sexes were represented (cf. Wolpoff 1973).

Another theory is that the graciles constituted the ancestral hominid lineage from which the robust forms diverged about 3 million
years ago. This theory, as shown in Figure 4-10, is based on the
assumption that the oldest known australopithecine bone, a piece of
jaw found at Lothagam Hill in Kenya, is from a gracile type. Other
early australopithecine bones, representing the span between 5 million and 3 million years ago, also can be interpreted as showing
gracile features. On the other hand, the oldest robust remains from
East Lake Rudolf in Kenya are probably only about 1.75 million years
old and definitely not older than 3 million years (Brock and Isaac
1974). This suggests to some experts that the gracile forms evolved

48

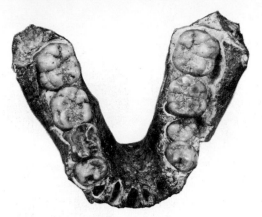

Figure 4-8. MAKAPANSGAT MANDIBLE.
(Photo by Alun R. Hughes, by permission of
Professor Phillip V. Tobias)

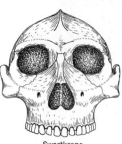

Swartkrans

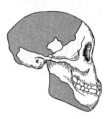

Taung

Figure 4-9. Australopithecines.

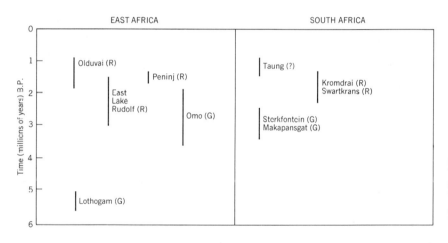

Figure 4-10. DISTRIBU-
TION OF ROBUST (R) AND
GRACILE (G) AFRICAN AUS-
TRALOPITHECINES IN TIME
AND SPACE (after Tobias
1973)

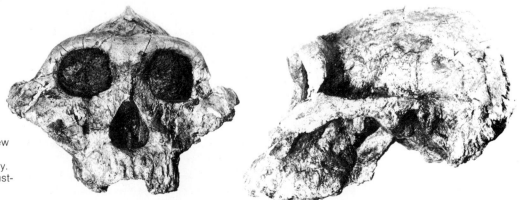

Figure 4-11. EAST
AFRICAN ROBUSTUS,
KNM-ER 406. Front view
(left) and lateral view
(right). (Richard Leakey.
Copyright Museum Trust-
ees of Kenya)

Figure 4-12. LOTHAGAM
MANDIBLE. Medial view
(left); occlusal view (right).
(Richard Leakey. Copyright
National Museum of Kenya)

into robusts or other hominids shortly to be discussed, and that they became extinct, whereas the robusts lingered on until about 750,000 years B.P. at Taung. The most serious drawback of this theory is that Dart's original Taung skull has long been regarded as a gracile type. But since the skull is that of a child, it may have been classified incorrectly (Tobias 1973; Partridge 1973).

The "Third Hominid"—The Habilines

Some experts hold the opinion that neither the gracile nor robust australopithecines were ancestral to the evolutionary lineage that led to the first human beings. This view itself represents a kind of "lineage," for it began with Louis Leakey's discovery in 1963 of a fossil that he called *Homo habilis* ("handy humans"), and it has been strengthened and expanded by discoveries made by Leakey's wife, Mary, and their son, Richard. The original habilines were found at the bottom of Olduvai Gorge in Northern Tanzania in the stratigraphic

Figure 4-13. LOOKING
DOWN INTO OLDUVAI
GORGE. (DeVore/Anthro-
Photo)

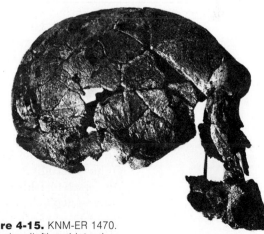

Figure 4-14. OH13. *Homo habilis,* mandible, side view (left), occlusal view (right). (Richard Leakey, Museum Trustees of Kenya)

layer known as Bed I, which has been dated by the radiometric potassium-argon decay method (K40/Ar40, for short) to about 1.75 million B.P. The Olduvai habilines were large hominids, lacking the crests and ridges of the robust australopithecines, with rounded crania and brain volumes that average out to 637 cubic centimeters (Holloway 1973).

In 1972 an expedition directed by Richard Leakey (1973b) discovered the remains of a remarkably advanced skull at East Rudolf in Kenya, known for the time being by its catalogue number—KNM-ER 1470 (Kenya National Museum–East Rudolf 1470). This skull is dated to 2.9 million years, over a million years older than the Olduvai habilines, and yet its volume, about 800 cubic centimeters, is considerably larger than that of *Homo habilis.* This early date for KNM-ER 1470 indicates that the habilines were contemporaries of both the gracile and robust australopithecines, and hence doubt is cast on the view that the graciles were the ancestors of the advanced hominids. Richard Leakey holds that the Lothagam mandible is not a gracile *Australopithecus;* that there never were any graciles in East Africa, only robusts; and that East African materials attributed to the graciles really belong to a lineage of advanced hominids extending

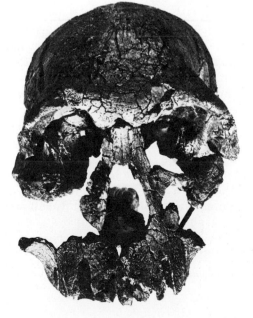

Figure 4-15. KNM-ER 1470. Front view (left) and lateral view (right). (Richard Beaty. Museum Trustees of Kenya)

0 1 2 3 4 5 cm

from Lothagam through KNM-ER 1470 and *Homo habilis* to modern species of the genus *Homo.* This interpretation is supported by F. Clark Howell's assignment of all or nearly all of the extensive hominid remains from Omo dating between 3 million and 1.4 million years to *Australopithecus robustus* (Howell and Wood 1974; Howell and Coppens 1974).* According to Louis Leakey, both robust and South African gracile australopithecines were evolutionary dead ends.

Richard Leakey's evidence for three or four separate phylogenetic lines of hominids living in the same general region for upward of 2 million years has upset traditional views of the forces responsible for the evolution of human beings. For a while, after the discovery of the first australopithecines, these forces seemed self-evident. The proto-humans were small-brained, bipedal animals who had left the safety of the forest to forage, scavenge, and hunt in the grasslands and savannahs. These relatively small animals with their conspicuously small canines had adapted to their habitat by means of manufactured tools and weapons. Dart, the first to discover the australopithecines, thought that they manufactured many different kinds of bone, horn, and tooth implements. With the discovery of very ancient and very simple stone tools—over a million years old—at Olduvai, Ain Henech, Algeria, and in East and South Africa, the probability that the australopithecines were tool-makers increased. Yet the fossil remains of the australopithecines and the stone artifacts were never united at a given site. And Dart's bone-horn-tooth tools were soon dismissed by many authorities as the remains of meal-eating by carnivores rather than tool-making by hominids.

At last, in 1959, Louis Leakey discovered a robust australopithecine skull ("Zinjanthropus") in Bed II at Olduvai, which was surrounded by a variety of choppers, scrapers, hammerstones, and other stone tools. This might have proven once and for all that the australopithecines were the makers of the most ancient tools except for the fact that Leakey also simultaneously discovered the remains of the first *Homo habilis* six inches below (and therefore older than) Zinjanthropus. From this he deduced that the habilines had made the tools and that they had used them to catch and eat Zinjanthropus (and other australopithecines). Stone tools dating much farther back than Olduvai, to 3 million years B.P., were soon found at East Rudolf and Omo. Since these tools were as much as a million years older than the Olduvai habilines, once again they were most plausibly attributed to the australopithecines whose remains were also found at Rudolf and Omo in geological strata of comparable or greater antiquity.

Figure 4-16. ZINJANTHRO-PUS. (Photo of cast courtesy of Wenner-Gren Foundation and with permission of owner, National Museum of Tanzania)

*In 1974 Karl Johanson and Maurice Taieb discovered the teeth and jaw bones of an advanced hominid type in the Awash Valley of Northern Ethiopia, tentatively dated to more than 4 million years B.P. This discovery if authenticated lends further weight to Leakey's theory that the hominid lineage leading to *Homo sapiens* had already emerged at the very beginning of the Pleistocene.

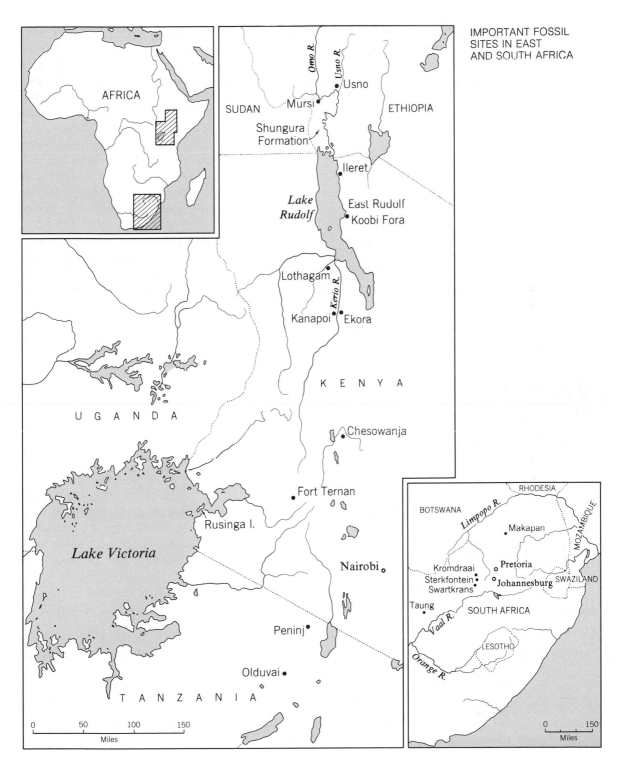

IMPORTANT FOSSIL
SITES IN EAST
AND SOUTH AFRICA

AFRICA

Omo R.

Usno R.

Usno

Mursi

SUDAN

ETHIOPIA

Shungura
Formation

Ileret

**Lake
Rudolf**

East Rudolf
Koobi Fora

Kerio R.

Lothagam

Kanapoi • Ekora

K E N Y A

U G A N D A

Chesowanja

Fort Ternan

Rusinga I.

Lake Victoria

Nairobi

Peninj

Olduvai

T A N Z A N I A

0   50   100   150
Miles

RHODESIA

BOTSWANA

Limpopo R.

Makapan

MOZAMBIQUE

Kromdraai

Sterkfontein
Swartkrans

Pretoria

Johannesburg

SWAZILAND

Taung

SOUTH AFRICA

Vaal R.

LESOTHO

Orange R.

0   150
Miles

Figure 4-17. EXCAVATED ARTIFACTS (ca. 2.0 million years). Lower Omo River Valley, Ethiopia. (H.V. Merrick)

Richard Leakey, however, continued to search for a habiline who was as old as the oldest tools. His discovery of KNM-ER 1470 is evidence that lends weight to his theory that the habilines alone were responsible for the manufacture of the ancient stone implements of East Africa. Nonetheless this interpretation raises more questions than it answers. It is difficult to understand how the australopithecines whose dentition was adapted for milling and grinding could survive in savannah and plain habitats. How did they protect themselves without tools against the predators that preyed upon the plains-dwelling herbivores? And, more puzzling, if the relationship between *Homo habilis* and the australopithecine was that of hunter to hunted, how did the australopithecines survive 2 million years of predation by their tool-using, meat-eating cousins?

One tempting solution to this puzzle is to deny that the difference between habilines and australopithecines ever amounted to a difference above the subspecies level. But this possibility now seems less likely because of the great length of time when the differences apparently remained stable—subspecies, unlike species, cannot remain unchanged for hundreds of thousands of years (see p. 109).

A basic principle of evolutionary ecology, the principle of *competitive exclusion,* states that two species that occupy a single habitat cannot have the same adaptive relationship to their common ecosystem; that is, they cannot feed themselves and live in fundamentally the same way. Whenever several species of primates occupying a common habitat are found, the way in which they exploit that habitat always differs in certain crucial respects. Howler, spider, capuchin, and squirrel monkeys, for example, all share overlapping living space in the rain forests of Colombia. Each species, however, has a distinctive feeding specialty with respect to insects, fruits, leaves, trees, and to the forest floor and canopy (Klein and Klein 1975). If the habilines and australopithecines were separate species or genera, one can assume that the principle of competitive exclusion applied to them. But no definite solution to this problem is presently available. In the meantime, some experts continue to present persuasive arguments in favor of the theory that habilines, robusts, and graciles all belonged to one species (Wolpoff 1974).

Tool Use among Contemporary Monkeys and Apes

Paleontological and archaeological data do not prove definitely that the earliest hominids used tools. But studies of modern-day animals

54

do allow inferences to be made that they did use tools. Such studies favor the conclusion that both the habilines and australopithecines made and used tools.

First, let me define what a tool is: a tool is an object, not part of the user's body, which the user holds or carries during or just prior to use and which is used to alter the form or location of a second object with which it was previously unconnected (cf. Beck 1973). By this definition, when a sea gull opens a clam shell by dropping it on a rock, the rock is not a tool. But when a vulture drops a rock on an egg, the rock, having been carried, is a tool. Similarly, a chimpanzee banging a fruit against a rock is not using a tool; but one that bangs a rock against the fruit *is* using a tool. Many animals will haul up or pull in objects attached to vines or strings. To constitute tool use, the animal itself must create the connection between the vine or the string and the object (by tying, wrapping, or hooking it).

Experimental approaches to behavior show that most mammals and birds are "intelligent" enough to learn to make and use simple tools, under laboratory conditions. Under natural, free-ranging conditions the capacity to make and use tools is expressed less frequently because most organisms can get along quite effectively without having to resort to artificial aids. Natural selection has adapted them to their particular habitat by providing body parts such as snouts, claws, teeth, hooves, and fangs. But natural selection has occasionally favored tool use as a normal mode of adaption even among insects. The wasp *Ammophilia urnaria,* for example, hammers the walls of its burrow with a pebble held in its mandibles. Several species of birds apparently have a predisposition to use tools as a supplement to their beaks. Galapagos finches, for example, break off small twigs and use them to push insects out of inaccessible holes and crannies. Jane Van Lawick-Goodall (1968) has observed Egyptian vultures breaking ostrich eggs by hurling stones at them with their beaks. The Satin bowerbird paints the inside of its nest with the aid of a bark wad held between the tips of its beak. Occasional tool use is reported among mammals: elephants scratching their backs with branches held in their trunks; and sea otters swimming on their backs and breaking shell fish against stones placed on their chests. It is highly probable that all tool-using performances among birds and mammals are dependent upon learning and socialization. Finches reared in isolation, for example, do not acquire the technique of using twigs (cf. Pronko 1969).

Although primates are intelligent enough to make and use tools, their anatomy and normal mode of existence discline them to develop extensive tool-using repertories. The primate's prehensile

Figure 4-18. PEBBLE TOOL AND CHOPPER. (American Museum of Natural History)

Tool Use among Contemporary Monkeys and Apes

Figure 4-19. CHIMPANZEE TERMIT-ING. A stick carefully stripped of leaves is inserted into the nest. The chimpanzee licks off the termites that cling to the stick when it is withdrawn. (Baron Hugo Van Lawick © National Geographic Society)

Figure 4-20. MACHIGUENGA TERMITING. Cultural nature of chimpanzee achievement is made more emphatic by reocurrence of termiting complex as a regular source of food among the Machiguenga Indians of Peru. Same technique is used except that termites are dropped into container. (Orna Johnson)

hand is admirably suited to perform many pushing, pulling, prying operations, but among primate quadrupeds commitment of the hand to tool use is inhibited by the importance of the forelimbs in locomotion. That is probably why the most common tool-using behavior among many different species of monkeys and apes is the repelling of intruders with a barrage of nuts, pine cones, branches, fruits, feces, or stones. Hurling projectiles requires only a momentary loss of the locomotor function of the forelimbs, returning the animal immediately thereafter to full locomotor capacity if flight is required.

Among free-ranging primates the most accomplished tool user is the chimpanzee. Over a period of many years Jane Van Lawick-Goodall has studied the behavior of a single population of free-ranging chimpanzees in the Gombe National Park in Tanzania. One of her most remarkable discoveries was that the chimpanzees "fished" for ants and termites. "Termiting" involves first breaking off a twig or a vine, stripping it of leaves and side branches, and then locating a suitable termite nest. Such a nest is as hard as concrete and impenetrable except for certain thinly covered tunnel entrances. The chimpanzee scratches away the thin covering and inserts the twig. The termites inside bite the end of the twig, and the chimpanzee pulls it out and licks off the termites clinging to it. Especially impressive is the fact that the chimpanzees will prepare the twig first and then carry it in their mouths from nest to nest while looking for a suitable

56

tunnel entrance. "Anting" is done by inserting a similar twig into an underground ant nest, but the ant twigs must be almost twice as long as the termite twigs.

Chimpanzees were also observed to manufacture "sponges" for sopping up water from an inaccessible hollow in a tree. They stripped a handful of leaves from a twig, put the leaves in their mouth, chewed briefly, put the mass of leaves in the water, let them soak, put the leaves to their mouths, and sucked the water off. A similar sponge was employed to dry their fur, to wipe off sticky substances, and to clean the bottoms of chimpanzee babies. Van Lawick-Goodall's chimpanzees also used sticks as levers and digging tools to pry off arboreal ant nests and to widen the entrance of a subterranean bee hive.

Elsewhere other observers have watched chimpanzees in their native habitats pound or hammer tough-skinned fruits, seeds, and nuts with sticks and stones. One subject in the Budongo Forest, Uganda, used a leaf on a twig to fan away flies (Sugiyama 1969).

Chimpanzees appear to go further than other primates in using weapons and projectiles. They hurl stones, feces, and sticks with considerable accuracy. Under semicontrolled conditions they have been observed to wield long clubs with deadly aim. One investigator (Kortlandt 1967) built a stuffed leopard whose head and tail could be moved mechanically. He set the leopard down in open country inhabited by chimpanzees and when the chimpanzees came into view he animated the leopard's parts. The chimpanzees attacked the leopard with heavy sticks, tore it apart, and dragged the remnants off into the bush.

It has long been known that chimpanzees in zoos and laboratories readily develop complex patterns of behavior involving tool use. Provided with a box on which to stand, sticks that fit together, and bananas out of reach, they quickly learn to push the box under the bananas, put the sticks together, stand on the box, and knock down the bananas. Captive chimpanzees will also spontaneously employ sticks to pry open boxes and doors and to break the mesh on their cages. A remarkable spontaneous pattern of social grooming has recently been observed in which Belle, a female chimpanzee at the Delta Regional Primate Station, cleaned her companion's teeth with a pencil-like object manufactured from a twig (McGrew and Tutin 1973).

In the context of the present discussion, the kinds of tool-using behavior that captive primates exhibit outside their native habitat is perhaps even more significant than what they normally do in their natural setting. In order for tool use to become an integral part of an animal's behavioral repertoire, it must contribute to the solution of

57

everyday problems that the animal cannot solve as efficiently by relying on its own body parts. The ease with which chimpanzees and other primates expand their tool-using repertory outside their normal habitat is thus extremely significant for assessing the potential for tool use among the australopithecines and habilines. It seems likely that no radical reorganization of the brain or sharp increase in intelligence was needed for the hominids to expand their tool-using behavior (cf. Beck 1975). The ancestral hominid need not have been one whit "smarter" than the average chimpanzee in order to make regular use of clubs and projectiles to repel predators, stones to smash bones and rip hides, and sticks to dig for roots and tubers. Give an animal the brain of a chimpanzee, free its hands of locomotor functions, grind down its canines and incisors to the level of its molars, and place it in an open savannah in sight of a pride of lions, and you have an animal that could make and use the first stone tools.

Infrahuman Culture

The great evolutionary novelty represented by culture is that the "capabilities and habits" of culture-bearing animals are acquired through social heredity rather than the more ancient process of biological heredity (see p. 164). By "social heredity" is meant the shaping of a social animal's behavior in conformity with information stored in the brains and neural circuits of other members of its society. Such information is not stored in the organism's genes. (Yet it must be stressed that actual cultural responses always depend in part upon genetically predetermined capacities and predispositions.)

There appears to be no specific genetic information that is responsible for chimpanzee termiting. In order for this behavior to occur, the genetically determined capacities for learning, for manipulating objects, and for omnivorous eating must be present in the young chimpanzee. But these general biological capacities and predispositions are inadequate for producing the response. Given nothing but groups of young chimpanzees, twigs, and termite nests, termiting will occur rarely if at all. The missing ingredient is the information about termiting that is stored in the brains and neural circuitry of the adult chimpanzees. This information is displayed to the young chimpanzees in actual termiting performances. Among the Gombe Stream chimpanzees, the young do not begin termiting until they are eighteen to twenty-two months old. At first their behavior is clumsy and inefficient, and they do not become proficient until they are about three years old. Van Lawick-Goodall witnessed many instances of

infants watching intently as the adults termited. Novices often retrieved discarded termiting sticks and attempted to use them on their own. There is thus little doubt that termiting is a habit or custom acquired by chimpanzees as members of society. According to Van Lawick-Goodall,

Figure 4-21. JANE VAN LAWICK-GOODALL. Making friends with a young chimpanzee in Gombe National Park, Tanzania. (Baron Hugo Van Lawick © National Geographic Society)

it seems probable that the use of sticks, stems, and leaves for specific purposes described here represents a series of primitive cultural traditions passed on from one generation to the next in the Gombe Stream area.   [1964:1266]

Examples of rudimentary infrahuman forms of culture are not confined to chimpanzees. As previously noted, experiments with the tool-using finches reveal that if the young birds are not permitted to watch older birds employing twigs as tools, they will not acquire the tool-using habit. Another example is the common white-crowned sparrow of California, which acquires a song dialect characteristic of extremely localized populations. If taken from the nest at birth and raised in pairs separately from their parents, the young fail to develop their parents' dialect. However, if captured between thirty and one hundred days of age and raised in pairs (they won't sing at all alone), their songs resemble the songs of their parents (Marler and Tamura 1964).

The most extensive studies of infrahuman culture have been carried out with Japanese macaques. Primatologists of the Primate Research Institute of Kyoto University have found among local

59

Figure 4-22. JAPANESE MONKEY CULTURE. A female monkey of Koshima troop washing a sweet potato. (Masao Kawai)

monkey troops a wide variety of customs and institutions based on social learning. The males of certain troops, for example, take turns looking after the infants while the infants' mothers are feeding. Such baby-sitting is characteristic only of the troops at Takasaki-yama and Takahashi. Other cultural differences have been noted too. When the monkeys of Takasaki-yama eat the fruit of the *muku* tree, they either throw away the hard stone inside or swallow it and excrete it in their feces. But the monkeys of Arashi-yama break the stone with their teeth and eat the pulpy interior. Some troops eat shellfish; others do not. Cultural differences have also been noted with respect to the characteristic distance that the animals maintain among themselves during feeding and with respect to the order of males, females, and juveniles in line of march when certain troops move through the forest.

The scientists at the Primate Research Institute have been able to observe the actual process by which behavioral innovations spread from individual to individual and become part of a troop's culture independently of genetic transmission. To attract monkeys near the shore for easier observation, sweet potatoes were set on the beach. One day in 1953 a young female began to wash the sand from the sweet potatoes by plunging them in a small brook that ran through the beach. This washing behavior spread throughout the group and gradually replaced the former rubbing habit. Nine years later, 80 to 90 percent of the animals were washing their sweet potatoes, some in the brook, others in the sea. When wheat was spread on the beach, the monkeys of Koshima at first had a hard time separating the kernels from the sand. Soon, however, one of them invented a process for desanding the wheat, and this behavior was taken over by the others. The solution was to plunge the wheat into the water: the wheat floats and the sand drops to the bottom (Itani 1961; Miyadi 1967).

Given the presence of rudimentary cultures among contemporary monkeys and apes, there seems little reason to deny that the australopithecines possessed fairly large repertories of socially conditioned responses including the making and using of tools. This conclusion is consistent with the view of nature that evolution is brought about by the accumulation of small innovations over a long period of time and that transitional forms connect all great transformations with their antecedents. Thus the australopithecines with their combination of small brains and bipedalism and their rudimentary cultures were protohuman not only anatomically but behaviorally as well. Their culture in its time undoubtedly represented an unprecedented degree of dependence upon social learning as a means to survival and reproduction.

Yet in assessing the significance of this early example of cultural adaption, there is no reason to equate rudimentary cultural achievements with the attainment of human status. As knowledge of the chronology of the Pliocene and Pleistocene epochs has improved, the conviction has spread among anthropologists that protohuman cultures persisted relatively unchanged for a staggeringly long time. Casual chimpanzeelike tool-making and tool-using were probably typical of many species of pongids and hominids during the Pliocene. Toward the middle of that epoch, some 5 million years ago, one or

Figure 4-23. JAPANESE MONKEYS WASHING WHEAT. Members of Koshima troop separating wheat from sand by placing mixture in water. Central figure in lower photograph is carrying the mixture in its right hand. Two monkeys in foreground are floating and picking up the wheat. (Masao Kawai — top; Mitsuo Iwamoto — bottom)

more species of bipedal hominids came to rely regularly on tools for food-getting and defense. These hominids, the ancestral australopithecines, were a highly successful evolutionary novelty. Indeed, they endured five times longer than our own species has thus far managed to endure. But during this vast stretch of time the cranial capacity of these creatures remained essentially unchanged. The inference is that the socially conditioned information contained in their neural circuitry was limited by genetic factors. Hence their culture could evolve only within a narrow range of local adaptations. In all probability they lacked the capacity for language behavior and therefore cannot be considered human.

Sexual Dominance and Canine Reduction

One of the most puzzling aspects of the hominid evolutionary trend is why our canines are virtually useless as weapons. One explanation of this phenomenon posits a kind of atrophy of the front teeth as the ground-dwelling hominids came to rely more and more on artificial tools and weapons. But why should the front teeth have lost their utility as weapons merely because cultural weapons became available? If brandishing a club could discourage predators, brandishing inch-long canines would enhance the effect. A simple but elegant solution to this problem is now available: large canines would have interfered with the rotary grinding and milling action of the hominid molars. Once the front teeth were no longer useful as tools and weapons, artificial substitutes would have been used more often. The reduction of the front teeth was therefore probably, like bipedalism, a precondition rather than an effect of the increased reliance on cultural tools and weapons.

The small size of the front teeth may have been connected with a general reduction in the height, weight, and strength difference between hominid males and females as compared with differences between terrestrial, anthropoid males and females. Baboon males, for example, weigh twice as much as the females. Furthermore, male baboons use their canines as much to intimidate females, juveniles, and subordinate male members of their own group as to defend the group against external dangers.

The small hominid canines may thus be part of a fundamental shift in social relationships between anthropoid males and females and between males and juveniles. The comparability of the front teeth of men and women is part of the general hominid trend away from genetically controlled expressions of dominance and subordination

62

Figure 4-24. YELLOW BABOON *(PAPIOCYNOCEPHALUS)*, SUBORDER *ANTHROPOIDEA*, SUPERFAMILY *CERCOPITHECOIDEA*. Baboons are of great interest to anthropologists because, like *Homo*, they have largely abandoned their ancestral arboreal habitat for life on the ground. (Mark Boulton/National Audubon Society)

characteristic of our pongid cousins. This in turn implies a heightened level of cooperative behavior between hominid males and females, especially in joint provisioning of infants and juveniles. As pointed out in Chapter 3, human beings are the only primates whose males regularly expend a significant portion of their energy in obtaining food that is eaten by females and juveniles. Chimpanzees come closest to us. As reported by Van Lawick-Goodall, chimpanzees frequently beg food from each other. But the outcome is uncertain:

A begging individual may reach out to touch the food or the lips of the possessor of the food, or he may hold out his hand toward him (palm up), sometimes uttering small whimpers. . . . The response to such gestures varied according to the individuals involved and the amount of food. Often the possessor pulled the food away from the begging individual or threatened him. . . . Almost always when chimpanzees held their hands to the mouth of the possessor, the latter eventually responded by pushing out a half-chewed lump of food. . . .   [1972:79]

In all known preagricultural human societies, food is shared regularly without "begging"; only advanced "civilized" societies have "beggars" (see Ch. 19).

Human food-sharing practices have obvious adaptive advantages for group survival during times of critical shortages. Human females continue to provision their children long after nursing ceases. And

63

instead of monopolizing available resources, the males continue to provision females and juveniles upon whom the breeding integrity of the group depends. Why, one wonders, should this system be so rare among primates? Part of the answer is that the entire social life of most primate species is regulated by elaborate dominance hierarchies that are based in turn on genetically determined expressions of dominance and subordination. These hierarchies control the level of intragroup violence and facilitate joint foraging and group defense, but they are incompatible with sharing and cooperative provisioning, especially when food is scarce. Although every human group has patterns of dominance and subordination, human hierarchies are based on factors other than the size of our teeth, the weight of our bodies, or the ferocity of our frowns. Among most primates the weaker animals in the hierarchy must give way to the stronger ones, infants and juveniles to adults, females to males. Hence food-sharing (nursing infants excepted) usually occurs only when weaker animals are forced to give up their food to stronger ones. Among hominids the remarkable reverse of this practice, whereby the strong regularly give to the weak, must have involved a profound change in the endocrine glands and the neural circuitry controlling aggression. This in turn was probably associated with the transference of intraspecies aggression from genetic to socially learned behavior. This corresponds in large measure to what women's liberationists mean when they declare: "anatomy is not destiny" (see p. 610). When humans, male or female, act in an intolerant, selfish, and brutal fashion it is for reasons that have little to do with human nature.

Loss of Instinctual Controls over Aggression

Most mammals on occasion exhibit aggressive behavior toward members of their own social group or species. Primates in particular indulge in much intragroup fighting; but under natural conditions aggressive encounters within monkey and ape societies seldom lead to fatalities. For the most part orderly relations within primate groups are maintained by displays of threatening behavior rather than by actual combat.

Among many primates aggressive displays include raising the hair on the back of the neck and arms so as to give the attacker an oversize appearance; specific cries or grunts indicating preparation for threat or attack; and shaking boughs, and hurling leaves, feces, or other objects in the direction of the offending animal. The transition from threat to attack is often postponed with instinctual signs of submis-

64

sion: vocal indications of fear and submission, running away, aversion of the eyes, and presentation of the rump as if for sexual intercourse. If these signals prove inadequate to prevent an aggressive charge, the attacker rarely presses the advantage to the point of incapacitating or killing the weaker animal. As Konrad Lorenz (1966) has suggested, aggression of this sort had a high survival value for the group: once the dominance order has been established, intragroup fighting and the amount of dead or injured individuals are kept to a minimum. The key to this result is that aggressive rage is switched off by built-in neural circuits when the victim shows signs of submission or injury. It is evident that at some point in the evolution of human nature, the genetic basis for both initiating and stopping aggressive behavior was either entirely lost or relegated to insignificance compared with socially acquired controls over aggressive behavior.

No one needs to be reminded of the ferocity that human beings sometimes exhibit in their attacks on one another. Nothing could be more misleading, however, than to attribute human sexual dominance, aggression, homicide, and war to instinctual mechanisms. To be sure, the rage we experience in certain kinds of combat is controlled by involuntary neural and hormonal systems similar to those of all mammals. When testosterone (male hormone) and adrenalin are mobilized within the body, patterns of aggressive action become probable. But the conditions that provoke the mobilization of our body's machinery of aggression are not closely related to any definite set of social situations. When an American housewife serves her dinner guests first and her husband last, the hair on the back of the host's neck remains unruffled. The mail carrier coming up the walk stirs the homeowner's dog to a display of aggressive barking, but the human residents do not bother to look up from their television sets. A female gorilla who stares too long into her mate's eyes risks being cuffed or stomped on. In certain human contexts staring is considered rude or dangerous, but children make a game of trying to outstare each other, and lovers find their ardor increased by prolonged staring into each other's eyes. The complete breakdown of innate controls over human aggressiveness can be witnessed in any dentist's office. Fully intact humans voluntarily seat themselves in the dentist's chair, open their jaws wide, and permit themselves to suffer excruciating pain, without giving so much as a nip to the offending hand. This result is possible because our interpretation of whether a situation calls for the mobilization of the body's machinery of rage and aggression has passed almost entirely under the control of complex, nonhereditary, learned patterns of thought and feeling.

Further evidence of the nonhereditary basis of human aggressive

65

behavior is found in the unique ability of human beings to kill one another without having been directly offended or threatened by their victims. Executioners, generals, and other specialists in killing human beings perform their socially defined functions best when they kill according to a plan rather than in response to atavistic emotions. Millions of Jews met their fate at the hands of Nazi technicians who turned valves and went about their business unruffled by any strong emotions. Blind "instinctual" rage is completely incompatible with the mass killing that modern warfare involves. A rifleman who is trembling with rage will not hit his target, and to fire rockets and mortars the artilleryman must remain cool.

The culmination of the unique human capacity to kill without instinctual rage occurs when aggressor and victim never come into each other's presence. Primate patterns of aggressive displays and attacks cannot be used to explain the behavior of bomber crews, who never see the people whom they annihilate.

Perhaps the most distinctively human consequence of the loss of genetic controls over aggression is the inability of the human victim to influence an aggressor by showing signs of submission. Monkeys and apes respond automatically to signals of defeat and appeasement, and when a subordinate chimpanzee is threatened by a dominant chimpanzee, it crouches, squeaks, whimpers, presents the rump, and walks backward toward the aggressor, grinning over its shoulder. The aggressor not only stops the attack but may even pat or embrace the subordinate animal. Under natural conditions, if a wounded or threatened primate makes a consistent attempt to flee, it is seldom if ever pursued and killed. There is nothing in the repertory of primate behavior comparable to the shooting of a mother and child on their knees begging for their lives to be spared. So, when we blame murder and war on our alleged aggressive instinct, we distort what is most fundamental in human nature viewed in evolutionary perspective. Monkeys and apes seldom commit anything resembling murder and never engage in anything resembling war precisely because their aggressive behavior is instinctual. Our problem is that our capacity to hurt and kill has passed beyond the control of instinct. Our aggressive behavior can only be turned on or off by culture. And that is why we are the world's most dangerous animal (Givens 1975).

Hunting and Human Nature

The theory that the earliest hominids derived a portion of their food supply from hunting other animals has inspired popular authors to ponder the significance of our alleged "hunting instincts." Playwright Robert Ardrey wrote a best seller entitled *African Genesis* on the theme that the australopithecines, unlike all previous "apes," were killers armed with lethal weapons. According to Ardrey, we are a "predator whose natural instinct is to kill with a weapon" (1961:316). In rebuttal it should be noted that the shift to hunting among the australopithecines or habilines need not have produced a nature any more fierce or bloodthirsty than that of contemporary apes and monkeys, most of whom readily take to diets that include meat. In addition, it is now known that chimpanzees as well as baboons and other primates occasionally attack and eat terrestrial animals. During a year of observation near Gelgil, Kenya, Robert Harding (1975) observed 47 small vertebrates being killed and eaten by baboons. Their most common prey were infant gazelles and antelopes. Over the course of a decade, chimpanzees of the Gombe National Park are known to have eaten 95 small animals—mostly infant baboons, monkeys, and bush pigs (Teleki 1973). Chimpanzee meat-eating and terrestrial-hunting has been observed in both forested and semi-forested habitats (Suzuki 1975). It is virtually certain therefore that the ancestral hominids were to some degree "hunters." But the extent and nature of this hunting remains very much in doubt, as does its significance for the evolution of culture.

The logical place to look for evidence of hunting as a major source of subsistence among the ancestral hominids is in their mouths. Mammals that consume large quantities of meat as part of their basic evolutionary adaptation have an unmistakable dental pattern: large canine teeth for puncturing and ripping; enlarged premolars shaped

Figure 4-25. CHIMPANZEE MEAT EATING. Two chimps devour a young baboon in Gombe National Park, Tanzania. (Geza Teleki)

like long, narrow blades for shearing and cutting; and small, narrow molars. For example, inspection of a convenient domestic cat (in the unlikely event that you can get it to open its mouth) will reveal only one small molar in each quadrant. Nothing could be more ill-suited to the needs of a "killer ape" than the set of twelve massive, high-crowned, flat "grinders" possessed by both habilines and australopithecines and, to a lesser extent, by *Homo sapiens.* These are clearly the dental features of an animal with superherbivore rather than supercarnivore affinities.

It has been said that the possession of tools and weapons rendered a carnivorous dental pattern superfluous, and this is obviously true for more recent phases of hominid existence. But what the "killer-ape" hunting theory asserts is that hunting and killing were the primordial forces shaping human nature. As shall be shown in a moment, for 3 million years, from the oldest tools at Rudolf and Omo to Bed II at Olduvai, there is no evidence of improvements in technology related to hunting. Hunting technology, in other words, remained rudimentary for millions of years. Hence if hunting were the primary adaptive mode of these ancestral hominids, it is inconceivable that their dentition would have evolved in a direction contrary to what would have been useful for puncturing, slicing, and chewing meat. As Clifford Jolly (1970) has put it: "The obvious way out of the dilemma is to set aside the current obsession with hunting and carnivorousness, and to look for an alternative activity which is associated with 'open-country' life but which is functionally consistent with the anatomy of the basal hominids."

As mentioned previously (p. 36), Jolly believes that the alternative activity was grass- and seed-eating. Like chimpanzees, our ancestors must occasionally have caught and eaten small vertebrates. But intensive patterns of hunting involving effective weaponry and the regular pursuit of big game may not have become a characteristic hominid activity until long after the protohumans had evolved into the first humans.

Studies of modern *Homo sapiens* hunting peoples also throw doubt on the theory of the hunting killer-ape. With the exception of the Eskimo and other arctic peoples, contemporary "hunters" are hunter-gatherers (one should really say, "gatherer-hunters,"), and by far the major share of food calories and most of the protein of these populations comes from the gathering and collecting of roots, fibers, seeds, fruits, nuts, grubs, frogs, lizards, and insects (see Ch. 12). Based on analogies with what is actually known about the way contemporary hunter-gatherers live, it is likely that the earliest expansion of hominid cultural technology involved improvements in items such as

68

containers (skin bags?) and digging implements rather than weapons of the hunt. Conceivably the earliest stone implements may have been used to manufacture *dibbles,* branches sharpened at one end for digging out wild roots and tubers. Lacking claws for digging or snouts for rooting, ground dwelling hominids could not have exploited this valuable source of food without tools. Unfortunately, because wood and skin are perishable, digging instruments and containers dating back to the Pliocene-Pleistocene boundary are unlikely to be found. Other wooden implements, such as clubs, spears, and levers, could also have been manufactured by the protohumans without leaving a trace in the fossil or archaeological record.

The possible importance of digging implements to the australopithecines can be extrapolated from the study of plains-dwelling baboons, the most fully terrestrial of the quadrupedal primates. Baboons fail to exploit rich sources of food to which a tool-using biped would have access. Observations of baboons living in relatively treeless country indicate that 90 percent of their food intake consists of grass. Baboons spend long hours during the dry season digging with their fingers to get at roots. Sometimes, when the surface grass has been heavily grazed by ungulates, these roots become critical to baboons for survival. To get at large bulbs and roots lying some fifteen inches below the surface, baboons must dig for as long as twenty minutes. "The use of a simple digging stick or a sharp stone would enormously increase their efficiency in extracting their food from the

Figure 4-26. BABOONS DIGGING FOR ROOTS. Baboon hands are poor digging instruments. Why don't they use a stick? (DeVore/Anthro-Photo)

69

Hunting and Human Nature

Figure 4-27. BUSHMAN HUNTER. Digging for roots after an unsuccessful day of hunting. (DeVore/Anthro-Photo)

ground, but no baboons were ever observed to use a tool in this or any other way" (DeVore and Washburn 1963).

Originally the theory of the hunting killer-ape relied on Dart's interpretation of bone fragments found at the South African australopithecine sites. Because of the preponderance of limb bones with jagged edges and sharp points, Dart concluded that they were hunting weapons. Subsequent research, however, has shown that similar assemblages of bone fragments can be produced by the combined action of scavengers, predators, and natural processes (Brain 1975).

Currently the best evidence concerning meat-eating during australopithecine and habiline times comes from Bed I at Olduvai. Animal bones found in association with stone tools leave no doubt that some or all of the protohuman hominids were eating meat. Most of the bones, however, are from medium-size antelopes and pigs, although some large animals such as giraffes, buffalo, and pachyderms are also represented. No one knows if the tool-makers killed all or any of these

Hunting and Human Nature

animals. If they killed the animals, no one knows how it was done. None of the tools are hunting weapons. There are no projectile heads. Yet so great is the urge among some of our fellow humans to believe that our ancestors were hunters and killers that they even imagine australopithecines attacking elephants by biting them in the leg. The most plausible interpretation of the earliest big-game butchery sites is that our ancestors scavenged carcasses left over from kills made by carnivores or attacked old and dying animals that had trapped themselves in the mud.

The best indication of hunting consists of stone artifacts in association with large numbers of bones from one or two species. Such sites can be interpreted as evidence of ancient drives or stampedes with animals mired in mud or trapped in cul-de-sacs; the hunters might then have clubbed or speared them to death. The earliest sites with these characteristics are Olduvai Bed II; Olorgesailie, Kenya; and Torralba and Ambrona, Spain. All of these, however, have Middle Pleistocene dates, 1.5 million years or considerably younger, and hence do not furnish evidence of hunting during the main stretch of protohuman existence. Moreover the interpretation of these sites as scenes of deliberate stampedes or entrapments is by no means unequivocal since the accumulation of bones in a swamp or bog might represent a low level of predation operating over decades or centuries. In this connection it is important to point out that many ancient tool

Figure 4-28. STONE TOOLS ON LIVING FLOOR AT OLORGESAILIE. Glynn Isaac on right. (DeVore/Anthro-Photo)

HUMAN EVOLUTION SITES

CHINA
1. Choukoutien, Hopei,
2. Kangwengling, Shenshi pro.
3. Yunnan province
4. Mapa, Kwantung province

BORNEO, Island of
5. Niah Cave, Sarawak

JAVA, Island of
6. Trinil and Djetis

INDIA
7. Siwalik Hills

IRAQ
8. Shanidar Cave

ISRAEL
9. Amud (Sea of Galilee)
10. Mount Carmel
11. Hazorea

EGYPT
12. Fayum

SUDAN
13. Singa

ETHIOPIA
14. Lake Omo

KENYA
15. Lake Rudolf
16. Fort Ternan
17. Olorgesaille
18. Lothogam Hill

TANZANIA
19. Olduvai Gorge
20. Gombe Stream Reserve

SOUTH AFRICA
21. Makapansgat
22. Kromdraii
23. Sterkfontein
24. Taung
25. Florisbad
26. Swartkrans
27. Nelson's Bay
28. Saldanha Bay

LIBYA
29. Hava Fteh

ALGERIA
30. Ternefine
31. Ain Henech

MOROCCO
32. Jebel Ighoud

SPAIN
33. Bañolas
34. Torralba-Ambrona

Areal Scale 1: 100.000.000²

GREECE
35. Petralona

YUGOSLAVIA
36. Krapina

HUNGARY
37. Vértesszőllős

ITALY
38. Monte Circeo
39. Quinzano
40. Saccopastore

CZECHOSLOVAKIA
41. Stranska
42. Gánovce

GERMANY
43. Ehringsdorf
44. Steinheim
45. Heidelberg
46. Neander Valley
47. Lehringen

FRANCE
48. Tautevel
49. Le Lazaret

50. Montmaurin
51. Orgnac-l'Aven
52. Fontechevade
53. Monsempron
54. La Chapelle-Aux-Saints
55. Le Moustier
56. Vallonet
57. La Chaise
58. St. Acheul

BELGIUM
59. Namur-Spy

ENGLAND
60. Clacton-on-Sea
61. Swanscombe

73

sites show few animal bones and that some have no bones at all. Thus the Olorgesailie and Olduvai instances may simply provide evidence of sporadic and intermittent activity dependent on the fortuitous conjunction of hunters, animals, and natural traps. In general, given the relative durability of bone and perishability of plant foods, the archaeological record inevitably tends to convey a picture of exaggerated carnivorous proclivities. Isaac (1971) concludes that "hunting has seldom if ever been in any exclusive sense the staff of hominid life":

The archaeological record, such as it is, appears more readily compatible with models of human evolution that stress broadly based subsistence patterns rather than those involving intensive and voracious predation.

The notion that hominids have an innate lust for hunting and killing is often used to explain such activities as hunting for sport, bull-fighting, gladiatorial spectacles, public torture, public execution, and war down through the ages. But none of these activities can be accounted for by invoking innate lusts. In the broad sweep of history and ethnography, opposite or contradictory patterns of behavior are just as characteristic of human behavior (cf. Montagu 1968). For every hunter there is bird-watcher; for every beef-eater, a vegetarian. The widespread practice of keeping animals for pets and of sometimes risking human life to preserve the lives of dogs and cats scarcely suggests the existence of a killer instinct. Moreover it is difficult to imagine how the first momentous steps toward the domestication of animals such as cattle, sheep, and goats could have taken place if *Homo sapiens* has uncontrollable urges to hunt and kill (see p. 194). For every act of torture and murder committed by human beings, there probably exists at least one other of kindness, love, and tenderness. It is doubtful that more people have been exhilarated by killing others or by watching others being killed than have found such events abhorrent, sickening, and terrifying. Human beings have an enormous potential for sympathizing with one another's painful experiences, especially if the suffering is directly observed and close at hand. The recent books that have attempted to assign responsibility for war and cruelty to our protohuman ancestors ignore the main facts of hominid evolution. Culture has not been brutalized by the ape in men and women; rather, the ape in men and women has been brutalized by culture. To end war and cruelty, it is culture and not human nature that must be changed.

THE FIRST HUMAN
BEINGS

When did the transition from protohuman to human status take place? No precise date can be given. But it can be narrowed down to some time within the past few "seconds" of geological time. The fossil record shows that between 300,000 and 100,000 years B.P., hominids with human-size brains were evolving in many parts of Eurasia and Africa. But these hominids had crania and vocal tracts unlike our own. Hence, the neural and anatomical bases of their language competence may not yet have reached human levels. But between 75,000 and 40,000 B.P. intensive selection for human language competence can be inferred from fossils and artifacts, and few would deny that by 30,000 B.P. people whose nature was no different from our own lived throughout Eurasia and Africa. By then our subspecies, *Homo sapiens sapiens,* had become, for better or worse, the sole surviving beneficiary and custodian of 15 million years of natural and cultural evolution within the family *Hominidae.* This chapter tells the story of how the hominids finally became human.

Cradles of Humanity and Gardens of Eden

The prominence of African localities in the study of protohuman species that lived between 3 and 1 million years B.P. has led to the popular idea that Africa was the "birthplace" or "cradle" of humanity. This idea, however, implies a lack of understanding of the adaptive processes responsible for hominid evolution. It neglects evidence that

Figure 5-1. CHRONOLOGICAL RELATIONSHIP OF PRINCIPAL PLEISTOCENE HOMINID FOSSILS

Million Years B. P.		European Glaciations	EUROPE: Fossil Beds	EUROPE: Fossils	SOUTH EAST ASIA: Fossil Beds and Caves	SOUTH EAST ASIA: Fossils	EAST ASIA: Caves	EAST ASIA: Fossils
.010	Upper Pleistocene	Warm						
.035		Cold		Cro-Magnon			Upper Cave	H. sapiens sapiens
.050		Warm			Niah Cave	H. sapiens sapiens		
.075		Cold		Classic Neandertals		Solo (Archaic H. Sapiens)		
.125	Middle Pleistocene	Warm		Archaic H. sapiens				Mapa (Archaic H. sapiens)
.145		Cold						
.300		Warm		Steinheim Swanscombe				
.400		Cold		Vértesszöllös (Homo erectus)			Lower Cave Choukoutien	Sinanthropus (H. erectus)
.700		Warm		Mauer (Homo erectus)	Trinil	Pithecanthropus I, II, III, VI, VII, VIII (H. erectus)		
1.		Cold		Prezletice (Homo erectus)				
1.3		Warm	Calabrian					
1.75	Lower Pleistocene	Cold				?		Lantian (H. erectus ?)
2.		Warm			Djetis	Pithecanthropus V (modjokertensis)		
2.5		Cold	Villafranchian			Pithecanthropus IV Meganthropus		
3.								
4.	Pliocene							
5.								

EAST AFRICA		SOUTH AFRICA		NORTH AFRICA	MIDDLE EAST		
Fossil Beds	Fossils	Caves	Fossils	Fossils	Fossils	European Glaciations	Million Years B. P.
							.010
				Singa	Skhūl		.035
					Amud		
					Tabūn		
					Shanidar		.050
						Würm	.075
							.125
	Omo-Kibish and Rhodesian (Archaic H. sapiens)		Saldanha (archaic H. sapiens)			Riss	.145
							.300
						Mindel*	.400
Olduvai IV	OH 12 (H. erectus)			Atlanthropus (H. erectus)	Hazorea (H. erectus)		.700
III							
	OH 9 (H. erectus)					Günz*	1.
II	Zinjanthropus (A. robustus)						1.3
I	Habilis	Kromdraai Swartkrans	Telanthropus (H. erectus)			Donau*	1.75
			Australopithecus robustus				2.
East Rudolf .							2.5
	KNM-ER 1470	Sterkfontein Makapansgat	Australopithecus africanus				3.
							4.
Omo (Shungura)	Lothagam						5.

*"These terms are so highly controversial that usage...should be discontinued." (Bützer 1971:23)

Figure 5-2. *HOMO MOD-JOKERTENSIS. Pithecanthropus V.* (Photo of cast courtesy of Wenner-Gren Foundation and with permission of owner, G.H.R. von Koenigswald)

indicates that from the beginning of the Miocene hominids were present on all the continents of the Old World. Given the occurrence of *Ramapithecus* in Spain, India, and China, as well as in Kenya, it is not unlikely that the first australopithecines and habilines had a similarly extensive range. At any rate, after 2 million years B.P. Africa ceases to have a monopoly on known protohuman sites. Primitive fossil hominids have been found in China and Java with dates roughly equal to Bed I at Olduvai (1,900,000 ± 400,000 B.P.). One of these called *Homo modjokertensis,* was found in Java and is an infant skull with a cranial volume in the 700–800 cubic centimeter range. It has been likened to the Olduvai and East Rudolf habilines. Another, represented by the fragment of a gigantic mandible with three teeth and two other mandibular fragments, is reminiscent of the robust australopithecines (Von Koenigswald and Tobias 1964). It bears the name *Meganthropus paleojavanicus* "giant from early Java." In East Central China a skull cap and upper jaw that may be as old as 1.5 million years has been found at Lantian, Shensi. Its endocranial volume—750–800 cubic centimeters—is suggestive of a habiline or more advanced phase.

After 1,500,000 B.P. the story of human evolution unfolds as much in East Asia and Southern Europe as in Africa. If the genus *Homo* had a "cradle," it was at least ten thousand miles long. And, if the species *Homo sapiens* had a "Garden of Eden," it occupied almost the whole of the Old World and was covered with ice and snow as well as tropical fruit trees.

Homo Erectus

Between 2,500,000 and 750,000 B.P. some of the australopithecines and habilines evolved into a bigger brained genus of hominids called *Homo erectus.* This evolution occurred gradually but at different rates in different parts of the Old World. The most obvious difference between *Homo erectus* and the earlier hominids is the increased cranial volume—an average of over 800 cubic centimeters as compared with about 650 cubic centimeters for the habilines and considerably less for the australopithecines. At the lower end, the *Homo erectus* endocranial volumetric range overlaps with that of habilines; at its upper end, it overlaps with that of *Homo sapiens.*

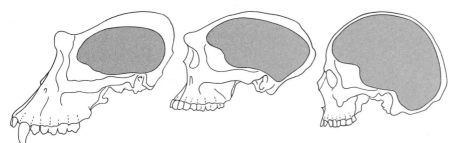

Figure 5-3. CRANIAL CAVITIES. Gorilla (left), *Homo erectus* (middle) and *Homo sapiens* (right).

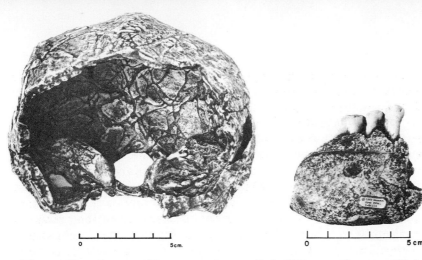

Figure 5-4. *PITHECAN-THROPUS IV* (left).
Figure 5-5. *MEGANTHRO-PUS* (right).
(Figures 5-4 and 5-5. Photos of casts courtesy of the Wenner-Gren Foundation and with permission of the owner, G. H. R. von Koenigswald)

The earliest known *Homo erectus,* called *Pithecanthropus IV,* is from the Djetis beds in Java. Unlike the australopithecines, this specimen has a marked canine diastema in its upper jaw—a distinctly pongid trait.

So marked are the primitive features of *Homo erectus,* that Eugene Dubois, the Dutch scientist who found the first skull cap in 1891, decided that it belonged to an ape rather than a hominid—hence the original nomenclature, *Pithecanthropus erectus* ("upright ape-man").

In Java, *Pithecanthropus I, II, III, IV, V, VI, VII,* and *VIII* are now known. All except *Pithecanthropus IV* and *V* are from Trinil beds (*V* is *modjokertensis*), which overlie the Djetis beds and date from 750,000 to about 500,000 B.P. (Pilbeam 1975). During this span *Homo erectus* underwent a significant cranial expansion culminating in *Pithecanthropus VIII,* the largest of the series, whose cranial volume is in excess of 1,029 cubic centimeters (Sartono 1975).

Homo erectus in China was originally identified as *Sinanthropus pekinensis.* About fifty individuals represented by cranial and dental fragments have been found at Choukoutien, near Peking; hence the name "Peking China man." Cranial volume starts toward the upper end of the Java pithecanthropine range. It averages about 1,050 cubic centimeters with an upper limit of 1,300 cubic centimeters, which is close to the present-day human average. The cranial vault bones are

Figure 5-6. *HOMO EREC-TUS.* Male from Java (left) and female from Peking (right).

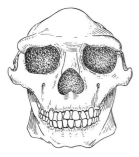
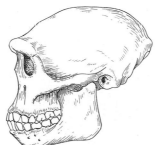
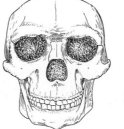
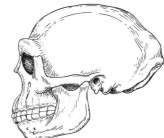

Java Homo erectus (male)   China Homo erectus (female)

thinner than those of the Java pithecanthropines; the brow ridges somewhat reduced; and the area behind the temple, less pinched. But other features clearly align the Choukoutien fossils with *Homo erectus* of Java and elsewhere: the low, elongated cranial vault; prominent brow ridges; heavy chinless jaw; and prognathic face. Although accurate dating has not been achieved, there is general agreement that these fossils are not as old as the Javanese and that they derive from the period between 700,000 and 300,000 B.P.

Homo erectus has been found in three different parts of Africa. In the north, large chinless jaws formerly assigned to the genus *Atlanthropus* were recovered at Ternifine, Algeria, with dates estimated to be no older than 800,000 B.P. Cranial volume of the North African *Homo erectus* is calculated to have been as high as 1,300 cubic centimeters.

For many years J. T. Robinson had argued that a mandible discovered at Swartkrans, and to which he gave the name *Telanthropus,* was more advanced than the robust australopithecines found at that site. *Telanthropus* was probably an early South African version of *Homo erectus* (Clarke, Howell, and Brain 1970). The date is uncertain, but it is possibly as early as *Pithecanthropus* in Java.

Olduvai Gorge is the third place in Africa where *Homo erectus* has been found. Olduvai Hominid 9 from upper Bed II (900,000 B.P. to 1,000,000 B.P.) has the characteristic thick vault bones, sloping forehead, and massive supraorbitals plus a cranial volume of about 1,067 cubic centimeters. In Bed IV the skull fragments of Olduvai Hominid 12 have also been assigned to *Homo erectus.* The thick vault bones and relatively small cranial volume of OH12, estimated at 727 cubic centimeters, present an unsolved problem since OH 12 may be as much as 500,000 years more recent than OH 9. Also from Bed IV is a femur (upper leg bone) that strongly resembles the Asian *Homo erectus* femur that dates to a comparable age, 500,000 B.P. (Day and Molleson 1973). *Homo erectus* has also been tentatively identified in the Middle East. While deep plowing in 1967, members of the Israeli kibbutz Hazorea uncovered cranial fragments that match those of *Homo erectus* in the Far East. These bones probably date somewhere between 700,000 and 500,000 B.P.

Finally, turning to Europe, there are several sites at which the bones of *Homo erectus* have been provisionally identified: Prězletice, Czechoslovakia (a tooth fragment); Vértesszöllös, Hungary (occipital fragments); Petralona, Greece (cranial fragments); and Mauer, Germany (mandible with teeth). Although stone tools found at the Grotte du Vallonet on the French Riviera indicate that hominids were active in Europe as early as 1,000,000 B.P., the bones of European *Homo*

80

erectus appear to date primarily from 700,000 to 400,000 B.P. More-over many authorities argue that some or all of the candidates for European *Homo erectus* status are more advanced than the Far Eastern pithecanthropines of comparable age and belong in a taxon intermediate between *Homo erectus* and *Homo sapiens.*

Homo Erectus Cultures

The spread of *Homo erectus* over so large a portion of Eurasia and Africa coincided with the gradual disappearance of the aus-tralopithecines and habilines as a result of evolutionary processes. The precise phylogenetic pathways and relationships among these protohuman species are not known. But it seems clear that *Homo erectus* possessed a higher capacity for cultural behavior than any of the habilines or australopithecines.The reduction in the number of separate hominid lineages by 500,000 B.P. suggests that the hominids were subject to intense selection for more complex and efficient tool use and socially acquired patterns of subsistence based on coopera-tion, division of labor, and food-sharing. With the spread of *Homo erectus* genes, culture began to evolve and to diversify, and became a source of adaptive change no less vital to hominid reproductive success than the hominid gene pool itself.

At Olduvai this new kind of evolution unfolds through successive beds containing changing inventories of stone implements and cul-tural debris. The culture represented in the oldest deposits (Beds I and II) is called the *Oldowan.* Some 537 stone tools have thus far been removed from Beds I and II, of which about half fall into the category called choppers, with eight other types accounting for the remainder.

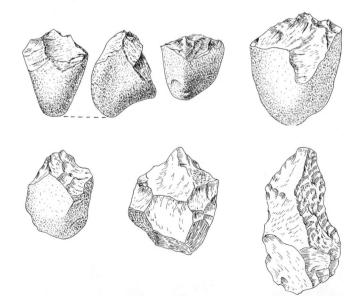

Figure 5-7. CHOPPERS (top), BIFACES (bottom left) AND ACHEULIAN HAND AX (bottom right). Found at Ol-duvai Gorge.

The choppers and other heavy-duty tools were made from waterworn lava pebbles. In the manufacture of choppers, one end of the pebble was smashed against a convenient rock, producing a sharp edge in the simplest and most effortless manner conceivable. Although Oldowan tool assemblages persist with relatively little change through Beds I through IV, a more advanced tool tradition makes its appearance starting in the middle of Bed II about 750,000 B.P. This is called the *Acheulian,* and its characteristic implements are *bifaces*—pebbles and/or large flakes that are worked on both sides to produce a variety of well-formed cutting, scraping, and piercing edges and points. Of these, the most typical is the *hand ax,* a multipurpose instrument that probably evolved out of the Oldowan chopper—although not necessarily at Olduvai itself (M. Leakey 1975).

While Oldowan toolmakers simply modified the circumference of pebbles in their effort to produce a tool, Acheulian craftsmen usually completely transformed pebbles, chunks, or large flakes so that it is now often impossible to determine on what kind or shape of object a finished hand-axe was made.   [Butzer 1971:437]

Figure 5-8. Olduvai Gorge. (DeVore/Anthro-Photo File)

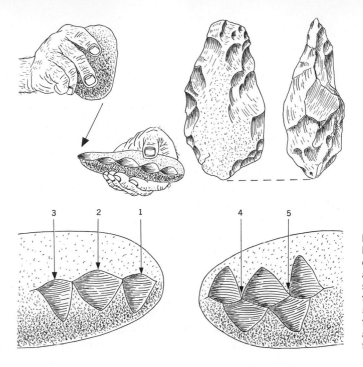

Figure 5-9. BIFACE MANU-FACTURE. Core is held in one hand and blows 1, 2, 3 are delivered with hammer stone held in other. Core is turned over and blows 4 and 5 are delivered creating cutting edge. Acheulian hand ax (upper right) was made in this manner.

Acheulian implements similar to those found at Olduvai Gorge form part of a widespread stone tool tradition, named after the site in France where such tools were first identified. Acheulian hand axes have been found over an enormous area extending throughout Africa, Northwestern, Southern, and Southeastern Europe, the Middle East, and Southern Asia as far east as the Indian states of Bihar and Orissa. They also occur sporadically in the Pajitanian culture of Java. Hand axes were probably multipurpose instruments that served to break soil and roots, to hack off branches, and to dismember game. The Acheulian tool kit usually also included smaller flake instruments for trimming wood, cutting meat and sinew, and scraping hides. Such flakes are the natural by-products of the manufacture of biface tools.

The advancing cultural achievements of *Homo erectus* are also indicated by the food refuse found at Acheulian sites; the bones of elephants, horses, wild cattle, and other large mammals are common. Some of these animals were probably killed with wooden spears fashioned by flake tools. At Clacton in Essex, England, the 300,000-year-old forepart of a yew-wood lance whose tip may have been hardened by fire is the earliest evidence of such spears. This fragment resembles a complete eight-foot yew-wood fire-hardened lance found at Lehringen embedded between the ribs of an extinct type of elephant that lived in West Germany at 125,000 B.P. There is also a resemblance to pieces of pine wood found at the Torralba site, whose age is comparable to the Clacton specimen (Butzer 1971).

83

Homo Erectus Cultures

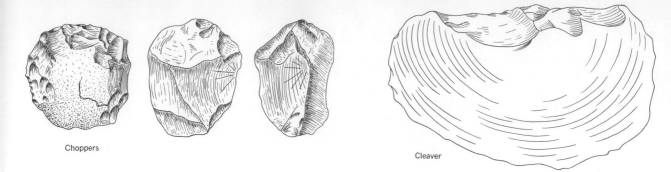

Choppers

Cleaver

Flakes

Figure 5-10. IMPLEMENTS FROM SINANTHROPUS LEV-ELS·OF CHOUKOUTIEN CAVE.

At Choukoutien *Homo erectus* also seems to have hunted large mammals. Here the debris includes bones of deer, bison, horse, rhinoceros, elephant, bear, hyena, and tiger. But hand axes are conspicuously absent at Choukoutien as in most of East and Southeast Asia. The stone tools at Choukoutien are in the tradition of rough and improvised flakes and choppers. It is not until the appearance of *Homo sapiens* that stone tools of workmanship comparable to the Acheulian are found in China and Southeast Asia.

Yet the Peking *Homo erectus* seems to have taken a cultural step even more important than carefully fashioned stone implements. Deep layers of charcoal fragments and pieces of carbonized bone indicate that the Choukoutien hominids were among the first to control the use of fire. The variety of animals found and the use of fire tend to counter the suggestion that Eastern *Homo erectus* groups were culturally more retarded than their Western hand-ax contemporaries. Hunting techniques using fire, pitfalls, traps, fire-hardened spears, bone and antler tools, and other relatively advanced technologies would not necessarily have been reflected in the inventory of stone tools. Moreover there are some equally old European sites that have a similar chopper and flake complex. Thus at Vértesszöllös (near Budapest) in Hungary there are thousands of chopper cores and flakes, indications of the early use of fire, and *Homo erectus* cranial fragments, but no hand axes.

Who's Human?

A majority of anthropologists believe that all pithecanthropines and some or all australopithecines or habilines should be included in the taxon *Homo.* In translation from Latin, *homo* means "man." Hence there are many anthropologists who regard all members of the genus *Homo* as human, reasoning that human = man = *homo.* This is an entirely unsatisfactory way of disposing of the problem of who's human. Bipedalism, big brains, and culture constitute a necessary but not sufficient set of diagnostics. Human beings process informa-

84

tion in a unique fashion—our brains contain unprecedented capacities for storage, retrieval, transmission, and reception of socially acquired knowledge. As a result of our unique communication capabilities, culture has replaced nature as the *primary* means of responding to the selective forces to which our species is exposed. The archaeological evidence of the cultural activities of archaic, big-brained hominids strongly suggests that for 2 or 3 million years populations classified as *Homo habilis* and *Homo erectus* did not exploit the evolutionary potential of cultural adaptations in a thoroughly human manner. The extraordinarily lethargic rate of cultural change throughout all but the last few "seconds" of the Pleistocene seems to have but one explanation: neuroanatomical structures for storing, retrieving, transmitting, and receiving socially acquired information operated at a level far below the modern standards of human language competence. Lacking that competence, the archaic members of the genus *Homo* should not be considered human.

This restriction should be applied to archaic members of *Homo sapiens* as well. A species is a taxon defined not by its communication behavior but by its actual or potential integrity as a breeding unit. There is no proof that all language-competent human beings were reproductively isolated from the protohuman forms of *Homo sapiens.*

A system of biological nomenclature that results in lumping humans and protohumans in the same species or genus is obviously not very satisfactory. Some might wish to argue that the difference between *Homo sapiens* and the other hominids is at least as great as a difference between phyla. Perhaps we deserve to be recognized not as the most advanced members of the *Chordata* but as the most primitive members of a new phylum, which might be called the *culturata:* organisms that adapt to nature primarily by means of cultural codes rather than genetic ones. But we ought not to fret too much about our taxonomic identity: the important thing is to understand the evolutionary processes that have led to *Homo sapiens.*

The Cultural Consequences of Big-Game Hunting

A number of lines of evidence converge toward the inference that *Homo erectus* was a more regular and more proficient hunter of large animals than either the habilines or australopithecines. As previously indicated, at such sites as Olorgesailie in Kenya, Terra Amata in

85

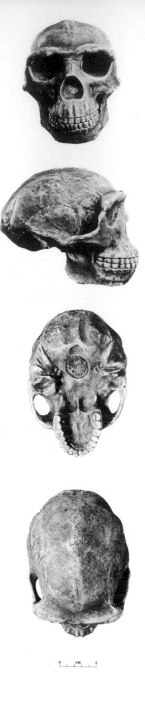

Figure 5-11. COMPARISON OF *HOMO ERECTUS* (above) AND NEANDERTAL (facing page)

France, and Torralba and Ambrona in Spain, large accumulations of bones of single species suggest that surrounds and drives were utilized. In addition, the presence of increasingly more numerous and concentrated animal deposits associated with relatively few tools points toward more efficient meat-procuring practices. Furthermore, control over fire would make drives and surrounds more effective and would have permitted the manufacture of fire-hardened wooden spears. Finally, the level of craftsmanship embodied in Acheulian stone implements suggests that effective hunting equipment such as bolas, wooden clubs, nets, lines, deadfalls, and hidden pits were not beyond the technological competence of *Homo erectus.*

Many anthropologists believe that the probable increase in hunting had a rather profound and specific effect upon the organization of *Homo erectus* social life. In hunting large mammals, local groups could not have moved as a unit in the fashion of monkey troops browsing together upon berries, fruits, and other vegetable foods. Children are an encumbrance to hunters, who must move swiftly and who must stalk and run down large animals capable of delivering mortal wounds.

Among modern hunting and gathering peoples the hunters of large game are invariably men. The kill usually occurs far from a "home base" or camp. The quarry is usually dismembered where it has fallen, and if it is very large, women and children are summoned to help carry the parts back to the campsite. Instead of accompanying the men on the hunt, women and children look for vegetable foods, grubs, insects, and small animals. All contemporary hunting groups exhibit this division of labor (but female gathering activities are more intensive in tropical and temperate regions than in the arctic). Hence it is assumed that *Homo erectus* hunting and gathering groups must have been organized in a similar fashion or at least that they were steadily selected for their ability to organize themselves that way. It is further often assumed that the organizational and communication problem posed by the prolonged absence of the males during hunting episodes would have led to selection for intelligent foresight and improved language behavior since departures, returns, and rendezvous would be facilitated by having a shared set of explicit expectations and plans.

This attempt to project the social organization and sex roles of contemporary hunting peoples back upon the *Homo erectus* population who lived 500,000 to 1,000,000 years ago merits extreme skepticism. There is absolutely no direct evidence that big-game hunting was carried out exclusively or primarily by males; nor is there any direct evidence that women alone did the baby-sitting. On physiological grounds it is of course "natural" to expect females who are in advanced pregnancy or who are nursing newborn infants to confine their economic contribution to relatively sedentary activities close to camp or home base. At other times, however, females can readily participate in far-ranging expeditions. Precisely this sort of shift has been observed among chimpanzees, among whom the extent to which females participate in heterosexual foraging groups depends on whether or not the individual is pregnant or nursing. (See J.K. Brown 1970; Williams 1971; Van Den Berghe 1972; Williams 1973). Moreover, there is evidence now steadily accumulating that in some contemporary hunting and gathering groups, the role of "woman the hunter" is not insignificant (Morren 1973). There is no biological imperative that *naturally* restricts big-game hunting to males. A home base populated exclusively by females and children is not theoretically more adaptive than a home base populated by nursing females, children, and males awaiting the return of hunting parties composed of both males and females. Selection for social bonding, cooperative planning behavior, and language proficiency would have been just as intense had both males and females participated in the hunt. The fact that males control the weaponry of hunting and warfare in all known contemporary human groups is not sufficient evidence for the belief that this was true of *Homo erectus* populations. Serious consideration must be given to the possibility that the beliefs and practices associated with male control of the technology of hunting and warfare originated in relatively recent times (see Ch. 13).

Studies of infrahuman social carnivores such as lions and wolves prove at least one thing: females can be effective hunters even though they weigh less and have smaller bodies than males. Anthropologists must make a special effort to prevent themselves from unconsciously projecting the male-centered stereotypes of their own cultures back upon the ancestors of our genus and thereby helping to perpetuate the myth that it is "human nature" for one sex to dominate the other.

The Neandertaloids

If cranial capacity could be considered a reliable indicator of the capacity for language, the threshold of humanity could be set no later than 100,000 B.P. By that time hominid types with average cranial capacities well within and even beyond the present-day human range had begun to appear in many different parts of the world. They are grouped together under the scientific colloquialism *neandertaloids,* derived from the specimen first identified in 1856 in the Neander-Tal

(From *Physical Anthropology,* 2 ed., by A.J. Kelso. By permission of the author and the publisher, J.B. Lippincott Company. Copyright © 1974).

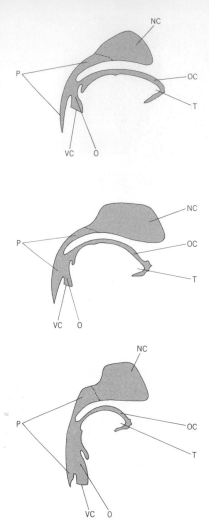

Figure 5-12. AIR PASSAGES OF CHIMP (top), NEANDERTAL (middle), AND HUMAN (bottom). P-pharynx; NC-Nasal cavity; OC-oral cavity; T-tongue; O-opening of larynx into pharynx; VC-vocal cords.

(Neander Valley), Germany.* A majority of experts agree that the neandertaloids were the first members of our species, *Homo sapiens.* Despite their large crania, neandertaloids in general possessed many features that gave them a more brutal or rugged appearance than any living human population.

Many specimens are markedly prognathic, with heavy brow ridges, robust, chinless jaws, and low brows reminiscent of *Homo erectus.* All authorities agree that the neandertaloids of Europe were members of the genus *Homo,* but a few experts continue to assign them to a separate species: *Homo neanderthalensis.* Others assign some or all of the neandertaloids to an archaic subspecies, *Homo sapiens neanderthalensis,* while placing all modern populations in a separate subspecies, *Homo sapiens sapiens.*

The main reason for doubting that some of the neandertaloids ought to be regarded as *Homo sapiens* is that their long, low cranial vaults and facial prognathism may be associated with a subhuman capacity for vocalizations. Philip Lieberman and his associates have shown that the human vocal tract has a unique ability to produce certain vowel and consonant sounds as a function of the enlarged size of our pharynx—the sound-resonating portion of our throats between the vocal cords and the back of the mouth (Lieberman, Crelin, and Klatt 1972). The comparatively small size of the chimpanzee's pharynx, for example, seems to explain why we have been able to teach them to communicate with us in the medium of sign language but not in the medium of spoken words (see p. 126). Reconstruction of the Classic Neandertal vocal tract (see left) closely resembles the chimpanzee vocal tract. This resemblance is related to the short neck and prognathic face characteristic of the neandertaloids. Lieberman concludes that it was only with the appearance of the fully rounded cranium and reduced prognathism of modern *Homo sapiens* that the hominid vocal tract achieved the shape needed to make sounds that are essential components in all human languages. This theory is especially appealing because it explains why the shape of the human cranium continued to change from the long, low, bulging neanderta-

*"In 1864, when King introduced the taxon *Homo neanderthalensis,* the spelling of the trivial name followed accepted German orthography. 'Thal' meaning valley, was spelled with an 'h,' although it was silent in pronunciation. Later, established German usage changed, and the silent 'h' in words like 'tal,' 'tor,' etc., was dropped. Thus, Neandertal man should be written without the 'h,' although, according to the International Code, the taxon *Homo neanderthalensis* must continue to be written as first proposed. Since English speakers tend to pronounce the 'h,' it is hoped that future discussions of the Neandertals will . . . write the term without an 'h.'" [Mann and Trinkaus 1974: 188]

[5] The First Human Beings

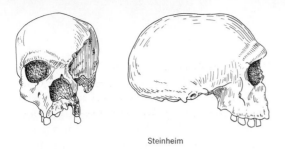

Steinheim

Figure 5-13. STEINHEIM. Intermediate between *Homo erectus* and Neandertal.

Figure 5-14. SWANSCOMBE. (Trustees of the British Museum—Natural History)

loid skull to the compact, globular skull of modern *Homo sapiens* even though the neandertaloids had already reached or exceeded us in cranial capacity. Other experts, however, challenge the validity of Lieberman's techniques for reconstructing the Neandertal vocal tract (Carlisle and Siegel 1974; Lieberman and Crelin 1974; Mann and Trinkaus 1974).

Neandertaloids in Europe and the Middle East

In Europe neandertaloids (or "pre-neandertaloids") may have been present as early as 250,000 B.P. This possibility is based primarily on two fragmentary fossils: *Swanscombe* from England, and *Steinheim* from Germany. Swanscombe and Steinheim are provisionally reckoned to have had cranial capacities within the *sapiens* range, but their cranial vaulting and the thickness of their bones suggest an intermediate stage between *Homo erectus* and archaic *Homo sapiens*. Between 250,000 and 150,000 B.P. other neandertaloid or archaic *Homo sapiens* flourished in Europe. The oldest series have been found in France at Arago cave (near Tautavel), La Chaise (near Charente), Le Lazaret (near Nice), Montmaurin, Orgnac-l'Aven, and Le Rafette.Between 150,000 and 75,000 B.P. archaic *Homo sapiens* or neandertaloid populations lived at Fontéchevade, Malarnaud, and Monsempron in France; Ehringsdorf in Germany; Saccopastore and Quinzano in Italy; Gănovce in Czechoslovakia; Bañolas in Spain; and Krapina in Yugoslavia. I mention all these sites in order to convey some idea of the complexity of the task that confronts physical anthropologists who attempt to sort these populations into taxons that were more or less directly ancestral to modern *Homo sapiens*. (de Lumley and de Lumley 1974)

It is only after 75,000 B.P. that the age of the original Neander specimen is reached. Some anthropologists insist that the term "neandertaloid" should be restricted to fossils that closely resemble

Figure 5-15. TWO NEANDERTALS.

Ehringsdorf

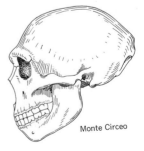

Monte Circeo

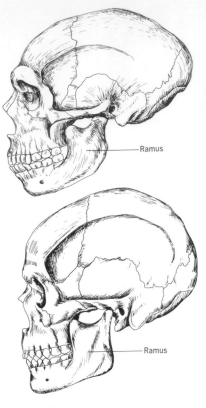

Figure 5-16. CLASSIC NE-ANDERTAL (top) AND *HOMO SAPIENS SAPIENS* (bottom). The third molar of *Homo sapiens sapiens* is behind ramus. (W.W. Howells 1973)

this "extreme" or "Classic" Neander type that flourished between 75,000 to 40,000 B.P. along the margins of the continental glaciers as, for example, at Spy in Belgium, Le Moustier and La Chapelle-aux-Saints in France, and Monte Circeo in Italy. The most important diagnostic of the Classic Neandertals is the extreme forward position of their teeth as compared both with earlier European archaic populations and modern *Homo sapiens*. In the Classic Neandertals, for example, the tooth row begins two to three centimeters further forward of the ascending portion (*ramus*) of the mandible than in either *Homo erectus* or *Homo sapiens sapiens* (Howells 1975).

Among humans, Eskimos have the most forward-jutting tooth rows. This feature is useful in arctic habitats where skin clothing is vital for survival. In order to prepare skins and to prevent them from becoming brittle, Eskimos chew them for many hours. In fact Eskimo women chew their husband's and children's boots every morning as a regular domestic chore. Since most of the Classic Neandertal sites were close to the edge of the continental glaciers, the extreme forward position of their teeth may reflect selection for jaws useful in chewing of animal hides and in other cold-climate industrial activities. Thus, according to some authorities, Classic Neandertals, despite their large cranial capacities, were not in the lineage that led to *Homo sapiens* but were a locally specialized species or subspecies that became extinct about 50,000 to 40,000 B.P.

According to other accounts, the Classic Neandertals were exterminated by true *Homo sapiens* who swept into Europe from the Middle East during a warm interval in the last continental glaciation. Even if this catastrophe (for the neandertals) did take place, it seems

Figure 5-17. ESKIMO WOMAN. Chewing family clothing is a daily chore. (American Museum of Natural History)

Figure 5-18. SHANIDAR NEANDERTAL. It rests on cave floor still embedded in the matrix. (Ralph S. Solecki)

unlikely that the neandertals would not have contributed their genes to their more modern replacements.

The events that led to the appearance of *Homo sapiens sapiens* must be seen in global rather than European perspective to be properly understood. From 125,000 to 50,000 B.P. many local populations throughout the world appear to have become progressively more sapienized. No doubt populations like the Classic Neandertals remained cut off for a time and developed their own anatomical specialties. But migrations and movements and countermovements must have broken such insularity again and again throughout the tens of thousands of years of the sapienization process. The neandertaloids were hunters of large migratory mammals in an environment subject to an enormous amount of local ecological variation. It is difficult to imagine them staying put long enough to produce a single inbred species, much less that such a species would endure for 100,000 years. It seems much more likely that the later stages of the sapienization process were accompanied by the repeated hybridization of local populations. European neandertaloids probably evolved into modern types of humans as a result of hybridization and natural selection at many different localities.

Evidence in support of this view comes from sites in Iraq and Israel. At Shanidar Cave in Iraq several neanderthaloid fossils have been recovered with radiometric ^{14}C ages of 47,000 B.P. or older. Some of the Shanidar specimens are similar to the Classic Neandertals (Solecki 1971). About 5,000 years later and 600 miles west at Tabūn Cave on Mount Carmel, Israel, a neandertaloid woman lived who might barely have "passed" as a Classic Neandertal. She had a low skull and heavy and continuous brow ridges but was considerably less robust than her Shanidar forerunner. One other roughly contemporaneous site in Israel, Amud near the Sea of Galilee, seems to

Figure 5-19. TABŪN I. Neandertal mandible. (Trustees of the British Museum—Natural History)

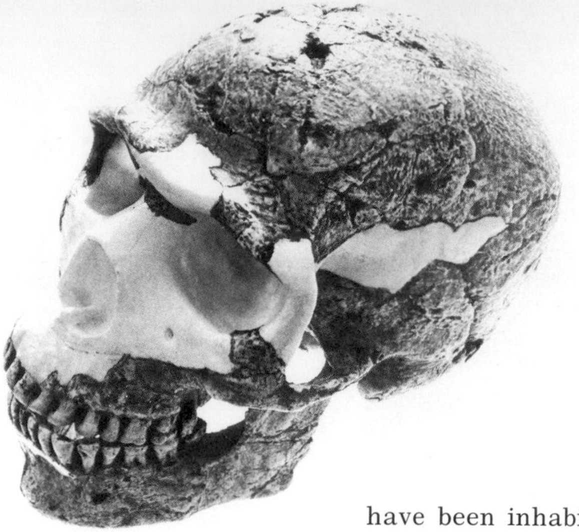

Figure 5-20. SKHŪL NEANDERTAL. (Photo of cast courtesy of Wenner-Gren Foundation and with permission of owner, Peabody Museum)

have been inhabited by populations very similar to the Tabūn neandertal (Suzuki and Takai 1970).

The next phase of the sapienization process has been recovered from another cave on Mount Carmel called Skhūl. Dated 36,000 B.P., the Skhūl fossils suggest the existence of a population closer to modern than to neandertaloid standards. As described by William Howells:

Their brain case was like ours in size and shape; high, flat-sided; and round, not projecting in the rear. The brows are marked and slightly neanderthal, though differing in being more like a pronounced shelf, not as heavy or bulbous as in neanderthal men. . . . It is hard to assess these people accurately. They are surely closer to us than to an average neanderthal, just as the Tabūn Woman is the opposite.   [1959:227–228]

However, Howells (1973) considers the lingering resemblance to the neandertals to be a result of genetic mixture rather than evidence of a late phase of transition.

By 30,000 B.P. the population of Europe from the Middle East to Spain and England had attained fully modern status. Thus in the sequence Shanidar-Tabūn-Skhūl there is evidence of about 15,000 years of sapienization, more than enough time for the relatively minor subspecies difference involved to have become established.

Studies indicating a gradual transition between the European neandertaloids and their modern descendants have been accumulating in recent years. In Yugoslavia, for example, a number of neandertaloid fossils from Krapina have been shown to be highly variable, resembling both the modern populations of Croatia and the Classic Neandertals (Jelínek 1969). Moreover restudies of a number of Classic Neandertal individuals and of such early European *sapiens sapiens* as *Cro-magnon* have revealed that some of the contrasts previously thought to exist were exaggerated (cf. Mann and Trinkaus).

92

Asian and African Archaic Homo Sapiens

During the initial period of anthropological inquiry into the origins of *Homo sapiens,* research was conducted mostly by European scientists who found it more convenient to work in Europe than elsewhere. As a result the number of European archaic *Homo sapiens* fossil specimens is much larger than the number of such specimens from any other region. As Buettner-Janusch points out, this has produced a biased picture of the sapienization process: "Europe is not the world and Europe was not the center of the major events, particularly the major transitional events, of primate and human evolution" (1973:258). Although the evidence from Africa and Asia is not as abundant as from Europe, there is enough to suggest that the processes of sapienization proceeded in a morphologically parallel and chronologically coordinated fashion throughout the Old World. Everywhere subhuman *Homo erectus* evolved into archaic sapiens types, some of which closely resemble the European and Middle Eastern Neandertals, and these types evolved further into modern populations. This does not mean that the African and Asian archaic sapiens possessed all the characteristics of the European and Middle Eastern archaic sapiens. Rather, there was a single, far-flung hominid population whose members were actually or potentially capable of interbreeding with each other—that is, a single polytypical species.

In Africa, from the Sahara to the Cape of Good Hope, *Homo erectus* populations were probably replaced or were being replaced by archaic sapiens populations at least as early as in Europe. Previous estimates of the dates of such relatively primitive types as "Rhodesian man," a rugged low-crowned skull with a capacity of 1,300 cubic centimeters, and "Saldanha man," a somewhat less brutal-looking contemporary

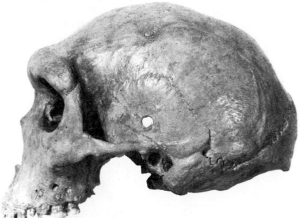

Figure 5-21. "RHODESIAN MAN." (Trustees of the British Museum—Natural History)

found ninety miles from the Cape of Good Hope, had led certain raciologists (see Ch. 6) to conclude that populations little different from *Homo erectus* were still alive in Africa as recently as 30,000 B.P. (Coon 1962). This view is almost certainly incorrect. Although the precise dates remain unknown, a reevaluation of the artifactual and faunal evidence suggests that the Rhodesian and Saldanha populations lived more than 125,000 years ago (Klein 1973). Moreover more advanced archaic sapiens are now known to have been present in the Kibish Formation, Omo, Ethiopia, with a tentative radiometric thorium date (Th/U) of 130,000 B.P. (Butzer 1971:444). As in Europe and the Middle East, archaic sapiens populations probably lived in Africa throughout the period 150,000 to 40,000 B.P. Large-brained but low-browed fossils have been found at Jebel Ighoud in Morocco, 43,000 B.P.; Hava Fteh in Cyranaica, Libya, 40,000 B.P.; and Florisbad, Orange Free State, 44,000 B.P. There is no evidence for the view that the development of African archaic sapiens was retarded; nor for the view that the archaic sapiens lingered on longer in Africa than elsewhere; nor for the view that *Homo sapiens sapiens* appeared significantly later in Africa than elsewhere. Fully modern *Homo sapiens sapiens* remains have been dated to 23,000 B.P. at Singa in the Sudan, roughly contemporary with Cro-magnon in Europe. Nelson's Bay, 300 miles east of Capetown, was occupied by generations of physically modern hunters and gatherers 18,000 years before the first European settlers set foot in South Africa.

In Asia, archaic *Homo sapiens* similar in many respects to those of Europe and Africa begin to appear in the fossil record at roughly contemporaneous levels. Perhaps the oldest is found at Mapa in Kwantung, China. Dated to about 125,000 B.P., the Mapa skull fragments indicate a strongly neandertaloid individual with a cranial capacity within modern range. The "Solo" population from Java, dated to levels roughly contemporary with the European neandertals, has heavy brow ridges, a sloping forehead, and rather a small cranial capacity (about 1,100 cc.) making it less reminiscent of the neandertals.

Figure 5-22. *HOMO SOLOENSIS.* Archaic *Homo sapiens* from Ngandong, Java. (Photo of cast courtesy of Wenner-Gren Foundation and with permission of owner, G.H.R. von Koenigswald)

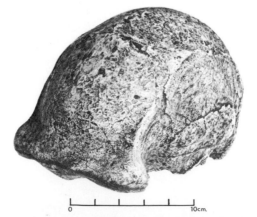

0   10cm.

In the Upper Cave at Choukoutien, local varieties of *Homo sapiens sapiens* were roughly contemporary with European Cro-magnon. One of the earliest *Homo sapiens sapiens* in the world is from Southeast Asia. A fully modern skull with a ^{14}C date of 40,000 B.P. has been found in Niah Cave on the island of Borneo. This is almost 10,000 years older than the oldest European *Homo sapiens sapiens*. But surely it would be absurd to claim that the first *Homo sapiens sapiens* arose in Borneo. Rather, it is clear that the process of sapienization unfolded in a synchronized fashion across all of Eurasia and Africa, and that no continent or region moved toward *Homo sapiens sapiens* status more rapidly than any other. Such differences as exist are certainly to be expected in a species which was spread so widely over the globe and which was adapting to so great a variety of habitats.

One Species, One World

In the perspective of millions of years of hominid evolution, no fact is more remarkable than the synchronized passage to *sapiens sapiens* status. Three forces explain the present-day unity of our species: natural selection, cultural selection, and migration and gene flow. Sapienization everywhere led to greater reliance upon culture as a source of adaptive innovations. Thus human beings were everywhere simultaneously selected for their ability to live as cultural animals, and this meant selection for expanded neural circuitry, vocal capability, and language competence.

The greater our dependence upon culture, the more important it became for us to enter into contact with neighboring groups in order to take advantage of innovations in the total pool of cultural adaptations. Cultural mechanisms for promoting the transmission of culture may have included some form of *exogamy*—systematic exchange of mates between local groups. Such an exchange would have promoted gene flow as well as the diffusion of cultural traits and would account for the remarkable continentwide uniformities in tool types and fossil species. When our ancestors finally crossed the threshold to fully human status they made the unity of *Homo sapiens* inevitable and unbreakable. There is only one human species, and no longer are there any parts of the world inhabited by hominids whose nature is less human than the rest.

THE ORIGIN OF RACIAL DIFFERENCES

During the past 35,000 years *Homo sapiens* has been the only living hominid species on earth. "Species" in this context means that barring pathological conditions any fertile *Homo sapiens* man will have fertile children if he mates with any fertile *Homo sapiens* woman, regardless of what each looks like and what part of the globe they come from. Evidence of humanity's oneness can be found at the boundaries of every more or less isolated human population. At such boundaries a certain number of children of mixed parentage are always present.

No new hominid species has arisen at least since the Upper Pleistocene, yet evolutionary forces have not ceased to act upon *Homo sapiens.* As groups of people moved to new habitats and as natural and cultural barriers prevented a free exchange of genetic material, populations appeared whose *gene pools* (see p. 15) exhibited markedly different frequencies of genes for one or more traits. Even though it would be perfectly sound taxonomically to refer to such breeding isolates merely as populations, most physical anthropologists still use the term *race.*

Although races may remain isolated for hundreds or even thousands of years and exhibit large numbers of distinctive gene frequencies, raciation represents a relatively insignificant biological phenomenon. As long as the accumulated genetic changes do not cross the threshold of speciation, racial differences can rapidly be reversed or obliterated by interbreeding or selection. Raciation therefore does not diminish the integrity of the species as an evolutionary unit.

After 14 million years of hominid evolution, contemporary racial differences might well be reckoned as trivial. But socially, raciation is one of the most debated and important issues of modern times. The superstitious and prejudiced nature of popular interpretations of racial differences place a grave burden upon anthropology. As the discipline most directly concerned with the process of hominid raciation, anthropology must shoulder a large share of the responsibility for providing an objective understanding of the causes and consequences of racial differences.

Raciation

Every species consists of populations whose frequencies of genes are to some extent distinctive from those of other populations. The taxonomic and evolutionary problem presented by these subspecific groupings, or races, is quite different from the problem of distinguishing species. To repeat, one species differs from another not merely because its repertory of genetic materials is distinctive, but because when and if individuals of one species mate with individuals of another, they will not normally produce fertile offspring. Once this criterion of speciation is accepted, the number of species at any given time is fixed and nonarbitrary. Discordant estimates of the numbers of species in a genus may be argued over, as you have seen, but in theory at least, everyone agrees that there is a fixed number at a given time. This is not so with subspecific categories. Since the criterion here is merely the frequency of genes in a population, there is no theoretically fixed limit to the number of different subspecific groupings. At one extreme, all mated pairs could be regarded as distinctive breeding populations and hence as different races because all individuals with the exception of identical twins (same ovum, same sperm) are genetically unique. Each individual has thousands of genes that in other individuals are absent or occur in different forms. Thus the particular combination likely to result from sexual pooling of the genotypes [see p. 13] of any two individuals will be in some respects an unprecedented combination. Racial groupings larger than mated pairs may be identified at the level of families, tribes, ethnic groups, nations, regions, or continents. The time span involved may be a single generation, two generations, hundreds or thousands of generations. And the number of possible combinations of genes for particular traits or their *alleles* [see p. 13] may range from one to hundreds to thousands. To demonstrate the existence of a scientifically valid race only two conditions need be fulfilled: (1) the individuals involved interbreed with a greater than random probability, and (2) the frequency with which one or more genes occurs among them is different from that of other populations. This means that from a genetic point of view there are as many races as there are genetic differences of interest to those who study human populations.

Frequencies versus Archetypes

The definition of race as a *breeding population* in which one or more genes occur with a particular frequency challenges popular and at one time scientifically accepted notions about the racial divisions of *Homo sapiens*. In the traditional raciological view *Homo sapiens* was divided into a fixed, natural, nonarbitrary number of races whose identity could be discovered by proper measurement and comparison. The same races that exist today were supposed to have existed in the past, from the very beginning of hominid evolution. Moreover every true member of a race was thought to possess a particular assemblage of hereditary traits that always made it possible to identify everyone's racial origin. While the number of such traits was assumed to be indefinitely large, the traditional raciologists insisted that some or all of a certain set of traits provided the main clue to the discovery of the fixed "natural" racial units.

These traditional race-defining traits consist of external characteristics that are readily noticeable but biologically of little or dubious significance. The main characteristics are: (1) coloration of the skin, hair, and eyes; (2) hair form; (3) amount of hair on body, face, and head; (4) thickness of nose and lips; (5) shape of the face and head; and (6) body mass and stature. In addition, a number of less generalized features are also frequently invoked: the *epicanthic fold* (the skin flap over the eyes), incisors shaped like a shovel, and a darkened area of skin at the base of the spine (the so-called "mongoloid spot").

The existence of several large breeding populations of regional or even continental scope can be inferred from the statistical "bundles" of these traits. Thus one population is the Europeans, who have a high frequency of pale skin, straight or wavy hair, large amounts of body hair, and noses of narrow to medium width. Marked prognathism is rare, and stature usually ranges from medium to tall. As everyone knows, individuals selected at random from European areas can be readily distinguished from individuals selected at random from Central Africa. The latter mostly have dark brown or black skin; their hair form is wiry and the amount of body hair is medium; lips and noses are relatively thick; and their faces are relatively prognathic. As

98

among Europeans, the stature of African populations is usually medium to tall. A different bundle of traits occurs with high frequency among East Asians. Here most people have pale to light brown skin, straight black hair, dark brown eyes, short to medium stature, and relatively hairless faces and bodies. There is also a relatively high incidence of epicanthic folds, mongoloid spots, and shovel-shaped incisors.

As informal, subspecific groupings, geographic races are legitimate, real, and useful concepts, *provided the limited nature of the phenomenon they are intended to designate is clearly understood.* The most important limitations arise from three aspects of the raciation process: (1) intraracial variation, (2) clinal variation, and (3) nonconforming variation. I shall discuss each in turn.

Intraracial Variations

One of the most serious misconceptions about race is that some individuals are more representative than others of the racial type or "essence." For example, there is a tendency to regard curly-haired, thick-lipped, dark-skinned Europeans as hybrids or less genuinely European than light-skinned, light-eyed Europeans. But it is very unlikely that increasingly more ancient samples of the population of Europe would be any less hybrid than modern samples. Of course one would expect the gene frequencies to be higher for some traits and lower for others, but modern genetics rules out the possibility that the individuals in any large population can have precisely similar genotypes for complex multigene traits such as skin color, hair form, lip form, and so forth.

The geographic races are statistical concepts that characterize population types rather than individuals; thus every individual whose genes are part of the population's gene pool is a member of that population. For example, when speaking of Europeans as having straight to wavy hair, one must not forget that many members of the European breeding population have quite curly hair. Similarly a small percentage of Europeans have shovel-shaped incisors, mongoloid spots, and epicanthic folds. Europeans who are less than five feet tall are no less European than those who are seven feet tall. A race is a concept built up out of the gene frequencies established by the existence of all these individuals. Similarly the four-and-a-half-foot Ituri Pygmy and the seven-foot Watusi are both Africans. If one ignores individuals who do not conform to what a "typical" African ought to look like, one destroys the scientific basis for the concept.

		4	10									
		5	11	17	21	25	29	34				
		6	12	18	22	26	30	35		39		
1	2	7	13	19	23	27	31	36	37	40		
		8	14				32		38	41	42	
	3	9	15				33					43
		16	20	24	28							

1 Mauritania
2 Tunisia
3 Eq. Guinea
4 Sweden
5 Denmark
6 Italy
7 Libya
8 Niger
9 Burundi
10 Finland
11 Hungary
12 Greece
13 Egypt
14 Sudan
15 Ethiopia
16 Zanzibar
17 Ukraine
18 Iraq
19 Yemen
20 Madagascar
21 USSR
22 Iran
23 Pakistan
24 Mauritius
25 USSR
26 Afghanistan
27 Pakistan
28 Maldive Is.
29 Tuva (USSR)
30 Nepal
31 India
32 India
33 India
34 Mongolia
35 China
36 Burma
37 Laos
38 Malaysia
39 Japan
40 Philippines
41 Indonesia
42 Ponape
43 Fiji

Figure 6-1. UNITY OF HUMANKIND. There are no sharp breaks in the distribution of racial types across Africa and Eurasia. (Consulate General of Denmark—5; Consulate General of Finland—10; Others courtesy of United Nations)

Because of enormous variation within the geographic races, many physical anthropologists have preferred to break these large units into subgroups. Schemes have been advanced, for example, to divide Europeans into Baltics, Nordics, Alpines, Dinarics, and Mediterraneans. Adding similar subgroups around the world yields classifications that have tens or even hundreds of groupings. But within all such subgroups, traits like hair form, skin color, and stature continue to vary widely. Even if one takes each of the two thousand or so "tribes" known to ethnographers and declares each a subgroup, no individuals could be found who would represent the true or pure type of their groups (cf. Hiernaux 1969).

Clinal Variations

Despite the internal variability of the major geographic races, it is usually easy to identify individuals drawn from European, African, and Asian populations. Given a random sample of individuals from Europe, East Asia, and Central Africa, one would make few mistakes in assigning them to the region of their birth. But if a random sample included individuals drawn from the remaining regions of the world, many mistakes would be made.

One of the most glaring difficulties of racial taxonomies is that they cannot be unambiguously applied to hundreds of millions of people not living in Europe, Central Africa, or East Asia. As recently as 1492 half the population of the world was distributed throughout Northern Africa, Southern Africa, the Middle East, Eastern Europe and Western Asia, India and Ceylon, Indonesia, New Guinea, Micronesia, Polynesia, Australia, and the New World. With the possible exception of the American Indians of the New World, random samples of people drawn from these regions cannot be definitely assigned to the European, African, or Asian race. All these regions are inhabited by peoples among whom there are bundles of traits not anticipated in popular stereotypes. For example, millions of people with thin lips and thin noses, wavy hair, but dark brown to black skin live in Northern Africa. The Bushmen-Hottentot, who have epicanthic eye folds, light brown to dark brown skin, and tightly spiraled hair, live in Southern Africa. India has millions of people with straight or wavy hair, dark brown to black skin, and thin lips and thin noses. On the steppes of Central Asia, epicanthic eye folds combine with wavy hair, light eyes, considerable body and facial hair, mongoloid spots, and pale skins. In Indonesia there is a high frequency of epicanthic folds, light to dark brown skin, wavy hair, thick noses, and thick lips. Throughout the

102

islands of Oceania is found every conceivable combination of brown to black skin, with contrastive forms and quantities of hair and facial features. One of the most interesting bundles of traits is found among the Ainu of Northern Japan, who have light skins, thick brow ridges, and are among the hairiest people in the world. Finally in Australia pale to dark brown skin color, marked prognathism, and wavy blond to brown hair are found.

For the most part, these variations are not distributed at random over the globe but occur in a definite pattern of gradually increasing and decreasing frequencies. Such patterns are called *clines*. For example, the frequency of the genes responsible for dark skin color gradually increases as one moves from Mediterranean Europe south along the Nile or across the Sahara and into Central Africa. There are no sharp breaks anywhere along the way. Similarly the incidence of epicanthic folds gradually increases from west to east across Asia, whereas the frequency of wavy hair gradually increases in the reverse direction, toward Europe.

There are three fundamentally different ways to interpret the high incidence of clinal distribution of gene frequencies throughout the Old World. First, the populations in the clinal regions can be regarded as hybrids produced by the mixture of European, African, and Asian genes through migration or some other form of "gene flow." The second possibility is that the clinal populations are not "hybrids" but races in their own right as old if not older than the others. Indeed, it is entirely possible that the "pure" races evolved fairly recently from populations that resembled the alleged "hybrids." I shall discuss the evidence for the antiquity of the races in a moment.

The third possibility is to regard segments of the clinal populations as parts of the major races. Narrow-nose, thin-lip, brown to black populations of the Sudan might be grouped with the Europeans—there is nothing to prevent it. But it would be no less defensible to classify them as Africans. Clearly if no strong reasons can be adduced for one rather than the other, it might be legitimately concluded that the whole enterprise isn't worth the effort. And that is precisely the conclusion reached by many physical anthropologists. This does not mean that there is any lessening of interest in the physical characteristics of these populations. On the contrary, there is more interest than ever in explaining why they manifest their distinctive gene frequencies. But the act of classifying a population as European, African, or Asian contributes not one whit to understanding the biological and cultural processes responsible for creating human racial differences and similarities.

The absurdity of trying to cram all populations into the mold of three or four racial types is well illustrated by the system of racial identity currently employed in the United States. In the American folk taxonomy, if one parent is "black" and the other "white," the child is "black" despite the fact that by the laws of genetics, half of the child's genes are from the black parent and half from the white. The practice of cramming people into archetypal racial pigeonholes becomes even more absurd when black ancestry is reduced to a single grandparent or great-grandparent. Under such circumstances there appears the astonishing phenomenon of the "white" who is socially classified as "black." The arbitrary nature of this practice extends to many ostensibly scientific studies of "blacks" and "whites." Most American blacks have received a significant portion of their genes from recent European ancestors. When samples of American blacks are studied (as in intelligence testing, see Ch. 22), the assumption that they genetically represent Africans is incorrect. In this matter both scientists and laymen would do well to emulate the Brazilians, who identify racial types not by three or four terms but by three or four hundred (M. Harris 1970).

The whole question of racial taxonomy from a biological viewpoint is a rather minor issue. It is impossible to set a limit to the number of races that could be identified. Each classification has its merits supplied by the kinds of research it is intended to serve. Unfortunately most systems of racial identity are not intended to serve scientific interests, but rather to provide the basis for the exploitation (see Ch. 19) of one group by another. Under these circumstances failure to emphasize the hybrid status of the major geographic races takes on added significance. Many raciological studies employing the major geographic races as basic taxonomic units reinforce popular but genetically false stereotypes about pure races and racial essences. Failure of scientists to distinguish between the scientific sense of geographic race and the popular, demagogic sense may reasonably be construed by concerned citizens as a political act (Fried 1965, 1968).

Nonconforming Gene Frequencies

So far I have discussed the taxonomic significance of genetic variation and clines with respect to the traits used to distinguish one geographic race from another. One conclusion is that although

Figure 6-2. BRAZILIAN PORTRAITS. The great variety of facial types in Brazil suggests that it is futile to think about human beings in terms of a small number of fixed and sharply distinct races.

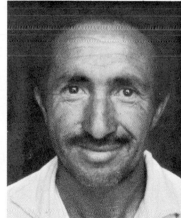

DISTRIBUTION OF ALLELES OF THE ABO BLOOD GROUP SYSTEM

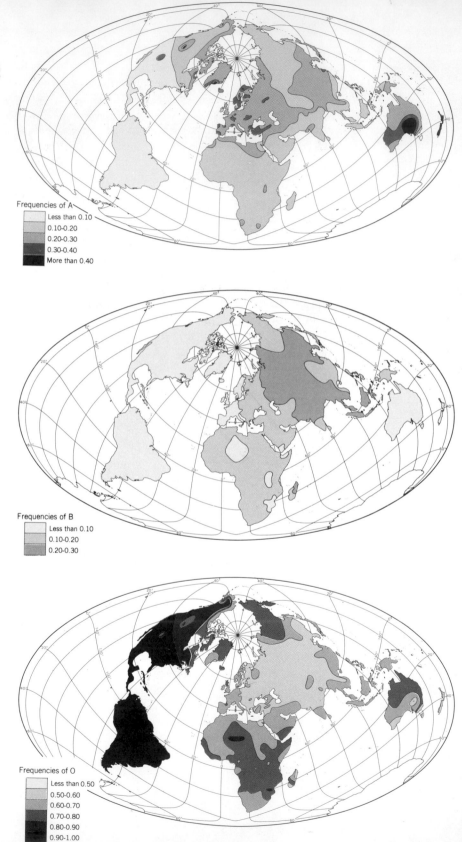

Frequencies of A
- Less than 0.10
- 0.10-0.20
- 0.20-0.30
- 0.30-0.40
- More than 0.40

Frequencies of B
- Less than 0.10
- 0.10-0.20
- 0.20-0.30

Frequencies of O
- Less than 0.50
- 0.50-0.60
- 0.60-0.70
- 0.70-0.80
- 0.80-0.90
- 0.90-1.00

106

European, Central African, and East Asian populations can readily be distinguished from each other, they cannot be distinguished from the populations of the rest of the world. Skin color and facial form provide the most widely used criteria for racial classifications. The real test of the utility and significance of the geographical races concerns the extent to which traits of skin color and facial form have distributions that conform to the distributions of other genetic traits. In other words, to what extent does the distribution of the other genes by which individuals differ from each other correspond to the distribution of the conventional geographic races?

The geographical races are confusing and inappropriate units of comparison for the study of many important genetic differences. Color blindness, for example, is a hereditary defect that afflicts human beings everywhere, but the incidence is higher among Europeans than among Africans. Shall it be inferred that this is a distinctively European racial trait? On the contrary, the higher frequency among Europeans is much more likely the result of the fact that color blindness has fewer adverse consequences in agricultural and industrial societies than in hunting and gathering societies. Since hunting for a living ceased to be important for Europeans earlier than for Africans, the accumulation of the defective genes can be expected to have reached greater proportions among Europeans than among Africans.

There seems little doubt that most alleles have distributions that cut across the geographic racial divisions as if these simply did not exist. Of highest interest in this regard are the genes controlling the immunochemical reactions of the blood. These genes at one time were thought to be the best possible source of a genetic classification of the races. Unlike traits such as skin color or hair form, the precise genetic mechanism for the inheritance of the blood groups is well understood, and thousands of controlled blood-group studies have been made throughout the world. The best-known series is the *ABO system.* Each human being has a genotype that puts us in either blood group A, B, AB, or O. (I shall ignore the complexities of the subtypes which, in any event, make the distribution even more erratic.) Type O has the widest distribution, occurring on all continents and crosscutting all racial divisions. For example, it occurs with a frequency of 70–80 percent in Scotland, Central Africa, Siberia, and Australia. Type A is equally unmindful of what the raciologists think the major divisions of mankind ought to be. Africa, India, and Southern and Northern China all have 10–20 percent frequencies, while Japan, Scotland, and much of aboriginal Australia are in the 20–29 percent bracket. Asians have frequencies of B ranging from 10–30 percent, yet the American Indians, whose ancestors were Asians, are in the 0–5 percent range, a frequency shared by the Australian aborigines. West Africa and Eastern Europe both show B frequencies of about 15–20 percent. Similar racially nonconforming distributions are characteristic of other blood systems such as MNS and Rh (cf. Hulse 1973; Kelso 1974).

It should be emphasized that the distribution of blood groups could very well serve as the basis for a taxonomy of major geographical races. Of course the resulting races would simply bear little resemblance to the races identified by the traditional criteria. Yet as biological taxons they would be no less valid, legitimate, or important. Indeed, at one time it was widely believed that they would be *more* valid, since their genetic properties are better understood and more amenable to objective methods of research.

DISTRIBUTION OF FALCIPA-
RUM MALARIA IN THE OLD
WORLD

DISTRIBUTION OF THE
SICKLE CELL TRAIT IN THE
OLD WORLD

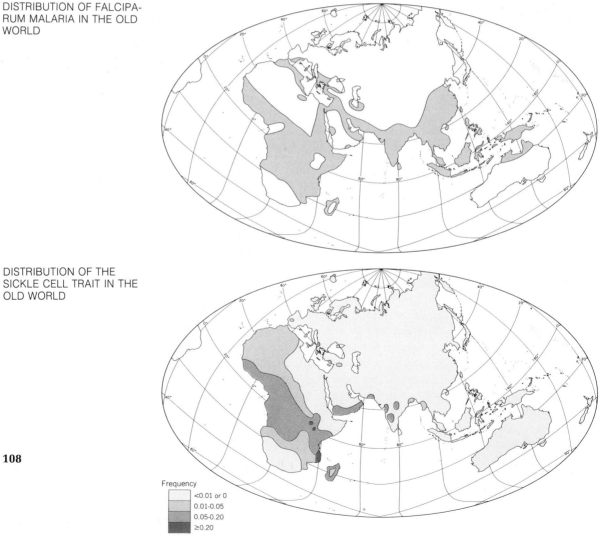

Frequency

<0.01 or 0
0.01-0.05
0.05-0.20
≥0.20

108

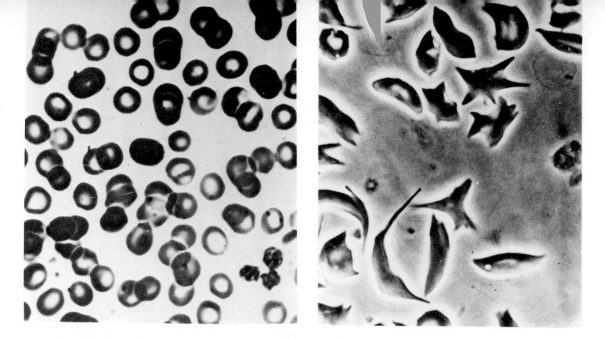

Among the most interesting racially nonconforming genes are those responsible for a disease known as *sickle cell anemia.* The red blood cells of persons afflicted with this congenital defect are sickle-shaped instead of round and are incapable of transporting normal amounts of oxygen. An individual falls victim to this potentially lethal defect only when both parents carry the gene for sickling (see p. 14). Individuals who have inherited the gene from one parent show only mild symptoms. The sickling gene was first noted among Africans and among Americans of African descent. Its highest frequencies, about 20 percent, occur in Central Africa, and so it was concluded that sickling was an "African trait." Yet it was discovered that the same gene also occurred in Greece, Turkey, Yemen, India, and Burma. Confronting such a distribution, the traditional raciologist concluded that the gene had somehow been introduced from Africa into these distant populations. The poverty of such reasoning, however, has been exposed by the further discovery that individuals who have the deleterious gene in its heterozygous form have a high degree of resistance to malaria. In areas of endemic malaria, the sickle gene in its heterozygous form protects more individuals from death due to malaria than it kills in its homozygous form as a result of anemia. Since the sickling gene outside of Africa is concentrated in malaria-infested areas, it seems likely that natural selection and not race is responsible for the distribution of the trait. Although processes involved are not yet completely understood, this case illustrates the intellectual sterility of the old raciological outlook. If sickling had been dismissed as an African trait, important questions involving the genetic mechanisms responsible for differential resistance to malaria would never even have been asked.

Figure 6-3. NORMAL BLOOD CELLS (left) and SICKLING BLOOD CELLS (right). (National Institute of Health)

109

Nonconforming Gene Frequencies

The Ephemerality of the Races

Many raciologists of the old school confer upon the races a permanency and inner integrity that not even species deserve. Some of these old-fashioned ideas can be traced back to pre-Darwinian times when biologists believed that species were unrelated to each other and that each species had its immutable nature fixed by God. Although modern raciologists do not propose that racial taxons are immutable, some nonetheless continue to argue that today's major geographic races were already in existence hundreds of thousands of years ago. According to Carlton Coon, for example:

> Over half a million years ago, man was a single species, Homo erectus, perhaps already divided into five geographic races or subspecies. Homo erectus then evolved into Homo sapiens not once but five times, as each subspecies, living in its own territory, passed a critical threshold from a more brutal to a more *sapient* state.   [1962:658]

Homo erectus is an extinct species. Therefore Coon in effect is proposing a theory that five subspecies within that species survived as separate entities while the species itself disappeared. The only way such subspecies could have maintained their integrity for 500,000 years would have been for them not to have exchanged genes. This, however, is the definition of a species not of a race. Thus in Coon's scheme there would actually be greater justification for regarding the geographic races as species than there is for regarding *Homo erectus* or *Homo sapiens* as species. But this is contrary to what is plain for all to see: after 500,000 years of supposed genetic isolation, all the races are today busily engaged in pooling their genes in most unspecieslike fashion.

As previously indicated, the geographic races are perfectly legitimate as long as one uses a small bundle of traits as their defining characteristics and does not expect these traits to correlate very well with each other nor expects too many other traits to conform to the same distribution. Especially prominent in the definition of the conventional geographic races are descriptions of features such as skin color, hair form, nose width, lip width, epicanthic fold, and amount of hair on face and body. It so happens that it is impossible to determine from a fossil any scientifically responsible description of such features of *Homo erectus*. These parts have simply not been preserved.

Thus the identification of the racial characteristics of *Homo erectus,* neandertaloids, and Upper Pleistocene moderns necessarily rests not on the most familiar major geographical racial traits but rather on facial dimension, head shape, and tooth shape. I shall not go into further detail concerning the lack of correlation between these features and skin color, hair form, lip and nose form, and so on. Let it

110

suffice to say that skilled physical anthropologists and medical pathologists dealing with well-preserved modern crania cannot reliably predict skin color even when there is foreknowledge that only a limited number of the total world inventory of anatomically contrastive populations is represented. No one knows what the total range of racial differences was like 500,000 or even 50,000 years ago. And next to nothing is known about the archaic clines and nonconformities. Modern-day images of what the races look like ought not to be projected back upon our remote ancestors. Most of our ancestors were probably neither blacks, nor whites, nor Asians, nor anything else that would be familiar to us.

The Causes of Racial Differences

The concept of a race as an archetype capable of enduring for untold millennia is further contradicted by consideration of what causes racial differences. The same processes that govern biological evolution in general probably operate in the establishment of some of the gene frequencies upon which human racial distinctions depend (see p. 15). In the partial or temporary isolates produced by geographical or other breeding barriers, genetic repertories are subject to local selective pressures. The frequency of adaptive genes will increase, while the frequency of nonadaptive genes will decline. As long as speciation does not take place, however, the breeding isolate is open to gene flow from the other races. If the racial specialties are not highly adaptive, a large amount of gene flow will alter the frequency of genotypes and destroy the phylogenetic continuity of the race. But if the racial specialties are highly adaptive, gene flow will destroy the phylogenetic continuity of the race without altering the gene frequencies since the same adaptive balance will be maintained. The case of the sickling gene will make this clear. Suppose a group with low sickling frequency moves into an area of endemic malaria. Within a number of generations (predictable by genetic equations) the frequency of sickling will increase among the immigrants, and after a relatively short time, the natives and the immigrants will become indistinguishable with respect to the sickling trait. However, in other respects they may continue to differ quite considerably.

Thus a bundle of racial differences that is strongly adaptive cannot be used as evidence for phylogenetic continuity. This fact raises grave doubts about the phylogenetic integrity of the major geographic races, for it is possible that several of the conventional diagnostics of racial descent may have been biologically adaptive in the not too distant past.

111

An even more rapid distortion of phylogenetic relationships will take place if there are cultural as well as natural forces at work in favor of one genotype at the expense of another. Cultural selection may come into play in the form of differential treatment of infants or potential mates on the basis of some trait that may be directly or indirectly linked to adaptive biological consequences.

To take a hypothetical example, suppose that epicanthic folds confer an adaptive advantage upon peoples who live and hunt amid the glare of arctic snows. The greater success of the heavy-lidded hunter might gradually receive recognition in the form of an aesthetic bias in favor of individuals with the epicanthic trait. Since infanticide was one of the most important means of population control during prehistoric times (see p. 266), this aesthetic bias might influence the decision not to rear a particular child. If cultural selection of this sort were added to the higher death rate among hunters who lacked the epicanthic fold, very rapid change in gene frequencies would follow, especially since archaic human populations were very small.

Distributions of several of the most important racial traits have been studied for clues concerning their possible adaptive significance. Results thus far have been inconclusive. A number of interesting suggestions have related racial features to temperature, humidity, and other climatological factors. For example, the long narrow noses of Europeans may have resulted from the need to raise extremely cold air to body temperature before it reached the lungs. The generally rounded squat form of the Eskimos is viewed as another type of adaptation to cold. There is a general biological principle known as *Bergman's Rule:* a spherical shape presents a maximum of body mass to a minimum of body surface, thereby linking maximum heat production to maximum heat conservation. A tall, thin body form, on the other hand, combines a minimum of body mass with a maximum of body surface leading to minimum heat production coupled with maximum heat loss. Bergman's Rule is sometimes also invoked to explain the characteristics of the tall Nilotic Africans who inhabit regions of intense arid heat. Coon even has an explanation for the tightly wound spirals known as peppercorns, the characteristic Bushman hair form. By leaving empty spaces on the head, the peppercorn "facilitates heat loss at high temperature" (1965:112).

The proposal that the geographic distribution of skin color genes has resulted from adaptive processes is one of the liveliest suggestions of this type. To a limited extent, darker skins are correlated with subtropical and tropical latitudes. The basis for these geographic distributions may involve a relationship between skin color and the ultraviolet component in solar radiation. Dark skin color results from the presence of the pigment *melanin*. When the skin is heavily pigmented it is resistant to the penetration of ultraviolet radiation. This radiation is useful or harmful, depending upon the dose. Without a certain minimal exposure to ultraviolet radiation, the human body cannot synthesize the hormone cholocalciferol (Vitamin D_3). A deficit of cholocalciferol results in turn in the crippling bone disease known as *rickets* (T.C.B.S. 1973). During the long, misty European winters, an adequate level of radiation may depend upon reducing the filtering effects of melanin; hence the pink-cheeked Northern European. On the other hand, an overdose of solar radiation may lead to the development of skin cancer (Blum 1964; Bakos and MacMillan 1973); hence the pigmentation of Africans, acquired as a result of the protection that melanin affords against the direct rays of the tropical sun.

Unfortunately the evidence in support of this theory is difficult to interpret. Americans of African descent and darker-skinned British Islanders from India and Pakistan do have higher rates of rickets than whites. Antiricketic substances occur in diets rich in fish, butter, and other sources of dietary Vitamin D. But since the poor tend to eat fewer such foods than the wealthy and since wealth in Great Britain and the United States tends to be correlated with skin color, no one knows how much of the incidence of rickets is due to genetic differences and how much is due to dietary differences. To complicate

Figure 6-4. MULLEN'S ALLEY, 1888. Lacking both sunlight and dietary sources of vitamin D, the children of the urban industrial slums fell victim to rickets, despite their light skin color. (Photo by Jacob A. Riis, the Jacob A. Riis Collection, Museum of the City of New York)

the picture still more, exposure to sunlight fluctuates with fashion, occupation, and disposable leisure time. Cases of rickets do occur in the tropics among populations that have dark skins. And hospital dosages of ultraviolet radiation have been found effective in the cure of dark-skinned victims of rickets entirely without dietary intervention. Finally it is by no means certain that Africans have lower rates of skin cancer per unit of ultraviolet radiation as compared with whites (Kendall 1972; Dent and others 1973).

Controlled tests have definitely shown, however, that dark skin is a disadvantage in at least one important respect for populations living in the tropics. Under the noonday sun, black skin absorbs as much as 15 percent more heat than sunburned white skin, rendering blacks more prone to heat stroke than Europeans (Baker 1958).

Other objections have been raised against using natural selection to explain skin color differences. It has been pointed out, for example, that Asians and American Indians have more or less the same pale to brown pigmentation whether they live in an arctic, desert, temperate, or tropical region. Countering this objection, it has been proposed that Asians, American Indians, and Eskimos are not pigmented the way they ought to be because they have migrated too recently for selection to have taken place.

L. L. Cavalli-Sforza (1972) has suggested an ingenious hypothesis for reconciling these anomalies with the Vitamin-D selection theory. Perhaps the development of white skin was a by-product of the spread of agriculture into northern Europe. As long as the populations who lived in the misty, short-day, long winter latitudes of Europe maintained a hunting and gathering way of life, their skin color could remain relatively dark since they could obtain their vitamin D from dietary sources. Thus, the Eskimos who consume large quantities of fresh fish and sea mammals have little need for solar radiation, and their skin color can remain relatively dark. But with the northward spread of farming from the Middle East (see p. 204), grains low in Vitamin D became the staple foods. One fascinating corollary of this explanation is that it places the origin of white skin color no further back in time than 10,000 B.P.

Perhaps the explanation for the anomalous distributions of skin color is to be found in the effects of cultural selection rather than natural selection. Following the line of conjecture used in the case of the epicanthic fold, natural selection in favor of differential pigmentation may have been intensified by a kind of cultural "resonance." If a preference for darker or lighter skin color became culturally established, it would influence differential survival and reproduction in contexts irrelevant to solar radiation such as infanti-

114

cide, illness, mating, and warfare. Once started, such a process of cultural selection would have a positive feedback effect of its own that might produce percentages of black or white phenotypes far in excess of what natural selection would have produced. In other words, if certain populations adopted the aesthetic standard "black is beautiful" and others adopted the aesthetic standard "white is beautiful," and if for reasons entirely unrelated to skin color, both kinds of populations were reproductively successful, geographic races could emerge in very short order. Frederick Hulse (1973) has suggested that the invention of agriculture may have provided the conditions that made it possible for certain small populations to contribute disproportionately to the gene pools of the continents of the Old World. Thus, even without conceding any adaptive advantages to skin color, the major races of the world, as they are known today, may have an antiquity no greater than 10,000 years.

Although each of the proposals concerning the selective processes responsible for racial traits is speculative, in combination they make it extremely unlikely that any of us really knows which early *Homo sapiens sapiens* populations contributed most to our individual genotypes. And this is apart from the genealogical ambiguities that are especially characteristic of all recent New World populations as a result of unprecedented migratory movements and race mixture (see p. 104).

I shall conclude this chapter without going into the question of the relationship between race, cultural performance, intelligence, and other behavioral phenomena. That discussion should never be attempted unless one has tried to understand the cultural causes of behavioral differences and similarities over adequate spans of space and time. Hence I shall postpone further consideration of racial factors until certain basic facts and theories concerning cultural causality can be taken into consideration.

7

LANGUAGE AND HUMAN NATURE

The assertion has repeatedly been made that language competence is a distinctive component of human nature. Now the moment has come to be more precise about the characteristics and consequences of being able to speak like a human being.

Despite the widespread occurrence among infrahuman organisms of complex communication systems, human language is a unique evolutionary product. Without exaggeration, one can contrast human language with infrahuman communication systems as one contrasts life with nonlife. With the emergence of human language, communication achieved a significance on earth as great as that of gravity, chemical bonding, natural selection, or any other force of nature (cf. Sebeok 1972).

The Uniqueness of Human Language

One way to sum up the special characteristics of human language is to say that we have achieved what the linguist Joseph Greenberg calls "semantic universality." A communication system that has *semantic universality* can convey information about all aspects, domains, properties, places, or events in the past, present, or future, whether actual or possible, real or imaginary, near or far.

Another way to express the same thing is to say that human language is infinitely *productive* semantically. This means that to every message that we send, we can always add another whose information is different from that in previous messages, and that we can continue to expand messages without any loss in the efficiency with which such information is encoded (although the "decoding"— the understanding of the message—may get progressively more difficult, as in the present sentence). Let me explain by way of contrast with systems that have a definite limit on their semantic productivity.

C. R. Carpenter found that gibbons have nine major types of calls. These calls convey socially useful information such as: "I am here"; "I am angry"; "Follow me"; "Here is food"; "Danger!"; "I am hurt." Because each call can be repeated at different volumes and durations the gibbon system possesses a certain amount of productivity. For example, the gibbon can say "Danger!" with different degrees of emphasis roughly equivalent to the series: "Danger!"; "Danger! Danger!"; "Danger! Danger! Danger!"; and so on. But this series exhibits a stunted amount of productivity because the amount of information conveyed does not increase at the same rate that the length of the utterance increases. A "danger" call repeated twenty times in succession is not much different from "danger" repeated nineteen times. In contrast, the productivity of human language is extremely efficient. In order to convey more and more specific information in a particular domain, our messages do not have to keep getting longer. We can say: "Be careful, there's a strange movement over there"; "I think I see a leopard"; "It's in that tree." Moreover these unique powers of productivity are not constrained to the small set of domains that gibbons and other anthropoids "talk about." Rather, we are capable of producing an infinite number of messages in an infinite number of domains.

Another component in the concept of semantic universality is the feature known as *displacement.* A message is displaced when either the sender or receiver has no immediate direct sensory contact with the conditions or events to which the message refers. We have no difficulty, for example, in telling each other about events like football games after they are over or about events like meetings and appointments before they take place. Human language is capable of communicating an infinity of details about an infinity of displaced domains. This contrasts with all other infrahuman communication systems. Among anthropoids, for example, usually only the receiver exhibits some degree of displacement, as when a "danger" message is understood at a distance. The sender must be in sensory contact with the source of danger in order to give an appropriate warning. A chimpanzee cannot say "Danger! There may be a leopard on the other side of this hill." On the other hand, in human communication both sender and receiver are frequently displaced, as when one tells another about how to behave in the future. Among humans most language behavior is displaced: we talk routinely about people, places, and things seen, heard, or felt in the past, present, or future, or that others have told us about, or that enjoy a completely imaginary existence.

Displacement is the feature usually in mind when human language is referred to as having the capacity to convey "abstract information." Some of the greatest glories of human life—including poetry, literature, and science—depend upon displacement; but so too do some of our species' greatest evils—lies and false promises.

Arbitrariness

How then does human language achieve its unlimited capacity for displacement and its unlimited productivity throughout an infinite series of semantic domains? One striking feature of human language is the unprecedented degree to which our information-bearing codes are constructed out of sounds whose physical shape and meaning have not been programmed in our genes. Most infrahuman communication systems consist of genetically stereotyped signals whose meaning depends on genetically stereotyped decoding behavior. For example, in communicating its sexual receptivity, a female dog emits chemical signals whose interpretation is genetically programmed into all sexually mature male dogs. Primate call patterns, like those of songbirds (see p. 57), are somewhat less tied to specific genetic programs and are known to vary among local groups of the same species. But the basic signal repertory of primate communication systems is species-specific. The facial expressions, hand gestures, cries, whimpers, and shrieks of chimpanzees constitute a genetically controlled repertory that is shared by all chimpanzees.

Not so with human languages. True enough, the general capacity for human language is also species-specific. That is, the ability to acquire semantic universality is genetically determined. Nonetheless the actual constituents of human language codes are virtually free of genetic constraints (not counting such things as the physiology of the ear and of the vocal tract). Take as an example populations in England and France. There is nothing in the genes of one population making it probable that utterances such as "water," "dog," or "house" should form part of their language, nor that once part of it they should convey the particular significance attributed to them. These code elements can be said to be biogenetically arbitrary because: (1) they do not occur in the language behavior of most human beings; (2) neighboring populations in France with whom there is considerable

118

gene flow utilize "eau," "chien," and "maison" to convey similar meanings; and (3) all normal human infants drawn from any population will acquire the English or French codes with equal facility depending upon whether they are *enculturated* (see p. 145) respectively in England or France.

There is another important sense in which human language is arbitrary. Human language code elements lack any physically regular relationship to the events and properties that they signify. That is, there is no inherent physical reason why "water" designates water. Many infrahuman communication systems, on the other hand, are based on code elements that resemble, are part of, or are analogous to the items they denote. Bees, for example, trace the location of sources of nectar by olfactory cues supplied by pollen grains that cling to the feet of their hive mates. (The extent to which the wiggles and waggles of scout bees also convey such information is under intense debate [Wells and Wenner 1973].) Chimpanzees communicate threats of violence by breaking off branches and waving or throwing them. Although we humans also frequently communicate by means of similar *iconographic* symbols—like shaking our fist or pointing to a desired object—the elements in spoken language seldom bear anything other than an arbitrary relationship to their meaning. Even *onomatopoetic* words (like "bow-wow" or "hiss") exhibit a rather striking degree of arbitrariness. "Ding dong" may sound like a bell to speakers of English but not to Germans, for whom bells say "bim-bam."

True semantic universality cannot be achieved unless some code elements are noniconographic. How else might one produce such logical and relational elements as "yes" and "no" and future, past and conditional tenses, as well as imaginary or hypothetical semantic ingredients? The fact that sounds constitute the medium of human language also guarantees the development of an essentially noniconographic code since many physical events or relationships vital for survival and well-being are not associated with conspicuous or distinctive noises. To appreciate this fact, try to play the game of charades by using sounds but no words or gestures.

Arbitrariness is a great advance in communication design. Codes constructed out of arbitrary elements are potentially capable of making use of meaningless signals to convey meaningful messages. Although at first glance this might appear to be a silly way to construct a communication system, the use of arbitrary meaningless code elements is the most efficient way to achieve semantic universality.

Duality of Patterning

The great paradox of semantic universality is that it can be achieved best by means of a very small number of arbitrary code elements. In language the smallest of these elements are called *phonemes.* Phonemes are distinctive sounds that are meaningless in isolation. But when phonemes are combined into prescribed sequences they convey definite meaning. The contrastive sounds in the utterance "cat" by themselves mean nothing; but combined they signify something about a feline animal. In reverse order the same sounds signify something about a small nail or a sailing maneuver. Thus the basic elements in the language code have *duality of patterning*: the same signals combine and recombine to form different messages.

Semantic universality can be achieved by a code that has duality of patterning based upon only two distinctive signals. This is actually the case in the dots and dashes of Morse Code and the binary + and − of digital computers. But a natural language having only two phonemes would require a much longer string of phonemes per average message than one having several phonemes. The smallest number of phonemes known in a natural language is thirteen in Hawaiian. English has between thirty-five and forty (depending on which authority is cited). Once there are more than ten or so phonemes, there is no need to produce exceptionally long strings per message. A repertory of ten phonemes, for example, can be combined to produce 10,000 different words consisting of four phonemes each. Now for a closer look at how phonemes can be identified and at how they combine to form meaningful utterances.

Phonemic Systems

In order to be effective as code elements the phonemes of a language must be clearly distinguishable. One way to achieve a well-defined set of discrete code units is to make each unit contrast as much as possible with every other unit. But when does one sound contrast with another? In the two-unit code of a digital computer, positive and negative electric charges are unmistakably distinctive. But no two acoustical events "naturally" contrast with each other. If we are able to distinguish one phoneme from another it is only because we have learned to accept and recognize certain sounds (*phones*) and not others as being contrastive. For example, the [t] in "ten" and the [d] in "den" are automatically regarded by speakers of English as contrastive sounds. (A symbol between brackets denotes a phone.) Yet these

120

two sounds actually have many *phonetic,* that is, acoustical features in common. It is culture not nature that makes them different.

One way to appreciate the similarity between [t] and [d] is to examine their *articulatory features,* that is, the manner in which they are produced by the vocal tract. Notice that when you produce either sound, the tip of your tongue presses against the *alveolar ridge* just behind the top of your teeth. Notice in addition that when either sound is made, the flow of the column of air coming from the lungs is momentarily interrupted and then released only in order to form the rest of the sounds in the utterance. In what way, then, are they different? The major articulatory difference between [t] and [d] consists of the way the column of air passes through the vocal chords. The vibration of the vocal chords produces a *voiced* effect in the case of [d] but not in the case of [t]. Both [t] and [d] are described phonetically as *alveolar stops,* but [d] is a *voiced alveolar stop,* whereas [t] is an *unvoiced alveolar stop.* The use of a voiced and unvoiced alveolar stop to distinguish utterances such as "ten"— "den," "tock"—"dock," "to"—"do," "train"—"drain," is an entirely arbitrary device that is characteristic of English but that is absent in many other languages. The phonemic system of a given language thus consists of sets of phones that are arbitrarily and unconsciously perceived by the speakers as contrastive.

The structure of a given language's *phonemic system*—its system of sound contrasts—is discovered by testing observed phonetic variations within the context of pairs of words that sound alike in all but one respect. The testing consists in part of asking native speakers if they detect a change in meaning. This is what is achieved in the comparison between "ten" and "den." By comparing similar *minimal pairs* of words we can detect most of the distinctive contrasts in English. For example, another instance in which voicing sets up a contrast is found in "bat"–"pat." Here the initial sounds are also stops. But this time they are made by pressing both lips together and are called *bilabial stops.* Again one of the stops, [b], is voiced, whereas the other, [p], is unvoiced.

Figure 7-1. PARTS OF ORAL PASSAGE

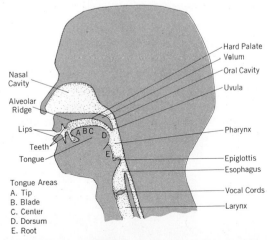

Tongue Areas
A. Tip
B. Blade
C. Center
D. Dorsum
E. Root

To the linguist's trained ear, many sound differences that escape the notice of the native speaker will appear as possible contenders for phonemic status. For example, the removal of the labial obstruction in the utterance "pat" is accompanied by a slight puff of air that is not found at the beginning of "bat." This phonetic feature is known as *aspiration* and can easily be detected by placing your hand close to your lips and pronouncing first "pat" and then "bat" several times in succession. A more precise phonetic description of the [p] in "pat" therefore is that it is an *aspirated bilabial unvoiced stop,* for which the phonetic symbol is [pʰ]. Both aspirated and nonaspirated /p/'s occur in English. (A symbol between slant lines indicates a phoneme.) Thus the bilabial stops in "sap," "flip," and "hip" are nonaspirated. Hence the question arises as to whether [p] and [pʰ] constitute separate phonemes. A search for a minimal-pair contrast between [p] and [pʰ] in English will fail. There are no meaningful English utterances in which the substitution of [p] for [pʰ] alters the meaning of an utterance. Instead [p] and [pʰ] are in *complementary distribution;* that is, they occur regularly in different sound environments. Closely resemblant but nondistinctive sounds like [p] and [pʰ] are called *allophones.*

In a sense every specific instance of any given phoneme is an allophone since no two utterances are ever exactly the same either in terms of articulation or acoustic effect. Allophones such as [p], and [pʰ], however, which occur in complementary distribution, are called *conditioned allophones,* whereas those that occur randomly and are not in complementary distribution are called *free allophones.* A given phoneme, then, consists of a range of sounds, which contrasts significantly with the range of sounds characteristic of at least one other phoneme.

Phones that regularly occur in one language may not occur at all in another. When the same phone does occur in two languages, it may be phonemic in one but not the other. And when similar phones are phonemic in two languages, they may have a different set of free and conditioned allophones.

Morphemes

Now is the time to see how the principle of duality of patterning applied to a language's phonemic repertory results in the production of meaningful utterance. The smallest units of language that have a definite meaning are called *morphemes.* Like each phoneme, each morpheme designates a class of sounds; hence there are allomorphs

122

just as there are allophones. Allomorphs, however, are grouped into a single morpheme on the basis of sharing a common meaning and a common function within the structure of different utterances. Un-/ (as in "unused") and /in-/ (as in insane) are allomorphs of a single morpheme whose meaning is "not" and which occurs as the *prefix* (initial sound) of many different English words. Similarly the English suffix (final sound) whose meaning is "two or more" has three allomorphs: /-s/ as in /kæt-s/; /-z/ as in /dɔg-z/; and /-əz/ as in /hɔrs-əz/.

Note that morphemes may consist of single phonemes or of strings of phonemes in many different combinations and permutations. It is here that you can see duality of patterning operating to produce thousands of code elements—each having a different meaning—out of a handful of code elements—none of which has any meaning.

Grammaticality

Now to the crowning achievement of human language: the rules that govern the combination of morphemes and allomorphs in the production of well-formed messages. To begin with, there are rules that determine which morphemes can occur as isolates as opposed to those which can occur only in conjunction with other morphemes. "Hello," "stop," "sheep" are *free* morphemes because they can constitute the entirety of a well-formed message. ("Are those goats or sheep?" "Sheep."). But the past-forming /ed/ of "talked" or "looked" and the /-er/ of "speaker" or "singer" are *bound* morphemes because they can never constitute well-formed messages on their own.

The grammatically competent speaker generates large numbers of words and strings of words by combining and modifying free and bound morphemes in conformity with grammatical rules. These rules govern the derivation of plurals, tenses, genders, and other related grammatical forms. They also define permitted, prohibited, and obligatory sequences of morphemes. The meaning of an utterance in human speech cannot be specified without some conscious or unconscious knowledge of grammatical rules.

Utterances constructed in conformity with grammatical rules are accepted as messages, even though the meaning may be obscure or the truth of the message may be in doubt. Thus, "Bit the Mary dog" leaves us with a feeling that there is something wrong with the speaker, whereas the improbable "Mary bit the dog" commands immediate attention. The question of whether an utterance is grammatical, that is, whether it is a well-formed message, has nothing to do with the question of whether it makes sense or whether we have

123

heard it before. As Noam Chomsky has suggested, native speakers of English identify one of the following sentences as grammatical even though they may never have heard either sentence before.

> Colorless green ideas sleep furiously.
> Furiously sleep ideas green colorless.

Native speakers can seldom state the rules governing the production of grammatical utterances. Even so simple a transformation as that from singular to plural nouns is hard to formulate as a conscious rule. As has been seen, adding an "s" converts "cat" into "cats," "slap" into "slaps," "fat" into "fats"; but something else happens in "house"—"houses," "rose"—"roses," "nose"—"noses"; and something else again in "crag"—"crags," "flag"—"flags," "hand"—"hands."

Human language is governed by a set of unconscious structural rules, and it is the sharing of these rules by the members of a speech community that makes it possible for them to produce and interpret a potentially infinite number of messages, none of which need precisely replicate any other previous message.

As Noam Chomsky has put it:

Normal linguistic behavior . . . as speaker or reader or hearer, is quite generally with novel utterances, with utterances that have no physical or formal similarity to any of the utterances that have ever been produced in the past experience of the hearer or, for that matter, in the history of the language, as far as anyone knows.   [1973:118]

How is it possible for us to create so many different messages and still be understood? No one is quite sure of the answer to this question. One of the most popular theories is that proposed by Chomsky. According to Chomsky, every utterance has a surface structure and a deep structure. Surface structures may appear dissimilar, yet deep structures may be identical. For example, "Meat and gravy are loved by lions" is superficially dissimilar to the sentence "Lions love meat and gravy." Yet both sentences take as their model a third sentence: "Lions love meat and lions love gravy." This third sentence more closely reflects the "deep structure" which can be transformed into various superficially different phrases. What is the deep structure of a sentence like "John knows a kinder person than Bill"? Note that the meaning of this sentence is ambiguous. Does John know a kinder person than Bill knows, or does John know a kinder person than Bill is? There must be two different deep structures that have gotten confused in the single ambiguous surface structure. Working backwards through a number of inferences, the linguist arrives at the two distinctive deep structures (Katz 1971: 79–81):

124

John knows a person/a person is kind/more than Bill is kind.
John knows a person/a person is kind/more than a person Bill knows.

Theoretically a knowledge of the transformation rules should also lead to the identification of the deep structures that underlie apparently dissimilar ways of saying the same thing. Unfortunately it has not yet proved feasible to identify all the transformation rules in any given language, and many linguists are convinced that there is a difference in meaning between deep structure sentences and their surface structure transforms (Silverstein 1972:376).

Much of what we regard as grammatical in novel speech behavior can be explained by the concept of analogy. Speakers of English recognize the grammaticality of Lewis Carroll's innovative verse "Twas brillig and the slithey Toves did gyre and gimble in the wabe" because it is put together in a way that resembles the way other utterances with which they are familiar have been put together. Its structure is analogous to sentences that have the form: It was [a certain time, season, or weather] and the [animate beings] did [perform some action] and [some other action] in the [place, region, or medium]. On a less complex level, one can see the principle of analogy operating when a child who has learned the plural forms "cats," "dogs," and "sodas" invents such plurals as "mens," "sheeps," and "mouses"; or when a child who has learned the past tense in "walked," "stopped," and "laughed" creates "ranned," "goed," and "taked." The notorious lack of consistency in rules governing the formation of plurals, tenses, genders, and other grammatical features suggests that grammar is always subject to modifications based on analogies introduced by individual speakers. This implies that no tidy set of deep structure rules will ever account for all the novel messages that we are capable of producing.

The view that grammars are complex and evolving systems of analogies stands opposed to the notion that there is one uniform intuition shared by all the members of a given speech community concerning whether or not a particular utterance is grammatical. As the linguist William Labov (1972b:203ff.) has noted, the existence of variation and of heterogeneous structures within speech communities is itself the rule not the exception. Obviously there must be an extensive core of agreement legitimizing many kinds of rules or analogies and condemning others; yet there must also be a considerable amount of individual variation with respect to many analogic constructions, as, for example: "he is"-"he isn't"; "I am"-"I ain't"; or "he has a car" - "he has no car; he's got a car" - "he got no car." Most linguists agree that a sentence like "I ain't got no car" is no less grammatical than "I have no car" since it occurs frequently and is perfectly intelligible to any native speaker of English. Of course, if you are applying for a job that requires you to speak the way your bosses speak, it will not help to argue that your competence is as good as theirs.

The Genetic Basis of Language

Many futile attempts have been made to teach infrahuman animals to speak in human fashion. After six years of intensive training, the chimpanzee Viki learned to say "mama," "papa," and "cup." With the demonstration that the vocal tract of these apes renders it anatomically impossible for chimpanzees to produce some phones necessary for human speech (see p. 88), attention has shifted toward attempting to teach them to use sign languages and to read and write. Washoe, a female chimpanzee, learned 160 different standard signs of the American Sign Language for the deaf. Moreover Washoe was capable of using these signs in a highly productive manner. She first learned the sign for "open" with a particular door and later spontaneously extended its use beyond the initial training context to all closed doors, then to closed containers such as the refrigerator, cupboards, drawers, briefcases, boxes, and jars (Bronowski and Bellugi 1970:670). When Susan, a research assistant, stepped on Washoe's doll, Washoe had many ways to tell her what was on her mind: "Up Susan; Susan up; mine please up; gimme baby; please shoe; more mine; up please; please up; more up; baby down; shoe up; baby up; please move up" (Gardner and Gardner 1971). Four additional chimpanzees have acquired the rudiments of this language (Fouts 1973).

David Premack (1971) used a set of plastic chips to teach a chimpanzee named Sarah the meaning of a set of 130 symbols with which they could communicate with each other. Premack could ask Sarah rather abstract questions such as: "What is an apple the same as?" And Sarah could respond by selecting the chips that stood for "red," "round," "stem," and "less desirable than grapes." Premack made a special effort to incorporate certain rudimentary grammatical rules into his human-chimp language. Sarah could respond appropriately to the plastic-chip command: "Sarah put the banana in the pail and the apple in the dish." Sarah herself, however, did not make such complex demands of Premack.

A third approach with a three-and-a-half-year-old chimpanzee

126

named Lana utilizes a keyboard controlled by a computer and a written language known as Yerkish. Lana knows 71 words and reads and writes such sentences as "Please machine make the window open," correctly distinguishing between sentences that begin appropriately and inappropriately and that have permitted and prohibited combinations of Yerkish words in permitted and prohibited sequence (Rumbaug, Gill, and Glasersfeld 1973).

Obviously some degree of grammaticality is involved in these languages. Yet the productivity of the grammars is very limited. The chimpanzees are still a long way from being able to say: "Why don't you get in here for a change and press some of these damn buttons yourself?" The level of grammaticality attained has certainly not gone beyond that of a two- or three-year-old human infant (R. Brown 1973; Slobin 1973).

Nonetheless these experiments prove that under suitable conditions—for example, life in cages controlled by behaviorist psychologists—chimpanzees are capable of acquiring communication systems that are closer to human language than had previously been thought possible. No longer is it valid to say that only humans are capable of symboling or of learning rules of grammar. The gap has been narrowed between semantic universality and infrahuman communication systems. One can readily see how that gap was bridged by slow degrees when populations such as the australopithecines were selected for neural circuitry that expanded their ability to encode and decode novel messages. As the volume of messages increased, duality

Figure 7-2. LANA USING YERKISH TO COMMUNICATE WITH A COMPUTER. She can read and write 71 cards. (Yerkes Regional Primate Research Center of Emory University)

127

of patterning would have become necessary to increase the rapidity of communication. Selection would then have focused on the ability of individuals to encode and decode novel messages based on analogies with the structure of messages whose meaning had become culturally standardized, much as Sarah analogizes "put the ——— in the ———" with different permutations and combinations of "banana," "dish," "apple," and "pail." The fact that chimpanzee grammatical competence stays below the level of a two- or three-year-old child and that a huge communication gap persists between chimpanzees and humans should cause no surprise. This gap is precisely what one should expect of an ape. There is no reason to conclude, however, that a similar gap existed between humans and our protohuman hominid ancestors. I cannot agree with Noam Chomsky when he writes: "there is no significant evidence of continuity, in an evolutionary sense, between the grammar of human languages and animal communication systems" (1973:123). No doubt Chomsky's sense of isolation from the rest of nature is an illusion created by the fact that all the creatures truly intermediate between us and the rest of the animal kingdom long ago became extinct. Once begun, there was no intermediate point at which the evolution toward semantic universality could be halted, no "niche" for a wide-ranging, ground-dwelling hominid whose "language" was less advanced than that of neighboring populations. Thus today all traces of the intermediate stages of language evolution have been obliterated.

The Equivalence of All Grammars

Contemporary human populations exhibit a wide range of technological, economic, and social accomplishments. For most anthropologists the cultural characteristics of contemporary hunters and gatherers, villagers, and other prestate peoples provide the basis for legitimate inferences concerning the life of prehistoric societies and the evolution of key aspects of extinct cultural systems. It would seem reasonable therefore to suppose that the languages spoken by contemporary preliterate peoples would show duality of patterning and grammaticality in a less perfect or less efficient stage of development than French, English, or some other favorite "civilized" language. European linguists of the nineteenth century were strongly convinced that this was indeed the case and that the languages of the world could be arranged in a hierarchical order. They invariably awarded the prize for efficiency, elegance, and beauty to Latin, mastery of whose grammar was long a precondition of scholarly success in the West.

128

One of the more influential schemes for evaluating the relative worth of different languages postulated that grammars evolve through *isolating, agglutinative,* and *inflective* stages. In the isolating stage there are few bound morphemes and few changes in roots in conformity with grammatical rules. Chinese is such a language. In the agglutinative stage, as in Turkish or Finnish, *affixes* or bound morphemes are attached to roots in long strings. Finally, in the inflective stage, as represented by Latin, there are numerous bound morphemes that themselves undergo regular variations in conformity with their semantic and grammatical function within an utterance.

Although it is true that some languages have overall grammatical profiles that correspond to these categories, most languages, like English, make use of all three types of constructions. The sentence "Last week all the deer cut through the road of the girl scout camp" is highly isolative. There are no inflectional endings; all the words consist of single morphemes; time is indicated by "last week"; number by "all"; possession by "of"; and sex by "girl." But inflectional and agglutinative constructions are also possible in English: "Butchers unthinkingly wandered into Pat's antivivisectionist head-quarters." Here all words consist of two or more morphemes. There are long agglutinative strings, for example, /un/ /think/ /ing/ /ly/; while inflectional affixes indicate tense, number, and possession.

Regardless of the appropriateness of the isolative-agglutinative-inflective distinction, there are neither functional nor historical reasons for rating one system as superior to the others. To classify Chinese as a "primitive" language is not only to ignore the complete and efficient nature of Chinese as a communication system but also the fact that both Chinese and English are today less inflective than they were in former times. Over thousands of years several alternations between isolative and inflective tendencies have probably occurred among most of the world's language families.

Furthermore, if morphological complexity is to be the criterion of superiority, then Latin can scarcely hold its own in comparison with many American Indian and other "primitive" languages that possess noun cases and verb tenses undreamed of by Cicero.

Beginning with the study of American Indian languages, anthropological linguists led by Franz Boas showed that the belief in the superiority of "civilized" grammars was untenable. It was found that syntactic and morphological rules run the full gamut from relatively simple to relatively complex systems among peoples on all levels of technological and political development. The conclusion of the great anthropological linguist Edward Sapir stands unchallenged: "When it comes to linguistic form, Plato walks with the Macedonian swine-

herd, Confucius with the head-hunting savages of Assam"
(1921:234).

Vocabulary Differences

Two other kinds of language differences are often cited as evidence
that one system is more "primitive" than another: (1) lack of general-
izing terms and (2) lack of specialized terms. Many observers have
noted the existence of numerous words for different types of parrots in
the Brazilian Tupi languages, and yet no term for parrots in general.
This has led to the assumption that the lack of a general term is
associated with a primitive intellectual and primitive linguistic capacity. The opposite side of this coin is the comparison that emphasizes a lack of specific terms. Thus many languages have no
specific terms for numbers higher than five. Larger quantities are
simply referred to as "many." From this it is concluded that the lack of
specific terms is associated with a primitive intellect and primitive
linguistic capacity. These evaluations fail to take into account the
fact that the extent to which discourse is specific or general reflects
the culturally defined need to be specific or general, not the capacity of
one's language to transmit messages about specific or general phenomena. For a Brazilian Indian there is little need to distinguish
parrots in general from other birds, but there is a need to distinguish
one parrot from another since each type is valued for its plumage.
English, which has terms for many special vehicles—"cart," "stretch-
er," "auto," "sled," "snowmobile"—lacks a general term for wheeled
vehicles. Yet this does not prevent one from communicating about
wheeled vehicles as distinguished from sleds and helicopters when
the need arises. Similarly the absence of higher-number terms usually
means that there are few occasions in which it is useful precisely to
specify large quantities. When these occasions become more common, any language can cope with the problem of numeration by re-
peating the largest term or by inventing new ones (cf. R. Brown 1958).

The question of the relationship between general and specific terms
and cultural conditions has been studied in considerable detail in the
domain of kinship. Most languages have a special term for mother's
brother as distinct from father's brother (see Ch. 16). English "uncle"
ignores this difference and for good reason, since there is no socially
defined difference in most English-speaking communities between a
mother's brother and a father's brother. But when it becomes useful
(as in the previous sentence) to distinguish varieties of "uncles" the
lack of special terms is readily overcome by using two or more words.

130

It is true of course that languages of industrial, state-level societies, which are spoken by millions of people, have a larger inventory of both generalized and specialized terms than the languages of preindustrial peoples who number only a few hundred per speech community. But much of this difference is associated with the lack of written records. It must be remembered that technical terms are locked up in dictionaries and textbooks. When it comes to the actual daily working vocabulary of a Bushman or an Eskimo and a Russian or an American, the difference may not be to the advantage of the latter. Vocabulary differences in any event are necessarily superficial. Semantic productivity is infinite in all known languages. When the social need arises, terms appropriate to industrial civilization can be developed by any language. This can be done either through the direct borrowing of the words of one language by another ("sputnik," "blitzkreig," "garage" or by the creation of new words based on new combinations of the existing stock of morphemes ("radiometric," "railroad," "newspaper"). We humans are never at a loss for words—not for long, that is.

Language and Social Class

A final form in which the claim for language superiority appears is associated with the dialect variations characteristic of stratified societies. Frequently mention is made of the "substandard" grammar or "substandard" pronunciation of a particular ethnic group or social class. Such perjorative allegations have no basis in linguistic science except insofar as one is willing to accept all contemporary languages as corrupt and "substandard" versions of earlier languages (see below).

When the dialect variant of a segment of a larger speech community is labeled "substandard," what is usually being dealt with is a political rather than a linguistic phenomenon (Hertzler 1965; Southworth 1969). The demotion of dialects to inferior status can only be understood as part of the general process by which ruling groups attempt to maintain their superordinate position (see Ch. 18). Linguistically the phonology and grammar of the poor and uneducated classes are as good as those of the rich, educated, and powerful classes. Of course a so-called substandard dialect is a definite handicap in certain competitive situations, but primarily because it is stigmatized and ridiculed by the superordinate group.

This point should not be confused with the problem of functional vocabulary differences. Exploited and deprived groups will lack many specialized and technical words and concepts as a result of their limited educational experience. This constitutes a real functional handicap in a competitive economy. But this has nothing to do with the question of the adequacy of the phonological and grammatical systems of lower-class and ethnic dialects.

Well-intentioned educators often claim that lower-class and ghetto children are reared in a linguistically deprived environment. In a detailed study of the actual speech behavior of blacks in Northern ghettos, William Labov (1972a, 1972b) has shown that this belief reflects the ethnocentric prejudices of middle-class teachers and researchers rather than any deficit in the grammar or logical structure of the ghetto dialect. The nonstandard English of the black ghetto contains certain forms that are unacceptable in white middle-class settings. Among the most common are negative inversion ("don't nobody know"); negative concord ("you ain't goin' to no heaven"); invariant "be" ("when they be sayin'"); dummy "it" instead of "there" ("it ain't no heaven"); and optional copula deletion ("if you're good . . . if you bad"). Yet the utilization of these forms in no way prevents or inhibits the expression of complex thoughts in concise and logically consistent patterns, as exemplified in a black teenager's discussion of life after death:

soon as you die, your spirit leaves you. (And where does the spirit go?) Well, it all depends. (On what?) You know, like some people say if you're good an' shit, your spirit goin' t'heaven . . . 'm' if you bad, your spirit goin' to hell. Well, bullshit! Your spirit goin' to hell anyway, good or bad. (Why?) Why? I'll tell you why. 'Cause, you see, doesn' no body really know that it's a God, y'know, 'cause, I mean I have seen black gods, pink gods, white gods, all color gods, and don't nobody know it's really a God. An' when they be saying' if you good, you goin' t'heaven, tha's bullshit, 'cause you ain't goin' to no heaven, 'cause it ain't no heaven for you to go to.   [Labov 1972a:214–215]

The grammatical properties of nonstandard language are not haphazard and arbitrary variations. On the contrary, they conform to rules that produce regular differences with respect to the standard grammar. All the dialects of English possess equivalent means for expressing the same logical content:

Whatever problems working-class children may have in handling logical operations are not to be blamed on the structure of their language. There is nothing in the vernacular which will interfere with the development of logical thought, for the logic of standard English cannot be distinguished from the logic of any other dialect of English by any test that we can find.   [Labov 1972a:229]

132

Language, Thought, and Causality

Any language or dialect possessing semantic universality has the capacity to receive and transmit any message that is intelligible in any other language. In other words, all human languages are mutually translatable. This statement must be carefully distinguished from the view that would say all languages are translatable with equal ease or facility. The latter is patently not the case. Ease of translation depends on the degree to which (1) the cultural and natural environments of two speech communities are similar; (2) their word inventories contain morphemes whose general and specific meanings coincide; (3) their grammars are similar.

In recent years an important controversy has arisen concerning the extent to which different word categories and grammars produce habitually incompatible modes of thought among peoples who belong to different language communities (cf. Hymes 1971). At the center of this controversy is the comparison made by the anthropological linguist Benjamin Whorf between American Indian languages and the Indo-European family of languages, to which English belongs. According to Whorf, when two language systems have radically different vocabularies and grammars, their respective speakers live in wholly different thoughtworlds. Even such fundamental categories as space and time are said to be experienced differently as a result of the linguistic "molds" that constrain thought.

The forms of a person's thoughts are controlled by inexorable laws of pattern of which he is unconscious. These patterns are the unperceived intricate systematizations of his own language—shown readily enough by a candid comparison and contrast with other languages, especially those of a different linguistic family. His thinking itself is in a language—in English, in Sanskrit, in Chinese. And every language is a vast pattern-system, different from others, in which are culturally ordained the forms and categories by which the personality not only communicates, but also analyzes nature, notices or neglects types of relationship and phenomena, channels his reasoning, and builds the house of his consciousness. [1956:252]

According to Whorf, English sentences are constructed in such a way as to indicate that some substance or matter is part of an event that is located at a definite time and place. Both time and space can be measured and divided into units. In Hopi sentences, however, events are not located with reference to time but rather to the categories of "being" as opposed to "becoming." English encourages one to think of time as a divisible rod that starts in the past, passes through the

133

present, and continues into the future; hence the English language's past, present, and future tenses. Hopi grammar, however, merely distinguishes all events that have already become manifest from all those still in the process of becoming manifest; it has no equivalent of past, present, and future tenses. Does this mean that a Hopi cannot indicate that an event happened last month or that it is happening right now or that it will happen tomorrow? Of course not. But Whorf's point is that the English tense system makes it easier to measure time, and he postulated some type of connection between the tense system of Indo-European languages and the inclination of Euro-Americans to read timetables, make time payments, and punch time clocks.

In rebuttal, other linguists have pointed out that the three-tense system that is supposed to color thinking about time really does not exist in English. First, there is no specific verb form indicating the future tense in English; one uses auxiliaries like "will" and "shall." Second, English speakers frequently use the present tense and even the past tense to talk about the future: *"I'm eating* at six this evening"; "If I *told* you, would you do anything?" This means that the use of tenses in English is a good deal more relaxed and ambiguous than high school grammars indicate. If one needed an opportunity to become confused about time, English provides no unusual obstacles (Haugen 1975).

A more important objection to Whorf's point of view is that it implicitly distorts the fundamental causal relationships between language and culture. No one would deny that the absence of calendars, clocks, and timetables must have given preindustrial societies like the Hopi an orientation to time very different from that of industrial-age societies. But there is no evidence to support the view that industrialization is in any way facilitated or caused by having one kind of grammar rather than another.

An interest in calendars and other time-reckoning devices is a recurrent feature of social and political development associated with peoples whose languages are as diverse as Egyptian and Maya. Indeed, the Chinese contributed as much to the invention of the modern mechanical clocks as did the Europeans (see p. 433). On the other hand, a lack of concern with counting time is a characteristic of preindustrial peoples in general, from Patagonia to Baffin Land and from New Guinea to the Kalahari desert—peoples who speak a thousand different tongues.

As it is with time-reckoning, so it is with other aspects of culture. The Aztecs, whose powerful empire marks the high point of political development in aboriginal North America, spoke a language closely related to that of the hunting and food-gathering Utes. Religions as

134

different as Hinduism, Catholicism, and Protestantism have flourished among peoples all of whom speak Indo-European languages. Malayo-Polynesian, Bantu, and Arabic have served equally well as media for the spread of Islam, whereas Chinese, Russian, and Spanish have served equally well for the spread of Marxism. Industrial capitalism in Japan and the United States share much in common, although the Japanese and English languages show few resemblances. To see grammar as a significant force in the evolution of cultural differences and similarities is to leave all these phenomena (and many more) utterly without explanation.

The causal process that determines cultural differences and similarities usually can be shown to operate not from language to social practice but from social practice to language. As suggested previously, kinship categories are a fertile source of evidence in this matter. For example, English makes no provision for distinguishing between mother's brother's child and mother's sister's child—one word, "cousin," is used for both (or sometimes "first cousin"). The Iroquois-speaking American Indians do make such a distinction, and so do the Bantu-speaking Zulu of South Africa, the Tupi-Guaraní-speaking Camayura of Brazil, the Malayo-Polynesian-speaking Dobuans of New Guinea, the Indic-speaking Vedda of Ceylon, and the Sino-Tibetan-speaking Chinese. These languages are entirely unrelated to each other and have no consistent structural similarities. However, the domestic life of each of these peoples is organized around kinship groups, called "sibs," and it is the presence of these groups that is probably responsible for the occurrence of this type of category in such widely dispersed quarters of the globe (see Ch. 16). The Bathonga of Mozambique provide another example: they use one word, "tatani," to signify both "father" and "father's brother." Obviously the Bathonga's way of looking at the world of domestic relationships is radically different from our own. But this is not because the Bathonga branch of the Bantu language family is different from English but rather because Bathonga domestic life is organized around lineages, polygyny, bride-price, the levirate, communal property, and many other institutions not found in most English-speaking communities.

The problem of translating words from the languages of people whose cultural life involves practices and relationships wholly different from one's own presents monumental difficulties. Vast domains of meaning having to do with property, work, money, law, crime, war, sickness, and religion require constant reference to the total cultural context if translation is to be achieved. It is a cardinal principle of anthropology that all exotic concepts and categories must be seen in

135

the full context of social practice if their semantic significance is to be grasped. Thus when Whorf insists that "we dissect nature along lines laid down by our native language," all anthropologists are in complete agreement. It is only when they start identifying what these lines are and what causes them that disagreement sets in.

Overliteral Translation

In assessing the degree to which the cognitive categories of one language correspond to the categories of another it must be remembered that grammar and vocabulary are never static. Failure to assess grammatical and vocabulary differences with respect to current, living contexts results in the blunder known as "overliteral translation."

Chinese evolved a word for "train" by combining *huo*, meaning "fire," and *ch'e,* meaning "cart." A translation of *huoch'e* as "fire cart" would be absurd since it would fail to take into account the altered technological conditions to which the new term is adapted. As Charles Hockett has suggested, a more correct translation is "train." This is shown by the word *tienli-huoche's,* which denotes the kind of train that runs on an electrified railroad—namely, an "electric train" not an "electric fire cart." English speakers are entitled to conclude therefore that the Chinese categorization of railroad phenomena is essentially similar to their own and is responsive to the same technological context. This is not to insist, however, that the meaning of *huoch'e* is precisely the same as "train," but rather that the difference is not sufficient to justify the use of "fire cart" as the translation. A more perfect translation would require a very lengthy ethnographic description of all the features of Chinese trains not found in trains elsewhere.

Another example of a vocabulary item that can no longer be literally interpreted is the Portuguese names of the days of the week. The ancient Romans had a week consisting of eight market days and one nonmarket day. After the introduction of Christian calendric reforms, Portuguese continued to denote Monday through Friday as second through sixth "market day" (*Segunda Feira . . . Seixta Feira*). There is no evidence, however, that these names reflect any economic or calendric specialty peculiar to the Portuguese. Thus an English translation of *Segunda Feira* as "Second Fair Day" is no more justified than a Portuguese translation of Monday as *Dia da Lua,* "Day of the Moon." The same cautions are in order with respect to the exotic grammatical categories found in non-Indo-European lan-

136

guages. Certain American Indian languages (e.g., Kwakiutl) have obligatory inflection to indicate whether or not an object is near or far from the speaker and whether or not it is visible or invisible. This grammatical device in all probability is not indicative of any active psychological tendency to be obsessed with the location of objects and people.

Obligatory Elitism and Sexism

It should not be concluded that grammatical conventions are always trivial. Certain obligatory grammatical categories do mirror social life quite faithfully. Consider the pronouns and verb forms for peers versus subordinates in the Romance languages. Because of the existence of a second person "familiar" form in the conjugation of Romance verbs, the speaker of French or Spanish is frequently obliged to evaluate and express the relative social standing of persons engaged in a conversation. Today these second person familiar forms (e.g., *tu hablas, tu parles*—in Spanish and French; roughly, "thou speaketh") are primarily applied to children, pets, very close friends, and loved ones. But another usage persists, especially in Spain, Portugal, and parts of Latin America, where landlords and officials apply the *tu* forms to servants, workers, and peasants as well as to children and pets. These forms clearly reflect an active consciousness of class and rank distinctions and bear a social significance that is far from trivial or merely conventional (cf. Southworth n.d.; Brown and Gilman 1960).

Similarly, certain obligatory categories in standard English seem to reflect a pervasive social bias in favor of male-centered viewpoints and activities. Many nouns that refer to human beings lack a sex gender—"child," "everybody," "everyone," "person," "citizen," "American," "human," and so on. Teachers of standard English prescribe masculine rather than feminine pronouns for these nouns. Thus it is considered "correct" to say: "Everyone must remember to take *his* toothbrush," even though the group being addressed consists of both males and females. Newspaper columnists are fond of writing: "The average American is in love with *his* car." And high school grammars insist that one must say: "All the boys and girls were puzzled but no one was willing to raise *his* hand" (Roberts 1964:382). Obviously a perfectly intelligible and sexually unbiased substitute is readily available in the plural possessive pronoun "their." In fact, almost everybody uses "their" in their (sic) everyday conversation (cf. Newmeyer 1975). So why bother to insist that "his" is correct?

137

Anthropologists face a particularly acute form of this problem in their dependence upon "man" as the vernacular term for "*Homo sapiens.*" Consider the following excerpt from a popular textbook:

A million or more years ago, man had become sufficiently differentiated from the other animals so that we can now look back on *him* as representing a new form of life. A feature of this differentiation was the elaboration of *his* nervous system . . . to the point where *he* could not only see, smell, and act but also symbolically represent a wide range of experience. *He* acquired the capacity to think and to speak. *He* could experience things and situations vicariously. . . . *He* learned how to communicate experience to *himself* and to others. . . . *He* began a process of self-organization. *He* began to see the universe about him. . . . *He* acquired the capacity. . . . *He* learned to create. . . . *He* began to shape. . . . *He* became imaginative.

It seems likely that the grammar of this passage reflects the fact that anthropology, like other learned professions in Western society, has been dominated by men. It seems just as likely that the use of "Him" and "He" as pronouns for God reflects the fact that men are the priests of Judaism and Christianity (see p. 553). The male-centered conventions of the English language may not be as benign and trivial as male anthropologists believe them to be (Lakoff 1973). But the fact that many women as well as men remain convinced that the obligatory male categories have nothing to do with the perpetuation of sexist stereotypes suggests that one ought to refrain from rendering definitive judgments about the relationship between grammar and cognition. It is certainly not my intention to imply that anthropologists who persist in the more conventional usage are necessarily dominated by unconscious sexist stereotypes. Moreover, as Frank Southworth (n.d.) has shown in his study of recent changes in the use of obligatory forms of address in India, mere linguistic changes are easy to make. So easy in fact that they sometimes function as "masks for power" by creating the superficial impression of democratization.

Phonological Evolution

As previously shown, the phonological elements of a language constitute an arbitrary although systematic arrangement of contrasting sounds. Like everything else, this system is subject to continuous change. Moreover, despite the fact that the native speakers are largely unconscious that any change at all is taking place, large parts of the phonological system change in unison. Indeed, the regularities of the changes are so great that it is possible to reconstruct the sound systems of entirely extinct languages.

138

Regularities of phonological change are expressed in terms of *phonetic laws.* Such laws describe the evolutionary transformation of a given language in terms of specific phonemes and allophones. For example, the sound of "ā" as in "cane" in Old English has become the sound of "o" as in "bone" in Modern English. This is shown in the following list of *correspondences* between the same words in Old English and Modern English (Sturtevant 1964:65):

bān	bone	mān	moan
bāt	boat	rād	road
gāt	goat	stān	stone
fām	foam		

Sound changes of this sort are common in the phonemic repertory of Modern English as compared with Old English. Accumulations of such changes eventually render a language as spoken by earlier generations incomprehensible to subsequent generations. In the case of English, virtually complete unintelligibility has been achieved in less than 1,000 years as the following passage from *The Anglo-Saxon Chronicle* for the year 1066 demonstrates:

On þissum ȝeare ... þe hē cyning wæs, hē fōr ūt mid scip-here tōȝēanes Willelme; and þā hwīle cōm Tostiȝ eorl intō Humbran mid 60 scipum. Eadwine eorl cōm mid land-fierde and drāf hine ūt; and þā butse-carlas hinc forsōcon, and hē fōr to Scotlande mid 12 snaccum, and hine ȝemētte Harald sē Norrena cyning mid 300 scipum, and Tostiȝ him tōbēag. And man cȳðde Harolde cyning hū hit wæs þær ȝedon and ȝeworden, and hē cōm mid miclum here Engliscra manna and ȝemētte hine æt Stæng-fordes brycge and hine ofslōg, and þone eorl Tostiȝ, and eallne þone here ēhtlīce ofercōm. And þā hwīle cōm Willelm eorl upp æt Hestingan on Sancte Michæles mæsse-dæȝ; and Harold cōm norðan and him wið feaht ær-þon þe his here cōme eall; and þær hē fēoll, and his twēȝen ȝebrōðra Gyrþ and Lēofwine, and Willelm þis land ȝeēode, and cōm tō Westminstre, and Ealdrēd arcebiscop hine tō cyninge ȝehālgode, and menn guldon him gold and gīslas sealdon, and siþþan hira land bohton. ...

In this year when he [Harold] was king, he went out with a fleet against William; and meanwhile Earl Tosti came into the Humber with sixty ships. Earl Edwin came with a land force and drove him out; and then the sailors forsook him [Tosti], and he went to Scotland with twelve small boats, and Harald, the Norwegian king, met him with three hundred ships, and Tosti submitted to him. And they told King Harold what had been done and had befallen there, and he came with a large army of Englishmen and met him [Harald] at Stamford Bridge and slew him and Earl Tosti, and courageously over-came the whole army. And mean-while Earl William came ashore at Hastings on Michaelmas; and Harold came from the north and fought against him before all his army came; and there he fell, and his two brothers Gyrth and Leofwin, and William conquered this land, and came to Westminster, and Archbishop Aldred consecrated him king, and men paid him gold and gave him hostages, and afterward redeemed their land.

The extent to which English has changed over the past 500 years is obscured by the standardization of spelling and hence by the maintenance of a common written form for words that are no longer pronounced as they were in the past. Although native speakers of English have little difficulty understanding Shakespeare's plays in written form, they would find a tape recording of a first night at the Globe Theater very difficult to follow.

When a community of people speaking a given language is dispersed or broken into smaller groups, the accumulation of sound changes results in the appearance of dialects. As the changes continue, languages emerge that differ not only from their ancestral forms but from each other as well. English and German, for example, are both modified versions of a language known as *Proto-West Germanic*. Just as there are regular sound correspondences between Modern English and Old English, there are also regular sound correspondences between English and German. For example, English /t/ corresponds to German /z/, as can be seen from the following words (after Sturtevant 1964:64–66):

tail	zagel	tin	zinn
tame	zahm	to	zu
tap	zapfen	toe	zehe
ten	zehn	tooth	zahn
tear	zehren		

In the 2,000 years that have elapsed since the Roman conquest of Western Europe, Latin has evolved into an entire family of languages of which French, Italian, Portuguese, Roumanian, and Spanish are the principal representatives. If linguists did not know of the existence of Latin through the historical records, they would be obliged to postulate its existence on the basis of the sound correspondences within the Romance family. It is obvious that every contemporary spoken language is nothing but a transformed version of a dialect of an earlier language and even in the absence of written records, languages can be grouped together on the basis of their "descent" from a common ancestor. Thus, in a more remote period, Proto-West Germanic was undifferentiated from Latin and a large number of additional languages including the ancestral forms of Hindi, Persian, Greek, Russian, and Gaelic. This group of languages constitutes the *Indo-European family* of languages. Inferences based upon the sound correspondences among the Indo-European languages have led linguists to reconstruct the sound system of the protolanguage from which they all ultimately derive. This language is called *Proto-Indo-European*.

140

The forces responsible for the regularity of phonetic laws are poorly understood. It is not known what conditions were responsible for the fact that Proto-West Germanic transformed itself into English in one place and into German in the next. One source of divergent phonological trends may be the contact experience with neighboring speech communities. In other instances, there is not the slightest clue as to why a particular phonological trend got started or even why once started it continued. Most phonological and grammatical changes seem to be analogous to "drift" (see p. 000) in biological evolution. Modern English is no more efficient or better adapted as a communication system than Old English; French is no more efficient or better adapted than Latin.

The phonological and grammatical changes that give rise to new languages have no significant consequences for human welfare associated with the particular direction in which the changes have taken place. Obviously it was of profound political and social significance that French, Italian, and the other Romance languages became mutually unintelligible. But the same profound significance would have resulted had the languages spoken by the people of Gaul evolved into Italian and had the language spoken by the people of the Italian peninsula evolved into French. Under certain circumstances people may want to kill each other over the question of which is to be the language used in public schools, in church, or in Parliament. But such struggles are not predicated upon the existence of any particular linguistic structures and can as easily develop in relationship to English, French, Swahili, or Hindi.

The Significance of Linguistic Change

There are two important ways in which the study of the evolution of new languages is relevant for an understanding of other aspects of cultural evolution. First, phonological and grammatical evolution shows how cultural forms, including those that are taken to be most permanent and enduring, are actually subject to continuous and relentless alteration. Individuals and groups dedicated to the preservation of the "purity" of French or English or Russian must reconcile their views with the fact that all contemporary languages are "corruptions" of previous languages. Attempts to prevent contemporary phonological and grammatical patterns from undergoing further change are doomed to failure. We can no more expect to terminate linguistic evolution than we can expect to terminate biological or geological evolution. Similar conclusions are valid in the other domains of cultural systems. The practices and beliefs regarded as most "pure" and most typical of a particular culture are products of active evolutionary forces. All social practices and beliefs are evanescent; change is not the exception but the rule.

Second, the evolution of new languages illustrates in a decisive fashion a principle that must be applied in the study of all cultural phenomena. The principle in question is that of the separation of consciousness and process. It should never be assumed that a people are aware of the nature of their own institutions or of the evolutionary pathways along which they are traveling. As stated long ago by Adam Fergusson, a great eighteenth-century Scottish philosopher, the forms of society "even in what are termed enlightened ages are made with equal blindness toward the future." Cultural systems are "indeed the result of human action, but not the execution of any human design." No individual or group of individuals ever sat down to plan the phonemic repertory of English or French or Kwakiutl. Not only does the average speaker of English find it difficult to reflect upon and correctly analyze the rules that form the structure of the English language, but linguistic specialists themselves, despite their prodigious labors, find it difficult to comprehend the system in its entirety. When it comes to the evolution of these systems, the "natives" are almost totally oblivious of what is really happening. Alfred Kroeber summed up the situation as follows:

The unceasing processes of change in language are mainly unconscious or covert, or at least implicit. The results of the change may come to be recognized by speakers of the changing language; the gradual act of change, and especially of the causes, mostly happen without the speaker being aware of them. . . . When a change has begun to creep in, it may be tacitly accepted or it may be observed and consciously resisted on the ground of being incorrect or vulgar or foreign. But the underlying motives of the objectors and the impulses of the innovator are likely to be equally unknown to themselves.   [1948:245]

Consciousness

The relationship between semantic universality and consciousness should not be overlooked. It is obvious that we are the only animals who are capable of talking about ourselves and of consciously analyzing our problems. We alone have conscious self-awareness. And that,

142

for many people, is the most important attribute of human nature. Yet there is something that is usually overlooked when consciousness is celebrated as our species' crowning glory. What is overlooked is that our minds are subject to restraints that do not affect the mental life of other organisms. Since we live by culture, our minds are shaped and channeled by culture. Hence the gift of semantic universality has many strings attached to it. Language does not necessarily give us freedom of thought; on the contrary, it often traps us into delusions and myths. Only human beings can suffer from the mental condition known as "false consciousness." Because we live by culture and because our minds are molded by culture, we have more to become aware of than any other creatures. We alone must struggle to understand how culture controls what goes on inside our heads. Without this additional level of awareness the human mind cannot be said to be fully conscious.

THE NATURE OF CULTURAL SYSTEMS

A culture is the total socially acquired life-way or life-style of a group of people. It consists of the patterned, repetitive ways of thinking, feeling, and acting that are characteristic of the members of a particular society or segment of a society. The ultimate goal of cultural anthropology is to describe the cultures of all human societies and to explain why they differ in some respects and are similar in others (cf. Weiss 1973).

In defining culture as consisting of patterns of behavior as well as patterns of thought, I am following the precedent set by Sir Edward Burnett Tylor, the founder of academic anthropology in the English-speaking world and the author of the first general anthropology textbook (1871:1).

Culture . . . taken in its wide ethnographic sense is that complex whole which includes knowledge, belief, art, morals, law, custom, and any other capabilities and habits acquired by man as a member of society. The condition of culture among the various societies of mankind, in so far as it is capable of being investigated on general principles, is a subject apt for the study of laws of human thought and action.

Some anthropologists restrict the meaning of "culture" exclusively to the mental rules for acting and speaking shared by the members of a given society. These rules are seen as constituting a kind of grammar of behavior in which the members of a society become competent, just as they become competent in the grammar of their language. The actual performances or behaviors that occur in a given society are then regarded as "social" rather than "cultural" phenomena. It is this distinction that some anthropologists seek to make when they write about social anthropology as distinguished from cultural anthropology (W. Goodenough 1970). No confusion can result if the more traditional definition is adhered to, taking care always to indicate whether the culturally determined ideas inside peoples' heads or the culturally determined activities of their bodies are being discussed.

One other kind of distinction between "social" and "cultural" is also quite common. Some sociologists and anthropologists employ the term "social" to refer to the relationship between the groups within a society. For these social scientists "culture" consists of the life-ways of the members of a society but not of the society's group structure. In the usage that I shall follow in this book, social groups will simply be treated as aspects of culture (mental and behavioral). The family, for example, is a social group that conforms to and exhibits a particular society's culture of domestic life.

What then is the definition of society? As employed in this book, the term *society* signifies a group of people who share a common habitat and who are dependent on each other for their survival and well-being. Because of culturally imposed restrictive mating patterns, societies need not constitute a single breeding population—although the boundaries between societies are usually characterized by breeding discontinuities and lowered rates of gene flow. No hard and fast rules exist for identifying the precise boundaries of societies or of subsocieties or of their corresponding cultures and subcultures. But it will seldom be necessary to define the precise limits of any particular society and culture in order to understand the processes that account for cultural similarities and differences.

Enculturation and Cultural Relativism

The culture of a society tends to be similar in many respects from one generation to the next. In part this continuity in life-ways is maintained by the process known as *enculturation*. Enculturation is a partially conscious and partially unconscious learning experience whereby the older generation invites, induces, and compels the younger generation to adopt traditional ways of thinking and behaving. Thus Chinese children use chopsticks instead of forks, employ tonal differences in their phonemic distinctions, and regard milkshakes as disgusting because they have been enculturated into Chinese culture rather than into the culture of the United States. Enculturation is primarily based upon the control that the older

145

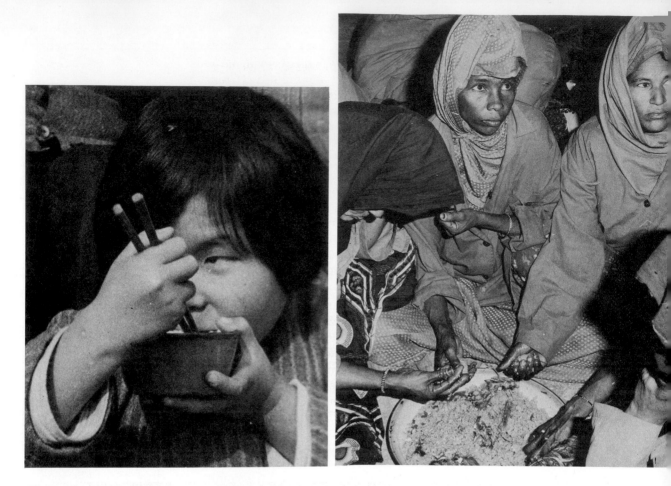

Figure 8-1. TECHNIQUES OF EATING. Power of enculturation is vividly apparent in diverse eating practices. Chinese girl (left) eating rice. Mauritanian factory workers (right) at lunch time. (FAO)

generation exercises over the means of rewarding and punishing children. Each generation is programmed not only to replicate the behavior of the previous generation but to replicate the replications. Each generation learns to reward behavior that conforms to the patterns of its own enculturation experience and to punish, or at least not reward, behavior that does not so conform.

The concept of enculturation (despite its limitations as discussed below) occupies a central position in the distinctive outlook of modern anthropology. Failure to comprehend the role of enculturation in the maintenance of each group's patterns of behavior and thought lies at the heart of the phenomenon known as *ethnocentrism*. Ethnocentrism is the belief that one's own patterns of behavior are always natural, good, beautiful, or important, and that strangers, to the extent that they live differently, live by savage, inhuman, disgusting, or irrational standards. People who are intolerant of cultural differences usually ignore the following fact. Had they been enculturated

146

with another group, all those supposedly savage, inhuman, disgusting and irrational life-styles would now be their own. Exposure of the fallacy of ethnocentrism leads to tolerance for and curiosity about cultural differences. Once having understood the enormous power that enculturation exerts over all human behavior, one can no longer rationally hold in contempt others who have been enculturated to different standards and practices different from their own.

All cultural anthropologists are tolerant of and curious about cultural differences. Some, however, have gone further and adopted the viewpoint known as *cultural relativism,* according to which each cultural pattern is regarded as being intrinsically as worthy of respect as all the rest. Although cultural relativism is a scientifically acceptable way of relating to cultural differences, it is not the only scientifically admissible attitude. Like everybody else, anthropologists make ethical judgments about the value of different kinds of cultural patterns. One need not regard cannibalism, warfare, human sacrifice, and poverty as worthy cultural achievements in order to carry out an objective study of these phenomena. Nor is there anything wrong with setting out to study certain cultural patterns because one wants to change them. In fact, when scientists fail to state clearly what values and motives have led them to undertake a particular study, they are more likely to bias their research than if they make their values and motives clear from the onset. The minimum requirement for a science of culture is honesty, not political or ethical neutrality (cf. Jorgensen 1971).

Figure 8-2. PASSING CULTURE ON. In Bali a man reads to his grandchildren from a script on narrow bamboo strips. (UPI Photo)

Continued on next page.

PASSING CULTURE ON
(continued). In Afghanistan
(above), father with son reading from Koran. In Taos, New
Mexico (above right), father
teaching child to dance. In
Moscow (below), a ballet
class. (Eugene Gordon—top
left; Museum of the American
Indian, Heye Foundation—
top right; UPI Photo—below)

Figure 8-3. CULTURE, PEOPLE, AND THE SUN. Relationship between people and the sun is mediated by culture. Sunbathing (above) is a modern invention. On the beach at Villerville in 1908,(left) only "mad dogs and Englishmen went out in the midday sun" . . . without their parasols. (Burk Uzzle/ Magnum—above; Jacques Henri Lartigue/Museum of Modern Art—below)

Limitations of the Enculturation Concept

Under present world conditions no special wisdom is required to realize that enculturation cannot account for a considerable portion of the life-styles of existing social groups. It is clear that replication of cultural patterns from one generation to the next is never complete. Old patterns are not always faithfully repeated in successive generations, and new patterns are continually being added. Recently the rate of innovation and nonreplication in the industrial societies has reached proportions alarming to adults who were programmed to expect crossgenerational continuity.

Today, nowhere in the world are there elders who know what the children know, no matter how remote and simple the societies are in which the children live. In the past there were always some elders who knew more than any children in terms of their experience of having grown up within a cultural system. Today there are none. It is not only that parents are no longer guides, but that there are no guides, whether one seeks them in one's own country or abroad. There are no elders who know what those who have been reared within the last twenty years know about the world into which they were born.   [Mead 1970:77–78]

Clearly enculturation cannot account for the "generation gap"; rather, it must be assumed that there has been a breakdown in the enculturative process and that increasing numbers of adults have not learned how to induce their children to replicate their own patterns of thought and behavior. Enculturation, therefore, accounts only for the

Figure 8-4. HIGH SCHOOL PROM, 1953. Dusk to dawn with chaperones. (UPI Photo)

Figure 8-5. ROCK FES
TIVAL. No chaperones, but
culturally determined. (Burk
Uzzle/Magnum)

continuity of culture; it cannot account for the evolution of culture.

Even with respect to replicated patterns, the mechanism of enculturation has important limitations. There is no evidence to support the view that every replicated pattern is the result of the programming that one generation experiences at the hands of another. Many replicated patterns are the result of the response of successive generations to similar conditions of social life. The programming received may even be different from the actual patterns; in other words, people may be enculturated to behave in one way but be obliged by situational or functional factors beyond their control to behave in another way. To take a trite example: enculturation is responsible for replicating the patterns of behavior associated with driving a car. Another replicated pattern consists of stalled traffic. Clearly automobile

151

Limitations of the Enculturation Concept

drivers are not programmed to make traffic jams; on the contrary, they are programmed to keep moving and to go around obstacles. Yet the situational result of this programming is a highly patterned cultural phenomenon.

Poverty, warfare, and crime require a similar analysis to which I shall return in later chapters. Here let it suffice to say that many poor people find themselves living in houses, eating food, working, and raising families according to patterns that replicate their parents' culture, not because they have been enculturated to these patterns but because they have been exposed to the same political and economic conditions (see Ch. 21).

The existence of cultural evolution and of situational or functional replication indicates that enculturation can never be invoked as an explanatory principle. A cultural pattern may not be replicated if there is evolution; on the other hand, it may be replicated even without enculturation. To say that a pattern has been enculturated, therefore, is to say that there existed a functional situation appropriate for replication rather than for evolution. In this world of endless flux, it is unrealistic to ask only why something has changed; one must also ask why it has not changed. Enculturation answers neither question. Enculturation is a universal tendency latent in all cultural situations. Variables cannot be explained merely by invoking constants such as aggressive "instincts," mother love, learning, or enculturation.

Cultural Systems: The Postulate of Functional Unity

Thus far I have been treating cultures as mere inventories of separate patterns, or "traits." One of the fundamental assumptions of anthropology is that cultural differences and similarities cannot be explained if they are looked upon merely as isolated entities. Something similar to this assumption was implied in the previous section when I said that the functional situation had to be considered in order to understand whether or not a particular trait would be replicated. Another way to express this aspect of cultural phenomena is to postulate that the items in a cultural inventory are parts of *cultural systems* (or *sociocultural systems*).

The nature of these systems can be grasped only in the perspective of the evolutionary career of our hominid ancestors. Culture is our

152

primary mode of achieving reproductive success. Hence particular cultural systems are arrangements of patterned behavior, thought, and feeling that contribute to the survival and reproduction of particular social groups. Traits contributing to the maintenance of a system may be said to have a *positive function* with respect to that system. A viable system may be regarded as consisting largely of positive-functioned traits since the contrary assumption would lead one to expect the system's extinction.

The *functional unity* of cultural systems is a basic postulate underlying all of cultural anthropology. It remains, however, a matter of empirical research to identify the functions of a given trait, that is, its precise contribution to the maintenance of the system, including always, first and foremost, the survival and reproduction of the group itself.

The postulate of functional unity does not imply that there are no completely useless and negative-functioned (system-destroying) traits. In the nineteenth century many anthropologists glibly spoke of *survivals,* traits that at one time were functional but that with the alteration brought on by cultural evolution had lost their utility. After considerable controversy it has come to be recognized that many cultural traits lose their original function and meaning, but few indeed can become utterly useless. Hunting with a bow and arrow, for example, does not contribute significantly to the protein ration of American sportsmen. But sports make an important contribution to the American economy, to physical and psychological well-being and to the stability of the U.S. political system. As another example, consider the celebration of Halloween, the evening before All Saints Day, formerly a time to pray for the dead and now an occasion for children to extort candy from adults by threatening them with "trick or treat." In addition to the obvious economic utility of this institution from the point of view of candy manufacturers, there may also be constructive social effects associated with the controlled expression of vandalism. Among the favorite candidates for a truly useless, vestigial survival are the sleeve buttons on a man's suit jacket, which were formerly used to keep shirt ruffles out of the inkwell. Even here, however, four extra buttons per jacket are not exactly useless from the point of view of the button manufacturer.

Negative-functioned traits are equally difficult to identify. Crime, the most likely contender, may have positive effects such as the redistribution of wealth and the deflection of rebellious impulses from more vital economic and political targets. I shall discuss many additional disruptive practices that probably also make positive contributions to the maintenance of stability. Witchcraft and warfare are examined in this perspective in Chapters 13 and 17. There are also many instances of apparent economic waste and irrational utilization of the environment that upon closer inspection turn out to be highly functional in the context of a given set of cultural and natural conditions. These too, as exemplified in wasteful feasts, the Hindu sacred cow complex, and food taboos, are discussed in later chapters.

In order to demonstrate that a given trait is truly negative-functioned, it must be shown that the society is heading toward extinction and that the trait in question is contributing to that result. Charles Wagley (1969) has described how the ideal of small families among the Tapirapé Indians of Brazil lost its positive function under the stress of European contact and thereafter contributed decisively to the extinction of the group. Instances of this sort are rare, however, because it seldom can be shown that extinction has resulted from unambiguously negative-functioned traits. Hundreds of American Indians social groups were wiped out during the past three centuries leaving behind neither progeny nor traditions. Yet these societies were smoothly functioning systems when first contacted by Europeans; their downfall was caused not by their negative-functioned traits but by their inability to withstand the combined attack of European armies and European diseases. They were overwhelmed by more powerful systems.

It should be clear therefore that the postulated functional unity of cultural systems has nothing in common with the notion that what exists cannot be improved upon. To say that a given cultural arrangement is functional is to make no prediction concerning its stability. Other arrangements of an even more functional nature are always imminent. Nor does the notion of functional unity imply that all the parts of the system are in perfect balance or harmony. Rather, there is always a considerable amount of stress as the system's components fluctuate above and below optimum levels. For example, it has been postulated that Melanesian religious rituals may act as homeostatic regulators of domestic animal populations. Up to a certain point, a rise in the animal population is convenient and useful; beyond this point, the animals press against the food resources available for people. This stress triggers a ritual slaughter of the animals. This reduces the animal population, producing a different form of stress, which is alleviated in turn by raising more pigs (see p. 273).

The functional unity of such systems is certainly not to be regarded as perfect or imperishable. Conditions external to the system— destruction of the forests or the arrival of colonial police patrols—may shatter its viability. And it may self-destruct from within if, for example, the human population grows too fast or slaughters too many

154

Figure 8-6. THE POWER OF CULTURE. There are no universal standards of pulchritude. The Ainu woman (left top) has a facial tatoo serving as a permanent form of lipstick. Body painting, something new that's very old (above), makes a comeback in U.S.A. The Senegal coiffure (left below) is one of endless numbers of culturally prescribed hairstyles. (American Museum of Natural History—left top; Leonard Freed/Magnum—above; United Nations—left below)

pigs. Minima and maxima in the homeostatic cycles always offer the possibility of evolutionary breakthroughs and the transformation or extinction of the system.

The Universal Pattern

In order to begin the task of describing and analyzing cultural systems, a classification of the parts of such systems is needed. Anthropologists have provisionally accepted one or another version of the *universal pattern* as adequate for a rough first-ordering of these research efforts. As formulated by Clark Wissler, the universal pattern consists of language, material traits, art, knowledge, society, property, government, and war. Many other versions exist. George Peter Murdock and his associates, for example, organized the Human Relations Area Files in terms of eighty-eight basic categories (Murdock, Ford, Hudson and others 1961). Others have operated, implicitly at least, with only a twofold scheme: *core* and *superstructure* (cf. Steward 1955). Core traits consist of the behavior patterns that most directly interact with the environment and that ensure the physical survival of the culture bearers; and superstructure consists of all residual patterns.

A universal pattern that has found favor among anthropologists of widely divergent theoretical interests will be used as the orienting framework for the rest of this book. It has three major functional sectors: (1) *ecology,* or the way the system is adapted to its habitat; (2) *social structure,* or the arrangements by which an orderly social life is maintained; and (3) *ideology,* or the mental characteristics that fit people to their ecology and social structure (cf. Radcliffe-Brown 1952). Let me elaborate.

1. *Ecology:* Ecology in a scientific sense is fundamentally a matter of the flow of energy among human and infrahuman populations in a habitat. The ecological adaptation of a particular culture depends upon the technology it has for obtaining, transforming, and distributing energy. Thus at the base of every culture are the tools, machines, techniques, and practices relating human existence to the material conditions of specific habitats. Through its technology each culture interacts with its natural habitat to obtain food, fuels, and other forms of disposable energy. Technological inventories and practices also provide each culture with protection against animal predators, disease, climatic extremes, and neighboring human populations (who are also to be counted as part of the environment). Additional technological inventories and practices regulate population size in relation-

156

ship to space, air, and other natural resources and dispose of human and industrial waste. All *technoenvironmental* transactions form part of the ecological pattern. Equally basic, however, are the size and density of population, the pattern of dispersal with respect to resources, the growth rates, and age and sex composition, insofar as all these *demographic* factors modify and regulate the relationship between a cultural system and its environment.

2. *Social structure:* The maintenance of an orderly social life is a necessity of all cultural systems. This necessity does not arise, however, from some abstract, aesthetic, or vindictive need for law and order but rather from the practical requirements of production and reproduction. The primary function of social structure therefore is the maintenance of orderly relationships among the individuals and groups responsible for the production of food, fuel, and other life-sustaining ecological transactions and for the breeding and care of children. Social structure is also concerned with the orderly transfer and distribution of energy and labor power among the various production and reproduction units. These aspects of cultural systems are sometimes grouped under the rubric *economy.*

I take the view that orderly processes of production, consumption, and exchange—that is, all *economic* transactions—cannot be understood apart from the structure of social groups, and vice versa, that the structure of social groups cannot be understood apart from their economic functions.

Domestic groupings and political groupings constitute the most important categories of social structure. To these correspond *domestic economy* and *domestic law and order; political economy* and *political law and order.* These concepts are clarified in Chapters 14 and 17.

Not every social grouping is necessarily organized directly around an economic (or demographic) function. Complex social structures contain many groupings that are directly concerned with law and order, such as police, military, legal, and political cadres. But other groupings are organized about ideological functions, such as churches and educational and scientific organizations. Nonetheless the postulate of functional unity requires one to look for functional connections among all elements in a system's social structure, its ecology, and its domestic and political economy. The nature of these relationships will also be made explicit in subsequent chapters.

3. *Ideology:* The development of semantic universality may be viewed as the adaptive response of a ground-dwelling, hunting, and food-gathering hominid to the problem of facilitating increasingly

complex levels of social and ecological activities. Language in this evolutionary perspective has an instrumental function that is as much a part of technoenvironmental, demographic, and technoeconomic transactions as are tools and work groups. With the achievement of semantic universality, however, language began to fulfill a new and unprecedented function, namely that of fitting the thoughts and feelings of individuals and groups to the ecological and structural conditions of their cultural life.

Although every social species is organized into groups that have ecological patterns and social structures, only human groups have ideologies. Animals undoubtedly have a mental life corresponding to the mental life of human infants before language competence is achieved. But infrahuman mental experience is forever locked up within the mind of the individual organism. Of course the psychological programs or "plans" governing an animal's response repertory can be formulated by observing its external behavior under controlled conditions. This is the main business of animal psychology. With human beings, however, anthropologists have the opportunity not only of observing external behavior but of being able to talk with people about their inner thoughts. Each of us knows that our own external behavior is preceded, accompanied, and followed by a ceaseless stream of mental and emotional experiences. Moreover we share these experiences with each other through talk, writing, and other modes of expression such as gestures, art, music, or dance.

Although these cognitive and emotional events and their verbal or other manifestations appear to originate in each individual's private inner being, it is a fundamental principle of anthropological analysis that most if not all of this inner behavior and its overt expression conform to definite culturally determined patterns, which originate outside the individual. Ideology thus embraces the entire realm of socially patterned thought. It includes the explicit and implicit knowledge, opinions, values, plans, and goals that people have about their ecological circumstances: their understanding of nature, technology, production, and reproduction; their reasons for living, working, and reproducing. Ideology also embraces all thoughts and patterned expression of thoughts that describe, explain, and justify the parts of social structure; that give meaning and purpose to domestic and political economy and to the maintenance of law and order in domestic and political relations; that describe, justify, and plan the delegation of authority, the division of labor, the exchange of products, and the sharing or nonsharing of resources. Finally, ideology also consists of the ideology of ideology, thoughts about thoughts, the explanation of itself as in formal systems of philosophy, science, art, and religion.

158

Emics and Etics

The existence of semantic universality and of the ideological sector of the universal pattern greatly complicate the task of describing and analyzing cultural systems. In studies of primate societies there is basically only one way in which the substance of group life can be scientifically observed. Primatologists cannot ask members of primate societies to give an account of their ecology, social structure, or ideology. There is no way to ask chimpanzees or baboons how they obtain their food supply. Telling a macaque "take me to your leader" would not advance the understanding of macaque authority patterns, and attempts to converse with a baboon about why baboons do not eat more meat or share their grass with each other or how they feel when they see a stranger would result in a useless monologue. A fundamentally different prospect confronts people who want to study people. By talking to people, anthropologists learn about a vast inner world of thought and feeling. This inner world exists on different levels of consciousness. First, there are patterns such as the grammatical or phonemic systems that are far below consciousness. Second, there are patterns that exist closer to consciousness and that are readily formulated when the proper questions are asked. For example, rules of conduct, values, and "norms" can usually be elicited for all cultural events. Thus people can usually formulate a proper code of conduct for activities such as weaning babies, courting a mate, choosing a leader, treating a disease, entertaining a guest, categorizing kinsmen, worshiping God, and tens of thousands of additional commonplace activities. They can formulate these rules more readily than the "deep structures" of phonemics and grammar. Yet such rules, plans, and values may not ordinarily be formalized or completely conscious. Finally, there are equally numerous, fully conscious, explicit, and formal rules of conduct and statements of values, plans, goals, and aspirations that may be discussed during the course of ordinary conversations, written in law codes, or announced at public gatherings (i.e., rules about littering, bank deposits, length of skirts, trespass, and so on).

Regardless of the level of consciousness, descriptions of cognitive and emotional patterns differ in a fundamental way from descriptions of actual behavior. When studying the inner world of plans, goals, values, meaning, rules, and codes, the task of the anthropologist is to achieve an explicit and orderly representation of what takes place "inside people's heads." The ultimate verification of whether an explicit and orderly representation of inner events is also an adequate or accurate representation depends upon the consent, opinion, or

159

affirmation of the people themselves. The nature of this verification process is best seen in the case of phonemic and grammatical analysis. Although English speakers are unaware of their phonemic repertory, the question of whether /p/ and /b/ in *pat* and *bat* constitute different phonemes cannot be answered independently of the native speakers' judgment. Only the native speakers are ultimately capable of judging whether /p/ and /b/ are distinctive signals. Not that the native speaker judges /p/ and /b/ to be different phonemes, but rather that the native speaker judges *pat* and *bat* to be different words, and on the basis of that judgment and others like it, the linguist decides that the initial sounds are contrastive. Similarly, although the linguist decides how the deep structure of a grammatical sentence ought to be described, the native speaker judges whether the sentences generated by that deep structure are grammatical (cf. Werner and Fenton 1973). As E.W. Bach (1964:34) points out:

> The data of linguists are not mere physical events, but physical events together with judgments of native speakers about these events. . . .
>   The fact remains that language as a cultural product cannot be adequately studied apart from the native speaker's judgments.

The relevance of the native speaker's judgment extends far beyond phonemic and grammatical distinction. It includes all conscious and unconscious culturally prescribed categorizations of culture, people, and nature; all realms of value, plans, rules, codes, goals, beliefs, and attitudes; and all descriptions of events from the native's point of view.

It was the linguist Kenneth Pike who first proposed to group all these phenomena under the general term *emic* (from phon*emic*). Pike went further and contrasted *emic* language and culture with what he called *etic* (from phon*etic*)language and culture. Etic phenomena are those that are identified and studied independently of the natives' cultural judgments. Thus in stating that many native speakers of English frequently form utterances that contain both bilabial voiced and bilabial unvoiced stops, the observer's statement is in no way influenced by whether or not the natives employ this distinction in judging words to be similar or different. Thus it is an etic rather than emic fact that there are two kinds of /p/ in the word "paper"; that Hindu farmers kill their cows by starving them to death (see p. 511); that 550,000 individuals own 21.2 percent of all the wealth in the U.S. (see p. 406); or that the !Kung Bushmen obtain 30 percent of their calories from mongongo nuts (see p. 237). Etic phenomena, in other words, lie outside the heads of the native actors.

One way to study emic phenomena is to attempt to describe the "program that native actors carry in their minds and that they employ in deciding whether an activity is appropriate. Just as a computer cannot ordinarily describe the program it uses in recognizing numbers or carrying out computations, so too native actors often cannot describe the rules they follow in making judgments about appropriate and inappropriate language and behavior. In dealing with computers, the programmers know what's "inside their heads" because the programmers have consciously designed the rules. In dealing with people, the rules people follow must be reconstructed by studying how they make judgments about what is similar or different or appropriate or inappropriate. But the study of emic phenomena need not always involve a search for the "deep structure" of cultural rules. Many aspects of ideology consist of conscious rules that can be elicited by direct questions ("cross on the green"; "thou shalt not kill"; "pay your taxes"). Note that a knowledge of the rules, conscious or unconscious, surface or deep, that people employ in judging what is significant, appropriate, or legitimate is not necessarily knowledge about how they will act. Emics is knowledge about competence rather than performance. In order to make predictions about how people will act, knowledge of both emic and etic phenomena is usually necessary. For example, many societies have rules against cannibalism; but when people go without food for a long time, these rules often cease to be reliable predictors of behavior.

Etics and Communication

One additional point remains to be cleared up. Etic studies need not be restricted to nonverbal behavior. Observers may make judgments concerning what people say to each other that need not depend upon native judgments of what was said or meant. It is possible to learn the rudiments of a human language and then to apply that knowledge to a description of the messages that people exchange. (Just as it is possible to interpret the meaning of messages that are exchanged when infrahuman organisms—chimpanzees—communicate without asking them what they are trying to say.) Obviously this level of meaning resembles the speaker-listener meanings in some respects but not in others. It is well known, however, that it is impossible to exhaust all the subtleties and individual nuances attached to any word or phrase in a person's mind even if one has total competence in a language (cf. Ikegami 1975).

The importance of an etic approach to human linguistic behavior arises from the fact that the daily life of any human group usually consists of a mixture of related verbal and nonverbal activities. An

Figure 8-7. NEW GUINEA BODY ADORNMENTS. These residents of Mount Hagen region insert feathers through their nasal septa. Modern American women follow a similar custom with respect to their ear lobes. (United Nations)

ethnography of performance as distinct from an ethnography of competence must therefore make provisions for identifying the meaning of utterances. For example, I have participated in an attempt to provide an etic description of how the members of households in the United States influence each other's behavior. One of the primary means by which household members exert such influence is by issuing verbal requests. In identifying requests and compliances to requests, the observers made use of videotape recordings of long sequences of household activities. They did not try to take into account what each member of the household subjectively intended in issuing a request or in complying with a request. They only took into account the level of meaning that was sufficient to obtain a high level of agreement among the observers that a particular request had been made and that it was or was not complied with. The team of observers agreed that between 70 and 80 percent of the requests were not complied with.

An emic study of influence or authority would be concerned with very different questions. It would be concerned with stating the rules inside the heads of the members of the household by which certain phrases are interpreted as appropriate or nonappropriate requests and certain activities as appropriate or nonappropriate responses to such requests. It would not take account, however, of the number of times dogs barking in the backyard, television sets blaring, water running in the sink, and other noises drowned out a request or gave an "excuse" for one member of the family not to "hear" what the other was saying. Nor would it take account of the fact that human beings who are members of the same society—indeed, members of the same household—frequently disagree concerning whether a request is legitimate, or "serious," or a response to a request is appropriate, or "satisfactory."

Emic descriptions and explanations frequently ignore or contradict etic descriptions and explanations. One of the basic points to be made in this book is that phenomena such as marriage, family, kinship, descent, exchange, authority, power, class, race, war, and religion can be adequately understood only by systematically separating their etic and emic aspects. There is no error more common or devastating than to confuse what people say, wish, dream, and believe they do with what they actually do. It must be emphasized, however, that the fundamental task of cultural anthropology cannot be served by neglecting either emic or etic phenomena. Both emic and etic phenomena form part of the adaptive process of human cultural systems (cf. M. Harris 1968; Burling 1969; Kay 1970; Pelto 1970).

Divergent, Convergent, and Parallel Evolution

The main objective of cultural anthropology is to state the conditions under which specific cultural phenomena are likely to occur. Another way of expressing this objective is to say that anthropologists seek the causes of cultural evolution: the explanation of why certain cultural systems have evolved along divergent, convergent, or parallel lines.

Divergent evolution is the appearance of increasing amounts of difference between two or more cultures as a result of different rates and directions of change. *Convergent evolution* occurs when the amount of difference between two or more cultures is decreasing. *Parallel evolution* denotes a situation in which two or more evolving cultures similar in certain respects undergo similar transformations at approximately the same rate.

All cultural differences and similarities have been produced by divergent, convergent, or parallel evolution. Hence to be able to explain cultural evolution is to be able to answer most of the causal questions that can be asked about cultural systems—that is, why they change and why they do not change, and why they change in certain directions and not in others.

163

Cultural versus Biological Evolution

Before embarking upon this venture, it is essential to discuss the extent to which cultural and biological evolution can be explained by similar principles. To this end it is useful to examine an analogy between cultural and biological structures and processes. Enculturation, for example, can be regarded as the analogue of genetic replication. Enculturation, like genetic reproduction, is imperfect, and hence innovations, the analogues of mutations, arise in the cultural system. Some of these innovations rapidly become extinct; others endure and become functional parts of the system. The differential survival of cultural innovations implies the existence of selective processes analogous to natural selection. However, natural selection itself does not account for the divergences, convergences, and parallelism of cultural evolution.

The analogy between biological and cultural evolution breaks down at a number of crucial points. First, the "traits" or "units" that evolve in biological evolution—namely, genes and organisms—replicate themselves in a fashion quite unlike the replication of cultural patterns. Biological reproduction consists of the replication of genes which govern the growth of new organisms. Cultural systems do not contain genes, and hence they do not undergo anything similar to biological reproduction. Of course the people whose behavior, thoughts, and feelings constitute the substance of a particular cultural system do reproduce, and without their reproduction their system would become extinct. But unlike the situation in biological evolution, in cultural evolution the adoption of innovations seldom depends upon the differential reproductive rates of the *individuals* who are associated with or who participate in the innovation.

The relationship between the adoption of a cultural innovation and its reproductive advantage is usually indirect and related to the reproductive advantage of the social group as a whole rather than to any particular set of individuals. Consider the case of the spread of electric lighting into the interior of Brazil. This innovation first made its appearance in the large cities and towns. It spread into the countryside as power lines were extended or as diesel generators were installed in remote places. Townspeople were given the option of having the lines brought into their houses. Those who could afford to pay for the installation, the bulbs, and the monthly service invariably adopted the innovation. Those who could not afford the new source of light continued to use their kerosene lamps. Decades have passed

164

since certain remote towns in Brazil began to acquire electricity, yet many townspeople still depend on smoky kerosene lamps made from tin cans and discarded ink bottles. If electric bulbs and kerosene lamps had been genetic traits, the only way by which one could have replaced the other would be for "kerosene lampers" to have had on the average fewer children who lived to reproductive age. But this is scarcely the case in Brazil. Those who have no electricity tend to mate early and to have large families. Electric lighting is thus actually spreading in a fashion contrary to what one would expect in a strictly biological model of natural selection. The solution to this paradox is that the spread of electricity does not require a reproductive act. "Kerosene lampers" become "electric lighters" during the course of their own lifetimes. An analogous event in the biological realm would have a bat take over the eye of an eagle, or a dog suddenly sprout an elephant's trunk.

The ability of cultural traits to spread from individual to individual within a single generation is one of the great advantages that cultural modes of adaptation possess over biological modes of adaptation. Human beings are the most adaptable of creatures precisely because we do not depend upon reproduction and differential survival in order to add innovations to our survival "kit." The spread of an innovation through learning is an intrinsically more efficient and flexible process than the spread of a gene through differential reproduction.

But it should not be concluded from the ability of cultural systems to adopt innovations within the span of a single generation that differential survival and reproduction are irrelevant to the course of cultural evolution. Evidence presented in following chapters indicates that because of the prevalence of warfare, innovations tend to be selected for their ability to increase population size, population density, and per capita energy production.

The mechanism of innovation does not always require actual testing of one trait against another to determine which contributes most in the long run to cultural survival. Given a choice of bow and arrow versus a high-powered rifle, the Eskimo adopts the rifle long before there is any change in the rate of population growth. In the short run the rifle spreads among more and more people not because one group expands and engulfs the rest, but because individuals regularly accept innovations that seem to offer them more security, greater reproductive efficiency, and higher energy yields for lower energy inputs. Yet it cannot be denied that the ultimate test of any innovation is in the crunch of competing systems and differential survival and reproduction. And that crunch may sometimes be delayed for hundreds of years. In the interim the basis for the selection

Figure 8-8. DIFFUSION. Can you reconstruct the diffusionary history of the objects and activities shown in these scenes? Brazilian woodsman (facing page left), Mongolian metropolis (facing page right), Tadzhik, USSR, farmers (facing page below), American nightclub (this page). (UPI Photo—facing left, below; Cartier-Bresson/Magnum—facing right; Burt Glinn/Magnum—this page)

of innovations must be sought in the immediate behavioral and psychic advantages and disadvantages experienced by individuals or dominant power groups (cf. Alland and McCay 1973; Ruyle 1973b).

Diffusion

The advantages of the cultural mode of adaptation are not restricted to the rapidity with which an innovation can spread and become established within a given population. Cultural innovations, unlike genetic mutations, also spread between populations. This process, known as *diffusion*, is so common that in any cultural system the overwhelming majority of traits has originated in other societies. In the United States, for example, large portions of religious life, political organization, and food technology originated in remote parts of the world. The Judeo-Christian forms of religious practice and thought diffused from the Middle East; parliamentary democracy was a Western European invention; and the food plants grown by United States farmers originated in major centers of domestication in the Middle East, the Mediterranean, Mesoamerica, Southeast Asia, and West Africa.

Among bioforms, the analogue of diffusion is sexual reproduction; the biological function of sex is to spread adaptive biological innovations within a population and from one population to another. But the spread of genes between populations is cut off by speciation. Perhaps the most decisive difference between cultural and biological evolutionary mechanisms is just this: there is no equivalent of speciation in the realm of culture. No matter how much two cultures may diverge from each other, contact between them invariably results in the exchange of some cultural features. The cultures of the Eskimo and of the Canadian fur traders, for example, were radically different in content, scale, and organization. Yet this did not prevent the Eskimo from adopting Christianity, canned food, and rifles, nor did it prevent the Canadians from adopting the dog sled, the fur parka, and snow-shoes.

Diffusion and Explanation

In the first half of the present century, diffusion was put forward as an independent explanatory principle. The lingering effects of this point of view are embodied in attempts to show that the civilization of one area is derived from that of another area—Polynesia from Peru, or vice versa; lowland Mesoamerica from highland Mesoamerica, or vice versa; China from Europe, or vice versa; the New World from the Old World. In recent years, however, diffusion has lost much of its reputability as an explanation of cultural differences and similarities. No one doubts that the probability of evolutionary convergences between different cultural systems is related to geographical proximity. In general the closer two societies are to each other, the greater will be the resemblances between them. But these resemblances cannot be regarded as the result of some automatic tendency for all traits to diffuse. Two societies in close proximity are likely to share similar natural environments (cf. Harner 1970). Hence the convergent and parallel developments between the societies may in part be accounted for by common response to a common set of environmental conditions. However, there are numerous cases of societies in

168

close contact that maintain radically different ways of life. For example, the Inca of South America achieved statehood while the nearby tropical forest peoples remained village-organized. Other cases are the Ituri forest hunters and their Bantu agriculturalist neighbors, and the sedentary Pueblo Indians of the Southwest and their nomadic, marauding Apache neighbors. Moreover, even when a cultural trait spreads from one culture to another, diffusion does not explain why it originated in the one or was accepted by the other. Finally, diffusion cannot account for the remarkably convergent and parallel transformations that have occurred on every continent among peoples who are known not to have been in close contact with each other.

In sum, diffusion is no more an explanation of cultural differences and similarities than enculturation is. If nothing but diffusion were involved, all cultural systems would be the same. Again it is a matter of not being able to explain variables by constants.

The task ahead therefore is to identify the general principles governing the appearance of cultural differences and similarities. These principles, by accounting for instances of divergent, convergent, and parallel evolution in terms of general conditions and general causal relationships, will account as well for diffusionary effects.

9

ARCHAEOLOGY AND THE EVOLUTION OF CULTURE: THE PALEOLITHIC

In the early phases of hominization the evolution of culture was closely associated with the evolution of learning ability. Natural selection favored individuals whose neural circuitry could handle grammatical speech and who could learn to respond in socially traditional ways. Our ancestors' neural circuitry became more complex the more they depended on culture. Eventually a cultural "take-off" occurred: the rate of cultural evolution began to outstrip the rate of biological evolution. The take-off probably occurred between 100,000 and 50,000 B.P. During the last twenty-five thousand years culture has been changing more and more rapidly. It is now evolving at an exponential rate, even though there have been no recent significant changes in cranial volume or shape.

The phenomenon of cultural take-off is of scientific and ethical significance. If the immense changes to be discussed occurred primarily as a result of cultural evolution rather than biological evolution, then it may reasonably be concluded that our species is capable of virtually unlimited amounts of additional cultural change. The further evolution of human nature will be almost entirely determined by the further evolution of culture.

The existence of a prehistoric cultural take-off point does not mean that culture has freed itself of the laws that govern other phenomena. Evolving past a certain point, human culture cast off its dependence upon the further evolution of the brain, but it did not rid itself of all biological and environmental restraints. The general and specific pathways of cultural evolution can only be understood in relation to the continuing interplay between culture, human nature, and relevant portions of the natural environment.

The anthropological study of cultural evolution rests upon the facts and inferences of prehistoric archaeology. Archaeology is to anthropology as paleontology is to biology. Without archaeology anthropologists could neither describe nor explain the course of cultural evolution. Because of the great sweep of time and space covered by archaeological research, anthropology enjoys a unique position among the social sciences. Anthropologists can observe the operation of long-range trends and formulate and test causal theories of cultural evolution.

Prehistoric Periods

Stone implements provide most of the evidence about the earliest phases of cultural evolution. Hence archaeologists divide the entire period of early prehistory into *lithic* (meaning "stone") ages. Three such ages are recognized in the cultural evolution of Europe: *Paleolithic* (old stone age), *Mesolithic* (middle stone age), and *Neolithic* (new stone age).

The Paleolithic was a phase of culture that once existed throughout the world. But archaeologists disagree concerning the extent to which the Mesolithic and Neolithic ages can also be identified on a worldwide basis. Most would agree that the Mesolithic was essentially restricted to Northern Europe and that the Neolithic or its equivalent can be identified in Asia and Africa as well as Europe. Some would extend the concept of Neolithic to include the early phases of the domestication of plants and animals in the New World as well. Anthropologists are interested in these ages not primarily for the stone tools themselves—the technological "traditions"—but rather for what these tools and their evolutionary modifications tell about the evolution of cultural systems.

On the most general level, Paleolithic cultures were based on hunting, fishing, and gathering rather than on farming or stock-raising. Group size was small, total population small, and the groups were widely dispersed. To make efficient use of available plant and animal resources, the hunting and gathering groups ranged over a wide territory and probably did not settle at any one campsite, cave, or shelter for more than a few weeks or months. In the same highly general perspective, one may characterize the Neolithic as the age of cultural systems based on domesticated plants and animals. Group size and total population were larger and settlement was more

171

nucleated. To make efficient use of the domesticated plants, permanent settlements or villages replaced the temporary camps of the Paleolithic hunters and gatherers. The Mesolithic was a time of transition between these two ages.

The Paleolithic, as the longest of the prehistoric ages, exhibits considerable local diversity and evolutionary change. Three subdivisions are generally recognized: (1) the *Lower Paleolithic,* dominated by simple pebble tools, core biface tools, and simple flake tools; (2) the *Middle Paleolithic,* characterized by an enlarged and refined repertory of core tools, flake points, and other flake tools; (3) the *Upper Paleolithic,* characterized by an enlarged and refined repertory of *blade* tools (see p. 180) and by many specialized ivory, bone, and antler implements and artifacts.

In the nineteenth century archaeologists assumed that in order to understand how the Paleolithic populations had conducted their lives, all that was necessary was to study the surviving groups of hunter-gatherers. Today archaeologists generally hold that some of the features of prehistoric sites can be interpreted by reference to the ethnography of contemporary hunting and gathering peoples. Yet it is now understood that extreme caution is necessary in all such extrapolations. Surviving hunting and gathering groups tend to be refugee populations who have moved into arid, frigid, or densely forested regions that could not easily be taken over by farming or stock-raising peoples. Consequently contemporary hunters and gatherers occupy only relatively marginal portions of the total spectrum of habitats. On the whole these habitats or their equivalents may have been left unused during the Paleolithic because the primordial hunters had access to more favorable regions. It is therefore likely that there are extinct cultural forms, just as there are extinct animal species, and that only archaeology can deal with them properly.

Lower Paleolithic Developments

The very earliest Oldowan and Omo industries have been examined previously (Ch. 4 and 5). The Oldowan pebble choppers can be seen as the logical antecedents of the first Acheulian hand axes, although all the steps in the transition have not yet been identified in terms of an actual series of tools from any one site (cf. Butzer 1971:437; M. Leakey 1975). Simple pebble choppers have also been found at some of the earliest European sites, especially at Vallonet cave on the French Mediterranean coast and at Vértesszöllös in Hungary. Pebble tools and Acheulian tools coexist at Olduvai and other African sites

Figure 9-1. ACHEULIAN HAND AX. (American Museum of Natural History)

for tens of thousands of years. In general, however, pebble traditions seem to have been gradually replaced by Acheulian traditions in Africa, Western Europe, the Middle East, and India. Acheulian tool kits include many different kinds of hand axes—often made from flakes rather than cores—*polyhedrals* (multi-faceted, rounded stones) of unknown function, knives, and scrapers made from cores, as well as significant numbers of large flake cleavers and scrapers and other small flake tools.

The absence of hand axes from European Lower Paleolithic sites such as Vértesszöllös in Hungary, Clacton, England, and Stranska, Czechoslovakia, have stimulated much discussion. Some archaeologists suggest that the Oldowan was succeeded by two great cultural traditions—the Acheulian and the Clactonian—which ran parallel but separate courses of development for several hundred thousand years (Collins 1969). Others, at a loss to explain how two such traditions could have shared common borders and overlapping territories throughout so many tens of thousands of years, propose that the presence or absence of hand axes reflects seasonal adaptation or variations in the nature of the tasks carried out at particular sites. Lewis Binford, for example, believes that in Africa, Lower Paleolithic hand axes and large knives were used in contexts unrelated to the butchering and processing of meat "and that the conditions obtaining when they were used were such that the probability of obtaining meat was very remote" (1972:274). By this hypothesis Lower Paleolithic small flake tool traditions like the Clactonian in England would simply reflect a higher degree of dependence on hunting than was true of populations who lived in warmer regions. Small flake tools, in other words, were probably all that were needed to cut through the hides of animals that had been hunted to death or that were being

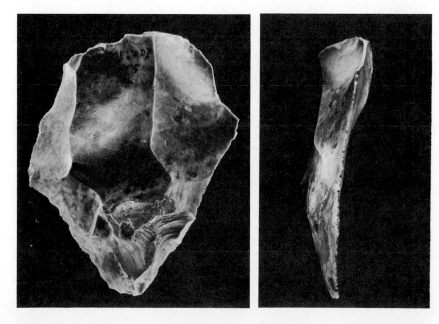

Figure 9-2. PALEOLITHIC SIDE SCRAPER. The long, almost straight right-hand edge of this 200,000-year-old tool is the working edge. Front view (left) and side view (right). (Lee Boltin)

ARCHAEOLOGICAL SITES

Briesemeister Projection

NORTH AMERICA
1. Alaska
2. Yukon
3. Calico Hills, California
4. Cahokia, Illinois
5. Pueblo Bonita, New Mexico
6. Bat Cave, New Mexico

MIDDLE AMERICA
7. Tamaulipas
8. Teotihuacán
9. Tula
10. Tenochtitlán
11. Cholula
12. Tehuacán Valley
13. La Venta
14. Chichén Itzá
15. Tikal, Guatemala

SOUTH AMERICA
16. Chanchan
17. Callejón de Huaylas
18. Ayacucho
19. Tiahuanaco
20. Fell's Cave, Straits of Magellan

ENGLAND
21. Star Carr
22. Clacton

FRANCE
23. St. Acheul
24. Vallonet Cave
25. Le Moustier
26. Terre Amata

SPAIN
27. Torralba and Ambrona

GERMANY
28. Lehringen

CZECHOSLOVAKIA
29. Strenska
30. Prezletice

HUNGARY
31. Vértesszőllős

GREECE
32. Argissa

TURKEY
33. Çatal Hüyük

ISRAEL
34. Mount Carmel
35. Mallaha
36. Nahal Oren

JORDAN
37. Jericho

SYRIA
38. Tell Mureybat

40°

20°

0°

160°

140°

20°

60. ● 60

● 59

58 ●

57 ●

55 ● ● 56

53 ●

54 ●

● 61

40°

0 ●
29 ●
31 ●

52 ●

32
33   38 39   40   45 44
       34   41   42   43
       36 35 37

80°

60°

60°

● 48

● 49

● 50

Areal Scale 1: 100,000,000²

● 51

60°

IRAQ
39. Zawi Chemi Shanidar
40. Karim Shahir
41. Jarmo
42. Uruk
43. Eridu
44. Al Ubiad

IRAN
45. Ali Kosh

ALGERIA
46. Ain Henech

MAURITANIA
47. Dar Tichit

ETHIOPIA
48. Omo Basin

TANZANIA
49. Olduvai Gorge

ZAMBIA
50. Kalambo Falls

SOUTH AFRICA
51. Fauresmith

PAKISTAN
52. Indus Valley

INDIA
53. Bihar state
54. Orissa state

THAILAND
55. Spirit Cave
56. Ban Chiang
57. Non Noktha

CHINA
58. Ordos
59. Pan-p'o
60. Choukoutien

JAVA
61. Patjitan

scavenged. Large bifacial tools like the hand ax would not be taken along on a hunting or scavenging expedition. Instead they would be used closer to the base camp and would be applied to such tasks as hacking off branches, cutting roots, and cutting edible bark from trees (cf. J. D. Clark 1975).

Acheulian tool-making techniques underwent a remarkably small number of changes considering the immense span of time and space within which they occur. Control over the cutting edge of hand axes and knives was improved by the utilization of soft-hammer techniques—blows delivered by bone or wood rather than by hammerstones (Fig. 9-3). Indirect percussion techniques involving resilient blows directed by punches made of wood, bone, or antler also resulted in further improvements. Finally, toward the end of the Lower Paleolithic, Acheulian assemblages were enriched by flake tools produced by an ingenious method known as the *Levallois* technique (Fig. 9-4). A tortoise-shaped core of flint was prepared as if one were about to produce a thick hand ax, except that shaping proceeded on only one side of the nodule. Next a transverse blow was struck at one

Figure 9-3. IMPROVED ACHEULIAN HAND AX AND TECHNIQUE. Blows may have been delivered by bone or wood hammers.

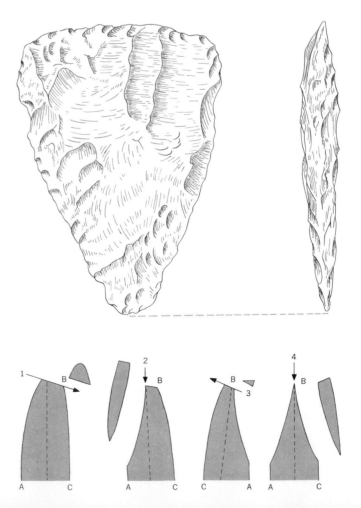

176

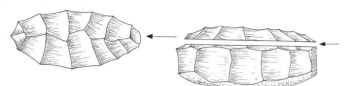

Figure 9-4. LEVALLOISIAN TORTOISE CORE TECHNIQUE. Left view shows Levalloisian flake. Right view shows (top to bottom) making platform, striking flake from nucleus, looking down on core after flake detached.

end of the core, creating a ledge, or *striking platform.* Then, a longitudinal blow was administered to the striking platform, detaching an extremely thin elongated flake with sharp, straight edges. Levalloisian cores and flakes have been found throughout Africa and Europe.

As previously indicated (p. 84), Acheulian assemblages are not found in China or Southeast Asia, where a separate tradition of choppers and chopping tools prevailed. Choppers have cutting edges flaked from one side only, whereas chopping tools have cutting edges produced by blows delivered to both sides and occasionally resemble hand axes (Butzer 1971). Asian Lower Paleolithic industries also include large tools called "hand-adzes" as well as a variety of flake knives and scrapers.

Evidence from Olduvai, Kalambo Falls in Zambia, Terra Amata in France, and Ambrona in Spain in the form of post-holes, circular arrangements of stones and elephant ribs, suggests that open-air dwellings—brush shelters or skin tents—were invented during the Lower Paleolithic. Thus there is no reason to suppose that the hominid hunters and gatherers of the Lower Paleolithic were primarily cave-dwellers (Kennedy 1975). Archaeological and paleontological evidence concerning cave life is more complete simply because cave sites are more likely to be sealed off and preserved than are open-air camps. Finally, it should be recalled (p. 84) that *Homo erectus* populations in Asia and Europe and, by inference, in Africa as well achieved control over fire and probably used fire in cooking and in the manufacture of hardened wooden tools such as spears and digging sticks.

These accomplishments indicate that Lower Paleolithic cultures evolved in a significant number of ways. Yet there are two outstanding enigmas about the Lower Paleolithic. Why, over a span of more than a million years, did technology change so little? And why was there such great uniformity in tool assemblages so that only two or three distinctive traditions can be identified throughout all of Eurasia and Africa.? These mysteries deepen when the fact is considered that throughout the Lower Paleolithic there must have been a steady increase in the number of localized hunting and gathering popula-

177

tions and therefore a steadily expanding potential for the development of distinctive local cultures. Perhaps the solution to both of these mysteries is that *Homo erectus* populations were, as I have previously suggested, infrahuman. Hence inferences about local cultural specializations based on knowledge of contemporary hunters and gatherers may not be applicable to the relationships that pertained between local groups during the Lower Paleolithic. This would seem to constitute another reason for being extremely skeptical of many currently popular notions about the social structure and ideology of *Homo erectus* and other pre-*Homo sapiens sapiens* populations (cf. Binford 1972:289).

Middle Paleolithic Developments

Euro-African Middle Paleolithic tool kits contain varying percentages of hand axes and other Acheulian-type implements. Points that might have been attached to spears make their appearance. They were fashioned from Levallois and other kinds of flakes and were light enough and sharp enough to have functioned as effective projectiles. In many regions Middle Paleolithic flake-tool assemblages conform to the type of industry known as *Mousterian.* These assemblages consist of small flakes removed from Levallois and other disc-shaped cores

Figure 9-5. MOUSTERIAN IMPLEMENTS.

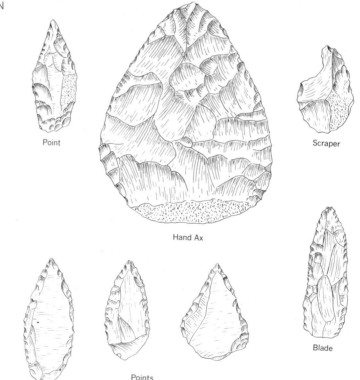

Point

Hand Ax

Scraper

Blade

Points

178

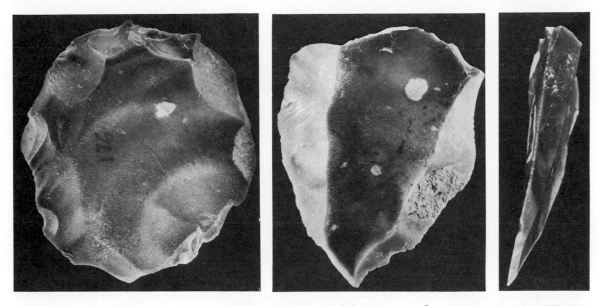

which were subjected to secondary flaking based on soft-hammer and pressure techniques (Fig. 9-5). (Some prehistorians use the term "Mousterian" to cover all Middle Paleolithic industries.) Middle Paleolithic tool kits thus usually included a few hand axes and numerous flake tools, including several varieties of points, scrapers, notched flakes for shaving wood, burins, and borers. A high degree of control had been achieved over the secondary flaking or retouching of working edges, and special bone instruments presumed to have been employed for this purpose are found at many Middle Paleolithic sites. It has recently been shown that excellent retouching and trimming can also be achieved by biting the edge of a flake with one's teeth (Gould, Koster, and Sontz 1971).

The transition from Acheulian industries to Middle Paleolithic industries occurred quite abruptly in Europe, the Middle East, and Africa and at approximately the same time—about 100,000 B.P. (cf. Beaumont and Vogel 1972; Deacon 1975; J.D. Clark 1975). This makes the Middle Paleolithic roughly equivalent to the period during which neandertaloid and other archaic varieties of *Homo sapiens* appeared throughout the Old World. Much of the archaeological knowledge of the European and Middle Eastern Middle Paleolithic is based upon artifacts found in association with neandertaloid fossils. It is known from the Mt. Carmel caves, for example, that the custom of burying the dead had already been established. The fifty-five-thousand-year-old skeletons from Skhül Cave had their knees drawn up toward the chest. One of the Skhül males had apparently been interred with the jaws of a wild boar resting on top of him, indicative of ritualized funerary practice. At Shanidar masses of bachelor buttons, hol-

Figure 9-6. MOUSTERIAN TORTOISE CORE. Trimmed in a shape reminiscent of a turtle's shell, the Mousterian core (left) was flaked across its flat-bottom face to detach materials for tools like the point shown in full view (middle) and profile (right). (Lee Boltin)

179

lyhocks, hyacinths, and other flowers were interred with a Neanderthal man who died sixty thousand years ago (Solecki 1971). Other Middle Paleolithic sites indicate that red ochre—a dye associated with blood and magical powers among many modern aboriginal populations—was also used in some kind of funerary ritual (Constable 1973).

At other Middle Paleolithic burials, hunting tools and the bones of meat offerings are also found, suggesting that death may already have been interpreted as a journey to a distant land. During this journey the meat would be needed to nourish the hunter, but upon arrival there would be plenty of game to hunt. The practice of provisioning the dead for life after death culminated fifty thousand years later in the literate and dynastic empires when wives and servants of powerful men were sacrificed and placed in carts or ships along with a full inventory of household supplies, in order that the deceased's journey might not be inconvenienced.

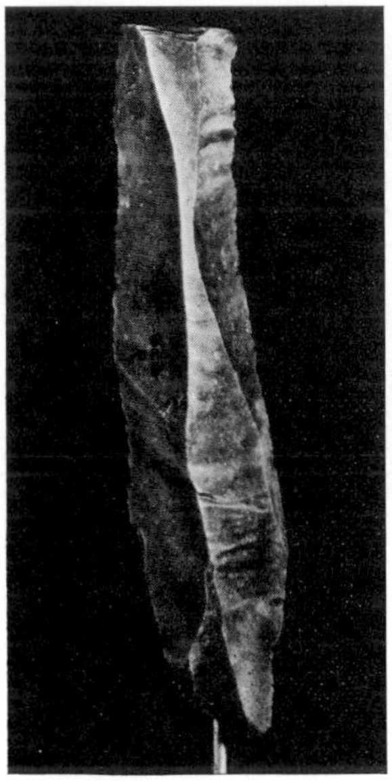

Figure 9-7. UPPER PALEO-LITHIC BLADE. Basic form of many Upper Paleolithic instruments. Specialized tools were made by retouching edges and ends. This blade is four inches long and only a quarter inch thick. (Lee Boltin)

The Upper Paleolithic

From observation of the cultural evolution of the Lower, Middle, and Upper Paleolithic alone, one can deduce something of the potential power and scope of culture as a life-sustaining and life-enriching adaptation. By now it was quite clear that the cumulative experience of millions of individuals could be tapped for new solutions to the technical problems of tool manufacture and tool use. At least forty thousand generations had passed since the smashing of the first river pebbles and the creation of the Olduvai tool kit. Yet in a sense an unbroken line of collaboration runs through all hominid generations, connecting the latest and most complex innovation with the earliest and most simple. Viewing the technological inventory of the Upper Paleolithic hunters, it becomes evident that the take-off point had been passed and that culture had embarked upon an evolutionary career of its own.

The Upper Paleolithic is characterized by a marked increase in blade tools and by a great florescence of ivory, bone, and antler implements. Flakes that have parallel edges and that are twice as long as they are broad are known technically as *blades*. Although uncommon, blade tools do occur during the Lower Paleolithic at scattered sites in Europe and Africa. Indeed, giant Levallois tools have been found together with delicate blades in East Africa, and a few blades have even been found in Oldowan assemblages.

The development of blade tools is of special interest since it exem-

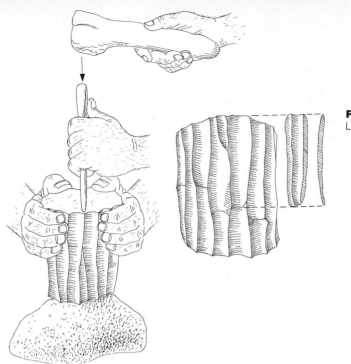

Figure 9-8. UPPER PALEO-
LITHIC BLADE TECHNIQUE.

plifies an important general Paleolithic trend: the conservation of
effort and of raw materials. Using Mousterian flake techniques, a flint
core could be made to produce forty inches of cutting edge. With the
Upper Paleolithic blade technique (see Fig. 9-8) ten to forty feet of
cutting edge could be produced from the same flint core (cf. Bordes
1968).

In Europe the Upper Paleolithic begins with the *Perigordian* industry, which (about 32,000 B.P. in Southwest France) is important
for its mixture of Middle Paleolithic tools together with pointed blade
knives, blade burins (for work in wood and bone), bone awls, and bone
points suitable for spears and arrows. Almost as early as the
Perigordian is the *Aurignacian,* characterized by fine blades, knives,
scrapers, and burins. Bone awls, pierced antlers thought to have been
used as arrow straighteners, and bone spearheads with a cleft base for
hafting are also common. Somewhat later and centered in Southern
Russia and Central Europe is the industry known as the *Gravettian,*
distinguished by small blade knives whose backs have been blunted,
perhaps to protect the user's fingers, bone awls, and various objects of
personal adornment such as bone beads, bracelets, and pins. Many of
the bone and ivory objects are decorated with incised geometric
designs. The most notable of the Gravettian artifacts are numerous
small figurines depicting pregnant women with enlarged breasts and
buttocks. The figurines, known as *Venus statues,* are carved in stone,
bone, and ivory, and they undoubtedly possessed some ritual signifi-

181

The Upper Paleolithic

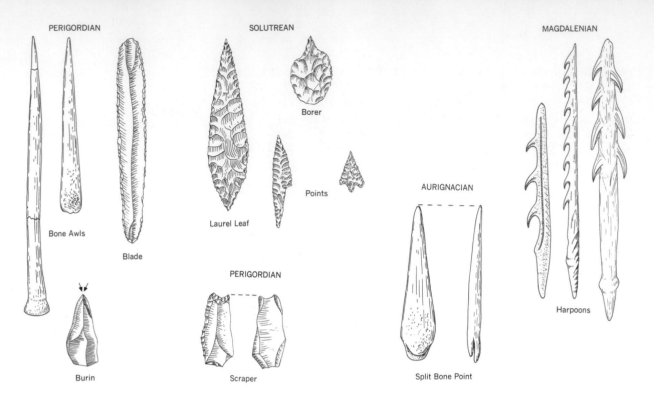

PERIGORDIAN

Bone Awls

Blade

SOLUTREAN

Laurel Leaf

Borer

Points

PERIGORDIAN

Burin

Scraper

AURIGNACIAN

Split Bone Point

MAGDALENIAN

Harpoons

Figure 9-9. UPPER PALEO-
LITHIC IMPLEMENTS.

cance associated with the fertility of women and animals. Some sixty
examples have been recovered from sites all the way from France to
Siberia. As indicated by skeletal remains, the Gravettians hunted
mammoth, horse, reindeer, bison, and other large herd animals. They
made their camps both in the open and at the mouths of caves and
rock shelters. In Southern Russia archaeologists have identified the
remains of a Gravettian mammoth hunter's animal-skin dwelling, set
in a shallow pit forty feet long and twelve feet wide. In Czechoslovakia round floor plans, reminiscent of American Indian tepees or
wigwams, have also been found.

At about 18,000 to 19,000 B.P. another Upper Paleolithic industry
known as the *Solutrean* is found throughout much of France and
Spain. The most famous Solutrean artifacts are magnificently flaked
symmetrical daggers and spear points made in the shape of long, thin
laurel leaves. The Solutreans also made finely worked stemmed and
barbed points. Eyed needles found at Solutrean sites indicate that skin
clothing must have been sewn to form-fitting shapes.

The richest of the European Upper Paleolithic industries is known
as the *Magdalenian* and ranges in time from about 16,000 B.P. to
10,000 B.P. (Bordes 1968). The Magdalenians added harpoons to the
inventory of hunting weapons. The barbed points of these harpoons
were made of bones and antler. Fine bone needles attest to the

182

probable importance of tailored clothing. For hunting, the early Magdalenians used the spear-thrower, a short rod or slat with a notch or hook at one end. The hook fits into the butt end of the spear. The extra length of the spear-thrower in effect increases the length of the hunter's throwing arm and adds to the force with which the spear can be hurled. Toward the end of the Magdalenian the bow and arrow were probably in use as depicted in some of the cave paintings of France and Spain. Magdalenian lance heads, harpoon points, and spear-throwers were often decorated with carvings of horses, ibex, birds, fish, and geometrical designs, some of which may be notations representing lunar cycles and seasonal changes.

The control achieved by Upper Paleolithic peoples over the techniques of tool manufacture in stone, bone, ivory, antler, and wood was reflected in their mastery of several ritualized art forms. On the walls and ceilings of deep caves in Spain and France, in hidden galleries far from the light of day, Upper Paleolithic peoples painted and engraved pictures of the animals they hunted. To a lesser extent similar paintings are found in caves as far across Europe as Russia. An occasional human figure—sometimes wearing a mask—outlines of hands, pictographs, and geometric symbols also occur, but the vast majority of the paintings and engravings depict horses, bison, mammoths, reindeer, ibex, wild boars, wild cattle, woolly rhinoceros, and other big-game animals. In spite of the magnificent economy of line

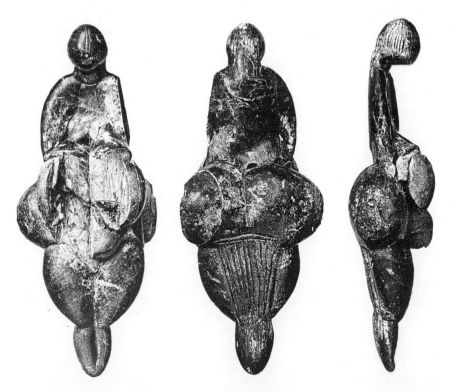

Figure 9-10. VENUS STATUE. Three views of the same statue from Lespugue, France. (American Museum of Natural History)

183

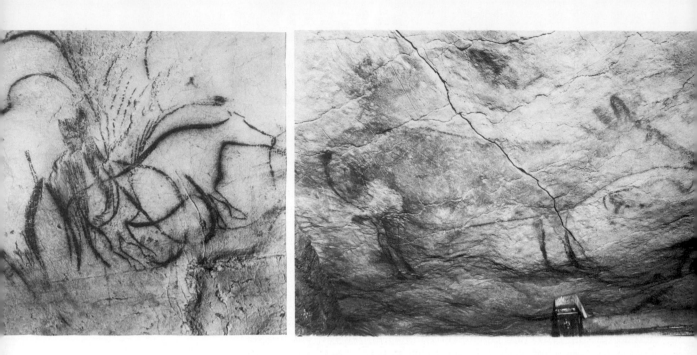

Figure 9-11. PALEOLITHIC MASTERPIECES. It is as if Picasso were to paint on a canvas already used by Rembrandt. Cabrerets, France (left) and Altamira, Spain (right). (French Government Tourist Office—left; Spanish National Tourist Office—right)

and color, so much admired today, Upper Paleolithic cave art must be considered at least as much an expression of culturally established ritual as of individual or cultural aesthetic impulses. The animals were often painted one on top of another even though unused surfaces were available, indicating that they were done first and foremost as ritual rather than art. It is generally assumed that the paintings were some form of hunting magic, but their precise function cannot be reconstructed reliably. All that can safely be asserted is that the hunters were impressed by the power and beauty of the animals whose death made their own lives possible (cf. Ucko and Rosenfeld 1967; Leroi-Gourhan 1968).

A number of attempts have been made to interpret various painted and incised geometric designs—dots, grids, scratches, lines—on Upper Paleolithic cave walls and on antler and bone implements. The theory has recently been advanced that the holes and lines found on certain antler and bone plaques and "batons" were records of the passage of days and phases of the moon (Marshack 1972a, b). Although these marks can be interpreted in other ways, I find no reason to doubt that the artists responsible for the amazingly realistic scenes on the cave walls would also have had the capacity to observe and record the phases of the moon and other celestial events, thereby preparing the way for the development of the first calendars.

184

The Significance of the Paleolithic

Sequences of Paleolithic industries similar to those in Europe occur in Africa and Asia. They also occur in Australia and North and South America but with much shorter time depth. Levallois techniques and Mousterian industries succeed Acheulian traditions at Fauresmith in South Africa and at many other African sites. There is even a Mousterian-like flake industry in North China, and by 40,000 to 30,000 B.P. bone, flake, and blade tools were being made on every continent. For the period 20,000–10,000 B.P., it is impossible to say that any particular region had achieved decisive technological advantages over the others. To be sure, there was a great deal of variation in the specific content of the tool kits of the Eurasian mammoth hunters, the Southeast Asian forest-dwellers, and the Australian hunters of marsupials, but this variation probably reflects local adaptation as much as it indicates levels of technological achievement. A general pattern of technological evolution characteristic of culture rather than of any particular race or region unfolded during the Paleolithic of each continent. This pattern may be viewed as a well-nigh inevitable consequence of the cultural mode of existence and is probably not limited to its one-time occurrence on earth. That is, if life has arisen in other solar systems, and if neural circuitry has crossed the threshold of language competence, it is highly probable that technology has evolved generally along the lines of the Paleolithic on earth, as follows:

1. The more recent the tool kit, the higher the standards of workmanship and control over raw materials, the finer the detail, the greater the symmetry, and the smoother the finish.
2. The number of different items in the tool kit increases slowly at first, but more rapidly as the basic techniques are mastered.
3. New additions to the tool kit perform functions previously performed by a few all-purpose tools; hence the tools are increasingly specialized.
4. The mode of manufacture of the tools exhibits a more efficient use of raw materials; more tools are made from the same quantity of primary substance (cf. Bordaz 1970).

The End of the Paleolithic

Despite the many technological triumphs of the Paleolithic, the basic mode of subsistence remained essentially what it had been since australopithecine times. All human groups continued to obtain food energy from hunting and fishing and the gathering of wild berries, fruits, tubers, and other plants. To be sure, neither the environmental opportunities for hunting and gathering nor the technological inventory available for exploiting the natural environment had remained constant. Throughout the hundreds of thousands of years of glacial advances and retreats, climatic zones underwent drastic changes. These changes in turn brought about a constantly changing succession of the plant and animal life upon which people depended for their livelihood. With each advance of the glaciers, warm-weather species of animals were driven south, tundras replaced plains, plains replaced forests, forests turned to deserts, and elsewhere deserts bloomed. The quality and nutritive value of the Paleolithic diet was determined as much by the local abundance of plants and animals as by the technological inventory by which the plants and animals were collected and hunted. Inefficient technology yielded a high standard of living when interacting with a great abundance of plants and animals, whereas even the most efficient hunting and collecting routines did not stave off hunger and population decline when game and plant resources became scarce. Abundance or scarcity of food was thus directly related to the response of animals and plants to natural conditions over which humans exerted little influence. However, Paleolithic peoples probably thought otherwise. Like contemporary hunters and gatherers, the Magdalenians probably believed they could increase the rate of reproduction of animals by the process of depicting them in murals or by other magico-religious techniques. But the basic weakness of the hunting and gathering way of life is precisely that intensive predation by expanding human populations can easily result in the extinction of the natural biota.

The basic insecurity of the hunting and gathering mode of subsistence is well illustrated in the transition from the Upper Paleolithic to the terminal Pleistocene cultures of Northern and Western Europe. Toward the end of the last glaciation, the region below the glaciers received a flow of meltwater favoring the growth of grassy plains on which enormous herds of horses, bison, mammoths, and reindeer grazed. As the glaciers retreated, lush virgin grasslands formed, into which these animals spread followed by their human predators. Both animal and human populations prospered, but unbeknown to either, their mutual way of life was doomed. The Eurasian grasslands were merely an evanescent phase of the Pleistocene's succession of biotic communities. At about 12,000 B.P. trees began to invade the European grasslands. Underneath the leafy forest canopy, no grass could grow. Thus trees began to kill the great European herds of mammals

186

as effectively as any weapons designed by human beings. By 10,000 B.P. much of the so-called *Pleistocene megafauna* had become extinct in Europe. Gone were the woolly mammoth and rhino, steppe bison, giant elk, and wild ass. No doubt the marvelously skilled Upper Paleolithic hunters themselves contributed to this ecological catastrophe, just as New World hunters probably played a role in the extinction of the Pleistocene megafauna in the New World (see p. 00). Elephants, rhinos, and other genera had survived numerous prior advances and retreats of grasslands and forests throughout the Pleistocene. What was new in the situation was the unprecedented efficiency of the Upper Paleolithic technology (cf. Butzer 1971; Kurtén 1972).

In Europe this period is called the Mesolithic. It was a time of intense local ecological change. Forests of birch and pine spread over the land, and the hunters made their camps in clearings along river banks and at lakesides, estuaries, and the seashore. The forests sheltered game such as elk, red deer, roe deer, wild cattle (aurochs), and wild pig. But to locate these animals, new tracking skills were needed. Forest-dwelling animals would disappear from view unless the kill was prompt and silent. Thus it is no accident that at a Mesolithic site, Star Carr in England, archaelogists have found the earliest European evidence, about 9500 B.P., of the long and successful symbiosis between people and dogs (Clutton-Brock 1969). In the forest the dog's sense of smell directed the hunter to within bowshot of evasive prey. But hunting under forested conditions, even with improved bows and hound dogs, could not yield the quantities of meat that were formerly obtained by following the herds of reindeer and bison. Thus the Mesolithic people turned increasingly to plant foods and fish, mollusks, and other riverine and maritime sources of food. Along the seacoast the heaped-up debris of centuries of Mesolithic shellfish-eating formed mounds called *kitchen middens.* Although clams, oysters, and mussels are good sources of protein, it took a lot of eating for a hungry person to fill up on such food.

It seems likely that the Mesolithic represented hard times for many of the descendants of the Aurignacian and Perigordian mammoth-hunters. The new technoenvironmental relationship also had rather drastic consequences upon the cave art. Both the herd animals and the ritual art depicting them disappeared at about the same time. The aesthetic component in Mesolithic rituals expressed itself in geometric designs and symbols incised on tools and weapons and painted on pebbles. In a very general sense the end of the cave art simply reflected the failure of ritual paintings to prevent the destruction of Upper Paleolithic ecosystems (cf. G. Clark 1967).

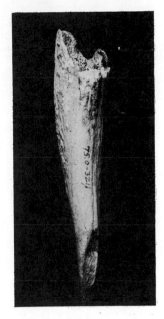

Figure 9-12. RETOUCHING INSTRUMENT. Fragments of bone or antler served as pressure flaker; this one, made of antler, dates from the Mesolithic. (Lee Boltin)

The End of the Paleolithic

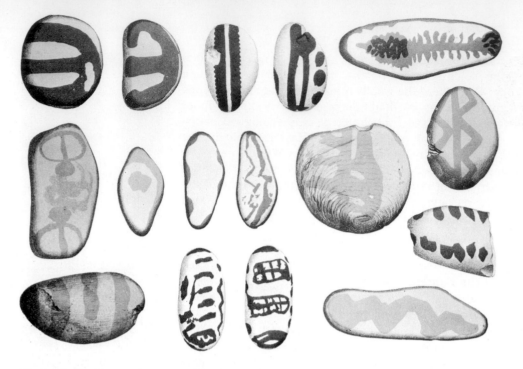

Figure 9-13. AZILIAN ART. Mesolithic painted pebbles. (American Museum of Natural History)

Because of the disappearance of the cave art, some prehistorians view the Mesolithic as a time of cultural decline or even degeneration. However, this view fails to give proper weight to the uninterrupted vitality of cultural innovation during the period. The domestication of the dog surely is an achievement no less significant than the cave paintings. Tool technology also continued to change in conformity with the four principles previously mentioned. Conservation of raw materials was carried to a new extreme by the development of cutting edges made from tiny blades and flakes known as *microliths*. To meet the challenge and the opportunity provided by the great abundance of trees, new techniques were developed for making and hafting woodworking tools. For the first time axes were produced by grinding rather than flaking processes. Fishhooks, fish spears, and harpoons were perfected; fish nets and bark floats, boats and paddles, sleds and skis, were also either invented or improved upon by the Mesolithic peoples of Europe. One of the most important experiments involved an increase in the amount of sedentism, as local groups camped for long periods of time near renewable resources such as shellfish beds or fishing streams. Thus, far from being degenerate, it was a time of great technological diversification and technological experimentation, as new ways to make the best of the altered natural circumstances were tried out. The stage was being set for momentous changes.

188

ARCHAEOLOGY AND THE EVOLUTION OF CULTURE: THE NEOLITHIC AND CITIES AND STATES

Between 10,000 and 2000 B.P. more changes of a fundamental nature were introduced into the total inventory of Old World cultural beliefs and practices than in all the previous millions of years of cultural evolution. The substitution of farming and stock-raising for hunting and gathering as the main mode of food production set in motion a complex adaptive process. With surprising swiftness this process drastically altered the ecology of the entire planet. It gave rise to an entirely new set of social and ideological limitations and opportunities and set the stage for the development of the cities and states of classical antiquity as well as for the development of all modern civilizations (P. Smith 1972a).

The Neolithic

Although *Neolithic* literally means "new stone age," it is not stone-working methods but rather the technology of food production that distinguishes this period from previous phases of cultural evolution. During the Neolithic, control over the rate of reproduction of plants and animals was achieved by the development of farming and stock-raising. The innovations leading to the development of domesticated species of plants and animals are regarded by anthropologists as among the most important ever made. Farming and stock-raising provided the material basis for high-density, sedentary settlements and gave rise to rapid population increase. During the Neolithic,

Homo sapiens changed from a rare to an abundant species. Farming and stock-raising also set the stage for profound alterations in social life, centering on access to land, water and other basic resources, and for the development of social structures characterized by profound differences in wealth and power. Without agriculture the development of cities, states, and empires could not have occurred. And all that is regarded today under the rubric of industrial society arose ultimately in response to that same great transformation.

Domestication involves a complex symbiotic relationship between human populations and certain favored plants and animals, called *domesticants*. The domesticators destroy or clear away undesirable flora and fauna from the domesticants' habitats. They adjust the supply of space, water, sunlight, and nutrients, and they interfere in the reproductive activity of the domesticants to ensure maximum use of available resources. Control over the reproductive activity of domesticants depends upon genetic changes wrought during the process of domestication. Thus a key difference between wild and domesticated varieties of wheat, barley, and other cereals is that wild grains break off upon ripening and fall to the ground on their own, whereas domesticated grains remain intact even when roughly handled. Indeed, the ripe domesticated grains must be pulled or beaten off if they are to be made available for human consumption. In the case of American Indian maize, this feature has evolved to the point where the ripe kernels do not fall off at all, and the plant is incapable of reproducing itself without human assistance. Other instances of this phenomenon are found in the banana plant and date palm. The final step in plant domestication occurs when the plant is removed from its natural habitat to an area that is markedly different, or when as a result of cultivation its original habitat is markedly transformed (Barrau 1967).

The Neolithic in the Middle East

The earliest archaeologically known transition from hunting and gathering to agriculture (involving both domesticated plants and animals) took place in the Middle East. This region extends from the Jordan Valley, northward to Southern Turkey, eastward to the headwaters of the Tigris and Euphrates rivers in Syria and Iraq, and southward along both flanks of the Zagros Mountains, which form the border between Iraq and Iran. Domesticated barley, wheat, goats, sheep, and pigs, dating to 11,000 to 9000 B.P., have been identified at a number of sites in this region. There is some evidence that the area

190

flanks of the Zagros Mountains, both dating from 12,000 to 10,000 B.P. (Solecki 1964). Very strong evidence of preagricultural village life, dating to 10,000 B.P., has been discovered at Tell Mureybat on the headwaters of the Euphrates River in Syria. Here clay-walled houses, grinding stones, and roasting pits have been found together with eighteen different types of wild seeds including wild wheat and barley. These preagricultural sedentary villages have revolutionized all previous theories concerning the origin of agriculture. Prior to 1960 it was generally believed that settled village life must have come after, not before, the development of domesticants. It is now known, however, that the hunters and gatherers were as much the domesticated as the domesticators (Braidwood 1969).

J. D. Harlan has shown that stands of wild wheat still grow thick enough in Turkey and other parts of the Middle East for an individual using a flint-bladed sickle to harvest a kilogram of grain per hour, or for a family of experienced plant-collectors working over a three-week period to gather more grain than they could possibly consume in a whole year. As Kent Flannery has remarked, "After all, where can you go with a metric ton of cleaned wheat? It requires storage facilities, and it requires that they be sufficiently waterproof so the grain does not sprout during the moist winter season" (1973:280).

The preagricultural villages grew up in order to store the grain, process it into flour, and convert it into flat cakes or porridge. The construction of houses, walls, roasters, grinders, and storage pits may be viewed as capital investment in grain futures. The people who made such an investment would be very reluctant to give it up in order to move to another site.

In order for their system of wild grain collection to remain viable for any length of time, the collectors must refrain from harvesting all the stalks in a particular field. Selective harvesting of this sort is practiced by many contemporary hunting and gathering peoples precisely to ensure future harvests from the same wild stands. Thus, with selective grain harvests supplemented by hunting and other collecting activities, the first villages were able to feed themselves indefinitely without having to move. But a number of technical and genetic problems had to be overcome. In their wild state, wheat and barley have heads that consist of a brittle axis to which the seed husks are affixed. When it is ripe, the axis (called a *rachis*) shatters easily. Harvesters may move through a field of wild grains, cutting off the entire ear or stripping the husk-encased seeds with their fingers. Either way, their activity shatters the most brittle heads (if the wind has not already done so), and these are the ones that reseed themselves. What the harvesters need are plants whose ripened seeds will

Figure 10-3. BARLEY EARS. Wild (a), 2-rowed cultivated (b), and 6-rowed cultivated (c). (Harlan 1975)

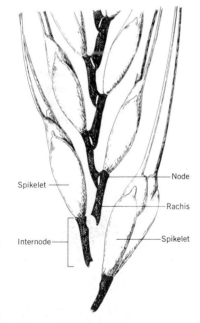

Figure 10-4. EMMER SPIKE.

not be dislodged by next year's winds before the harvesters can get to them. Yet these are the ones they take home to eat. And so the people would seem to be unconsciously selecting *against* the very feature that is most essential for the breeding of domesticated grains. How was this selection reversed? One theory is that when sheaths of tough-rachis grain were brought to the village to be threshed and winnowed, tough-rachis seeds would accidentally be scattered in the area around the houses where human waste and garbage provided ideal growing conditions. The next step would be deliberate planting of these tough-rachis seeds in the favored area around the village. Finally it would be recognized that sowing seeds from a few plants with good harvesting qualities produced whole fields of tough-rachis plants. Another change involved selection for husks that did not adhere firmly to the seeds and that could easily be detached during threshing. In the wild varieties the husks had to be heated and then pounded and winnowed in order to get at the grain. This may explain the presence of roasting pits and subterranean earth ovens in the earliest villages (see above). Other desirable genetic changes—leading to larger ears with multiple rows of seeds—were easily achieved by following one simple rule: don't eat the seeds from plants that have the most desirable features; plant them.

The Domestication of Animals

Which came first—the domestication of sheep and goats or the domestication of wheat and barley? No definite answer can or should be given. The animal and plant domesticants and the people who depended on them were part of a single ecosystem. As the human components began to obtain their food energy in a new way, other plants and animals were forced into new relationships with each other. For example, the wild grasses—including the ancestors of wheat and barley—had been a major food source for the wild sheep and goats. But as permanent villages more and more often came to be located in the middle of dense fields of grain, herds of wild sheep and goats would be forced into closer and closer contact with people. With the aid of dogs, the people could begin to control the movements of these herds, keeping the sheep and goats permanently on the margins of the grain fields, allowing them to eat the stubble but keeping them away from the ripe grain. Hunting, in other words, had suddenly become greatly simplified. The hunters no longer had to go to the animals; the animals, finding the lush fields of concentrated vegetation irresistible, came to the hunters. Indeed the ripening grain was so

194

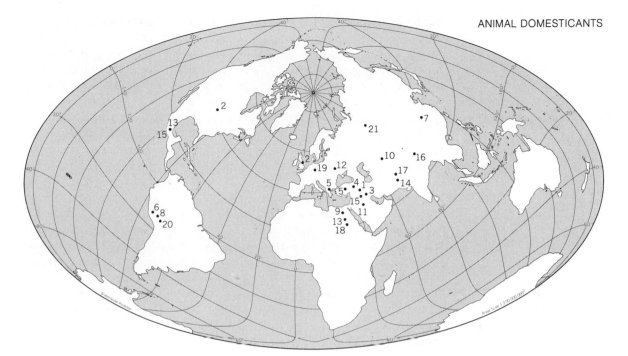

ANIMAL DOMESTICANTS

	1. SHEEP (9000 B.C.) Zawi Chemi Shanidar, Iraq			
	2. DOG Jaguar Cave, Idaho (8400 B.C.) Star Carr, England (7500 B.C.)		12. HORSE (3000 B.C.) Ukraine, U.S.S.R.	
	3. GOAT (7500 B.C.) Ali Kosh, Iran		13. HONEY BEE Nile Valley, Egypt (3000 B.C.) Mexico (? B.C.)	
	4. PIG (7000 B.C.) Cayönü, Turkey		14. WATER BUFFALO (2500 B.C.) Indus Valley, Pakistan	
	5. CATTLE (5500 B.C.) Thessaly, Greece; Anatolia, Turkey		15. DUCK Near East (2500 B.C.) Mexico (? B.C.)	
	6. GUINEA PIG (6000 B.C.) Ayacucho Basin, Peru		16. YAK (2500 B.C.) Tibet	
	7. SILK MOTH (3500 B.C.) Hsi-yin-t'sun, China		17. DOMESTIC FOWL (2000 B.C.) Indus Valley, Pakistan	
	8. LLAMA (3500 B.C.) Andean Highlands, Peru		18. CAT (1600 B.C.) Nile Valley, Egypt	
	9. ASS (3000 B.C.) Nile Valley, Egypt		19. GOOSE (1500 B.C.) Germany	
	10. BACTRIAN CAMEL (3000 B.C.) Southern U.S.S.R.		20. ALPACA (1500 B.C.) Andean Highlands, Peru	
	11. DROMEDARY (3000 B.C.) Saudi Arabia		21. REINDEER (1000 B.C.) Pazyryk Valley, Siberia, U.S.S.R.	

irresistible that the animals probably threatened to destroy the crops. This gave the hunters a double incentive as well as a double opportunity to increase their production of meat. But unrestricted predation inevitably threatens extinction. Comparative ethnographic research indicates that there is an inverse relationship between the spread of agriculture and the availability of wild game (Harner 1970). Hence the domestication of animals may be viewed essentially as a massive conservation reflex that prevented useful endangered species from becoming extinct.

The actual mechanisms for achieving the genetic modification requisite for animal domesticants were readily available. Many modern-day hunters and gatherers and simple horticulturalists keep animals as pets. It was not lack of knowledge about animals that prevented pre-Neolithic peoples from raising large numbers of such pets and making use of them for food and other economic benefits. Rather, the principal limitation was that human populations would soon run out of food for themselves if they had to share it with animal populations (see p. 243). The raising of grains opened new possibilities: sheep and goats thrive on stubble and other inedible portions of domesticated plants. They could be penned, fed on stubble, and milked and slaughtered selectively. Breeding for desirable features, unlike the initial phases of plant domestication, would have been quite straightforward. Animals that were too aggressive, or that grew too slowly, or that were too delicate would have been eaten before they reached reproductive age. On theoretical grounds therefore, it is likely

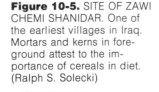

Figure 10-5. SITE OF ZAWI CHEMI SHANIDAR. One of the earliest villages in Iraq. Mortars and kerns in foreground attest to the importance of cereals in diet. (Ralph S. Solecki)

that the domestication of plants and animals in the Middle East occurred synchronously as part of a general regionwide process of cultural and ecological change. This seems to be confirmed by the approximately equal early dates at which plant and animal domesticants begin to appear.

At Zawi Chemi Shanidar, one of the earliest villages in Iraq, domesticated sheep appeared shortly after 11,000 B.P., and the earliest domesticated goats have been found at Ali Kosh in Iran, dating to 9500 B.P., along with domesticated wheat and barley; at Jericho in Jordan there were domesticated varieties of wheat, barley, and goats by 9000 B.P., and the same complex is found at Jarmo in Iraq by 8800 B.P. (Higgs and Jarman 1972; Herre and Röhrs 1975; Harlan 1975; Protsch and Berger 1973). Many other Neolithic sites of similar antiquity have been excavated, and new ones are being brought to light every year. A pre-Neolithic grain-eating complex in the Upper Nile Valley, with a date of 15,000 B.P., suggests that the search for the earliest Neolithic communities must be broadened to include areas where the ancestral plants and animals are no longer found in their wild state (Wendorf, Schild and Rushdi 1970). And new discoveries concerning domesticated wheat at Nahal Oren, Israel, may push the date of cereal domestication back to 11,000 B.P. (Flannery 1973:275).

The Neolithic and Urban "Revolutions"

Once the threshold to full Neolithic status was crossed, new domesticants, tools, productive techniques, and forms of social life appeared with explosive rapidity. True this "explosion" lasted from 10,000 to

197

Figure 10-7. JERICHO. The ruins lie near permanent springs, 700 feet below sea level. (UPI Photo)

5000 B.P., but during those five thousand years technology, social organization, and ideology changed more drastically than during the preceding 2 or 3 million years.

For reasons probably related to an increase in warfare, walled towns were built shortly after the appearance of domesticated plants and animals. The most astonishing of these towns was Jericho, whose earliest walls and towers date to 10,000 B.P. Situated in an oasis, Jericho probably controlled the Dead Sea salt trade; it covered ten acres and had a population estimated at two thousand (Hamblin 1973). By 8750 B.P. adobe-brick towns covering thirty or more acres were in existence. One such site in Southern Turkey, Çatal Hüyük, contains a dazzling array of art objects, woven cloth, decorative murals, and wall sculpture (Mellaart 1967).

At about 7500 B.P. cattle joined the list of domesticated animals. Because of their bulk and power, they constitute a major ecosystem breakthrough in their own right. Harnessed to plows, which were invented by 5500 B.P. or earlier, cattle made it possible to farm a

198

variety of virgin soil zones. As population increased, village settlements spread out over the fertile but rainless southern portion of the Tigris-Euphrates Valley. Confined at first to the margins of the natural watercourses, dense clusters of villages and towns came increasingly to rely on artificial irrigation to water their fields of wheat and barley. By 6350 B.P. monumental mud-brick temples reared up from the center of major towns such as Eridu and Al Ubaid. Finally, as at Uruk between 5800 and 5200 B.P., there appeared the first cities whose streets, houses, temples, palaces, and fortifications covered hundreds of acres and were surrounded by thousands of acres of irrigated fields.

The catalogue of technological achievements now included spinning and weaving (earlier Neolithic inventions) as well as ceramics, smelting and casting of bronze, baked brick, arched masonry, the potter's wheel, sailing ships, the first wheeled vehicles, writing, calendrical time-reckoning, weights and measures, and the beginnings of mathematics. Here, for the first time, human communities became divided into rulers and ruled, rich and poor, literate and illiterate, townspeople and peasants, artists, warriors, priests, and kings.

The general processes responsible for the emergence of the cities and states of ancient Mesopotamia, the area between the Tigris and Euphrates rivers, seem fairly clear. As the population increased in the areas of deficient rainfall, irrigation was used to expand and intensify agricultural productivity. But as density increased further, competition within and between local settlements for access to and control over the water needed for irrigation also increased. This laid the basis for the rise of centralized priesthoods and governments concerned

Figure 10-8. ÇATAL HÜYÜK. Early adobe brick town in Southern Turkey. (Ralph S. Solecki)

199

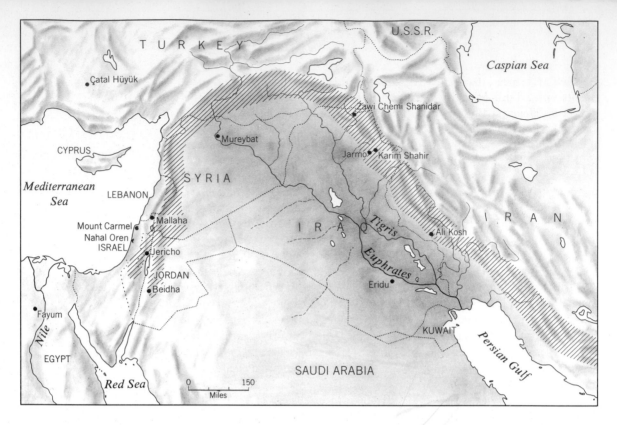

FERTILE CRESCENT RE-
GION. Cross hatching indicates zone of early sites.

with regulating the distribution of water and the storage of harvest surpluses. Although these elite groups provided services in the form of calendrical calculations, provision of emergency rations, support of artisan specialists, and religious ceremonials, they eventually developed into exploitative classes whose despotic power rested on control over police-military force. By imposing various forms of taxation, the dynastic ruling classes succeeded in diverting a substantial portion of the farming population's harvests into state enterprises, thereby preventing the peasant food-producers from cutting back on their productive efforts or from enjoying the leisure or security that are intuitively but erroneously associated with the adoption of advanced technologies. More and more intensive irrigation merely provided additional means of consolidating and intensifying the ruling elite's power over people and nature. I shall take a closer look at these processes in Chapter 18 (cf. Childe 1952; Wittfogel 1957; Braidwood and Willey 1962; R. McC. Adams 1966, 1972; Mitchell 1973).

The Causes of the Neolithic

Early attempts to understand the transition to the Neolithic were hobbled by a belief that hunters and gatherers led "nasty, mean,

200

brutish" lives and that they engaged in a grim, never-ending search for game and edible morsels. Since pre-Neolithic peoples were seen as perpetually verging on starvation and near exhaustion from their unrelenting food quest, it seemed self-evident that they would opt for the Neolithic mode of production in order to achieve greater ease, comfort, security, health, and general well-being. Anthropologists now agree, however, that there could not have been any such self-evident advantage in the initial phases of the transition in the Middle East. In fact, the archaeological and ethnological evidence points in the opposite direction. Under sedentary Neolithic conditions, people probably worked at least as hard as before, but continuously over longer stretches and more routinely, in conformity with the demands of agricultural cycles (see p. 252). It is doubtful that they enjoyed any substantial improvement in their per capita intake of protein and calories even in the short run. And it is certain that in the long run, as the population pushed closer to the limit of the new ecosystem—filling up grazing lands with people, intensifying the use of each acre, shortening fallow periods, double cropping, and irrigating—the consumption of animal protein fell below Paleolithic levels. As I shall explain later on, preindustrial farming peoples usually find it impossible to raise large numbers of animal domesticants primarily as a source of meat protein (ch. 12).

Why then did the people of the Middle East adopt a system that obliged them to work harder simply in order to have more mouths to feed? The solution to this puzzle lies in a better understanding of the means by which hunters and gatherers maintain their high levels of leisure and high standards of living. These means involve not only a system of production, but a system of reproduction. Abundant leisure is coupled with high levels of health and well-being among hunters and gatherers only to the extent that their population is regulated well below the *carrying capacity* of their ecosystems.

Regulation of hunting and gathering population is achieved by a complex of factors, all of which impose certain penalties and deprivations upon the people who use them. The most important population-limiting practices among hunters and gatherers are abortion (with risk to the survival of the mother; see p. 266); female infanticide and systematic neglect of female infants; contraception by prolonging lactation; and death of mothers in childbirth (cf. Birdsell 1968; Polgar 1972; Divale 1972). Certain demographic facts provide the basis for strong inferences if not absolute proof that some or all of these measures were employed throughout the Upper Paleolithic. Calculations by Ferki A. Hassan (1973) show that with a generous spacing period of 3.5 years, 20 percent infant mortality from "natural" causes, a fertile life span for women of only 18 years (out of a theoretical maximum of 30 years, i.e., from about age sixteen to age forty-six), and generous allowances for women who are infertile or who die before giving birth to their first child, an average of 2.16 children will survive for each woman in the population. Under such a system of "natural" regulation, population will grow at the rate of 0.4 percent per year, which is sufficient to produce a doubling every 180 years. Starting with 2 people in the year 30,000 B.P., this rate of doubling would have produced populations in the Middle East at the end of the Paleolithic in the order of 10^{31}, or as many people as there are grains of sand on all the beaches of the world.

The actual rate of growth during the Upper Paleolithic is estimated to have been only 0.0007 percent per year, yielding a population in the Middle East of about 100,000 in the year 10,000 B.P. (Carneiro and Hilse 1966; cf. Coale 1974). Any new means of food production that reduced the necessity for physically hazardous abortion, female infanticide, or systematic neglect of infants and juveniles would tend to be adopted provided that the initial "trade-off" with the old system did not lead to an immediate marked reduction in the general standard of living. Reduction in leisure time and standards of living associated with peasant farming did not occur until thousands of years after the beginning of the Neolithic. One way to envision the ecological pressures for and against the adoption of the Neolithic mode of production is to think of population increase in terms of the "costs" that adults have to "pay" for rearing additional children (see p. 458). These costs are prohibitive in most hunting and gathering ecosystems because the availability of game per capita rapidly falls off with each increase in the density of the human population. For this reason hunting and gathering populations are usually stabilized at about 30 percent of their ecosystem's theoretical carrying capacity (Lee and DeVore 1968; Casteel 1972, 1975). A closer approach by a population to carrying capacity as a result of more intensive hunting jeopardizes the natural biota at the same time that it produces rapidly diminishing returns per unit of labor input. Additional children are therefore very "expensive."

An entirely different situation confronts people who switch over to domesticants. The more people there are, the more plants and animals that can be taken care of. Children can be put to work at an early age in a number of simple tasks connected with planting, weeding, and herding and can easily "pay" for themselves—at least as long as there is plenty of land available (or game where there are no domesticated animals; see p. 458).

Another relative cost that probably entered into the "trade-off"

202

involves the differential consequences for women of rearing addition-al children in sedentary villages instead of seminomadic camps. Women in hunting and gathering societies expend a relatively enor-mous amount of energy simply carrying their infants from one place to another. In permanent village situations there is less need for long-distance travel and hence more incentive to shorten the span of years between the rearing of one infant and another per woman. Perhaps it was this reduction in "cost" per child per woman more than any other that was responsible for the initial concentration on seed-gathering even before plants and animals were domesticated (Suss-man 1972; Sengel 1973).

A lively discussion is now underway concerning the possibility that population pressure increased *before* the beginning of the Neolithic during the initial stage of sedentism based on wild-seed-gathering. Some anthropologists say that it was this pressure that stimulated the switch to more intensive modes of production based on domesti-cants (Binford 1972; Smith, and Young 1972). Others disagree (Bronson 1975). This argument seems to me unnecessary since the equilibrium enjoyed by preindustrial societies has always involved severe penalties to women connected with infanticide and other population-regulating mechanisms. Once the Neolithic mode of pro-duction was adopted the population increased rapidly, and this even-tually raised "population pressure"—that is, returned it to the level of the pre-Neolithic ecosystem. However, the rate of population growth in the Middle East never returned to the level that had been character-istic of 99 percent of hominid history. It is estimated that the rate averaged .1 percent between 10,000 and 6000 B.P. This amounts to a doubling of population every 700 years. Thus starting with 100,000 people in 10,000 B.P., the population of the Middle East probably reached 3.2 million shortly before 6000 B.P.—a thirtyfold increase in four thousand years. By this time the original domesticants and Neolithic techniques could no longer maintain the same high per capita rate of return for labor input that had been characteristic of the years when land was abundant and population was small. Hence a steadily expanding list of plant and animal domesticants and new agricultural implements and techniques were added to the system. But each such addition to or intensification of the system only produced a further rise in the rate of population increase (Hassan 1973:539). Finally, between 5500 and 5000 B.P. the fundamental paradox of human history had assumed tangible form: despite the achievement of high rates of return per capita of labor input in food production, the standard of living of the food-producers began to decline (see ch. 19). And despite this decline, the population continued to increase. Essentially the same paradox exists today, and it remains the single most important problem confronting the human species (see p. 459).

The Spread of the Neolithic

The enormous geographical distribution of Paleolithic core, flake, and blade tools demonstrates the powerful effects of cultural diffusion. All great technological innovations have tended to spread to every portion of the globe to which they are ecologically suited. Throughout the Paleolithic the rate of diffusion of important technological developments exceeded the rate of innovation. The Neolithic breakthrough, however, opened up so many new cultural and ecological possibilities that this relationship was reversed. For the first time in the history of the world, new cultural-ecological systems followed one another in rapid succession, faster than they could diffuse to potentially receptive regions. Thus the period from 10,000 to 5000 B.P. marked the beginning of drastic inequalities not only within social systems but between them as well. As a matter of fact, agriculture was still spreading in the direction of such remote regions as Patagonia and Australia when the wave of Neolithic traits was overwhelmed everywhere by the convulsive effects of Euro-American colonialism and industrialization.

The spread of the Neolithic complex was slowed and complicated by the fact that the original domesticants had to be removed from their natural habitats and made to function in entirely new environments. The ecosystem of the Mesolithic European hunters, for example, was basically different from the one that gave rise to the Middle Eastern domesticants. The latter, with the exception of the pig (see below), could not be transferred directly into forested regions. (Actually the pig may have been domesticated in Greece as early as anywhere else [Protsch and Berger 1973].) Hence the spread of agriculture into Europe involved substantial modifications in the original Neolithic system. For this reason Europe followed a course toward urbanization that was fundamentally different from that of the Middle East (see p. 432). Even the grains, as in the case of rye, oats, and millet, had to undergo considerable modification in order to survive in the generally colder and damper European climate. By 8500 B.P. farming communities were well established in Greece. In the next millennium they had advanced into the Hungarian plains and up the Danube River. Extensive burning of the Central and Northern European forests accompanied further penetration of the Neolithic complex. By 6000

204

B.P. agriculture had reached Spain, the North Sea, and Southern England, but not until 5500 B.P. was the Neolithic way of life general throughout the British Isles (Murray 1970; Herre and Röhrs 1975; Renfrew 1973).

The East Asian Neolithic

The Middle Eastern Neolithic moved eastward with the same deliberate speed. It reached Afghanistan and Pakistan by about 5000 B.P. and the Indus Valley in India by 4500 B.P. (Vishnu-Mittre 1975). Beyond this point, however, the role of diffusion becomes obscure. There is mounting evidence that China and Southeast Asia were the centers of one or more Neolithic food-producing "revolutions" based on a complex of domesticants different from those of the Middle East and largely or entirely independent of Middle Eastern influences.

Recent radiometric studies have pushed the beginnings of sedentary village life in China back before 6000 B.P. One of the earliest sites is at Pan-p'o in the semiarid loess highlands bordering the upper reaches of the Yellow River. Here there were village settlements employing a form of field agriculture involving domesticated millet and domesticated pigs. The well-patterned graveyards, painted pottery, and prototypes of the characters used in the Chinese form of writing indicate that still earlier Neolithic and protoagricultural sites remain to be discovered. Like the earliest Middle Eastern argicultural sites, Pan-p'o and the other early villages of China are found away from the principal watercourses and the most fertile river valleys. This circumstance makes it difficult to interpret the millet at Pan-p'o as anything other than the product of an independent development. For if the millet had been obtained through diffusion, one would expect to find it applied first in regions of more abundant rainfall or in the river valleys. Although the virgin loess soils of China are highly fertile, they have the drawback of requiring a year of exposure to the air before they become productive. Moreover, the major varieties of millet found at Pan-p'o have wild ancestors that grew both in China and Europe. The earliest domesticated millet in Europe has been found at Argissa, Greece, with a date of 7500 B.P. Considering the length of time it took wheat and barley to reach India, it seems highly unlikely that there was any connection between the onsets of European and Chinese millet-farming. It is even more improbable that the domestication of the pig in the West had anything to do with its domestication in the East. The pig has always been a marginal component in the agricultural complex of the Middle East but in China the pig has always played a central role. Since the pig is the only major animal domesticant that cannot be milked, the fundamentally opposed attitudes toward the consumption of animal milk in the Middle East and China also appear to confirm the separate origins of the Chinese and Middle Eastern Neolithic. Millet apparently provided the energy basis for the first Chinese cities, which were located along the central floodplains of the great bend of the Yellow River, dating to about 4000 B.P. Eventually, in the period 3300 to 3000 B.P., wheat and barley reached China and were incorporated into the agricultural system. But by that time two additional important crops, rice and soybeans, unknown in Europe and the Middle East, were also being used. The Middle Eastern plow and oxen arrived even later—2200 B.P.

All this indicates that the early North China system of field agriculture and stock-raising had developed independently of the Middle Eastern Neolithic (Ping-ti 1975, 1974; Harlan 1975; Chang 1973). Large-scale state-managed flood control and irrigation works became prominent in the period 3000–2500 B.P. Life in the despotic dynasties of China, despite the independent origins of Chinese civilization, bore many remarkable similarities to life in dynastic Mesopotamia and Egypt (see p. 435).

The Neolithic in Southeast Asia and Africa

The Neolithic in China and the Middle East was based upon the domestication of grains whose wild ancestors were adapted to semi-arid temperate upland habitats. The possibility must be kept open that the transition to settled Neolithic village life was also independently achieved in humid semitropical habitats of Southeast Asia through the domestication of root crops, especially yams and taro (Harlan 1975; D. Harris 1975). Remains of such crops decompose more readily than grains and are difficult to recover archaeologically. There is no doubt that a concern with broad-spectrum plant-gathering extends about as far back in time in Southeast Asia as in the Near East. At Spirit Cave in Northwest Thailand 11,500-year-old remains of almonds, candle nuts, betel nuts, peppers, gourds, Phaseolus beans, peas, cucumbers, and other edible plants have been identified. Some of these plants may have been domesticated, but expert opinion is divided (Gorman 1969, 1975; Solheim 1970; Vishnu-Mittre 1975).

The role of rice in the development of a distinctive Southeast Asian Neolithic is still poorly understood. Species of wild rice occurred in almost all the riverine deltas and estuaries of South and Southeast

206

Asia, but it is possible that the first cultivated varieties were grown in interior savannah habitats and other dry-land settings (Chesnov 1975). One theory is that the first Southeast Asian cultivated plants were taro and yams. Taro grows wild in swampy areas, and yams grow wild in forest areas. Transfer of yams into swampy areas would have required mounding and drainage. Thus rice would have grown initially as a weed in the irrigated upland taro fields rather than in the yam mounds and drainage ditches (Condominas 1972). Thus far, however, the earliest archaeological evidence for rice cultivation in Asia is found at two sites on the low-lying Northeastern plateau, or piedmont, of Thailand. At Non Nok Tha elaborately incised cord-marked pottery, domesticated cattle, and dry-rice agriculture seem to have been present at about 6500 B.P. (Bayard 1968). At the second site, Ban Chiang, wet-rice farming seems to date from 5500 B.P. (Gorman 1975). This evidence suggests that if taro and/or yams were actually the first crops grown in the region, then the beginnings of agriculture in Southeast Asia may have taken place at about 9000 B.P.—or roughly at the same time as in the Middle East. Chester Gorman (1975) has proposed that rice itself may have been the earliest Southeast Asian domesticant and that the beginning of the Neolithic in that region was related to the rise in sea level at the end of the last glaciation. This rise in sea level reduced the land area of Southeast Asia by one-half, subjecting the Upper Paleolithic hunters and gatherers to population pressure analogous to the pressures experienced at the end of the Pleistocene by the big-game hunters of Europe and the Middle East. There seems little reason to doubt that Southeast Asia was a third independent center of plant domestication in the Old World.

Less confidence can be placed in the proposal that Africa was a fourth independent center of Neolithic transformations. Agreement does exist concerning the fact that several important food crops were originally domesticated in Africa. These include sorghum, African rice, African yams, teff (the major grain crop of Ethiopia), and eleusine (finger millet). Opinion is divided, however, concerning the effect of the known early spread of domesticated Middle Eastern plants and animals into Egypt, Morocco, and Ethiopia. Independent transitions based on yams may have occurred in West Africa but not much before 4500 B.P. (Munson 1972; Ellis 1975). An essentially Middle Eastern complex of walled villages and domesticated animals had reached Dar Tichitt in Mauretania by 3150 B.P., but there is no definite evidence of grain cultivation from the Nile to the Atlantic before 3100 B.P. (J. D. Clark 1972).

11

ARCHAEOLOGY AND THE EVOLUTION OF CULTURE: THE SECOND EARTH

The ancestors of the American Indians must have reached *Homo sapiens* status in the Old World. No fossil pongids have been found in the Americas, nor does anyone expect them to be found. The dental formula of the New World ceboidean monkeys indicates they diverged from the Old World hominoid line 30 to 40 million years ago.

No subject has greater strategic importance for an understanding of cultural systems and processes than the evolution of culture in the New World. In fact archaeological research into the developmental trajectories of New World cultures has recently yielded information of decisive importance for all the social sciences.

The Discovery of America

Intense controversy surrounds the question of how long humans have been living in the New World. Fractured flints with an antiquity of more than fifty thousand years have been found at Calico Hills, California, but their status as tools is in doubt (Leakey and Goodall 1969; Haynes 1973). A single bone tool with a radiocarbon date of 27,000 B.P. is known from the Canadian Yukon (Irving and Harington 1973). As for physical remains, the oldest bones may be the cranial and rib fragments unearthed by a steam shovel in Southern California, which have recently been dated by new amino acid techniques to 48,000 B.P. (Bada et al. 1974). If substantiated, this would make the earliest people of the New World contemporaries of the last of the European Neandertals.

The most likely origin of all the ancestral American Indian populations was Asia. This seems probable, first of all, because American Indian populations phenotypically resemble Asiatic populations. Like East Asians, many American Indians have straight black hair, epicanthic folds, and very little body hair. Although I have argued that such traits are evanescent and are thus unreliable for deep phylogenetic reckoning, the time involved is short enough to suggest at least that the American Indians did not originate in either Europe or Africa. Moreover the question of how they traveled from the Eastern to the Western Hemisphere must be considered. If the migrations had begun during the late Pleistocene/Upper Paleolithic, this would have been long before the invention of ocean-going craft. Hence it is extremely improbable that the American Indians crossed either the Atlantic or Pacific oceans. On the other hand, they could easily have crossed to the New World at the Bering Straits across which, on a clear day, one can see Alaska from Siberia. At several periods during the last continental glaciation, there was no water at all between Siberia and Alaska. At the maximum glacial advance an amount of moisture sufficient to reduce the level of the oceans by at least three hundred feet was held on land in the form of ice. Since the Bering Straits are less than three hundred feet deep, the earliest migrants had to neither swim nor hop from one iceberg to another in order to enter the Western Hemisphere. The first unsung "Discoverers of America" could easily have walked across on dry land, and they probably did so on more than one occasion. Others undoubtedly followed at frequent intervals, since when the sea was down only one hundred and fifty feet, they could have walked across on a "bridge" over one hundred miles wide. At its maximum, Beringia, as this now submerged land is called, was a thousand miles wide.

Even without the land bridge, the Bering Straits would not have been much of a barrier. From time to time the straits still freeze over solid enough for people and animals to walk across on the ice. Moreover, there was no lack of motive for such crossings. Like other Upper Paleolithic peoples, the first American Indians were hunters of migratory herbivores, especially of mammoths, horses, caribou, bison, and musk oxen. These and other large mammals abounded in great unexploited herds from Alaska to Tierra del Fuego.

The Beringia Bridge was above water from about 36,000 to 32,000 years ago, under water from about 32,000 to 28,000 years ago, above water from 28,000 to 13,000 years ago, and under water ever since. But hunters who used the bridge confronted an additional obstacle: mile-high walls of ice covered most of Alaska, blocking the way south. The blockage was not total, however. At various intervals there existed an ice-free corridor that connected the North coast of Alaska with the great plains east of the Rockies. This corridor was open from 36,000 to 32,000 B.P., from 28,000 to 20,000 B.P., and from 13,000 B.P. on. Migrations southward of people and animals must have taken place during at least one of these intervals, and it is not unlikely that all three opportunities were utilized.

The New World Paleolithic

The precise nature of the earliest American Indian tool kit has not yet been determined. There seems to have been a widespread technological horizon in the New World that lasted from about 35,000 to 14,000 B.P., which suggests that the first American Indian came equipped with discoidal-core and edge-retouch techniques similar to those employed throughout the Eurasian Upper Paleolithic, but with especially strong resemblances to certain Central Siberian complexes. Traces of this initial horizon have been found both in Northwest Alaska and near Ayacucho, Peru, with dates centering on 16,000 B.P. After about 12,000 B.P. a period of divergent American cultural growth ensued, yielding tool complexes having little specific resemblance to Old World artifacts (Lanning 1970; MacNeish 1972; Patterson 1973; Forbis 1974).

In North America these more advanced traditions have as their mainstay pressure-flaked blade projectile points with fluted surfaces or thinned basal edges. These projectile points have no precise parallels in the Old World and are presumed to have been shaped to facilitate hafting on spears. Two such traditions, known as Llano and Plano, have been identified: Llano lasting from 11,500 to 9000 B.P., and Plano from 9000 to 7000 B.P. *Llano* is associated with intense hunting of Pleistocene megafauna. It has two major North American assemblages, Clovis and Folsom. *Clovis* is characterized by large fluted points (see Fig. 11-1) found at sites where mammoths were killed and butchered on the high plains of Oklahoma, Colorado, New Mexico, and Southern Arizona (although Clovis points are also found in the prairie and Eastern woodlands as well). *Folsom* assemblages are characterized by Folsom and Sandia points (see Fig. 11-2), which were used to kill now extinct species of bison on the Central plains from Montana to Texas. The *Plano* tradition consists of many local assemblages of finely worked points and knives found in association with modern forms of bison and antelope (Jennings 1968; Patterson 1973). Separate but possibly related regional big-game traditions of comparable age have also been found in the Valley of Mexico, in the Andes from Argentina to Chile, and in Venezuela. One of the most

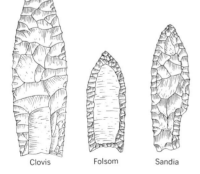

Clovis   Folsom   Sandia

Figure 11-1. NEW WORLD PALEOLITHIC PROJECTILE POINTS.

Figure 11-2. FOLSOM POINT EMBEDDED IN RIBS OF AN EXTINCT BISON. An historic discovery, altering the conception of the antiquity of the American Indian presence in the New World. (American Museum of Natural History)

interesting assemblages is that of Fell's Cave near the Strait of Magellan at the Southern tip of South America. Here stone tools, including Llano-like fluted points, were found with the remains of extinct ground sloths and American horses, revealing that the big-game hunters had completed their invasion of the New World no later than 11,000 B.P.

The rapid expansion of the second wave of early American Indian big-game hunters may have been one of the major causes of the extinction of several of the large Pleistocene species such as the mammoth, big-horned bison, camel, and horse (Martin and Wright 1967). The early American Indians hunted these animals by stampeding them over cliffs or by bottling them up in ravines. They probably set fire to the grassy plains in order to influence the movement of the herds or to facilitate their own travels. These activities contributed to the ecological stresses associated with the terminal phases of the glaciations and probably tipped the balance against several Pleistocene species that fortuitously managed to survive in the Old World. Thirty one genera of the New World Pleistocene fauna became extinct at the end of the last glaciation. Since most of these have not been found in definite association with kill or butchering sites, some experts have discounted the importance of hunting "overkills" as an explanation of their disappearance. However, Paul S. Martin (1973) has proposed that the extinction of the megafauna occurred so rapidly that the total of kill and butchering sites was actually very small and hence difficult to find archaeologically. According to Martin's calculations, if a band of 104 people, doubling in population every twenty years, set out from Edmonton, Canada, and migrated southward, they could easily have destroyed the entire big-game population between Canada and the Gulf of Mexico in three hundred years if one person in four killed only one 450-kilogram animal per week. Although one need not accept this scenario as an accurate representation of what actually happened, Martin's calculations point up the extreme fragility of big-game ecosystems subject to human predators who permit their own population to expand at a rate significantly higher than the rate of expansion of their animal prey.

One thing seems certain: the American Indians later paid a cruel and ironic penalty for their ancestors' failures as conservationists. The horse was destined to return to the New World as an avenging engine of war. More than anything else, the possession of cavalry explains how a handful of sixteenth-century Spanish soldiers conquered the most powerful American Indian peoples of Mexico and Peru and enslaved and despoiled their descendants.

The New World "Neolithic"

The discovery of the origins of New World agriculture constitutes an outstanding scientific achievement. Many details remain unknown, but there is one overwhelming, indeed stupendous, fact: the domestication of plants and animals by the American Indians did not depend on diffusionary influences emanating from any of the Old World centers of domestication. This means that diffusion is also unlikely to account for the other remarkable cultural convergences between the Old and the New World such as the development of sedentary village life, cities, states, empires, monumental architecture, writing, and metallurgy. The independent origins of New World agriculture prove that there is a tendency for human cultures to evolve with considerably higher probabilities in some directions rather than in others. It indicates that the explanation for both convergences and divergences in human history must be sought in the study of lawful processes that tend to produce similar consequences under similar conditions.

There had always been strong circumstantial evidence for postulating an independent American Indian development of agriculture. The inventory of New World crops consists almost entirely of domesticants found only in North and South America. At the time of contact with the first Europeans, this inventory was as diverse and nutritionally satisfactory as that of the combined Middle Eastern and Southeast Asian plant complex. It included grains such as maize, amaranth, and quinoa. It also included legumes like black beans, string beans, peanuts, and lima beans and other important vegetables like squash, melons, and tomatoes. Among the root crops were manioc, potatoes, and sweet potatoes. There were also condiments such as chili peppers, cacao, and vanilla; narcotics and stimulants such as coca and tobacco; and useful fiber-yielding plants such as henequen, maguey, cotton, and sisal. Cotton was independently domesticated in the Old World and the New World.

212

The joining of these native American domesticants with those of the Old World after 1492 had massive consequences all over the world. Sugar combined with cacao yielded chocolate. Sugar cane, which had been domesticated first in Southeast Asia, was planted in Brazil and the Caribbean islands to make sugar for chocolate and to sweeten coffee and tea. The attempt to find cheap labor for the sugar plantations led to the development of the slave trade and the forced migration of tens of millions of African blacks to the New World. Maize was taken to China where it provided extra calories for a population explosion in the sixteenth century. Manioc became a staple food crop of tropical populations throughout Africa. The potato was taken to Ireland, where it produced a population explosion followed by crop failures, a famine, and a mass exodus to America. And tobacco was taken to Europe, then sent back to Virginia, where it provided the impetus for the development of plantation slavery in the United States.

Several respected authorities were unwilling to concede that the American Indians had been able to domesticate these important plants without help from the Old World. This view persisted until quite recently largely because of the apparent chronological priority of plant domestication in the Middle East and East and Southeast Asia. Thus it was argued that a boatload of post-Neolithic migrants from across the Atlantic or Pacific had washed up in Mexico, Brazil, or Peru, bringing with them the *idea* of plant domestication. Some archaeologists even argued that the voyagers must have brought maize with them since the wild ancestors of maize had not yet been identified.

Diffusionist theories of New World agricultural origins have been decisively refuted by the identification of the ancestral forms of maize and of the entire sequence of modifications that these forms underwent as they were domesticated. The most important discoveries were made by Richard S. MacNeish in the highlands of the Mexican State of Tamaulipas and in Tehuacán Valley in the State of Puebla in 1958 and 1964, respectively. MacNeish showed that in both of these rather arid upland areas the domestication of maize and other native American plants was the product of a series of cultural and ecological interactions that were determined by specific local conditions not found in the Middle East. It now appears likely that the ancestor of maize was a plant called *teosinte,* a grass that still grows wild in the highland valleys of Mesoamerica and that is still used as a source of flour by modern seed-collectors (Flannery 1973; cf. Mangelsdorf 1974). Its domestication must antedate 7000 B.P. because the people who lived in the Tehuacán Valley at that time were already growing a

213

primitive form of maize that had a small cob with two or three rows of soft-husked seeds and toughened rachis (see p. 193).

Over the next 3,000 years further selection and hybridization produced varieties more closely resembling the ones now in use. So the American Indians on their own not only domesticated maize, but they subjected it to the greatest amount of selection and morphological change and adapted it to the widest geographical range of any major food plant (Flannery 1973). In this process there is simply no place at which Euro-Asian or African "ideas" about other crops could have played a significant role. The domestication of New World plants and animals was an independent development governed by the particular conditions of nature and culture in the Western Hemisphere.

At 10,000 B.P. the Mexican highlands were occupied by hunting and gathering peoples whose way of life was probably similar to that found elsewhere in North America at approximately the same time level. But the animals hunted in Tamaulipas and Tehuacán seem not to have been as large or as abundant as those that the Clovis and Folsom big-game hunters depended on.

After 9000 B.P. the horse was extinct in the New World, including highland Mesoamerica. Subsistence came to depend upon many different kinds of small animals, such as deer, rabbits, gophers, rats, turtles, and birds, plus a wide variety of plants, including the ancestors of domesticated squash, avocados, maize, and beans.

Although completely different in terms of the species involved, the ecological conditions in these highland Mexican valleys bear some resemblance to the pre-Neolithic situation in the centers of domestication in the Middle East. In both instances the extinction of the Pleistocene megafauna was followed by a broadening of the subsistence base to include a wide spectrum of smaller animals and wild plants. The appearance of seed-grinding equipment in Mexico at this time parallels the increased use of such equipment among the Middle Eastern Natufians during the incipient phases of plant domestication. Another striking parallel is the early date at which protein-rich legumes like beans were combined with the basic grains in both areas (Zohary and Hopf 1973).

This is how MacNeish (1972) views the developments in the Tehuacán Valley from 9000 B.P. onward: From 9000 to 7000 B.P. the people aggregated and disaggregated into larger and smaller semimigratory groups, depending on the season. They obtained 54 percent of the food from wild animals, 40 percent from wild plants, and about 6 percent from domesticated plants such as squash, amaranth, chili peppers, and avocados. They had mortars and pestles, milling stones, baskets, and nets but no permanent house sites. From 7000 to 5400 B.P. meat

214

provided 34 percent, wild plants provided 52 percent, and domesticants including squash, amaranth, maize, beans, gourds, chili peppers, and avocados provided 14 percent of the food supply. From 5400 to 4300 B.P. the proportion had changed to 25 percent meat, 25 percent domesticated plants, and 50 percent wild plants. During this period the Tehuacán people built permanent structures in hamlets that served as their main residence throughout much of the year. Large permanent villages, however, did not appear in Tehuacán until after 2850 B.P.

In other highland valleys, villages containing over 300 persons who lived in wattle and daub huts began to appear shortly after 3500 B.P. (Flannery 1973). In Tehuacán, as in several other highland valleys, large villages seem to be related to the development of some kind of irrigation, which brought reliance on agriculture up over 60 percent and reliance on meat down below 25 percent (all these figures must be considered educated guesses). In the transition to still larger aggregates of villages and states in the highlands, the studies at Tehuacán "strongly indicate that a major causal factor was the development of water control and various kinds of irrigation agriculture" (MacNeish 1972:93).

At some point after 4000 B.P. maize was brought down from its native highland habitat and adopted by lowland tropical forest peoples in Veracruz and Guatemala. These lowlanders may already have achieved some form of village life based on tropical root crops and exploitation of the abundant riverine and coastal fauna. It was in the lowlands, shortly after 3500 B.P., that the earliest Mesoamerican ceremonial center was constructed (see below). But it is in the highlands, where irrigation agriculture was practiced, that the greatest parallels with the Middle East are to be found.

Thus the major difference between the period of incipient agriculture in the Middle East and Mesoamerica was that the American Indians retained their seminomadic way of life for a much longer time after they had begun to domesticate their basic food crops. Sizeable Mesoamerican villages that predate 3500 B.P. have not yet been found. The ecological basis for this difference seems quite clear. First of all, teosinte and wild amaranth are far less productive than the wild ancestors of wheat and barley (Flannery 1973). Second, New World opportunities for animal domestication were limited by a lack of suitable wild species. The only New World animal at all comparable to sheep, goats, or cattle is the llama. But this marginally useful beast did not occur in association with the basic plant repertory of Mexico. Although the ancient Peruvians did eventually domesticate the llama, their chief source of animal protein was the domesticated guinea pig.

215

The Mexicans ultimately domesticated the turkey, the muscovy duck, and the honey bee, but these species were of no significance in the incipient agricultural phase and never did amount to much in later periods.

The strength of the Middle Eastern Neolithic consisted in the mutual reinforcement provided by the domestication of both plants and animals. Sedentary village life increased the productivity of plant domesticants, which increased the productivity of animal domesticants, which increased the productivity of sedentary village life, and so on. In highland Mexico, however, the need to retain animal protein in the diet worked against the abandonment of hunting since there were few animals suitable for domestication as a food source. Hence, compared with the Middle East, the development of village sedentism in Mesoamerica did not precede the first phases of cultivation but followed it after a lapse of three or four thousand years.

The Development of New World States, Cities, and Empires

As in the case of the Middle East, once the threshold of full sedentary village life based on agriculture was crossed in the New World, population density increased and larger units of social structure came into existence. Parallel and probably mutually related transformations to multicommunity, stratified states took place throughout Mesoamerica and the Andean region during the period 3500 to 2000 B.P. During subsequent phases of growth several of the New World developmental sequences culminated in states of imperial dimensions containing millions of inhabitants. These empires were ruled from capital cities, which contained as many as 150,000 residents and great concentrations of monumental architecture including temples, palaces, and gigantic pyramids (E. Wolf 1959; Gorenstein and others 1974).

Olmec and Maya

As in the Middle East, the earliest manifestation of the thrust toward statehood can be seen in the construction of large ceremonial and civic centers. Huge earth mounds, plazas, pyramids, and temples made their appearance; stone idols depicting gods and rulers were set up in the public spaces. In Mesoamerica two varieties of such ceremonial centers begin to appear shortly after 3500 B.P.

In the lowland, forested areas of Veracruz and in Southern Yuca-

216

Figure 11-3. OLMEC HEAD, SAN LORENZO, MEXICO. The massiveness and abundance of Olmec monuments indicate the existence of state-level institutions. (Gordon Ekholm and American Museum of Natural History)

tán, the growth of state-level societies was based on the type of agriculture known as *slash and burn.* This technique involved controlled periodic burning of patches of forested land to clear crop space and to provide fertilizer in the form of ashes. Although it is highly productive, slash and burn is thought to be incompatible with the growth of densely nucleated cities since it requires large amounts of land in various stages of cultivation and forest regeneration (see p. 239). The civic and ceremonial centers of lowland Mesoamerican states may have been relatively empty most of the year, filling up with people only on ceremonial occasions when they also probably served as market centers for the dispersed populations (cf. Vogt 1969). The claim by some archaeologists that lowland ceremonial centers such as Tikal in Guatemala attained densities of 45,000 people in an area of 123 square kilometers (about 367 people per square kilometer) are disputed by others (Haviland 1970; cf. Sanders 1972).

The earliest examples of Mesoamerican lowland civic centers occur in the piedmont and coastal districts of Veracruz and Tabasco and are known collectively as the *Olmec* culture. One of the best-known Olmec sites, La Venta, has an earth-fill pyramid shaped like a volcano with gullied slopes. It is 105 feet in height and 420 feet in diameter. Construction was under way by 3000 B.P. As at several other Olmec localities, nine-foot-high round-faced stone heads, stone altars, tombs, and stelae (monolithic carved columns) also occur. Basalt for

217

Olmec and Maya

Figure 11-4. MAYAN TEMPLE, TIKAL, GUATEMALA. (George W. Gardner)

these constructions had to be transported from quarries over fifty miles away (cf. Coe 1968; Heizer 1960).

The *Maya* of the Yucatán Peninsula achieved the zenith of state formation in the lowlands. The beginning of Maya stone construction dates back to about 2100 B.P., but between A.D. 300 and 900, Maya ceremonial centers were at their maximum. Elaborately ornamented multiroom buildings were constructed on top of supporting platforms and grouped symmetrically around plazas. Ball courts for ceremonial games, stelae and altars incised with hieroglyphics, and massive statuary were also part of the plaza complexes. Towering over all were great, truncated pyramids, with stone facing and flights of steps leading to temples at their crests (Coe 1966; Weaver 1972). There were "at least a dozen gigantic ceremonial-civic centers, scores of smaller but still imposing ones, hundreds of small ceremonial centers, tens of thousands of hamlets, and a population that must have numbered in the millions" (Sanders 1972:121).

Although the lowland Maya area is heavily forested, it is subject to an annual dry season. Moreover, because the bedrock forming the Yucatán Peninsula is limestone, almost all surface water sinks into the ground and disappears during the dry spell. All the lowland Maya civic centers are therefore located in the vicinity of natural water

218

holes or are associated with artificial reservoirs. Thus it is possible that the Maya ruling class controlled access to sources of drinking water, which were critical for survival during years of drought. Barring this means of control, it is unlikely that Maya social life was initially afflicted by extreme difference in power, since the dispersed villagers could not easily be taxed or rounded up for *corvée* (forced labor). This would mean that much of the labor input in the lowland areas was voluntarily donated or at least compensated for in food or trade goods rather than coerced (Vogt and Caucian 1970).

The single most important factor triggering the growth of lowland Mesoamerican populations and the subsequent evolution of the Maya ceremonial centers was probably the spread of maize in its developed form from its native highlands after 4000 B.P. Maize, planted with beans and squash and lowland crops such as the nut from the *ramon* tree, rapidly transformed the forested lowlands into an extremely productive ecosystem. The potential of this ecosystem for state formation and for urban nucleation, however, was not as great as that of early dynastic Mesopotamia or highland Mexico and Peru. The main limitation seems to have been the technical and environmental obstacles to the development of irrigation agriculture under the auspices of the rulers of the temple centers. In the highlands, where irrigation was introduced as early as 3500 B.P., political organization continued to evolve far beyond the Maya level.

Not only did the Maya ceremonial centers fail to evolve into imperial systems, but after reaching their maximum population, they suddenly collapsed. Between A.D. 800–1000 Tikal and the entire

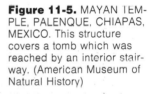

Figure 11-5. MAYAN TEMPLE, PALENQUE, CHIAPAS, MEXICO. This structure covers a tomb which was reached by an interior stairway. (American Museum of Natural History)

central area of classic Maya civilization was abandoned. The resulting population vacuum in the central area has lasted into modern times. A theory that accounts for all the relevant facts is that as the population increased, the ruling class attempted to intensify agricultural production by stepping up its tax and labor demands on the peasantry. The peasants responded by intensifying their agricultural efforts, progressively shortening the fallow periods until infestations of weeds and grass and soil exhaustion made it impossible to sustain high yields.

The evidence we now have leads to the conclusion that agriculture as constituted under the slash-burn system could just barely supply with corn the probable peak population of the Maya empire, although it was adequate for the depleted populations of the post-classic era.   [Cook:1972:32]

The last act of this scenario probably involved rebellions in which the bulk of the peasants became fugitives and migrated to other ceremonial centers, whose carrying capacities were in turn pushed over their limits (cf. Cowgill 1964; Sanders 1972; Cook 1972).

Teotihuacán and Tenochtitlán

In the highlands a fundamentally different kind of population growth curve is associated with the rise and fall of various states and empires. Here the developmental sequence of cultures displays certain remarkable parallels to what transpired during the urbanization of the Middle East.

At Teotihuacán, located twenty-five miles northeast of Mexico City, there was an initial period of rainfall farming beginning some time after 3500 B.P. For over a thousand years villages clung to the moist flanks of the mountains. But between 2300 and 2000 B.P. the people shifted to the alluvial plain, adopted irrigation techniques, and began to coalesce into a huge sprawling city. The immediate support area of this city covered some 200 square miles and contained a population over 100,000. The city itself probably had at least 85,000 inhabitants, most of whom were tillers of the soil. There was formal planning of the city's residential and civic precincts as indicated by the grid pattern of the avenues and alleys, markets in various districts, and exclusive quarters allotted to craft specialists (Millon 1970). In the middle of Teotihuacán there is a complex of public buildings and monuments that, by comparison, dwarf even those of Tikal and render the Olmec sites puny. The central monument is the so-called Pyramid of the Sun, still among the world's largest artificial struc-

220

tures. Measuring 200 feet in height and over 700 feet on a side, this edifice contains 840,000 cubic meters of fill. A second, smaller pyramid contains 210,000 cubic meters, which makes it about twice as big as the Olmec pyramid at La Venta. The civic buildings of Tikal cover only a small fraction of the area of Teotihuacán's ceremonial complex (Sanders and Price 1968; Millon 1973). With the emergence of Teotihuacán the Mesoamerican highlands entered a period of imperial rivalry and extensive warfare.

At about A.D. 700 Teotihuacán began to distintegrate, probably under the impact of military defeats. But a succession of neighboring highland imperial centers arose to take its place. The first of these was centered at Cholula, where there is an unexcavated pyramid whose dimensions dwarf even those of the Pyramid of the Sun. Then from A.D. 968–1156 the reigning empire was that of a people called the Toltecs, whose capital was at Tula. Their influence extended as far as Chichen Itza in the Yucatán.

The final and greatest of the empires in the native imperial lineage of Mesoamerica was that of the Aztecs, whose capital, Tenochtitlán, contained well over 100,000 inhabitants when Cortes' disbelieving eyes first glimpsed its gardens, causeways, markets, pyramids, and temples (E. Wolf 1959; Coe 1962; Vaillant 1966). There is no reason to suppose that the highland American Indian empires had reached the limits of their potential population growth and political development at this fateful date. (This can be seen more clearly perhaps in the case

Figure 11-6. PYRAMID OF THE SUN, TEOTIHUACÁN. (George W. Gardner)

221

Teotihuacán and Tenochtitlán

Figure 11-7. RUINS OF TULA, HIDALGO, MEXICO. This was the capital city of the pre-Aztec people known as the Toltecs. It was destroyed by invaders in 1160 A.D. (George W. Gardner)

of the Inca of Peru, which I shall discuss in Ch. 18). It took something like an invasion from "outer space" to halt the indigenous development of the American Indian civilization. At least that's how the Aztecs explained it. They mistook the Spanish horsemen for gods.

Developments North of Mexico

Just as the Neolithic spread from the Middle Eastern center of domestication into Europe, India, and Africa, so too, in the New World, the basic Mesoamerican farming complex gradually affected the life-styles of people living in remote parts of North America. And again, as in the Old World, as the farming complex spread, it encountered diverse environments and was adapted and readapted by hundreds of different local cultures. Primitive varieties of corn were being planted in the vicinity of Bat Cave in Southwest New Mexico as early as 3000 B.C. But, as at Tehuacán, agriculture did not lead immediately or inexorably to sedentary village life. Almost three thousand years elapsed before the first permanent villages appeared in the Southwest. These consisted of small clusters of pit houses found in the valleys of the Mogollon Mountain Range in New Mexico at about 300 B.C. Larger villages associated with a culture called Hohokam soon appeared in the valleys of the Salt and Gila rivers in Southern Arizona. The Hohokam peoples built extensive irrigation

222

systems fed by canals thirty miles long, reared pyramid mounds, and constructed Mexican-style ball courts.

The third great Southwestern culture based on agriculture is called the Anasazi. These were the "pueblo" peoples of Arizona, New Mexico, Utah, and Colorado. At Pueblo Bonito, long before the coming of the first Europeans, they built an apartment house five stories tall containing eight hundred rooms. The Anasazi were forced to abandon many of their pueblos as a result of a prolonged drought that gripped the Southwest during the thirteenth century A.D.

Maize cultivation moved up the Mississippi and Ohio River valleys beginning about 1000 B.C., creating profound transformations in the life-styles of the seminomadic inhabitants. The three main phases, known as Adena, Hopewell, and Mississippian, were marked by the construction of thousands of earth mounds, some containing burials and others that served as platforms for temples or residences. Dense populations appeared during the Mississippian phase, giving rise to urban nucleations and elaborate temple-priest-idol cults that exhibited strong Mesoamerican influences. The greatest expression of this trend toward monumentality, urbanism, and state formation occurred at Cahokia near East St. Louis between A.D. 900 and 1100. Here, with energy derived from the Mexican plant food "trinity"—maize, squash, and beans—the Mississippians built a mound that was one hundred feet high and covered fifteen acres. Numerous additional large and small mounds, supporting houses and temples, surrounded the main structure.

The effects of the introduction of maize agriculture were less spectacular in the Eastern woodlands where people like the Iroquois and Delaware continued to live in small villages and rely on hunting and gathering for a major source of their food supply. Elsewhere in North America there were vast regions into which agriculture never penetrated. The peoples of the entire Pacific Coast from California to Alaska, for example, never abandoned their reliance on hunting, wild-seed-gathering, and intensive forms of fishing and shellfish-collecting. One can only conclude that the initial phases of farming offered no conspicuous advantages over the existing subsistence practices in these regions.

The Development of States in South America

The Andean region of South America may also have been the center of an independently developed complex of domesticated animals and plants. This complex almost certainly provided the basis for an

223

Figure 11-8. TIAHUANA-CO. Ruins of the pre-Inca civilization near Lake Titicaca, Bolivia. (UPI Photo)

essentially independent rise to cities, states, and empires. Although maize eventually became the principal crop of the Inca Empire, and although the Andean region shared many other domesticants in common with Mesoamerica, several important New World plants and animals were specialties of the Andes. Chief among these are high-altitude tubers like the potato and high-altitude grains like quinoa. The recent discovery of two kinds of domesticated beans at Callejón de Huaylas, Peru, dating between 7680 and 10,000 B.P. suggests that domestication was under way at least as early in the Andes as in Mesoamerica (Kaplan, Lynch, and Smith 1973). The earliest maize in South America, dating between 6300 and 4800 B.P., has been found at Ayacucho in Peru, again indicating an antiquity almost as great as for the maize that MacNeish discovered in the Tehuacán Valley. (Incidentally, MacNeish also found the Ayacucho maize.)

The first signs of agriculture began to appear along the Peruvian coast by about 5000 B.P., at first consisting mostly of squash, gourds, and peppers, which were tied in with a subsistence economy heavily dependent on fishing, shellfish-collecting, and sea-mammal-hunting. As additional domesticated plants were added to the agricultural repertory, settlements grew up in the floodplains of the Peruvian coastal rivers and were inhabited by as many as three or four thousand people in the period 1900–1750 B.C. (Mark Cohen 1975). Before and after the introduction of irrigation and maize, the coastal population underwent rapid growth. Canal systems extending across

224

whole valleys were constructed, and the first small states made their appearance by 350 B.P to A.D. 1. Thereafter a series of wars and conquests led to the emergence of larger states, which united coastal valleys and highland valleys into single political units. These in turn expanded, reaching imperial scope with the Tiahuanaco and Huari empires (A.D. 550–800), followed by the Chimu Empire with its huge mud-walled city of Chan Chan and finally by the Inca Empire, 1438–1525 (Lanning 1974).

It is impossible to survey the prehistory of the New World without experiencing a great sense of loss at the premature termination of the

Figure 11-9. CHIMU EMPIRE (top). Ancient irrigation canal with culvert under Chimu road. Despite absence of wheeled vehicles, pre-Inca roads were built with great skill. (Barbara J. Price)

Figure 11-10. CHANCHAN, CAPITOL OF THE CHIMU EMPIRE (bottom). Ruins of cisterns inside the city walls. (Barbara J. Price)

225

Figure 11-11. MACHU PICCHU, PERU. Ruins of an Inca fortress-city. (Sergio Larrain/Magnum)

various largely independent trajectories of cultural growth as a result of the European conquest. Perhaps if Columbus had been delayed only a few hundred years more, that conquest would never have taken place.

The Meaning of the "Second Earth"

Until the Spanish conquest, technology in the New World had been evolving along lines remarkably parallel to the Middle Eastern sequence. Nonetheless American Indian technological change was definitely proceeding at a slower rate. Much of the "lag" can be attributed to the differential natural endowments of the Middle Eastern and nuclear American regions. I have already pointed out

226

how the extinction of potential domestic animals among the Pleistocene megafauna rendered the American Indians vulnerable to military conquest by European adventurers mounted on horseback. The same megafauna extinction deprived the American Indians of potential animal domesticants that might have served to provide traction for plows and for wheeled vehicles. For the purposes of later discussions of the role of "intelligence" in cultural evolution, let me emphasize the fact that the American Indians lacked these items not because they were any less intelligent or inventive than the Europeans or Asians. The Incas actually did have a form of plow that people pushed and pulled. And the preconquest Mesoamericans understood the principle of the wheel at least to the extent of putting them on children's toys. Presumably, given more time, these inventions and their applications would have been improved upon and extended.

A similar situation existed with respect to the development of metallurgical skills. Lack of steel tools placed the American Indians at a great disadvantage during the European invasions. But the development of American Indian metallurgical techniques had already passed beyond the hammering of sheet copper to the smelting and casting of copper, gold, silver, and several alloys. Just before conquest, bronze mace heads and knives were being made, and it would seem reasonable to conclude, given the two-thousand-year interval separating the bronze and iron ages in the Middle East, that

Figure 11-12. CROW INDIANS. One of the numerous seminomadic peoples of the Great Plains whose way of life was completely altered by the reintroduction of the horse into the New World. (Museum of the American Indian, Heye Foundation)

Figure 11-13. MAYAN GLYPHS. On Stela from Monte Alban (above). Symbols in form of stylized human faces and mythical animals, from Palenque (below). (George W. Gardner—above; Walter R. Aguiar—below)

228

had the American Indians been left alone they too would have eventually discovered the superior qualities of iron and steel.

My confidence in this perhaps untestable prediction is based on the independent achievement of items far more complex than plows, wheeled vehicles, or iron smelting. Like their Middle Eastern counterparts, the American Indian priests and rulers were concerned with the regulation of agricultural production. Under state and temple auspices, astronomical observations were carried out which led to the development of calendars. Indeed, the Maya calendar was more accurate than its Egyptian counterpart. To keep calendrical records, as well as records of agricultural production, taxes, and other state affairs, hieroglyphic writing systems were invented by several Mesoamerican peoples. Of special interest is the Maya system of vigesimal numeration, which incorporated the principle of the zero. This feature was absent in the Middle Eastern, Greek, and Roman number systems. Without the concept of a zero quantity to mark the absence of the base number or its exponents, it is extremely difficult to perform arithmetical operations involving large numbers. In this respect at least the American Indians appear to have been more precocious than their Middle Eastern contemporaries.

Given the fact that the ecosystems of the Middle East and Mesoamerica were initially quite different, precise parallels in the evolutionary trajectories leading toward urban and imperial societies in the two hemispheres should not be expected. Again and again, however, the peoples of the two hemispheres independently achieved convergent solutions to similar problems when the underlying technological, environmental, and demographic conditions were approximately similar. The meaning of the "second earth" therefore is that human affairs are subject to determining forces that select innovations and shape the course of cultural evolution as surely as biological evolution is determined by natural selection. This does not mean that all cultures must evolve through the same stages of evolution any more than that the principle of natural selection means all organisms must have similar phylogenetic experiences. The determinism that governs cultural systems produces both similar and dissimilar trajectories of evolutionary transformation. It does this because the conditions under which the interaction between culture and nature takes place are quite diverse. Nonetheless, what the geological time-perspective of archaeology teaches is that even when cultures diverge, their differences can usually be understood in terms of orderly, scientifically intelligible processes (cf. Coe and Flannery 1966; R. M. Adams 1966; Sanders and Price 1968; Parsons and Price 1971; Binford 1972; P. Smith 1972b; Plog 1974; Thomas 1974b).

12
ENERGY AND ECOSYSTEMS

Archaeological evidence presented in previous chapters indicates that there is a strong tendency for major technological innovations to be diffused or to be reinvented over wide portions of the globe. Furthermore, there is a general chronological order in which major inventions tend to appear that results from the fact that certain inventions depend upon or actually incorporate previous inventions. For example, in both the Old World and the New World the sequence of inventions that led up to metallurgy depended upon the prior achievement of high-temperature ovens and furnaces for baking ceramics, and this obviously depended on learning how to make and control fire in cooking and other contexts. Low-temperature metallurgical experience with copper and tin almost of necessity had to precede the development of iron and steel, and mastery of these metals in turn had to precede the development of the countless tools and machines spawned by the industrial revolution.

Major technological inventions alter the means of subsistence and influence the structural and ideological sectors of culture. Yet both archaeology and ethnology attest to the fact that the convergence of technologies through parallel growth and diffusion does not produce globally uniform "stages" of cultural evolution. At any given point in time there is a great diversity of cultures even among those that possess similar technologies. This diversity arises first and foremost from the fact that technology always interacts with specific natural environments, each of which has its own special features. The aim of this chapter is to show how the interaction between technologies and environments establishes specific modes of production upon which many other features of cultural life depend.

Other Sources of Diversity

Before moving on to an examination of the consequences of particular interactions between technology and environment, let me clarify one important point: environment is not the only source of variables that modify and influence technologies. Other causes of diversity in technology must not be overlooked. Nonenvironmental factors associated with total political and economic organization are especially important among industrial cultures. For example, Third World underdevelopment is closely associated with political and military domination and exploitation, which are integral parts of modern imperialist systems. In addition, the differential spread and development of technological complexes is influenced by the preexisting mode of production. In the short run, for example, people accustomed

Figure 12-1. SCHEMATIC REPRESENTATION OF RANGES OF LABOR PRODUCTIVITY OF BASIC FOOD PRODUCTION TECHNOLOGIES. Dotted vertical lines indicate wide degree of variation associated with technological applications as a result of environmental and political contexts.

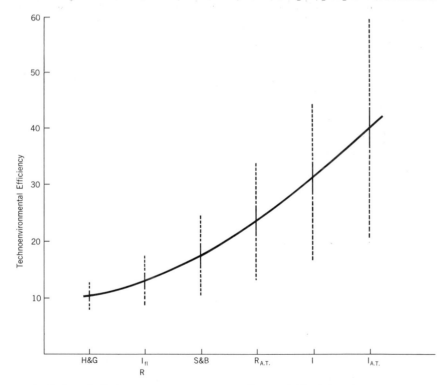

H & G = Hunting and gathering

I_{fl} = Irrigation in natural floodplains without animal traction plow

R = Rainfall agriculture in savannah and parklands without animal traction plow or animal manure

S & B = Slash-and-burn forest gardens

$R_{A.T.}$ = Rainfall agriculture with animal traction plow and animal manure

I = Irrigation with canals and terracing but no animal traction

$I_{A.T.}$ = Irrigation with canals, terracing, and animal traction

230

to plowing with horses can adopt mechanized forms of agriculture more easily than pastoral nomads (see p. 246). Preexisting demographic conditions also influence the rate of technological change. In India, for example, organizational problems associated with vast numbers of people greatly complicate efforts to raise productivity. And more efficient technologies may be resisted by densely populated capitalist countries because labor-saving devices can lead to increased unemployment, and by densely populated socialist countries because labor is less costly than machines. These additional sources of diversity will be discussed in later chapters.

The Influence of Environment

Soils, climate, topography, rivers, lakes, seashores, forests—all these interact with the invention and diffusion of technology. Thus agriculture obviously does not penetrate as readily into arctic or desert environments as it does into river valleys and areas of abundant rainfall. The yield from rice planted in irrigated terraces far surpasses the yield from rice planted in gardens dependent upon rainfall. To repeat: any item of technology must interact with a specific natural environment. Similar kinds of technologies in different environments may entail very different amounts and types of labor, which may in turn influence the social structure and system of economic management. Small, semimigratory villages may arise when maize is planted in the tropics and great tracts of forest are available for burning. Entirely different settlement patterns will form where the forests are limited in extent. Irrigation farming is not definable in abstract terms. Its influence upon social life varies according to the size and dependability of the water supply, the availability of flat terrain, the amount of minerals in the water, and many other conditions.

In industrial societies, the influence of environment often appears to be subordinate to the influence exerted by prior modes of production and by demographic, political, and ideological factors. This statement must be carefully distinguished from the often repeated but dangerously incorrect belief that industrial societies have liberated themselves from the influence of the environment or that our species now dominates or controls the environment. It is true that replicas of American suburbs have been built in the deserts of Saudi Arabia and in Alaska and that they can also be constructed on the moon. But the energy and material that such efforts are premised upon derive from definite interactions between technology and environment carried out

Figure 12-2. IRRIGATED PLAINS. Rice paddies near Ahmedabad, Gujarat, India. (United Nations)

at mines, factories, and farms in various parts of the world. The rate of depletion of irreplaceable reserves of oil, water, soil, forests, and metallic ores remains in part a function of the availability of these resources as natural "givens" at particular times and places. Similarly, at all sites where modern technology extracts or processes natural resources or where any form of industrial construction or production takes place there are differential capacities for disposal of industrial wastes, pollutants, and other biologically significant by-products. Recently, widespread publicity has been given to the ecological hazards of industrialization, and efforts are under way in several industrial nations to reduce air and water pollution and to prevent the depletion and poisoning of the environment. The costs of these efforts testify to the continuing importance of the interaction between technology and environment in industrial contexts. These costs will continue to mount, for this is only the very beginning of the industrial era. In the centuries to come, the inhabitants of specific regions will pay for industrialization in ways as yet uncalculated. There will be restraints upon production, social structure, and other aspects of culture as definite and far-reaching as those imposed by the extinction of the American horse through overkill or by the introduction of the potato into Ireland.

232

Energy

The system of relationships among the organisms in an environment is known as an *ecosystem.* The most important aspect of any ecosystem is the pattern of energy flow characteristic of its organic and inorganic components. A full understanding of a human ecosystem requires much more than an analysis of its energy pathways. Factors such as population size and density, sex ratio, age distribution, fertility control, and other demographic variables also play an independent role in giving different systems their particular characteristics. Similarly, certain economic variables involving the organization of the production, distribution, and consumption of goods and services will also have to be considered. However, the relationships among these additional variables cannot be understood unless the basic pattern of the system's flow of energy has been described. And this description must involve quantitative measures.

Every human population participates in an ecosystem whose energetic patterns are unique. In order to explain the general role that energetic variables play in the evolution of culture, I shall have to simplify and omit many pertinent measures. But in view of the huge number of different cultures, this is the only way to achieve the desired level of generality.

One of the assumptions that can be made in order to simplify is that the most influential feature of the energy flow in preindustrial societies is the manner in which human metabolic food energy is obtained from plants and animals. In describing preindustrial systems, in other words, energy obtained from wind power or from the burning of wood and other fuels can be treated as of secondary importance. On the other hand, in describing industrial systems, nonmetabolic energy involving fuels, wind, and water power have to be given equal weight with food energy.

Energy and Factors of Production

The basic characteristics of preindustrial energy flow patterns can be set forth by means of a simple equation relating crucial aspects of food production to energy output: food energy (E), or the number of calories that a system produces annually, equals the number of food-producers (m) times the hours of work per food producer (t) times the calories expended per food producer per hour (r) times the average number of calories of food produced for each calorie expended in food production (e).

233

$$E = m \times t \times r \times e$$

The last term in the equation, e, must have a value greater than one in order for the energy produced to be greater than the energy expended in producing it. This factor reflects both the technological inventory of food production and the application of that technology by the food-producers to the tasks of food production in a specific environment. The larger the value of e, the greater the labor productivity or techno-environmental efficiency enjoyed by the food-producers in their attempt to derive food energy from the environment. That is, the larger the value of e, the larger the number of calories produced for each calorie expended on food production.

A Hunting and Gathering Food-Energy System

This formula can be applied to the food-energy system of the Kalahari Desert hunting and gathering !Kung Bushmen studied by Richard Lee (1968). Lee estimated that the average daily production of food energy in a Bushman camp was 64,200 calories.* To achieve this level of production, an average of 7.4 food-producers were needed per working day. Lee estimates that the average Bushman's working day was 6 hours long. So, 7.4 workers worked 6 hours each to produce a total of 64,200 calories. (Note that this figure does not take into consideration the work expended in preparing and cooking the food after it has been brought into camp.) If the rate of work was moderate, each worker expended about 150 calories per hour above basal metabolism. Hence, the calorie cost of a day's work for the work force was:

$$7.4 \text{ workers} \times \frac{6 \text{ hours}}{\text{worker}} \times \frac{150 \text{ calories}}{\text{hour}} = 6,660 \text{ calories}$$

Thus, 6,660 calories were invested in an average day of hunting and collecting activities, and this investment yielded an average output of 64,200 calories. The ratio 64,200/6,660 = 9.6 is the value of e, the technoenvironmental advantage or labor productivity of the Bushmen's mode of production.

The formula for E during what was presumably an average year can be completed as follows: if the daily calorie output is 64,200 calories, then annual output is $365 \times 64,200 = 23,433,000$ calories.

---

*Kilogram calories. A kilogram calorie is the amount of energy needed to raise 1 kilogram of water one degree centigrade.

Figure 12-3 BUSHMAN WOMEN RETURNING TO CAMP. They have been out gathering wild vegetables. (Richard B. Lee)

This is the value of *E*. The formula now reads:

$$\frac{E}{23,433,000} = \frac{m}{?} \times \frac{t}{?} \times \frac{r}{150} \times \frac{e}{9.6}$$

Over a period of several weeks an average of 20 different adults participated in food production either through hunting or collecting activities. Inserting 20 as the value for *m*, the formula now reads:

$$\frac{E}{23,433,000} = \frac{m}{20} \times \frac{t}{?} \times \frac{r}{150} \times \frac{e}{9.6}$$

Solving for *t,* the completed formula (in round numbers) is:

annual calories	food-producers	hours per food-producer	calories expended per hour	techno-environmental efficiency
23,000,000 =	20 ×	805 ×	150 ×	9.6

Although this formula is constructed from several "guesstimates," correspondences with the data from other societies increase my confidence in its basic accuracy. The most problematical factor is the value of 150 calories per hour for *r*. It is very difficult to measure calorie expenditure per time unit under natural field conditions. A study carried out in West Africa (see below) indicated an overall average of 157 calories per hour on the basis of field tests and estimates. Since comparable data are seldom available, I shall use the value 150 calories per hour throughout the subsequent discussion. This procedure is justified because the rate of work is probably the least variable of preindustrial input factors. Work can be "speeded up" under industrial conditions or whenever there is close surveillance of the individual worker by overseers and managers. But most preindustrial work tends to take place at a rate that is physiologically comfortable, so that the worker does not become overheated or out of breath, except during brief periods when the nature of the productive process requires bursts of intense effort.

A Comparison with Hoe Agriculture

How can the quantitative levels of the Bushman food-energy system be explained? Is the annual per capita total of working hours of the Bushman labor force small or large? Is the labor efficiency of their mode of production low or high? Is their ratio of food-producers to nonfood-producers usual or unusual? Only by comparing one food-energy system with another can the most important features of particular systems be identified and judgments rendered concerning their place in the range of cultural behaviors.

A well-studied comparative case is that of Genieri Village in Gambia, West Africa (Haswell 1953). Here the basic mode of subsistence is agriculture involving the cultivation of peanuts and several varieties of cereals. The Genieri villagers till their fields with iron hoes, practice a fallowing routine to maintain soil fertility, and depend on rainfall to provide water for their crops. A team of agronomists and anthropologists kept detailed figures on the hours spent by all members of the village in every phase of food production, including the time spent by adolescents in scaring off birds and the time spent in threshing and winnowing the grain. As in the case of the Bushmen, however, I shall omit consideration of energy expended in food preparation and cooking. The Genieri food-energy formula in round numbers is as follows:

annual calories	food-producers	hours per food-producer	calories expended per hour	techno-environmental efficiency
460,000,000 =	334 ×	820 ×	150 ×	11.2

The most striking difference between the Genieri and the Bushman food-energy systems is the twentyfold increase in total calorie output in the former. Most of this difference is accounted for by the increase in the size of the labor force. The population of Genieri Village is about five hundred. Note that this population is sustained by a value of e that is practically the same as that enjoyed by the Bushmen. This

236

feature accords well with the view of the origin and spread of the Middle East Neolithic (p. 200). Sedentary village life need not be associated with sharp differences in labor productivity as compared with hunters and gatherers. The use of domesticants, however, does permit people to live in larger and denser settlements. Such settlements tend to replace hunting and gathering groups wherever cultivation or stock-raising can be practiced. I shall discuss the reasons for this trend in the next chapter. But first something must be said about why the Bushmen, whose labor productivity and hours of work are essentially the same as those of the Genieri villagers, live in settlements that contain on the average one-fifteenth the population of Genieri.

Environmental Limits and Restraints

In order to understand why the Bushmen do not build villages, it is necessary to consider certain environmental factors not included in the energy formula. These factors set limits to the number of people who can operate the hunting and gathering technology within walking distance of a permanent camp without lowering labor productivity or without permanently impairing the life-sustaining capacity of the environment. For the Bushmen, water supply and abundance of game are the most important environmental restraints.

Throughout the dry season each Bushman band is obliged to camp close to a permanent water hole. From this camp the hunters and food-gatherers set out each day, returning in the evening with whatever they have killed, rooted up, or gathered. About one-third of the Bushman calorie ration is derived from a high-protein nut produced in great abundance by the *mongongo* tree. Indeed there are enough mongongo nuts to provide 100 percent of the Bushmen's calorie needs at present population levels. Unfortunately the mongongo groves are far from the permanent water holes. During the rainy season the Bushmen make camp in or near the groves; but during the dry season, they must carry the mongongo nuts a considerable distance back to the water hole. In an area of 15,000 square kilometers there are only ten water holes that can be counted on to hold water throughout the year (Lee 1973). It is clear that the scarcity of water away from permanent water holes is the critical factor limiting the size of the Bushman band during most of the year. At the height of the dry season people must congregate at the largest holes and restrict their range of hunting and foraging. But they cannot stay together for long

237

Figure 12-4. COOKING MONGONGO NUTS (left). After the exterior fruit is eaten, the nut itself is cracked to get at the edible nut meat. (Richard B. Lee)

Figure 12-5. CONSERVING WATER (right). Bushman women filling ostrich egg shell canteens at a seasonal water hole. (Richard B. Lee)

without depleting the surrounding area of plants and animals and all but the largest holes of water (Lee 1969b, 1972a, b).

The Bushman's problem of water supply cannot be regarded as typical of pre-Neolithic hunting and food-gathering groups who lived in the favored areas now everywhere occupied by agriculturalists. But wherever migratory herds or widely dispersed animals had to be pursued in order to obtain essential proteins, density per camp would have had to be kept quite low. Under other ecological conditions, considerable nucleation is perfectly compatible with the hunting and food-gathering modes of production. Archaeological examples of sedentary incipient agriculturalists are known from coastal Peru as well as the Middle East. In addition, there are several well-known examples of contemporary village-dwelling hunters and food-gatherers. Along the coastal region extending from Northern California to Southern Alaska, there were nonagricultural American Indian peoples who lived in plank-house villages that contained at least a core of permanent residents. These people earned their subsis-

238

tence primarily from great fish-spawning runs. Marine animals and a variety of wild tubers, roots, and berries filled out their calorie- and protein-rich diet. In all likelihood the technoenvironmental efficiency of the nonagricultural Northwest Coast peoples exceeded that of the Genieri villagers. Unfortunately little quantitative information is available about their food-energy system.

Environmental restraints upon human food-energy systems are not always immediately apparent even to the expert. Extreme caution must be exercised before concluding that a particular culture could "easily" raise its total energy flow by increasing the size of its labor force or by increasing the amount of time put into food production. Allegations of untapped environmental potential are especially dubious when based upon short periods of observation. Many puzzling features of human ecosystems result from adaptations that are made to recurrent but infrequent ecological crises such as droughts, floods, frosts, hurricanes, and cyclical epidemics of animal and plant diseases.

A basic principle of ecological analysis states that communities of organisms adapt to the minimum life-sustaining conditions in their habitats rather than to the average conditions. One formulation of this principle is known as *Liebig's Law of the Minimum:* growth is limited by the minimum availability of any one necessary factor rather than by the abundance of all necessary factors. The short-time observer of human ecosystems is likely to see the average condition, not the extremes, and is likely to overlook the minimum factor when confronted with apparently unrestricted abundance. Liebig's law applies as well to seasonal minima such as the availability of water among the Bushmen. As Richard W. Casteel (1975) has shown, the population of many subarctic North American hunters and gatherers was closely adjusted to the amount of fish available during the winter months rather than to land animals available throughout the year.

A Slash-and-Burn Food-Energy System

Roy Rappaport (1968) has made a careful study of the food-energy system of the Tsembaga Maring, a clan living on the northern slopes of the Central Highlands of Australian New Guinea. The Tsembaga, who number about 204, plant taro, yams, sweet potatoes, manioc, sugar cane, and several other crops in small gardens cleared and fertilized by the slash-and-burn method. Rappaport calculates the technoenvironmental efficiency (e) to be about 18 for the production of plant foods. He also estimates that the annual food-energy con-

239

Figure 12-6. "COOKING" THE GARDEN. Tsembaga Maring woman during the burning phase of swidden cycle. (Roy Rappaport)

sumption of the Tsembaga is 150,000,000 calories. If the work force is taken to include everyone age ten or older, the value of m is 146. The completed formula for Tsembaga plant-food energy is:

$$\underset{150,000,000}{E} = \underset{146}{m} \times \underset{380}{t} \times \underset{150}{r} \times \underset{18}{e}$$

The slash-and-burn mode of production permits the Tsembaga to satisfy their calorie needs with remarkably small investment of working time—only 380 hours per year per food-producer in the cultivation process. High productivity of slash-and-burn techniques partially accounts for the continuing importance of this form of agriculture in the tropics. I must point out, however, that all the labor productivity data on slash-and-burn systems is derived from studies of peoples who enjoy the use of steel axes obtained through trade before the anthropologists got to them. Experiments have shown that it requires five times more calories to chop an inch of wood with a stone ax than a steel ax (Saraydar and Shimada 1971). Unfortunately it is not known how this affects work patterns and productivity under actual gardening conditions.

240

Two environmental limits and restraints are especially pertinent to tropical slash-and-burn ecosystems. First, there is the problem of forest regeneration. Because of leaching by heavy rains, and because of the invasion of insects and weeds, the productivity of slash-and-burn gardens drops rapidly after two or three years of use, and additional land must be cleared to avoid a sharp reduction in labor efficiency and output (Janzen 1973). Optimum productivity is achieved when gardens are cleared from a substantial secondary growth of large trees. If gardens are cleared when the secondary growth is very immature, only a small amount of wood-ash fertilizer will be produced by burning. On the other hand, if the trees revert to climax-forest size, they will be very difficult to cut down. Optimum regeneration may take anywhere from ten to twenty years or more, depending on local soils and climates.

Thus, in the long run, slash-and-burn cultures use up a considerable amount of forest per capita, but in any particular year only 5 percent of their total territory may actually be in production (Boserup 1965:31). The Tsembaga, for example, had only 42 acres planted in 1962–1963. Nonetheless about 864 acres in their territory had been gardened. This is about the amount of forest that the Tsembaga would need if their population remains at about 200 people and if they burned secondary-growth garden sites every 20 years. Rappaport estimates that the Tsembaga had at their disposal an amount of forest land sufficient to support another 84 people without permanently damaging the regenerative capacities of the forest. However, the bulk of this land lay above or below the optimum altitude levels for their major crops and thus would probably somewhat diminish their labor productivity if put into use. In the words of the Mnong-Gar of Vietnam (Condominas 1957), all slash-and-burn peoples confront the ultimate spectre of "eating up their forest" by shortening the fallow period to a point where grasses and weeds replace trees—remember the Maya (p. 220). At least this is what has happened to other New Guinea peoples not too far from the Tsembaga (Sorenson 1972; Sorenson and Kenmore 1974). Nonetheless there are situations, such as in the Amazon jungle, where such vast untapped reserves of trees remain and where population densities are so low that the supply of burnable trees cannot be the operative factor limiting the size of the population and work force.

Many tropical slash-and-burn energy systems, however, confront another problem that sets limits to the expansion of their population and work effort. This problem is especially acute where the main staples are protein-deficient root crops such as sweet potatoes, yams, manioc, and taro. Natural tropical forest ecosystems produce a vast

241

Figure 12-7. SLASH AND BURN (right). Amahuaca Indians of Peru burning felled tree in their garden. (Cornell Capa/Magnum)

Figure 12-8. PLANTING IN A SWIDDEN (left). This Amahuaca woman is using a digging stick to plant corn in a recently burned garden. (Robert Carneiro and American Museum of Natural History)

amount of plant biomass per acre, but they are very poor producers of animal biomass as compared, for example, with grasslands and marine ecosystems (Richards 1973). The animals that inhabit tropical forests tend to be small, furtive, and arboreal. As human population density rises, these animals quickly become very scarce and hard to find. The total animal biomass—the weight of all the spiders, insects, worms, snakes, mammals, and so on—in a hectare of Central Amazon rain forest is 45 kilograms. This compares with 304 kilograms in an East African thorn forest. In East African savannah grasslands 254 kilograms of large herbivores are found per hectare, far outweighing all the large and small animals found per hectare in the Amazon (Fittkau and Klinge 1973:8). Although plant foods can provide nutritionally adequate amounts of proteins if eaten in variety and abundance, meat is the most effective source of all the amino acids necessary for nutrition. Hence one of the most important limiting factors in the growth of slash-and-burn energy systems is the availability of animal protein.

242

The High Cost of Pigs

Like most slash-and-burn agriculturalists, the Tsembaga crave meat as a supplement to their starchy plant diet. This craving is not a matter of whim, since animal proteins have a definite nutritional advantage over vegetable proteins, and their ingestion in even small amounts leads to improvements in health and physical well-being. The Tsembaga, whose population density has risen to 67 persons per square mile, have very few sources of wild animal fat and protein left to them in their territory. But they have compensated for this lack by stocking their land with a domestic animal—the pig. The Tsembaga's pigs root for themselves during the day but come home to a meal of sweet potatoes and food scraps in the evening. An average Tsembaga pig weighs as much as an average Tsembaga human, and Rappaport estimates that each pig consumes almost as much garden produce as each person. Pigs gain about 50 pounds per year in Maring land. There were 160 pigs at the pig maximum. Therefore these pigs gained a total of $160 \times 50 = 8,000$ pounds. This converts to a food calorie value of 5,252,000 calories, which can be taken as the value of E. Additional data provided by Rappaport indicate that 66 Tsembaga women engaged in pig-raising and that their labor productivity (e) was 0.7 (Rappaport 1968:62). Solving for t, the formula for pig-raising when pigs are at a maximum is:

$$\frac{E}{5,252,000} = \frac{m}{66} \times \frac{t}{758} \times \frac{r}{150} \times \frac{e}{0.7}$$

Figure 12-9. A KAIKO PARTY. Tsembaga Maring on the way to a pig slaughter. (Roy Rappaport)

Figure 12-10. DISPATCHING A PIG. Pigs have great ritual significance throughout New Guinea and Melanesia. The people in this scene are the Fungai Maring, neighbors of the Tsembaga Maring. (Cherry Lowman)

Thus when the Tsembaga pig herd is at its maximum, almost as much time and energy is devoted to feeding pigs as to feeding people. Like many New Guinea cultures, the Tsembaga allow their pig population to increase over a number of years, slaughtering pigs only on ceremonial occasions. When the effort needed to care for the pigs becomes excessive, a huge pig feast is held, resulting in a sharp decline in the pig population. This feast, as will be shown in the next chapter, is also closely related to the cycle of reforestation in the Tsembaga's gardens and to the regulation of war and peace between the Tsembaga and their neighbors.

Thus the Tsembaga do not have quite as easy a time of it as the energy formula for plant production might seem to indicate. The more pigs they raise, the harder they must work. But if they raised more people instead of more pigs, they would have to work just as hard, and their health would suffer.

Irrigation Agriculture

The labor productivity associated with advanced forms of irrigation agriculture is higher than in any other preindustrial system. Among irrigation farmers the Chinese have excelled for thousands of years. A detailed study of the labor inputs and weight yield of agricultural

244

production in precommunist times was carried out by the anthropologists Fei Hsiao-t'ung and Chang Chih-i (1947) in the village of Luts'un, Yunnan Province. Considering only the energy costs and yields associated with rice production, the Luts'un energy formula looks like this:

$$\frac{E}{2,841,000,000} = \frac{m}{418} \times \frac{t}{847} \times \frac{r}{150} \times \frac{e}{53.5}$$

Rice constituted about 75 percent of Luts'un output; other crops such as soybeans, corn, manioc, and potatoes were planted along the margins of the rice paddies and were probably also associated with highly favorable energy advantages. The formula for all crops, therefore, might very well be as follows:

$$\frac{E}{3,788,000,000} = \frac{m}{418} \times \frac{t}{1129} \times \frac{r}{150} \times \frac{e}{53.5}$$

The total population of Luts'un was about 700 people. A liberal calorie ration of 2,500 calories per day per person would require an annual production of 638 million calories. For lack of data these estimates do not include energy costs associated with the care and feeding of draft animals and the construction and maintenance of the irrigation facilities, but I do not believe that the labor productivity factor would be substantially different if these costs were included. Draft animals reduce human labor inputs in agricultural tasks such as threshing, hauling, and milling. These savings probably cancel out the costs of

Figure 12-11. TERRACED IRRIGATION. Intensive irrigation agriculture of this type is not associated with the formation of the state. Compare Figure 12-2. (Harold C. Conklin)

feeding and caring for the animals. As for the irrigation facilities, these are typically built over many generations and require relatively little input per capita per year.

What happened to the more than 3 billion calories per year that were not eaten up by the people of Luts'un? Here I must point out that Luts'un was merely a tiny part of a vast state-level society. The population of China includes several hundred million people who live in cities and towns and do not participate at all in food production. In brief, the energy in question was diverted from the village to towns and cities; it was exchanged via markets and money into nonfarm goods and services; it was taxed away by the local, provincial, and central governments; it went into rent as payment for use of land; and it was used to raise large numbers of children and to sustain a high rate of population increase.

Pastoral Nomadism

The loss in caloric efficiency associated with the processing of plant food through domesticated animals accounts for the relatively infrequent occurrence of cultures whose mode of food production is that called *pastoral nomadism.* Full pastoral nomads are peoples who raise domesticated animals and who do not depend upon hunting, gathering, or the planting of their own crops for a significant portion of their diet. Pastoral nomads typically occupy arid grasslands and steppes in which precipitation is too sparse or irregular to support rainfall agriculture and which cannot be irrigated because they are too high or too far from major river valleys. Exploitation of these ecological zones by sedentary farmers through a system of mixed farming and stock-raising can be attempted only to a limited extent when the grasslands are not too distant. Deep penetrations of the pastoral zone by flocks tended by members of the farmer's household lowers farming efficiency by diverting labor into calorically inefficient tasks. By specializing in animal husbandry, the full pastoral nomads can move their herds about over long distances and take advantage of the best pasture without having to worry about the crops at home.

It has long been recognized, however, that pastoral peoples must obtain grain supplements to their diet of milk, cheese, blood, and meat (the last always being a relatively small part of the daily fare). The labor efficiency of herding alone is not adequate to support dense populations. Grains are usually obtained through trade with agricultural neighbors who are eager to obtain hides, cheese, milk, and other animal products that are in short supply wherever intensive

246

preindustrial agricultural systems support dense populations. Pastoralists frequently attempt to improve their "bargaining position" by raiding the sedentary villagers and carrying off the grain harvest without paying for it. They can often do this with impunity since their possession of animals such as camels and horses makes them highly mobile and militarily effective. Continued success in raiding may force the farming population to acknowledge the pastoralists as their overlords. Repeatedly in the history of the Old World, relatively small groups of pastoral nomads—the Mongols and the Arabs being the two most famous examples—have succeeded in gaining control over huge civilizations based on irrigation agriculture. The inevitable outcome of these conquests, however, was that the conquerors were absorbed by the agricultural system as they attempted to feed the huge populations that had fallen under their control (Lattimore 1962; Salzman 1971; Lees and Bates 1974).

247

Population Density and Agricultural Intensity

There is no simple correlation between technoenvironmental efficiency and population density. The chief reason for this is that as population density increases there is often a tendency for technoenvironmental efficiency to decline. This decline results from the application of the food-producing technology to less and less favorable portions or phases of the habitat in order to accommodate the need for larger total output. Thus every cultural food-energy system has room in it for the *intensification* of production.

Hunters and gatherers may increase the length of their per capita hunting time (t in the formula) and raise their total output and hence their population density simply by going out to hunt more often. But this will make the game scarce and harder to find. For example, by increasing t by a factor of 2, they may unavoidably reduce e by a reciprocal factor almost as large—say, $2/5$. In other words, the closer the system moves toward the carrying capacity of a particular habitat, the less efficient a given mode of food production will tend to become. In a system of rainfall agriculture, for example, sparse populations mean that land may be used *extensively*—that is, gardens and fields can be left fallow for long periods of time, and only the most fertile and accessible soils need be put into production. In fact it has been suggested that the difference between slash-and-burn gardening, rainfall farming, and irrigation farming is really only a matter of increasing intensification of the same basic technoenvironmental relationships under increasing population pressure (Boserup 1965; Netting 1969). As population increases, people cut down and burn the forests faster and faster until there are no more trees left. Then they cut down and plow under shrubs and bushes faster and faster until there are no more shrubs and bushes left. And as population increases still further, the farmers work harder and harder to bring nutrient-laden irrigation water to their plots, which get smaller and smaller and are cropped and double-cropped more and more often.

There is much to be learned from this viewpoint. For example, the relative low labor productivity of the Genieri villagers in relation to their relatively high population density, as shown in the following table, can be interpreted as a result of the intensification of what was formerly a slash-and-burn system.

As I have already mentioned, many of the savannah grasslands of Africa and other continents have been created by shortening the fallow periods in slash-and-burn cycles beyond the limits of forest regeneration. Thus the Genieri villagers practice a form of bush

248

	Population Density (persons per square mile)	Technoenvironmental Efficiency
!Kung	.5	10
Tsembaga	64.0	18
Genieri	88.0	11
Luts'un	500.0	53

fallowing with hoes and without benefit of plows or animal manure. And consequently their labor productivity is scarcely higher than that of the Bushmen.

However, this kind of overlap must not be permitted to obscure the fact that in the long run agricultural technology has been selected for greater labor productivity. The available data show that most slash-and-burn systems have greater labor productivity than most hunting and gathering systems. And most rainfall systems using animal traction and animal manure are more efficient than slash-and-burn systems. The data are particularly conclusive with respect to the difference between irrigation agriculture and all other preindustrial systems. Irrigated rice, for example, is one-and-a-half to three times more productive per unit of labor expended than unirrigated rice even when land is scarce and the system involves intensive transplanting operations (Bronson 1972: Tables 8.1, 8.2, 8.3; Hanks 1972: Tables 4.2, 4.5).

But each of these technologies may be intensified—that is, applied with greater labor input per year per acre—and this intensification

Figure 12-13. PHILIPPINE SWIDDENS. Partly consumed felled timber remains to be burned in three swiddens set in advanced secondary forest. (Harold C. Conklin)

may lead to diminished return and ultimately to the permanent depletion or destruction of resources necessary for the maintenance of the system. When the latter occurs, the environment is said to have been *degraded.* Thus the evolution of food-producing technologies cannot be described simply as a matter of ever-increasing intensification of labor input nor as a matter of ever-increasing labor productivity. There are advances and declines in labor productivity, and both are related to increasing population density. Faced with high densities and environmental degradation, some food-producing systems develop new technologies and move on to higher levels of productivity; others remain locked into a degraded environment with consequent severe cutbacks in the people's standards of living. But even those that move on to more productive alternatives eventually seem to find themselves confronted with the threat of environmental degradation and declining productivity as population density once again approaches carrying capacity (see Fig. 12-1, p. 230).

Efficiency in Agro-Industrial Food-Energy Systems

It is difficult to estimate the labor efficiency of industrial agriculture because the amount of indirect labor put into food production exceeds the amount of direct labor. An Iowa corn farmer puts in 9 hours of work per acre, which yield 81 bushels of corn with an energy equivalent of 8,164,800 calories. This gives a nominal productivity factor of 6,000 calories for every calorie of input! But this is a very misleading figure. First of all, three-quarters of all the crop lands in the United States are devoted to the production of animal feeds with a consequent 90 percent reduction in caloric output. The livestock population of the United States consumes enough food calories to feed 1.3 billion people (Cloud 1973). Second, enormous amounts of human labor are embodied in the tractors, trucks, combines, oil and gas, pesticides, herbicides, and fertilizers used by the Iowa corn farmer. Fifteen tons of machinery, 22 gallons of gasoline, 203 pounds of fertilizer, and 2 pounds of chemical insecticides and pesticides are invested per acre per year. This represents a cost of 2,890,000 calories of nonfood energy per acre per year (Pimental, Hurd, and others 1973). It is not known how much human labor input is expended in the process of making this amount of machinery, fuels, and chemicals available to the farmer.

Perhaps a comparison of the labor efficiency in preindustrial and postindustrial systems can be gained by asking the question: How

250

Figure 12-14. INDUSTRIAL AGRIBUSINESS WORKERS, NORTH DAKOTA. (United Nations)

many hours do people have to work in order to obtain their calorie ration for one year? In 1970 the average blue collar worker in the United States earned $3.42 an hour, and the average per capita food bill was about $600. Therefore United States workers had to work about 180 hours per year to obtain their annual food supply. Luts'un farmers "earned" on the average 7,500 calories per hour ($150 \times 50 = 7500$). If they consumed 2,500 calories per day, they would earn their annual food ration in only 122 hours. Of course industrial workers consume more animal fat and protein and about 500 more calories per day. Nonetheless it cannot be said that industrial workers work less than preindustrial farmers in order to obtain their food supply.

Another deceptive aspect of industrial food production is the apparent reduction in the percentage of farm workers in the work force. Thus it is said that less than 3 percent of the United States labor force is employed in agriculture and that one farmer can now feed fifty people. But there is another way to view this ratio. If farmers are dependent on the labor input of workers who manufacture, mine, and transport fuels, chemicals, and machines employed in food production, then these workers must also be considered food-producers. In other words, industrial agriculture does not so much reduce the agricultural work force as disperse it away from the farm. The individuals who remain on the land to operate the high-powered agro-industrial machinery resemble (etically speaking) workers in an automobile factory more than they do peasant farmers. Farmers in the United States consume more than 12 percent of the total industrial energy flow. For each person who actually works on the farm, at

251

Figure 12-15. THE FIRST ASSEMBLY LINE. Ford's Highland Park, Michigan, magneto assembly line, saved 15 minutes per unit and initiated the era of mass production in 1913. But the workers worked harder than ever. (Wide World Photos)

least two farm-support workers are needed off the farm. In a broader sense almost all industrial and service workers make some contribution to the support of agro-industrial production. "Yesterday's farmer is today's canner, tractor mechanic, and fast food carhop" (Steinhart and Steinhart 1974). Like everyone else, farmers now get their own food at the supermarket check-out counter. If all this be granted, then it is more accurate to say that it takes fifty people to feed one agro-industrial worker than to say that one modern farmer feeds fifty people.

Potentially a sizeable increment in food-energy productivity could be achieved by applying modern technology to the task of maximizing the return per human calorie input. But thus far industrial technology has been applied primarily toward increasing total output per acre and toward decreasing the portion of farm labor that is expended on the farm. The flow of energy in the average industrial system has increased by several orders of magnitude. But the efficiency of the system, in human energy terms, may have scarcely advanced at all.

The Myth of Increased Leisure

The data presented so far lend no support to the widespread belief that "civilization" is associated with a general increment in "leisure

252

time." On the contrary, except for a very small percentage of the very rich and the very poor, higher productivity is associated with increasing amounts of subsistence work time per individual. Indeed the main trends in cultural evolution can only be understood in relation to the fact that food-producing systems are selected as much for their potential to increase the time per worker devoted to food production as for their higher labor productivity. In hunting and gathering systems, lengthening t, as previously discussed, leads quickly to overkill. In slash-and-burn systems, it leads to both overkill and deforestation. In contrast, canal irrigation systems that tap major rivers like the Nile, Mekong, Indus, and Yellow have enormous potentials for absorbing more and more labor without degrading the environment since the critical limiting condition for such systems is the amount of nutrient-bearing water that can be sluiced onto the fields.

Similar principles apply to the intensification of work input under industrial conditions, although the explanation for why people do it is far more complicated. Let me note simply that with a forty-hour week and a three-week vacation, the typical factory worker puts in close to 2,000 hours per year under conditions that any sane Bushman would have to regard as "inhuman."

Figure 12-16. LABOR SAVING DEVICES THAT DON'T SAVE WORK. All work and no play in a Russian television factory. (UPI Photo)

Admittedly this statement should not be taken too literally. As previously indicated, additional inputs of considerable magnitude pertaining to food-processing have been disregarded for want of comparative data. And I do not want to give the impression that time devoted to the food-energy system necessarily adds up to the total amount of work that an individual performs. Obviously preindustrial peoples are not merely idle when they are not sleeping or processing or producing food. In every culture much time and energy are devoted to additional tasks and activities, some of which are essential to the survival of the population. Unfortunately anthropologists have seldom collected the appropriate data, and hence it is very difficult to generalize about how time is allocated to various tasks and activities in different cultures. I do not believe, however, that a broader definition of "work" would give the middle-class industrial wage earner or office worker an advantage over hunters and gatherers or other prestate peoples as far as leisure is concerned.

One of the few attempts to quantify daily activity patterns for a whole population has been carried out by Allen Johnson (1974) among the Machiguenga, a slash-and-burn village people who live on the Upper Urubamba River on the eastern slopes of the Andes in Peru. Johnson randomly sampled what the members of thirteen households were doing between the hours of 6 A.M. and 7 P.M. throughout an entire year. His results, given in the table below show that food production plus food preparation plus the manufacture of essential items such as clothing, tools, and shelter consume only 6.0 hours per day for married adult males and 6.3 hours per day for married adult females.

TIME DEVOTED TO VARIOUS ACTIVITIES PER DAY BY MACHIGUENGA MARRIED MEN AND WOMEN

	Married Men	Married Women
Food Production	4.4 hours	1.8 hours
Food Preparation	0.2	2.4
Manufacture	1.4	2.1
Child Care	.0	1.1
Hygiene	.3	.6
Visiting	1.0	.8
Idle	2.3	2.5
	9.6	11.3

SOURCE: Johnson 1974

It seems clear that when labor leaders boast about how much progress has been made in obtaining leisure for the working class, they have in mind the standard established in "civilized" nineteenth-century Europe when factory workers put in 12 hours a day or more in basic subsistence instead of the standard of 6 hours or less established by hunters and gatherers, and other prestate peoples. This leads to the question of why the great labor-saving potential of technology has been devoted to the ever-greater expansion of energy systems rather than to the achievement of an ever-greater amount of leisure based on a constant population and a constant level of production and consumption. And that is the subject of the next chapter.

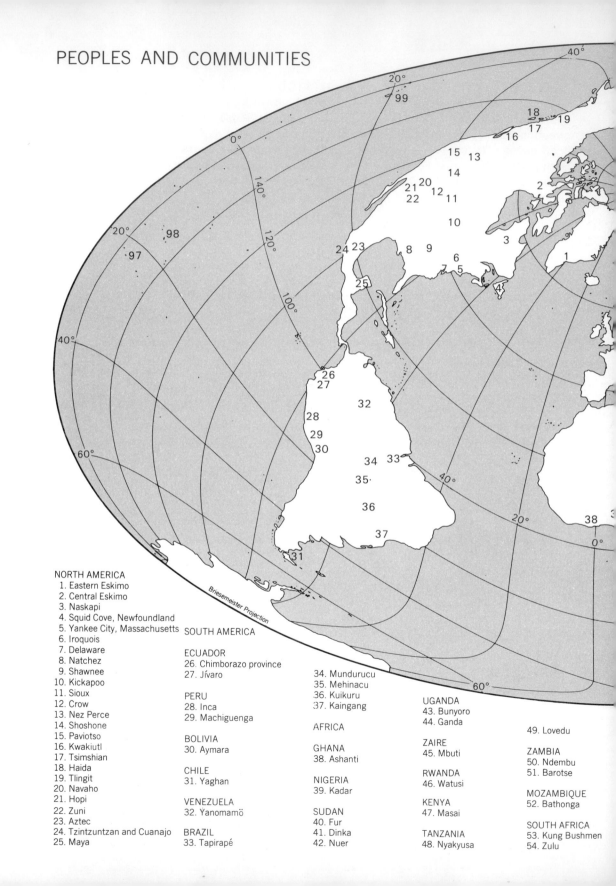

PEOPLES AND COMMUNITIES

Briesemeister Projection

NORTH AMERICA
1. Eastern Eskimo
2. Central Eskimo
3. Naskapi
4. Squid Cove, Newfoundland
5. Yankee City, Massachusetts
6. Iroquois
7. Delaware
8. Natchez
9. Shawnee
10. Kickapoo
11. Sioux
12. Crow
13. Nez Perce
14. Shoshone
15. Paviotso
16. Kwakiutl
17. Tsimshian
18. Haida
19. Tlingit
20. Navaho
21. Hopi
22. Zuni
23. Aztec
24. Tzintzuntzan and Cuanajo
25. Maya

SOUTH AMERICA

ECUADOR
26. Chimborazo province
27. Jívaro

PERU
28. Inca
29. Machiguenga

BOLIVIA
30. Aymara

CHILE
31. Yaghan

VENEZUELA
32. Yanomamö

BRAZIL
33. Tapirapé

34. Mundurucu
35. Mehinacu
36. Kuikuru
37. Kaingang

AFRICA

GHANA
38. Ashanti

NIGERIA
39. Kadar

SUDAN
40. Fur
41. Dinka
42. Nuer

UGANDA
43. Bunyoro
44. Ganda

ZAIRE
45. Mbuti

RWANDA
46. Watusi

KENYA
47. Masai

TANZANIA
48. Nyakyusa

49. Lovedu

ZAMBIA
50. Ndembu
51. Barotse

MOZAMBIQUE
52. Bathonga

SOUTH AFRICA
53. Kung Bushmen
54. Zulu

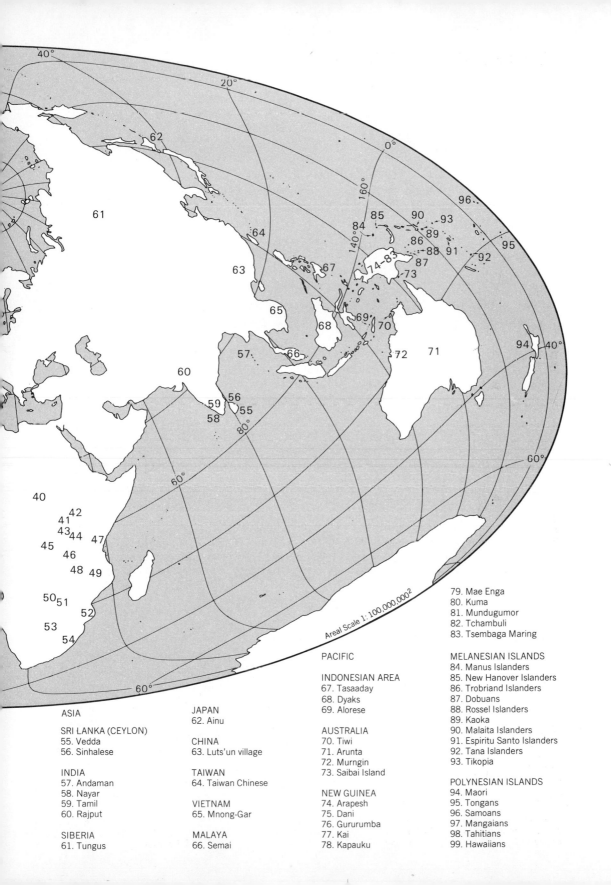

Areal Scale 1:100,000,000²

79. Mae Enga
80. Kuma
81. Mundugumor
82. Tchambuli
83. Tsembaga Maring

PACIFIC

INDONESIAN AREA
67. Tasaaday
68. Dyaks
69. Alorese

AUSTRALIA
70. Tiwi
71. Arunta
72. Murngin
73. Saibai Island

NEW GUINEA
74. Arapesh
75. Dani
76. Gururumba
77. Kai
78. Kapauku

MELANESIAN ISLANDS
84. Manus Islanders
85. New Hanover Islanders
86. Trobriand Islanders
87. Dobuans
88. Rossel Islanders
89. Kaoka
90. Malaita Islanders
91. Espiritu Santo Islanders
92. Tana Islanders
93. Tikopia

POLYNESIAN ISLANDS
94. Maori
95. Tongans
96. Samoans
97. Mangaians
98. Tahitians
99. Hawaiians

ASIA

SRI LANKA (CEYLON)
55. Vedda
56. Sinhalese

INDIA
57. Andaman
58. Nayar
59. Tamil
60. Rajput

SIBERIA
61. Tungus

JAPAN
62. Ainu

CHINA
63. Luts'un village

TAIWAN
64. Taiwan Chinese

VIETNAM
65. Mnong-Gar

MALAYA
66. Semai

POPULATION, WAR,
AND SEXISM

The Wapituil are like us to an extraordinary degree. They have a kinship system which is very similar to our kinship system. They address each other as "Mister," "Mistress," and "Miss." They wear clothes which look very much like our clothes. They have a Fifth Avenue which divides their territory into east and west. They have a Chock Full o'Nuts and a Chevrolet, one of each. They have a Museum of Modern Art and a telephone and a Martini, one of each. The Martini and the telephone are kept in the Museum of Modern Art. In fact they have everything that we have, but only one of each thing.

We found that they lose interest very quickly. For instance they are fully industrialized, but they don't seem interested in taking advantage of it. After the steel mill produced the ingot, it was shut down. They can conceptualize but they don't follow through. For instance, their week has seven days—Monday, Monday, Monday, Monday, Monday, Monday, and Monday. They have one disease, Mononucleosis. The sex life of a Wapituil consists of a single experience, which he thinks about for a long time.

Donald Barthelme: *City Life*, p. 140

The question posed at the end of the last chapter would never have occurred to Thomas Malthus, founder of modern population studies. Malthus assumed that populations would always tend to get bigger because there was no way to stop people from having children. Any small population would naturally tend to grow at a geometric rate—2, 4, 8, 16, and so on—and it would keep right on growing until it ran out of food at which point people would die from wars, famines, plagues, and other lamentable but necessary consequences of their carnal impulses. Malthus did not allow for the possibility that population would stop growing because people might decide to limit their fertility

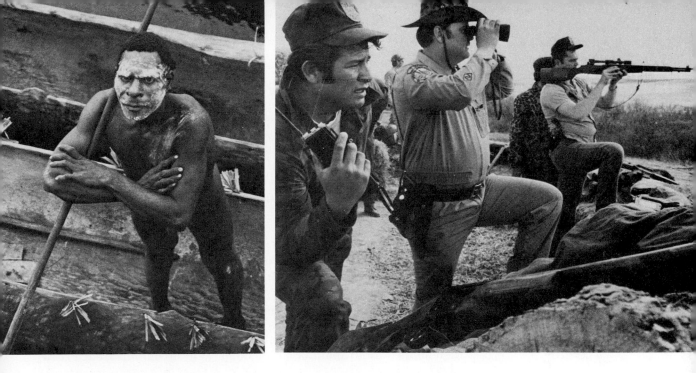

Figure 13-1. WARRIORS. Asmat, New Guinea man (left) prepares for war and U.S. marshalls (right) keep watch. (Eugene Gordon—left; UPI Photo—right)

by means of contraception, abortion, or infanticide. These were "unnatural" things to do and hence had no role to play in Malthus's attempt to understand nature.

To the anthropologist the reason why populations tend to grow is not so obvious. It is obviously *not* natural for populations always to keep on growing because for tens of thousands of years during the Paleolithic densities remained below one person per square mile (p. 202). Moreover, like the Bushmen and the Tsembaga, most preindustrial peoples have populations that appear to be stabilized at levels considerably below what would be possible under a regimen of maximum intensification. Even preindustrial peoples are perfectly capable of significant degrees of control over their demographic situation without leading sex lives like those of the imaginary Wapituil. Humanity has never been completely at the mercy of the propensity to "delve and spawn." Nonetheless the restriction of preindustrial population growth involved penalties and costs that deeply influenced the quality of life (cf. Hayden 1972).

War and Power

In evolutionary perspective there is one obvious reason why technology has been used to expand population and build ever larger energy systems. Natural selection favors greater population density among societies that persistently try to annihilate each other (Otterbein

259

1970) Where food is the primary source of energy, and spears, clubs, and bows and arrows constitute the chief engines of destruction, the more food, the more warriors and the greater the chances of surviving attacks and killing enemies. Where warfare is based on muscle power, the groups that raise more muscles by increasing food production whenever they can will inevitably destroy, disperse, or absorb groups that fail to increase production and food supply. After the invention of gunpowder and industrial weaponry, muscle power declined in importance, but control over other sources of energy became more important. It remains true to this day that as a result of warfare, powerful, high-energy societies tend to replace weak, low-energy societies. This is a sad but unassailable fact of which every anthropologist familiar with the history of contact between Europe and the aboriginal peoples of Africa, Oceania, and the New World is painfully aware. Hence, where there is war, territorial groups tend to maximize their strength by getting as close as possible to their habitat's carrying capacity. But why do people like the Tsembaga Maring and their neighbors want to annihilate each other? Why do human groups go to war?

Warfare among Hunters and Gatherers

War is defined as armed combat between groups of people who constitute separate territorial teams or political communities (cf. Otterbein 1972). Most hunting and food-gathering peoples are organized into small, open groups called "bands." Such bands frequently lack sharp territorial boundaries, and their membership changes from season to season, and even day to day, as kin arrive, depart, and visit each other over a wide geographical area. This "openness" of the hunting and food-gathering band is made possible by pervasive networks of marriage alliances. Hence the identification of individuals with territories is often blurred (see p. 341). When armed conflict occurs and people take sides, it is often impossible to determine whether or not territorial teams are involved. This makes it difficult to evaluate the claim that hunting and gathering cultures such as the Andaman Islanders, the Shoshoni, the Yahgan, the Mission Indians of California, and the Tasaday of the Philippines lack warfare (Lesser 1968; Macleish 1972). If warfare is absent among some hunters and gatherers, by far the greater number of such peoples do practice group forms of armed combat that fall close to or well within the definition of war. William Divale (1972) lists thirty-seven hunting and gathering cultures in which warfare is known to have been practiced.

Attempts to assess the frequency of warfare among hunters and

260

gatherers during the Paleolithic on the basis of archaeological evidence have led to inconclusive results. Mutilated skulls found in Paleolithic caves have sometimes been interpreted as indicating prehistoric head-hunting and cannibalism. Such evidence is equivocal because it is not known how the individuals died; nor is it necessarily true, even if cannibalism was practiced, that the individuals were enemies. Processing and eating of the skulls and brains of deceased kin as part of ritual mortuary practices is an ethnographically well-known custom. The earliest strong archaeological evidence for warfare is found in Neolithic Jericho in the form of defensive walls, towers, and ditches. It is generally agreed that warfare rapidly increased in scope and frequency after the development of states and cities in both the Old and New Worlds (Roper 1969, 1973; Bigelow 1975).

It seems likely on both ethnological and theoretical grounds that some form of warfare preceded the Neolithic. However, after the development of permanent villages with large capital investments in crops, animals, and stored foods, the form of warfare changed. Among nonsedentary hunters and gatherers warfare involved a higher degree of individualized combat directed toward the adjustment of real or imagined personal injuries and deprivations. Although the combat teams may have had a temporary territorial base, the organization of battle and the consequences of victory or defeat reflected the loose association between people and territory. It is doubtful that the victors gained territory by routing their enemies, since neighboring hunting and gathering groups normally have free or relatively unrestricted access to each other's resources. Warfare among village-dwelling cultivators, however, frequently involves a total team effort in which definite territories are fought over and in which defeat may result in the rout of a whole community from its fields and dwellings.

The slippery line between warfare and personal retribution among hunters and gatherers is well illustrated in the example of armed conflict among the Tiwi of Bathurst and Melville Islands, Northern Australia. As recounted by C. W. Hart and Arnold Pilling (1960), a number of men from the Tiklauila and Rangwila bands developed personal grievances against a number of men who were residing with the Mandiimbula band. The aggrieved individuals, together with their relatives, put on the white paint of war, armed themselves, and set off, some thirty strong, to do battle with the Mandiimbula.

On arrival at the place where the latter, duly warned of its approach, had gathered, the war party announced its presence. Both sides then exchanged a few insults and agreed to meet formally in an open space where there was plenty of room.   [1960:84]

Warfare among Hunters and Gatherers

During the night, individuals from both groups visited each other, renewing acquaintances. In the morning the two armies lined up at opposite sides of the battlefield. Hostilities were begun by elders shouting insults and accusations at particular individuals in the "enemy" ranks. Although some of the old men urged that a general attack be launched, their grievances turned out to be directed not at the Mandiimbula band, but at one or at most two or three individuals.

Hence when spears began to be thrown, they were thrown by individuals for reasons based on individual disputes.   [ibid.]

Marksmanship was poor because it was the old men who did most of the spear-throwing.

Not infrequently the person hit was some innocent noncombatant or one of the screaming old women who weaved through the fighting men, yelling obscenities at everybody, and whose reflexes for dodging spears were not as fast as those of the men. . . .
    As soon as somebody was wounded, even a seemingly irrelevant crone, fighting stopped immediately until the implications of this new incident could be assessed by both sides.   [ibid.]

The ethnographic evidence is equivocal concerning what portion of the overall death rate among hunters and gatherers is due to combat deaths in warfare. Although hunters and gatherers seldom try to annihilate each other and often retire from the field after one or two casualties have occurred, the cumulative effect may be quite considerable. Remember that the average Bushman band has only about thirty people in it. If such a band engages in war only twice per generation and each time with the loss of only one adult male, casualties due to warfare would account for more than 10 percent of all adult male deaths. This is an extremely high figure when one realizes that less than 1 percent of all male deaths in Europe and the United States during the twentieth century have been battlefield casualties. In contrast, Lloyd Warner estimated that 28 percent of the adult male deaths among the Murngin, a hunting and gathering culture of Northern Australia, were due to battlefield casualties (Livingstone 1968).

Among hunters and gatherers the importance of male deaths due to combat is shown by a statistical comparison of the ratio of males per 100 females in junior age categories compared with the same ratio in senior age categories among hunters and gatherers who were censused before the colonial authorities extinguished the practice of warfare. This ratio was 128:100 for juniors and 101:100 for seniors. Although some of this discrepancy may have been due to casualties in hunting, a fair conclusion is that the much higher death rate among men as compared with women was largely due to combat casualties.

262

(I shall soon discuss the significance of the huge disproportion in the junior age sex ratio.) There seems to be little basis for the view to which I myself subscribed in the previous edition of this book, that war is essentially a post-Neolithic phenomenon (Divale and Harris 1975).

Warfare among Village Agriculturalists

Although village peoples were not the first to practice warfare, they did expand the scale and ferocity of military engagements. Village houses, food-processing equipment, crops in the field, domestic animals, secondary-growth forests, and prime garden lands represent capital investments closely identified with the arduous labor inputs by specific groups of individuals. The defense of this investment laid the basis for the development of stable, exclusive territorial identities. Villages often oppose each other as traditional enemies, repeatedly attack and plunder each other, and often expropriate each other's territories. Archaeologically the onset of territoriality is suggested by the practice of burying deceased villagers beneath the houses that they occupied during life (cf. Flannery 1972). Ethnologically the intensification of local identities is found in the development of systems of reckoning kinship based upon descent through a single line of fathers and sons or uncles and nephews (see Ch. 16). The development of the concern with descent and inheritance, as Michael Harner (1970) has shown, is closely related to the degree to which agricultural populations cease to depend on hunting and gathering for their food supply (see p. 341).

Warfare among village cultivators is likely to be more costly in terms of battle casualties than among seminomadic hunters and gatherers. One of the reasons for this is the greater vulnerability of people who live in permanent settlements to surprise attacks and ambushes. Unfortunately there is a dearth of reliable comparative data. Among the Dani of West Irian, New Guinea, warfare has an open-field, ritualistic phase (which resembles the encounters described for the Tiwi) in which casualties are light. But there are also sneak attacks resulting in a hundred fatalities at a time and in the destruction and expulsion of whole villages. Karl G. Heider (1972) estimates that the Dani lost about .5 percent of their population per year to warfare, and that 29 percent of the men and 3 percent of the women died as a result of battle injuries incurred primarily in raids and ambushes. Among the Yanomamö of Brazil and Venezuela, who are reputed to have one of the world's "fiercest" and most warlike cultures, sneak raids and ambushes account for about 33 percent of

Figure 13-2. "THE FIERCE PEOPLE." Yanomamö warriors ready for a raid. (Napoleon Chagnon)

adult male deaths from all causes and about 7 percent of adult female deaths from all causes (Chagnon 1968). Like hunters and gatherers, the sex ratios of warring village cultivators are markedly skewed in the junior age categories in favor of males, whereas their senior age categories approach a more even balance. Among the Tsembaga Maring, for example, in the group 0–15 years of age there are 46 boys and 31 girls, a ratio of 146:100. In the age group 25 and older there are 40 men and 42 women, a ratio of 95:100. "This change in the Tsembaga male-female ratio at estimated age twenty-five is quite clearly an effect of differences in casualty rates" (Rappaport 1968:16).

Warfare and the Regulation of Population Density

Given the prevalence and deadly seriousness of warfare in preindustrial societies, the relationship between warfare and population density must now be considered. Under certain conditions (to be clarified later on), warfare exerts a stabilizing influence on population and helps to prevent the overexploitation of critical resources. It may seem obvious that since people kill each other in warfare, that warfare restrains population growth. But the matter is not so simple. In fact it is easier to show that war-makers like the Yanomamö and Tsembaga Maring cannot control the growth of their population by killing each other at the rates reported above. The problem is that the people who

264

are killed in battle are mostly males. Deaths due to warfare among the Yanomamö, for example, have no long-run effect on the size of the Yanomamö population because, like almost all war-making preindustrial societies, the Yanomamö are polygynous (i.e., each man has several wives, see p. 312). This means that any woman whose husband is killed is immediately remarried to another man. As few as twenty men can maintain high annual rates of pregnancy among one hundred or more women. The reported death rates from female battle casualties is almost everywhere insignificant—below 10 percent (cf. Polgar 1972:206). As discussed in Chapter 10, any reasonably healthy human population living well below its carrying capacity and not practicing fertility control can easily double its number every twenty-five years. The rate of female battle casualties indicated by ethnographic studies of preindustrial war might alter the doubling period, but it would scarcely produce a no-growth population. Similar conclusions about the ineffectuality of combat deaths as a population control device have been reached with respect to warfare in industrial contexts. Catastrophes like World War II "have no effect on the population growth or size" (Livingstone 1968:5). This can be seen vividly in the case of Vietnam, where population continued to increase at a phenomenal 3 percent per year during the decade 1960–1970.

A clue that may relate warfare to population control is that there is a strong correlation between the presence of warfare and the unbalanced junior age sex ratios mentioned above. These ratios change in the direction of a more even balance in proportion to the amount of time during which groups have been forced to stop engaging in warfare as the result of the interposition of colonial governments.

	Young males per 100 females
Warfare Present	128
Stopped 5–25 years before census	113
Stopped over 25 years before census	109

SOURCE: Divale and Harris 1975

These data show that with the suppression of warfare, proportionately more females are reared to reproductive age. What mode of population control can produce such an effect?

Warfare and the Regulation of Population Density

Technology of Preindustrial
Population Control

Preindustrial, low-energy societies possessed few techniques for controlling population growth. One technique, universally available, is the limitation of heterosexual contact through taboos and other ideological prescriptions. Many cultures, for example, taboo sexual intercourse with a woman while she is nursing a child. Other common taboos prohibit sexual intercourse with women who are not married or with women who are menstruating. The rate of heterosexual intercourse can also be influenced by encouraging abstinence as a virtuous or holy state and by tolerating or encouraging coitus interruptus, masturbation, and homosexual relations rather than full heterosexual relations. None of these measures occurs widely or regularly enough to account for the huge discrepancy between observed population densities and the densities that healthy hunters and gatherers and village cultivators are potentially capable of achieving within a few generations (cf. Polgar 1972; Kolata 1974; Frisch and Williams 1974).

Preindustrial peoples in general lack effective chemical or mechanical means of preventing conception. They do, however, possess a large repertory of chemical and mechanical means for inducing abortion. Numerous plant and animal poisons that produce generalized physical traumas or that act directly on the uterus are employed throughout the world to terminate unwanted pregnancies. Many mechanical techniques for inducing abortions are also employed in virtually every known culture. These include tying tight bands around the pregnant woman's abdomen, or punching her abdomen, or jumping on it. These techniques are effective but they are almost as dangerous to the pregnant woman as to the fetus (Devereux 1967; Nurge 1975). Undoubtedly abortion contributes significantly to the control of population density among hunters and gatherers and village cultivators. But it cannot produce a distortion in the junior age sex ratio, since it affects male and female fetuses indifferently. The only population control technique that can account both for the overall low density and a male to female junior sex ratio of 146:100 is some form of female infanticide.

Infanticide not only involves direct killing by blows to the head, suffocation, strangulation, or exposure to the elements, as reported for the Yanomamö and many other cultures; it also includes various forms of neglect and indifference ranging from the malign to benign in intent and to more or less rapid death in practice. Hundreds of variables affecting an infant's security, comfort, diet, and health are

266

substantially under the control of an infant's mother and family and determine its ability to survive. These range from how often a mother feeds a child to how quickly its cries of distress get attention, to the degree of care exerted in preventing it from falling out of a hammock, or from getting stepped on or dropped or kicked or rolled over on during sleep.

Female infanticide thus denotes the sum total of homicide and acts of malign and benign aggression and neglect that consciously or unconsciously favor the survival of male children over female children. Information regarding all forms of infanticide is difficult to acquire since many cultures try to hide or disguise their treatment of unwanted children, especially if inquiries are made by authorities whose cultures treat infanticide as a crime. Despite these difficulties it is significant that where infanticide of any sort is reported as common, the junior age sex ratio of males to females is 133:100 as compared with 104:100 where it is rare (Divale and Harris 1975). Clearly, in many of the cultures for which no infanticide at all is reported, some form of female infanticide is practiced. The Tsembaga, for example, deny that they practice any kind of infanticide but this does not prevent them from having a junior age sex ratio of 148:100.

In order to achieve the net reproduction rate necessary to maintain a stable population as many as 50 percent of the females born per generation under a regimen of modest fertility and health must be prevented from reproducing. This estimate follows from the assumption that each woman has four children who can live to reproductive age, two of whom are females. In order for the population to remain stable, however, each woman must rear only one female to reproductive age (cf. Birdsell 1968; Polgar 1972:206; Coale 1974).

Warfare and Male Dominance

How does warfare result in the killing and neglect of female babies and the rearing and preferential treatment of male babies? Warfare achieves this result in the preindustrial era by conferring survival advantage on groups that maximize the numbers of males who can be put into combat (see p. 260). Thus war may be responsible for creating or intensifying the widespread cultural devaluation of women. Certainly this devaluation cannot be regarded as "natural." A very powerful cultural force is needed to convince parents that male infants are more valuable than female infants, especially in the context of post-Neolithic agricultural villages where women do most of the gardening. To the women, little girls represent help in the

267

garden, whereas to the men they represent producers of food, children, and sexual satisfaction. In an energy-cost sense, women are almost universally a better energy bargain than men. In cultures that practice intensive warfare, however, the number of males available may become the most critical factor determining the survivability of the entire population. Male children become critically valuable in the

Figure 13-3. CAN THE GAP BE CLOSED? Comparison of Male and Female Olympic Records.

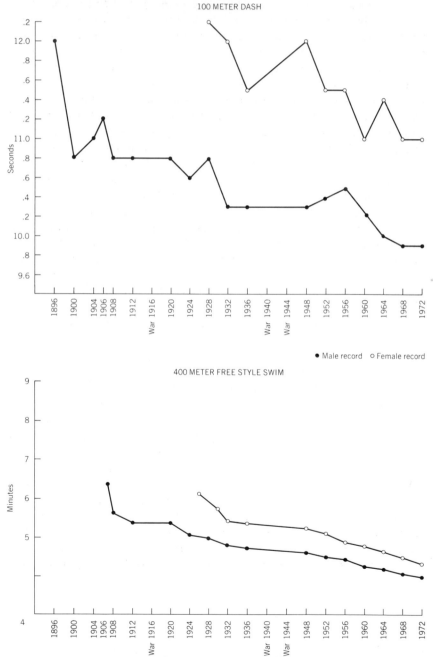

context of intensive war because men have heavier musculature, longer arms, greater weight, and sprint-adapted pelves.

It is well known that in Olympic competitions males hold a considerable edge over females in sports such as javelin-throwing, running, and weight-lifting—sports that are most closely related to the kinds of performances relevant to success in warfare involving hand-to-hand combat and muscle-powered missiles. This comparison is not intended to prove that the differences involved are completely biologically determined and unchangeable. Perhaps with earlier training and greater emphasis on competition with male athletes, women may eventually narrow or entirely eliminate the present gap. As Figure 13-3 shows, in some sports, such as swimming, this has already taken place to an extent previously regarded as biologically impossible. When Shane Gould set a new world's record of 4 minutes, 19.04 seconds, in the 1972 400-meter freestyle swimming event for women, she bettered John ("Tarzan") Weismuller's 1924 Olympic championship time by over 45 seconds. Similarly Lia Manoliu's javelin throw of 191 feet, $2\frac{1}{2}$ inches, in the 1968 women's competition would have won her a medal had she been competing against the male javelin-throwers in the 1906 and 1908 Olympic games. Although there is obviously an important genetic component in the dimorphism of males and females, there is no reason to suppose that women in the future will not also increase their average height and weight relative to men. It seems plausible to infer that the present degree of sexual dimorphism is a result of selection against tall, heavily muscled women in the past. As a result of this selection, male infants up till now have been more valuable in a military-cost sense.

In virtually all preindustrial societies only males are taught how to become proficient in the use of clubs, bows and arrows, spears, and other weapons of war. Women are generally not permitted to participate in war as front-line combatants because (1) the occasional military success of large and powerful females against smaller males would subvert the sex hierarchy and loosen the restraints on population growth; and (2) in order to rear fierce and aggressive warriors, males are rewarded with sexual privileges that depend on women being passive and submissive. Therefore females are prohibited from acquiring a knowledge of weaponry and martial skills.

War-linked, male-centered institutions, prerogatives, and ideologies seem to be present in the great majority of ethnographically known cultures. Thus the males in many cultures believe that they are spiritually superior to females and that females are dangerous and polluting, weak and untrustworthy. Males repeatedly denigrate women's work and confer prestige on their own—the relative prestige

269

Figure 13-4. AGGRESSIVE MALE GAMES. There is evidence of a close correlation between warfare and aggressive male sports. Afghan game (above) requires daring feats of horsemanship. Mock combat in Indonesia (above right). Brazilian boys (below) play soccer, the Brazilian national sport. On the facing page, the gentle art of football, U.S.A. (left) and the sporting life in England—rugby (right). (Eugene Gordon—above left and right; UPI Photo—below and facing, right; George Gardner—facing left)

of hunting versus collecting being the prime example. As George Morren (1973) has shown, women may contribute significant amounts of protein through the hunting of small animals, yet their role as hunters seldom receives recognition. Extreme skepticism is warranted concerning the extent to which women consciously or unconsciously share these values. In many cases it is now becoming clear that they do not (cf. Kaberry 1970; Sacks 1971; Leacock 1975; Menge-Kalman 1974). Nonetheless reversals of these values in favor of women seem rarely to exist in any pronounced form even among women. In many cultures both males and females do glorify male sexual appetites and aggressive masculine displays. And there are many etic behavioral manifestations of the complex of male supremacy. Marriages in which males marry several wives—polygyny—occur a hundred times more frequently than marriages in which women marry several husbands (see Ch. 15). By requiring men to be trained to be fearless and aggressive, war sustains an almost universal interest in male-centered dangerous and competitive sports and games such as wrestling, foot-racing, dueling, and various forms of mock fighting, many of which are direct preludes to actual combat (Sipes 1973, 1975). The masculine male-war complex leads further to the control over gardens and property by male members of domestic groupings, to

271

Warfare and Male Dominance

the prevalence of ideologies in which descent through males is more important than descent through females, to the prevalence of patriarchy, and to the virtual absence of matriarchy (see Ch. 16). It should be remembered, however, that males have a price to pay for all this: they constitute the bulk of the victims of warfare in preindustrial societies.

It has been suggested that this male supremacy complex contributes to the maintenance of attitudes and practices that lead to selective infanticide and benign and malign neglect directed by parents against their daughters rather than against their sons. This leads to the raising of sons who find themselves in a world where there is an actual shortage of women, and this shortage is intensified by the culturally induced standards of masculine sexuality and by the practice of polygyny. Thus it is not mysterious that peoples like the Yanomamö, Dani, and Maring attribute their wars to disputes over women. But such explanations cannot be accepted at face value, for there would be no shortage of women if half of them were not killed off as infants. On the other hand, if preindustrial peoples did not limit their population, they would probably soon find themselves without food as well as without women. Warfare, in other words, may be the price the Yanomamö, Dani, and Maring and many other preindustrial groups pay for persisting in raising sons when they cannot raise an equal number of daughters. But persist they must, because once the war complex gets started, groups that rear equal numbers of male and female children will tend to be driven from their lands and destroyed (Divale and Harris 1975).

Distribution of Population with Respect to Resources: The Maring

Local groups frequently share overlapping portions of a habitat containing resources essential to human welfare. Such groups will seldom achieve precisely the same population density. Some will press close to carrying capacity, whereas others remain far below it. A more even spread of population with respect to resources permits a larger number of people to occupy the habitat and at the same time protects critical resources from becoming permanently depleted in areas of high density. Warfare frequently fulfills this function: it often distributes people over a habitat in a manner that prevents the degradation of ecosystems in which several local groups participate (cf. Vayda 1970; Graham 1975). Roy Rappaport's classic study (1968) of the role of warfare in the ecology of the Tsembaga Maring and their neighbors sheds light on how this effect is achieved.

272

Maring clans believe that they need the support of their ancestors in order to win wars. But the ancestors will only lend support if they are thanked with offerings of pigs. Such offerings are made at a series of feasts when most of the clan's pigs are slaughtered and eaten in a few months' time. Allies are invited to these feasts to help thank the ancestors and to enjoy the delicious meat and fat. With the ancestors properly thanked and allies pledged to render assistance, hostilities begin. The fighting is usually directed against traditional enemy clans who have previously shed each other's blood or expropriated portions of each other's territory. Fighting escalates through several phases, beginning with regulated encounters like those described for the Tiwi (p. 261). But if one side begins to feel that it has a decisive advantage over the other, it may launch a sneak attack directly at the enemy's village—burning the houses; killing as many men, women, children, and pigs as possible; and routing any survivors out of their home territory. When such a rout occurs, the survivors seek refuge in the villages of their allies. But the victorious clan does not immediately occupy the central portion of the vacated territory. Its members say they fear the ghosts of slain enemies who remain near the scene of destruction. But there is also an ecological reason for not occupying the central garden lands from which the enemy has been routed. These are the lands that have been most intensively cultivated and therefore most in need of fallow. The victors clear gardens in fallow forests in what were formerly boundary and no-man's lands. And the defeated clan does the same. It plants gardens on the edge of its former territory but in those portions that are close to the friendly villages where it has sought refuge. Thus the central gardening areas containing the best garden sites are put into fallow as the result of a rout.

As soon as the war is over, both sides separately hold ceremonies in which each plants a sacred tree, vowing that until the tree has grown tall and as long as it stays in the ground they will not engage in further fighting. At the same time they address themselves to the ancestors and promise that they will work industriously to rebuild the pig herd so that the ancestors can be thanked properly for preserving their lives or for giving them victory.

As I indicated in the previous chapter, an adult pig eats as much garden produce as an adult person. With the increase in the pig population, more and more effort goes into feeding pigs rather than people. The people soon find themselves working harder and harder and in need of expanding their garden lands. The women, upon whom the burden of the extra gardening and pig-raising effort falls most severely, begin to complain. Other sources of tension also increase.

Pigs knock down fences and break into gardens. The village becomes filled with bickering and suspicion. People accuse each other of witchcraft. Some women have more than the average number of pigs and children to take care of. Rappaport notes that it is these over-worked women who are the first to agitate for the pig slaughter. Thus in every population there will be individuals who feel the stress of approaching population limits before that limit is experienced by the entire group.

As Rappaport points out, increases in the causes of frustration or anger in a population increase geometrically with respect to population growth. Many social and biological processes may take their toll. For example, mothers who are under stress may deliver underweight and sickly babies; continued stress may affect quantity and quality of the mother's milk. Even if there has been no physiological impairment of mother or infant, stress may interfere with the mother's ability to devote herself to the care and protection of her child. Under such circumstances only a very fine line separates premature death through neglect from outright infanticide. The women in effect find themselves killing their babies in order to feed their pigs! Finally it becomes clear that the basic source of trouble is the failure to thank the ancestors. The men go out to inspect the sacred tree. If it is tall enough, they all grab hold of it and pull it up by its roots. Everyone now begins to prepare for the pig feast. Allies are invited, the pig herd is slaughtered, the ancestors thanked, and hostilities are renewed. Soon another sacred tree is planted establishing another interim of peace based upon another reapportionment of garden lands among the warring clans. If the same clan is routed again, its fallow former central garden area will be taken over by its enemies and replanted; but if the tables are turned, the new victors will reoccupy their former territory and reestablish their gardens in the secondary growth that has matured during their absence.

How long does it take before the people decide that the sacred tree is tall enough to be uprooted? Rappaport indicates that the great pig slaughters usually occur about every ten to twelve years. This period corresponds to the minimum period necessary for the replenishment of secondary growth. That the war and peace cycle is governed by the height of a growing tree is both a symbolic and practical measure of the link between warfare and the conservation of the life-sustaining forest. If the sacred tree is too small, the secondary growth in the temporarily vacated lands will not be mature enough for replanting. But if the sacred tree gets too big, the men will have trouble uprooting it—just as they will have trouble in handling the trees that have grown too tall in the fallow gardens (see p. 241). Thus the sacred tree functions as a kind of calendar that records the passage of ecologically significant intervals.

But what about the pigs? Why raise them in such numbers only to slaughter them all at once? Rather than regard this as an inexplicable and irrational practice, certain probable ecological functions should be considered. Rappaport counted 169 pigs and 200 Tsembaga just before the beginning of the pig feast that he witnessed in 1963. Seven-eighths of all the pigs by weight were eaten up during the festivities. The formula on page 243 shows that almost as much effort was going into the feeding and care of these pigs as into the production of garden foods for people. Then why not raise fewer pigs and more people? The answer may be that the pig population can easily be cut back when it places too great a strain on the gardens and threatens the system with reduced fallow periods, scarcity of secondary growth, and ecological degradation. Since the various Maring clans are continuously engaged in testing each other's capacity to defend their territories (Vayda 1971), rearing more pigs and fewer children may permit rapid upward and downward adjustments of the pressure exerted by each local group as its territorial base expands and contracts with victory or defeat. Furthermore groups that have many pigs per capita can attract allies, are better nourished, and hence are better prepared to defend and expand their territory. In the long run, energy invested in raising pigs may be better spent than in raising people. Remember that the burden of raising pigs rests mainly on the women. In energy terms the pigs embody the temporarily "surplus" calories that the women could have invested in rearing additional daughters. But when daughters grow up and threaten to "eat up" the forest, they cannot be sacrificed and eaten in turn. This theory may help to explain why pigs are widely regarded as sacred animals among the Maring. The ancestors eat them instead of eating people (see Ch. 24).

Psychological Explanation of War

Motives that the belligerents themselves cite for going to war do not explain the etic conditions under which wars recur. The most common explanation for war among those who do the fighting is revenge for injuries or insults received. Such injuries or insults include homicide, trespass, poaching, adultery, and abduction of women. Often the manifest provocation involves an accusation of witchcraft. It is frequently asserted that such-and-such group went to war "to bring back scalps" or "to obtain human flesh" or "to test manhood" or even "to indulge in an exciting sport." These motivational factors, goals, and values do play an important role in the timing and conduct of particular conflicts. But unless one can state the general conditions under which people will seek revenge, steal women, trespass, practice witchcraft, crave enemy flesh, and so on, the causes of war remain obscure. It may seem strange that the people who lose their lives in armed combat seldom accurately understand why they do so. But the masking of deeper causes by superficial psychological motives is advantageous for people who depend on war for their well-being. To understand the causes of war is to relieve the enemy of the onus of guilt, making it impossible to mobilize the adrenalin and other hormones necessary for effective hand-to-hand combat. The group that is burdened by doubts is subject to annihilation. Only those who are psychologically convinced that they must kill their enemies have a chance of surviving (cf. Moskos 1969; Givens 1973).

The point I wish to stress here is that humans have the potential to quickly reach the limit of their ecosystem's carrying capacity. When a particular group appears superficially not to be pressing against its resources and yet engages in warfare, a careful inquiry must be made to determine if the practice of war is itself partially responsible for the maintenance of the population below carrying capacity or if, in fact, carrying capacity is actually not being threatened.

The Case of the Yanomamö

The Yanomamö are regarded as among the world's fiercest and most male-centered cultures. Their style of life seems to be entirely dominated by incessant quarreling, raiding, dueling, beating, and killing. Yet they derive their main source of food calories with little effort from the plantains and banana trees that grow in their forest gardens. Like the Maring, they burn the forest to get these gardens started. But bananas and plantains are perennials that provide high yields per unit of labor input for many consecutive years. Since the Yanomamö live in the midst of the world's greatest tropical forest, the little burning that they do scarcely threatens to "eat up the trees." A typical Yanomamö village has only one hundred to two hundred people in it, a population that could easily grow enough bananas or plantains in nearby garden sites without ever having to move. Yet the Yanomamö villages are constantly on the move—splitting up, moving their gardens—at a much higher rate than other slash-and-burn Amazon forest peoples. There is evidence that the Yanomamö have "eaten" a very important resource as a result of population expansion. Unlike the Maring, the Yanomamö have no domesticated food animals. They

276

Figure 13-5. YANOMANÖ QUARREL. Guests who have come to the village were accused of adultery. The indignant husband has just been hit over the head. (Napoleon Chagnon)

obtain their meat protein from hunting. In this they are different from other populous Amazon cultivators who live on large rivers and obtain their meat protein from fish and aquatic animals. The shortage of forest animals—always a precarious resource, as I have already indicated—can be deduced from the fact that Yanomamö hunters must range far from their villages in order not to return empty-handed.

Game animals are not abundant, and an area is rapidly hunted out, so that a group must keep constantly on the move. Furthermore, hunting depends as much on luck as it does on skill and is not a very reliable way to supply nourishment. I have gone on five-day hunting trips with the Yanomamö in areas that had not been hunted for decades, and had we not brought cultivated foods along, we would have been extremely hungry at the end of this time—we did not collect even enough meat to feed ourselves. On other trips, we often managed to collect enough game in one day to feed the entire village.   [Chagnon 1968:33]

Since the typical Yanomamö village is less than a day's walk from its nearest neighbor, extended expeditions inevitably cross and recross hunting territories that are used by villages other than one's own. These villages compete for the same scarce forest animals.

The Yanomamö exhibit signs of a culture that is adapting to a new ecosystem. They do not know how to construct or paddle canoes, although their main settlements are now on the banks of or close by the Orinoco and Mavaca rivers. They do little fishing (Wilbert 1972:43) although such waters are rich in fish and aquatic animals. Most villages lack knowledge of how to make cooking pots, although

277

The Case of the Yanomamö

plantains are best prepared by boiling. And finally, they do not know how to manufacture stone axes, although they are now dependent upon axes for making their plantain gardens (Wilbert 1972:30).

Estimates of total Yanomamö population range between 7,500 and 35,000. There is no doubt that they have undergone an explosive population growth during the past one hundred years.

> The indigenous settlements were traditionally established far from navigable rivers and one had to walk several days through dense forests in order to find them. . . . It is only recently, following an astonishing expansion into unoccupied areas due to fissioning, war, hostilities, and a remarkable demographic increase, that some groups . . . began to establish themselves on the Orinoco River and its tributaries.   [Lizot 1971:34–35]

In the area studied by Chagnon, one group has gone from two hundred people or less to over two thousand in four or five generations. This expansion is likely to have begun when the Yanomamö increased their dependence on plantains and bananas—neither of which existed in South America before the arrival of Europeans. Plantains and bananas are important in the explanation of Yanomamö warfare

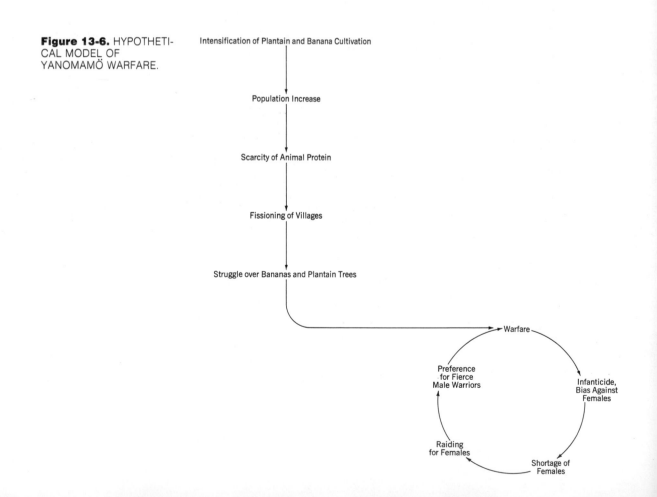

Figure 13-6. HYPOTHETICAL MODEL OF YANOMAMÖ WARFARE.

Intensification of Plantain and Banana Cultivation

Population Increase

Scarcity of Animal Protein

Fissioning of Villages

Struggle over Bananas and Plantain Trees

Warfare

Preference for Fierce Male Warriors

Infanticide, Bias Against Females

Raiding for Females

Shortage of Females

because these are tree crops that yield for several years in a row. When a village becomes too large in relation to the supply of game animals, the segment that fissions off suffers a significant loss of capital investment. The segment that moves away must transport heavy loads of banana and plantain cuttings and take up a dependent position in some ally's village while waiting for its new gardens to mature.

A plausible ecological explanation of the incessant warfare among the Yanomamö therefore is that the Yanomamö may formerly have obtained much more of their food supply from hunting and gathering. By intensifying their plantain gardens they increased their population density to the point where they permanently depleted the forest's animal resources. And they are now struggling with each other to gain access to the remaining hunting areas on the margins of their former territory (Meggers 1971; Morrey and Marwitt 1975; D. Harris 1974; Ross and Ross n.d.).

Adaptive and Maladaptive Aspects of Warfare

To recognize the general adaptive value of the population control aspects of some forms of warfare is not to concede that in any given instance the entire pattern of warfare is explicable in terms of ecological consideration nor even that the function of population control itself is always well served. Warfare at best is a poor solution to a difficult problem. That is, even if only the bare minimum of individuals were killed while population was maintained at an optimum level below carrying capacity, from a human point of view such a system clearly leaves much to be desired. Any ecological adaptation requiring the sacrifice of human lives is an unwelcome feature of the ecosystem. Warfare can be escalated to the point where the whole texture of life is dominated by raiding and killing, counter-raiding and counterkilling. Under these circumstances not only may there be an increase in suffering but the system may get out of hand. By inducing more infant female deaths than necessary for equilibrium and by interfering with the efficiency of food production, war may cause many unnecessary deaths even among preindustrial village cultivators. The Yanomamö may very well represent such a case. Chagnon himself is convinced that "Yanomamö warfare is not related to . . . ecological parameters" (1974:195) and has contradicted his earlier statements about the unreliability and the scarcity of meat by writing of "enormous tracts of land abounding with game" found between villages (1974:127). Certainly their war system has none of the elaborate feedback controls that in the case of the Maring guarantee that there will be long intervals of peace.

Nothing in the relation between people, nature, and culture guarantees that all cultural systems will stabilize themselves at the highest possible levels of productive and reproductive efficiency. Excessive warfare is an ecological trap into which humanity has probably fallen again and again.

Nonetheless, in general, as long as the cultural mechanisms for intensifying labor input depend upon more or less uncoordinated, voluntary efforts responsive to what "feels comfortable" to the individual food-producer, warfare will tend to stabilize or reduce population density. With the rise of political institutions, however, it becomes possible to induce or coerce food-producers to work harder for the same return or less. Under such conditions warfare will have the effect of increasing rather than stabilizing population density. It will do this because if there is political control, production and population density can be raised and threats to the ecosystem can be avoided by continuously expanding into adjacent territories. This implies that there is a close relationship between warfare and the rise of stratified societies, states, and empires. Indeed, under certain circumstances discussed later, war may be a cause of stratification and of the evolutionary emergence of the state. Once in existence, states in turn have been selected for their ability to intensify production and reproduction in support of military engagements involving more and more combatants, equipment, and supporting facilities. But I shall postpone further discussion of the origins and expansionist nature of states to Chapter 18.

The question of the relationship between warfare and population pressure among industrial societies is too important to be postponed, however. It should be obvious from what I have just said and from the archaeological evidence presented earlier that as long as the state has been in existence, warfare has been a central part of the system that is responsible for the explosive expansion of production and population. (The Wapituil could only exist in a world without war.) Warfare exercises no homeostatic influences whatsoever in the modern world. Furthermore, it should be obvious that unlike the Maring and the Yanomamö, industrial societies have no ecologically determined need for any form of population control that involves injury or risk to any infant or mother. Therefore the causes of modern wars and of the threat of nuclear catastrophe must be sought in variables that are specific to state-level ecosystems.

280

14

ECONOMY

An economy is a set of institutionalized activities which combine natural resources, human labor, and technology to acquire, produce, and distribute material goods and specialist services in a structured, repetitive fashion.

[Dalton 1969:97]

To study economy in an anthropological sense is to study the etics and emics of production, consumption, and exchange. It is to study who works at doing what, who consumes valuables of various kinds, and who gives valuables to or takes them from each other. It is to study these activities and relationships both as they appear to the observer and as they appear to and are experienced by the participants.

Economic organization mediates between ecology on the one hand and social organization on the other. Some aspects of economic organization form a "seamless" unity with the ecosystem; other aspects blend imperceptibly with the organization of domestic life and political law and order. In this chapter certain facts and concepts basic to a comparative study of economic systems will be introduced. I will show that economic organizations differ in the extent to which individuals share equally in the tasks of production and the rewards of consumption; that systems of distribution and exchange maintain characteristic levels of economic equality and inequality; and that these features are adapted to ecological constraints and opportunities. Additional aspects of economy will be dealt with in other chapters.

Egalitarian Economies

It used to be said that "except for sex and age differences" preindustrial societies could be regarded as having egalitarian—even communistic—economies. It remains true that in societies such as those of the Bushman and other low-energy hunters and gatherers, the economy has a marked communistic bent: everybody works at food production tasks; no one is systematically denied access to natural resources vital for survival; people tend to consume more or less the same quantities and qualities of valuables; and no individuals accumulate valuables produced by the labor of others. Anthropologists have become increasingly sensitive, however, to the extent to which this formulation masks the occurrence of important differences in economic duties and privileges apportioned according to sex. Even among the Bushmen, women probably work harder than men, carry more burdens, and contribute more calories and protein to the food supply. Where warfare is intense, as among the Maring and the Yanomamö, the economic role of women may closely approximate that of an exploited caste or class (see p. 402). Women are assigned the dull, arduous, and repetitious economic tasks: fetching water and firewood, cooking, carrying the children, weeding and harvesting, carrying heavy baskets of harvested products from the garden to the house. Women who do not perform these functions to the satisfaction of their husbands are beaten or even killed. The men, who work less, are entitled to choice morsels of food, especially to choice parts of slain animals; they frequently monopolize available supplies of intoxicants and drugs; and they accumulate valuable adornments such as armbands, necklaces, masks, and headdresses.

Economic inequalities such as these are certainly not to be minimized; they render invalid many depictions of band and village societies as egalitarian paradises. Nonetheless even in militaristic village cultures, where females constitute an economically exploited sex, within-sex economic relationships tend to be markedly different from those characteristic of class-structured preindustrial societies.

Reciprocity

One of the most striking features of the economic life of band and village societies is the prominence of exchanges that are conducted between members of the same sex according to the principle known as *reciprocity.* In reciprocal exchanges the flow of labor products and services does not appear to be contingent upon any definite counterflow. Each adult appears to take according to need and to give according to whim. Yet there is an underlying expectation of return.

Richard Lee has written a succinct description of this form of exchange as it occurs among the !Kung Bushmen. In the morning

Figure 14-1. BUSHMAN
RECIPROCITY. Men awaiting
the distribution of meat from
a small wart hog. (Richard B.
Lee)

anywhere from one to sixteen of the twenty adults in the !Kung band
leave camp to spend the day collecting or hunting. They return in the
evening with whatever food they have managed to find. Everything
brought back to camp is shared equally regardless of whether the
recipients have spent the day sleeping or hunting:

Not only do families pool the day's production, but the entire
camp—residents and visitors alike—shares equally in the total quantity of
food available. The evening meal of any one family is made up of portions
of food from each of the other families resident. Foodstuffs are distributed
raw or are prepared by the collectors and then distributed. There is a
constant flow of nuts, berries, roots and melons from one family fireplace to
another until each person resident has received an equitable portion. The
following morning a different combination of foragers moves out of camp
and when they return late in the day, the distribution of foodstuffs is
repeated.   [1969b:58]

Eventually all the adults will have gathered or hunted and given as
well as received food. But wide discrepancies in the balance of giving
and receiving may exist between individuals over a long period
without becoming the subject of any special talk or action.

Reciprocity is not unknown to people who live in industrial societies.
In the United States, for example, husbands and wives, friends,
brothers, sisters, and other kin regulate and adjust their economic
lives to a minor degree according to informal, uncalculated, give-

and-take transactions. Perhaps the clearest modern instance of reciprocity is to be found in the practice of giving Christmas gifts. In any given year the value of the gifts exchanged can be quite unequal. Persistent discrepancies, however, are a source of acute embarrassment or disappointment and will lead to mutual attempts to balance the account despite the fact that there is no legal or even informal recognition of the need for such a balance.

The Problem of the Freeloader

Among hunters and food-collectors the maintenance of permanently asymmetrical exchange also does not go entirely unnoticed. Thus some individuals will come to enjoy reputations as diligent gatherers or outstanding hunters, whereas others acquire reputations as shirkers or malingerers. No specific mechanisms exist, however, for obliging the debtors to even up the score. Yet it should not be concluded that there are no sanctions against becoming a complete freeloader. Such behavior generates a steady undercurrent of disapproval. Freeloaders are eventually subject to collective sanctions. They may meet with violence because they are suspected of being bewitched or of bewitching others through the practice of sorcery (see p. 363).

What is distinctive about reciprocal exchange, therefore, is not that products and services are simply given away without any thought or expectation of return, but rather that there is (1) no immediate return, (2) no systematic calculation of the value of the services and products exchanged, and (3) an overt denial that a balance is being calculated or that the sums must come out even.

Pure Gifts

Is there no exchange then corresponding to what Bronislaw Malinowski called "pure gift"? Are we always to look for hidden, self-seeking, material motives whenever labor products are moved from one individual or group to another? Nothing of the sort is implied. Rather, the bestowal of gifts without any tangible reciprocity in services or products is a universal phenomenon. Pure gifts consisting of everything necessary for the maintenance of life and well-being may flow unidirectionally to receivers throughout the entire lifetimes of givers. Indeed, this relationship is becoming increasingly common throughout the industrial world. In preindustrial contexts, parents generally

284

expect and receive material reciprocity for their child-rearing efforts. Children begin to reciprocate by working at agricultural and household tasks at an early age, and this relationship continues into the old age of the parents, who frequently end their lives with a net favorable balance of labor and products. But all contemporary industrial states display a trend toward a lifetime exchange balance between parents and children that is favorable to the younger generation. Parents must increasingly rely on their own savings and state aid in the form of insurance, pensions, old-age social security, and other public welfare schemes to maintain themselves during periods of sickness and senility.

There is no question that human beings under certain conditions will voluntarily give away their most valued possessions and expect nothing material in return. Yet it is obvious that an entire system of exchange cannot operate exclusively on such principles. An exchange system that does not provide pressure for a reverse flow of goods and services during periods of lowered individual productivity, sickness, incapacity, or old age menaces its own population with starvation and premature death. This is merely another way of saying that cooperation is adaptive for social species and that gift-giving is maladaptive unless it is reciprocal. Thus there is no need to get involved with the question of whether human nature is inherently selfish or altruistic in order to explain why, as a matter of ethnographic record, no exchange system depends entirely upon pure gifts. What does occur, especially on the level of small hunting and food gathering societies, is that goods and services are reciprocally exchanged in such a way as to keep the notion of material balance, debt, or obligation in an ideologically subordinate position. As in the case of modern Euro-American intrahousehold exchanges, this is accomplished by expressing the reciprocal exchanges as kinship obligations. These kinship obligations establish reciprocal expectations with respect to food, clothing, shelter, and other economic goods.

Kinship-embedded transactions constitute only a meager portion of modern exchange systems, whereas among band and village peoples almost all exchanges take place between kin, or at least intimate associates, for whom the giving, taking, and using of goods is drenched with sentiments and personal significance.

Problems of Trade

Reciprocity is practiced primarily where exchange is kinship-embedded. Even hunters and gatherers, however, want valuables

such as salt, flint, obsidian, red ochre, reeds, and honey that are
produced or controlled by peoples with whom they have no kinship
ties. In the absence of state-controlled markets, economic dealings
between nonkin must be based on the assumption that every individual will try to get the best of an exchange through chicanery and theft.
As a result, trading expeditions are likely to be hazardous in the
extreme.

One interesting mechanism for getting around this problem is
known as *silent trade*. The objects to be exchanged are set out in a
clearing, and the traders retreat out of sight. The other group inspects
the wares and lays down what it regards as a fair exchange of its own
products. The first group returns and, if satisfied, removes the traded
objects. If not, it leaves the wares untouched as a signal that the
balance is not yet even. In this fashion the Pygmies of the Ituri Forest
trade meat for bananas with the Bantu agriculturalists, and the
Vedda of Ceylon trade honey for iron tools with the Sinhalese.
Herodotus reports that this was the manner in which the Carthagini-
ans obtained gold from the African tribes living south of the Strait of
Gibraltar.

More developed trade relations are occasionally found among prestate agricultural groups. Conditions for the occurrence of markets

seem to have been especially favorable in Melanesia where, as in Malaita in the Solomon Islands, women regularly traded fish for pigs and vegetables under the armed guard of their menfolk. Among the Kapauku of Western New Guinea (see p. 305), full-fledged price markets involving shell and bead money may have existed before the advent of European control. Generally speaking, however, marketing as a regular mode of exchange is associated with the evolution of the state and with the enforcement of order by means of police and soldiers.

Perhaps the most common solution to the problem of trading without kinship ties or state-supervised markets is the establishment of special *trade partnerships.* In this arrangement members of different bands or villages come to regard each other as metaphorical kin. The members of trading expeditions deal exclusively with their trade partners who greet them as "brothers" and give them food and shelter. Trade partners attempt to deal with each other in conformity with the principle of reciprocity, deny an interest in getting the best of the bargain, and offer their wares in the form of gifts (Heider 1969).

The Kula

The classic anthropological example of trade partnerships is described in Bronislaw Malinowski's *Argonauts of the Western Pacific.* The argonauts in question are the Trobriand Islanders who trade with the neighboring island of Dobu by means of daring canoe voyages across the open sea. The entire complex associated with this trade is known as the *Kula.* According to the men who risk their lives in the voyages, the purpose of the Kula trade is to exchange shell ornaments with their trade partners. The ornaments, known to the Trobrianders as *vaygu'a,* consist of armbands and necklaces. In trading with the Dobuans, who live to the southeast, the Trobrianders give armbands and receive necklaces. In trading with the people who live to the southwest, the Trobrianders give necklaces and receive armbands. The armbands and necklaces are traded in opposite directions from island to island and finally pass through their points of origin from the direction opposite to the one in which they were first traded.

Participation in the Kula trade is a major ambition of youth and a consuming passion of senior men. The vaygu'a have been compared with heirlooms or crown jewels. The older they are and the more complex their history, the more valuable they become in the eyes of the Trobrianders. Nothing is done with them except that on ceremonial occasions they are worn as adornments; otherwise they

287

remain in the house where they are occasionally inspected and admired in private. Although regarded as a man's most valuable possessions, they can be used only to obtain other armbands or necklaces.

Each Kula expedition requires extensive social and ritual preparation. Minor gifts as well as vaygu'a are brought along to please the trade partners. These partnerships are usually handed down from one kinsman to another, and young men are given a start in the Kula trade by inheriting or receiving an armband or a necklace from a relative. When the expedition reaches shore, the trade partners greet each other and exchange preliminary gifts. Later the Trobrianders deliver the precious armbands, accompanied by ritual speeches and formal acts concerned with establishing the honorable giftlike character of the exchange. As in the case of reciprocal transactions within the family, the trade partner may not be immediately able to provide a necklace whose value is equivalent to the armband just received. Although the voyager may have to return home empty-handed, except for some preliminary gifts, he does not complain. He knows that his trade partner will work hard to make up for the delay by presenting him with an even more valuable necklace at their next meeting.

Why all this effort in order to obtain a few baubles of sentimental or aesthetic value? As is often the case, the Kula activities that are overtly emphasized and that possess the greatest motivational significance are the least significant ecologically. The boats that take part in the Kula expedition turn out to be loaded with trade items of great practical value in the life of the various island peoples who participate in the Kula ring. While other members of the expedition barter for necessities, the trade partners fondle and admire their priceless heirlooms. As long as everyone agrees that the expedition is not really concerned with such mundane necessities as coconuts, sago palm flour, fish, yams, baskets, mats, wooden swords and clubs, green stone for tools, mussel shells for knives, creepers and lianas for lashings, these items can be haggled over with impunity. Although no Trobriander would admit it, or even conceive how it could be true, the vaygu'a are valuable not for their qualities as heirlooms but for their truly priceless gift of trade (cf. Uberoi 1962).

Redistributive Exchange

Generalized reciprocity is associated with low and irregular work inputs adjusted to production levels and population densities that are far below carrying capacity. Much of the evolution of economic

288

systems consists of the development of more coercive organizational and ideological arrangements, which supplement or almost entirely replace generalized reciprocity. More coercive systems did not appear in sudden full-blown opposition to general reciprocity. Rather, they first achieved coercive effects through what was regarded merely as an intensification of familiar reciprocal principles.

The exchange system known as *redistribution* enabled this transition to occur. In redistributive exchange the labor products of several different individuals are brought to a central place, sorted by type, counted, and then given away to producers and nonproducers alike. Considerable organizational effort is required if large quantities of goods are to be brought to the same place at the same time and given away in definite shares. This coordination is usually achieved by individuals who act as *redistributors.* Typically the redistributor consciously attempts to increase labor input. This attempt is closely related to the expansion of population density, increased warfare, and the emergence of classes and the state. Thus egalitarian and stratified forms of redistribution must be distinguished.

As an egalitarian system of exchange, redistribution is carried out by a redistributor who has worked harder than anyone else producing the item to be given away, who takes the smallest portion or none at all, and who, after it is all over, is left with fewer material possessions than anyone else. In its egalitarian form, therefore, redistribution appears to be merely an intense example of reciprocity; the generous provider gives everything away and expects nothing in return.

In the stratified form, however, the redistributor withholds labor from the production process, retains the largest share, and ends up with more material possessions than anyone else.

Redistributive exchange, like reciprocal exchange, is usually embedded in a complex set of kinship relations and rituals that may obscure the ecological significance of the exchange behavior. From the point of view of the rank-and-file producers, redistribution is often a feast held to celebrate some important event such as a harvest, the end of a ritual taboo, the construction of a house, a death, a birth, or a marriage. A common feature of Melanesian redistributive feasts is that the guests gorge themselves with food, stagger off into the bush, stick their fingers down their throats, vomit, and then return to eating with renewed zest. Another common feature of redistributive feasting is the boastful and competitive attitude of the redistributors and their kin with respect to other individuals or groups who have given feasts.

Reciprocity versus Redistribution

Boastfulness or acknowledgment of generosity is incompatible with the basic etiquette of reciprocal exchanges. Among the Semai of Central Malaya, no one ever says "thank you" for the meat received from another hunter. Having struggled all day to lug the carcass of a pig home through the jungle heat, the hunter allows his prize to be cut up into exactly equal portions, which are given away to the entire group. As Robert Dentan explains, to express gratitude for the portion received indicates that you are the kind of person who calculates how much you are giving and taking.

In this context saying thank you is very rude, for it suggests first that one has calculated the amount of a gift and second, that one did not expect the donor to be so generous.   [1968:49]

Thus to call attention to one's generosity is to indicate that others are in debt to you and that you expect them to repay you. It is repugnant to egalitarian peoples even to suggest that they have been treated generously. Richard Lee tells how he learned about this aspect of reciprocity through a revealing incident. To please the Bushmen with whom he was staying, he decided to buy a large ox and have it slaughtered as a Christmas present. He spent days searching the neighboring Bantu villages looking for the largest and fattest ox in the region. Finally he bought what appeared to be a perfect specimen. But one Bushman after another took him aside and assured him that he had been duped into buying an absolutely worthless animal. "Of course, we will eat it," they said, "but it won't fill us up—we will eat and go home to bed with stomachs rumbling." Yet when Lee's ox was slaughtered, it turned out to be covered with a thick layer of delectable fat. Lee eventually succeeded in getting his informants to explain why they had claimed that his gift was valueless, even though they certainly knew better than he what lay under the animal's skin.

Yes, when a young man kills much meat he comes to think of himself as a chief or a big man, and he thinks of the rest of us as his servants or inferiors. We can't accept this, we refuse one who boasts, for someday his pride will make him kill somebody. So we always speak of his meat as worthless. This way we cool his heart and make him gentle.   [1968:62]

In flagrant violation of these prescriptions for modesty in reciprocal exchanges, redistributive exchange systems involve public proclamations that the host is a generous person. This boasting is one of the most conspicuous features of the *potlatches* engaged in by the Indian tribes who inhabit the Northwest Pacific Coast of the United States and Canada. In descriptions made famous by Ruth Benedict in

290

Patterns of Culture, the Kwakiutl redistributor emerges as a virtual megalomaniac. Here is what the Kwakiutl chiefs had to say about themselves:

I am the great chief who makes people ashamed.
I am the great chief who makes people ashamed.
Our chief brings shame to the faces.
Our chief brings jealousy to the faces.
Our chief makes people cover their faces by what he is
    continually doing in this world,
Giving again and again oil feasts to all the tribes.

I am the only great tree, I the chief!
I am the only great tree, I the chief!
You are my subordinates, tribes.
You sit in the middle of the rear of the house, tribes.
I am the first to give you property, tribes.
I am your Eagle, tribes!

Bring your counter of property, tribes, that he may try in vain to count the
    property that is to be given away by the great copper maker, the chief.
                                        [Benedict 1934:190]

In the potlatch the guests continue to behave somewhat like Lee's Bushmen. They grumble and complain and are careful never to

Figure 14-3. KWAKIUTL VILLAGE CA. 1900. The signs over the doors read: "Boston. He is the Head chief of Arwœtc. He is true Indian. Honest. He don't owe no trouble to white man" and "Cheap. He is one of the head chief of all tribes in this country. White man can get information." (American Museum of Natural History)

291

appear satisfied or impressed. Nonetheless there has been a careful public counting of all the gifts displayed and distributed. Both hosts and guests believe that the only way to throw off the obligations incurred in accepting these gifts is to hold a counter potlatch in which the tables are reversed.

The Cultural Ecology of Rivalrous Redistribution

Why do the Bushmen esteem a hunter who never draws attention to his generosity, whereas the Kwakiutl and other redistributor peoples esteem a man who can boast about how much he has given away?

Unfortunately potlatching came under scientific scrutiny long after the Northwest Coast peoples had entered into trade and wage-labor relations with Russian, English, Canadian, and American nationals. Declining populations and a sudden influx of wealth had combined to make the potlatches increasingly competitive and destructive by the time Franz Boas began to study them in the 1880s (cf. Rohner 1969). At this period the entire tribe was in residence at the Fort Rupert trading station of the Hudson's Bay Company, and the attempt on the part of one potlatch-giver to outdo another had become an all-consuming passion. Blankets, boxes of fish oil, and other valuables were deliberately being destroyed by burning or by throwing them into the sea. On certain occasions, made famous by Benedict in *Patterns of Culture,* entire houses burned to the ground when fish oil was poured on the fire. Potlatches that ended in this fashion were regarded as great victories for the host potlatchers.

Many years of painful theoretical reformulation have been required in order to place these events within the comparative perspective of redistribution exchange systems. The astonished observers of the burning blankets and fish oil saw only the destructive and wasteful aspects of these exchanges. Thus it came to be widely accepted that potlatching had originated in the lust for prestige. The potlatch simply proved that the desire to obtain prestige had overwhelmed the desire to conserve input and maximize productivity. Now there is no doubt that the men who competed in the potlatches were motivated by the hope that they would be esteemed and praised by their fellows. But the search for esteem and praise is always part of the motivation behind human behavior. For the Swiss Calvinist, esteem and praise depend upon conservative dress, a discreet bank account, and the refusal to indulge in costly pleasures. On the other hand, the Eskimo hunter is esteemed and praised for skill and bravery in bringing down

292

Figure 14-4. POTLATCH. Spokesman for Kwakiutl chief making speech next to blankets about to be given away. (American Museum of Natural History)

polar bears. Among the members of "hippie" communes, esteem and praise is given to those whose drug "trips" result in deeper personal insights. The point is that prestige is gained only by behavior that is culturally defined as prestigious. Thus the question that must be answered with respect to potlatch is: Why did the cultures of the Northwest Coast peoples define potlatching as the means of obtaining prestige?

The answer may be that before the coming of the Europeans, the Kwakiutl potlatch more closely resembled the Melanesian and the New Guinea redistributive feasts. These feasts, in turn, despite their rivalrous aspects, are ecologically adaptive and economically maximizing forms of exchange. In the absence of coercive sanctions capable of forcing food-producers to increase their input, egalitarian societies must substitute noncoercive mechanisms. Rewarding an individual's extra productive effort with prestige is a common institutional "trick" for establishing higher levels of input and output. Thus, although rivalrous feasts may contain elements of waste, the net increment in total production exceeds the loss due to gorging and spoilage. Moreover, at large redistributive feasts, after the visitors have eaten to their satisfaction, there still remains much food, which they carry back home with them.

The Cultural Ecology of Rivalrous Redistribution

The fact that guests come from distant villages leads to additional important ecological and economic advantages with respect to the regional population. First, feasting rivalry between groups raises productivity throughout the region more than if each village feasts only its own producers. Second, as has been suggested for the Northwest Coast region by Wayne Suttles (1960) and Stuart Piddock (1965), rivalrous intervillage redistributions may be ecologically adaptive as a means of overcoming the effects of localized, naturally induced production failures. Failure of the salmon runs at a particular stream could threaten the survival of certain villages while neighbors on other streams continue to catch their usual quotas. Under such circumstances the impoverished villagers would want to attend as many potlatches as they could and carry back as many vital supplies as they could get their hosts to part with by reminding them of how big their own potlatches had been in previous years. Intervillage pot-latches were thus a form of savings in which the prestige acquired at one's own feast served as a tally. The prestige was redeemed when the guests turned hosts and sought to put themselves into the position of prestige creditor rather than debtor. If a village was unable year after year to give potlatches of its own, its prestige credit would disappear.

In this connection, Thomas Hazard (1960) suggests a third ecological function for rivalrous redistributions, namely the shifting of popula-tion from less productive to more productive villages. When an impoverished and unprestigious group could no longer hold its own potlatches, the people abandoned their defeated redistributor-chief and took up residence among relatives in more productive villages. From this point of view the boasting and the giving away and displaying of wealth were advertisements that helped to recruit additional labor power into the work force gathered about a particu-larly effective redistributor. Incidentally, if this hypothesis is correct, it is easier to understand why the Northwest Coast peoples lavished so much effort in the production of their world-famous totem poles. These poles bore the redistributor-chief's "crests" in the guise of carved mythic figures; title to the crests was claimed on the basis of outstanding potlatch achievements. The larger the pole, the greater the potlatch power, the more the members of poor villages would be tempted to change their residence. Thus the aboriginal potlatch pattern may have been an ecologically adaptive example of redis-tributive exchange.

With the coming of the Europeans, however, this pattern underwent an intelligible but maladaptive evolution. The impact of European diseases had reduced the population of the Kwakiutl from 23,000 in 1836 to about 2,000 by the end of the century. At the same time the trading companies, canneries, lumber mills, and gold-mining camps pumped an unprecedented amount of wealth into the aboriginal economy. The percentage of people prepared to claim the crests of achievement rose, while the number of people available to celebrate the glory of the potlatcher dropped. Many villages were abandoned; hence rivalry intensified for the allegiance of the survivors. With the population declining and with food obtainable at the trading post, a whole new ecosystem had come into existence. The increasing destructiveness and wastefulness of the potlatch represents the attempt of a changing culture to adapt to a new ecosystem with its old institutions.

The Semai and Bushmen's reluctance to say thank you and their dislike of economic boasting may also be rooted in ecological conditions. Labor intensification poses a grave threat to such populations in the form of faunal overkills. To encourage the Bushman hunter to be boastful is to endanger the group's survival. On the other hand, the Kwakiutl, as long as they used the aboriginal fish net, could never deplete the spawning runs of the salmon and candlefish no matter how hard they worked.

Money

The idea and practice of endowing a material object with the capacity of measuring the social value of other material objects, animals, people, and labor occurs almost universally. Such standard-of-value "stuffs" are widely exchanged for goods and services. Throughout much of Africa, for example, a young man gives cattle to his father-in-law and gets a wife in return (see p. 324). In many parts of Melanesia, shells are exchanged for stone implements, pottery, and other valuable artifacts. Elsewhere beads, feathers, shark teeth, dog teeth, or pig tusks are exchanged for other valuable items and are given as compensation for death or injury and for personal services rendered by magicians, canoe-builders, and other specialists. With rare and still controversial exceptions, however, these "money stuffs" lack some of the major characteristics of the money stuffs found in state-organized price-market economies. In such economies money is commercial or market money, an all-purpose medium of exchange. It has the following features:

1. *Portability:* It comes in sizes and shapes convenient for being carried about from one transaction to the next.
2. *Divisibility:* Its various forms and values are explicit multiples of each other.

295

Figure 14-5. SHELL AND DOG TEETH MONEY. Manus dance and display their ceremonial money prior to exchange with trade partners. (American Museum of Natural History)

3. *Convertibility:* A transaction completed by a higher-valued unit can be made as well by its lower-valued multiples.
4. *Generality:* Virtually all goods and services have a money value.
5. *Anonymity:* For most purchases, anyone with the market price can conclude the transaction.
6. *Legality:* The nature and quantity of money in circulation is controlled by the state.

Although some of these traits may be associated with money in band and village economies, collectively the traits depend upon an economy in which selling and buying in a price market is a daily, lifelong occurrence. Where reciprocity, egalitarian redistribution, and trade-partner relations are the dominant modes of exchange, money in the modern dollar sense does not and cannot exist.

For example, cattle that are exchanged for wives are not the kind of currency that you would want to take to the supermarket check-out counter, being neither very portable nor readily divisible. As employed in *bride-price* (see p. 324), cattle are frequently not convertible; that is, a large, beautiful, fat bull with a local reputation cannot readily be substituted for by offering two smaller but undistinguished animals. Furthermore cattle lack generality since only wives can be "purchased" with them, and they lack anonymity because any stranger who shows up with the right amount of cattle will find that he cannot simply take the woman and leave the cattle. Cattle are exchanged for women only between kinship groups who have an interest in estab-

296

lishing or reinforcing preexisting social relationships. Finally, cattle are put into circulation by each individual household as a result of productive effort that is unregulated by any central authority.

In other instances noncommercial money-stuff bears a greater resemblance to commercial money. For example, among the inhabitants of Rossel Island, which lies off the east coast of New Guinea, a type of shell money-stuff occurs that has sometimes been confused with commercial money. The shells have portability, and they occur in 22 named units of value, that is, 1 to 22. These units, however, fall into 3 classes: numbers 1 to 10, numbers 11 to 17, and numbers 18 to 22. A person who borrows a no. 1 shell must return a no. 2. A person who borrows a no. 2 must repay with a no. 3. This continues through to no. 9. But a person who borrows a no. 10 cannot be obliged to return a no. 11. Thus the series 1 to 10 is divisible. Moreover the series 1 to 10 has a considerable amount of generality, being used to buy such items as baskets and pots. But the two series 1 to 10 and 11 to 17 are neither divisible nor convertible with respect to each other. Similarly the series 18 to 22 stands apart. There are only 60 shells in this series in circulation, and they are inconvertible with respect to each other and to the other series. For example, a no. 18 is the only shell that can be used for wife-purchase or for sponsorship of a pig feast. A no. 20 is the only shell that can be used as indemnity for ritual murder. As George Dalton (1965) observes, "It is about as useful to describe a pig feast on Rossel as buying a pig with a no. 18 *ndap* as it is to describe marriage in America as buying a wife with a wedding ring."

Money, like all other economic phenomena, has no existence apart from the kinship and political institutions that it is embedded in.

Political Economy

With the intensification of production and the rise in population density, economic organization fell increasingly under the control of state-administered institutions that set production quotas and carried out lopsided redistributions based on labor conscription, taxation, and control over price-market exchanges. These administered systems of production and exchange involved a high level of compulsion. They obliged people to increase their work input not merely by promising them prestige but by threatening them with socially imposed material sanctions (as distinct from those naturally imposed) leading ultimately to physical annihilation. Such systems conform to local and regional conditions and are highly variable in detail. But everywhere the common irreducible element is the existence of a class of rulers who have the power to compel others to do their bidding. The expression of this power in the realm of production and exchange results in the economic subordination of the labor force and their partial or total loss of control over production and exchange. Specifically the labor force loses control over:

1. Access to land and raw materials
2. The technology of production
3. Work time and work schedules
4. Place and mode of production activity
5. Disposition of the products of labor

Forms of production and exchange that depend upon the coercive effects of power can be understood only within the framework of a combined political and economic analysis. All the concepts appropriate to the analysis of contemporary economic systems, such as wages, rent, interest, property, and capital, have a political dimension to them. Just as production and exchange in egalitarian societies are embedded in kinship institutions, the processes of production and exchange of state-level societies are embedded in institutions of political control.

Landownership

Ownership of land and resources is one of the most important political-economic relationships. This relationship is as much political as it is economic because people do not voluntarily renounce their material interests in the environment. Unequal restriction of access to the environment implies some form of coercion applied by political superiors against political inferiors.

It is true that forms of land and resource ownership also occur in classless and stateless societies. Ownership of garden lands is often claimed by kin groups smaller than the local population; but everybody belongs to such kin groups, and hence no adult male or female can be deprived of an essentially equitable share of the habitat.

Certainly no adults can be deprived to the extent of making it impossible for them to carry out necessary, life-sustaining economic activities. Landownership by landlords, rulers, or the state, however, means that individuals who lack title or tenure may be barred from using land even if it leads to death through starvation.

Ownership of land and resources does not result merely from the selfish drive for wealth and power of a few ambitious individuals. It results also from systemic processes that select for more dense and

298

more productive populations. Landownership is a great stimulus to production because it forces food-producers to work longer and harder than they would if they had free access to resources. Landownership raises production mainly through the extraction of rent from the food-producers. *Rent* is a payment in kind or in money for the opportunity to live or work on the owner's land. This payment automatically compels the tenants to increase their work input. By raising or lowering rents the landlord exercises a fairly direct measure of control over work input and total production.

Because the extraction of rent is evolutionarily associated with an increase in productivity, some anthropologists regard the payment of rent as indicative of the existence of a *surplus* product—an amount greater than what is needed for immediate consumption by the producers. But it is important to note that the "surplus" that the landowner takes away as rent is not in any sense a *superfluous* quantity from the producers' standpoint. The producers can very well use the full amount of their output to increase the size of their family or to raise their own standard of living. If they surrender their produce, it is because they lack the power to withhold it. In this sense all rent is an aspect of politics, because without the power to enforce property titles, rent could not and does not exist. Thus there is a close resemblance between rent and taxation. The state stands behind the landlord, ready to use force if necessary in order to protect the owners' property and to make the tenants pay their rent.

Alternatively, as in the ancient irrigation civilizations, agents of the state collect the land tax and then deliver it over to the ruling class to be used in culturally prescribed ways (see p. 383). Where the state is very powerful, it obtains a monopoly over the means of exploiting its food-producers. Under such circumstances the effective landlord is the state itself and "rent" is extracted wholly in the form of taxes on produce, trade, and markets. In the centralized empires associated with irrigation systems, these tributes are supplemented by massive compulsory labor service known as *corvée*. All these forms of compelling extra effort and of diverting food and other valuables away from the food-producers are based on political systems that deprive the food-producers of free access to land and resources. The food-producers who are subject to such politico-economic systems are called "peasants."

The Political Economy of Peasant Life

Peasants are preindustrial food-producers who pay rent or taxes. Many different types of rent or taxes are extracted from peasants in conformity with local demographic, technoenvironmental, and technoeconomic possibilities. But "peasants of all times and places are structured inferiors" (Dalton 1972:406). The kind of rent or taxes extracted from a peasantry defines the essential features of that structured inferiority.

Each of the major types of peasant political economies is the subject of a vast research literature. Anthropological studies of peasants have usually taken the form of "community studies." Anthropologists have studied peasant communities more than they have studied tribespeople or hunters and gatherers (Pelto and Pelto 1973). In order to understand these studies (cf. E. Wolf 1966, 1969) it is essential to classify the principal varieties of peasant types based on their relationship to specific forms of rent, taxation, and political control (cf. Riegelhaupt and Forman 1970).

1. *Feudal peasants:* They are subject to the control of a decentralized hereditary ruling class whose members provide military assistance to each other but do not interfere in each other's territorial domains. Feudal peasants, or "serfs," inherit the opportunity to utilize a particular parcel of land; hence they are said to be "bound" to the land. For the privilege of raising their own food, peasants render unto the lord rent in kind or in money. Rent may also take the form of labor service in the lord's kitchens, stables, or fields.

Some anthropologists, following the lead of historians of European feudalism, describe feudal relationships as a more or less fair exchange of mutual obligations, duties, privileges, and rights between lord and serf. George Dalton (1972:390–391), for example, lists the following European feudal lord's services and payments to peasants:

1. Granting peasants the right to use land for subsistence and cash crops
2. Military protection (e.g., against invaders)
3. Police protection (e.g., against robbery)
4. Juridical services to settle disputes
5. Feasts to peasants at Christmas, Easter; also harvest gifts
6. Food given to peasants on days when they work the lord's fields
7. Emergency provision of food in times of disaster

Dalton chides some anthropologists for calling the material transactions between lord and peasant "exploitation" because it cannot be taken for granted that "the peasant paid out to the lord much more than he received back" (see p. 402). In rebuttal I would point out that the reason why the peasants are "structured inferiors" quite unlike any Bushman or Maring is that the feudal ruling class deprives them of free access to the land and its life-sustaining resources. This form of deprivation is antithetical to the principle of reciprocity and egalitarian redistribution. The counterflow of goods and services listed by Dalton merely perpetuates the peasants' structured inferiority. The one gift that would alter that relationship—the gift of land (free of rent or taxes)—is never given. There is no need to argue in the abstract concerning whether the exchange between feudal lords and tenants is "fair" or not. History demonstrates that the structured inferiority of peasant societies leads to a highly volatile situation. Over and over again the world has been convulsed by revolutions in which peasants struggled in the hope of restoring free access to land (E. Wolf 1969). This phenomenon becomes utterly irrational and unintelligible if one supposes that peasants voluntarily accept the lord's gifts and services as a fair return for their rent and taxes and are satisfied with their "structured inferiority."

2. *Prebendal peasants:* They are people who fall under the sway of nobles or officials who rule over them at the pleasure of the state. Prebends are awarded for specific service to the state, usually in recognition of military or bureaucratic exploits, and are not necessarily heritable thereafter. In other respects the prebend lord proceeds

Figure 14-6. PERUVIAN PEASANTS Man's wife is planting potatoes as he plows. (Walter Aguiar)

as a feudal lord, extracting rent in the form of labor service and tribute. This arrangement often represents a partial sacrifice of sovereign power in order to establish effective rule in remote territories. The Spanish Crown, for example, awarded prebends known as *encomiendas* to Cortes and Pizarro and the other conquistadores in return for their conquest of the peoples of Mexico and Peru. The attempt by these privileged subjects to convert their holdings into heritable, feudal domains led to a prolonged struggle with the Spanish Crown, during which the peasants were squeezed by uncontrolled labor and tax demands. This resulted in a precipitous decline in the American Indian population in Peru and Mesoamerica. Because of the temptation to "mine" prebendal peasants for all they are worth in get-rich-quick schemes, the status of such peasants is sometimes worse than that of slaves who can be bought and sold (Dobyns 1966; C. T. Smith 1970; M. Harris 1974b; also see p. 462).

3. *State-owned peasants:* Preindustrial societies in Peru, Egypt. Mesopotamia, and China developed into highly centralized, despotic, managerial states. The mass of peasants in these states were controlled by national laws and policies. Unlike the feudal peasants, they were subject to frequent conscription for labor brigades drawn from villages throughout the realm to build roads, dams, irrigation canals, palaces, temples, and monuments. In return the state made an effort to feed its peasants in case of food shortages caused by droughts or other calamities. The pervasive bureaucratic control over production quotas and life-styles has often been compared with modern forms of preindustrial socialist welfare states.

4. *Capitalist peasants:* In Europe, Japan, Latin America, India, and Southeast Asia, feudal and prebendal types of peasantries were frequently replaced by peasants who enjoyed increased opportunities to buy and sell land, labor, and food in competitive price markets. Most of the existing peasantries of the world outside of the communist block belong to this category. The varieties of structured inferiority within this group defy any simple taxonomy. Some capitalist peasants are subordinate to large landowners; others are subordinate to banks that hold mortgages and promisory notes. Capitalist peasants pay rent in the form of cash, head taxes, or chores (sharecroppers) and interest on mortgages and loans.

When the crops in production enter the international market, holdings are of the large, or *latifundia,* type, and the real landowners tend to be the commercial banks. Elsewhere in more isolated or unproductive regions holdings may be very small, giving rise to postage-stamp

302

Figure 14-7. ECUADORIAN PEASANTS. Note the postage stamp minifundia on the steep hillsides. See page 462. (United Nations)

farms known as *minifundia* and to the phenomenon that Sol Tax has aptly called "penny capitalism."

Capitalist peasants correspond to what Dalton calls "Early Modernized Peasants." They display the following features:

1. Marketable land tenure
2. Predominance of production for cash sale
3. Growing sensitivity to national commodity and labor price-markets
4. Beginnings of technological modernization

Although many capitalist peasants own their own land, they do not escape payment of rent or its equivalent. Many communities of landowning peasants constitute labor reserves for larger and more heavily capitalized plantations and farmers. Penny capitalists are frequently obliged to work for wages paid by these cash-crop enterprises. Penny-capitalist peasants cannot obtain enough income to satisfy subsistence requirements from the sale of their products in the local market. Hence they are obliged to work for wages as seasonal migrants on cash-crop latifundia and plantations, and they find themselves as much under the control of dominant landowning or mercantile classes as their landless counterparts from whom rent is extracted in a more direct form (Wolf and Mintz 1957).

303

Figure 14-8. ALBANIAN PEASANTS (above). Commune members plowing. (Eastfoto)

Figure 14-9. CHINESE PEASANTS (right). Water control is still one of the main functions of the Chinese state. Some of the 25,000 workers employed in construction of Shih Man Tan Reservoir on Huai River are shown with their earth moving equipment. (Eastfoto)

304

[14] Economy

5. *Communist peasants:* Food-producers in China, Albania, Eastern Europe, Cuba, and the Soviet Union continue to carry out their productive activities by means of preindustrial techniques. Since the state in these situations is all-powerful—setting production quotas, controlling prices, extracting taxes in kind and in labor—the official view that rent or its equivalent is not being extracted from the peasant laborer is unacceptable. Much depends, of course, on the extent to which peasants may exchange their lot with party bosses and bureaucrats and vice versa. In China a considerable effort is being made to destroy the class nature of peasant identity and to merge all labor—intellectual, industrial, and agricultural—in a single working class. To the extent that this effort proves successful, one might no longer wish to consider agricultural workers in China as peasants even though their technology may remain on a preindustrial level and even though they may remain subject to a bureaucratic ruling class. On the other hand, some analysts insist that the political economy of the food-producing class in China amounts to little more than the restoration of the despotic managerial state socialism that had existed for thousands of years under the Ming, Han, and Chou Dynasties.

Capitalism without the State:
The Kapauku Case

The following economic features are associated with capitalism: private property in land; private ownership of the technological means of production; interest on loans; profits on capital; wage labor; price making markets in which virtually all resources, products, and services can be exchanged for a single standard unit of value (i.e., money). There is no doubt that *in general* band and village societies lack these forms of economic organization. In some cases, however, egalitarian reciprocal and redistributive systems may have certain features strongly reminiscent of contemporary capitalist arrangements. Upon closer inspection, as in the case of the Rossel Island "money," such resemblances usually can be shown to be superficial. Nonetheless these cases are of special interest precisely because they reveal the abiding limitations imposed upon production, exchange, and consumption when there is no state and hence where differential access to resources and technology cannot be sustained.

The Kapauku Papuans of West New Guinea (today, West Irian, Indonesia) are a case in point. According to Leopold Pospisil (1963), the Kapauku have an economy that is best described as "primitive capitalism." All Kapauku agricultural land is said to be owned

305

individually; money sales are the regular means of exchange; money, in the form of shells and glass beads, can be used to buy food, domesticated animals, crops and land; money can also be used as payment for labor. Rent for leased land and interest on loans are also said to occur. A closer look at the land tenure situation, however, reveals that there are fundamental differences between the political economy of Kapauku and capitalist-peasant societies. To begin with, there is no landowning class. Instead, access to land is controlled by sublineages (see p. 338). No individual is without membership in such a group. These sublineages control communal tracts of land, which Pospisil calls "territories." It is only within sublineage territories that one may speak of private titles, and the economic significance of these titles is minimal on several counts. (1) The price of land is so cheap that all the gardens under production in 1955 had a market value in shell money less than the value of ten female pigs. (2) Prohibition against trespass does not apply to sublineage kin. (3) Although even brothers will ask each other for land payments, credit is freely extended among all sublineage members. The most common form of credit with respect to land consists merely of giving land on loan, that is, in expectation that the favor will shortly be returned in kind. (4) Each sublineage is under the leadership of a *headman* (see p. 365). But the headman's authority depends upon his generosity, especially toward the members of his own sublineage. A rich headman does not refuse to loan his kinsmen whatever they need to gain access to the environment since "a selfish individual who hordes money and fails to be generous, never sees the time when his word is taken seriously and his advice and decisions followed, no matter how rich he may become" (Pospisil 1963:49). Obviously, therefore, the wealth of the headman does not include the power of ownership associated with true peasant capitalism. In Ecuador or Brazil (see Ch. 21) the peasant who is tenant or sharecropper can be barred from access to land and water regardless of the landlord's reputation. Under the rules of true private landownership, it is of no significance whatsoever to the sheriff and the police officers who evict tenants that the landlord is being "selfish."

Pospisil argues that differences in wealth are correlated with striking differences in consumption of food and that Kapauku children from poor homes are undernourished while neighbors are well fed. However, the neighbors are not members of the same sublineage, since Pospisil insists that sublineage kinsmen "exhibit mutual affection and a strong sense of belonging and unity" and that "any kind of friction within the group is regarded as deplorable" (1963:39). It need cause no surprise that certain sublineages may be poorer than others.

306

Sickness and misfortune of various sorts frequently lead to inequalities in physical well-being among the several kinship units that are the building blocks of stateless societies. It would be unusual, however, if such misfortune were to perpetuate itself so that the Kapauku poor people came to form a permanent class as they do under true peasant capitalism. Without the political economy of the state, marked economic inequalities are always ephemeral because the rich cannot defend themselves against the demand of the poor that they be given credit, money, land, or whatever is necessary to end their poverty. Under aboriginal conditions some Kapauku villagers might have starved while neighbors ate well; but it is extremely unlikely that those who starved did so because they lacked access to land, money, or credit.

Pospisil provides dramatic evidence as to why this could not have happened very often. The truth of the matter is that the Kapauku rich man is an egalitarian redistributor rather than a capitalist. He has capital, but he does not control its disposition; *he cannot afford not to give it away on demand.* Were he able to withhold it from those who need it more, then he would cease being a mere headman. He would

Figure 14-10. TOKYO STOCK EXCHANGE. The public sale and purchase of shares in companies and corporations is a fundamental feature of capitalist economies. (UPI Photo)

then be a member of a ruling class. But this cannot happen among the Kapauku, because in New Guinea, and elsewhere, people do not voluntarily suffer poverty in order that others stay rich. A stingy redistributor in a stateless society is a contradiction in terms for the simple reason that there are no police to protect such people from the murderous intentions of those whom they refuse to help. As Pospisil tells it:

Selfish and greedy individuals, who have amassed huge personal properties, but who have failed to comply with the Kapauku requirement of "generosity" toward their less fortunate tribesmen may be, and actually frequently are, put to death. . . . Even in regions such as the Kamu Valley, where such an execution is not a penalty for greediness, a non-generous wealthy man is ostracized, reprimanded, and thereby finally induced to change his ways.   [1963:49]

Wage Labor, Money, and the Affluent Society

Increased population densities and higher technoenvironmental efficiency coupled with class control over access to land and technology yield more and more precise control over the time, quantity, quality, and place of labor input. As previously indicated, the industrial wage earner works longer and harder than most prestate hunters

308

or farmers. Lacking access both to land and to the tools of production, wage workers pay for the privilege of staying alive by selling their labor. The modern wage laborer is relatively free to change jobs (provided there is little unemployment, few travel restrictions, and no educational qualifications). Once on the job, however, tasks are rigorously defined and work schedules are closely supervised. The degree of supervision and control exerted over industrial work rhythms has been exceeded only in such labor systems as plantation and galley slavery.

The saving grace of wage-labor systems, of course, is that the producers are paid in money that can be used to purchase subsistence requirements and luxury items in a relatively sporadic, intermittent, and impulsive fashion. Markets and stores filled with dazzling varieties of products offer the wage earner (capitalist and communist) an exciting and unparalleled range of usable products. Perhaps the shopping expedition restores some of the zest and freedom that have been drained from the wage worker's daily life as a result of the routinization of work. This at least is the theory of "consumerism"— the belief that people find happiness in proportion to the amount of goods they buy and consume. The only problem is that unless one is very rich, shopping expeditions will frustrate as often as they will satisfy a consumer's desire to consume. This problem is especially acute in capitalist economies. The rate of capitalist production depends upon the rate at which people purchase, use, wear out, and destroy goods and services. Hence an enormous effort is expended on extolling the virtues and benefits of products in order to convince consumers that they should make additional purchases. Prestige is awarded not to the person who works hardest or gives away the greatest amount of wealth, but rather to the person with the highest standard of living. For the average wage earner, consumerism is thus a lifelong burden, an insatiable hunger and thirst, a mighty itching that has no remedy. Is it possible, therefore, that scarcity is never so great as in a culture that sets no limits to the desire to consume? Under such circumstances, as Marshall Sahlins has argued, perhaps there can be no true affluence.

The market makes available a dazzling array of products, good things in unlimited quantity and variety, each with its clarion price-tag call: "this is all it takes to have me." A man's reach is then inevitably beyond his grasp, for one never has enough to buy everything. Before the judgement of the market, the consumer stands condemned to scarcity, and so to a life sentence at hard labor. . . . To participate in a market economy is an inevitable tragedy; what began in inadequacy will end in deprivation—of something else that could have been had instead. To buy one thing is to deny yourself another.   [1968:77]

309

THE ORGANIZATION OF
DOMESTIC LIFE

Domestic activities involve preparation and consumption of food; cleaning, grooming, and disciplining of the young; sleeping; and adult sexual intercourse. These activities take place within an architectural setting—a residence or domicile—which provides protection against natural and cultural impediments to the domestic routine: buildings to control moisture, heat, wind, and animal pests; fences, palisades, and walls to keep out unwanted human and animal visitors. Domestic scenes can be identified by the presence of certain kinds of people, including preeminently infants, children, and adult caretakers of these infants and children. Many different combinations of domestic personnel and domestic activities occur. In this chapter domestic life-styles will be seen as adaptations to specific ecological and economic conditions.

The Nuclear Family

It was formerly believed that domestic life everywhere was organized around a married pair and their offspring. This combination of people, called the *nuclear* family, is still popularly regarded as a minimal panhuman unit of social organization. According to Ralph Linton, the combination of father, mother, and child is the "bedrock underlying all other family structures." Linton predicted that "the last man will spend his last hours searching for his wife and child" (1949:21). George Peter Murdock found the nuclear family in each of 250

310

Figure 15-1. JAPANESE NUCLEAR FAMILY. Industrialization in Japan is producing convergence toward pattern of nuclear family life in the United States. (Consulate General of Japan)

societies. He concluded that it was universal because it fulfills vital functions that cannot be carried out as efficiently by other means. The functions identified by Murdock are: (1) the sexual, (2) the reproductive, (3) the educational, and (4) the economic (sexual division of labor).

1. The nuclear family satisfies sexual needs and diminishes the disruptive force of sexual competition.
2. The nuclear family guarantees the protection of the female during her relatively long pregnancy and during the months and years of lactation.
3. The nuclear family is essential for enculturation. Only the co-resident adult man and woman possess knowledge adequate for the enculturation of children of both sexes.
4. Given the behavioral specialties imposed upon the human female by her reproductive role, and given the anatomical and physiological differences between men and women, a sexual division of labor is required for the most efficient utilization of subsistence effort.

The nuclear family thus guarantees heterosexual sex, reproduction, heterosexual enculturation, and heterosexual economic support.

Despite the cogency of these arguments, the weight of opinion has shifted in recent years against the proposition that the nuclear family is the elementary building block of social structure (cf. Richard Adams 1968). It has been found that husband-wife-child are not always co-resident; that even when co-resident they may share do-

311

The Nuclear Family

mestic functions with larger domestic groupings; and that other nondomestic groupings and extradomestic activities are frequently more important than the nuclear family in fulfilling the functions of sex, reproduction, enculturation, and economy.

Polygamy and the Nuclear Family

Some form of plural marriage (*polygamy*) occurs in 90 percent of the world's cultures. In one form, called *polygyny,* a husband is shared by several wives; and in another, much less common form called *polyandry,* a wife is shared by several husbands. Now it is logically possible to think of a man or a woman as creating another nuclear family each time he or she marries another wife or husband. But to do so would be to ignore the fact that plural marriages create domestic units that are behaviorally and psychically very different from those created by *monogamous* (one husband, one wife) marriages.

Polygamous sexual arrangements are, to begin with, obviously quite different from those characteristic of monogamous marriages. Second, the reproductive function is different, especially with polygyny, because the spacing of births is easier to control when husbands have several wives. Also distinctive patterns of nursing and infant

Figure 15-2. POLYGYNOUS HOUSEHOLD, SENEGAL. Islamic law permits this man to take one more wife to fill his quota of four, providing he can take good care of her. (United Nations)

care arise when the mother sleeps alone with her children while the father sleeps with a different wife each night (see p. 597). From the point of view of enculturation, there are special psychological effects associated with a father who divides his time among several mothers and who relates to his children through a hierarchy of wives. The monogamous American nuclear family, with its narrow focus of adult attention resting on a small group of full siblings, cannot be regarded as the psychological and emotional equivalent of a polygynous household in which a dozen or more half-siblings must share the affection of the same man. Furthermore the presence of co-wives or co-husbands drastically alters the portion of the enculturation process that devolves upon a particular parent. For example, the American nuclear family is structurally tortured by the question of what to do with children when both parents are preoccupied with adult-centered activities; whereas every polygynous situation has a built-in solution to the baby-sitting problem. Turning finally to economic functions, the minimal polygamous economic unit consists of the entire co-resident production team and not each separate husband-wife pair. Under polygyny, for example, domestic tasks—nursing, grooming, cleaning, fetching water, cooking, and so on—frequently cannot be satisfactorily performed by a single wife. Indeed, in polygynous societies, one of the main motivations for marrying a second wife is to spread the work load and to increase domestic output.

Figure 15-3. SITTING BULL. This famous Sioux chief is shown with two of his wives and three of his children. Polygyny was widespread among American Indian peoples. The photo was taken in 1882 at Fort Randall, South Dakota. (Museum of the American Indian, Heye Foundation)

313

Polygamy and the Nuclear Family

Segregation of Nuclear Family Functions

Contrary to popular opinion, there is no scientific basis for the application of Euro-American concepts of family, house, home, or household to the entire known spectrum of human domestic arrangements. Cooking, eating, sleeping, enculturation, and sexual relations are not carried out in any single pattern of adjacent rooms, houses, or groups of houses. In the case of the American nuclear family this is evident with respect to enculturation and education. Although the continuity of many essential patterns is dependent upon domestic family routines, survival of modern industrial populations depends upon patterns of thought and behavior acquired in nondomestic settings. Enculturation in contemporary life is increasingly a nondomestic affair carried out in special buildings—schools—under the auspices of specialist nonkinspeople—teachers. Paradoxically Euro-Americans attribute more important educational effects to nuclear family upbringing than to the vast apparatus of formal education. Others believe that the schools could easily outweigh family experience if given the chance to do so. Increasing use of kindergarten, nursery, and prenursery grades and the growing number of people attending colleges and universities suggest that the nuclear family is as important as a means of allocating privileges as it is as a means of providing cultural continuity.

Many village and band societies also temporarily separate their children and adolescents from the domestic scene in order to enculturate them with respect to traditional knowledge, sexual competence, and the military arts. With this separation the entire domestic routine of infancy and childhood sometimes comes to an abrupt end. Among the Gusii of Kenya young men move into bachelor huts, never to return to their former residences. A more drastic development of this alternative is found among the Nyakyusa of Southern Tanzania. At the age of about six or seven, Nyakyusa boys begin to put up reed shelters or playhouses on the outskirts of their village. These playhouses are gradually improved upon and enlarged, eventually leading to the construction of a whole new village. Between the ages of six and eleven, Nyakyusa boys sleep in their parents' house; but during adolescence they are permitted to visit only during daylight hours. Sleeping now takes place in the new village, although the mother still does the cooking. The founding of a new village is complete when the young men take wives who cook for them and begin to give birth to the next generation (Wilson 1963).

Another rather famous variation on this pattern is found among the Masai of East Africa where unmarried men of the same ritually

314

defined generation (*age-set*) establish special villages or camps from which they launch war parties and cattle-stealing raids. The mothers and sisters of these men cook and keep house for them.

The common English upper-class practice of sending sons six years of age or older to boarding schools should also be noted. Like the Masai, the English aristocracy never dreamed of letting the major burden of maintaining their society rest upon the educational resources of the nuclear household.

Togetherness

A precise examination of how members of domestic groups are deployed in time and space in relation to specific activities may lead to the conclusion that those involved are anything but "living together" in the sense appropriate to a modern suburban nuclear family household. In many societies married men spend a good deal of time in special men's houses. Food is handed in to them by wives and children who are themselves forbidden to enter. Men also sleep and work in these "clubhouses," although they may on occasion bed down with their wives and children. Under these circumstances much of the sexual activity between husband and wife takes place in the bush. An essentially similar pattern is reported for the Fur of the Sudan. Fur husbands usually sleep apart from their wives in houses of their own and take their meals at an exclusive men's mess. One of the most interesting cases of the separation of cooking and eating occurs among the Ashanti of West Africa. Ashanti men eat their meals with

Figure 15-4. MEXICAN PEASANT FAMILY. The mother is making tortillas on a skillet made from an oil drum. Note the manufactured items that cannot be produced in the household. (FAO)

315

their sisters, mothers, nephews, and nieces, not with their wives and children. But it is the wives who do the cooking. Every evening in Ashanti land there is a steady traffic of children taking their mother's cookery to their father's sister's house (cf. Barnes 1960; Bender 1967).

The ethnographic literature does not lack for even more dramatic infringements upon the spatial and functional unity of the nuclear family. Thus there is at least one famous case—the Nayar of Kerala—about which anthropologists believe that husband and wife do not live together. Nayar women formerly stayed with their brothers and sisters. Their mates were men who visited overnight. Children born of these sexual associations were brought up as part of a domestic scene dominated by their mother's brother.

For many years the Nayar have served anthropologists as a kind of exception that proves the rule—the rule of the universality of the nuclear family. But the pattern of Nayar domestic life fits within a continuum of adaptive family forms, none of which stands in splendid isolation or constitutes a quantum leap apart from all the others.

The Extended Family

In a significant proportion of the societies studied by anthropologists, domestic life is dominated by groupings larger than simple nuclear or polygamous families. Probably the majority of contemporary cultures still carry on their domestic routines in the context of some form of *extended family,* that is, a domestic group consisting of siblings, their spouses, and their children and/or parents and married children. Extended families may also be polygynous. A common form of extended family in Africa, for example, consists of two or more brothers, each with two or three wives, living with their adult sons, each of whom has one or two wives. Among the Bathonga of Southern Mozambique domestic life fell under the control of the senior males of the polygynous extended family's senior generation. These prestigious and powerful men in effect formed a board of directors of a family-style corporation. They were responsible for making managerial decisions about the domestic group's holdings in land, cattle, and buildings; they organized the subsistence effort of the co-resident labor force, especially of the women and children, assigning fields, crops, and work tasks on a daily and seasonal basis. Their explicit concern was to increase the size of their cattle herds, augment the available supplies of food and beer, obtain more wives, and increase the size and strength of the entire unit. (They differed from the directors of Euro-American family-owned corporations in that there

316

Figure 15-5. BILATERAL EXTENDED FAMILY ON A MINNESOTA FARM, 1895. The demand for labor was high (see Chapter 20.) (The Bettmann Archive)

were no purely monetary profits, cost balances were not precisely calculated, and work schedules reflected approximate and customary modes of time-reckoning.) The younger brothers, sons, and grandsons in the Bathonga extended families could reach adulthood, marry, build a hut, carry out subsistence tasks, and have children only as members of the larger group, subject to the policies and priorities established by the senior males. Nuclear families—if such can be said to exist—were never emically or etically independent units.

The corporate nature of extended family domestic units is also apparent in the case of Chinese households. Usually a monogamous senior couple carries out calculations regarding household size, domestic labor force, and marriage rates. Women brought into the household as wives for the senior couple's sons are placed under the direct control of their mother-in-law, who supervises almost their entire domestic routine, including cleaning, cooking, and raising children. Where there are several daughters-in-law, cooking chores are often rotated so that on any given day a maximum contingent of the domestic labor force can be sent to work in the family's fields (Myron L. Cohen 1975). The degree to which the nuclear constellation is submerged and effaced by these arrangements is brought out by a custom formerly found in certain Taiwanese households: "adopt a daughter-in-law; marry a sister." In order to obtain control over their son's wife, the senior couple adopts a daughter. They bring this girl into the household at a very early age and train her to be hardworking

317

and obedient. Later they oblige their son to marry this stepsister, thereby preventing the formation of an economically independent nuclear family within their midst while at the same time conforming to the socially imposed incest prohibitions (A. Wolf 1968).

Among the Rajputs of Northern India, extended families take similar stern measures to maintain the subordination of each married pair. A young man and his wife are even forbidden to talk to each other in the presence of senior persons, meaning in effect that they "may converse only surreptitiously at night" (Minturn and Hitchcock 1963:241). Here the husband is not supposed to show an open concern for his wife's welfare; if she is ill, that is a matter for her mother-in-law or father-in-law to take care of. "The mother feeds her son even after he is married . . . she runs the family as long as she wishes to assume the responsibility."

As a final brief example of how extended families modify the nuclear constellation, there is Max Gluckman's wry comment on the Barotse of Zambia: "if a man becomes too devoted to his wife he is assumed to be the victim of witchcraft" (1955:60).

Is Marriage Universal?

The question of the universality of the nuclear family is closely bound up with the question of the universality of marriage. If the functional significance of the nuclear family depends on the larger context, so too does the meaning of marriage. Among the many ingenious attempts to define marriage as a universally occurring relationship, the definition proposed by Kathleen Gough, who has studied the Nayar, merits special attention. Here it is (you will have to read it more than once):

Marriage is a relationship established between a woman and one or more persons, which provides that a child born to the woman under circumstances not prohibited by the rules of the relationship, is accorded full birth-status rights common to normal members of his society or social stratum. [1968:68]

According to Gough, for most if not all societies this definition identifies a relationship "distinguished by the people themselves from all other kinds of relationships." Yet Gough's definition seems oddly at variance with English dictionary and native Western notions of marriage. First of all, there is no reference to rights and duties of sexual access, much less to simple sexual performance. More remarkable, if Gough's definition is accepted, the conclusion drawn would have to be that marriage need not involve a relationship between men

318

and women. She merely specifies that there must be a woman and "one or more other persons" of undefined sex! What accounts for these omissions?

The main reason for omitting mention of sexual rights and duties is, once again, the case of the Nayar. In order to bear children in a socially acceptable manner, pubescent Nayar girls had to go through a four-day ceremony that linked them with a man whom Gough identifies as a "ritual husband." Completion of this ceremony was a necessary prerequisite for the beginning of a Nayar woman's sexual and reproductive career. Henceforth she was free to have sexual relations with as many "visiting husbands" as she wished, provided that she did not violate the rules of caste and of incest. These visiting husbands spent one night at a time with her, leaving their weapons at the door to warn each other that they were inside. If a Nayar girl had a child without first acquiring a ritual husband, and if she could not get one of her visiting husbands (or any other male of suitable caste status) to acknowledge paternity, she was subject to punishment. Yet neither the ritual husband nor the visiting husbands exercised any control over the disposition of their wife's sexual favors.

Gough's reasons for defining marriage as a relationship between a woman and "persons" rather than between "a woman and a man" are based on several additional well-known ethnographic facts. It is clear, first of all, that polyandrous marriages involve a relationship between a woman and men, not *a* man. Second, there are several instances among African peoples—the Dahomey case is best known—in which a woman is said to marry one or more women. This is accomplished by having a woman who herself is already married to a man pay bride-price (see p. 324). The female bride-price payer becomes a "female husband." She founds a compound of her own by letting her "wives" become pregnant through relationships with designated males. The offspring of these unions fall under the control of the "female father" rather than the biological *genitors* (see p. 332).

Yet Gough's definition ignores the equally marriagelike relationships that have no women at all. Some anthropologists would like to include man-man relationships as marriage. For example, among the Kwakiutl, a man who desires to acquire the privileges associated with a particular chief can marry the chief's male heir. If the chief has no heirs, a man may marry the chief's right or left side, or a leg or an arm. In Euro-American culture, stable relationships between co-resident homosexual men are also often spoken of as marriage. It has been suggested that all reference to the sex of the people involved in the relationship should be omitted in the definition of marriage in order to accommodate these additional cases (Dillingham and Isaac

319

1975). But what is left of the concept of marriage after it is deprived of any necessary reference to the sex of the participants?

Legitimacy

The essence of the marital relationship, according to some anthropologists, is embodied in that portion of Gough's definition dealing with the assignment of "birth-status rights" to children. Children born to a married woman "under circumstances not prohibited by the rules of the relationship" (e.g., adultery) are legal or legitimate children. Children born to unmarried women are illegitimate. As Malinowski put it: "marriage is the licensing of parenthood."

The case for the universality of marriage rests on the claim that in the ideology of every society a distinction is drawn between legitimate or legal child-rearing and illegitimate or illegal child-rearing. I agree that in all societies women are discouraged from attempting to rear children or dispose of their newborn infants according to their own whim and capacities. But the concept of legal or legitimate childbirth is highly ethnocentric. Behind this concept lies the assumption that every society has a single, well-defined set of rules that identify legitimate and illegitimate births. There is the further assumption that those who violate these rules will be subject to punishment or disapproval. This view is ethnographically wrong on both counts. Many societies have several different sets of rules defining permissible modes of conception and child-rearing. Frequently enough some of these alternatives may be esteemed more highly than others, but the less esteemed modes do not necessarily place children in a status analogous to that of Western illegitimacy (Scheffler 1973:754–755). For example, among rural Brazilians there are four kinds of relationships between a man and a woman that provide children with full birthrights: church marriage, civil marriage, simultaneous church and civil marriage, and consensual marriage. For a woman the most esteemed way to have children is through simultaneous church and civil marriage. This mode legally entitles her to a portion of her husband's property upon his death. It also provides the added security of knowing that her husband cannot desert her and enter into a civil or religious marriage elsewhere. The least desirable mode is the consensual marriage, because the woman can make no property claims against her consort nor can she readily prevent him from deserting her. Yet the children of a consensual arrangement can make property claims against both father and mother while suffering no deprivation of birthrights in the form of

320

Figure 15-6. DAHOMEY FAMILY AT MEALTIME. They are eating manioc and mice. (FAO)

legal disadvantages or social disapproval (as long as the father acknowledges paternity).

Among the Dahomey, Herskovits (1938) reported thirteen different kinds of marriage determined largely by bride-price arrangements. Children enjoyed different birthrights depending on the type of marriage. In some modes the child was placed under the control of the father's domestic group, and in others, under the control of a domestic group headed by a "female father" (see above). The question here as elsewhere is not whether the child is legitimate but rather the specific type of rights, obligations, and groupings that emanate from different modes of sexual and reproductive relations. Most of the world's peoples are not concerned with the question of whether a child is legitimate but rather with the question of who will have the right of controlling the child's destiny. Thus failure to follow the preferred mode of conception and child-rearing rarely results in the child's economic deprivation or social ostracism. Western society has been a lamentable exception in this regard.

More frequently various degrees of punishment and disapproval are administered to the woman who fails to fulfill the preferred conditions for motherhood. Even in this respect, however, it is false to assume that women are everywhere subject to some form of disapproval if they depart from the normal course of child-rearing. Everything depends on the larger domestic and social context in which the woman has become pregnant. No society grants women complete "freedom of conception," but the restrictions placed on motherhood and the occasions for punishment and disapproval vary enormously.

Where the domestic scene is dominated by large extended families and where there are no strong restrictions on premarital sex, the pregnancy of a young unmarried woman is rarely the occasion for much concern. Under certain circumstances the birth of a child to an "unwed mother" may even be a source of comfort rather than an occasion for remonstrance. Among the Kadar of Northern Nigeria, as reported by M. G. Smith (1968), most marriages result from infant betrothals. These matches are arranged by the fathers of the bride and groom when the girl is three to six years old. Thus ten years or more may elapse before the bride goes to live with her betrothed. During this time a Kadar girl is not unlikely to become pregnant. This event will disturb no one even if the biological father is a man other than her future husband:

Kadar set no value on premarital chastity. It is fairly common for unmarried girls to be impregnated or to give birth to children by youths other than their betrothed. Offspring of such premarital pregnancies are members of the patrilineage . . . of the girl's betrothed and are welcomed as proof of the bride's fertility.   [1968:113]

Analogous situations are quite common among other societies whose domestic groups value children above chastity.

Functions of Marriage

Every society regulates the reproductive activities of its sexually mature adults. One way of achieving this regulation is to set forth rules that define the conditions under which sexual relations, pregnancy, birth, and child-rearing may take place and that allocate privileges and duties in connection with these conditions. Each society has its own sometimes unique combination of rules and rules for breaking rules in this domain. It would be a rather futile exercise to attempt to define marriage by any one ingredient in these rules—such as legitimation of children—even if such an ingredient could be shown to be universal. This point can be illustrated by enumerating some of the variable regulatory functions associated with institutions commonly identified as "marriage." The following list incorporates suggestions introduced by Edmund Leach.

322

1. To establish the legal father of a woman's children
2. To establish the legal mother of a man's children
3. To give the husband or his extended family control over the wife's sexual services
4. To give the wife or her extended family control over the husband's sexual services
5. To give the husband or his extended family control over the wife's labor power
6. To give the wife or her extended family control over the husband's labor power
7. To give the husband or his extended family control over the wife's property
8. To give the wife or her extended family control over the husband's property
9. To establish a joint fund of property for the benefit of children
10. To establish a socially significant relationship between the husband's and the wife's domestic groups

As Leach remarks, this list could be greatly extended, but the point is "that in no single society can marriage serve to establish all these types of rights simultaneously, nor is there any one of these rights, which is invariably established by marriage in every known society" (Leach 1968:76).

Too much effort has been expended on trying to arrive at a minimum definition of marriage. More important tasks are first, to describe the actual arrangements, domestic and extradomestic, through which sexual relations, birth, child-rearing, and the labor and reproductive power of the younger generation are controlled and regulated; second, to relate these actual arrangements to the various kinds of rules, sentiments, and beliefs about sex, birth, child-rearing, and control over children; and third, to explain the actual arrangements and their ideological concomitants in terms of the wider conditions of cultural life.

Nonetheless the term "marriage" is too useful to drop altogether. I shall employ it therefore in an ample rather than restrictive sense to mean the behavior, sentiments, and rules concerned with heterosexual mating and reproduction in domestic contexts. To accommodate the various sensitivities that may be injured by using this concept exclusively for heterosexual domestic mates, a simple expedient is available. Let such other relationships be designated as man-man marriages, woman-woman marriages, or by any other appropriate specific nomenclature. It is clear that these marriages have different ecological, demographic, economic, and ideological implications. Hence nothing is to be gained by arguing about whether they are "real" marriages.

Marriage in Extended Families

In extended families, marriage must be seen in the context of group as well as individual interests. Individuals serve the corporate interests of the domestic groups. Thus husbands in male-dominated extended families are assigned the task of closely supervising the productive and reproductive contributions of one or more specific women. For these services the husband is rewarded with the right to dispose of his wives' sexual favors. The larger domestic group, however, never loses interest in nor totally surrenders its rights to the productive, reproductive, and sexual functions of each husband's wives and children. Similarly the domestic groups from which wives are drawn (wives are rarely born in the same domestic units as their husbands for reasons shortly to be discussed) maintain a lasting, if relatively minor, interest in the productive, sexual, and reproductive functions of the same women and children. Marriage under these circumstances is aptly described as a "contract" between groups. This contract varies in content, and it influences not only present but future matings involving other members of both groups.

Among many herder-farmer peoples of Eastern and Southern Africa, the contractual relationship between extended families is expressed in the institution known as *bride-price*. These extended families exchange their daughter-sisters for wife-mothers. Of course the exchange of women is not equivalent to the selling and buying of automobiles or refrigerators in Euro-American price-market societies. The wife-receivers do not own their woman in any total sense; they must take good care of her or her brothers and "fathers" (i.e., her father and father's brothers) will demand that she be returned to them. Nonetheless the amount of bride-price is not fixed; it fluctuates from one contract to another. The traditional medium for wife-exchange was cattle, although other valuables such as iron tools were also used. (Nowadays government-fixed cash payments are the rule.) A family that had many daughter-sisters was in a favorable position. By trading women for cattle they could trade cattle back for women. The more cattle, the more mother-wives; the more mother-wives, the larger the reproductive and productive labor force and the greater the corporate material welfare and influence of the extended family. One of the most interesting aspects of bride-price is that the transfer of wealth from one group to another is carried out in installments: so much on initial agreement, more when the woman goes to live with her husband, and another, usually final, payment when she has her first child. Frequently enough failure to have a child voids the contract; the woman goes home to her brothers and fathers, and the

324

cattle are returned to her former husband's extended family (cf.
Goldschmidt 1973). Marriage under these circumstances is not a
sudden shift from one status to another completed in a half-hour
ceremony that confers exclusive sexual rights upon a conjugal pair
and legitimacy upon their offspring. Rather, it is the gradual detachment of a woman from one group and the gradual transfer to another
of her reproductive and productive capacities. Bride-price does not
confer legitimacy upon children; it merely transfers control over a
child's future from mother's family to father's family—from the
wife-givers to the bride-price-payers.

These examples reveal that the native Western view of marriage
and legitimacy suffers from the obsession that children cannot be
properly reared unless a specific male is legally encumbered with
exclusive responsibility for each child's welfare. United States marriage laws presume that fathers regard the raising of children as
burdensome and that men must be coerced into accepting this responsibility. These sentiments are not mere fantasies; they arise instead
from definite features of economy and social organization. But they
are not universally applicable. Assignment of paternity is important
among most peoples not because the burden of child-rearing must be
shouldered by the offending male, but because one corporate extended
family vies with another to give birth to and to rear as many children
as possible.

325

Marital Reciprocity between Domestic Groups

Bride-price is one of many forms of economic exchanges associated with marriage that reveal the corporate interests of domestic groups in the productive and reproductive value of their women. Bride-price prevails where women are scarce and where ecological conditions permit domestic groups to intensify production by putting more women and children to work.

A common alternate form of bride-price is known as *bride-service*. The groom or husband compensates his in-laws by working for them for several months or years before taking his bride away to live and work with him and his extended family. Rare by comparison is the transfer of valuables to the groom's family, known in Western civilization as *dowry*. This usually occurs where women and children are economic liabilities and where there are large numbers of unmarried women. Dowry should not be confused with "groom-price," a logically conceivable but ethnographically nonexistent compensation to a man's family for the loss of a valuable able-bodied male (Goody and Tambiah 1973:6). This form does not occur because even when males go to live with their wife's family, they usually remain in effective control of the domestic groups in which they were reared (see p. 345). The nonexistence of groom-price is closely related to the nonexistence of matriarchies and the pervasiveness of male supremacy, a matter to which I shall give special attention later on. What does occur quite frequently, however, is a two-way symmetrical exchange of token-valuables between the bride's family and the groom's family. One side thus acknowledges the economic importance of the woman it has received while the other side makes known its intention not to lose interest in the daughter-sister it has lost nor in the children she may bear. Also common is the practice of *sister-exchange* in which reciprocity between two domestic groups is maintained not by exchanging valuables but by exchanging the groom's sister for his bride.

Domestic Groups and the Fear of Incest

All these exchanges point to the existence of a profound paradox in the way human beings find mates. Instead of marrying the women who are born within the domestic group—their sisters and daughters—males export these women, thereby imposing upon themselves the task of finding replacements. This practice of "marrying out" is known as *exogamy*. The opposite practice—"marrying in"—is known as *endogamy*. Certain forms of endogamy are universally prohibited:

326

father-daughter and mother-son marriages. Sister-brother marriage is also almost universally prohibited except for the ruling class among highly stratified states such as the Inca, the ancient Hawaiians, and ancient Egypt. In the emics of Western civilization, sister-brother, father-daughter, and mother-son marriages are called "incest." Why are these marriages so widely prohibited?

Here I shall try to answer that question only with regard to band and village societies. Contrary to popular opinion, close inbreeding in small populations is not necessarily deleterious for the population. Individuals homozygous for deleterious recessive genes will suffer higher death rates and lowered fertility, but as Frank Livingstone (1969) has pointed out, inbreeding may also lead to the gradual elimination of deleterious recessive genes. In other words, if a small inbreeding group is able to overcome the higher rate at which deleterious homozygotes initially appear, it will eventually reach a genetic equilibrium involving a lowered percentage of deleterious genes. It has often been pointed out that the effects of close inbreeding in a small group depend upon the original frequency of deleterious genes. Theoretically a succession of nuclear families could practice inbreeding for several generations without adverse effects. Cleopatra, Queen of Egypt, was the product of eleven generations of brother-sister marriage within the Ptolemaic dynasty. This should not be passed on as a recommendation to friends and relatives since the odds (in modern populations) appear to be very much against such felicitous results (Adams and Neil 1967).

But modern populations are carrying a much greater load of harm-

Domestic Groups and the Fear of Incest

ful recessives than is found in small groups of demographically stable band and village peoples. The chances of genetic catastrophes arising among groups that are highly inbred to begin with is much less than in a modern heterozygous industrial society. Indeed, Livingstone makes the point that many of the smallest, most inbred village groups, such as the Kaingang of Central Brazil, have remarkably low frequencies of deleterious recessives. The reason for this is twofold: first, harmful recessive genes are more likely to occur in the homozygous condition when the choice of mates is restricted to one hundred people rather than a million or more; second, because of the practice of infanticide, small band and village groups seldom permit homozygous carriers of deleterious genes to live to reproductive age.

Infanticide is a much more direct and efficient solution to the problem of homozygous misfits than is the development of abstract rules of exogamy and incest avoidance. Through infanticide a small inbreeding group could rapidly reduce its load of nonlethal recessives below that of a comparable exogamous group. Finally, a purely biological theory of exogamy is hard to reconcile with the widespread occurrence of endogamous practices that are carried out simultaneously and in support of the exogamic arrangements. Members of exogamous extended families frequently are involved in marriage systems that encourage them to mate with one kind of first cousin (*cross cousin*) but not another (*parallel cousin*, see p. 335). The difference between these two forms of inbreeding cannot be explained by selection for heterozygosity. Furthermore the widespread preference for some form of cousin marriage itself weighs against the conclusion that exogamy expresses a principle established by fear of biological inbreeding.

The explanation of the prohibition on father-daughter, mother-son, and sister-brother marriages in band and village cultures probably lies in the advantageous demographic and ecological consequences of exogamy. Bands rely on marriage relationships to establish networks of kinspeople over many hundreds of square miles. Any group that formed a completely closed breeding unit would be denied the mobility and territorial flexibility that are essential to the subsistence strategy of groups like the Eskimo and Bushmen. Territorially restricted, endogamous bands of twenty to thirty people would also run a high risk of extinction as a result of sexual imbalances caused by an unlucky run of male births and adult female deaths, which would place the burden for the group's reproduction on one or two aging females. Exogamy is thus essential for the effective utilization of a small population's productive and reproductive potential. Once a band begins to obtain women from other bands, the prevalence of

328

reciprocal economic relations leads to the expectation that the receivers will reciprocate with a sister or daughter of their own. The taboos on mother-son, father-daughter, and brother-sister marriages defend these reciprocal exchange relationships against the ever-present temptation to keep one's children for oneself.

Among village horticulturalists, exogamy also increases the total productive and reproductive strength of the intermarried groups. It permits the exploitation of resources over a larger tract or region than the constituent groups could manage on an individual basis; it raises the upper limit of the size of groups that can be formed to carry out coordinated activities (e.g., communal game drives, harvests, and so on); and it allows several different kinds of task groups to carry out specialized subsistence activities simultaneously in a variety of microenvironments. Furthermore where intergroup warfare poses a threat to group survival, the ability to mobilize countervailing numbers of warriors is decisive. Hence in militaristic, highly male-centered village cultures, sisters and daughters are frequently used as pawns in the establishment of shifting alliances. These alliances do not necessarily promote peace, as might be expected from the presence of sisters and daughters in the enemy's ranks (Tefft 1975); but they are an integral part of the whole warfare system whose profound demographic and ecological consequences have already been discussed (Ch. 13).

Preferential Marriages

Because of exogamy, corporate interests of domestic groups are protected by rules that stipulate who is to marry whom. Having given a woman away in marriage, most groups expect either material wealth or women in exchange. Consider two domestic groups, A and B, each with a core of resident brothers. If A gives a sister to B, B will have to reciprocate by giving a woman to A. This reciprocity is often achieved, as I have said, by a direct exchange of one of B's sisters. But it is also frequently achieved by having B's sister's daughter marry one of A's sons. The bride in such a marriage will be her husband's father's sister's daughter, and the groom will be his wife's mother's brother's son. Bride and groom are each other's cross cousins (see p. 335). If A and B have a rule that such marriages are to occur whenever possible, then they are said to have *preferential cross-cousin marriage.*

Reciprocity in marriage is sometimes achieved by several intermarrying domestic groups that exchange women in cycles. For example, A → B → C → A; or A↔ B and C↔ D in one generation and A↔ D and

B$\longleftrightarrow$C in the next, and then back to A$\rightarrow\leftarrow$B and C$\rightarrow\leftarrow$D. These exchanges establish domestic alliances that are known as *circulating connubia.* They are enforced by preferential marriage with appropriate kinds of cousins, nephews, nieces, and other kin types.

Another common manifestation of corporate domestic interest in marriage is the practice of supplying replacements for in-marrying women who die prematurely. To maintain reciprocity or to fulfill a marriage contract for which bride-price has been paid, the deceased woman's brother may permit the widower to marry one or more of his wife's sisters. This custom is known as the *sororate.* Closely related to this practice is the preferential marriage known as the *levirate,* in which the services of a man's widows are retained within the domestic unit by having them marry one of his brothers. If the widows are old, these services may be minimal and the levirate then functions to provide security for women who would otherwise not be able to remarry.

To sum up: the organization of domestic life everywhere reflects the fact that husbands and wives originate in different domestic groups that continue to maintain a sentimental and practical interest in the marriage partners and their children.

KINSHIP

The comparison of the domestic life of hundreds of cultures all over the world has led anthropologists to conclude that there are two universally held cognitive principles that influence the organization of domestic life everywhere. The first of these is the principle of *affinity,* or of relationships through marriage. The second is the principle of *descent,* or parentage. All persons whose relationship to each other can be described in terms of a combination of affinity or descent or a combination of both are kin to each other. The domain of ideas constituted by the beliefs and expectations that kin share with each other is called *kinship.* Kinship is the paramount ideology of domestic life.

Descent*

Kinship relationships must not be confused with biological relationships. The cultural meaning of marriage and descent is not the equivalent of biological mating and descent. As I have pointed out (p. 319), marriage may explicitly establish "parentage" with respect to children who are biologically unrelated to their culturally defined "father." Even where a culture insists that descent must be based on actual biological fatherhood, domestic arrangements may make the

*British social anthropologists restrict the term "descent" to relationships extending over more than two generations and use "filiation" to denote descent relationships within the nuclear family (Fortes 1969).

identification of the biological father extremely difficult. For these reasons anthropologists have come to distinguish between the culturally defined "father" and the *genitor,* the actual biological father. A similar distinction is necessary in the case of "mother." Although the culturally defined mother is usually the *genetrix,* the widespread practice of adoption creates many discrepancies between emic and etic motherhood.

The separation of biological and cultural kinship must also take into account the great gulf that separates folk concepts of the procreative process from the modern biological understanding of reproduction and heredity. The meaning of descent varies enormously from culture to culture. As a matter of fact, if one tries to give a universally valid definition of descent one can say no more than that it is the belief that married people play a distinctive role in the formation and birth of their culturally designated children. Any attempt to become more graphic and to "flesh out" the contents of the beliefs, conscious and unconscious, that justify and organize descent relationships immediately runs into difficulties. Different cultures profess remarkably different theories about how human procreation occurs. Nonetheless, "so far as we know, no human society is without such a theory" (Scheffler 1973:749).

In Western folk traditions, married pairs are linked to children on the basis of the belief that male and female make equally important contributions to the child's being. The male's semen is regarded as analogous to seed, and the woman's womb is analogous to the field in which the seed is planted. Blood, the most important life-sustaining and life-defining fluid, supposedly varies according to parentage. Each child's veins are thought of as being filled with blood obtained from mother and father. As a result of this imagery "blood relatives" are distinguished from relatives who are linked only through marriage. This led nineteenth-century anthropologists to denote descent relationships by the unfortunately ethnocentric term *consanguine* (of the same blood).

Obviously descent need not depend upon the idea of blood inheritance, nor need it involve equal contributions from both father and mother. The Ashanti, for example, believe that blood is contributed only by the mother and that it determines only a child's physical characteristics. An Ashanti child's spiritual disposition and temperament is the product of the father's semen. The Alorese of Indonesia believe that the child is formed by a mixture of seminal and menstrual fluids, which accumulate for two months before beginning to solidify. Many people share this idea of a slow growth of the fetus as a result of repeated additions of semen during pregnancy. For the polyandrous

332

Tamil of Malabar, the semen of several different males is believed to contribute to the growth of the same fetus. The Eskimo believe that pregnancy results when a spirit child climbs up a woman's bootstraps and is nourished by semen. But the Trobrianders profess a famous dogma denying any procreative role to the semen whatsoever. Here also, a woman becomes pregnant when a spirit child climbs into her vagina. The only physical function of the Trobriand male is to widen the passageway into the womb. The Trobriand "father" nonetheless has an essential social role, since no self-respecting spirit child would climb into a Trobriand girl who was not married.

A similar denial of the male's procreative role occurs throughout Australia; among the Murngin, for example, there was the belief that the spirit children live deep below the surface of certain sacred water holes. For conception to take place, one of these spirits appears in the future father's dreams. In the dream the spirit child introduces itself and asks its father to point out the woman who is to become its mother. Later, when this woman passes near the sacred water hole, the spirit child swims out in the form of a fish and enters her womb.

Thus, despite the many different kinds of theories about the nature of procreative roles, there is worldwide acknowledgment of some special contributory action linking both husband and wife to the reproductive process, although they may be linked quite unevenly and with vastly different expectations concerning rights and obligations.

Descent Rules

Duties, rights, and privileges with respect to many different aspects of social life are assigned to individuals by reckoning their descent relationships. A person's name, family, residence, rank, property, and basic ethnic and national identity may all depend on such *ascriptions* independent of any validating *achievements* other than getting born and staying alive.

Two great classes of descent rules have been identified by anthropologists: the *cognatic* and the *unilineal.* Cognatic descent rules are those in which both male and female parentage is used to establish any of the above-mentioned duties, rights, and privileges. Unilineal rules accomplish the same results by restricting parental links either exclusively to males or exclusively to females. The most common form of *cognatic rule* is *bilateral descent,* the reckoning of kinship evenly and symmetrically along maternal and paternal lines in ascending and descending generations through individuals of both sexes (Fig. 16-2).

333

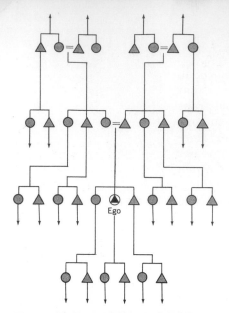

Figure 16-2. BILATERAL DESCENT. Everyone on the diagram has a descent relationship with Ego.

Figure 16-3. AMBILINEAL DESCENT. Ego traces descent through both males and females but not equally and not simultaneously.

△ MALE

○ FEMALE

= IS MARRIED TO

| IS DESCENDED FROM

⌐⌐ IS THE SIBLING OF

▲ EGO WHOSE GENEALOGY IS BEING SHOWN

Figure 16-1. HOW TO READ KINSHIP DIAGRAMS.

The second main variety of cognatic rule is called *ambilineal* descent (Fig. 16-3). Here the descent lines traced by *ego* ignore the sex of the parental links, but the lines do not lead in all directions evenly. As in bilateral descent, ego traces descent through males and females but the line twists back and forth, including some female ancestors or descendants but excluding others and including some male ancestors or descendants and excluding others. In other words, ego does not reckon descent simultaneously and equally through mothers and fathers.

There are also two main varieties of unilineal descent: *patrilineality* and *matrilineality*. When descent is reckoned patrilineally, ego follows the ascending and descending genealogical lines through males only (Fig. 16-4). Note that this does not mean that the descent-related individuals are only males; in each generation there are relatives of both sexes. However, in the passage from one generation to another only the male links are relevant; children of females are dropped from the descent reckoning.

When descent is reckoned matrilineally, ego follows the ascending and descending lines through females only (Fig. 16-5). Once again, it should be noted that males as well as females can be related matrilineally; it is only in the passage from one generation to another that the children of males are dropped from the descent reckoning.

One of the most important logical consequences of unilineal descent is that it segregates the children of siblings of the opposite sex

334

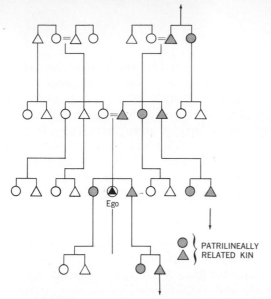

Figure 16-4. PATRILINEAL DESCENT. Descent is traced exclusively through males.

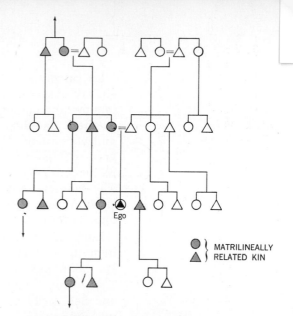

Figure 16-5. MATRILINEAL DESCENT. Descent is traced exclusively through females.

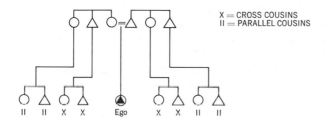

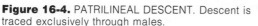

X = CROSS COUSINS
II = PARALLEL COUSINS

Figure 16-6. CROSS COUSINS AND PARALLEL COUSINS.

into distinct categories. This effect is especially important in the case of cousins. Note that with patrilineal descent, ego's father's sister's son and daughter do not share common descent with ego, whereas ego's father's brother's son and daughter do share common descent with ego. In the case of matrilineal descent, the same kind of distinction results with respect to ego's "cousins" on the mother's side. In view of the large number of cultures in which distinctions of this sort occur, anthropologists apply the terms *cross cousin* to children of brother and sister and *parallel cousin* to children of brother and brother or sister and sister (Fig. 16-6).

Anthropologists distinguish an additional variety of descent rule, called *double descent,* in which ego simultaneously reckons descent matrilineally through mother and patrilineally through father.

Many other combinations of the aforementioned descent rules may also occur. In all cultures, for example, there is some degree of

335

bilateral descent in the reckoning of rights and obligations. If a society observes patrilineal descent in the grouping of people into landowning corporations, this does not mean that ego and mother's brother's daughter do not regard each other as having special rights and obligations. Euro-American culture is strongly bilateral in kin group composition and inheritance of wealth and property; yet family names are *patronymic*—that is, they follow patrilineal descent lines. The point is that all varieties of descent may theoretically occur simultaneously within a given society as long as the descent rules are applied for different purposes.

Each of the above descent rules provides the logical basis for mentally aligning people into abstract or ideal kinship categories. Of special interest are the alignments of people into emic kinship groups. These groups have an important influence on the way people think and behave in both domestic and extradomestic situations. I shall proceed now to a description of the principal varieties of such groups.

Cognatic Descent Groups: Bilateral Variety

If bilateral descent is applied to an indefinitely wide span and to an indeterminate number of generations, there results the logical outline

Figure 16-7. KINDREDS. Children have kindreds that are different from either parent's kindred.

Figure 16-8. COGNATIC LINEAGE. Descent is traced to an apical ancestor through males and/or females.

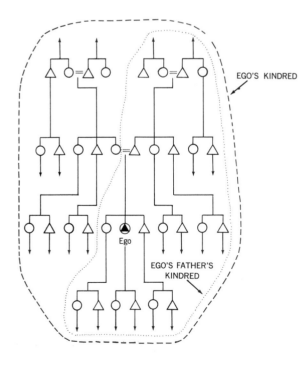

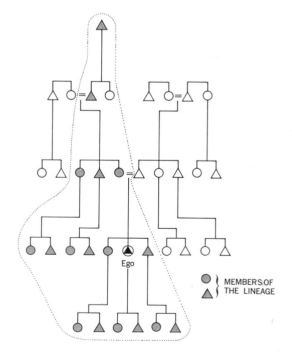

of the *kindred.* This group is familiar to Euro-Americans as the "family" when something other than the nuclear family is being referred to. The main characteristic of the kindred is that the span and depth of bilateral reckoning is open-ended. Relatives within ego's kindred can be judged as "near" or "far" depending on the number of genealogical links that separate them, but there is no definite or uniform principle for making such judgments or for terminating the extension of the kinship circle. An important consequence of this feature, as shown in Figure 16-7, is that egos and their siblings are identified with a kindred whose membership cannot be the same for any other persons (except for ego's *"double cousins"*—cousins whose parents are two brothers who have exchanged sisters). This means that it is practically impossible for co-resident domestic groups to consist of kindreds and very difficult for kindreds to maintain corporate interests in land and people.

Cognatic Descent Groups: Ambilineal Variety

The open-ended, ego-centered characteristics of the bilateral kindred can be overcome by specifying one or more ancestors from whom descent is traced either through males and/or females. The resultant grouping has a logical membership that is potentially the same regardless of which ego carries out the reckoning. Because the characteristics of ambilineal descent began to be identified only in the 1950s, a considerable amount of disagreement still reigns concerning what to call such groups. The name *cognatic lineage* (the terms *ramage* and *sept* are also in use) perhaps best describes the logical status involved (Fig. 16-8).

The cognatic lineage is based on the assumption that all members of the descent group are capable of specifying the precise genealogical links relating them to the lineage founder. A common alternative, as in the ambilineal "clans" of Scotland, is for the descent from the lineage founder to be *stipulated* rather than *demonstrated.* This can be done easily enough if the name of the founder gets passed on ambilineally over many generations. After a while many of the persons who carry the name will belong to the group simply by virtue of the name rather than because they can trace their genealogical relationship all the way back to the founding ancestor. An appropriate designation for such groups is *cognatic clan.*

Unilineal Descent Groups

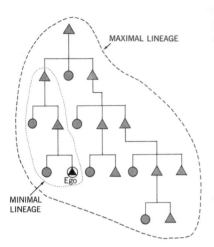

Figure 16-9. PATRILIN-EAGES. Everyone on the diagram belongs to the same maximal lineage.

When unilineal descent is systematically demonstrated with respect to a particular ancestor, the resultant kin group is called a *matrilineage* or a *patrilineage*. All lineages contain the same set of people regardless of the genealogical perspective from which they are viewed. This makes them ideally suited to hold joint interests in persons and property. Because of exogamy, however, both sexes cannot remain co-resident beyond childhood. Some lineages include all the generations and collateral descendants of the apical ancestor. These are *maximal* lineages. Lineages that contain only three generations are *minimal* lineages (Fig. 16-9).

When unilineal descent from a specific ancestor is stipulated rather than demonstrated, the group that results is known as either a *patriclan* or a *matriclan* (the terms *patrisib* and *matrisib* are also in use). There are many borderline cases, however, in which it is difficult to decide whether one is dealing with a lineage or a clan. Just as lineages may contain lineages, clans may contain clans, usually called *subclans.* Finally it should be noted that clans may also contain lineages.

Factors Promoting Bilateral Descent

In the view of the great pioneer of cross-cultural kinship research, Lewis Henry Morgan, descent principles and descent groups formed a simple evolutionary series. According to Morgan and many other nineteenth-century theorists, matrilineality everywhere preceded patrilineality. Morgan reasoned that the most primitive cultures were endogamous and promiscuous. Under such circumstances one could never be sure of paternity. Hence descent could only be reckoned matrilineally. While "savages" were still in a matrilineal phase they invented the clan, which Morgan interpreted essentially as a device for extending the biological benefits of exogamy. Hence the first clans were matriclans. Later, with the development of greater concentrations of wealth, patrilineality and patriclans replaced the institutions of the matrilineal stage. Finally, with the growth of "civilization" and a more "rational" outlook, both the matrilineal and patrilineal principles received equal emphasis, leading to the Euro-American bilateral family.

In modern perspective Morgan's attempt to order the appearance of descent rules in an evolutionary progression has been totally invalidated. (Not all of Morgan's ideas have suffered the same fate.) To

338

begin with, bilateral descent is the main ideological kinship principle in the domestic life not only of contemporary Euro-American industrial societies but also of the great majority of the world's band-organized hunters and gatherers. This fact does not mean that kinship phenomena are whimsical fantasies nor that domestic organizations have not evolved in an orderly fashion. It means rather that the domestic patterns of band-organized and of industrial societies possess certain functional similarities. These have to do with the mobility of family units, their constant shifting from one domestic context to another, in and out of open local communities.

The ecological and economic basis for this mobility is quite different for Euro-Americans as compared with the Eskimo or the Bushman. In the hunting and gathering context, people move from one set of bilateral kin to another. The entire world for these hunters is peopled with kin, and all aspects of life—from subsistence to ceremony—are mediated by the web of kinship relations created through nuclear and extended family exogamy and bilateral descent. Bilateral descent and kindreds therefore help to smooth the way for the ecologically imposed social arrangements of many hunting and gathering peoples.

The hunter-gatherer local group commonly has a genealogical core consisting of females *and* males. According to Richard Lee, mother-daughter bonds predominate followed by sister-sister and brother-sister; but father-son, and brother-brother bonds are also common. The key to band structure is not the maintenance of exclusive rights to land by a core of jealous males, "but the maintenance of the flexibility to adapt to changing ecological circumstance." Among the Bushmen about 15 percent of the people make a relatively permanent shift from one camp to another each year, while another 35 percent divide their time equally between periods of residence at two or three different camps (Lee 1972b).

In the Euro-American case the nuclear family is not only highly mobile, it is also in a permanent state of physical and social detachment from almost all other kin. This is reflected in the fact that the typical newly married Euro-American couple lives neither with the wife's family nor the husband's family—postmarital residence is *neolocal.* Hunters and gatherers like the Bushmen, on the other hand, usually reside alternately with the wife's or the husband's family or both—a residence practice known as *bilocality* (see p. 342).

Obviously the mobility and detachment of Euro-American nuclear families does not arise from the fluctuating supply of springbok and wild yams. It arises mainly from the pervasive individualizing and isolating effects of wage labor, industrial production, and commercial markets. The Detroit production-line worker does not need a brother-

339

in-law to get a job; wage labor is done as efficiently by complete strangers as by relatives. To obtain food from the local supermarket, no one asks who your father is. Furthermore it is obvious that enormous economic interests depend upon and sustain the practice of neolocality. The modern nuclear family is not so much a production unit as it is a consumption unit; the bulk of nonmilitary, agricultural, and industrial consumption takes place through and within the nuclear domestic sphere. Each nuclear family has its own house or apartment; it does its own cooking and rides in its own automobile. Maintenance of the rate of formation of independent nuclear households is essential to the stability of the price-market economy.

Neolocality is so firmly embedded in modern Euro-American social and economic life that government planners and business people scarcely give it a second thought. For the same reason, it appears completely "natural" to reckon descent bilaterally. If Americans are asked why they practice neolocality, they respond by pointing to the problem of living with a mother-in-law or of having two women in one kitchen and to the importance of raising one's own children. It is clear, however, that these are rationalizations for patterns whose causes lie at a deeper level. Most of the world's cultures have found living with a mother-in-law, several women in the kitchen, and joint family residence to be perfectly feasible and "natural."

Determinants of Cognatic Lineages and Clans

Cognatic lineages and cognatic clans are associated with *ambilocality.* This is a form of postmarital residence in which the married couple elect to stay on a relatively permanent basis either with the wife's or the husband's domestic group. Ambilocality differs from the neolocality of the American family since residence is established with a definite group of ambilineal kin. Ambilocality also differs from the bilocality of hunting and gathering bands in that the shifting from one domestic group to another occurs less frequently. This implies a relatively more sedentary form of village life and also a somewhat greater potential for developing exclusive corporate interests in people and property. Yet all cognatic descent groups, whether bilateral or ambilineal, have less potential for corporate unity than unilineal descent groups, a point to which I shall return in a moment.

One example of how cognatic lineages work has already been discussed. Such lineages occurred among the Pacific Northwest Coast potlatchers. You will recall (p. 294) that the Kwakiutl potlatch chiefs sought to attract and to hold as large a labor force as they

340

possibly could. Among the Kwakiutl the production of salmon, fish oil, seals, and other sea mammals was essentially a matter of labor input. The more people a village put to work during a salmon run, the more fish they would catch.

The core of each village consisted of a chieftain and his followers, usually demonstrably related to him through ambilineal descent and constituting a cognatic lineage known as a *numaym*. The chieftain claimed hereditary privileges and noble rank on the basis of ambilineal reckoning from his noble forebears. Validation of this status depended upon his ability to recruit and hold an adequate following in the face of competition from like-minded neighbor chieftains. Notice the importance placed upon individual choice and the uncertainty surrounding the group's corporate estate.

Cognatic versus Unilineal Groups

Although there is no basis for reviving nineteenth-century notions of universal stages in the evolution of kinship, certain well-substantiated general evolutionary trends must be acknowledged. Hunting and gathering band societies tend to have cognatic descent groups and/or bilocal residence because their basic ecological adjustment demands that local groups remain open, flexible, and nonterritorial. With the development of horticulture and more settled village life, the identification between domestic groups or villages and definite territories increased and became more exclusive. Population density increased and warfare became more intense, for reasons already discussed (Ch. 13), contributing to the need for emphasizing exclusive group unity and solidarity. Under these conditions, unilineal descent groups with well-defined localized membership cores, a heightened sense of solidarity, and an ideology of exclusive rights over resources and people became the predominant form of kinship groups. Using a sample of 797 agricultural societies, Michael Harner (1970) has shown that a very powerful statistical association exists between an increased reliance on agriculture as opposed to hunting and gathering and the replacement of cognatic descent groups by unilineal descent groups.

This is not a one-way process, however. Reversion to cognatic forms can be expected if warfare is eliminated and/or population declines precipitously. Kwakiutl cognatic descent groups probably represent such reversions from formerly unilineal organizations. As will be recalled, the Kwakiutl population was decimated as a result of contagious diseases introduced by Euro-American and Russian traders.

Horticultural village societies that are organized unilineally out-number those that are organized cognatically 380 to 111 in Harner's sample. Moreover almost all the unilineal societies display marked signs of population pressure as measured by the extent to which they have exhausted their wild plant and food resources.

Unilineal Descent and Locality Practices

Unilineal lineages and clans show a close correspondence with unilocal residence. There are two basic patterns of unilocal residence: (1) *patrilocality:* brothers and sons remain in their fathers' domestic unit, sisters and daughters move out, wives move in; (2) *matrilocality:* sisters and daughters remain in their mothers' domestic unit, brothers and sons move out, husbands move in.

PRINCIPAL VARIETIES OF POST-MARITAL RESIDENCE RULES

Name of Rule	Place Where Married Couple Resides
neolocality	apart from either husband's or wife's kin
bilocality	alternately shifting from husband's kin to wife's kin
ambilocality	some couples with husband's kin, others with wife's kin
patrilocality	with husband's father
matrilocality	with wife's mother
avunculocality	with husband's mother's brother
amitalocality	with wife's father's sister (This rule has no empirical example and is important only as a theoretical possibility.)
uxorilocality	with the wife's kin (Several of the above may be described as uxorilocality.)
virilocality	with the husband's kin (Several of the above may be described as virilocality.)

One other kind of residence pattern is also closely related to the formation of unilineal descent groups. This type is called *avunculo-cality.* Here mother's brothers and sister's sons form the core of the

Figure 16-10. AVUNCU-LOCALITY.

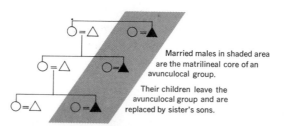

Married males in shaded area are the matrilineal core of an avunculocal group.

Their children leave the avunculocal group and are replaced by sister's sons.

domestic unit; sister's sons are born in her husband's mother's brother's household, but as juveniles or adults, sister's sons leave this household and take up residence with their own mother's brother (Fig. 16-10). The way in which avunculocality works will become clearer in the discussion of its functions with respect to male supremacy in matrilineal societies (see below).

The Prevalence of Patrilocality and Patrilineality

It should come as no surprise after the discussion of female infanticide and the male-centered warfare complex (Ch. 13) that the overwhelming majority of known societies have male-centered residence and descent patterns. Seventy-one percent of 1,179 societies classified by George Murdock (1967) are either patrilocal or virilocal; and in the same sample, societies that have patrilineal kin groups outnumber societies that have matrilineal kin groups 588 to 164. The factors that account for most of the patrilocal-patrilineal cases have already been discussed. These include high population density, limited land and resources, frequent warfare, and concentrated forms of wealth such as standing crops, garden plots, animal herds, or granaries. Under such conditions residence will tend to be patrilocal. Patrilocality concentrates the male strength of the domestic unit; it physically aligns father and sons and brothers with respect to common interests in property and people. And this commonality of material interests in turn gives rise to the ideology of patrilineal descent and fraternal solidarity. Since the development of horticulture and sedentary village life, patrilocality and patrilineal ideologies have been the statistically "normal" mode of domestic organization. They have been predominant not only, as was once thought, in societies that have plows and draft animals or that practice pastoral nomadism but in simple horticultural and slash-and-burn societies as well (Divale 1974).

Matrilocality and Matrilineality

Matrilineal descent groups will not form independently—that is, in the absence of matrilineal neighbors—unless matrilocality is the postmarital residence practice. Until recently it was believed that most cases of matrilocality arose when women exercised a predominant economic role with respect to vital subsistence activities. Ma-

343

trilocality was thought to be likely where women produced most of the food supply, especially where gardening predominated over hunting and where males did not operate animal-drawn plows. It has been shown conclusively, however, that there is no greater association between horticulture and matrilocality than between horticulture and patrilocality (Ember and Ember 1971; Divale 1974). In view of the evidence presented in previous chapters that women are almost always more productively and reproductively valuable than men in low-energy band and village societies, it makes little sense to look for the explanation of matrilocality in the relative value of female and male subsistence activities. If female labor value was crucial, then most of the world's societies would be matrilineal rather than patrilineal. There may actually be a negative correlation between the contribution of women to subsistence and their status in relation to men (Sanday 1973). Where women work harder, they are likely to nurse their children for shorter periods, have children more often, and suffer from poorer health (cf. Nerlove 1974).

The development of matrilocality and matrilineal domestic units is probably closely tied in with a number of factors (to be identified in a moment) that oblige males to spend much of their time away from the domestic scene. When patrilocal males leave a village for extended periods they leave behind their patrilineal kin group's corporate interests in property and people to be looked after solely by their wives. The allegiance of their wives however is to their own patrilineal kin groups. The local group's women are drawn from different kin groups and have little basis for cooperative activity when they are unsupervised by the male managers of the corporate domestic units into which they have married. There is no one home, so to speak, "to mind the store." Matrilocality solves this problem because it structures the domestic unit around a permanent core of resident mothers, daughters, and sisters who are trained in cooperative labor patterns from birth and who identify the "minding of the store" with their own material and sentimental interests.

Matrilocality releases women from the dominance of their husbands. The in-marrying males remain "strangers" in their wive's domestic unit. Indeed, they are rather like temporary visitors. Since a man's children do not "belong" to him, divorce is easy. If friction begins to develop between him and his wife, he bundles up his personal effects and goes "home" to his sisters. Or, as among the Hopi, the wife may take the initiative and put her husband's belongings outside the door. But matrilocality does not prevent women from being dominated by males. Rather, it usually merely renders them subordinate to their brothers instead of their husbands. It is a wo-

344

man's brothers who exercise authority over the woman's children and who make the crucial decisions affecting the matrilineal kin group's property and personnel (Schlegel 1972).

Whereas some anthropologists argue that there are, or have been truly egalitarian societies . . . and all agree that there are societies in which women have achieved considerable social recognition and power, none has observed a society in which women have publicly recognized power and authority surpassing that of men. . . . Everywhere we find that women are excluded from certain crucial economic or political activities, that their roles as wives and mothers are associated with fewer powers and prerogatives than are the roles of men.   [Rosaldo and Lamphere 1974:3]

Contradictions within Matrilineal Systems

Due to the continuing vitality of the male supremacist complex within matrilocal and matrilineal societies, matrilineal domestic groups are highly unstable structures. In masculinized matrilineal societies, males are reluctant to relinquish control over their own sons to the members of their wives' kin groups, and they are not easily reconciled to the fact that it is their sons rather than their daughters who must move away from them at marriage. Because of this contradiction, matrilocal-matrilineal systems tend to revert to patrilocal-patrilineal systems as soon as the forces responsible for keeping males away from their natal village and domestic groups are removed or moderated.

A statistical indication of the continuing strength of the male complex within matrilocal-matrilineal systems is that matrilocal marriages are usually village-endogamous, whereas patrilocal marriages are usually village-exogamous (cf. Divale 1974). This is best explained on the assumption that it is advantageous for the male to have his sister and wife in the same village. With village endogamy the male members of the matrilineal corporation need experience little inconvenience in personally supervising the affairs of their joint estate.

One other way to solve the same dilemma is to loosen the male's marital obligations (already weak in matrilocal societies) to the point where he need not live with his wife at all. This is the path followed by the Nayar. The Nayar matrilineal-matrilocal descent group, the *taravad,* reproduced itself through visiting "husbands" who spent the night and nothing more. Taravad men had no home other than their natal domestic unit; they were untroubled by what happened to their children—whom they were scarcely able to identify—and they had no

345

difficulty keeping their sisters and their nephews and nieces under proper fraternal and avuncular control.

Why is this type of matrilineal system so rare? (Even the Nayar no longer practice it [cf. Mencher 1965].) It is rare because the Nayar come perilously close to giving up all the benefits of exogamy without enjoying any of the benefits of incest. Although Nayar men do not keep their sisters entirely to themselves, they establish only the flimsiest of kinship networks among neighboring taravads. This form of matrilineality is opposed by all the structural forces that compel male-dominated domestic kin groups to export and import women.

Avunculocality is by far the most common solution to the conflicts experienced by male chauvinists in matrilineal societies. It is a remarkable fact that there are more matrilineal descent groups that are avunculocal than there are matrilineal descent groups that are matrilocal.

RELATIONSHIP BETWEEN RESIDENCE AND DESCENT
IN THE ETHNOGRAPHIC ATLAS

| Kin Groups | Postmarital residence | | | | |
	Matrilocal or Uxorilocal	Avunculocal	Patrilocal or Virilocal	Other	Total
Patrilineal	1	0	563	25	588
Matrilineal	53	62	30	19	164

Source: Murdock 1967; Divale and Harris 1975.

Under avunculocality a male eventually goes to live with his mother's brothers in their matrilineal domestic unit. His wife will join him there. Upon maturity a male ego's son will in turn depart for ego's wife's brother's domestic unit (ego's daughter, however, may remain resident if she marries her father's sister's son). Thus the core of an avunculocal domestic unit consists of a group of brothers and their sisters' sons. The function of this arrangement is to reinsert a male fraternal interest group as the residental core of the matrilineal descent group.

Avunculocality occurs because males continue to dominate the affairs of matrilineal groups. This interpretation accords well with another remarkable universal fact: the logical opposite of avunculocality never òccurs. The logical opposite of avunculocality is *amitalocality* ("aunt-locality"). Amitalocality would exist if brother's daughters and father's sisters constituted the core of a patrilineal domestic unit. Women, however, have never been able to control patrilineal kin groups in the way men have been able to control matrilineal kin groups. Hence males, not females, constitute the resident core of virtually all patrilineal kin groups as well as most of the known cases of matrilineal kin groups.

A rather thin line separates avunculocality from patrilocality. If the resident group of brothers decides to permit one or more of its sons to remain with them after marriage, the residential core will begin to resemble an ambilocal domestic group. If more sons than nephews are retained in residence, the locality basis for a reassertion of patrilineal descent will be present. In this way fraternal and filial solidarity constantly reassert themselves against maternal and nepotic solidarity.

Causes of Matrilocality and Matrilineality

What kinds of forces are capable of rupturing the unity of male-centered patrilocal domestic groups in favor of matrilocality? Some matrilocal cases may be due to subsistence activities that require males to be absent on long expeditions. Among the contemporary Navajo, for example, both men and women own sheep, but the women are the shepherds. Men raise horses and work for wages. Both tasks require them to leave their homesteads for long periods. The Navajo women are less mobile, and sheep-herding is carried out close to their matrilocal homestead without disrupting other essential domestic tasks. These are probably some of the factors that have kept the Navajo matrilineal during the past century despite many drastic changes in their subsistence practices. Analogous considerations may explain the matrilineal tendencies of the nonagricultural Northwest

Figure 16-11. NAVAJO SHEPHERDS. A woman's specialty. (Museum of the American Indian, Heye Foundation)

Coast Tlingit and Haida. Here women were responsible for exploiting perennial beds of shellfish while the men engaged in far-ranging sea mammal hunts (Ingilis 1970).

By far the most common and powerful reason for long expeditions by males is warfare. Warfare in general obviously cannot explain matrilocality because it lies at the root of the patrilocal-patrilineal complex. But there is a strong correlation between matrilocality and one particular kind of warfare that is quite different from the warfare practiced by the Yanomamö or Maring. Among patrilocal, patrilineal villages, the belligerent territorial teams consist of patrilineally related kin who constitute competitive fraternal-interest groups. These groups make shifting alliances with neighboring villages, exchange sisters, and raid each other. Most combat takes place between villages that are about a day's walk from each other. The warfare that has been found to be highly correlated with matrilineal cultures, on the other hand, involves far-ranging invading and raiding societies and the villages that are the common victims of such long-distance raids and invasions. Such villages tend to form permanent alliances; they are bonded not by the exchange of women but by the in-marrying of males from different domestic groups. Thus warfare against a common external enemy can lead both to the prolonged absence of males on military expeditions and to the need for breaking up competitive fraternal-interest groups by scattering fathers and brothers into several different households.

It has long been noted that matrilocal-matrilineal societies like the Iroquois of New York enjoy a degree of internal peace that contrasts markedly with the constant bickering, feuding, and raiding of groups like the Tsembaga Maring or Yanomamö. But most matrilineal societies like the Iroquois have a history of intense warfare directed outward against powerful enemies. The Nayar, for example, were a soldier caste in the service of the kings of Malabar. Among the matrilocal Mundurucu of the Amazon, conflict between villages was unheard of and interpersonal aggression was suppressed. But the Mundurucu launched raids against enemies hundreds of miles away, and unrelenting hostility and violence characterized their relations with the "outside world" (Murphy 1956).

An additional reason for the suppression of internal hostility among matrilocal groups is that matrilocality is incompatible with polygyny. The males who are in charge of the matrilineal estate are not interested in marrying several of their sisters to one male, and they themselves will not benefit from having many wives and children. Conflict over women, one of the major causes of war between neighboring villages, is thus reduced.

348

After a society has adopted matrilocality and developed matrilineal descent groups, changes in the original conditions may lead to a restoration of the patrilocal-patrilineal pattern. At any given moment many societies are probably in some transitional state between one form of residence and another and one form of kinship ideology and another. Since the changes in residence and descent may not proceed in perfect tandem at any given moment—that is, descent changes may lag behind residence changes—one should expect to encounter combinations of residence with the "wrong" descent rule. For example, a few patrilocal societies and quite a large number of virilocal societies have matrilineal descent, and one or two uxorilocal societies have patrilineal descent (see table, p. 346). But there is now ample evidence for a very powerful strain toward consistency in the alignment between domestic groups, their ecological, military and political functions, and their ideologies of descent.

To sum up: the ideology of descent embodies a culture's attempt to understand, normalize, and regularize its residence, exogamic, and subsistence practices. The principal function of the rules of descent may be described as the establishment and maintenance of networks of cooperative and interdependent kinspeople aggregated into ecologically adapted domestic production and reproduction units. In order for such units to act effectively and reliably they must share an organizational ideology that interprets and validates the structure of the group and the behavior of its members.

Kinship Terminologies

Every culture has a special set of terms for designating types of kin. The terms plus the rules for using them constitute a culture's *kin terminological system*.

In describing and analyzing kin terminological systems every effort must be made to avoid using one's own kin terms as translations of the terms found in other systems. To reduce the possibility of imposing ethnocentric preconceptions upon terminological systems that have no kin types in common, minimum use should be made of words like "uncle," "aunt," or "cousin." Even terms like "father," "mother," "sister," "brother," "son," and "daughter" cannot be used without the risk of distorting the way in which other cultures categorize and designate their kinfolk.

Lewis Henry Morgan was the first anthropologist to realize that despite the thousands of different languages over the face of the globe and despite the immense number of different kinship terms in these languages, there are only a handful of basic types of kin terminological systems. These systems can best be defined by the way in which terms are applied to an abbreviated genealogical grid consisting of two generations, including ego's siblings of the same and opposite sex and ego's cross and parallel cousins.

One way to cope with the task of categorizing the sixteen possible kin types on this grid is to give each of the sixteen kin types a separate term (see Fig. 16-12). This logical option is fulfilled in only a handful of cases, which exhibit what are known as *Sudanese* terminologies. Out of 862 societies in Murdock's *Ethnographic Atlas,* only 7 have Sudanese terminologies.

Figure 16-12. SUDANESE TERMINOLOGY.

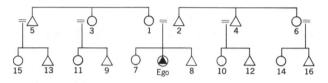

Clearly there must be powerful and widespread selective forces operating against the application of a separate kin term to every position on the genealogical grid. Most of the world's cultures have kin terminologies that lump several kin types under a single term. One of anthropology's most important discoveries is that the lumping of kin into kin types usually reflects a society's domestic organization and larger social structure, sometimes in rather precise detail. Because the effects of material conditions on this realm cannot be grasped intuitively, the study of kinship terminologies provides important lessons about the relationship between ideology, social structure, and technoeconomic and technoenvironmental conditions.

Eskimo Terminology

The kind of kin terminological systems with which Euro-Americans are most familiar is known as Eskimo, shown in Figure 16-13. Two important features of this system are: first, that none of the terms

Figure 16-13. ESKIMO TERMINOLOGY.

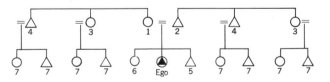

applied to ego's nuclear relatives—1, 2, 6, 5—are applied outside the nuclear family; and second, that there is no distinction between the

350

maternal and paternal sides. Thus there is no distinction between cross and parallel "cousins" or between cross and parallel "aunts" or "uncles." These features reflect the fact that societies using Eskimo terminology generally lack corporate descent groups. In the absence of such groups, the nuclear family tends to stand out as a separate and functionally dominant productive and reproductive unit. For this reason its members are given a terminological identity separate from all other kin types. On the other hand, the lumping of all "cousins" under a single term (7) reflects the strength of bilateral as opposed to unilineal descent. The influence of bilateral descent is also reflected in the failure to distinguish terminologically between "aunts" and "uncles" on the maternal side as compared with "aunts" and "uncles" on the father's side. The theoretical predictions concerning Eskimo terminology are strongly confirmed by the tabulations of Murdock's *Ethnographic Atlas* (1967). Of the 71 societies having Eskimo terminology, only 4 have large extended families and only 13 have unilineal descent groups. In 54 of the 71 Eskimo terminology societies descent groups are entirely absent or are represented only by kindreds.

Eskimo is the terminological system of Euro-America. But as the name "Eskimo" implies, the same pattern is frequently found among hunters and gatherers. The reason for this is that any factors that isolate the nuclear family increase the probability that an Eskimo terminology will occur. Among hunting and gathering groups the determining factors are associated with low population densities and the need for maximum geographical mobility in relationship to fluctuations in the availability of biotic resources. Among the industrial "Yankees" the same terminological pattern reflects the intrusion of state and market institutions into the domestic routine and a high level of wage-induced social and geographic mobility.

Hawaiian Terminology

Another kin terminological system that occurs among highly stratified state-level societies as well as among hunters and gatherers is known as Hawaiian. This is the easiest system to portray since it has the least number of terms (see Fig. 16-14). In some versions even the distinction between the sexes is dropped, leaving one term for the

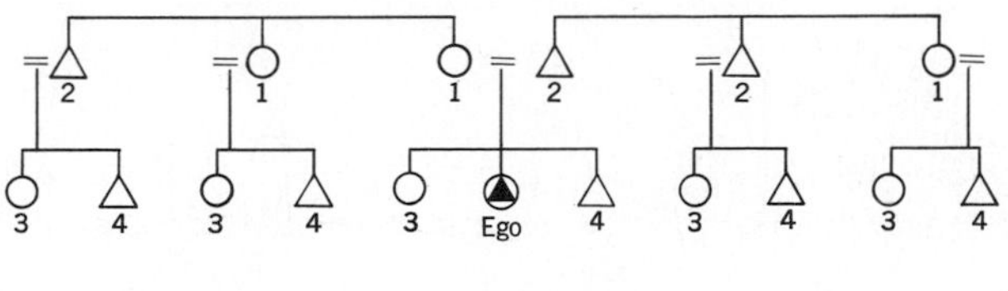

Figure 16-14. HAWAIIAN TERMINOLOGY.

members of ego's generation and another term for the members of ego's parents' generation. The most remarkable feature of Hawaiian terminology, as compared with Eskimo, is the application of the same terms to people inside and outside the nuclear family. Hawaiian is thus compatible with situations where the nuclear family is submerged within a domestic context dominated by extended families and other corporate descent groups. In Murdock's *Ethnographic Atlas* 21 percent of the Hawaiian terminology societies do indeed have large extended families. In addition, well over 50 percent of Hawaiian terminology societies have some form of corporate descent group other than extended families.

Theoretically most of these descent groups should be cognatic descent groups rather than unilineal descent groups. The reason for this prediction is that the merging of relatives on the maternal side with those on the paternal side indicates an indifference toward unilineality. An indifference toward unilineality is logically consistent with either ambilineal or bilateral descent.

Data from Murdock's ethnographic sample only partially support this prediction: there are indeed many more Hawaiian terminology societies that have cognatic as opposed to unilineal descent. But there are many exceptions for which as yet no generally accepted explanation is available.

Iroquois Terminology

In the presence of unilineal kin groups there is a worldwide tendency terminologically to distinguish parallel from cross cousins (previously noted, p. 335). This pattern is widely associated with a similar distinction on the first ascending generation whereby father's brothers are distinguished from mother's brothers and father's sisters are distinguished from mother's sisters.

An Iroquois terminology exists where—in addition to these distinctions between cross and parallel cousins and cross and parallel aunts and uncles—mother's sister is terminologically merged with mother, father's brother is terminologically merged with father, and parallel cousins are terminologically merged with ego's brothers and sisters.

Figure 16-15. IROQUOIS TERMINOLOGY.

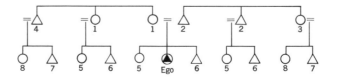

This pattern of merging occurs in large part as a result of the shared membership of siblings in corporate unilineal descent groups and of the marriage alliances based on cross-cousin marriage between such groups. Thus in Murdock's ethnographic sample there are 166 societies having Iroquois terminology. Of these, 119 have some form of unilineal descent group (70 percent).

Crow Terminology

Iroquois and Eskimo terminologies reflect an even balance between the assignment of kinship identity on the basis of lineal descent and generation differences. Hawaiian systems, on the other hand, stress generation differences over lineal descent differences. Many cultures have terminological systems in which the influence of lineal descent overwhelms generation criteria. These systems occur in both matrilineal and patrilineal versions. The matrilineal variety is called Crow, and the patrilineal variety is called Omaha. Since these systems are mirror images of each other, I shall describe only Crow.

Note that several of the features of the Iroquois pattern are maintained (see Fig. 16-16). Parallel cousins are equated with siblings (5

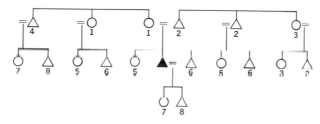

Figure 16-16. CROW TERMINOLOGY, MALE EGO.

and 6); father's brother is equated with father (2) and mother's sister with mother (1); cross aunts (3) are separated from parallel aunts (1); cross uncles (4) are separated from parallel uncles (2); and cross cousins (7, 8, 3, 2) are separated from parallel cousins (5 and 6). All these features are carry-overs from the influence of descent group identity already present in the Iroquois system. The novel feature in the Crow system involves the distinction between patrilateral and matrilateral cross cousins. These "cousins" are not only distinguished from each other but the female patrilateral cross cousin is equated with father's sister (3) and the male patrilateral cross cousin is equated with father (2). There is also the curious fact that the matrilateral cross cousins are equated with ego's daughter and son (7 and 8). The basic reason for these terminological mergings is that father's sister (3) and father's sister's daughter (3) are members of one matrilin-

353

eage; father (2) and father's sister's son (2) are also members of that patrilineage. Moreover, since ego and his mother's brother are also in one matrilineage, they are likely to marry women who come from the same matrilineage, hence their children (7) and (8) are called by the same terms. The further importance of lineage identity and lineage marital alliances can be seen by the fact that both Crow and Omaha systems are different from the point of view of a female ego versus a male ego. In the Crow system, female ego speaking (see Fig. 16-17), mother's brother's children are not merged with ego's own

Figure 16-17. CROW TERMINOLOGY, FEMALE EGO.

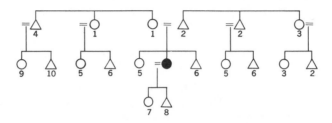

children. They are merged instead with ego's brother's children (not shown on diagram). In order to give a complete explanation of this difference, the nature of the marital alliances between the various matrilineages in Crow-type societies would have to be discussed. Because of its technical complexity, I shall not pursue this matter further.

Most authorities agree that Crow/Omaha terminologies represent the mature product of social systems in which unilineal descent groups play a preponderant role in the organization of productive and reproductive tasks and other vital functions. The correlation between Crow/Omaha terminologies and the presence of unilineal descent groups is very high. Thus, in Murdock's ethnographic sample, 102 societies have Crow/Omaha terminologies. Of these, 90 percent have some kind of unilineal descent group.

Kin terminological systems comprise a vast field of ongoing research into which anthropologists have poured much time and ingenuity. I regret that I have only skimmed the surface of a few of the many fascinating and important problems that this field contains. But perhaps enough has been said to establish at least one point: kin terminological systems possess a remarkable logical coherency. Yet, like so many other aspects of culture, kin terminological systems are never the planned product of any inventive genius. Most people are unaware that such systems even exist. Clearly the major features of these systems represent recurrent unconscious adaptations to the prevailing conditions of domestic life. Yet there are many details of kin terminologies as well as of other kinship phenomena that are as yet not well understood.

354

17

LAW AND ORDER

As Europeans began to make contact with the aboriginal denizens of the American forests and the remote islands of Oceania, much thought was given to what the original "state of nature" must have been like. Two interpretations were offered. There were those who shared the views of Sir Thomas Hobbes, the British philosopher, that people lacking a sovereign capable of compelling their obedience would destroy themselves in a "war of all against all." Others, partial to the philosophical speculations of Jean Jacques Rousseau, argued that in "the state of nature" people were peaceful, orderly, honest, and courageous. According to Rousseau, this noble natural endowment was destroyed by the rise of civilization.

Firsthand study of life in small village and band societies has provided little support for Rousseau's idyll. Anthropologists have yet to find a culture that is completely harmonious, peaceful, and happy. Although modern anthropological research has led to the rejection of the myth of the noble savage, it nonetheless has confirmed the existence of a remarkable contrast between the way prestate and state-level societies prevent internal conflicts from threatening the survival of their respective populations. Both Rousseau and Hobbes were wrong, but of the two, Hobbes was further from the truth.

The whole enormous apparatus of "law and order" associated with modern life is absent among village and band-level cultures. Yet there is no "war of all against all." The Eskimo, the Bushmen of the Kalahari, the Australian aborigines, and many other cultures enjoy a high degree of personal security without having any "sovereign" in

Hobbes's sense. They have no kings, queens, dictators, presidents, governors, or mayors; police officers, National Guard soldiers, sailors, or marines; CIA, FBI, Treasury agents, or federal marshals. They have no written law codes and no formal law courts; no lawyers, bailiffs, bondsmen, judges, district attorneys, juries, or court clerks; and no patrol cars, paddy wagons, jails, or penitentiaries. People managed to get along without these means of law enforcement for tens of thousands of years. Why are contemporary state-level societies so dependent upon them?

Equality and Order

The maintenance of order in prestate societies is rooted in a commonality of material interests. The greater the amount of common interests, the less need there is for law-and-order specialists. Among band-level cultures law and order stem directly from the relations between people and the natural habitat from which subsistence is derived. All adults usually have open access to this habitat: the rivers, lakes, beaches, oceans; all the plants and animals; the soil and the subsoil. Insofar as these are basic to the extraction of life-sustaining energy and materials they are communal "property."

Anthropologists have occasionally reported the existence of nuclear family or even individual ownership of hunting and gathering territories among band-level cultures. Careful analysis or further research has shown each of these to conform to the general pattern. It was argued a number of years ago that fur-trapping Canadian Indians had family-owned hunting territories (Speck 1915). Subsequent research by Eleanor Leacock (1954, 1973) and Rolf Knight (1965, 1974) has shown that these family territories, if they existed at all, were associated with the introduction of the fur trade, and that private or family property in land probably did not occur aboriginally.

Misunderstandings concerning the existence of family territories within band areas stem from a failure to distinguish between ideological claims and actual behavior. The report that a family regards a particular area as its "own" is not conclusive. The crucial information concerns the conditions and consequences of trespass. If permission is always freely granted, and if use without permission results merely in some muttering or name-calling, "ownership" is the wrong term to use. Thus water holes among the Bushmen are sometimes reported as being owned by particular individuals. Yet it is also reported that the people who use the water holes do not feel that they are obligated to the owner. As Morton Fried (1967:87–88) has put it, it seems clear

356

that the owners "comprise all the persons in proximity to the re-sources."

Wherever there is inequality of access to vital natural resources, especially to land, there is a marked increase in the number of law-and-order specialists. As I pointed out in Chapter 14, peasants must pay either rent or taxes to gain access to agricultural land. Landlords, rulers, and bureaucrats prefer to extract the peasants' "surplus" (see Ch. 18) with a minimum of force. They believe and they want the peasants to believe that the payment of rent and taxes is a law of the universe. They prefer to have the peasants pay their rent and taxes voluntarily as a matter of duty, conscience, and faith. But inevitably some peasants fail to accept the belief that lands properly

Figure 17-1. YANOMAMÖ CLUB FIGHT. Egalitarian peoples are not without problems of law and order. Another phase of the fight pictured in Figure 13-5. (Napoleon Chagnon)

357

Equality and Order

belong only to "lords" and other privileged persons. The owners of the land must therefore be prepared to use physical force to back up their "rights." They must be prepared to do so by sending in soldiers, police, lawyers, or other law-and-order specialists to evict "squatters." Thus the payment of "rent" is always a source of animosity and is unthinkable in the absence of ultimate police-military backing.

Today in many industrial societies marked inequalities in access to air represent an exquisite refinement of private property in land. Such inequalities demand constant armed vigilance against trespass. In the slums of New York City there are as many as five thousand people to an acre, while a few miles away, amid the rolling hills and swimming pools of the country-club suburb, there are two people to an acre. On a hot, smoggy summer night people who lack access to land must also do without a proper supply of the fresh air on which humans depend for oxygen and body comfort. Without the police and the vast apparatus of law enforcement, such drastic inequalities could not exist for any length of time. (Note that I am not saying that the police cause the inequality in these situations.) Even more volatile inequalities exist in many parts of the world. Many a traveler has peered up at the great shantytowns perched on the hillsides above the luxury apartments of Rio de Janeiro or Caracas and wondered aloud, "What keeps those people up there?" In Calcutta two hundred thousand people nightly sleep on the sidewalks. It is evident that under these circumstances the maintenance of law and order constitutes a challenge that has no true analogue among band-level egalitarian societies.

Students often find it difficult to understand why some bully does not come along sooner or later to take over the "ownership" of a band's basic resources. Given the absence of police-military specialists, why don't those individuals who are naturally stronger and more crafty than the rest try to exclude others from the richest hunting lands and most prolific fields of tubers or wild grains? The crux of the matter is that under certain circumstances communal tenure fulfills the material self-interest of the "strong" as well as the "weak" more effectively than private tenure does.

The rudimentary nature and accessibility of available weapons has a great deal to do with this situation. A single individual armed with nothing more than a spear can scarcely hope to intimidate a half-dozen people also armed with spears. Combinations of four or five against three or two might be attempted with some hope of success. But a conflict of this sort will merely result in the fissioning of the group into two parts. Thus internecine band-level struggles never result in the subordination of one social segment to another (with the

358

possible exception of women to men). Those who find their access to basic resources encumbered by the aggressive behavior of others have the simple option of gathering up their belongings and walking off to any of perhaps a dozen camps where they have ties of descent or affinity. As long as people have the freedom to move to areas that can be made to yield subsistence with no loss of efficiency, they cannot be dominated.

The absence of differential access to basic resources at the band level is a most significant aspect of cultural evolution. The distinction between rich and poor, ruler and ruled, evolved simultaneously from this base as a result of cumulative changes in the ecological and economic spheres of culture. This evolution was not a result of any sudden conspiracy of the strong against the weak, nor of any sudden collapse of the charitable components of human nature. It was rather the result of recurrent evolutionary forces that I have been discussing in previous chapters and to which I shall return again in a moment.

"Primitive Communism"

Much effort has been expended by anthropologists in disproving a doctrine known as "primitive communism." According to this doctrine there was a universal stage in the development of culture marked by the complete absence of private property (cf. Epstein 1968). It is important to establish the fact that many material objects of band-level societies are effectively controlled ("owned") by specific individuals. This applies especially to items that the user has produced. The members of even the most egalitarian societies usually believe that weapons, clothing, containers, ornaments, tools, and other "personal effects" ought not to be taken away or used without the consent of the "owner." Given the basic band-level ecological adaptation, however, the chance is remote that theft or misappropriation of such objects will lead to serious conflicts demanding the intervention of law-and-order specialists.

First of all, the accumulation of material possessions is rigidly limited by the recurrent need to break camp and travel long distances on foot. In addition, most utilitarian items may be borrowed without difficulty when the owner is not using them. If there are not enough such items to go around (arrows, points, nets, bark or gourd containers), easy access to the raw materials and possession of the requisite skills provide the have-nots with the chance of making their own. There is considerable evidence that for most human beings the intrinsic rewards of creative craftsmanship are superior to the re-

359

wards gained by substituting theft for work. Moreover, among cultures having no more than a few hundred people, thieves cannot be anonymous. If stealing becomes habitual, a coalition of the injured parties will eventually take action. If it is only an occasional item that is coveted, better to ask for it openly. Most such requests are readily obliged since reciprocity is the prevailing mode of exchange. Finally, it should be pointed out that contrary to the experience of the successful modern bank robber, no one can make a living from stealing bows and arrows or feather headdresses since there is no regular market at which such inedible items can be exchanged for food (cf. p. 287).

Sexual Communism

Band and village cultures depart farthest from total communism in the sphere of sex and marriage. Complete sexual sharing of wives by husbands and of husbands by wives is unknown. Indeed, marriage by definition implies that there are restrictions on sexual access. I have already indicated that conflict leading to violence, the splitting of groups, and warfare are associated with artificially induced shortages of women caused by female infanticide and polygyny. Band-level peoples are quite surprisingly antipathetic to polyandrous arrangements, whereas the practice of some degree of polygyny is almost universal among them. In several of the Australian groups, older men actually seem to hoard women, a practice scarcely promoting commonality of interest. (On the other hand, there is some indication that the best-known example—the Tiwi—have adopted their extreme form of wife-collecting as a response to the recent willingness of foreign sailors to pay for sexual favors [cf. Hart and Piling 1960].) Even in groups like the Yanomamö, however, a husband's sexual monopoly is far from total. Although adultery is condemned, there is seldom any objection to sex between a married woman and another man provided the husband's permission has been obtained. In this matter as in all else reciprocity prevails. Band-level societies usually have provisions for reciprocal *wife-lending*. A husband offers his wife to visitors who need a mate for the night, and he expects similar favors in return. As in the case of theft, therefore, it is easier for a man who has a hankering for someone else's wife merely to come right out and ask for the favor rather than to arrange a tryst. A fair amount of this sort of sharing also takes place on ritual occasions.

Conflict Resolution

In small societies conflict can be controlled by mechanisms that are similar to the peace-keeping strategies of modern domestic groups. Although families are not entirely free of disruptive hostility and violent clashes (most homicides in the United States are carried out by a spouse or relative of the victim), the members of small domestic groups generally conduct their affairs peacefully and harmoniously. Each individual's position and function within the group is based on unambiguous criteria (married or unmarried, male or female, younger or older). Since the group is small, the common advantage of maintaining harmonious relations is easily grasped by all members. Finally, since most of the members of the domestic unit are reared together from infancy, specific interpersonal adjustments can be made an integral part of the enculturation process. Each new member of the household is not only trained to be a "sister" or "son" or "younger brother," but each is also taught to perform these roles with respect to a specific set of teammates; that is, children are trained for specific personality adjustments as well as for the roles of abstract statuses.

Even in the world's most egalitarian societies conflicts arise that threaten the maintenance of orderly social life. Such conflicts usually involve individuals who were born in or who reside in different domestic units. To prevent disruption and loss of life, every society possesses at least rudimentary procedures for deescalating hostilities and for the peaceful resolution of interdomestic conflicts.

The most important requirement for the control of interdomestic disputes in prestate contexts is the temporary insulation of one or both of the disputants from the corporate response of their respective kin group. As long as both parties feel that they have the backing of their kin groups they will continue to press their claims and counterclaims. The members of these kin groups, however, never act with zombielike partisanship. They are eager not to be caught in a situation where they are opposed by a majority of people in the community. Public opinion, in other words, is a decisive factor in diminishing or enhancing the support that disputants can expect from their kin groups.

The Song Contest

Because of the importance of aligning potential kin group supporters with the drift of public opinion, band and village adjudication processes frequently exhibit a peculiar indifference to abstract principles of

361

justice. What matters is not so much who is morally right or wrong; or who is lying or telling the truth. The important thing is to mobilize public opinion on one side or the other decisively enough to prevent the outbreak of a feud.

The classic example of how such mobilization can be achieved independently of abstract principles of equity is the song contest of the Central and Eastern Eskimo. Here it frequently happens that one man claims that another man has stolen his wife. The counterclaim is that she was not stolen but left voluntarily because her husband "was not man enough" to take good care of her. The issue is settled at a large public meeting that might be likened to a court. But no testimony is taken in support of either version of why the wife has left her husband. Instead the "litigants" take turns singing insulting songs at each other. The "court" responds to each performance with differential degrees of laughter. Eventually one of the singers gets flustered, and the whooping and hollering raised against him becomes total—even his relatives have a hard time not laughing.

> Something was whispered
> Of a man and wife
> Who could not agree
> And what was it all about?
> A wife who in rightful anger
> Tore her husband's furs,
> Took their canoe
> And rowed away with her son.
> Ay-ay, all who listen,
> What do you think of him
> Who is great in his anger
> But faint in strength,
> Blubbering helplessly?
> He got what he deserved
> Though it was he who proudly
> Started this quarrel with stupid words.
> [Adapted from Rasmussen 1929:231–232]

The Eskimo have no police-military specialists to see to it that the "decision" is enforced. Yet chances are that the man who has lost the song duel will give in since he can no longer count on anyone to back him up if he chooses to escalate the dispute. Nonetheless, the defeated party may choose to go it alone.

Wife-stealing does occasionally lead to murder. When this happens, the man who has lost public support may stay alive for quite a while on the strength of his own vigilance and fighting skill. He will probably have to kill again, however, and with each transgression the coalition against him becomes larger and more determined until finally he falls victim to an ambush.

362

Witchcraft, Shamans, and Social Control

Among egalitarian societies, part-time magico-religious specialists known as *shamans* frequently play an important role in eliminating persistent sources of conflict. Most cultures reject the idea that misfortune can result from natural causes. If animals suddenly become scarce, or if several people fall sick, it is assumed that somebody is practicing witchcraft. It is the shaman's job to identify the culprit. Normally this is done through the shaman's art of divination or clairvoyance. Putting themselves into trances with the aid of drugs, tobacco smoke, or monotonous drumming, shamans ascertain the name of the culprit. The people demand vengeance and the evildoer is ambushed and murdered.

It might be thought that this sequence of events would lead to more rather than less internal conflict. Even if the accused had actually been practicing witchcraft, the disruptive consequence of magico-religious forms of aggression would seem to be considerably less dangerous than those resulting from actual murder.

But the chances are that the murdered individuals never even attempted to carry out the witchcraft of which they were accused or indeed any witchcraft at all! In other words, the witches are probably wholly "innocent" of the crime with which they have been charged. Nonetheless the shaman's witchcraft accusations usually conserve rather than destroy the existing condition of law and order.

Consider the case reported by Gertrude Dole (1966) for the Kuikuru—an egalitarian, village-dwelling group of Brazilian Indians. Lightning had set fire to two houses. The shaman divined that the lightning had been sent by a man who had left the village some years

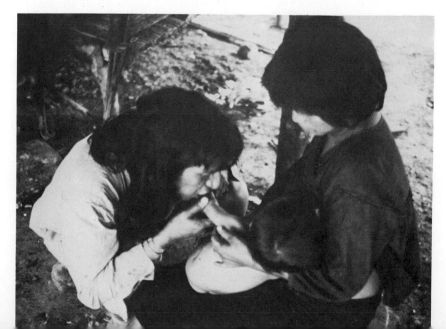

Figure 17-2. ACHUARA SHAMAN. The supernatural "dirtiness" is being sucked from this baby. See Chapter 23 (Michael Harner)

363

previously and had never returned. This man had only one male relative, who was also no longer living in the village. Before the accused witch had left the village, he had become engaged to a young girl. The shaman's brother had persuaded the girl's mother to break the betrothal and to permit him to marry the girl.

During the course of the divining ceremony, the shaman carried on dialogues with various interested members of the community. When he finally disclosed the identity of the culprit, it created considerable anxiety. One after another, several individuals stood apart in the plaza and spoke in long monologues. . . . In the heat of the excitement, the shaman's brother left with a few companions to kill the man suspected of witchcraft.   [Dole 1966:76]

The ethnographer points out that a change of residence from one village to another usually indicates that there is trouble brewing and that, in effect, the individual has been ostracized. (The Kuikuru suspected Dole and her anthropologist husband of having been "kicked out" of their own society.) Thus the man accused of sorcery was not a randomly chosen figure, but one who fulfilled several well-defined criteria: (1) a history of disputes and quarrels within the village; (2) motivation for continuing to do harm (the broken engagement); (3) weak kinship backing.

Thus the shaman's accusation was not based on a spur-of-the-moment decision; there had been a long incubation period during which the shaman in or out of trance had ample opportunity to sound out his fellow villagers on their attitude toward the accused. As Dole indicates, the supernatural authority of the shaman allows him to make public indictments. But shamans are not in control (as in the movie and television versions of the sinister medicine man turning the "natives" against the friendly European explorers). Rather they are largely constrained by public opinion. Although the act of divination appears to put the onus of the judicial process on the shaman, clearly the shaman actually "deduces, formulates, and expresses the will of the people" (ibid.). Shamans abuse their supernatural gifts if they accuse people who are well liked and who enjoy strong kin group support. If they persist in making such mistakes, they themselves will be ostracized and eventually murdered.

The peculiar thing about witchcraft as a means of social control is that its practitioners, if they exist at all, can seldom be detected. The number of persons falsely accused of witchcraft probably far exceeds the number who are justly accused. It is clear, therefore, that nonpractice of witchcraft is no safeguard against an accusation of witchcraft. How then do you protect yourself from such false accusations? By acting in an amiable, open, generous manner; by avoiding

364

quarrels; by doing everything possible not to lose the support of your kin group. Thus the occasional killing of a supposed sorcerer results in much more than the mere elimination of a few actual or potential antisocial individuals. These violent incidents convince everyone of the importance of not being mistaken for an evildoer. As a result, as among the Kuikuru, people are made more amiable, cordial, generous, and willing to cooperate.

The norm of being amiable deters individuals from accusing one another of delicts, hence in the absence of effective political or kin-group control, interpersonal relations have become a kind of game, in which almost the only restrictive rule is not to show hostility to one another for fear of being suspected of witchcraft. [ibid.:74]

This system is not "fail-safe." Many cases are known of witchcraft systems that seem to have broken down, involving the community in a series of destructive retaliatory witchcraft accusations and murders. The interpretation of these cases, however (especially in situations of intensive colonial contact, as in Africa and Melanesia), must be carefully related to the underlying conditions of communal life. In general the incidence of witchcraft accusations varies with the amount of community dissension and frustration. When the traditional ecological balance has been upset by exposure to new diseases, increased competition for land, and recruitment for migratory wage labor, an epoch of increased dissension and frustration can be expected. This period will also be characterized by great activity among those who are skilled in tracking down and exposing the malevolent effects of witches. Later on I shall discuss the great European witch craze as a reaction to the breakup of feudal society (see Ch. 24).

Headmanship

The maintenance of orderly relations in simple egalitarian societies is usually facilitated by individuals who are the analogues or prototypes of state-level specialists in the administration of political power. To the extent that political leadership can be said to exist at all among simple egalitarian societies, it is exercised by leaders of the "headman" variety. The headman, unlike such state-level specialists as king, president, or dictator, is a relatively powerless figure incapable of compelling obedience to his commands. He lacks control over a decisive quantum of organized physical force. When he gives a command he is never certain of being able to physically punish those who disobey. (Hence if he wants to stay in "office," he gives few direct commands.) In contrast, political power at the state level rests firmly on the ability of the political specialist to muster punitive forces sufficient to expel or exterminate any readily foreseeable combination of nonconforming individuals and groups. In turn, the control over decisively superior force rests upon differential access to basic resources and the tools and weapons useful for hurting or killing people. But as I have said before, a headman or any other bully alone or in combination with a segment of his band or village cannot achieve or maintain a decisive superiority in police-military power without destroying the basic ecological adjustment upon which everyone's life depends (p. 358).

Among the Eskimo, leadership is especially diffuse, being closely related to success in hunting. A group will follow an outstanding hunter and defer to his opinion with respect to choice of hunting spots. But in all other matters the "leader's" opinion carries no more weight than any other man's. The Kalahari Bushmen have more definite forms of headmanship replete with a rule of succession from father to son. Although the Bushman headman is identified with rights over desert water holes and wild vegetable patches, actual access, as you have seen, is free and easy. Theoretically it is the headman who decides when camp is to be broken and what line of march is to be followed. In practice, however, all critical moves are undertaken through consensus (Fried 1967:88).

A similar pattern of headmanship is reported for the Semai of Malaya. Despite recent attempts by outsiders to bolster up the power of Semai leaders, the headman is merely the most prestigious figure among a group of peers. In the words of Robert Dentan, who carried out field work among these egalitarian shifting horticulturalists in 1962–1963:

[The headman] keeps the peace by conciliation rather than coercion. He must be personally respected. . . . Otherwise people will drift away from him or gradually stop paying attention to him. Moreover, the Semai recognize only two or three occasions on which he can assert his authority: dealing as a representative of his people with non-Semai; mediating a quarrel, if invited by the quarreling parties to do so but not otherwise; and . . . selecting and apportioning land for fields. Furthermore, most of the time a good headman gauges the general feeling about an issue and bases his decision on that, so that he is more a spokesman for public opinion than a molder of it.   [1968:68]

The term "chief" is also often applied to leaders who are incapable of compelling obedience among their followers. Claude Lévi-Strauss refers to the Nambikwara Indians of Brazil as having "chiefs." Yet he states firmly:

It should be said at once that the chief cannot seek support either in clearly defined powers or in publicly recognized authority. . . . One or two malcontents may throw the chief's whole programme out of joint. Should this happen, the chief has no powers of coercion. He can disembarrass himself of undesirable elements only in so far as all the others are of the same mind as himself.   [1963b:303]

Headmanship is likely to be a frustrating and irksome position. The cumulative impression given by descriptions of leadership among Brazilian Indian groups is that of an overzealous scoutmaster on an overnight cookout. The first one up in the morning, the headman tries to rouse his companions by standing in the middle of the village plaza and shouting, "Everybody up for the fish-poisoning expedition! Let's get those women into the manioc gardens! Anyone for roof-thatching?" The headman seems to cajole, harangue, and plead from morning to night. If a task needs to be done, it is the headman who starts doing it; and it is the headman who works at it harder than anyone else. Moreover, not only must the headman set an example for hard work, but *noblesse oblige,* he must also set an example for generosity. After a fishing or hunting expedition, he is expected to give away more of the catch than anybody else; if trade goods are obtained, he must be careful not to keep the best pieces for himself.

Thomas Gregor, who studied the Mehinacu Indians of Brazil's Xingu National Park in 1967, describes the Mehinacu headman as follows:

The most significant qualifications for Mehinacu chieftainship are learned skills and personal attributes. The chief, for example, is expected to excel at public speaking. Each evening he should stand in the center of the plaza and exhort his fellow tribesmen to be good citizens. He must call upon them

Figure 17-3. MEHINACU CHIEFTAINSHIP. In front of the men's house the chief is redistributing presents given to him by the ethnographer. (Thomas Gregor)

to work hard in their gardens, to take frequent baths, not to sleep during the day, not to be angry with each other, and not to have sexual relations too frequently. . . . In addition to being a skilled orator, the chief is expected to be a generous man. This means that when he returns from a successful fishing trip, he will bring most of his catch out to the men's houses where it is cooked and shared by the men of the tribe. His wife must be generous, bringing manioc cakes and pepper to the men whenever they call for it. Further, the chief must be willing to part with possessions. When one of the men catches a harpy eagle, for example, the chief must buy it from him with a valuable shell belt in the name of the entire tribe. . . . A chief should also be a man who never becomes angry in public. . . . In his public speeches he should never criticize any of his fellow tribesmen, no matter how badly they may have affronted the chief or the tribe as a whole.   [Gregor 1969:88–89]

It is pertinent at this point to recall the plight of the ungenerous Kapauku headman (p. 307). Even the most generous headman in good standing cannot force obedience to his decisions. According to Pospisil:

If the principals are not willing to comply, the authority becomes emotional and starts to shout reproaches; he makes long speeches in which evidence, rules, decisions, and threats form inducements. Indeed, the authority may go as far as to start *wainai* (the mad dance), or change his tactics suddenly and weep bitterly about the misconduct of the defendant and the fact that he refuses to obey. Some native authorities are so skilled in the art of persuasion that they can produce genuine tears which almost always break the resistance of the unwilling party.   [Pospisil 1968:221]

One wonders if the Kapauku headman does not shed tears more because he is frustrated than because he is skilled.

The Population Limits of Egalitarian Organizations

In the absence of a powerful leader or governing class, how large a population can be mobilized for cooperative activity? Nineteenth-century theories of the origin of the state surmised that egalitarian organizations could function effectively only within a single village or at most a group of villages—perhaps one or two thousand people at best. The reasons advanced were essentially sound: beyond a certain point it is simply mechanically impossible for headmen to intuit public opinion and act on behalf of a firm consensus. Yet modern ethnographic research has substantially qualified this view. It has been found that for *limited* purposes, especially for warfare, remarkably large numbers of people can join together in temporary alliances completely without centralized political leadership.

368

The prime ethnographic case is that of the Nuer, a pastoral and farming people who live astride the marshy grasslands of the Upper Nile in the Sudan. There is no doubt about the absence of law-and-order specialists throughout Nuerland:

The lack of governmental organs among the Nuer, the absence of legal institutions of developed leadership, and generally, of organized political life is remarkable. . . . The ordered anarchy in which they live accords well with their character, for it is impossible to live among Nuer and conceive of rulers ruling over them. . . . The Nuer is a product of a hard and egalitarian upbringing, is deeply democratic, and is easily roused to violence. This turbulent spirit finds any restraint irksome and no man recognizes a superior. Wealth makes no difference. A man with many cattle is envied but not treated differently from a man with few cattle. Birth makes no difference. . . . There is no master or servant in their society but only equals who regard themselves as God's noblest creation. . . . Among themselves even the suspicion of an order riles a man . . . he will not submit to any authority which clashes with his own interest and he does not consider himself bound to anyone.   [Evans-Pritchard 1940:181–182]

The largest emic political units among the Nuer are the "tribes," some of which contain as many as thirty to forty thousand people. The Nuer are organized according to the following kinship principles. Each political unit is a huge patriclan that is divided into numerous lineages. Generally speaking, genealogical distance increases with geographical distance, so that adjacent villages usually have lineage cores belonging to the same major lineage. What is distinctive about the Nuer organization is that varying depths and spans of lineage kin can be brought into military alliance, ranging all the way from the members of a single minimal lineage to all the maximal lineages. The extent of the activation of these segments depends entirely upon the size and nature of the opposing forces. Sometimes the opposition arises among the Nuer themselves; each segment then calls upon kin up to the level and span of the opposition or until a common ancestor is reached. When the threat originates among the non-Nuer, the call for assistance spreads up and out through wider and wider segments until all Nuer have the opportunity to be involved. Indeed, the very existence of the segments can be said to depend on the opposition that they confront. To give the phenomenon its technical name, the segments exist by virtue of their *complementary opposition.*

Complementary opposition seems to be related to the Nuer's expansion into their present habitat at the expense of groups that had previously occupied the region. The habitat itself is distinguished by a regular alternation of immense floods and severe droughts. Large, permanent, year-round settlements are impossible. During the rainy season, the low-lying areas are completely under water, isolating the various territorial segments. During the droughts the cattle must be dispersed in search of water holes. There is no ecological basis, therefore, for the centralization of power and leadership. Yet by the "massing effect" of complementary opposition the Nuer have been able to drive out and displace neighboring peoples, especially the Dinka, against whose remaining territory they continue to press with unrelenting zeal (cf. Sahlins 1961).

Blood Feud and Complementary Opposition

The ever-present danger confronting egalitarian societies is that kinship groups tend to react as units to real or alleged aggression against one of their members. In this way disputes involving individuals may escalate to include whole villages or groups of villages. The worst danger, of course, arises from disputes that lead to homicide. Among egalitarian kinship-organized peoples there is intense adherence to the conviction that the only proper reaction to a murder is to kill the murderer or any convenient member of the murderer's kin group.

One of the most important measures of political organization is the ability of a social system to prevent this pendulum of revenge from continuing its deadly swing. The ultimate evolutionary solution to this problem was the development of the state. Given a sufficiently powerful ruling class, blood feuds may be interdicted by forcefully isolating the slayer from kin group support and by threatening the murdered person's kin group with additional misfortune should they persist in an independent course of action. It is in this sense that the state is often referred to as the institution claiming a monopoly over the use of force to settle disputes.

Some theoreticians, continuing the line of thought initiated by Hobbes, explain the evolution of the state primarily as a response to the need for maintaining law and order. The case of the Nuer, however, once again suggests that the maintenance of order among as many as forty thousand people can be achieved without a state apparatus to put down feuds.

All Nuer dread the danger of an escalating feud. The main reason for this is the principle of complementary opposition: wider and wider lineage segments are activated by virtue of their opposition under conditions of stress. But at each escalation more and more people who are interested in a peaceful settlement are brought into the quarrel. Thus, in Evans-Pritchard's words, "fear of incurring a blood-feud is,

370

Figure 17-4. LEOPARD SKIN CHIEF. (E. E. Evans-Pritchard and Clarendon Press)

in fact, the most important legal sanction within a tribe and the main guarantee of an individual's life and property" (Evans-Pritchard 1940:150).

Among many prestate societies the formal mechanisms for preventing homicide from flaring into a protracted feud include the transference of substantial amounts of prized possessions from the slayer's kin group to the victim's kin group. This practice is especially common and effective among pastoral peoples whose animals form a concentrated repository of material wealth and for whom bride-price is a regular aspect of kin group exogamy. The Nuer settle their feuds (or at least deescalate them) by transferring forty or more head of cattle to the victim's lineage. If a man has been killed, these animals will be used to buy a wife whose sons will fill the void left by his death. The dead man's kin are obliged to resist the offer of cattle, demanding instead a life for a life. However, members of the lineage segments standing next in line to become involved are under no such compulsion. They do their best to convince the injured kin group to accept the compensation. In this effort they are aided by certain semisacred arbitration specialists. The latter, known as Leopard Skin Chiefs, are

371

usually men whose lineages are not represented locally and hence who can more readily act as neutral intermediaries.

The Leopard Skin Chief is the only one who can perform the ritual of ablution for a murderer. Hence, if a homicide takes place, the killer flees at once to the Leopard Skin Chief's house. The Leopard Skin Chief's house is a sanctuary respected by the slain individual's lineage. Nonetheless the Leopard Skin Chief lacks even the rudiments of political power; the most that he can do to the reluctant members of the slain man's lineage is to threaten them with various supernatural curses. Yet the determination to prevent a feud is so great that the injured lineage eventually accepts the cattle as compensation. Note that the ability of the Nuer to compose feuds through cattle compensation is simply the obverse of their ability to mass lineage segments in response to outside threats.

The Nuer are an important case because of the light they shed on the conditions responsible for state formation. It must be conceded that as an egalitarian population expands it becomes increasingly difficult to act by consensus in the disposition of crimes involving members of different kin groups. The larger the population, the more difficult it will be to achieve consensus by divination, intervention of shaman and headman, drum dance, and so on. Yet the threat of anarchy is never so great that egalitarian relationships must be sacrificed for law and order merely to maintain law and order. In other words, the state does not arise merely as the result of the need to preserve law and order; rather, it arises under certain conditions that render stratification adaptive. The state is not the instrument of preserving law and order in general, not even among large populations in general. Rather, the state is the instrument for maintaining law and order in stratified societies.

LAW AND ORDER
IN STRATIFIED
SOCIETIES

Modern anthropological opinion is divided concerning the nature of the evolutionary sequence that led from egalitarian to stratified political systems. It seems doubtful that any single developmental trajectory was followed in all cases. Nonetheless in recent years much progress has been achieved in formulating testable hypotheses concerning this greatest of all cultural transformations.

The Origin of Social Stratification

Certain aspects of the developmental trajectory leading toward stratification are not in dispute. Stratification is associated with dense populations and large harvests. Part of the food-producers' output is taken by or given to a ruling class. Taxation, rent, serfdom, corvée, and slavery are the principal mechanisms for gaining control over peasant production (see p. 299). Given control of production, a ruling class can perform a number of functions that enhance the adaptive capacity of the entire population.

Specialists in science, mechanics, weaving, and manufacture can be freed from the agricultural routine and fed from government granaries. Large groups of men and women can be assembled and put to work on public projects, which in turn may lead to increased food production. As I have already indicated, the self-reinforcing nature of the relationship between a ruling class and agricultural productivity is especially clear in the case of societies dependent on large-scale

373

flood control, irrigation, and other hydraulic projects (p. 199). Here the government specialists form an elaborate bureaucracy that intervenes at every stage of the cycle of production and distribution. The government directs the construction of dams and canals for irrigation and drainage; regulates the flow of irrigation waters; sets production quotas for villages and farms; patronizes astronomical and mathematical specialists who earn their keep by foretelling the seasons, predicting rains and floods, regulating the time for planting and the time for harvest. All this increases the food-energy output and permits the ruling class to employ more police-military specialists to maintain law and order in the face of ever-increasing differences in wealth and power. Once this situation comes into being, population densities increase. To relieve the pressure against resources, territorial expansion is attempted. Soon all remnant egalitarian peoples dwelling in adjacent high-yield habitats are either incorporated or exterminated. Eventually there is a military clash with a neighboring state. The result is incorporation of one by the other, still larger populations, more massive output, larger levies of labor conscripts, larger police-army forces, and a more powerful and privileged ruling class.

It is clear that once in existence the state is adaptively superior to primitive egalitarian organizations. But how the state came into existence remains a great puzzle. During the transition from egalitarian society to stratified society those who became the governing class were rewarded with unprecedented privileges and material luxuries. But what were the rewards of those who were cut off from the ancient universal heritage of free access to basic resources? Expropriation of the producer's output frees the governing class from food-producing activities, but it binds the food-producing class to unprecedented forms of drudgery and exploitation. How did vast segments of humanity get cut off from access to the earth's natural resources? Why was control of the soil, water, and even the air yielded up into the hands of a relatively small group of people?

As suggested in Chapter 14, the phenomenon of redistribution provides a possible link between egalitarian chieftainship and the earliest known stratified societies. It is time to take a closer look at this relationship.

The Egalitarian Redistributor

I left the "social director" egalitarian headman exhorting his people to increase production and setting an example by his own strenuous efforts. Intense collecting and hunting in most habitats may simply

374

kill off next year's source of calories and protein. In horticultural or exceptionally high-yield fishing and hunting contexts, however, increased work effort will raise production without damaging the habitat, and under such conditions extra individual input may substantially raise a small village's standard of living. As long as everyone shares in the extra products, the headman and his helpers will receive the admiration and encouragement of the entire community.

Numerous redistributive systems in which the redistributor, known in the Oceanian ethnographic literature as a *big man,* acquires a definite political status have now been studied (cf. Sahlins 1971). Typically this status is achieved in connection with rivalrous public feasting (see p. 290). The aspiring big man and the people who have helped him give away the results of their extra productive effort to invited guests from their own and neighboring settlements. In general the big man cannot secure his position by means of a single giveaway feast; numerous repetitions escalating in lavishness are needed. A careful study of this process has been made by Ian Hogbin (1964) among the Kaoka-speaking people of Guadalcanal in the Solomon Islands.

The would-be big man in Guadalcanal begins his career by cultivating larger gardens. He solicits help from his kin and neighbors, rewarding them with meals at the end of the day. He also begins to raise more pigs, begging sows from litters owned by relatives, and farming out additional animals to his sisters and other members of his kin group. When crops on several acres are flourishing and about ten fat pigs are available, the aspiring big man undertakes the construction of a larger-than-usual dwelling. Once again he has the assistance of his kin and neighbors, who are rewarded throughout the construction period with meals and promises of large-scale feasting. When the house has been completed a group of supporters, including kinsmen from several different hamlets, combine for a series of fishing expeditions.

In the case of a big man named Atana, the fishing expeditions lasted for ten days. While the men were away, Atana's kinswomen busied themselves in the yam gardens. Four more days were devoted to collecting banana leaves, firewood, and coconuts to be used in the preparation of yam and coconut layer cakes. On the day of the feast, 250 pounds of dried fish, 3,000 yam and coconut layer cakes, 11 large bowls of yam pudding, and 8 pigs were displayed in front of Atana's new house. All this was the direct result of the extra effort of Atana and his kin. But the invited guests also brought their own food, bringing the total up to 300 pounds of fish, 5,000 layer cakes, 19 bowls of pudding, and 13 pigs. Atana now proceeded to make up 257 portions of varying sizes and quality and redistributed them among

375

the various categories of people who had helped him or who had brought contributions to the feast. "Only the remnants were left for Atana himself." Hogbin explains this by means of a local adage: "The giver of the feast takes the bones and the stale cakes; the meat and the fat go to others" (ibid.: 66).

This first feast must be followed by several others. Larger gardens, more pigs, more help from kin, bigger displays of generosity, and larger feasts and entertainments mark the difficult path. The aspiring big man must build a clubhouse for the men of the hamlet, provide pigs for ceremonials, and, if a sorcerer is to be killed, reward the warriors who do the killing.

If he goes on doing all these things there is little doubt about his becoming headman of his village. But no matter how much food and other things he has given away, he can never rest on his laurels. As soon as his gardens begin to shrink in area and his herds cease to multiply, as well may happen when he becomes advanced in age and less active, he subsides into insignificance.   [ibid.:69–70]

Redistribution, Productivity, and Stratification

An important advance in understanding the evolutionary significance of redistribution is owed to Marshall Sahlins' study of stratification differences among the island societies of Polynesia. Sahlins (1958) showed that variations in Polynesian redistributive systems are associated with variations in the stratification hierarchies found on each island. In general the greater the amount of energy and materials flowing through the economy the greater the degree of social stratification. On small atolls or islands with improverished soils or poor fishing grounds, redistributive activities were confined to small networks of kin and involved relatively small amounts of produce. In the larger, better-endowed islands, such as Tonga, Hawaii, and Tahiti, complex networks involving production quotas and taxation concentrated huge amounts of food and materials into the hands of a powerful full-time governing class. At the apex of these stratified, state-level systems, there were a king and royal family who abstained from ordinary subsistence tasks. In Hawaii the Alii Nui, like the Inca of Peru (see p. 386) and the Pharaoh of Egypt, claimed descent from the sun. He was carried around on a palanquin, lest the touch of his foot render the ground permanently taboo to commoners; his holiness was so great that only his sister was suitable to be his wife. The Alii Nui lived in a palace that was staffed by specially trained attendants,

376

and he controlled the services of full-time warriors and religious specialists drawn from the royal family.

Although there is no proof that the various forms of Oceanian redistribution systems actually evolved one from the other, certain inferences about one of the processes that might lead to stratification seem justified. The key to the situation is control over the producers' harvests, which are conveniently collected together in every redistributive performance. Increasing delays in disbursement and prolongation of the collection phase combined with technologically induced increments in productivity (such as the introduction of irrigation techniques or new crops) provide the egalitarian redistributor with the material basis for becoming the owner of all nature. Under certain conditions to be made clear in a moment, kin and neighbors can be satisfied with less than a total redistribution and a portion of the food supply can be held back permanently to constitute the rudiment of a royal treasury for the maintenance of police-military forces and other specialists.

Figure 10-1. IMMORTAL PHARAOH. The temple of Abu Simbel was moved out of the way of the rising waters of the Aswan Dam. Thus, Ramses II, who has just gotten his head back, continues obliging others to do his bidding, three thousand years after his death. (UPI Photo)

377

Redistribution, Productivity, and Stratification

On the Threshold of Stratification:
The Trobriand Islands

Some aspects of this hypothetical process seem to be present in the Trobriand Islands. Trobriand society is organized primarily along kinship lines. There are four major matriclans, each consisting of several landowning subclans. The women live away from their subclan lands and hence do not work on their own subclan gardens. (Their husbands live avunculocally.) At yam harvest time the men of each subclan send their absent sisters gift baskets of yams. Now the Trobrianders have a fairly powerful ruler—a paramount chief—whose most distinctive characteristic is that he is married to sixty wives, most of whom are drawn from different clans and subclans. Moreover each wife is usually the sister of a clan or subclan headman. At yam harvest time these headmen call upon their clansmen to help collect gift yams for their absent sisters, the chief's wives. These yams are then put in baskets and delivered to the paramount chief's village where they are placed on display in special yam racks. A portion of this display is redistributed in elaborate feasts. Another portion, however, is held back and used to feed canoe-building specialists and other artisans and retainers. The Trobriand paramount chief participates in the work process only in a ritual capacity; he performs ceremonies to initiate the planting of gardens and "pays" for magicians who signal the various phases of the agricultural cycle by the performance of suitable rites.

Despite his sixty wives, the Trobriand chief stands midway between a big man and a genuine state-level ruler. The paramount chief is dependent upon the voluntary contributions of his kin; he has no police-military specialists; he cannot set production quotas or enforce obedience except by common consent or the threat of black magic. As for the sixty wives, it should be recalled that even egalitarian redistributors enjoy the privilege of polygyny. Moreover the large number of wives reported by Malinowski probably reflected the effects of European contact. It seems likely that the Trobriand chief's harem underwent a rapid expansion after European companies began to use him as an intermediary in copra production and labor recruitment, thus greatly increasing the wealth under his control (Uberoi 1962).

On the Threshold of Stratification: Tikopia

Another famous ethnographic case is Tikopia, a Polynesian "outlier" in the Solomon Islands. Here the chief's pretensions and claims were greater than those of the Trobriand chief, but the actual power available was considerably less than what the Trobriand chief disposed. Thus the Tikopian chiefs claimed that they "owned" all the land and sea resources, yet the size of the redistributive network and of the harvests under their control made such claims unenforceable. Despite an elaborate ideology of special descent, Tikopian chiefs enjoyed few sumptuary privileges. Nominally they claimed control of their cognatic kin group's gardens; but in practice they could not restrict their kin from any unused sites. Labor for their own gardens was in scarce supply, and they themselves worked as any "commoner" in the fields. To validate their positions they were obliged to give large feasts, which in turn rested upon the voluntary labor and food contributions of their kin. Ties of kinship tended to efface the abstract prerequisites and etiquette of higher rank. Raymond Firth describes how a classificatory "brother" from a commoner family could exchange bawdy insults with the island's highest ranking chief:

On one occasion I was walking with the Ariki (chief) Kafika . . . when we passed the orchard of Pae Sao . . . all the principals present were "brothers" through various ties, and with one accord they fell upon each other with obscene chaff. Epithets of "Big testicles!" "You are the enormous testicles!" flew back and forth to the accompaniment of hilarious laughter. I was somewhat surprised at the vigor of the badinage for the Ariki Kafika, as the most respected chief of the island, has a great deal of sanctity attached to him. . . . However, this did not save him and he took it in good part. . . .   [Firth 1957:176–177]

Conditions Promoting Stratification

The further evolution of big man and paramount chief into kings and other state-level rulers depends on four factors: (1) a mode of production that can be intensified so that the imposition of taxes, rents, and production quotas will yield greater energy flow and higher population densities; (2) a redistributive system whose scale exceeds that which is characteristic of prestate political systems such as Tikopia or the Trobriands; (3) intensive warfare, which gives the redistributor permanent control over police-military specialists; and (4) an *impacted* habitat (Carneiro 1970).

An impacted habitat exists when people cannot avoid production quotas, rents, and taxes by fleeing to virgin areas where they can work less and eat as much. Impaction is especially likely in fertile river valleys surrounded by arid lands. It is probable that the very first states arose in such habitats in the Middle East and East Asia and Peru. Impaction can also be produced in groups that depend on irrigation in highland valleys, as in the case of Mexico, and it can also occur, but with less likelihood, in restricted tropical forest habitats that are closed off by mountains and oceans, as in the case of the Yucatan Peninsula. But the most important source of impaction is the expansion of the state itself. That is, once the first states come into existence they themselves constitute barriers against the flight of people who seek to maintain egalitarian systems. Moreover, with states as neighbors, egalitarian peoples find themselves increasingly drawn into warfare and are compelled to increase production and to give their redistributor-chiefs more and more power in order to prevail against the expansionist tendencies of their neighbors. Thus most of the states of the world are produced by a great diversity of specific historical and ecological conditions (Fried 1967).

An African Kingdom: Bunyoro

Africa south of the Sahara is a particularly rich repository of stratified societies where control over redistribution led to effective control over access to basic resources. States ranging in size from tens of thousands to millions of people were widely distributed throughout West and Equatorial Africa, the Sudan, East Africa, and the Rift Valley Lake Regions.

Bunyoro, a medium-sized state in Uganda with a population of about a hundred thousand people and an area of about five thousand square miles, will serve as a convenient example. Supreme power over the Bunyoro territory and its inhabitants was vested in the Mukama, scion of a royal lineage that reckoned its descent back to the beginning of time. The use of all natural resources, but especially of farming land, was a dispensation specifically granted by the Mukama to a dozen or more "chiefs" or to commoners under their respective control. In return for these dispensations, quantities of food, handicrafts, and labor services were funneled up through the power hierarchy into the Mukama's headquarters. The Mukama in turn directed the use of these goods and services on behalf of state enterprises. The basic redistributive pattern was still plainly in evidence:

In the traditional system the king was seen both as the supreme receiver of goods and services, and as the supreme giver. . . . The great chiefs, who themselves received tribute from their dependents, were required to hand over to the Mukama a part of the produce of their estates in the form of crops, cattle, beer or women. . . . But everyone must give to the king, not only the chiefs. . . . The Mukama's role as giver was, accordingly, no less stressed. Many of his special names emphasize his magnanimity and he was

380

traditionally expected to give extensively in the form both of feasts and of gifts to individuals.   [Beattie 1960:34]

However great the Mukama's reputation for generosity, it is clear that he did not give away as much as he received. He certainly did not follow Atana, the Guadalcanal headman, and keep only the stale cakes and bones for himself. Moreover much of what he gave away did not flow back down to the peasant producers. Instead it remained in the hands of his genealogically close kin, who constituted a clearly demarcated aristocratic class. Part of what the Mukama took away from the peasants was bestowed on nonkin who performed extraordinary services on behalf of the state, especially in connection with military exploits. Another part was used to support a permanent palace guard and resident staff who attended the Mukama's personal needs and performed magico-religious rites deemed essential for the welfare of the Mukama and the nation. The following regalia keepers and palace officials were still functioning in 1951–1955 when Beattie did his field work: custodian of spears, custodian of royal graves, custodian of the royal drums, custodian of royal crowns, "putters-on" of the royal crowns, custodians of royal thrones (stools) and other regalia, cooks, bath attendants, herdsmen, potters, barkcloth makers, musicians, and many others. Many of these officials had several assistants. In

Figure 18-2. AFRICAN ROYALTY. Members of the ruling class of Dahomey. (Marc and Evelyne Bern heim/Rapho Guillumette)

An African Kingdom: Bunyoro

addition there was a loosely defined category of advisers, diviners and other retainers who hung around the court, attached to the Mukama's household or dependents, in the hope of being appointed to a chieftainship. To this must be added the Mukama's extensive harem, his many children, and the polygynous *ménages* of his brothers and of other royal personages. To keep his power intact, the Mukama and portions of his court made frequent trips throughout Bunyoro staying at local palaces maintained at the expense of his chiefs and commoners. (In precontact times, he may not have had any permanent headquarters.)

Feudalism

As Beattie points out, there are many analogies between the Bunyoro state and the "feudal" system existing in England at the time of the Norman invasion (1066 A.D.). Like England after the Norman conquest, Bunyoro stratification involved a pledge of fealty on the part of the district chiefs ("lords") in return for grants of land and of the labor power of the peasants who lived on these lands ("serfs"). The English king, like the Mukama, could call upon these chiefs to furnish weapons, supplies, and warriors whenever an internal or external threat to the king's sovereignty arose. The survival of the English feudal royal lineage, as in Bunyoro, was made possible by the ability of the king to muster larger coalitions of lords and their military forces than could be achieved by any combination of disloyal lords. But there are important differences in demographic scale and in the ruler's role as redistributor that must also be noted. While redistribution was continued through a system of royal taxation and tribute, the police-military function of the English king was more conspicuous than among the Bunyoro. The English sovereign was not the "great provider." He was, instead, the "great protector." With a population numbering over a million people, and with agricultural and handicraft production organized on the basis of self-sustaining independent local estates, the redistributive function of Europe's feudal kings was wholly asymmetrical. It was not necessary for William the Conqueror to cultivate an image of generosity among the mass of serfs throughout his kingdom. Although he was careful to be generous to the lords who supported him, the display of generosity to the primary producers was no longer an important concern. A vast gulf had opened between the styles of life of the primary producers and their overlords. And the maintenance of these differences no longer rested mainly on the special contribution that the overlords made to

382

production, but largely on their ability to deprive the serfs of subsistence and of life itself. Of course, on the European Medieval manorial estates, feudal lords were well advised not to push the exploitation (see p. 402) of their serfs beyond certain limits, lest they undermine their reproductive capacity or lower their productivity through illness or rebelliousness.

In comparing African with European political development, it must be remembered that there were two periods of feudalism in Western and Northern Europe. The first, about which little is known, preceded the growth of the Roman Empire and was cut off by the Roman conquest. The second followed the collapse of the Roman Empire. Although the latter period provides the standard model of feudalism, the Bunyoro type of polity is actually a much more widely distributed form and probably closely resembles the political systems that the Romans encountered and overran in their conquest of Western Europe (cf. Bloch 1964).

Because of the Roman Empire the feudalism of Medieval Europe rested on a technology far in advance of the technology found in even the most populous kingdoms south of the Sahara. The product taxed away by the Bunyoro ruling class was infinitesimal compared to what was expropriated by the English feudal aristocracy. Metallurgy, textiles, weaponry, and other manufactures were far more advanced in Medieval Europe. The great European cathedrals, castles, and palaces of the tenth to thirteenth centuries embody an investment of technology and labor power that has no quantitative parallel among even the largest of the Arab-influenced West African kingdoms, such as Songai, Ghana, and Mali (see p. 496).

An American Indian Empire

Under feudalism the highest governing class plays a relatively indirect and insignificant role in the organization of production. The primary producers are peasant serfs, who are controlled by local lords whose contribution to the productive process does not extend much beyond controlling access to land and raw materials. The king tours the countryside making sure that his vassals are loyal and that appropriate amounts of wealth are siphoned off into his own treasury or, as in Europe, into the hands of religious ministers. Some effort is made to use taxation to improve the distribution of agricultural and industrial products, as in road-building, standardization of weights and measures, and the control of coinage. But there is very little centralized involvement in the actual routines of production. For the most part, taxes and tribute in the form of goods and labor power allotment are not reinvested in basic production but are expended instead in nonproductive activities such as wars or the construction of gigantic and complex cathedrals, palaces, and castles.

Under certain ecological conditions, however, a feudal governing class can intervene directly in the production process itself. As previously indicated, this intervention may have far-reaching consequences when the basic mode of production is irrigation agriculture (see also p. 199). Irrigation is known to have played an important role in the development of the Inca Empire, the largest and most powerful of the New World political systems. Over a thousand years prior to the emergence of the Incas, vast amounts of labor had been invested in the construction of canals, aqueducts, and hillside terraces. These irrigation facilities provided subsistence for an increasingly dense population in areas where rainfall agriculture is either precarious or impossible. Thus the Inca rulers not only owned the land but they could, in a sense, turn the "rain" on and off as if from a central spigot. As a result the state was more powerful and monolithic than in Feudal Africa or Medieval Europe, and it controlled a larger territory and greater numbers of people. At its prime the Inca Empire stretched fifteen hundred miles from Northern Chile to Southern Colombia and contained possibly as many as six million inhabitants.

Because of government intervention in the basic mode of production, agriculture was not organized in terms of feudal estates but rather in terms of villages, districts, and provinces. Each such unit was under the supervision, not of a feudal lord who had sworn fealty to another slightly his superior and who was free to use his lands and manpower as he saw fit, but of government officials, appointed by the Inca and responsible for delivering government-established quotas of laborpower, food, and other material. Village lands were divied into three parts, the largest of which was probably the source of the

Figure 18-3. SACSA-HUAMAN. Two views of the principal fortress of the Inca Empire near Cuzco, Peru. (Barbara Price)

workers' own subsistence; harvests from the second and third parts were turned over to ecclesiastical and government agents who stored them in provincial granaries. The distribution of these supplies was entirely under the control of the central administration. Likewise when laborpower was needed to build roads, bridges, canals, fortresses, or other public works, government recruiters reached directly into the villages. Because of the size of the administrative network and the density of population, huge numbers of workers could be placed at the disposal of the Inca engineers. In the construction of Cuzco's fortress of Sacsahuaman, probably the greatest masonry structure in the New World, thirty thousand people were employed in cutting, quarrying, hauling, and erecting huge monoliths, some of which weigh as much as two hundred tons. Labor contingents of this size were rare in Medieval Europe. One has to turn to ancient Egypt and the Middle East for analogous systems for it must be remembered that the Inca lacked metal tools, wheeled vehicles, and pulleys (see p. 227).

Control over the entire empire was concentrated in the hands of the Inca sovereign, first born of the first born, descendant of the God of the Sun, a celestial being of unparalleled holiness. This God-on-Earth enjoyed power and luxury undreamed of by the poor Mehinacu chief in his plaintive daily quest for respect and obedience. Ordinary people could not approach the Inca face to face. His private audiences were conducted from behind a screen and all who approached him did so with a burden on their back. When traveling he was carried on an ornate palanquin by special crews of bearers. Several hundred men were required to clear the path ahead and to handle the palanquin (Mason 1957:184). A small army of sweepers, water carriers, woodcutters, cooks, wardrobemen, treasurers, gardeners, and hunters attended the domestic needs of the Inca in his palace in Cuzco, the capital of the empire. According to the chronicles of Garcilaso de la

Vega, if members of the staff offended the Inca, their entire village would be destroyed. The Inca ate his meals from gold and silver dishes in rooms whose walls were covered with precious metals. His clothing was made of the softest vicuña wool, and he gave away each change of clothing to members of the royal family, never wearing the same garment twice. The Inca enjoyed the services of a large number of concubines who were methodically culled from the empire's most beautiful girls. His wife, however, to conserve the holy line of descent from the God of the Sun, had to be his own full sister. When the Inca died, his wife, concubines, and many other retainers were strangled during a great drunken dance in order that he suffer no loss of comfort in the afterlife. Each Inca's body was eviscerated, wrapped in cloth, and mummified. Women with fans stood in constant attendance upon these mummies ready to drive away flies and to take care of the other things mummies need to stay happy.

Control in Stratified Societies

Inequalities in the form of differential access to basic resources, asymmetrical redistribution, lopsided work loads and consumption standards, confront every state-level society with an unrelenting organizational challenge. The achievement of law and order under these conditions always absorbs a considerable portion of the total energy flow. Even when the state provides the mass of citizens with a measure of security and well-being superior to that of egalitarian peoples, the expropriation of the peasant's output, the sealing off of habitats, and the demand for obedience to authority place the governing class in an essentially unstable and vulnerable position. The evolutionary viability of the state rests in large measure on the perfection of institutional structures that protect the ruling class from confrontation with coalitions of alienated commoners. These structures fall into two basic categories: (1) institutions that control the content of ideology; and (2) institutions that physically suppress the subversive, rebellious, and revolutionary actions of alienated individuals and groups.

Thought Control

Every state, ancient and modern, has its cadres who perform ideological services in support of the status quo. Often enough these services are rendered in a manner and in contexts that seem unrelated to

Figure 18-4. STRATIFI-
CATION: THE KING OF
MOROCCO. Social inequality
cannot endure without the
use or threat of force. (UPI
Photo)

political issues. And often enough the cadres are quite ignorant of or
uninterested in the political consequences of their behavior. Contemporary state societies deploy large numbers of government-
supported censors, press officers, media men, and public relations
specialists whose explicit task is to manipulate people's ideas about
society and the world. Yet the main body of thought-control specialists
still consists of cadres that operate in what are emically classified as
"nonpolitical" contexts.

The thought-control apparatus of all preindustrial state systems is
directed by state-supported magico-religious specialists. The elaborate priesthoods of the Incas, Aztecs, ancient Egyptians, and other

Thought Control

preindustrial civilizations sanctified the privileges and powers of the ruling elite. They upheld the doctrine of the divine descent of the Inca and the Pharaoh and promulgated through doctrine and rite the idea that the entire balance and continuity of the universe required the subordination of commoners to persons of noble and divine birth. Among the Aztecs the priests were convinced that the gods must be nourished with human blood; and as they personally pulled out the beating hearts of the state's prisoners of war on top of Tenochtitlán's pyramids, they made it difficult for anyone to believe that the Aztec state was not one and the same as the structure of the world (see p. 544). Elsewhere, through elaborate, administered doctrines, priesthoods have tried to condition large masses of people to accept relative deprivation as necessity, to look forward to material rewards in the afterlife rather than in the present one, and to be grateful for small favors from superiors lest ingratitude call down a fiery retribution in this life or in a hell to come.

To deliver messages of this sort and demonstrate the truths that they are based on, state societies invest a large portion of national wealth in various types of monumental architecture. From the pyramids of Egypt or Teotihuacán in Mexico to the Gothic cathedrals of Medieval Europe, state-subsidized monumentality in religious structures has had a common theme: to make the individual feel powerless and insignificant. The great edifices, whether seeming to float as in the case of Amiens Cathedral or to press down with infinite heaviness as in the case of the pyramids of Khufu, teach all who come before them the futility of discontent and the invincibility of those who rule.

Thought Control in Modern Contexts

A considerable amount of thought control is achieved not by frightening or threatening the masses but rather by inviting them to identify with the governing elite and to enjoy vicariously the pomp of state occasions. Public spectacles such as religious processions, coronations, and victory parades work against the alienating effects of poverty and exploitation. As everyone knows, during Roman times the hostility of the masses was kept under control by letting them watch gladiatorial contests and other circus spectaculars. In the movies, television, radio, organized sports, sputnik orbitings, and lunar landings, modern state systems have infinitely more powerful techniques for distracting and amusing their citizenry. Through modern media the consciousness of millions of listeners, readers, and watchers is

388

often manipulated along rather precisely determined paths by government-subsidized specialists. But "entertainment" delivered through the air directly into the shantytown house or tenement apartment is perhaps the most effective form of "Roman circus" yet devised. Television and radio not only prevent alienation by exercising the spectator's powers of vicarious participation but they also keep people off the streets. In a very real historical sense, the modern urban poor have given up forests of pine, oak, and redwood and received in return forests of aluminum television antennas.

Yet the most powerful modern means of thought control may not lie in the electronic opiates of the entertainment industry, but rather in the state-supported apparatus of universal education. Teachers and schools obviously serve the instrumental needs of complex industrial civilizations by training each generation in the technical and organizational services necessary for cultural survival and well-being. But teachers and schools devote a great deal of time to noninstrumental instruction—civics, history, citizenship, social studies. These subjects are loaded with implicit or explicit assumptions about culture, people, and nature indicative of the superiority of the political-economic system in which they are taught. In the Soviet Union and other highly centralized communist countries, no attempt is made to disguise the fact that the function of universal education is political indoctrination. Western capitalist democracies are generally less open in acknowledging their educational systems as instruments of political control. Many teachers are probably unaware of the extent to which their books, curricula, and classroom presentations are devoted to the support of the dominant political forms. Elsewhere, however, in school boards, boards of regents, and punitive legislative committees, the political functions of education are well understood and explicitly demanded. As a result, much of what passes for education, even at the college level, may consist of official historical axioms and myths, devoid of technological or scientific value and useful only for their advocacy of conformity to a particular system of stratification (Wax et al. 1971; Ianni and Story 1973; Gearing and Tindale 1973).

Modern universal educational systems from kindergarten to graduate school operate with a politically induced double standard. In the sphere of mathematics and the biophysical sciences, every encouragement is given to students to be creative, persistent, methodical, logical, and independently inquisitive. On the other hand, curricula dealing with cultural phenomena systematically avoid "controversial subjects" (e.g., concentration of wealth, hegemony of corporate business, the tax structure, involvement of banks and real estate interests in urban blight, ethnic and racial minority viewpoints,

389

ownership of mass media, military defense budget, overseas corporate investment, economic imperialism, viewpoints of underdeveloped nations, alternatives to capitalism, alternatives to nationalism, and so on.) But these curricula go beyond mere avoidance of controversial subjects. Certain political viewpoints are deemed so essential to the maintenance of law and order that they cannot be entrusted to objective methods of instruction; instead they are implanted in the minds of the young through appeal to fear and hatred. The visceral reaction that many American youth experience against "godless communists," "Marxists," and "radicals" is not a result of open thought and study but of cultivation of prejudices. Equally visceral techniques are utilized to condition minimally acceptable degrees of identification with a loyalty to the given system of political economy. Flag-saluting, oaths of allegiance, patriotic songs, and patriotic rites (assemblies, plays, pageants) are some of the familiar ritualized political aspects of primary school curricula.

Jules Henry, who went from the study of Indians in Brazil to the study of high schools in St. Louis, has contributed to the understanding of some of the ways by which universal education molds the visceral pattern of national conformity. In his *Culture against Man,* Henry shows how even in the midst of spelling and singing lessons, there can be basic training in support of the competitive "free enterprise system." Children are taught to fear failure; they are also taught to be competitive. Hence they soon come to look upon each other as the main source of failure, and they become afraid of each other. As Henry observes: "School is indeed a training for later life not because it teaches the 3R's (more or less), but because it instills the essential cultural nightmare—fear of failure, envy of success. . . ."

Figure 18-5. THOUGHT CONTROL IN THE SOVIET UNION. May Day in Moscow. (Wide World Photos)

390

Figure 18-6. THOUGHT CONTROL IN CHINA (above). The Red Guard lined up in front of a portrait of their leader. (Wide World Photos)

Figure 18-7. THOUGHT CONTROL IN USA (left). (Wide World)

Henry concludes that U.S. schools, despite their ostensible dedication to creative inquiry, punish the child who has intellectually creative ideas with respect to cultural phenomena:

Learning social studies is, to no small extent, whether in elementary school or the university, learning to be stupid. Most of us accomplish this task before we enter high school. But the child with a socially creative imagination will not be encouraged to play among new social systems, values, relationships; nor is there much likelihood of it, if for no other reason than that the social studies teachers will perceive such a child as a poor student. Furthermore such a child will simply be unable to fathom the absurdities that seem transparent *truth* to the teacher. What idiot believes in the "law of supply and demand"? Learning to be an idiot is part of growing up or, as Camus put it, learning to be absurd. Thus the child who finds it impossible to learn to think the absurd the truth . . . usually comes to think himself stupid.   [1963: 287–288]

Physical Coercion: Oriental and Communist Despotisms

Law and order in stratified societies depends upon an infinitely variable mixture of physical compulsion through police-military force and thought control based on the kinds of techniques discussed in the previous section. In general the more marked the social inequalities and the more intense the labor exploitation, the heavier must be the contribution of both forms of control. The regimes relying most heavily on brutal doses of police-military intervention are not necessarily those that display the greatest amount of visible social inequality. Rather, the most brutal systems of police-military control seem to be associated with periods of major cultural transformations, during which the governing classes are insecure and prone to overreact. Periods of dynastic upheaval and of prerevolutionary and postrevolutionary turmoil are especially productive of brutality.

The most enduring of the world's despotisms have displayed their powers of coercion in coiled readiness rather than in active flagellation. As long as the Chinese emperors felt politically secure, they needed to give only an occasional demonstration of physical destruction in order to represent disloyal factions. Karl Wittfogel (1957) has provided a vivid account of the coiled terrors at the disposal of ancient despotisms. He writes of "total loneliness in the hour of doom" awaiting those who gave the slightest cause for apprehension to the sovereign. In the torture rooms and at the execution blocks, the vast power of the state, symbolized so perfectly in colossal public monuments and edifices, routinely obliterated potential troublemakers.

392

Some of the most brutal episodes in the career of the state occurred in the aftermath of the Russian revolution, when millions of people suspected of "counterrevolutionary" thoughts and attitudes were executed or sent to slower deaths in a vast system of slave labor camps (Solzhenitsyn 1974). The Chinese revolution was also followed by waves of unrestrained attacks against millions of persons suspected of bourgeois sympathies, and evidence of an extensive system of political forced labor camps within contemporary China has recently come to light (Bao and Chelminski 1973).

Many Western observers believe that the communist states are merely an industrial form of oriental despotism and that the consolidation of the Chinese communist revolution will be followed by a system of police-military control technologically more perfect than that of any previous tyranny (cf. Wittfogel 1960). More optimistic interpretations of communist political coercion stress the fact that, according to no less an authority than Karl Marx, communism is not only antithetical to despotism but to any form of the state whatsoever. Marx was convinced that the state had come into existence only to protect the economic interests of the ruling class. If economic equality can be restored, the state will "wither away." The very notion of a "communist state" is a contradiction in terms from the point of view

Figure 18-8. CHINESE HYDRAULIC AGRICULTURE. Spring plowing on a commune in Yunnan Province. The construction, maintenance, and management of waterworks continues to be a major focus of governmental concern in modern China. (Eastfoto)

393

Figure 18-9. NIKOLAI
LUKIN, STAKHANOVITE
LUMBERMAN. Stakhanovites
are workers in the Soviet
Union who carry out prodi-
gious feats of production.
Like egalitarian redis-
tributors, they are given
largely honorific rewards.
(See p. 375) (Sovfoto)

of Marxist theory (Marx and Engels 1948; Lichtheim 1961). The anomaly of the communist state is officially attributed to the need to protect the people who are building a communist order from the aggression of the capitalist states or the lingering threat of the remnant bourgeoisie. An equally plausible interpretation, however, is that the ruling classes in the Soviet Union and China will neither voluntarily surrender their control over the means of production nor voluntarily dissolve the still rapidly growing apparatus of state coercion.

Physical Coercion: Parliamentary Democracies

During the early phases of the struggle for the control of the state in postfeudal Europe, the parliamentary democracies engaged in repressive violence on a scale equal to that of Stalin's reign of terror. In England, for example, millions of people were driven out of the countryside in order to make room for sheep (whose wool provided the basis for the industrial revolution). These people crowded into the cities where they formed vast armies of unemployed and totally alienated wage workers. As the feudal forms of control grew increasingly unreliable, a complete breakdown of law and order threatened the propertied classes. The slogan "Bread or Blood" spread throughout the English factory districts in 1810. After the end of the Napoleonic Wars, the crisis reached its apogee. "Throughout the first half of the nineteenth century, behind the picture of growing starvation, immorality, and drunkenness we find the threat of revolution. The newly created proletariat was ready at any moment for rebellion and

394

violence" (Rusche and Kirchheimer 1939:95). More and more the impoverished masses were driven to steal for a living. Between 1805 and 1833 the number of annual convictions for larceny in England increased by 540 percent. To meet this threat the propertied classes availed themselves of three main types of punishment: banishment to Australia or the other colonies, imprisonment, and hanging. Some notion of the scale of this repressive activity can be gained from the following statistic: between 1806 and 1833, 26,500 people were hanged in England, mostly for the theft of minor sums of money.

During similar periods of transition in the United States, vast numbers of people have been killed, maimed, lynched, and clubbed as the struggle for control of the state passed through its successive phases: slavery, the Indian Wars, white supremacy, the right to strike, and most recently the struggle between the military-industrial complex on the one hand and minorities and the urban poor on the other.

Today in the United States acceptance of economic inequality depends on thought control more than on the exercise of naked repressive force. Children from economically deprived families are taught to believe that the main obstacle to their achievement of wealth and power is their own intellectual merit, physical endurance, and will to compete. The onus of poverty is individualized and resentment engendered by failure is directed primarily against oneself or against those with whom one must compete and who stand on the same rung of the ladder of upward mobility. In addition, the economically deprived portion of the population is taught to believe that the electoral process guarantees redress against abuse by the rich and powerful through legislation aimed at redistributing wealth. And finally, most of the population is kept ignorant of the actual workings of the political-economic system and of the disporportionate power exercised by lobbies representing corporations and other special interest groups.

Nonetheless, as many college students, blacks, Puerto Ricans, Mexican-Americans, and rural and urban poor came to realize from direct experience during the 1960s, those who actively protest the unequal distribution of wealth and privilege must be prepared to encounter numerous instances of police-military aggression, arbitrary imprisonment, mass arrests, frame-ups, dirty tricks, electronic surveillance, and other forms of physical coercion. More recently, as a result of the Watergate scandals, increasing numbers of United States citizens have been obliged to ponder the question of whether the state rests on the consent of the governed or on a decisive quantum of force held by those who do the governing.

STRATIFIED GROUPS

The rich man in his castle
The poor man at his gate
God made them, high or lowly
And ordered their estate.

"All Things Bright and Beautiful," by C.F. Alexander
Nineteenth-Century Protestant Hymn

In this chapter I shall identify and describe the principal varieties of stratified groups found in state-level societies. People who live in state-level societies think and behave in ways that are determined to a great extent by their membership in stratified groups and by their position in a stratification hierarchy. Responsible scientific studies of the culture of state-level societies must include an analysis of the different values and conflicting material interests of stratified groups.

Class

All state-level societies are organized into a hierarchy of segments known as *classes.* It is difficult to offer a definition of class that will correspond to the many ways this term has been used by anthropologists, sociologists, historians, and economists. But the most important feature of class is the asymmetrical distribution of *power.*

A class is a group of people who possess similar amounts of power and who exert similar forms of control (or lack of control) over basic resources, the tools and techniques of production, and the flow of socially available energy. All state societies have at least one superordinate and one subordinate class.

Class structures need not consist exclusively of superordinate and subordinate classes arranged in a single hierarchy like rungs on a ladder. Classes that have distinctive patterns of production and consumption and that relate to the natural environment in distinctive ways may possess approximately equal amounts of power per capita and be equally powerful (or powerless) as groups. For example, fishermen and neighboring peasant farmers are sometimes usefully regarded as two separate classes because of different life-styles, although neither has a clear-cut power advantage or disadvantage with respect to the other. Similarly, anthropologists often speak of an urban as opposed to a rural lower class, although the quantitative power differentials between the two may be minimal.

Power

The nature of the power differentials defining class hierarchies should be made as explicit as possible. Power in human affairs, as in nature, consists of the ability to control energy. Control over energy is mediated by the tools, machines, and techniques for applying that energy to individual or collective enterprises. To control energy in this sense is to possess the means for making, moving, shaping, and destroying minerals, vegetables, animals, and people. Power is control over people and nature (cf. Richard Adams 1970).

The power of particular human beings cannot be measured simply by adding up the amount of energy that they regulate or channel. If that were the case, the most powerful people in the world would be the technicians turning the switches at the Bratsk and Grand Coulee dams, or the commercial jet pilot opening the throttle on four engines each of which has the power of forty thousand horses. Military field officers in the armed forces, with their enormous capacity for killing and maiming, are not necessarily powerful people. The crucial question in all such cases is: Who obliges these technicians, civil servants, and executioners to turn their "switches" on or off? Who tells them when, where, and how to fly? Who and when to shoot and kill? Or, equally important, who has the power to determine where and when a Grand Coulee Dam or a space shuttle will be built, or how large a police-military force is to be recruited and with what machinery of destruction it is to be equipped?

The calculation of the differential power of whole classes (as distinct from per capita amounts) must proceed with the same caution. One cannot simply add up all the energy in the form of food, chemicals, and kinetic forces that flow through the masses of the Inca

Figure 19-1. CARACAS SHANTYTOWN. Squatters in Latin American cities often enjoy the best views since apartment houses were not built on hilltops due to lack of water. But this means that the squatters have to carry their water up the hill in cans. (UPI Photo)

commoners as compared with the Inca nobility and arrive at an assessment of their relative power positions. The fact is that much of the energy expended by the subordinate masses in stratified societies is expended under conditions and on behalf of tasks that are stipulated or constrained by the superordinate group. In other words, the question of whether or not such tasks are carried out depends on whether or not their performance enhances the power and well-being of the superordinate group. This does not mean that the subordinate masses will derive no benefit, but simply that the performance will not take place if the superordinate group does not also derive an important and usually disproportionately greater benefit.

Sex, Age, and Class

It is a matter of convention that sex hierarchies are excluded from the definition of class. Class refers to stratified groups that contain both men and women and that occur only in state-level societies. Sex hierarchies occur in prestate societies as well as in state societies. This distinction does not mean that sex hierarchies are any less real or important than class hierarchies. Yanomamö men are as tyrannical with Yanomamö women as Oriental monarchs are with their slaves. In the United States the exploitation of women (see below) is as real as the exploitation of blacks or migrant farm workers. It is only with the rise of the state, however, that both men and women became the victims of systems of differential distribution of power.

Although the role of women in various non-Western societies has been discussed by anthropologists . . . and the position of women in European societies has been discussed by some social historians, the sexual dichotomy rarely appears in sociological works on stratification. That this criterion has been largely ignored or dismissed by stratification theorists is attributable to several factors not the least of which is no doubt that members of the privileged sex have authored most of the work and to them such ranking has not been a problem and hence has not been apparent. Also, their culturally derived biases have been such that this kind of ranking was taken for granted as a manifestation of biological differences.   [Berreman 1972:402]

Both state and prestate societies exhibit another form of power hierarchy that is also sometimes associated with brutal and exploitative practices. This is the age hierarchy.

Age groups within both state and prestate societies are often associated with drastically unequal distributions of power. One age hierarchy, that of mature adults versus juveniles and infants, is universal. Here, too, traditional usage obscures the extent to which the treatment of children by adults sometimes involves highly exploitative and physically and mentally punitive practices. One might argue that age hierarchies are fundamentally different from class and sex hierarchies because the maltreatment and exploitation of children is "for their own good." Superordinate groups of all sorts, however, always say this of the subordinate groups under their control. The fact that some degree of subordination of juveniles and infants is necessary for enculturation and population survival does not mean that such hierarchies are fundamentally different from class and sex hierarchies. Since brutal treatment of children can result in permanent damage to their health and well-being, it is clear that age hierarchies are not *always* for the good of the subordinate age group. The resemblance between age hierarchies and class hierarchies is even stronger in the cases in which old people constitute a despised and powerless group. In many societies senior citizens are victims of punitive physical and psychological treatment comparable to that which is meted out to criminals and enemies of the state. Descriptions of class structure therefore must never lose sight of the differences in power and life-style that are associated with sex and age groups within each class.

Class Consciousness

People do not normally conceive of their system of social stratification in terms of power groups. Numerous studies have shown that class differences in the United States are not thought of in terms of access to basic resources; control over tools and techniques of production, energy, and supplies; and control over governance of the state. Instead people rank each other by wealth, education, family connection, neighborhood, race, religion, social clubs, and even manners and etiquette (West 1945). Led by Lloyd Warner, an anthropologist who turned to the study of U.S. culture after doing field work among the aborigines of Australia, anthropologists and sociologists have emphasized how people tend to conceptualize the stratification phenomena that affect their lives. Warner said that the most important point to remember in investigating a class hierarchy is that the criteria:

Must reflect how Americans feel and think about the relative worth of each job, the sources of income which support them, and the evaluations of their houses and the neighborhoods in which they live. For it is not the house, or the job, or the income, or the neighborhood that is being measured so much as the evaluations that are in the backs of all our heads—evaluations placed there by our cultural traditions and our society.   [Warner, Meeker, and Ells 1949:40]

By combining the opinions of various informants, Warner attempted to develop a single composite picture of social class. For example, he depicted the class structure of Yankee City (pseudonym for Newburyport, Massachusetts) in terms of the diagram shown in Figure 19-2.

Some social scientists are inclined to accept class distinctions as real and important only when consciously perceived and acted upon by the people involved. Others believe that the significant contours of

Figure 19-2. CLASS HIER-ARCHY-YANKEE CITY. (Adapted from Warner et al. 1949:42)

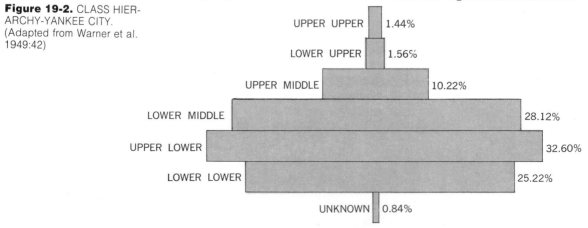

UPPER UPPER 1.44%

LOWER UPPER 1.56%

UPPER MIDDLE 10.22%

LOWER MIDDLE 28.12%

UPPER LOWER 32.60%

LOWER LOWER 25.22%

UNKNOWN 0.84%

a stratification system exist independently of the self-appraisal or consciousness of the subordinate and superordinate segments.

In the former view, in order for a group to be considered a class, its members must have a consciousness of their own identity, exhibit a common sense of solidarity, and engage in organized attempts to promote and protect collective interests. Many sociologists (cf. Bendix and Lipset 1966) believe that classes only exist when persons with similar forms and quantities of social power organize into solidary collective associations. In anthropological perspective, however, this view seems to assign an exaggerated significance to formal organization and consciously perceived interests.

The definition of class given above readily allows for a lack of understanding of the origin and structure of cultural patterns. Absence of a sense of class solidarity and of class consciousness, and the presence of antagonistic and competitive struggles within a class, do not by themselves necessarily alter the actual distribution of social power within a society's stratification system.

Subordinate classes without class consciousness are scarcely exempt from the domination of ruling classes. Similarly ruling classes containing antagonistic and competitive elements nonetheless dominate those who lack social power. Ruling classes need not form permanent, hereditary, monolithic, conspiratorial organizations in order to protect and enhance their own interests. There is no empirical validation for the theory that a struggle for power within the ruling class necessarily results in a fundamentally altered balance of power between the classes. The struggle for control of European mon-

Figure 19-3. LIFE ON THE STREETS OF CALCUTTA. These people have their residences on the sidewalk. They cook, eat, sleep here. (Moni Nag)

Class Consciousness

archies, Chinese dynasties, the Soviet party apparatus, and modern multi-national corporations all testify to the fact that class structure does not depend on a sense of class identity or class solidarity.

Of course there is no disputing the importance of a people's belief about the shape and origin of their stratification system. Consciousness of a common plight among the members of a downtrodden and exploited class may very well lead to the outbreak of organized class warfare. Consciousness is thus an element in the struggle between classes, but it is not the cause of class differences.

Economic Exploitation

The control over large amounts of power by one class relative to another permits the members of the more powerful class to *exploit* the members of the weaker class. There is no generally accepted meaning of the term *exploitation,* but the basic conditions responsible for economic exploitation can be identified by reference to the previous discussion of reciprocity and redistribution. When reciprocity prevails or when the redistributors keep the "stale cakes and bones" for themselves, there is no economic exploitation. But when the redistributors start keeping the "meat and fat" for themselves, exploitation may soon develop. One cannot say, however, that every inequality in power and in consumption standard necessarily establishes exploitation. If, as a result of the rewards given to or taken by the ruling class, the economic welfare of *all* classes steadily improves, it would seem inappropriate to speak of the people responsible for that improvement as exploiters. For exploitation to exist four other conditions must prevail: (1) the subordinate class experiences deprivations with respect to basic necessities such as food, water, air, sunlight, leisure, medical care, housing, and transport; (2) the ruling class enjoys an abundance of luxuries; (3) the luxuries enjoyed by the ruling class depend upon the labor of the subordinate class; and (4) the deprivations experienced by the subordinate class are caused by the refusal of the ruling class to apply its power to the production of necessities instead of luxuries and to redistribute these necessities to the subordinate class (cf. Ruyle 1973; Boulding 1973).

Some anthropologists insist that *exploitation* is a term that can only be defined emically. George Dalton, for example, states:

A true believer who gladly gives one tenth of his income to his church does not feel exploited. He approves of his religion, his church, and the services he gets from both. For an outside observer who disapproves of religion to call the true believer "exploited" is merely to register a prejudice. [1972:413–414; see also Dalton 1974]

402

This objection is valid only if one offers an exclusively emic definition of exploitation. In rebuttal I would stress the importance of quantitatively measuring the four etic factors mentioned above. It is true that heavily exploited subordinate groups do not always express dissatisfaction with their status. Nonetheless it is considerably more than a mere "prejudice" that the etic deprivations and inequalities associated with exploitation have often been the prelude to massive rebellions and revolutions. Moreover the psychological acquiescence of some exploited groups is more apparent than real and disappears when the members of such groups are asked different questions in contexts not controlled by their superiors (see pp. 301, 419, and 425). It is socially irresponsible to deny that different political, economic, and domestic organizations are associated with different degrees of exploitation. Because of the relationship between exploitation and human suffering, the study of exploitation is an important responsibility of social scientists who are concerned with the survival and well-being of our species. Of course it is also everyone's responsibility to see to it that the study of exploitation is conducted empirically and with due regard to both emic and etic components.

The Ruling Class in the Soviet Union and the United States

The nature of contemporary class structures and the facts of exploitation are the object of elaborate ideological manipulation by the ruling classes of all modern industrial states. Both the United States and the Soviet Union, for example, have ruling classes that foster the illusion that they do not exist. The governing elites of both countries claim that the people are the source of all power. Both ruling classes claim to be democratic, and, to a considerable extent, the mass of Soviet and U.S. citizens appear to accept these illusions as accurate accounts of actual conditions in their own but not the other country.

According to Soviet ideology, classes in the Soviet Union began to disappear after 1917 as a result of the transfer of the ownership of the means of production to the people under the leadership of the Communist party. The latter proceeded to organize the productive resources of the nation allegedly in order to maximize the material and spiritual well-being of the entire population. The task of organizing and carrying out this enterprise was turned over to a newly created government, all of whose top leaders were also Communist party members. The party elected its own top leadership. This leadership then filled out the top posts in government through appointments and sham elections. Despite the fact that the entire apparatus of party and government had quickly fallen under the control of a single man (or small group, after Stalin's death), the system's ideologues insisted that there was no ruling class (cf. Djilas 1957). During the Stalinist period, millions of citizens who were suspected of believing that the party and its government bureaucracy were indeed a ruling class suffered banishment, forced labor, torture, intimidation, and loss of life. Yet, today, despite systematic censorship of artistic, literary, and scholarly work, despite direct state control over all communications media, and despite the complete absence of opposition parties, the Soviet Union continues to represent itself as a socialist democracy (Rothberg 1972). Although it is easy enough for Westerners to "see through" this charade, it is very difficult to adjust to the fact that large numbers of Soviet citizens probably do not (cf. Inkeles 1966; Feldmersen 1966; Fainsod 1967).

In the case of the United States the publicly visible segments of the ruling class also claim to be responsible to the will of the people. It is widely believed that the electoral process assures the continuation of a form of government described by Abraham Lincoln as "of the people, by the people, for the people." According to schoolbooks, the acid test of democracy is whether or not there are regular, multiparty, one-person-one-vote, closed ballot elections. Yet it is well known that the actual selection of political candidates and the financing and conduct of election campaigns are controlled through special interest groups rather than by the "people." Small coalitions of powerful individuals working through law firms, legislatures, the courts, executive and administrative agencies, and the mass media decisively influence the course of elections and of national affairs. Elections are only the tip of the iceberg; the great bulk of the decision-making process consists of responses to pressures, ranging from subtle hints

Figure 19-4. A MEMBER OF THE UNITED STATES' RULING CLASS. J. Paul Getty, U.S. oil magnate, participates in bidding for British offshore oil rights. (UPI Photo)

about the next election to outright gifts and emoluments. Even in presidential elections, about 40 percent of the eligible electorate does not vote, and few among those who do cast ballots have detailed, special knowledge of whom and what a particular candidate will actually represent once elected (Aron 1966; Dahl 1961).

Nonetheless there is much opposition to the notion that the United States has a "ruling class." This opposition maintains that power is dispersed among so many different contending blocs, lobbies, associations, clubs, industries, regions, income groups, ethnic groups, states, cities, age groups, legislatures, courts, and unions that no coalition can form among them powerful enough to dominate all the others. In the terminology of the economist John Kenneth Galbraith (1958, 1967) there is no ruling class; there is only "countervailing" power (cf. Roach et al. 1969). However, there is considerable evidence to indicate that in an etic sense there is a ruling class in the United States and that it is the most powerful ruling class that has ever existed.

The Concentration of Wealth

Official government research on the distribution of wealth and power in the United States usually takes the form of income studies. Thus the President's Council of Economic Advisors (1974) reported that in 1972 the top 5.1 percent of the families in the United States earned $28,837 before taxes. This group of families accounted for 15.9 percent of all the personal income in the United States. Although these figures do suggest a lopsided distribution of income, they obscure the actual extent to which wealth is concentrated. Among the very richest families, annual income is an insignificant part of the increment in wealth achieved each year. Capital gains—increments in the value of stocks, bonds, and real estate—do not show up as income unless the properties held are sold or inherited (Peckman and Okner 1974). The statistical relationship between income and net worth therefore is unknown and there is little effort being made to find out what it is. ("Because of the extreme difficulties involved, no effort was made to compute the distribution of capital gains or losses among families" [President's Council of Economic Advisors 1974:144.]) Even so, in 1968 4,000 families in the United States reported incomes greater than $500,000. The total earned by these families was the equivalent of the budget for one million families living on welfare and exceeded all the money that the government spent on education in that year (Parker 1972:130–131). It is no accident that additional information about the assets of these top

405

4,000 families is difficult to come by. At least 160 of them are worth more than $150 million. "The fact is that wealth is surprisingly concentrated" (*Wall Street Journal,* Feb. 20, 1974:1).

An attempt to measure the degree of concentration of wealth as distinct from income has been carried out by The Urban Institute (Smith, Franklin, and Wion 1973) using data on estate inheritance "grudgingly provided by the IRS [Internal Revenue Service] after a five-year effort to withold it and after some data had been destroyed." This study indicates that less than 5 percent of individual adults who have a net worth of $60,000 or more possess 35.6 percent of the nation's wealth. Their average wealth per individual was $200,000. In contrast 53 percent of the adult population would be worth less than $3,000 if they sold all their possessions and paid all their debts.

Four percent of the population owned over a quarter of the nation's real estate, three-fifths of all privately held corporate stock, four-fifths of the state and local bonds, two-fifths of the business assets (excluding business real estate), a third of the cash and virtually all of the notes, mortgages and foreign and corporate bonds. After subtracting their debts, they were worth over a trillion dollars, enough to have purchased the entire national output of the United States plus the combined output of Switzerland, Denmark, Norway and Sweden, in 1969. [J. Smith 1973:44]

The same study shows that the one percent of richest adults—about 550,000 individuals—own 21.2 percent of all the wealth. There are about 2,500 individuals who possess more than $10 million with an average of almost $20 million per head! Although these figures show more about class in the United States than do income studies, they obscure the structural significance of the concentration of wealth by failing (through no fault of the authors) to show the extent to which the top one percent of wealthy individuals are actually members of the same households or families. Herman Miller of the U.S. Bureau of the Census states that 22 percent of the wealth in the United States is possessed by a group of households that constitutes less than one-half of one percent of the country's "consumption units" (1971:156). But there are reasons to regard this as a conservative estimate.

The fact that about 30 million U.S. citizens own stock is frequently used as an argument against the existence of a ruling class. But the average stockholder owns only trivial amounts of stock compared with the top managers and the major stockholders. Fewer than 90,000 individuals —.3 percent of all stockholders—own over 25 percent of all the stock in private hands. Fewer than 23,000 individuals—.1 percent—own *all* the tax-free state and municipal bonds in private hands. The same top .1 percent of wealthy individuals own 40 percent of all Treasury bills, notes, and mortgages. Once again no one knows for certain how this handful of large-scale investors is related by descent and marriage.

There is one certainty, however: "Because in many cases a small proportion of a firm's outstanding stock is sufficient to control the firm's total assets, ownership of corporate stock may confer power over assets far greater in value than the stock itself" (Smith et al. 1973:16). For example, if ownership of a billion-dollar corporation is divided between one person who owns $100 million of its stock and 10,000 small shareholders who together own $900 million of its stock, the power of the corporation is not divided up into 10,001 parts. Rather, the person who has $100 million of stock may control the entire operation; that one stockholder therefore possesses not $100 million but $1 billion worth of power. Far from exerting countervailing power against the top managers and owners of the top companies, the average small stockholder actually contributes to or further reinforces the power of the handful of large stockholders (Lundberg 1968:13). If the top owners owned 100 percent of investment assets, the power that they exercise would not necessarily be any greater. In fact it might even be less, since wealth so conspicuously concentrated would be a standing invitation for political attack.

According to Robert Heilbroner (1966:19) there are about 11 million business enterprises in the United States ranging from candy stores to giant steel-making corporations. Over 90 percent of these businesses are small and, from the point of view of national influence, inconsequential. This can be seen from the fact that the remaining 10 percent of all companies do 85 percent of all business. Of these the 500,000 that are corporations do 75 percent of all business, and of these .1 percent—the 500 largest corporations—do 33 percent of all business in the corporate field.

Who controls the largest corporations? For the 150 corporations with assets or sales of more than $1 billion, there are about 1,500 to 2,000 top managers. But these managers may ultimately be controlled in turn by as few as the 200 to 300 supermillionaire families who own 5 to 10 percent of the voting stock (Heilbroner 1966:26).

Stratification means control over access to basic resources, control over productive processes, and control over social energy. Control over corporate business activity is control over all three of these dimensions of stratification. Business corporations do in fact control access to almost every conceivable natural resource. They own outright or otherwise restrict the use of vast quantities of land, forests, subsoil, water, and air. They also control access to the production facilities necessary for the maintenance of life and well-being. Thus even without considering the relationship between corporate business interests and government policy, it is clear that the daily routines of U.S. culture must to a large extent be controlled by those who control the corporations.

407

Figure 19-5. WHAT WENT WRONG? High technology and low quality of life. (Charles Gatewood)

To complete the case for the existence of a U.S. ruling class, it needs to be shown that the corporations exert a decisive influence on American politics in such spheres as taxation (oil depletion allowances, capital gains privileges, expense account privileges, stock option privileges, and so on); military spending (defense contracts, weapons research, and so on); subsidies (mineral stockpiling, soil bank payments, air transport, maritime shipbuilding, third-class bulk mailing rates, national auto road network, and so on); foreign relations (protection of U.S. business investments in South America, Africa, and Asia; protection of domestic industries through tariffs and import quotas; worldwide diplomatic and military intervention against anticapitalist regimes). It was President Dwight D. Eisenhower who coined the phrase "military-industrial complex" while drawing attention to the influence of what he regarded as a new development in U.S. life. Speaking of the "conjunction of an immense military establishment and a large arms industry," he noted that "the total influence—economic, political, and even spiritual—is felt in every city, every office of the federal government" (Farewell Address, January 18, 1961). But other presidents had previously found equal cause for alarm at the total influence of the corporate industrial complex even when it was not so conspicuously linked to the military. Woodrow Wilson, for example, while campaigning for the presidency in 1913, declared: "The masters of the government of the United States are the combined capitalists and manufacturers of the United States" (cf. Domhoff 1970).

Class and Life-Style

Classes differ from each other not only in amount of power per capita but also in broad areas of patterned thought and behavior called

408

"life-style." The differences in life-style between peasants, urban industrial wage workers, middle-class suburbanites, and upper-class industrialists permeate every activity. Cultural contrasts between class-linked life-style specialties are as great as contrasts between life in an Eskimo igloo and life in a Pygmy village of the Ituri forest.

Classes in other words have their own *subcultures,* made up of distinctive work patterns, architecture, home furnishings, diet, dress, domiciliary routines, sex and mating practices, magico-religious ritual, art, ideology. In many instances classes even have lexical, syntactic, and phonetic specialties that render a considerable portion of their speech behavior mutually unintelligible. Because of work routines involving the exposure of body parts to sun, wind, and callus-producing friction, certain classes tend to be associated with distinct physical phenotypes. Further distinctions are the result of dietary specialties. Throughout almost the entire evolutionary career of stratified societies, class identity has been as explicit and unambiguous as the distinction between male and female. The Han dynasty peasant, the Inca commoner, the Russian serf, could not expect to survive to maturity without knowing how to recognize members of the "superior" classes. Doubt was removed in many cases by state-enforced standards of dress: only the Chinese nobility could wear silk clothing; only the European feudal overlords could carry daggers and swords; only the Inca rulers could wear gold ornaments. Violators were put to death. In the presence of their "superiors" commoners still perform definite rituals of subordination, among which lowering the head, removing the hat, averting the eyes, kneeling, bowing, crawling, and maintaining silence unless spoken to occur almost universally.

Throughout much of the world, class identity continues to be sharp and unambiguous. Among most contemporary nations differences in class-linked life-styles show little prospect of diminishing or disappearing. Indeed, given the increase in luxury goods and services available to contemporary elites, contrasts in life-styles between metropolitan-based oligarchies and the denizens of peasant villages or urban shantytowns may be reaching an all-time high. During the recent epochs of industrial advance, governing classes throughout the world have gone from palanquins to Cadillacs to private jets, while their compatriots in increasing numbers find themselves without a donkey or a pair of bullocks with which to carry out their subsistence routines. While the governing elites now take advantage of health care at the world medical centers, increasing numbers of their compatriots have never heard of the germ theory of disease and will never be treated by modern medical techniques. While governing elites attend the ranking institutions of higher learning on every

409

continent, the decade 1960–1970 saw the world population of illiterates (fifteen years or older) increase by 60 million (*New York Times,* Oct. 19, 1969:8).

Despite the potential availability of mass-produced clothing, the quality and condition of the garments that people can afford to purchase still widely signal class differences.

In Latin America, shoes, suits, and neckties are unambiguous indices of class identity. Other sure signs of class status are the condition of a person's hands, refusal to be seen in public with a package under the arm, graduation rings. Writing of the situation in his native state of Bahia, the Brazilian anthropologist Thales de Azevedo points out that members of the lower class must employ special terms of address when conversing with "superiors": *Dona* for women; *O Senhor* for men. The "inferior" must be careful not to use *vôce,* the term ordinarily employed between equals. When upper-class women meet, they kiss, and upper-class men embrace and pat each other on the back. When the relation of the greeters is asymmetrical (even after many years of acquaintance) these forms are not employed. Superiors at most permit an inferior to shake their hand, which is offered as if it were a dead fish on a string.

410

Figure 19-6. CLASS AND LIFE-STYLE. Shanties in Bombay (left) going up next to railroad tracks and across from middle-class housing. Alley where children play, New York City (right). (United Nations—left; Charles Gatewood—right)

Other mechanisms regulate the spatial positions and limit the use of intimate gesture and words. Members of the inferior group are received into the house of an upper- or middle-class person, but rarely do they seat themselves in the living room or at the dinner table. If a meal is offered, they eat in the kitchen, in the pantry, or sometimes at the table, but either before or after the others.

The members of the subordinate class are expected to show proper respect or courtesy to a member of the elite, even if the latter has committed a crime:

A *pobre* (lower class person) caught at a crime by a policeman is taken to a comfortless prison where he may be treated brutally and where his companions are criminals, bums, alcoholics, and beggars. The individual of the higher group in the same circumstances almost always finds a way to avoid immediate imprisonment. If he is taken prisoner he is brought to the police station discreetly in an automobile. He may be taken to the hospital rather than to prison, while persons with (college) degrees are *legally* entitled to be put in special prisons.   [Azevedo 1956]

Class and Life-Style

The Problem of the Self-Effacing Elites

During the present century a remarkable change in interclass etiquette has taken place among the advanced Euro-American industrial nations. Mass production of clothing and ornamental jewelry, expansion of white-collar desk work, easing and cleansing of blue collar and agricultural tasks, and the general anonymity of city life tend to obscure class identity in public contexts. Demands for ritual expressions of respect and subordination have almost entirely disappeared from public view. Many of the world's most powerful figures are careful to project an image of modulated comfort rather than of luxury and great power. This self-effacement of the elites has its roots in a pervasive blurring of all class boundaries. The vast spread of income and property rights characteristic of modern price-market economies has produced an ambiguous system of stratification in which it is said that everyone claims to be "middle class." Because of the apparent democratization of the elites, and because of the middle-class spread, many people seem to be convinced that class differences have lost their former behavioral importance.

It should be pointed out, however, that the ritual acknowledgment of superordinate status is not an essential feature of stratification. Profound class-linked power differentials and associated life-style specialties do not necessarily lead to or depend upon public validation. Vast power and life-style differences continue to be characteristic of all capitalist countries and, to a somewhat lesser degree, of most socialist countries as well. To appear in public in shirt sleeves or sports clothes and drive one's own car is not to alter the per capita distribution of power within the superordinate classes. In the industrial "democracies" of both East and West the ruling classes seek to create the impression that such ruling classes do not exist. This has the obvious advantage of confusing people who are being exploited about who is to blame for their misery and poverty.

Closed and Open Classes

Classes differ greatly in the manner in which membership is established and in the rate at which membership changes. When class membership is established exclusively through hereditary *ascription*—through the inheritance of durable power in the form of money, property, or some other form of wealth—there is necessarily a low rate of mobility in or out. Such a class is spoken of as being "closed" (it is

412

also sometimes referred to as being a *caste* or as being "castelike," see below). The ruling classes of the Oriental despotic states, the nobility of seventeenth-century Europe, and the highest echelons of contemporary supermillionaire elites in the United States are examples of superordinate closed classes.

An essential diagnostic of the structure of these closed classes is that they are endogamous. Among superordinate groups, endogamy is practiced as a means of preventing the dispersal of power; marriage alliances among the superordinate families consolidate and concentrate the lines of control over the natural and cultural sources of power. For the subordinate classes, endogamy is almost always an imposed condition that prevents men and women of humble birth from changing their class identity and from sharing in the power prerogatives of the superordinate segments.

In modern industrial "democracies" great importance is attributed to the achievement of mobility from the subordinate to the superordinate classes. In the United States official encouragement is given to the notion that by diligent effort anyone can work their way up from poverty to riches within a lifetime. It is clear, however, that only a tiny fraction of the population can hope to move into the ruling class. As in many realms of nature and culture, the latecomer's chance for success in a particular niche is always smaller than what it was for those who competed for success when the niche was relatively empty. The roster of supermillionaires in the United States consists overwhelmingly of persons who inherited substantial wealth from their forebears.

At the lower levels the U.S. stratification system is fairly open—but not as open as most people seem to believe. One of the conclusions reached in a definitive study of U.S. class mobility is that the main factor that determines a person's chances of upward mobility is the level on which one starts. "There is much upward mobility in the United States, but most of it involves very short social distances" (Blau and Duncan 1967:420). This can be seen from the rate at which men setting out from different occupational starting lines rise to the professional and technical "elite" of the U.S. work force. The rate at which members of the manual (menial) working class rose to this level in 1962 was 9 percent, whereas the rate at which middle-class men (white collar workers) rose to this level was 21 percent (ibid.). Incidentally the "elite" in these calculations must not be confused with the corporate ruling class discussed previously. The U.S. "professional and technical elite" had a median income of $12,048 in 1962 and constituted about 11 percent of the population, whereas the corporate ruling class numbers less than 1 percent of the population.

The chance of entering the corporate elite starting from the bottom of the class hierarchy is certainly less than one in a million.

The Limits of Class Mobility

Will it ever be possible to produce a completely open class structure? What would such a system look like? If there were only two classes, complete mobility could be achieved if each person spent half of their lifetime in the upper group and the other half in the lower group. Aside from the incredible confusion that this transfer of wealth, power, and leadership would create, there is another reason intrinsic to the nature of class stratification that makes a completely open class system improbable. It is in the very nature of a ruling class that it tends to consolidate its power and to have fewer members than its subordinates. For a class system to be completely open, the members of the ruling class must voluntarily abdicate their power positions. But in the entire evolutionary career of state-level societies no ruling class has been known voluntarily to surrender its decisive power advantages simply out of a sense of obligation to ethical or moral principles. Of course individuals may do so, but there will always be a residue who will use their power to stay in power. One interpretation of the recurrent upheavals in China, known as "cultural revolutions," is that they are designed to prevent government bureaucrats from showing favoritism to their own children with respect to educational opportunities and exemptions from labor battalions. These cultural revolutions, however, are obviously not designed to destroy the power of those who command each successive upheaval to start and stop. Perhaps a completely open class system is a contradiction in terms; the best that can be hoped for are relatively high rates of mobility.

In the great world museum of exotic ethnographic forms, at least one society made an ingenious attempt to create a maximally open class system through special rules of marriage and descent. The Natchez of the Lower Mississippi were organized into two classes—rulers and commoners. The early French explorers called the latter *Stinkards.* The members of the ruling group were further divided into three grades known as *Suns, Nobles,* and *Honored People.* All members of the ruling group were obliged to marry commoners (but since there were more commoners than rulers, most commoners married commoners). Children of female members of the ruling class inherited the position of their mothers, but children of the male members of the ruling class dropped down a grade with each marriage. Thus a male *Sun* had a *Noble* male child, who in turn had a

414

Stinkard male child. The female *Sun's* children, however, remained *Suns;* the female *Noble's* children remained *Nobles,* and so on. This system might be compared to a custom that would oblige all male millionaires to marry paupers; it would not put an end to the distinction between millionaires and paupers, but it would certainly reduce the social distance between them. The exogamy of the Natchez ruling class probably indicates a fairly recent emergence from an unstratified form of organization (C. Mason 1964). Under other circumstances, however, there are no structural reasons for expecting a ruling class to accept power-dispersing exogamic marriage prescriptions.

Minorities

The British aristocracy was convinced that the manners, thought, and speech of authentic gentlemen and gentlewomen were dependent upon noble "breeding" (i.e., descent). George Bernard Shaw's *Pygmalion,* in which a cockney flower girl is transmuted into an elegant lady through linguistic reprogramming, intrigued British theatergoers long after the British aristocracy had been thoroughly penetrated by bourgeois upstarts. Thus the capacity of a ruling class to present its subordinates as consisting of "kinds" of people different from itself should never be underestimated, even when the population is essentially homogeneous from a racial and cultural point of view.

On the other hand, it is no less characteristic of the state as an emergent social form that people with substantially different racial or ethnic backgrounds are regularly incorporated into the stratification system: These groups, which I shall call *racial and ethnic minorities,* differ from classes in two main respects: (1) some of their cultural specialties derive from traditions associated with alien cultural systems; and (2) they are internally stratified in their own right, that is, they have superordinate and subordinate classes whose power characteristics are analogous to or even parallel with the power structure of the host society.

No definition of minorities can be applied to the vast spectrum of stratified groups found in contemporary state societies without a considerable amount of "hemming and hawing" over the different degrees to which racial and cultural specialties are linked. *Ethnic minorities* such as the Jews, Greeks, Italians, Irish, and Polish groups in the United States are all primarily Euro-Americans and hard to tell apart physically. *Racial minorities* such as the blacks in the United States, the *colored* in the Union of South Africa, and the *mixtos* of Angola and Mozambique are usually easy to identify on the

Figure 19-7. ETHNIC IDENTITY. All of these people identify themselves as Jews. The man was born in Yemen and the girl in India (top left and right). The girl was born in Morocco and both boys in Israel (bottom left and right). (Israeli Information Service)

416

basis of racial differences. But the distinction between *racial minorities* and *ethnic (or cultural) minorities* is often difficult to make since racial differences are attributed to or claimed by minorities that lack them. Similarly cultural differences, for reasons to be made clear in a moment, are often attributed to or claimed by minorities whose behavior is largely undifferentiated from the rest of the population at a particular class level. Even groups that have lost almost all their distinctive cultural traits and that manifest no readily apparent racial differences may nonetheless linger on as minority enclaves. This effect is produced in the case of the Eta of Japan by making membership in the group detectable only through a descent rule (De Vos and Wagatsuma 1968). The extent and nature of a particular minority's etic cultural and racial differences place limits on the kinds of strategies that the minority can follow in seeking to defend itself against the hostility of the rest of the population.

Assimilation versus Pluralism

Like classes, minorities occur in both relatively open and closed versions. Some minorities are almost completely endogamous, and of these many are endogamous by "choice." The Jews, Chinese, and Greeks in the United States, the Hindus in Guyana, the Moslems in India, and the Japanese in Brazil are examples of groups for whom endogamy is a practice valued as much by the minority as by the rest of the population. Other minorities, such as the Eta of Japan, the blacks of the United States, and the coloreds of South Africa, lack strong endogamic preferences of their own but find intermarriage blocked largely by the hostility of the rest of the population. Still other minorities neither possess internal barriers to exogamy nor encounter external resistance. Such groups (e.g., the Germans or Scots in the United States and the Italians in Brazil) usually move toward *assimilation*—the loss of separate identity as a minority group.

Where endogamy prevails, either by choice of the minority or by imposition of the "majority," a *pluralistic* condition may endure for centuries or even millennia. Assimilation may also fail to take place even when a certain amount of intermarriage occurs if there is a form of descent rule that assigns the mixed offspring to the minority or if the rate of intermarriage is not very high relative to the rate of population increase.

What accounts for these variations? Any attempt to explain why a minority will develop along pluralistic rather than assimilationist lines requires a broad evolutionary and comparative approach. The most important fact to consider is this: minorities enter a particular state society under disadvantageous circumstances. They enter as migrants seeking relief from exploitative class systems in their native lands; they enter as defeated peoples who have been overrun during wars of conquest and expansion; or they enter as defeated peoples transferred from colonial outposts to serve as indentured servants or slaves.

Each minority brings with it a unique *adaptive capacity* to survive and prosper in the particular situation in which it finds itself. This capacity is based on its prior experiences, history, language, and

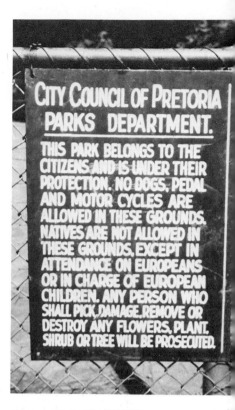

Figure 19-8. APARTHEID. (United Nations)

417

culture. Wherever the class structure of the majority's social system is marked by individualized competition for upward mobility and a corresponding lack of class identity or class solidarity, the minority may derive advantages from the practice of endogamy, settlement in restricted regions or neighborhoods, and pursuit of pluralistic goals.

The reasons for the development of pluralistic goals are as diverse as the adaptive capacities of the world inventory of minorities and the structure of state societies in which they live. Some groups appear to be more likely than others to benefit from the preservation of their traditional cultural patterns because these patterns have a high adaptive capacity. Jews, for example, long excluded from land-based means of earning a living in Europe, arrived in the rapidly urbanizing society of late nineteenth-century United States "preadapted" to compete for upward mobility in occupations requiring high levels of literacy. Contemporary Japanese migrants to Brazil bring with them special skills related to intensive agriculture and truck farming. Chinese migrants in many parts of the world achieve outstanding success by adhering to traditional family-based patterns of business activity.

Conspicuous forms of pluralism in which differences in language, religion, and other aspects of life-styles are employed to increase the minority's sense of identity may have considerable utility in impersonalized, class-structured, competitive contexts. Informal networks of Jewish, Chinese, Japanese, Greek, Syrian, Hindu, or Moslem merchants and businesspeople frequently provide important commercial advantages in highly competitive situations. Yet minority solidarity carries with it the danger of overexposure and reaction. In maintaining and increasing their own solidarity, minorities run the risk of increasing the sense of alienation of the larger population and hence of becoming the scapegoats of genocidal policies. The fate of the Jews in Germany and Poland, the Hindu Indians in East and Southern Africa, the Chinese in Indonesia, and the Moslems in India are some of the better known examples of "successful" minority adaptations that have been followed by mass slaughter and/or expulsion.

Another important reason for the perpetuation of pluralist goals is that the wealthier and more powerful segments of the minority often derive economic and political strength from the maintenance of a separate identity for their subordinates. Roger Sanjek (1972) studied the relationship between twenty-three different "tribal" groups who live in the city of Accra, Ghana, and found that in terms of language, behavior, dress, residence, and facial markings there was little to distinguish one group from another. Nonetheless politicians relied

418

heavily on their tribal identities in competing for political office. Based on his study of the relation between Afro-Americans and Hindus in Guyana, Leo Despres (1975) suggests that ascribed ethnic (cultural and/or racial) identities will follow upon the differential adaptation of population segments and persist to the extent that the assertion of ethnic identities serves to confer competitive advantage in respect to environmental resources.

Pluralism and "Black Power"

By remaining identified as a minority enclave, especially with a strong locality base, minority groups minimize the psychological tensions to which they are exposed in their obstacle-strewn attempt to achieve upward mobility. Living with their "own kind" they are less likely to suffer from the psychological effects of the defamatory stereotypes and discriminatory practices that greet any stranger's attempts to find a decent place within the class hierarchy.

The association of minority members in ghettos, neighborhoods, and regions is primarily a result of the prejudice and discrimination of the "host majority." But residential segregation (with its attendant consequences in schools, businesses, and other institutions) is usually a double-edged sword. On the one hand, the confinement of people within segregated areas provides opportunities for intensive exploitation in the form of low wages, high rents, price gouging, and sub-standard health and welfare services. But residential concentration may also provide new adaptive possibilities for the minority. Segregation may intensify the group's sense of solidarity, increase its capacity to organize politically and economically, and encourage it to defend itself against prejudice and discrimination in opposition to or at the expense of competitive class and minority groups (cf. Safa 1968).

In the decade 1960–1970 the double-edged nature of segregation among Afro-Americans became one of the most important factors in U.S. political life. Millitant leaders, rallying their constituencies under the banner of "black power," substantially altered the status quo within many large cities and regions.

Throughout the first century following the end of slavery, Afro-Americans accommodated themselves to violence and the threat of violence by avoiding political confrontation. Leaders such as Booker T. Washington argued that the problems of his people would be solved only by convincing the whites to be more benevolent toward their black servants and black workers. In the meantime blacks were to avoid the worst effects of prejudice and discrimination by leading a

Figure 19-9. BLACK POWER.
(George W. Gardner)

419

life of exemplary moral purity and of patience and loyalty to their white employers.During this period antiblack sentiments were internalized by the blacks themselves. Members of the Afro-American elite sought to minimize their racial distinctiveness: they straightened their hair, stressed lighter skin as desirable in a mate, and aspired to live in white middle-class neighborhoods and to attend white middle-class schools.

A reversal of this assimilative strategy was made possible by the migration of blacks to the principal urban centers. A new militant leadership now disputes the century-old belief that equality can be achieved only by appeal to the benevolent values of the white majority. It is now argued that equality can be achieved only by intensifying the political and economic pressures whose objective base already exists in the segregated black ghettos. This new pluralist strategy is effective to the extent that the black "community" is brought to act in a solidary fashion on behalf of its collective defense and advancement. Thus measures strengthening the sense of identity and racial self-esteem assume great importance as ideological components in the struggle to overcome the black minority's historically conditioned competitive disadvantages. "Afro" hair styles signify a new-found pride in African descent; "soul food" is presented as a superior culinary tradition; black men are urged to consider black women as more beautiful than white women; and black heroes of slave revolts, champions of sports contests, and black geniuses in the arts and the professions are collected together into a new pantheon of culture heroes for black children to emulate. "Black power" now pits itself against "white power" much to the uncomprehending dismay of the liberal white integrationist leaders. The latter are usually the first victims of the new militant pluralism since they are the most visible and most vulnerable representatives of the old assimilative strategy (Kupferer and Rubel 1973).

Minority Consciousness versus Class Consciousness

In the United States the intensity and clarity of racial and ethnic struggles present a curious counterpoint to the generally amorphous and confused nature of class confrontations. Racial and ethnic minorities and majorities rather than classes are the stratified groups that manifest a sense of their own identity, consciousness of a common destiny, and solidary purpose. These phenomena are not unrelated. The persecution, segregation, and exploitation of minority

420

enclaves by solidary racial and ethnic majorities, and the solidary activism of minority enclaves on their own behalf, reduce the possibility of class confrontations. The reason for this is that the revolutionary power of the underprivileged classes is dissipated in interethnic and interracial struggles (cf. Bottomore 1966).

There is little evidence that the pluralist ethnic situation in the United States has arisen as the result of any conscious conspiratorial effort. The formation of solidary ethnic and racial segments took precedence over the formation of solidary class units because of the high rate of interclass mobility enjoyed by the great majority of the white immigrants. Class consciousness did not develop because it seemed disadvantageous for the white working class, with its relatively high mobility, to make an alliance with the black working class. The blacks were abandoned (and actively persecuted) by working-class whites; they were left behind to suffer the worst effects of low wages, unemployment, and exploitation because by doing so large numbers of whites increased their own chances of rising to middle-class status. In the long run, however, working-class whites have had to pay an enormous economic penalty for failing to unite with the black poverty and working class (see p. 490).

Castes in India

The term *caste* is frequently applied to closed endogamous classes, such as the European aristocracies or the Oriental despotic ruling classes. It is also used often to refer to groups, such as Afro-

421

Americans in the United States or the American Indians in Peru (Berreman 1960). To complete the confusion, there are those who argue that, properly speaking, castes exist only in India.

The Indian system of social stratification is extremely complicated, and some of its features are unique to India. Hinduism, the major religion of India, explicitly concerns itself with the origin, maintenance, and regulation of an ideal stratification hierarchy. This hierarchy consists of the four major *varnas,* or grades of being. According to the earliest traditions (e.g., the Hymns of Rigveda) the four varnas correspond to the physical parts of Purusa, who gave rise to the human race through dismemberment. His mouth became the *Brah-*

Figure 19-11. WASHER-MEN AT WORK IN BOMBAY. (Myron L. Cohen)

mans (priests), his arms the *Kshatriyas* (warriors), his thighs the *Vaishyas* (merchants and craftsmen), and his feet the *Shudras* (menial workers) (H. Gould 1971). According to Hindu scripture an individual's varna is determined by a descent rule; that is, it corresponds to the varna of one's biological parents and is unalterable during one's lifetime.

The basis of all Hindu morality is the idea that each varna has its appropriate rules of behavior, or "path of duty" (*Dharma*). A system of supernatural rewards and punishments via transmigration of the soul (*Karma*) regulates assignment to the various grades. Those who follow the "path of duty" will find themselves at a higher point of Purusa's body during their next life. Deviation from the "path of duty" will result in a lowering of the soul's next incarnation into outcaste or even animal rank.

One of the most important aspects of the "path of duty" is the practice of certain taboos regarding marriage, eating, and physical proximity. Marriage below one's varna is a defilement and pollution; acceptance of food cooked or handled by persons below one's varna is also a defilement and pollution; mere bodily contact between Brahman and Shudra has similar consequences.

Although the general outlines of this system are agreed upon throughout Hindu India, there are enormous regional and local differences in the finer details of the ideology and practice of caste relationships. The principal source of these complications is the fact that it is not the varna but rather thousands of internally stratified subdivisions known as *jatis* (or subcastes) that constitute the emic endogamous units. Moreover, even jatis of the same name (e.g., "washermen," "shoemakers," "herders," and so on) further divide into local etic endogamous subgroups.

The New Look in Caste Studies

Edmund Leach (1960) states that Indian castes are not like racial or ethnic minorities or classes in other societies because in Indian society the upper castes compete among themselves for the services of the lower castes. Traditionally each subordinate caste was linked with a definite hereditary profession or economic activity, enjoyed a considerable amount of security, was not exploited, and believed that its place in the hierarchy was divinely ordained. Joan Mencher (1975) has disputed this view, attributing it to the habit of interpreting the Indian caste system according to the ideology of the dominant castes. Viewed from below, caste is an exploitative arrangement of super-

423

ordinate and subordinate groups. The lowest castes are not satisfied with their station in life and do not believe that they are treated fairly by their caste superiors. As for the security allegedly provided by the monopoly over such professions as smiths, washermen, barbers, potters, and so on, such castes taken together never constituted more than 10 to 15 percent of the total population, and even within such castes, the caste profession never provided basic subsistence for the majority of people. Among the Chamars, for example, who are known as leatherworkers, only a small portion of the caste engages in leatherwork, and in the countryside almost all Chamars are a source of cheap agricultural labor. When questioned about their low station in life, many of Mencher's low-caste informants explained that they had to be dependent on the other castes since they had no land of their own. Did landowners in times of extreme need or crisis actually give free food and assistance to their low-caste dependents? ". . . to my informants, both young and old, this sounds like a fairytale" (Mencher

Figure 19-12. UNTOUCH-ABLES. Caste in India must be seen from the bottom up to be understood. (UPI Photo)

1975). Note the resemblance between the "upside" and "downside" view of caste and the different interpretations of feudal serfdom on page 301.

Anthropological studies of actual village life in India have yielded a picture of caste relationships that is drastically opposed to the ideals posited in Hindu theology. One of the most important discoveries is that local jatis recurrently try to raise their ritual status. Such attempts usually take place as part of a general process by which local ritual status is adjusted to actual local economic and political power. There may be low-ranking subcastes that passively accept their lot in life as a result of their Karma assignment; such groups, however, tend to be wholly lacking in the potential for economic and political mobility. "But let opportunities for political and economic advance appear barely possible and such resignation is likely to vanish more quickly than one might imagine" (Orans 1968:878).

One of the symptoms of this underlying propensity for jatis to redefine their ritual position to conform with their political and economic potential is a widespread lack of agreement over the shape of local ritual hierarchies as seen by inhabitants of the same village, town, or region.

As the sociologist Bernard Barber (1968) has noted, the study of caste "dissensus" is now a central concern of village India research. Kathleen Gough (1959) indicates that in villages of South India the middle reaches of the caste hierarchy may have as many as fifteen castes, whose relative ritual ranks are ambiguous or in dispute. Different individuals, even in the same caste, give different versions of the rank order of these groups. Elsewhere even the claims of Brahman subcastes to ritual superiority are openly contested (Srinivas 1955). The conflict among jatis concerning their ritual position may involve prolonged litigation in the local courts and if not resolved may, under certain circumstances, lead to much violence and bloodshed (cf. B. Cohn 1955; Berreman 1974).

Low-caste Hindus who achieve economic success are thus in a position analogous to the plight of American blacks, Jews, or American Indians who rise within the U.S. class sytem. In all these circumstances wealth is not fully or immediately convertible into power. In the United States prejudices analogous to notions of ritual pollution and defilement set limits to the things that money can buy. In both instances minorities are excluded from social situations— neighborhoods, clubs, dinner parties—even though they can afford the requisite life-styles. Unlike their upper-caste Hindu counterparts, white Anglo-Saxon Protestant Americans (WASPs) lack an explicit religious justification for their prejudice and discrimination. Yet

425

Christianity cannot be said to be explicitly and unequivocally opposed to stratification involving classes or minorities because it has coexisted with such phenomena for almost two thousand years. Whatever may be their formal religious beliefs on the subject of cultural and racial differences, WASPs keep blacks, American Indians, Jews, Mexicans, Puerto Ricans, Italians, Chinese, Japanese, and many other minority groups out of their living rooms and away from their daughters. In doing so they certainly act as if they might have something like the Hindu's notion of pollution and defilement at the back of their minds. In fairness to the much maligned WASPs, however, it must be said that the notion of pollution and defilement is equally attributable to many of the excluded minorities, especially those prescribing endogamy as a moral and ethical duty.

In comparing Indian castes with minorities in other parts of the world, it should be emphasized that substantial cultural differences amounting to ethnic traditions are frequently associated with each local jati. Subcastes may speak different languages or dialects, have different kinds of descent and locality rules, different forms of marriage, worship different gods, eat different foods, and altogether present a greater contrast in life-style than that which exists between New Yorkers and the Zuñi Indians. Moreover many castes of India are associated with racial differences comparable to the contrast between whites and blacks in the United States.

In view of all these resemblances, it might very well be argued that either the term "caste" or "minority" could be eliminated without dealing any great blow to the understanding of stratification phenomena.

The stratification system of India is not noteworthy merely for the presence of endogamous descent groups possessing real or imagined racial and cultural specialties. Every state-level society has such groups. It is rather the extraordinary profusion of such groups that merits our attention. Nonetheless the caste system of India is fundamentally similar to that of other countries that have closed classes and numerous ethnic and racial minorities: like the blacks in the United States or the Catholics in Northern Ireland, low castes in India "resist the status accorded them, with its concomitant disabilities and discrimination, and strive for higher accorded status and its attendant advantages. High castes attempt to prevent such striving and the implied threat to their position. In this conflict of interests lies the explosive potential of all caste societies" (Berreman 1966:318).

426

UNDERDEVELOPMENT AND COLONIALISM

One of the most important differences among present-day cultures is the contrast between so-called developed and "less developed" or "underdeveloped" or "developing" state societies. Anthropologists have much to contribute to the explanation of these differences because of their firsthand experience with peasant farmers, urban lower classes, and other poor and exploited groups all over the world. Anthropologists can also make an important contribution to the evaluation of plans aimed at ending underdevelopment and poverty by showing how such plans affect the lives of ordinary people.

Development and Underdevelopment Defined

Development is a characteristic of contemporary national states whose cultures have been transformed by the industrial revolution. Developed societies enjoy high standards of health and bodily comfort based on a relatively high per capita consumption of the full inventory of mid-twentieth-century industrial and agro-industrial goods and services. Underdevelopment is a condition restricted to the context of the industrial era. The underdeveloped nations are contemporary state-level societies that have been in close contact with the industrializing nations, but that have achieved per capita consumption of only a small fraction of the world supply of industrial and agro-industrial goods and services. The people of the underdeveloped nations suffer from poor health and bodily discomfort.

Disparities between high- and low-energy societies and levels of sociopolitical organization have been present since the emergence of the state. Thus one might in a different sense speak of more or less developed preindustrial societies. For example, in terms of energy levels and sociopolitical organization, the ancient Romans might be thought of as having been more developed than the peoples of northern Europe. Or the Incas might be thought of as having been more developed than the village Indians of the Amazon basin. But the postindustrial development-underdevelopment contrast goes beyond such differences. It contains three novel ingredients: (1) the relatively high- and low-energy societies of the present era maintain close, even pervasive contact with each other; (2) industrialization is ecologically practicable over a wide spectrum of climatological and geophysical environments; and (3) development in the modern sense involves drastic improvements in the health and bodily comfort of common citizens.

These characteristics appeared only with the spread of the industrial revolution. The Neolithic food-producing revolution was carried out through sporadic contacts between self-contained and essentially isolated societies. Moreover the planting of basic food crops was limited by rainfall, temperature, and soil conditions. Finally, the introduction of grain or tuber staples and the emergence of exploited peasantries led to a lowering of protein intake and a worldwide decline rather than rise in health standards. One can scarcely compare the Eskimo, Iroquois, and Aztecs in terms of development or underdevelopment. They had nothing to do with each other; each occupied a special ecological niche; and the differences in their productivity did not lead to significantly different levels of health and well-being. If anything the Eskimo were probably healthier than the people of Tenochtitlán as a result of their higher protein intake. Similarly, between ancient Romans and the "tribal" peoples of Northern Europe, where contact was more intense, it is difficult to speak of development and underdevelopment. The culture of the Roman *plebs* offered no clear-cut advantage in individual health and well-being over a village way of life. The life expectancy of the average Roman citizen is estimated to have been about thirty-five years. Epidemics, malaria and other parasitical infections, calorie and protein deficiencies, high infant mortality, high death rates in childbirth, were probably more common in Rome than in the less densely populated areas of Europe.

The situation in the world today is quite different. The development-underdevelopment relationship applies to large state-level societies whose people have been intensively buying and selling goods from each other and buying, selling, or conscripting labor from each

428

other for as long as two or three hundred years. Indeed most of the underdeveloped nations were formerly colonial dependencies of the developed nations and so have had extensive opportunity to learn about and to become at least partially involved in industrial technology. Moreover the peoples of underdeveloped countries believe that severe penalties in health, life expectancy, and bodily comfort are paid by those who fail to achieve developed status.

Finally, popular misconceptions notwithstanding, it is technically no more difficult to maintain a factory on the equator than it is to run one in New York City. (Temperate climates demand winter heating for survival, and in summer, air conditioning is needed at least as badly in New York as in Calcutta.) Thus both the cultural demand and the ecological opportunity for development appear to be present throughout the underdeveloped world.

A rough measure of the unequal way in which postindustrial development has taken place is provided by the annual gross market value of goods and services produced per capita. As the table on page 430 shows, some countries produce as much as seventy times more gross national product per capita than others. These differences are associated with rates of infant mortality that are three to fifteen times higher in the underdeveloped countries (table, p. 431) and with markedly different nutritional standards (Figs. 20-1 and 20-2). About 70 percent of the world's population live in the less developed countries. What is more noteworthy about this situation is that the rate of economic growth of the developed countries exceeds the rate of economic growth of the underdeveloped countries, creating an ever-widening gap between the richest and poorest nations, as can be seen from the graph in Figure 20-3. Especially alarming in this regard is

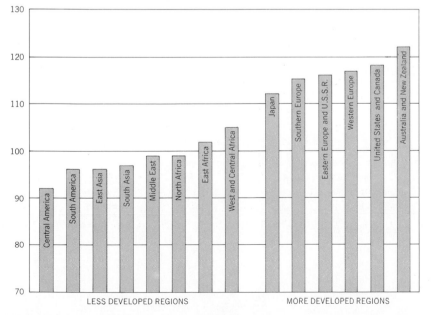

Figure 20-1. CALORIE SUPPLY PER CAPITA AS PERCENTAGE OF ESTABLISHED STANDARDS, BY MAJOR REGIONS AND SELECTED COUNTRIES, 1970. (*Trends in Developing Countries*, World Bank, 1975)

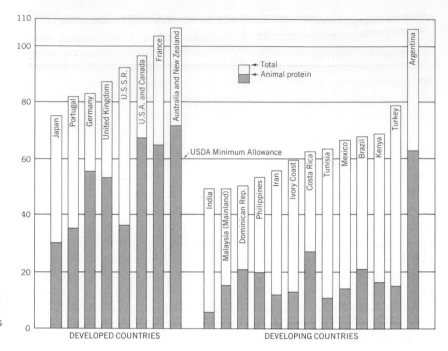

Figure 20-2. NET PROTEIN SUPPLY PER CAPITA BY SELECTED COUNTRIES (Grams per day).

the fact that during the decade 1960–1970 agricultural output in the underdeveloped countries increased at an average annual rate of 2.7 percent per year while the population of these countries increased at an annual average rate of 2.8 percent (United Nations 1973), creating an absolute deterioration in their living standards.

If the annual increase in gross national product were evenly distributed among the underdeveloped peoples, they could look forward

GROSS NATIONAL PRODUCT PER CAPITA IN SELECTED DEVELOPING AND DEVELOPED COUNTRIES

Developing Countries		**Developed Countries**	
Mexico	$670	United States	$4760
Dominican Republic	350	Sweden	4040
Colombia	340	France	3100
Turkey	310	Germany (West)	2930
Ivory Coast	310	Australia	2820
Egypt	210	United Kingdom	2270
India	110	Japan	1920
Pakistan	100	U.S.S.R.	1790
Tanzania	100	Italy	1760
Upper Volta	60	Ireland	1360

Source: World Bank, 1973

430

Developing Countries		Developed Countries	
Dominican Republic	64	Sweden	12
Mexico	69	Japan	13
Colombia	76	France	15
Egypt	118	Australia	18
Malawi	119	United Kingdom	18
Ivory Coast	138	United States	19
India	139	Ireland	19
Pakistan	142	U.S.S.R.	24
Tanzania	162	Germany (West)	24
Upper Volta	182	Italy	24

Source: World Bank, 1973

to an increment in income of two or three dollars per year per capita. At the present rate of growth of many of these countries it will take them fifty to seventy years to double their per capita incomes from $100 to $200! But per capita income tells only part of the story. Income in most of the underdeveloped countries is distributed in the same lopsided fashion as world income is distributed. This means that many countries, such as Brazil or Mexico, which have shown relatively high rates of per capita growth, nonetheless contain steadily increasing numbers of people who are almost entirely cut off from the health and welfare benefits of the industrial era. What has caused this imbalance in world development?

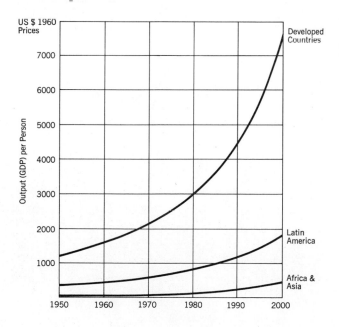

Figure 20-3. THE WIDEN-ING GAP. (Columbia University Conference on International Development)

The Causes of the Industrial Revolution

Despite the fact that industrialization first took place in Europe, it is wrong to think of the industrial revolution as an essentially European achievement. The basis for modern technology was laid down millions of years ago when the first Oldowan chopper tools were fashioned out of river pebbles by the prehistoric hominids. An unbroken sequence of technological evolution connects our most complex machines with the earliest stone, wood, and bone tools of the Paleolithic. The tools, techniques, and knowledge providing the foundation of the industrial epoch were developed over the course of millennia by slow accretion and the combined efforts of thousands of now extinct and forgotten peoples. The rate of technological innovation was at first extremely slow; at the onset of the Neolithic this rate began to increase; and with the appearance of the first large cities in the 4th

Figure 20-4. MUSCLE ENERGY. By shifting his weight, this Indian farmer near Tanjore raises the water to the level of his field. (United Nations)

and 3rd millennia B.C., inventions began to breed inventions at a still faster rate.

From 9000 B.C. to 500 B.C. Europe was a technologically retarded region; the centers of technological advance were in Egypt, Anatolia, Mesopotamia, the Indus valley, and China. Europe's basic crop inventory—wheat and barley—was taken over from non-European peoples. Europe's transport and traction animals—horses, oxen, donkeys—were likewise first domesticated outside of Europe. Europe's architectural inventory—fired bricks, cut stone, the arch—were also imports. All of Europe's basic metallurgical and chemical techniques originated in the Middle East. Ceramic and glass containers, bronze, iron, and steel tools—these were all invented outside of Europe. So were wheels, gears, screws, levers, pulleys, pumps, drills, pistons, presses, bellows, kilns, and looms. Carts, chariots, and sailing ships were also non-European inventions. And, of course, so were the alphabet, writing, books, the calendar, and the basic principles of arithmetic, algebra, geometry, and astronomy (see p. 199).

With the Greeks and Romans, Europe began for the first time to make significant technical and scientific innovations; during the Middle Ages the gradual perfection of geared wind- and water-driven mills was especially significant. Advances in metallurgy and mechanics culminated in the invention of the watch—the preindustrial world's most complicated machine. Yet up to A.D. 1500 Europe still had not achieved a decisive technological advantage over Persia, India, and China (see p. 495).

Technology in China

China probably retained an edge in ceramics, metallurgy, textiles, and explosives as late as 1500. The Europeans made a prodigious effort to carry on trade with the East. They wanted the spices, silks, ceramics, and other luxury goods that they were unable to produce themselves. But when the European merchants finally reached China ("Cathay") by way of the Cape of Good Hope, they found that the Chinese did not want to trade with them. As late as the eighteenth century, England was sending delegations to plead with the Chinese for trade concessions. The most famous was the expedition under George Macartney, which arrived in Peking in 1793. Macartney's party enjoyed the sights but the mission ended in total failure. The Emperor Ch'ien-lung explained that there was no need to expand trade between China and the "red-faced barbarian" people of England. China was already well endowed with all that Europe could

Figure 20-5. CH'IEN-LUNG, EMPEROR OF CHINA. "We possess all things." (Metropolitan Museum of Art, Rogers Fund. 1942)

possibly offer. Ch'ien-lung's words, addressed to George III, king of England, merit careful study:

As to your entreaty to send one of your nationals to be accredited to my Celestial Court and to be in control of your country's trade with China, this request is contrary to all usage of my dynasty and cannot possibly be entertained. . . .

Our Celestial dynasty possesses vast territories, and tribute missions from the dependencies are provided for by the Department for Tributary States, which ministers to their wants and exercises strict control over their movements. . . .

Swaying the wide world, I have but one aim in view, namely, to maintain a perfect governance and to fulfill the duties of the state: strange and costly objects do not interest me. If I have commanded that the tribute offerings sent by you, O King, are to be accepted, this was solely in consideration for the spirit which prompted you to dispatch them from afar. Our dynasty's majestic virtue has penetrated unto every country under heaven, and kings of all nations have offered their costly tribute by land and sea. As your Ambassador can see for himself, we possess all things.   [Schurmann and Schell 1967:105–113]

In the field of mechanics, fifteenth-century China matched the main advances of fifteenth-century Europe. Modern historical research has demonstrated that the Chinese were responsible for developing a crucial element of the watch, namely the escapement, the part that prevents the spring from unwinding faster when it is tightly wound. Ironically it was the Chinese who had invented gunpowder, which the Europeans used in their conquest of the Orient. Because of investment in government-controlled dams, canals, and irrigation systems, the Chinese excelled the Europeans in many types of water mills. Joseph Needham, the great historian of Chinese science and technology, regards the Chinese water-powered metallurgical blowing-machine as the direct ancestor of the steam engine. Needham also credits the Chinese with the invention of the first computer, the canal lock gate, the iron chain suspension bridge, the first true mechanical crank, the stern-post rudder, and the man-lifting kite (Needham and Ling 1959; Needham 1970). As long ago as A.D. 1313 the Chinese were experimenting with water-driven spinning machines that were the direct prototypes of the European spinning jennies (Elvin 1974:196).

In the last quarter of the eighteenth century China was still technologically on a par with Europe. In terms of transport, agricultural productivity, population size, and population density, the tiny European nations scarcely merited comparison. The Manchu Empire stretched from the Arctic Circle to the Indian Ocean and three thousand miles inland. It had a population of 300 million all under the

434

control of a single, centralized bureaucracy. It was the biggest and most powerful empire the world had ever seen.

Yet in less than fifty years after Ch'ien-lung's arrogant dismissal of the "red-faced barbarians" from England, Chinese imperial power was destroyed, its armies humiliated by handfuls of European troops, its seaports dominated by English, French, German, and American merchants, its peasant masses gripped by famine and pestilence. It was in those fifty years (1775–1825) that Europe had for the first time achieved a decisive technological advantage. The technological gap widened all during the nineteenth and first half of the twentieth century while China lay politically prostrate. With the central government under the control of European trading interests, the provinces seethed with rebellion, and China spent the nineteenth century regressing to earlier technoeconomic and technoenvironmental levels.

Oriental Despotism and Industrialization

If the Chinese were so inventive, why didn't the industrial revolution take place in China instead of Europe? A definitive answer to this question cannot as yet be given, but it seems likely that differences in the political economies of the two regions must be taken into consideration. And these differences in political economy were ultimately rooted in the differences between the European and Chinese ecosystems. China was a prime example of what Karl Wittfogel has called "hydraulic civilization." Its wealth and prodigious population, so fabulous in the eyes of Renaissance European observers, were based upon intensive irrigation agriculture. This agriculture was made possible by a national system of dikes, dams, canals, artificial lakes, and reservoirs that controlled the floods of the Yellow (Hwang Ho) and Yangtze rivers and supplied water to the fields of millions of peasant farmers. Vast amounts of labor were needed to construct and maintain the hydraulic installations. The prime function of the Chinese imperial bureaucracy was to organize, coordinate, and direct these public works. Like the analogous systems in the valleys of the Indus, Tigris-Euphrates, and Nile rivers, the Chinese political economy focused on a single apex of total authority.

In contrast, the basic political economy of Europe before industrialization was feudalism. Europe's crops depended on rainfall, the proper rotation of fields, and the right balance between stock-raising, dairying, and agriculture. About the best contribution the state could

435

Figure 20-6. CHINESE WATERWORKS. Importance of reservoirs like this, and of canals and aqueducts, has led Karl Wittfogel to classify China as an "hydraulic civilization." (China Photo Service)

make was to build roads, and even in this endeavor the European feudal kings were glaring "underachievers." European agriculture could not match China's in productivity per acre. Yet this weakness had an immense hidden strength: it prevented the formation of a centralized agrarian bureaucracy. It seems likely that the absence of a centralized bureaucracy ruling over a vast population set the stage for the rise of capitalism and the political adjunct of capitalism—parliamentary democracy.

Capitalism and Technology

Under capitalism, production, distribution, and all technoeconomic and technoenvironmental relationships are dominated by business "companies" that crystallize around capital—accumulated supplies of money. This "capital" is applied freely to the productive or distributive tasks that the company's entrepreneurs deem to be most profitable.

It was the competitive action of the extraordinarily numerous,

436

diverse, and energetic European manufacturing and trading companies that pushed Europe across the threshold of the industrial revolution. As these units competed with each other they increasingly sought technological solutions to the problem of profitability. As everybody knows, science and engineering were harnessed to this task, and a spectacular increase in technological innovation ensued. The scientific and technological superiority of the Euro-American capitalist countries gave them a decisive military and political edge over the rest of the world and brought into being the worldwide distinction between developed and underdeveloped nations.

In China capitalism remained incomplete. The Chinese had a money economy; they sold their agricultural and manufactured goods in price markets for a profit; there were numerous rich merchants and a network of banks and merchant associations. The peasant households participated in the local markets and sought to make their family farms yield maximum profits. But significant capital accumulation in China never came to depend on technological innovation. Profitability was a function of bureaucracy. Without the proper imperial connections, profits were insecure; they could be taxed away by corrupt officials; licenses to trade could be arbitrarily suspended; and the most lucrative businesses were constantly being taken over and swallowed up by the dynastic hierarchy. Competitive business units existed, but they competed with each other mainly for access to some bureaucrat's ear, not for lower prices. Scientific and technological innovations were encouraged, but only in relationship to the needs of imperial power. The imperial bureaucracy was indeed interested in increasing profitability and labor efficiency. But since it controlled vast amounts of peasant labor, it rarely felt compelled to substitute machines for people. The whole system was caught in what Mark Elvin (1974) has called a "high-level equilibrium trap." The system of handicrafts, agriculture, transport, and administration operated on a scale so vast that it was difficult to improve upon its efficiency by tinkering with wheels and gears.

To sum up: in China the growth of private trade and manufacture followed upon the growth of the political structure and remained an important but strictly subordinated aspect of imperial political economy (Chu'u 1964). However, in Europe private industry and commerce grew up simultaneously with the emergence of such kingdoms as England, France, and Prussia. The power of the throne and the power of the merchant emerged out of a common substratum of feudal restriction and limitations; both king and merchant competed for control over the postfeudal political economy. In comparison with the Chinese emperors, the European kings were petty princes. When they

437

tried to claim divine mandates and absolute authority, the nascent capitalist classes in France and England would have none of it. Europe's "heavenly emperors" of the seventeenth and eighteenth centuries either signed away their divine rights to parliaments or ended up under the guillotine. Europe's experience with the divine right of kings was not comparable to what Wittfogel (1957) calls the "total power" of the Oriental despots. (Fascism under Hitler and communism under Stalin are another story, but they did not last for two thousand years.)

Capitalism and the Protestant Ethic

In contrasting the developed and underdeveloped nations, much has been written on the role of the European "spirit" of enterprise. Many attempts have been made to link this "spirit" with European religious beliefs. According to the German sociologist Max Weber, Protestantism—especially in its Calvinist and Puritanical forms—gave religious sanction to forms of social behavior that were most likely to lead to business success. Protestantism emphasizes individual initiative and responsibility; it encourages hard work and thrift. Individuals search their own conscience to discover their proper calling in life. God intends the world for human use. By our calling, hard work, and frugal husbandry, we can reap an abundance of material satisfactions. Worldly success is a sign of God's blessing and a portent of salvation. But one who flaunts material rewards in ostentatious display risks both earthly and heavenly retribution. Thus by making hard work, modesty, and frugality sacred virtues, Protestantism provided an "ethic" admirably suited to the life goals of the capitalist entrepreneur: hard work and the sober reinvestment of profits.

In one guise or another, theories linking entrepreneurial success to Protestant values have achieved great popularity (cf. Eisenstadt 1968). These theories seek to explain not only why capitalism arose first in Europe but also why so many countries of the world have remained underdeveloped. Thus a popular stereotype of underdeveloped peoples is that they are held back by their unwillingness to work hard and steadily; that they lack a propensity to save; that they dissipate their capital in wasteful and conspicuous displays and festivals and in the consumption of luxury goods; and finally that they are tradition-bound and superstitious (see p. 475).

This view of the causes of underdevelopment has little scientific merit. Weber himself did not claim that it was the Protestant ethic that *caused* the rise of capitalism. He merely suggested that by adopting Protestantism, Northern Europeans had acquired an en-

438

trepreneurial advantage over the Southern Europeans, who remained Catholic. But Weber did not answer the question of why it was the Northern Europeans who adopted Protestantism (cf. Samulsson 1964).

Anthropology provides little support to the notion that the root cause of underdevelopment is the absence of an ethic of hard work, frugality, reinvestment, and openness to novelty. Indeed, as shown in the next chapter, this ethic is actually present in many of the non-Protestant regions where underdevelopment is most conspicuous. The problem is that hard work, frugality, reinvestment, and open-mindedness are by themselves no guarantee of entrepreneurial growth. If these attitudes are expressed in a political economy that systematically prevents the formation of capital and that fails to reward even the most energetic efforts, they will have little effect upon raising per capita income.

Colonialism and Underdevelopment

The phenomenon of underdevelopment has not arisen because the peoples of the underdeveloped world have been lazy. If anything they have worked too hard. But their labor has been wasted on producing tropical and semitropical plantation crops—sugar, cotton, tea, tobacco, sisal, hemp, copra—which steadily brought lower prices per man-hour relative to the value of industrial products in international trade. (This relationships shows signs of changes during the 70's). Ironically, crops like sugar, cotton, coffee, and tobacco were once among the most valuable bulk items per pound in international trade. Yet the countries that grew these crops were unable to accumulate capital during the initial period of high prices. This lost opportunity was not the consequence of a lack of a spirit of enterprise and initiative.

Most of the regions and countries that gave themselves over to the tropical and semitropical plantation crops did so as a result of being conquered and made into colonies. The wealth produced in these colonies was used to further the development of Europe rather than the development of the lands where the crops were grown and the work performed. This happened in several ways: through taxation, through interest on bank loans to buy slaves and milling machinery, and through one-sided trade relations that compelled colonies to purchase metropolitan commodities above world market prices. Even when the colonists accumulated capital, they were frequently forbidden by law or by the tax structure from establishing businesses that

439

might compete with those of the metropole. It was to end such colonial restrictions that the thirteen North American colonies took up arms against the king of England in 1776.

At the beginning of Europe's expansion, the more tropical the land, the more desirable it was as a colony. The most lucrative crops were those that could not be grown at home. Moreover the planting of tropical crops was less likely to disturb the politically powerful landed aristocracies at home. The precocious economic development of the United States derives in no small measure from the relative lack of profitability of the Northern temperate zone colonies. It is doubtful that the British would have let go of the thirteen colonies if they had contained anything as lucrative as the sugar plantations of the British West Indies. On the other hand, it was precisely because New England was useless for growing tropical crops that it had become the dumping ground for England's religious malcontents, criminals, paupers, and other "surplus elements." Even in the slave and tobacco areas of Virginia, the English yeoman homesteaders and indentured servants far outnumbered the slaves in 1776. It was this situation that made it possible to organize a fairly effective rag-tag army and to convince the British that it was not worth the effort to keep such troublesome and unrewarding territories within the Empire. Once again what appeared to be the least promising area actually contained the greatest evolutionary potential. Because the thirteen colonies were more suited to homesteading than to making quick profits, the colonial yoke was broken before the mother country could permanently block the road to industrialization.

Labor and Capital in Colonial Contexts

As new colonial regions were brought into production for the world market, the prices of tropical and semitropical crops declined in relationship to manufactured goods. One way to compensate for declining prices is to increase labor productivity. This is what has happened in the agricultural sectors of the Euro-American industrial nations. But in the colonial dependencies of these nations, it was profitable to grow the same cheap crops for export for hundreds of years without raising productivity. Instead of investing in machinery, fertilizers, and other production facilities, colonial entrepreneurs made profits by keeping labor costs down to the barest possible minimum. Protected colonial landowners need not invest in improved production facilities in order to stay in business. With the assistance

440

of the metropole's police-military forces, they can merely lower the price of labor. As wages get down to subsistence or below subsistence, entrepreneurs still can obtain all the labor they need to produce at a profit. Slavery is one means of accomplishing this rather miraculous result. There may come a time, however, when even the cost of maintaining slaves is prohibitive with respect to the value of the product. A widespread alternate solution may then be sought through corvée systems. The corvée labor force spends most of its time earning its own subsistence on small farms. Through the imposition of a tax per number of people in a household (head tax), which must be paid in cash, or through a law that specifies that every man must work so many months of the year for wages, or through outright impressment into labor crews, cheap labor is drawn at will into the production of the undervalued export commodity (see p. 383).

All these arrangements were especially prevalent in Africa after the period of slavery came to an end and before independence. They flourished most recently in the Portuguese colonies of Mozambique and Angola and are still found in the Reserve and "Bantustan" areas of the Republic of South Africa. In Mozambique, Africans who were unable to prove that they had worked for wages on European plantations or in other European-dominated businesses were conscripted into labor brigades and put to work on the docks and roads. Their salaries were lower than the already below-subsistence salaries they would have obtained had they dutifully "volunteered" for work. Another common colonial solution to the problem of making inefficient tropical agriculture profitable is to award buying concessions to protected companies and then to force every "native" in a given area to grow a fixed minimum of a designated crop. In Mozambique and Angola millions of people were forced to divert a portion of their subsistence plots to the cultivation of cotton, even in areas where such cultivation was ecologically risky and prone to complete failure. Such experiments cost the concessionaires nothing; only the peasant family pays in the form of a lowered calorie ration or in outright starvation.

Indonesia and Japan

The magnitude of the economic disaster inherent in colonialism can best be understood by comparing areas that experienced colonial rule with those that partially or totally escaped it. The comparison initiated by the anthropologist Clifford Geertz (1963) between Japan and Java is especially instructive in this regard.

Java, the most populous island in the modern Republic of Indonesia, resembles the larger Japanese Islands in certain important ecological and historico-political respects. When first contacted by Europeans, both Japan and Java had feudal organizations based on wet-rice agriculture. Irrigation was essential in both instances, but the hydraulic networks were small by comparison with the Chinese system. Both Java and Japan have relatively small land masses, broken into relatively small valleys by numerous volcanic peaks and mountains. In the early sixteenth century, when European influence first began to spread into the Western Pacific, Java was the more appealing colonial target because of its tropical products. Moreover the conquest of Java was easier than the conquest of Japan. Java was fragmented into warring kingdoms, each of which was fragmented into feudalities. Japan, on the other hand, was nominally a single kingdom, headed by an emperor; the Japanese feudal subdivisions thus tended to be larger and militarily better organized than those of the independent Javanese kingdoms. The first attempts at European penetration were carried out in both cases by Portuguese and Spanish merchants and priests.

By the last quarter of the sixteenth century, regular trade relations had been established between Japan and Spain via Nagasaki and Manila, and between Japan and Portugal via Nagasaki and Macao. The Portuguese gained entrance to the Japanese markets through the missionary work of the Jesuit order under the leadership of the Italian, Francis Xavier. The vanguard of the Spanish penetration, on the other hand, were missionaries of the Franciscan order. The mix of rival missionaries, rival European traders, rival feudal princes, and the clash of commercial, feudal, and peasant interests culminated in 1614 in a political event of supreme importance to Japanese development. I shall return to it in a moment.

In Java the early missionary work of the Portuguese was impeded by the spread of Islam, and it seemed for a while as if the Europeans were about to be driven from the East Indies. Under Islamic influence a vigorous class of Indonesian traders and businessmen held their own in competition with the Portuguese. However, the Dutch, newly emancipated from Spanish tutelage, formed the United East India Company in 1602 and pursued a policy of armed conquest intended to assure monopoly control over the entire East Indies trading area. Maneuvering between the rival Javanese kingdoms and their feudal principalities, the Dutch steadily expanded their politico-economic domination of Java and the Outer Islands (Sumatra, Borneo, the Celebes).

As the conquest was enlarged, the defeated ruling families were

442

Figure 20-7. JAVA RICE TERRACES. Intensive labor input into irrigation agriculture under colonial conditions yielded population growth without economic development. (United Nations)

converted into agents of the "Company." Profits were made in a variety of ways: by forced planting of export crops (indigo, coffee, sugar) over which the Company exercised monopoly privileges; by simple tribute taxation in kind (rice, timber, cotton, thread, beans); by money taxes; and by exports from sugar and coffee plantations worked by forced laborers. This phase of Dutch colonial rule lasted from 1602 to 1798. Its main economic consequence was the destruction of the Javanese trader class, which had almost succeeded in getting the upper hand over the Portuguese.

Between 1798 and 1825 there was an interlude during which the East India Company went bankrupt from paying dividends at an annual rate of 40 percent. The English took over temporarily during the Napoleonic Wars. The Dutch returned in 1816 but, in the face of mounting unrest among the Javanese peasants, were unable to

443

Indonesia and Japan

Figure 20-8. JAKARTA, IN-DONESIA. No green revolution here. (Eugene Gordon)

continue as before. A bloody war for independence was fought between 1825 and 1830, in which some two hundred thousand Javanese lost their lives to no avail. (Four thousand deaths in contrast had secured the freedom of the Thirteen Colonies.) At the end of this war, the Dutch intensified their efforts to make profits from compulsory crop quotas. Through massive corvées they planted a large proportion of Java's remaining nonirrigated lands with coffee—300 million trees between 1837 and 1850 (enough to make the phrase "a cup of Java" a household substitute for "a cup of coffee" in many parts of the world). At the same time, in order to encourage the villagers to plant sugar cane in their paddy fields, the Dutch authorities undertook a vast expansion of irrigation facilities, again through the use of forced laborers. The official policy called for having the peasants themselves rotate the planting of sugar and rice in their own paddy fields. Sugar production climbed steadily but so did population. By taking advantage of the extra water made available from the sugar projects, and by working more intensively in their paddies, the Javanese peasants produced enough rice to raise their population by 700 percent during the nineteenth century (from 4 to 30 million). Despite this population increase, much capital was being accumulat-

444

ed out of sugar and coffee; but these installations and funds remained wholly under the control of Dutch rather than Indonesian entrepreneurs. In 1870 the government gave direct control of the sugar industry to private hands, all of whom were Dutch.

In an attempt to preserve the peasant economy, while continuing to guarantee profits to the Dutch corporations, the government prohibited the sale of village paddy lands. Sugar cultivation was carried out on lands secured through twenty-one-and-a-half-year lease contracts between the villages and the sugar corporations. Given the enormous population increase, the sugar corporations never lacked for labor to plant and cut the cane; yet the system of leasing preserved the illusion of ownership and thus reduced the political hazards of creating agro-industrial landless laborers. The net result of all this "development" is that when independence finally came in 1949, the Javanese peasants were demonstrably worse off than they had been at the beginning of the 350 years of Dutch rule. *No significant beginnings had been made toward industrialization;* the population had swollen from 4 million to 60 million; caloric intake had never risen above 2,000 a day; the entire island, with its millions of tiny holdings, had been converted into "one vast rural slum." Practically all its capital had been drained off to build the economy of Holland and Europe.

Japan

Return now to that fateful point in Japanese history: the Europeans seeking entry to Japanese trade were stirring up the usual internecine wars and carrying out rival missionary programs. Momentarily, toward the end of the sixteenth century, it appeared that Japan would not escape the fate of Java. Indeed, missionization under Francis Xavier had been remarkably successful; but Japanese feudalism was more centralized than the Javanese counterpart. Under the threat of a European takeover, the Japanese feudal lords further consolidated their national organization and dedicated themselves to the task of evicting the missionaries, stamping out Christianity, and controlling their own trade. The Jesuits and their Japanese allies fought back but were defeated; large numbers of Christians were massacred, and trade with one European country after another was cut off.

In 1614, under the victorious warlord Tokugawa Ieyasu, the process of consolidating Japanese nationhood was accelerated. Foreign commercial interests were vigorously combated; soon even the Japanese themselves were forbidden to build ships for foreign trade. By 1637, except for a small group of Dutch traders maintained in quarantine on

Figure 20-9. CENTRAL CONTROL ROOM IN A JAPANESE STEEL PLANT. It used to be said of the Japanese that they could only copy the achievements of others. Now European and American manufacturers visit Japan to learn latest automation techniques. (George W. Gardner)

an island in Nagasaki harbor—Japan's "window on the west"—Japan became totally cut off from the "assistance" of European administrators, missionaries, and businessmen. This state of affairs lasted until 1853. During the 250 years of "isolation," however, Japanese social organization evolved in a direction convergent with that taken by the earlier European transition from feudalism to capitalism (Bloch 1961, 1964; Jacobs 1958). Entrepreneurial activity expanded at the expense of feudal privileges, and by the time Commodore Perry arrived in 1853 to force Japan to open its doors to international trade, the doors were about to burst open on their own due to pressure generated among the Japanese merchant capitalists.

Moreover, despite their "isolation," the Japanese had assiduously been studying the development of Western technology as depicted in Dutch books passed through the "window" in Nagasaki habor. Even before Perry's arrival they had been experimenting with everything from the telegraph to steel mills by following the directions in these books. Special laboratories had been established to explore the practical application of all branches of "Dutch" learning—photography, cotton spinning, sugar refining, metal plating, and the manufacture of acids, alcohol, and glass (T.C. Smith 1955:3).

Most important, the opening of Japan to the West began only after Japan had succeeded in casting its own large-bore cannon in its own

446

foundries. Of course, after the restoration of international trade, Japanese government officials and businessmen turned increasingly to foreign technological advice. They imported technicians and engineers and went on overseas inspection tours. But the decisive difference between this kind of technological assistance and many modern aid programs to underdeveloped nations is that the beneficiaries were Japanese industries, protected by a Japanese government relying on Japanese guns. With the establishment of the Meiji government in 1868, the protection of Japanese entrepreneurial activity was guaranteed by an emerging centralized state committed to rapid industrialization and the encouragement of all forms of capital accumulation as long as the beneficiaries were Japanese.

Japan today is the world's third ranking industrial power (Abegglen 1970). Its shipbuilding, automotive, steel, optical, electronic, textile, and plastics industries are envied throughout the world. In comparing Japan's emergence as a developed nation with what Geertz has called the "anthology of missed opportunities" and the "conservatory of missed possibilities" represented by Java, it is difficult to avoid the conclusion that the difference lies in Japan's unique exemption from colonial bondage. As Geertz concludes: "The existence of colonial government was decisive because it meant that the growth potential inherent in the traditional Javanese economy . . . was harnessed not to Javanese (or Indonesian) development but to Dutch" (1963:141).

Underdevelopment in the Postcolonial Phase

Why has underdevelopment persisted and even grown worse now that so many countries have won their independence? No general formula can hope to explain all the predicaments of the postcolonial tropical and semitropical peoples. Great differences in developmental potential are associated with: (1) different endowments of natural resources; (2) population size and population density; (3) the degree of capitalization under colonialism; (4) the extent to which independence is merely a word for a more subtle form of political and economic subordination to the same or new Euro-American powers; (5) the conditions under which freedom was obtained (e.g., whether through unifying wars of liberation or through voluntary withdrawal of a bankrupt administration); and (6) the degree of cultural and linguistic unity of the emergent political entity. One basic problem of the developing countries is the handicap of the late start. They are like the bicycle manufacturer who wants to start making automobiles or

447

the kite manufacturer who would like to produce airplanes. As the Swedish sociologist Gunnar Myrdal points out, once a certain level of technological and organizational competence has been reached in a particular sector of market-connected enterprises, entry becomes increasingly difficult for new organizations (1957:26).

An obvious solution to this problem is for the underdeveloped countries to sever the connection between their infant industries and the destructive forces of the world market. To go it alone in this manner, however, means that stern political measures must be enacted to control or extirpate the usually small, but nonetheless powerful, classes whose wealth and livelihood already are linked to established foreign investments. Governments that attempt to erect barriers against the further penetration of foreign capital run grave political risks since their internal security is ultimately in the hands of their police-military establishments, which in turn are inevitably dependent upon the developed nations for military hardware. These risks are well illustrated in the opposition to and final overthrow of the Chilean government under Salvador Allende.

Another obvious solution is to throw the country open to foreign capital and to actively encourage a maximum of foreign investments. However, this process has shown little prospect of raising per capita income fast enough to outpace population growth. In many instances, such as in the contrast between the industrial and agricultural regions of Brazil, the principal effect of large-scale foreign investment is a lopsided distribution of income and an intensification of internal differences in standard of living. The reason for this is that the type and size of the industrial sector is limited by what is convenient to the multinational corporations with respect to their previously established enterprises. Profits of multinational corporations are withdrawn as dividends and costs to the parent company. Since the underdeveloped countries are usually politically unstable, it is clearly imprudent for a company to tie up too much capital in any one country. Despite such development programs as the Alliance for Progress, the amount of capital withdrawn from underdeveloped countries in the form of profits, payments on loans, and trade deficits is greater than the amount invested. The total amount of foreign aid received in Latin America during 1960–1970 was exceeded by the net loss attributable to a decline in the price of exported agricultural products relative to necessary manufactured imports (Frank 1964, 1967; Furtado 1965; Kolko 1969: 68–78). Since 1970 the commodities exported by most of the developing countries have suffered a further deterioration in price relative to the value of commodities exported by the developed countries, crude oil being the most important exception

448

(United Nations 1974a). Between 1955 and 1972 these terms of trade had deteriorated by 15 percent, which was

Figure 20-10. NEOCOLONIAL PHASE. Arch erected in 1962 to celebrate the independence of Rwanda. The colonial powers left little to build on. (United Nations)

equivalent to a loss, in 1972, of about 10 billion dollars, or rather more than 20 percent of these countries' aggregate exports, and considerably exceeding the total official development assistance from developed market economy countries to developing countries in Africa, Asia, and Latin America (some $8.4 billion in 1972). In other words there was, in effect, a net transfer of real resources, over this period, from developing to developed countries, the flow of aid being more than offset by the adverse trend in the terms of trade of the developing countries. [United Nations 1974b:4]

It is understandable therefore why the underdeveloped nations are now desperately trying to raise the price of their raw materials. This effort is obviously an important factor in the worldwide inflationary spiral.

The Green Revolution

All too often development is viewed as a narrow production problem that can be solved simply by the application of engineering and other technological inputs. In fact, however, development is a problem that requires an understanding of politico-economic and ecological process-es on an anthropological scale. The Green Revolution well illustrates the calamitous possibilities inherent in development approaches that disregard the relationship between technology and environment on the one hand and between politics and economy on the other.

449

Figure 20-11. RICE HARVEST, JAVA. Harvesting (left) is done with a small hand-knife, known as the *ani-ani*. Each stalk is individually cut, but with the large supply of labor, a single morning is enough for all but the very largest plots to be harvested. The paddy is bound in bundles (right) and carried to the home of the owner where one-tenth portions are given to the harvesters. No other wage is paid. (Richard W. Franke)

The Green Revolution had its origin in the late 1950s in the dwarf varieties of "wonder wheat" developed by Nobel prizewinner plant geneticist Norman Borlaug at the Rockefeller Foundation's Ciudad Obregón research center in Northwest Mexico. Designed to double and triple yields per acre, wonder wheat was soon followed by dwarf varieties of "miracle rice" engineered at a joint Rockefeller and Ford Foundation research center in the Philippines. The significance of the dwarfed forms is that short, thick stems can bear heavy loads of ripe grain without bending over. On the basis of initial successes in Mexico and the Philippines, the new seeds were hailed as the solution to the problem of feeding the expanding population of the underdeveloped world and were soon planted in vast areas of Pakistan, India, and Indonesia.

Despite initial successes, per capita production of wheat and rice is now falling throughout the underdeveloped regions, and the world is faced with a grain crisis of unprecedented dimensions. In some countries the new varieties are actually partly responsible for this crisis. The main problem with the first generation of the miracle seeds is that they were engineered to outperform native varieties of rice and wheat only if grown in fields that have been heavily irrigated and treated with enormous inputs of chemical fertilizers, pesticides, insecticides, and fungicides. Without such inputs, the first high-yield varieties performed no better, and sometimes worse, than the native varieties, especially under adverse soil and weather conditions.

450

The question of how these inputs are to be obtained and how and to whom they are to be distributed immediately raises profound ecological and politico-economic issues. Irrigated crop lands form only 30 percent of Asian crop lands (Wade 1973). Most peasants in the underdeveloped world not only lack access to adequate amounts of irrigation water but they are unable to pay for expensive chemical fertilizers and the other chemical inputs. This means that unless extraordinary counterefforts are made by the governments of countries switching to the miracle seeds, the chief beneficiaries of the Green Revolution will be the richest farmers and merchants who already occupy the irrigated lands and who are best able to pay for the chemical inputs.

Richard Franke (1973, 1974) studied the Green Revolution in Central Java. He describes three different phases of the Indonesian government's attempt to distribute miracle rice. In Phase I the government gave loans to individual peasants for the purchase of the high-yield rice seeds and the chemical inputs. The poorest peasants, desperately in need of cash, sold the fertilizers on the black market; others defaulted on the loans; corruption and mismanagement among the officials who disbursed the loans and seeds created additional problems; and the program was stopped.

Phase II began in 1969. The government, having lost faith in its own ability to distribute the miracle seeds, contracted for a number of multinational corporations to do the job. For each hectare converted

451

to miracle rice the corporations received $54. Peasants were again given loans by the government to pay for the seeds and chemicals, to be repaid with one-sixth of the rice harvest. The loans were to be collected by the army. To make certain that prescribed amounts of insecticides were applied on schedule, the corporations hired planes and pilots to spray a million hectares from the air, endangering the fish in the ponds and the water buffalo, not to mention the peasants themselves. At harvest time the peasants underreported the quantity of rice they had grown in order to lower the amount they would have to hand over to the army in repayment of their loans; and the army overestimated the amount produced in order to enlarge their personal cut of the one-sixth due the government. Phase II ended when it was discovered that the corporations were getting $2 for every $1 worth of rice that the army said it was getting from the peasants. Miracle rice was costing $305 a ton to produce when the world market price of ordinary rice was $130 a ton (Hansen 1972).

Phase III began in 1970. The government shipped the seeds and chemicals to local warehouses, and peasants took out low-cost loans and were "free" to use the seeds and inputs as they saw fit. Despite the fact that yield increases of up to 70 percent were being obtained, in the village studied by Franke only 20 percent of the farming households had joined the program. The chief beneficiaries were the farmers who were already better off than average, owned the most land, and had adequate supplies of water. The poorest families did not adopt the new seeds. They make ends meet by working part-time for well-to-do farmers who lend them money to buy food. The rich farmers prevented their part-time workers from adopting the new seeds. The rich farmers feared that they would lose their supply of cheap labor, and the poor farmers feared that if they cut themselves off from their patrons, they would have no one to turn to in case of sickness or drought. Franke concludes that the theories behind the Green Revolution are primarily rationalizations for ruling elites which are trying to find a way to achieve economic development without the social and political transformation which their societies need.

Why has there been so much public enthusiasm for miracle seeds that cannot be used by the great mass of ordinary peasants? From the point of view of the poor peasant farmer, these seeds, with their tremendous water and chemical input requirements, are anti-miracles. If the seeds were miracles, they would require less water and fertilizer, not more. But the authorities and technicians responsible for promoting the Green Revolution sought to convert peasant farming into agribusiness systems modeled after high-energy agricul-

452

ture in the developed countries. It was hoped that by stimulating the development of agribusiness in the tropics the productivity of agriculture will be raised fast enough to catch up with the rate of population growth. This transformation obviously requires the virtual destruction of small peasant holdings—just as it has meant the destruction of the small family farm in the United States. There are grave penalties associated with this transformation even in the industrial nations where the former farm population can be employed as car hops, meat packers, and tractor mechanics (see p. 252). But in the underdeveloped countries, where there are few jobs in the manufacturing and service sectors of the economy, it is hard to see how migration to the cities can result in higher standards of living for the hundreds of millions of peasants who are about to be forced off their lands.

Much of the push for the Green Revolution originates in the board rooms of the multinational corporations that sell the chemical inputs and the industrial hardware essential for agribusiness systems. In the Philippines, for example, Esso Standard Fertilizer and Agricultural Company played a key role in the introduction and marketing of high-yield rice. This company installed 400 stores throughout the Philippines and hired a sales staff of hundreds of agent-representative-entrepreneurs who served as extension agents to promote the rice program and train farmers (US-AID 1971). The Philippine government, for its part, provided the loans with which the farmers bought the packages containing the fertilizers and other chemicals produced by Esso at a government-subsidized factory.

The association between the miracle seeds and agribusiness was present at the very start of the Mexican wheat experiment. Ciudad Obregón in Sonora was the center of huge wheat farms that depended upon extensive government irrigation projects in the Yaqui River Valley. The former peasant inhabitants of this valley—the Yaqui Indians—had been evicted from their lands in a series of military engagements, the last of which occurred in 1926 when the Yaquis tried unsuccessfully to kidnap Mexico's President Obregón. They were replaced by medium- and large-scale farmers who were the beneficiaries of $35 million of public funds expended on dams alone. As in the case of the Philippines, the Mexican government also subsidized the growth of the petrochemical industry, which supplied the fertilizers for the new seeds. Further subsidies were given to the miracle wheat producers in the form of government support prices pegged 33 percent above world market prices. Much has been made of the fact that the wonder wheat made Mexico into a wheat-exporting nation. Yet the price of Mexican wheat is so high that it must be exported—the average Mexican peasant cannot afford to eat it. Poor

453

Mexicans eat corn and beans, which remain the basic Mexican staples. Meanwhile, in 1969 miracle wheat that had been produced at a cost of $73 a ton, the support price, was being sold at $49 a ton to foreign buyers. "Mexico thus lost $30.00 a ton, or 80¢ on each bushel exported" (Paddock and Paddock 1973:218).

At the outset of the Green Revolution both industry and government spokespeople assured the developing nations that ample supplies of fertilizers were available for the foreseeable future. At the point at which 40 million hectares of prime irrigated lands were planted with the chemical-hungry high-yield plants, the worldwide energy crisis was "discovered." Rising prices and outright shortages of the petrochemical inputs constitute what might be called Phase IV of the Green Revolution—a phase during which the underdeveloped countries are finding themselves more and more at the mercy of multinational oil corporations for their basic food supply.

Leaving aside political economic factors, it is quite clear that in energy terms alone, U.S. agribusiness methods of producing food cannot be exported intact to the rest of the world. This system, as discussed in Chapter 12, is the most energy expensive mode of food production that has ever been devised. If U.S. methods of food production were used to feed the entire world, almost 80 percent of the world's current total annual expenditure of energy would be required just for the food system (Steinhart and Steinhart 1974:312).

Population and Development

Among two-thirds of humanity, population is rising faster than food production, and living standards and vast numbers of people daily experience the deprivations and suffering that inevitably result when population levels approach too close to carrying capacity.

Recognizing that continued population growth poses a grave threat to world peace, the developed countries are paying increasing attention to the possibility of slowing down the rate of growth of the populations of underdeveloped nations. The main approach to the problem has been to reduce fertility through the introduction of contraceptive devices and techniques. Getting people to use these devices and techniques has thus far proven extremely difficult. Adoption of fertility control has been left to the discretion of domestic units—so-called family planning programs. Yet it is generally recognized that family planning programs by themselves are an ineffectual means of population control. As Kingsley Davis has put it:

454

Current programs will not enable a government to control population size. In countries where couples have numerous offspring that they do not want, such programs may possibly accelerate a birth-rate decline that would occur anyway, but the conditions that cause births to be wanted or unwanted are beyond the control of family planning, hence beyond the control of any nation which relies on family planning alone as its population policy.   [1967:734]

For example, it has been found in India that millions of men are willing to be sterilized—but only *after* their wives have given birth to five or six children. It has been said quite bluntly: "In no underdeveloped country has a government undertaken, or been allowed to undertake, a really effective fertility-control policy" (Spengler 1969:1235).

In the absence of more vigorous and effective government-directed policies, it is reasonable to conclude that many underdeveloped nations are not wholly committed to reducing their rate of growth. Although it cannot be denied that high rates of population growth impede development, there is another dimension to this issue seldom presented by those seeking to extend the benefits of contraception to the underdeveloped nations. Population expansion must be seen in the perspective of the worldwide evolutionary relationship between population size and political power previously discussed (Ch. 13). It is only in the last few hundred years that size of population has ceased to be a reliable index of political-military strength. Given the uncertainties of military strategy in an age of nuclear weapons, there is no evidence to indicate that the correlation between population size and the ability to withstand military aggression has been decisively changed. For example, a Nigeria with 60 million people represents a totally different political-military entity from a Nigeria of 200 million people, as may very well occur by A.D. 2050. Many leaders of underdeveloped countries are quite conscious of this difference and do not share the enthusiasm for population control now being exhibited by government agencies and private foundations. In many small or middle-sized underdeveloped nations the campaign to reduce population growth is viewed as an attempt on the part of the former colonial powers to ensure the continued political-military subjugation of the countries upon whom they depend for cheap raw materials.

The Population Explosion

Many factors must be considered in explaining the rapid growth of population in the underdeveloped countries. Although each country must be studied as a separate case, some popular notions about which

455

factors are generally most important need to be qualified. For example, it is often said that the explosive rate of increase derives from the introduction of modern medical techniques. Better health care, it is said, lowers infant mortality and promotes longevity. People continue to have children at the former rate, and the widened gap between birth rate and death rate produces the explosion. This explanation fails to take into account the fact that the population explosion began in most countries before the introduction of improved medical care. The populations of India, Indonesia, Egypt, and Mexico, for example, began to zoom during the nineteenth century, and the increment may even have been associated with an average shortened life-span and deteriorating health conditions. The view that modern medicine caused the population explosion also fails to take into account the proven ability of preindustrial human populations to stay far below carrying capacity for millions of years. It cannot be assumed that peasant families were the helpless victims of a sudden improvement in the survivability of their children. Rather, it is much more probable that the birth rate was adjusted to immediate practical and mundane conditions. An extremely important consideration, for example, concerns the probability that a given rate of raising children to adulthood will provide enough survivors to take care of aged parents who can no longer work in the fields. The decline in the death rate associated with improved medical care has not been sufficient in many countries to ensure parents that they will have a living heir when they need support in old age (Polgar 1972:211). There is considerable evidence that when the peasant class death rate comes down far enough and parents have good odds that most of their children will survive to adulthood, then they have fewer children. Thus, contrary to popular opinion, improving the diet and health of infants and children is not necessarily a self-defeating activity that results in greater suffering for all (Brown and Wray 1974).

There is also considerable evidence to indicate that peasant families in many underdeveloped countries increase the number of children per domestic unit as part of an attempt to improve their economic position or to prevent its deterioration. The fact that this behavior leads in the aggregate to a declining per capita income puzzles many outsiders. It seems irrational for poor people to have so many children. Yet from the point of view of each domestic unit, the only hope of improving one's standard of living or even of holding on to what one has, meager as it may be, often depends on increasing the size of the domestic work force (Mamdani 1973). Responses of this sort are especially common among peasants who practice irrigation agriculture where labor can be intensified many times over per hectare

456

Figure 20-12. CHILD LABOR. In a Balinese village, six-year-olds can make important labor contributions. This little girl is helping her mother pound rice for the family meal. (Eugene Gordon)

without a loss in productivity per worker, provided there is enough water. The original impetus for intensification may be an increase in taxes or rents or the introduction of cash crops. If the peasants intensify their efforts to meet the new demands and opportunities, they soon find themselves being taxed even more and are obliged to respond by further intensification. Population growth in such a situation is not a suicidal, irrational "involution" but rather a rational response to the demand for labor.

Seeking an explanation for the disastrous tenfold increase in the population of Java between 1820 and 1920, Benjamin White (1973) has suggested that peasant families were responding to colonially

457

Figure 20-13. NEW YORK STATE FARM FAMILY, 1940. The need for family labor was high. The virtual disappearance of the small family farm has probably affected rate of population growth in the United States more than the invention of contraceptive pills. Also see Figure 15-5. (The Bettmann Archive)

imposed needs and opportunities for greater labor input into agriculture per household. The Dutch, as just described (p. 444), established sugar plantations, expanded the irrigation networks, and enlarged the sphere of commercial agriculture. At the same time they imposed various forms of rents, taxes, and corvée. To meet these taxes and labor obligations the peasant family faced the threat of having to take a cut in its standard of living. The peasants sought to avoid such a cut by increasing the number of children put to work in an expanded range of economic activities. By putting more children to work the peasant family sought to preserve its standard of living (much as middle-class families in the United States as a result of inflation are now finding it necessary for both husband and wife to work in order not to suffer a deterioration in their standard of living). The Javanese peasants raised as many children as they could, as long as the cost of raising each child was more than compensated for by the value of the food and handicrafts that each child produced. In a study of the labor contribution of Javanese children to the domestic economy White (1975) has provisionally shown that the cost of rearing children is still a major determinant of family size in neocolonial Javanese villages. The more children a family has, the more children it can free from

458

household chores and put to work weaving mats or working for wages in the fields.

This approach helps to explain why middle-class families in Europe, Japan, and the United States are more likely to want fewer children than do peasant families in underdeveloped parts of the world. The more children a modern middle-class couple have, the closer to bankruptcy they must live. In the developed countries children are prohibited from entering the labor force until they are fourteen or sixteen; their lifetime economic contribution to their parents consists largely of occasional household chores and small income-tax deductions. The drain for child support may last for as much as thirty years in the case of students educated for professional specialties, and most modern parents have no expectation of a return flow of support for their old age.

Colonialism has probably also contributed to the present population explosion by suppressing the practice of overt forms of abortion and infanticide. This has been achieved both by more effective police-military supervision on the village level and by the spread of religious doctrines opposed to infanticide. Regardless of the ethical and moral pros and cons of abortion and infanticide, it should be kept in mind that it was to the benefit of every nineteenth-century colonial power that the population of its colonies increase as rapidly as possible. With the suppression of the more overt forms of abortion and infanticide it is conceivable that colonial peasant populations for the first time in history actually found themselves without effective means for adjusting numbers of children to the demand for labor, old age insurance, and other domestic requirements. This possibility makes it imperative that cheap and reliable contraceptive techniques and medical abortions be made available as quickly as possible to all the countries of the underdeveloped world that have instituted programs of population control.

For Whom the Bell Tolls

It is increasingly evident that the high standard of living enjoyed by Japan and the Euro-American industrialized nations is causally related to the continuing poverty of the underdeveloped nations. In other words, one of the reasons why the advanced industrialized powers are so rich is that they have been systematically looting the natural resources and exploiting the labor of the underdeveloped peoples. This looting and exploitation has been made possible in no small measure by political-military conquest and control. The underdeveloped nations can be expected to intensify their struggle for a larger share of the world's industrial wealth by confiscating foreign investments and by actions aimed at forcing up the price of raw materials and tropical products. Ultimately they may resort to war to force a redistribution of wealth. The reliance of the developed nations upon military strength to maintain international inequality is hazardous for all of us. The threat of war will not be removed until (1) international inequalities in standards of living are abolished; (2) population size is brought under control everywhere through medical abortions or contraception; and (3) a system of mutual security based upon internationally supervised disarmament is created. Given the catastrophic potential of nuclear weaponry, additional delays in achieving these fundamental changes in world culture may very well result in the extinction of our species. Ignorance is the sole ground for being optimistic about our chances. As George Gaylord Simpson has warned, the ability of any species to survive is exceptional.

The vast majority of all multitudes of minor sorts of organisms that have appeared in the history of life have either changed to forms distinctly different or have disappeared absolutely, without descendants.   [1949:196]

CULTURE AND POVERTY

We carry manures and improved seeds in a trailer and offer to deliver them right at the door-step to induce these cultivators to use them. We offer them loans to buy the seeds and manures. We go to the fields and offer to let in the water for them. We request them to try it out first in two acres only if they are not convinced. They could quadruple their yields if they would only take our advice and at least experiment. Still they are not coming forward.
Kussum Nair, *Blossoms in the Dust*

Human beings inevitably acquire values and attitudes that are a product of their experience. Peasants and other subordinate groups, such as the urban and rural poor, acquire values and attitudes that explain, rationalize, and ward off the demeaning and harmful aspects of their subordinate position. Anthropologists have carried out many studies aimed at determining the extent to which the values and attitudes of subordinate classes, castes, and ethnic groups trap the members of such groups into subordinate and exploited statuses. This chapter attempts to assess the importance of values and attitudes in the perpetuation of such statuses.

Peasant Conservatism: Ecuador

Peasant populations are often highly conservative and are suspicious of those outside their small circle of neighbors and kinfolk. Well-intentioned government health officers, peace corps volunteers, and development technicians are frequently unable to secure the confidence of the peasant communities that they wish to help. Technical

461

assistance specialists conclude, therefore, that the prime obstacle to development is the peasants' irrational aversion to novelty. In most cases, however, this conclusion depends upon wrenching the peasants' conservative values and attitudes out of the colonial and postcolonial context in which such attitudes and values are realistic and perfectly rational.

A highly conservative American Indian peasantry is found in Ecuador, living in isolated villages at altitudes between 9,000 and 12,000 feet on the treeless slopes of Chimborazo Province. Visitors to Chimborazo villages are unwelcome; at their approach men, women, and children untie their watchdogs and lock themselves into their walled compounds and windowless houses. The dogs are trained to attack and will lunge at anyone, even a fellow villager who crosses the boundary of the house plot. Persistent attempts to penetrate these villages may provoke more energetic countermeasures. During the national Ecuadorian census, Chimborazo peasants earned a reputation for stoning the census takers. Questions having to do with land tenure arouse great fear and hostility among the peasants. Inquiries concerning the size and location of a family's property are regarded as a dire threat calling for immediate evasive action, such as suspending all work in one's fields until the stranger goes away (see Figure 14-7).

The historical conditions responsible for the growth of this fear-ridden complex center on the loss of the best valleys and irrigated hillside terraces during a four-hundred-year-old process of conquest, expropriation, theft, and legal trickery. In the sixteenth century the Indians of Ecuador became the prebendal peasants (see p. 301) of the Spanish conquerors. The Spanish awarded themselves corvée and tribute rights (*encomiendas*) over designated areas, but the Indians were left with nominal "ownership" of the productive valleys. After independence was won from Spain, however, the Indians were set "free" and hence became legally eligible to own their traditional holdings provided they obtained private title. However, the Indians were seldom told about the new law, lacked access to legal advice, and were subjected to violence and threats of violence by the white and *Mestizo* (part Indian, part Spanish) colonists when they sought to obtain titles. Hence they were rapidly driven out of the best valley lands. In other instances whole villages suddenly found their traditional holdings had become a *hacienda* (ranch) owned by a white colonist. The *hacendado* (rancher) permitted the Indians to plant crops on "his" land provided the Indians paid rent in the form of labor services (E. Wolf 1959:230; Harris 1974a).

The Indians also had cash obligations that they had to meet for taxes, clothing, salt, tools, and medicine. They were encouraged to

462

avail themselves of their new landlord's generosity and quickly fell into debt, which no amount of saving or hard work could expunge since the hacendado kept the books. Ostensibly to teach the Indians that going into debt was a serious matter, children were declared responsible for the debts of their deceased parents; furthermore, no one who was in debt to a particular hacendado could leave the hacienda without permission. This system, known as *debt peonage,* lasted in Ecuador until 1920. After that the Indians were once again declared "free" and told they could go wherever they wanted. But there was no place to go, since the hacendados controlled the bottom lands and all the upper slopes had long since been occupied by Indians who had managed to avoid debt peonage. These "free" upper-slope Indians eke out a living by planting potatoes and barley and by raising sheep on the stubble. To hold on to their lands is their one overriding passion. In this context it cannot be doubted that hostility and fear are adaptively correct responses to the modern-day strangers (international development experts) who have suddenly appeared promising freedom if the Indians consent to build roads into their villages and windows in their houses.

Peasant Realism

There is very little evidence that development proposals now being urged upon many peasant peoples are the rational products of a scientific understanding of cultural processes. Many international aid programs are piecemeal ad hoc measures designed primarily to alleviate the threat of political instability. They do not attempt to provide permanent and substantial change in the relationship between the peasantry and the landlord class. It is difficult to assess the importance of peasant conservatism as an obstacle to development when the innovations offered are objectively impractical, dangerous, or counterproductive. Yet many planned technological innovations may actually be useless or ill-advised when examined within the full context of the adaptive potential of peasant life.

An example of what can go wrong when peasant conservatism is broken under the piecemeal importunings of development specialists is the case of the Chimborazo merino sheep. With the best of intentions, Australian sheep experts persuaded a "progressive" Indian to breed his ewes with a high-yield merino stud, furnished gratis. The promise was that the crossbred flock would have twice as much meat and wool as the native one. That part of the promise was easily fulfilled. But the Chimborazo Indians live in a strictly regulated caste-structured society. Mestizo farmers who live in the lower valleys resented the attention being paid to the Indians; they began to fear that the Indians would be emboldened to press for additional economic and social gains, which would undermine their own position. The unusually fine sheep caught someone's attention, and the whole flock was herded into a truck and stolen. The rustlers were well protected by public opinion, which regarded the animals as "too good for the Indians anyway." Thus the "progressive" innovator was left as the only one in his village without sheep.

Forestry experts in the same area were constantly baffled by the Indians' refusal to accept eucalyptus seedlings. With the entire area denuded of its natural cover, nothing would seem more rational than to use some of the commons land for reforestation. In thirty years an acre of eucalyptus could make a whole village "rich." All the Indians had to do was build a little fence around each seedling and water it until it was firmly rooted; then nature would do the rest. The Indians were keenly aware of the potential value of such trees. They had little confidence, however, that the men who were giving away the seedlings were simply going to forget about them. Nothing could be certain until the fateful moment thirty years hence when the trees were full grown and ready to cut. Who could tell if the experts would not suddenly reappear and claim their timber? How could they be sure the whole thing was not merely a scheme to trick them into taking care of someone else's trees? Given the history of Indian-Mestizo relations in Ecuador, it is difficult to dismiss these doubts as illogical or unrealistic.

The way to test the importance of peasant conservatism as an obstacle to development is to offer innovations that are unambiguously associated with immediate, secure, and tangible rewards. Anthropologists have yet to meet peasants who would rather walk than ride to market, who would hesitate to direct water into their parched fields (if they could be certain they would not be shot), who would be reluctant to switch from hoe to plow if appropriate stretches of hacienda bottom lands were to be deeded over, or who would not accept higher prices for their barley and corn. Political economy, not peasant conservatism, is what usually stands in the way of these innovations.

Wages, Work, and Values

An important source of misunderstanding concerning values and underdevelopment is the response of peasant populations to oppor-

464

Figure 21-1. POVERTY AND FORCE. Welfare demonstrator is arrested for breaking windows in protest aimed at obtaining allowance for home furnishings. The maintenance of inequality is costly. (UPI Photo)

tunities in the wage-labor market. Historically the rise of wage labor as the predominant form of labor contract was closely associated with the creation of a landless urban proletariat. In Europe the wage-labor force was a product of population increase and "enclosure," whereby peasant farmers were forced off the land to make room for sheep. The European wage-labor market during the early phases of industrialization consisted of a mass of urban poor who either worked for wages under the precise conditions specified by their employers or starved.

Subsequent attempts to create wage-labor work forces in non-European settings have usually taken place in the context of colonialism. Because of problems of military and political control, colonial and neocolonial administrations discourage the formation of urban proletariats. Colonial and neocolonial wage systems, therefore, frequently preserve the subsistence base of peasant or tribal villages, drawing off wage workers as temporary migrants to industrial and agro-industrial centers. Because of the high cost of capital, transportation, and equipment in colonial areas, industrial and agro-industrial enterprises can be profitable only if labor costs are kept far below the market value of labor in the developed countries. Yet, paradoxically, the most important inducement for wage labor is absent; that is, the target labor force continues to enjoy the alternative of subsistence agriculture on family homesteads.

In order to overcome this paradox, employers resort to politico-economic measures that are the analogues but not precise equivalents of the European "enclosures" of the fifteenth to seventeenth centuries. (1) Head taxes are imposed at a level calculated to be above what the subsistence farmer can possibly earn from the sale of

465

surplus subsistence crops. (2) The traditional homestead land is expropriated to make way for colonists, while the native populations are crowded into ecologically marginal "reservations" or "reserves" where their agricultural output falls below subsistence. Thus huge numbers of people are forced into migratory wage work. (3) Where an especially ruthless form of control can be exercised, the subsistence farmers are simply told: "it is illegal not to be working for wages."

Obligatory work contracts compel peasants to remain for periods of six months to two years in the wage relationship specified and supervised by the authorities. In order to justify these politico-economic measures, the government administration and business interests picture themselves as the victims of the native's stubborn primitive reluctance to work. The labor codes of the British, French, Belgian, and Portuguese colonies of Africa and Oceania, as well as the Spanish New World colonies, all emphasized the "high moral duty" of the conquerors to teach their dependent populations, the "value of hard and regular work"—a value that the dependent populations were uniformly said to lack, as demonstrated by their reluctance to volunteer for wage labor. All too often, however, this reluctance was a perfectly rational decision influenced by (1) the availability of subsistence alternatives in the traditional agricultural sector; (2) the inconsequentiality of the wages offered in relation to the possibility of substantial modification in consumption or production standards and processes; and (3) the danger, monotony, or loneliness of the work conditions (cf. Gregson 1971; Curtain 1975; Magubane 1971, 1975).

"Volunteers" for the Mines of South Africa

The system of migratory labor responsible for the development of the great gold-mining complex of the Transvaal in the Union of South Africa illustrates many of the paradoxes of wage labor and peasant values. Discovery of the gold along the "Rand" in 1886 produced an instantaneous demand for large numbers of African laborers. The reason for this is that, contrary to what might be supposed of the world's "richest" gold mines, the ore in the South African gold fields is of very low quality. The gold fields around Johannesburg consist of low-grade ore requiring elaborate, large-scale mining (Morrell 1968). Prodigious numbers of miners in the Rand mines bring up huge volumes of rock that, when processed, produce only a small amount of gold. By 1899 over 100,000 Africans, mostly migratory wage laborers, were working in the Rand mines in shafts that had already gone below

466

Figure 21-2. MIGRANT
MINERS. Their work is arduous and dangerous over two
miles beneath the surface of
the earth. (Optima)

3,000 feet. Agreements between the Portuguese Colonial Administration and the mining companies raised the total to 160,000 African
laborers by 1910. Most of these "volunteers" were brought in under
unbreakable international contracts. Today over 375,000 Africans
work on the mines in shafts that have reached 12,000 feet below the
surface and that are projected to go down to 15,000 feet. At these
depths the temperatures of the rocks are above 125° F. As William
Hance has pointed out:

If the gold reefs (of the Rand) were situated in the United States, they
probably would be of interest only to students of geology; they would not be
worked.   [1964:523]

The gold of the Rand, in other words, is not gold, but cheap African
labor. During the first seventy-five years of mining, the main labor
force was "recruited" out of Portuguese Mozambique by the following
method. African men were required to prove that they had worked for
wages for six months of each year either within Mozambique or in the
Rand mines. Men who could not prove that they had been employed in
this manner were rounded up in great nighttime raids and put to work
as conscripts on plantations, docks, and roads within Mozambique.
Rather than risk becoming wageless conscripts, most African men
"volunteered" for some form of wage labor. Moreover, since the mines
paid more than other types of wage labor, most men permitted themselves to be rounded up by the special mine recruiters who were
stationed throughout the territory. Wages at the mines, however,

remained below subsistence; a man could not maintain his family with what he was paid at the mines. Instead, during his absence, sometimes lasting up to two years, his family had to continue to grow their own staples or starve.

A very specific set of values developed among the Mozambique people with respect to the trip to the mines. It came to be believed that those men who had not yet gone to the Rand were unmanly and not suited for marriage. The recruiting agents from the mines did their best to spread and reinforce this idea. They further embroidered it with the explanation that mining had been substituted for the battlefield as a test of manhood. Many well-intentioned Europeans found this a conscience-saving explanation of why such vast numbers of men were willing to "volunteer." The casualties produced by the mines were indeed very much like those of the battlefields. From 1890 to 1926 80,000 Africans died on the Rand from accidents, lung failure, and exhaustion—exclusive of the tens of thousands who died when they returned home. This is a higher rate of injuries than on the battlefields of Europe during World War I. Moreover African girls did prefer to marry men who had gone to "Joburg"; but this preference must be seen in the full context of the labor system. The man who did not "volunteer" was exposed to forced labor conscription; other things being equal, a man who showed initiative and courage by going to the mines made a better husband than one who let himself get caught in a forced labor raid. This value was the product not the cause of the labor system (cf. M. Harris 1958; Mondlane 1969; Magubane 1975).

The Image of Limited Good

In a review of the factors holding back the economic development of the Tarascan Mexican village of Tzintzuntzan, George Foster suggests that suspicion and conservatism are "basic . . . in preventing villagers from taking advantage of opportunities that already exist" (1967:350). According to Foster the peasants of Tzintzuntzan suffer from a complex of values that he calls the "Image of Limited Good"—the belief that life is a dreary struggle, that very few people can achieve "success," and that they can improve themselves only at the expense of other people. Foster is uncertain as to the significance of this complex. On the one hand he indicates that this conception of life must be "at or near the top of the list of factors which hold back the village," but on the other hand he supplies evidence that this "Image of Limited Good" is a highly realistic outlook for the villagers to have.

468

Figure 21-3. IMAGE OF LIMITED GOOD. Peasant women of Tzintzuntzan with their homemade pottery. (United Nations)

The evidence consists, first, of the tribulations of a UNESCO-sponsored community development project called CREFAL (Regional Center for the Development of Fundamental Education in Latin America). This organization attempted to change production patterns and raise the standard of living in five sectors of Tzintzuntzan's economy: (1) tourist pottery, (2) tourist textiles, (3) tourist furniture, (4) tourist embroidery, and (5) chicken ranching.

1. CREFAL technicians persuaded four potters to experiment with brick kilns fired by a power-driven kerosene burner. The new kiln overfired and blackened the pottery. The grate collapsed and broke all the pots. By 1957 all four were saddled with individual debts of more than 6,000 pesos, the equivalent of two years of gross income.

2. CREFAL taught a number of people who had never seen a loom how to weave cloth for tourists. The cost of production, however, was twice as much as in neighboring villages. Initially there was no trouble in selling at higher prices since people came from all over to see what CREFAL had accomplished. When the technician who had provided the initial construction left Tzintzuntzan, no one came to buy any more cloth. Meanwhile the weavers continued to turn out hundreds of meters of fine cloth, which piled up in the workshops.

3. CREFAL established a cooperative and taught twenty-one youths to make woven-palm furniture. The product sold amazingly well, but its price had been set above that of neighboring villages. As in the case of the cloth, most of the sales were to CREFAL employees or their

469

Figure 21-4. TZINTZUNT-ZAN. Traditional pottery market. (United Nations)

friends. When the technician left, sales stopped. Meanwhile the cooperative had piled up a debt of 136,000 pesos, and the National Cooperative Development Bank stopped all further credit.

4. Twenty-five girls began to embroider cloth on small looms loaned by CREFAL. When the instructor left, some of them continued to earn spare money by trading with tourists. Foster considered this "the most successful of the CREFAL projects" because girls without other ways of earning money could now "pick up small sums."

5. CREFAL loaned money to six people to build hen houses for 125 birds each. Complaints were soon heard that CREFAL buyers short-weighed the eggs. Also CREFAL withheld all funds for further investment. "Then during a cold wet winter many birds died." One woman succeeded in running a "small egg business."

The most remarkable aspect of these failures is the alacrity with which the CREFAL technicians were able to find peasant "guinea pigs" for their well-intentioned but ill-advised schemes. It is clear

470

that, if anything, these desperately poor people of Tzintzuntzan were less suspicous and conservative than they should have been. The alleged conservatism is also contradicted by the fact that the principal source of income in Tzintzuntzan is from migrant farm work in the United States. The men of Tzintzuntzan bribe, cajole, and scheme to get a chance to work across the border. By 1960, 50 percent of the men had succeeded in getting through, "many of them ten times or more" (277). Foster himself elsewhere retracts his own emphasis upon peasant conservatism and suggests that the "Image of Limited Good" is not a crippling illusion but rather a realistic appraisal of the facts of life in a society where economic success or failure is capricious and hinged to forces wholly beyond one's control or comprehension (as, for example, when the United States unilaterally terminated the *bracero* program).

For the underlying, fundamental truth is that in an economy like Tzintzuntzan's, hard work and thrift are moral qualities of only the slightest functional value. Because of the limitations on land and technology, additional hard work does not produce a significant increment in income. It is pointless to talk of thrift in a subsistence economy, because usually there is no surplus with which to be thrifty. Foresight, with careful planning for the future, is also a virtue of dubious value in a world in which the best laid plans must rest on a foundation of chance and capriciousness.   [150–151]

With the passage of time it has become clear that many of the heavily staffed development schemes in the Tarascan area have been less successful than development efforts made by the people themselves when they had accumulated some capital from working as *braceros* and the government had brought in electricity and roads. As James Acheson, who studied the community of Cuanajo, has argued, unless one has economic opportunities, development will not occur, and if opportunities do present themselves, some individuals will always take advantage of them.

It is one thing to say that Tarascans are suspicious, distrustful, and uncooperative; it is another to assume that this lack of cooperation precludes all possibility for positive economic change.   [Acheson 1972:1165; cf. Foster 1974; Acheson 1974]

Sisal in Brazil

Contrary to popular notions of the causes of underdevelopment and poverty, peasant populations can be readily induced to surrender their traditional ways if substantial improvements in cash income and heightened security seem clearly associated with the innovations.

471

Figure 21-5. OLD MAN OF THE NORDESTE. (Daniel Gross).

Unfortunately the peasants' impressions are often inaccurate and their trust in local officials or businesspeople unjustified. Another case worth considering in this context has been studied by Daniel Gross. It concerns the shift from subsistence farming to sisal farming in Brazil.

In the great hinterland of Brazil's Atlantic bulge, there is a drought-ridden section of the country known as the *Nordeste* where some 30 million people have a per capita income of about $200. This region has traditionally been given over to open-range ranching and to subsistence farming, activities rendered precarious by a cycle of droughts that have been repeating themselves about every eleven years over the past three centuries. During the droughts, hundreds of thousands of refugees can be seen trekking along the dusty roads toward the coastal cities seeking temporary shelter and employment. When the rains come, they trek back to plant two or three acres of corn, beans, and manioc.

Sisal, a plant that yields a high-quality fiber suitable for twine, had been cultivated in the region for many years, although it was grown more as hedgerow fencing than for its fiber. During World War II, however, Asian sources of natural fiber were cut off and Brazilian sisal came into great demand. During the 1950s the price climbed steadily, apparently in response to the worldwide spread of hay-baling machinery for which natural twine has certain advantages over synthetics and wire (animals can digest it). The Brazilian ranchers began to plant sisal, and in a few years millions of sisal plants stood where previously there had been nothing but shrubs and cactus. Once planted, sisal practically takes care of itself. If it rains, it grows; if it doesn't rain, it vegetates. Its extensive roots and thorny leaves make it practically indestructible.

472

Many of the large-scale planters benefited from this conversion. A small group of sisal buyers and truckers also prospered. These individuals in the middle financed and distributed decorticating motors—diesel-driven mechanical rasps that strip away the green portion of the sisal leaf leaving the useful fibers. The quantity of sisal that could profitably be planted and sold depended upon the amount that could be decorticated; hence those in the middle lent money for the purchase of these motors at favorable rates.

Between 1955 and 1965 some 800 decorticating motors were introduced into Victoria, a typical sisal county in the State of Bahia. Meanwhile the subsistence farmers began to plant sisal on their own small plots. As a matter of fact, the more miserable the farmer, the higher percentage of land planted in sisal. The peasants hoped to be favored with loans to purchase decorticating motors. In the meantime they cut and stacked the leaves, put them through the rasp, cleaned away the debris and dried and weighed the fibers, earning a subsistence wage of less than 50 cents a day.

Despite the thorny leaves, the danger of getting one's hands caught in the rasp, and the monotonous steady work paced by the insatiable motor, the Nordestino subsistence farmers unhesitatingly opted for wage labor and a cash crop. Unfortunately there were things about sisal that they could not possibly know. Between 1951 and 1969 the

Figure 21-6. REFUGEES FROM THE DROUGHT. Hundreds of thousands of people flee the Brazilian Northeast during years of drought. (FAO)

Figure 21-7. SISAL WORKER. Five thousand calories to make fifty cents. (Daniel Gross)

world market price of sisal declined from $600 per metric ton to $170 per metric ton.

In 1968 the total output of an eight-man crew working from dawn to dusk was worth about $16 on the world market. Yet production continued, since the owners of the motors owed the people in the middle, and the erstwhile subsistence farmers had their fields full of virtually indestructible plants. A time and motion study of the men who fed the sisal into the rasp showed that they expended as much as 5,000 calories per day to make 50 cents. With all this money expended on food, the only way that a man could eat enough calories to work at the required rate was to put his wife and children on a diet of less than 2,000 calories each. Additional nutritional studies showed that for the class of subsistence farmers as a whole, the fifteen years of "development" that people believed was taking place actually resulted in increased nutritional deficits as reflected in lowered height and weight averages (Gross and Underwood 1969; Gross 1970).

The Culture of Poverty and Ethnocentrism

Maladaptive attitudes and values are often attributed not only to underdeveloped peasant populations but also to the rural and urban poor in both developed and underdeveloped countries. Some anthro-

474

pologists believe that the contrasts between the ideologies of the poor and the middle class are sharp enough and systematic enough to warrant thinking about the way of life of the poor as a subculture—as a "lower-class culture" or a "culture of poverty." It should occasion no surprise that the inhabitants of an urban slum have some values different from those held by the affluent middle class. But the extent to which values play a role in perpetuating poverty is the center of much controversy.

Sociologist Walter Miller contends that poverty is a way of life supported by its own set of self-perpetuating values and attitudes. Miller regards these values and attitudes not simply as the reverse of middle-class values and attitudes but as part of a culture that has its own inner justification, its own strength and weaknesses, just like any other "design for living": "lower class culture is a distinctive tradition many centuries old with an integrity of its own" (1968:270).

The implications of this view are that poverty is largely the responsibility of the poor; that the poor, in effect, have achieved a cultural adaptation for which the ruling and middle classes need feel no guilt. Indeed, by feeling guilty and by attempting to extirpate poverty, the middle class may actually be engaging in a form of ethnocentrism in which middle-class standards are arbitrarily forced upon people who have their own way of doing things.

Anthropologists who have studied the culture of poverty have also warned against assuming that merely because a practice is associated with low-income levels that it is necessarily inferior. Helen Icken Safa (1967) has shown, for example, that high-rise public housing destroys the sense of community and patterns of neighborly cooperation that frequently exist in established slums and shantytowns. Betty and Charles Valentine (1970) stress the resourcefulness, sense of humor, and informality of black ghetto culture. Oscar Lewis's (1961, 1966) remarkable documentaries of ghetto life, as told in the tape-recorded words of the people themselves, show that many individuals who are trapped in poverty nonetheless achieve a great nobility of spirit.

The Culture of Poverty and the Causes of Poverty

Oscar Lewis has written of the culture of poverty as consisting "both of an adaptation and a reaction of the poor to their marginal position in a class-stratified, highly individuated, capitalistic society" (1966:21). Although he recognizes that many of the traits attributed

475

Figure 21-8. SQUATTERS IN KARACHI. The rope bed is their most valuable possession. (United Nations)

to the poor are "local spontaneous attempts to meet needs" produced by poverty, he also believes that once the culture of poverty comes into existence it tends to perpetuate itself:

By the time slum children are six or seven they have usually absorbed the basic attitudes and values of their subculture. Thereafter they are psychologically unready to take full advantage of changing conditions or improving opportunities that may develop in their lifetime.

Lewis carefully hedges his estimate of the self-reinforcing power of ideology. He proposes that only 20 percent of the urban poor actually have the culture of poverty, implying that 80 percent fall into the category of those whose poverty results from ecological and structural conditions rather than from an ideological heritage or "design" for poverty living (cf. Valentine 1970; Leeds 1970; Parker and Kleiner 1970).

The traits attributed to the culture of poverty closely resemble the previously discussed sterotypes concerning peasant conservatism. Lewis, for example, pictures the poor as being fearful, suspicious, and apathetic toward the major institutions of the larger society: they tend to hate the police and to mistrust the government and are "inclined to be cynical of the church." When seen in a larger context, however, these attitudes are quite rational and have their analogues in middle-class subcultures.

Being suspicious of government and of politicians is certainly not a

476

working-class specialty. The undoubtedly greater fear of the police among the poor, on the other hand, need not be explained as a centuries-old tradition. By the time ghetto children reach six years of age, they have witnessed enough instances of arbitrary, prejudiced, and menacing police behavior to begin to make up their own minds as to whether the police officer is a friend or foe (cf. Chevigny 1969). It would probably make as much sense to discuss the fear of police in terms of the traditional prejudices and hostilities of the police toward the poor, especially toward the ethnically and racially distinct poor. But the main obstacle to the improvement of police and community relationships is the active hardship and tension of poverty, not the tradition of poverty.

Poverty and Deferred Gratification

Another important aspect of the culture of poverty, according to Lewis (1966:21), is "a strong present-time orientation with relatively little disposition to defer gratification and plan for the future." This implies that poor people are less willing to save money and are more interested in "getting mine now" in the form of hifi sets, color television, latest style clothing, and gaudy automobiles. It also implies that the poor "blow" their earnings by getting drunk or by going on buying sprees.

Figure 21-9. SQUATTERS IN LIMA. Life on a garbage heap. (United Nations)

Considerable skepticism is warranted, however, with respect to the actual difference between middle-class and poor people's valuations of savings and spending. The general propensity to consume is constantly heightened by the immense persuasive resources of mass media advertising. Debt is even regarded as a patriotic duty, as when President Eisenhower pleaded with the nation to step up consumer purchases in order to prevent a business recession. Banks are more eager to provide loans for people who will use the money to pay for luxury vacations than to consolidate their installment debts. Waste is engineered into the entire capitalist economy through planned obsolescence, disposable containers, deliberate downgrading of quality, and style changes.

Good business practice requires "write-offs" of usable plants and machinery for tax benefits; to be in debt to banks and mortgage companies, far from being frowned upon, is regarded as an important achievement. Credit companies prefer clients who are already in debt over those who have no record of borrowing. In sum, there is little

478

evidence that the middle class as a whole lives within its income more effectively than poor people do. The only certainty is that when the poor mismanage their incomes the consequences are much more serious. If the male head of a poor family yields to the temptation to buy nonessential items, his children may go hungry or his wife may be deprived of medical attention. But these consequences result from being poor, not from any demonstrable difference in the capacity to defer gratification.

The sterotype of the improvident poor masks an implicit belief that the impoverished segments of society ought to be more thrifty and more patient than the members of the middle class. This is an essentially vindictive judgment. It is conscience-saving to be able to attribute poverty to values for which the poor themselves can be held responsible.

Deferred Gratification and Work

Why then are the poor unable to earn as much money as the middle class? Why don't the poor work their way out of poverty? These questions obviously do not apply to the mentally and physically sick, the disabled, or those who, by current standards, are deemed too old to work. That these people live in poverty is clearly the result of inadequate welfare practices for which the middle and upper classes are certainly responsible. The controversy surrounding the culture of poverty concept concerns rather the able-bodied poor who manifestly seem not to be prevented from competing for or from being successful in middle-class occupations.

Once again there is a widespread belief that the principal difficulty confronting lower-class wage earners is the complex of values and attitudes concerning work that their own subculture of poverty imposes on them. This view is especially prominent as an explanation of why black males fail to rise above the poverty level. It is frequently asserted that lack of proper motivation to seek and hold a job is the main cause of the plight of the ghetto male. In fact more Americans attribute black poverty to inadequate effort than to racial inferiority (Schuman 1969). This aspect of the theory of the culture of poverty closely resembles the theories upon which compulsory colonial labor laws are based. The heart of the issue is whether black youth and the poor in general are any more reluctant to work than the rest of the population. Only if wages, working conditions, and prospects for

479

advancement are held constant can one say that differential rates of absenteeism, unemployment, and job turnover reflect fundamentally different evaluations of the importance of work. If, as with the Mozambique mine workers, clear evidence exists that one group is being paid less to do more under more difficult conditions for a longer time and with less prospect of advancement, then different values are not the explanation for not wanting to work. Under such circumstances, as in the case of the peasants of Tzintzuntzan or Chimborazo, skepticism concerning long-run prospects for economic success is the only rational attitude one can have.

When the conditions and prospects of wage-labor available to the urban poor are specified, the question of why some people have a high rate of absenteeism and job instability gives way to the question of why they should work at all. For example as a result of a combination of functional processes built into the structure of the U.S. economy, blacks especially find fewer openings in well-paying jobs with promotion possibilities. Historically the dregs of the job market in the U.S.A. have been left for blacks and other minorities: jobs whose conditions and prospects are the mark of failure, which are demeaned and ridiculed by the rest of the labor force, and which do not pay enough for a man to get married and have a family or even to pay rent and food bills exclusive of children; jobs that are dull—as in dishwashing or floor polishing, dirty—as in garbage collecting and washroom attending, or backbreaking—as in truck loading or furniture moving.

The duller, dirtier, and more exhausting the work, the less likely that extra diligence and effort will be rewarded by anything but more of the same. There is no "track" leading from the night maid who cleans the executive's office to the executive; from the dishwasher to the restaurant owner; from the unskilled, unapprenticed construction worker to journeyman electrician or bricklayer. These jobs are dead ends from the beginning. To expect people not to be apathetic, lethargic, and uninterested under such conditions is once again to expect more of the poor than of the affluent.

The Futility of Work

In his book *Tally's Corner* (1967), Elliot Liebow, an ethnographer who has studied the black streetcorner men of Washington D.C., provides a vivid account of the material conditions shaping the work patterns of the unskilled black male. The streetcorner men are full of contempt for the menial work that they must perform, but this is scarcely a result of any special tradition that they acquire from the

480

culture of poverty. As Liebow points out, no one is more explicit in expressing the worthlessness of the job than the boss who pays for it. The boss pays less than what is required to support a family. The rest of society, contradicting its professed values concerning the dignity of labor, also holds the job of dishwasher or janitor in low esteem.

So does the streetcorner man. He cannot do otherwise. He cannot draw from a job those social values which other people do not put into it.   [1967:59]

An additional mark of the degradation involved in these jobs is that wages for menial work in hotels, restaurants, office and apartment buildings are frequently predicated on the assumption that the workers will steal food, clothing, or other items in order to bring their take-home pay above subsistence. The boss then sets the wages so low that stealing must take place. While implicitly acknowledging the need for theft, the boss nonetheless tries to prevent it and will call the police if someone is caught stealing.

Many young men are apathetic at the outset of their employment careers and quickly gravitate toward the streetcorner life: occasional jobs, borrowing from girlfriends, short-lived marriages followed by abandonment of wife and children, drugs, crime. Many others, however, struggle toward the vision of a better life.

Liebow tells the story of Richard, a black man in his twenties who had tried to support his family by extra jobs ranging from shoveling snow to picking peas and who had won the reputation of being one of the hardest working men on the street. "I figure you got to get out there and try. You got to try before you can get anything," said Richard. After five years of trying Richard pointed to a shabby bed, a sofa, a couple of chairs, and a television set, and gave up:

I've been scuffling for five years from morning til night. And my children still don't have anything, my wife don't have anything, and I don' have anything.   [1967:67]

At one point along the road leading to his entry into the ranks of the streetcorner men, Richard took a job with a fence company in Virginia at $1.60 an hour. Like many of the nonunion construction jobs, the work required was greater·than most of the streetcorner men could physically manage. Richard, crying out in his sleep about the "God-damn digging," could not keep it up long enough to save any money. Construction jobs, whose high hourly wage would seem to be a way out for at least some of the streetcorner men, also tend to be seasonal and are subject to interruption by rain or snow. Moreover most of the nonunion jobs offered in construction are located far outside of town and can seldom be reached by public transportation. Liebow sums up

481

The Futility of Work

the etic conditions regulating the work pattern of the streetcorner men as follows:

> . . . the most important fact is that a man who is able and willing to work cannot earn enough money to support himself, his wife and one or more children. A man's chance for working regularly are good only if he is willing to work for less than he can live on, and sometimes not even then. On some jobs, the wage rate is deceptively higher than on others, but the higher the wage rate, the more difficult it is to get the job, and the less the job security. Higher paying construction work tends to be seasonal and, during the season, the amount of work available is highly sensitive to business and weather conditions and to the changing requirements of individual projects. Moreover, high-paying construction jobs are frequently beyond the physical capacity of some of the men, and some of the low-paying jobs are scaled down even lower in accordance with . . . the assumption that the man will steal part of his wages on the job.   [1967:50–52]

Now Whose Fault Is That?

The tendency to blame the poor for being poor is not confined to relatively affluent members of the middle class. The poor or near-poor themselves are often the staunchest supporters of the view that people who really want to work can always find work. This attitude forms part of a larger world view in which there is little comprehension of the politico-economic conditions that make poverty for some inevitable. What must be seen as a system is seen purely in terms of individual faults, individual motives, individual choices. Hence the poor turn against the poor and blame each other for their plight.

In a study of a Newfoundland community called Squid Cove, Cato Wadel (1973) has shown how a structural problem of unemployment caused by factors entirely beyond the control of the local community can be interpreted in such a way as to set neighbor against neighbor. The men of Squid Cove earn their living from logging, fishing, and construction. Mechanization in logging, depletion of the fishing grounds, and upgrading of construction skills have left most of the men without a steady, year-round means of making a living. A certain number of men, especially those who have large families and who are past their physical prime, place themselves on the able-bodied welfare rolls. In doing so they must be prepared to wage a desperate struggle to preserve their self-esteem against the tendency of their neighbors to regard them as shirkers who "don't do nothin' for the money they get." What makes the plight of the Squid Cove welfare recipients especially poignant is that Newfoundlanders have long been noted for their intense work ethic. Many welfare recipients formerly worked at

482

extremely arduous unskilled jobs. For example, Wadel's principal informant, George, was a logger for twenty-nine years. George stopped logging only when he partially slipped a disk in his spine. The injury was sufficient to prevent him from competing for the better paying unskilled jobs but insufficient to place him on the welfare roles as a disabled worker. George says he is willing to work, provided it is not too heavy and does not require him to leave the house he owns in Squid Cove: "Now who's fault is that?" he asks. "I'm willin' to work but there's no work around." Others disagree. In Squid Cove welfare is thought of as something "we," the taxpayers, give to "them," the unemployed. There is no generally accepted feeling that it is the responsibility of the government or the society to secure appropriate work; the responsibility for finding a job falls upon the individual and no one else.

For a welfare recipient to say outright that if work is not available, it is only proper for the government to provide adequate assistance, is not approved. Recipients thus have to be careful not to talk about their "rights". . . . On the other hand, if a recipient does not complain at all, this might be taken as a sign that he is satisfied with being on welfare, that he, in fact, is unwilling to work. Whatever the recipient does, complain or not, he is likely to be sanctioned.   [38]

In explaining why he chose to study the plight of people on welfare, Cato Wadel writes: "From what has been said so far, it should be clear that I am not much in doubt about 'whose fault it is.'"

It is *not* the fault of the unemployed individual. If this study were summarized into a simple and clear statement, it would be that it is unemployment itself which produces behavior on the part of the unemployed which makes people blame the unemployment on the individual, and *not* the other way around: that a special attitude or personal defect produces unemployment.   [127]

Getting Drunk in Denver

One of the few quantitative studies of the relationship found in the culture of poverty between personality traits and economic success has yielded some surprising results. Theodore Graves (1974) selected three personality attributes that occupy a central place in discussions of the culture of poverty: (1) future-time perspective and delayed gratification, (2) control over one's destiny (internal locus of control), and (3) drive for achievement. Graves attempted to measure the extent to which these attributes contributed to the success or failure of Navajo Indians who had migrated to Denver in search of work.

483

Graves formulated a specific hypothesis: those migrants who possess the above attributes will do significantly better economically in the city than those who do not possess them. A second hypothesis concerned with the high rates of drunkenness and disorderly conduct associated with poor Indian migrants to urban centers was also formulated: those migrants who possess the above traits would have lower rates of drunkenness and would be arrested less frequently.

To determine the strength of each of the three attributes in a sample of Navajo migrants, Graves had them take three tests. The first test measured their future-time orientation by asking them to name five things that they expected to do or expected to happen to them. They were then asked to say when they thought these events were going to occur—the average time cited in the future being the measure of their future-time orientation. The second test measured their degree of belief in their ability to control their own destiny by asking the migrants to choose from among paired statements that expressed feelings of fatalism or personal control. For example: "When I make plans, I am almost certain that I can make them work" versus "I have usually found that what is going to happen will happen regardless of my plans." Finally, in the third test, the migrants were shown six drawings of Navajos in everyday scenes and asked to tell what was happening in the pictures, what led up to it, what the people in it were thinking about or wanted, what would happen next, and how it would end. The answers were then rated for the extent to which they revealed a psychological concern with achievement, getting things done, and overcoming obstacles. The results of all three tests were then compared with data about how successful the migrants had been in getting jobs at various wage levels and at holding on to them. Only one of the success measures showed even a low positive correlation with the personality attributes, while half of the success measures showed correlations (statistically insignificant) in the direction opposite from that predicted by the first hypothesis. "We conclude that our data provide *no* empirical support for the thesis that an absence of middle class personality traits is contributing to Navajo marginality in the economic sphere."

The second hypothesis was tested by comparing the arrest rates of migrants who had the culture of poverty attributes with those who did not. Different correlations were found with the different attributes. Migrants who received poor wages and who lacked a feeling of being in control got arrested about twice as often (almost always for alcohol-related offenses) than those who had the *same* poor jobs but believed they were more in control. Graves suggests that the reason for this is that some people are resigned to failure and see no sense in not getting drunk. The others, who are not so resigned, refrain from getting drunk, but this does not help them get ahead. The other two attributes—future-time orientation and achievement motivation—are also correlated with arrest rates among people who have low wages, but in the opposite direction from that anticipated in the hypothesis. Those with middle-class values get arrested more, not less frequently! Graves suggests that migrants who do poorly and have a future-time orientation tend to berate themselves and to be more anxious than those who live from day to day. Similarly migrants who do poorly and have a high achievement drive feel their economic failure more keenly. Both types drink more often, which causes them to be arrested more often. Graves concludes:

A middle-class personality is adaptive only within a structural setting which permits the attainment of middle-class goals. Otherwise such psychological traits tend to be *maladaptive* and to create additional adjustment problems for those who have acquired them. [83]

Values and the Matrifocal Family

A persistent explanation of poverty among blacks of the urban ghettos focuses attention on the high incidence of so-called "fatherless," or *matrifocal,* families. In 1965, with the release of a report by Daniel P. Moynihan, then U.S. Assistant Secretary of Labor, matrifocality received official recognition as the prime cause of the perpetuation of black poverty. According to Moynihan the failure of black youth to be properly motivated for the jobs that are actually available results from the lack of a male father figure in poor black households. Many black youth are reared in households where only the women are regularly employed. Adult males drift in and out of these households, and thus black youths grow up without the aid and inspiration of a stable male figure holding a steady job and providing comfort and security for his wife and children. Moynihan indicated that this experience accounts not only for poverty but for crime, drug addiction, and urban rioting as well.

Explanations of poverty that appeal to the enculturation experience within the matrifocal household must be rejected because the phenomenon of matrifocality is itself an adaptive response to poverty.

The main structural features of matrifocality are as follows: the domestic unit consists of a mother and her children by several different men. Some of the woman's co-resident adult daughters may also have children. The fathers provide only temporary and partial

485

maintenance. Men who move in and out of the domestic unit are etically "married" to the mothers—they act out all of the typical husband/father roles. Yet emically the relationship is distinguished from "true marriage," and the children are legally regarded as "illegitimate" (cf. Gonzalez 1970).

Added to these central features are a number of speculative attributes for which there is no supporting evidence. Thus Moynihan (1965) assumes that the matrifocality is the equivalent of matriarchy, and he pictures the female "head" of the household as bossing the males and being dominant. Detailed studies of authority and behavior in matrifocal households indicate that there are well-defined and separate spheres of authority for both male and female adults (De Havenon 1970; cf. Hannerz 1970; Kriesberg 1970; Valentine 1972).

Moynihan also regards the matrifocal family as "pathological" and "disorganized." Unless you believe that having more than one husband is itself a sign of pathology and disorganization, there is little basis for concluding that the actual day-to-day routines in such households are any more disorganized than in other poor or middle-class households.

Like all domestic arrangements, the matrifocal family arises under specific and known material conditions, and represents an adaptive achievement that is no more or less "pathological" than any other family form. The conditions in question are: (1) males and females lack access to strategic resources, that is, they own no significant property; (2) wage labor is available to both males and females; (3) females earn as much or more than males; and (4) male wages are insufficient to provide subsistence for a dependent wife and children.

Matrifocal families were common among European urban poor during the nineteenth century. Today they occur throughout broad areas of the Caribbean, Northeastern Brazil, and Central America, as well as in the black and Puerto Rican ghettos of the United States.

In the United States the high incidence of matrifocal families among the black poor is made virtually inevitable. First of all, most black males find employment only at the very bottom of the wage scale in jobs that have the least amount of security and chance for advancement. Second, as a result of the structure and ideology of the welfare system in the United States, poor households that seek welfare support cannot contain able-bodied "fathers." Mothers whose husbands or children's fathers do not earn enough money to support the household can claim Aid to Families with Dependent Children (AFDC) allotments, provided the fathers are not co-resident with their children. The reason why this expedient is built into the national and state welfare laws is that it is far cheaper for the government to

486

Figure 21-11. UNEM-
PLOYED. Down and out in
Detroit. (Burk Uzzle/Magnum)

provide such payments than to establish a high-quality system of child day-care centers that would free mothers to help their husbands by going to work. Since fathers cannot stay home with their children and claim AFDC allotments, the law confers upon women an extra economic value that makes it inevitable that they will become the center of domestic organization as long as the men cannot earn enough to make the AFDC allotments unnecessary.

In her study of the Flats, a black ghetto in a Midwestern city, Carol Stack (1974) has provided a vivid account of the adaptive strategies that poverty-level black families follow in attempting to maximize their security and well-being in the face of the AFDC laws and the inadequate wages of the unskilled black male. Nuclear families on the middle-class model do not exist because the material conditions necessary for such families do not exist. Instead the people of the Flats are organized into large female-centered networks of kinfolk and neighbors. The members of these networks engage in reciprocal economic exchanges, take care of each other's children, provide emergency shelter, and help each other in many ways not characteristic of middle-class domestic groups. As Stack points out:

Attempts by those on welfare to formulate nuclear families are efficiently discouraged by welfare policy. In fact, welfare policy encourages the maintenance of non-coresidential cooperative domestic networks.   [127]

487

Values and the Matrifocal Family

The Functions of Poverty

The failure to eliminate poverty in the United States has led increasing numbers of observers to conclude along with Stack (1974:128) that the present welfare programs are not merely passive victims of underfunding and conservative obstructionism, but "active purveyors of the status quo, staunch defenders of the economic imperative that demands maintenance of a sizable but docile impoverished class" (cf. Piven and Cloward 1971).

Why does so much poverty continue to exist in the United States? Clearly it has little to do with the amount of effort people make to work themselves out of poverty. Perhaps individuals who work harder, save more, and consume less do have a better chance of raising their standard of living. But this effort merely determines *who* will be poor. It does not determine *how many* will be poor. Those who blame poverty on the culture of poverty forget or deliberately attempt to make others forget one simple point: poverty will end the day after everyone who wants to work is guaranteed a job that pays more than poverty wages.

Failure to achieve this result leads inevitably to the conclusion that poverty is the result not of the failure of the poor but of the contribution that the poor make to the success of the wealthy. The poor contribute to the success of the wealthy because they constitute a

Figure 21-12. POOR PEOPLE'S PROTEST. Demonstrators mass at the state capitol in Albany to protest proposed cut in welfare payments. (UPI Photo)

reserve labor pool that enhances corporate profits. The poor enhance corporate profits because they inhibit demands for higher wages among the employed members of the working class. The poor do this by putting pressure on the group of underskilled and underemployed workers who are one step above them in the class hierarchy. The poor make this group expendable if they push too hard for a larger slice of the pie. The existence of the poor puts pressure on those just above them to conform and work hard. And this pressure gets transmitted through each successive level of the labor force, dragging back the entire wage-push emanating from the working class. The poor are then very valuable to the rich. Because the tax burden falls primarily on the working class, the rich pay very little to keep the poor alive. This is doubly valuable because the working class feels that it is being ripped off by those below them who live on the dole rather than by those above them who make money from the dole (cf. Blauner 1973; Bell et al. 1974).

If this analysis is correct, then one can understand why a system ostensibly dedicated to "welfare" continues to have such a corrosive and dehumanizing effect on its clients. From studies such as those of Wadel and Stack, it is clear that the welfare system deliberately intensifies the psychological significance of the narrow gap between poverty incomes and the lowest incomes of the working class. By demeaning and humiliating the poverty class, the welfare system makes it possible to keep the lowest paid working-class jobs a mere

Figure 21-13. PRUITT-IGOE. To avoid charges of coddling the poor for whom this huge high-rise project was built in St. Louis, elevator exits were installed only on alternate floors and water pipes were run through the corridors. Vandals broke the corridor windows, the pipes froze and burst, water cascaded down the stairwells and then froze. This rendered the stairs unusable and trapped hundreds of people on alternate floors in waterless and heatless apartments. Plagued by vandalism and crime and unable to obtain funds for security and maintenance, the housing authority decided to dynamite the buildings and level the entire project despite the acute shortage of low-income housing. (St. Louis Post-Dispatch)

The Functions of Poverty

notch ahead of the poverty income. If the people on welfare were not punished for their "failure," the morale and discipline of the working class would collapse. Millions of people might opt for welfare rather than the low-paying monotonous jobs they now hold. Yet the millions who are unemployed or underemployed through no fault of their own cannot be left to starve without risk of massive unrest. The function of welfare therefore is to prevent people from starving while at the same time making their life-style undesirable to the people who are just one step above them. AFDC does this by making it impossible for able-bodied males to receive welfare supplements to their own wages and at the same time to participate in the raising of their children within a nuclear family household. By destroying the nuclear family among the urban poor, AFDC transmits the stern warning to those tempted to withdraw from the labor market: you will not starve, but you will live without self-esteem. For in mainstream U.S. culture the nuclear family is a well-nigh sacred institution, regarded as essential for the moral and economic well-being of all "normal" men and women. And this warning is doubly effective because a large portion of the urban poverty class is black. Trained to prejudice, the whites who are just one step above poverty cannot sympathize with blacks who receive welfare. They thus fail to identify common interests, to unite politically, and to force the system to change in the direction of greater equity for all (cf. Piven and Cloward 1971).

HEREDITY AND INEQUALITY

To what extent is inequality the result of racial and other heritable genetic factors? Are underdeveloped nations poor because they are genetically less capable of inventing and using complex technologies? Do the poor live in poverty because they are less intelligent than the wealthy? Are the differences between the income levels of blacks and whites genetically determined? These questions were not brought up earlier in the book because they cannot be answered without the aid of the basic facts and theories of general anthropology. I will now turn to them, keeping in mind that only in the context of the full temporal and geographic range of human social and cultural phenomena can one attempt to identify the causes of inequality among nations, races, and classes.

Scientific Racism

In the nineteenth century almost all educated Westerners were firm adherents of the doctrines of *scientific racism.* They believed that Asians, Africans, and American Indians could achieve industrial civilization only slowly and imperfectly. Nineteenth-century scientists insisted that they had scientific proof that Europeans were intellectually superior and that an unbridgeable biological gulf separated Europeans from the rest of humanity (Haller 1971). They conceded the possibility of an occasional American Indian, Asian, or African "genius." But for the most part they denied that the hereditary capabilities of the "inferior" races overlapped with the hereditary

491

capabilities of the "superior" races. A typical opinion from one of the most learned scientists of the nineteenth century, Thomas H. Huxley, went as follows:

It may be quite true that some Negroes are better than some white men; but no rational man, cognisant of the facts, believes that the average Negro is the equal, still less the superior of the average white man. And if this be true, it is simply incredible that, when all his disabilities are removed, and our prognathic relative has a fair field and no favour, as well as no oppressor, he will be able to compete successfully with his bigger-brained and smaller-jawed rival, in a contest which is to be carried on by thoughts and not by bites.   [quoted in Birch 1968:50–51]

Race and Cultural Evolution

Huxley's racism was influenced in no small measure by the fact that Europeans had fought, tricked, and traded their way to control over almost the entire human species. The apparent inability of Asians, Africans, and American Indians to resist the encroachment of European armies, businesspeople, missionaries, and administrators continues to be widely accepted as proof of the innate superiority of the white race.

As everyone knows, these economic and political triumphs were associated with the mastery of industrial and military technology. This mastery has also been widely interpreted as evidence that the white race is the vanguard branch of *Homo sapiens*. Contemporary racist doctrines rely heavily on this interpretation of the differential achievements of the major social groups.

An anthropological perspective and an interest in the fullness of history and prehistory are prerequisites for any attempt to evaluate the significance of differential rates of cultural evolution. Very different implications can be extracted from the status of technological, political, and aesthetic development, depending on the particular slice of time being inspected. Prior to 12,000 B.P. it is difficult to associate any major geographical area with greater or lesser degrees of technological achievement. The basic Upper Paleolithic tool kits of Africa, Asia, and Europe are essentially equal from the point of view of precision, strength, virtuosity, and efficiency (Ch. 9). Everywhere technological achievements rested on an extensive inventory of wood, bone, and stone tools; this inventory varied in response to particular ecological opportunities, but no major geographical area can be said to have been consistently more advanced in basic Paleolithic techniques (see p. 185).

At 12,000 B.P. no population anywhere had yet crossed the threshold

492

Figure 22-1. BRONZES OF CHOU DYNASTY. The Chinese developed metallurgical skills far in advance of Western Europe. The top four bronzes date from late 11th to early 10th century B.C.; the bottom two date from 5th century B.C. (Smithsonian Institution, Freer Gallery of Art, Washington, D.C.)

to state organization. The great organizational achievements of this period probably consisted of kinship-mediated groupings such as lineages, sibs, and circulating connubia, which in all likelihood were invented repeatedly in different parts of the world among all the major races in response to local conditions. Hence no geographical area can be said to have been politically more advanced than any other prior to 12,000 B.P.

It is true that during the period 25,000 to 12,000 B.P. European artists achieved realistic cave art paintings of animals for which there is no known parallel on other continents. But by 12,000 B.P. most of the cave art had already been abandoned in favor of quite undistinguished geometric designs. Applying the logic of racial determinism one would have to conclude that the Western European whites (if they were white!) had suffered some form of genetic damage and had lost their capacity for cultural achievement (what they actually lost, as you saw in Ch. 9, were the herds of reindeer, bison, and horse). The next 5,000 years would have confirmed this interpretation, for the descendants of the cave artists were to contribute little to the advance of technology and political organization.

The populations of Mesopotamia and Anatolia took the lead in the transition from hunting and gathering to settled village life. These same populations led in the development of the first urban centers and imperial dynasties. In the year 2000 B.C. a racial determinist would have had to conclude that the East Asians were an inferior branch of humanity, since at that time "civilization" had been achieved only by the Middle Easterners, South Asians, and Egyptians. In the Middle East metallurgy had been practiced for 2,500 years and the Great Pyramid at Giza was already 800 years old when the first stirrings of similar developments began to be felt in Shang China. But racist observers, had they been Sumerian, Egyptian, or Syrian, would probably have been even more impressed with the cultural lag of Europeans living in Germany and Scandinavia, who in 2000 B.C. had barely crossed the threshold to settled village life. Noting that these illiterate, semisedentary peoples had fallen at least 2,500 years behind the vanguard of civilization, Middle Eastern racists would probably have denied that Europeans were bona fide members of the white race. But let another 2,000 years elapse. With the conquests of Alexander the Great (334–323 B.C.) the relative positions of the Middle Easterners and the "barbarians" of Southern Europe underwent a complete inversion.

The change in the status of the Chinese was equally dramatic. The florescence of Greece and Rome was paralleled by the rise of the Han dynasty. After Rome collapsed, plunging most of Europe back into

494

feudalism, China emerged in the latter part of the sixth century as the largest, most powerful, and technologically most advanced empire in the world. China held this position for at least one thousand years. Remember that as late as the eighteenth century the Chinese emperor was convinced that the "red-faced" peoples of Europe were an inferior barbarian race.

The irony of the modern racist explanation of inequality is that the Northern Europeans, among whom the doctrines of scientific racism arose, would have to be included among the world's most backward races during all but 1,000 of the last 12,000 years of human history.

Had Julius Caesar or one of his contemporaries been asked whether by any sane stretch of fantasy he could imagine the Britons and the Germans as inherently the equals of Romans and Greeks, he would probably have replied that if these northerners possessed the ability of the Mediterraneans they would long since have given vent to it, instead of continuing to live in disorganization, poverty, ignorance, rudeness and without great men or products of the spirit.   [Kroeber 1948:202]

Today the emergence of Japan as the Asian match of Great Britain and Germany, China's return to first-rank technological status as signaled by its independent development of the hydrogen bomb, and the military stalemates suffered by the United States in Korea and Vietnam effectively discourage white racial determinists from demeaning the cultural achievements of Asia.

Africa and Empire

But what of the Africans? White supremacists point out that no equivalent of the Roman, Mesopotamian, Indic, or Chinese empires developed south of the Sahara. To combat these views, historians and social scientists often draw attention to the existence of indigenous African kingdoms, especially in the Sudan and in West Africa.

Perhaps the most impressive of the pre-European African states were Ghana, Mali, and Songhay. These kingdoms succeeded each other from A.D. 300 to about A.D. 1500 and covered a region equivalent to and ultimately larger than Western Europe. Notable centralization of power was achieved. There were populous capital cities (e.g., Songhay's Timbuktu) with palaces, temples, and universities; armies consisting of tens of thousands of foot and horse soldiers equipped with iron lances; centralized taxation and corvée; and divine kings who ruled with the assistance of nobles and bureaucrats. The Neolithic had arrived later in West Africa than in Europe (see p. 207). Nonetheless in the year A.D. 500 the feudal kingdoms of West Africa

495

Figure 22-2. WEST AFRICAN HORSEMAN. The Sultan of Meiganga, Cameroons. European armies did not gain a decisive military advantage over West African kingdoms until the mid-19th century. (United Nations)

resembled the feudal kingdoms of Northern Europe and of the Iberian Peninsula. Like their feudal counterparts in Europe, the West African states were based on rainfall agriculture and stock-raising. As the European kingdoms consolidated and grew, the African kingdoms also became larger and more centralized. During the eighth century A.D. the Iberian Peninsula and the Sudan were simultaneously invaded by Arab armies—one across the Straits of Gibraltar, the other across the Sahara Desert. The Sahara, however, impeded the southward flow of Arabic influence. Lacking the previous exposure to Roman influence and cut off from the main trade routes in the Mediterranean area, the sub-Saharan kingdoms fell behind the pace of European development. Perhaps the most important difference was that Ghana, Mali, and Songhay traded by land across the Sahara, whereas the Europeans turned more and more to maritime commerce. By the fourteenth century the technological and military advantages of the Europeans had reached decisive levels.

496

With the arrival of the Portuguese along the Guinea coast in the fifteenth century, the fate of Africa was sealed for the next five hundred years. At first the West African states were too strong for outright conquest by European expeditionary forces. Unlike the inhabitants of Mexico or Peru, the Africans were mounted and possessed iron weapons capable of piercing European armor. Rather than invade the interior, the Europeans stayed on the coast. Trade relations were established with the indigenous rulers, but the principal items of trade were slaves destined for the New World plantations. In order to obtain these slaves, the Africans enlarged the scope of warfare, raiding, and internecine struggle. The Songhay empire was split into a hundred warring tribes and microkingdoms. Thus the arrival of the Europeans cut short the trajectory of African political development and turned vast portions of the interior into warring communities whose chief export became the human crop used for slavery (Birmingham 1966; Trimingham 1959; Harris 1972; Derman 1975).

Again and again in world history those who lag furthest behind in one period move furthest ahead in the next. For the first time since the geological formation of the Sahara Desert at the end of the Pleistocene, Africa is now in full contact with the centers of technological and political advance. To attribute Africa's present state of underdevelopment to racial factors is to reveal a profound incapacity to learn from the past 12,000 years of cultural evolution.

Ethnography and Race

Previous chapters have presented likely explanations for the occurrence of matrilineality, patrilineality, cognatic descent groups; nuclear and polygamous families, kinship terminologies, reciprocity, redistribution, feudalism, oriental despotism, and many other cultural traits and complexes. In none of the relevant hypotheses or theories has it been found necessary or even useful to contemplate that such phenomena are caused by genetic differences. Anthropologists are virtually unanimous in this matter. The spectrum of world cultural differences is correlated neither geographically nor temporally with identifiable racial specialties. Murdock's *Ethnographic Atlas* clearly demonstrates that marriage and residence patterns, descent groups, and social and political systems are not the exclusive possession of any one of the geographic races. Each of the main racial groups is culturally far more heterogeneous than can be accounted for by any rational scheme of genetic causality. Contemporary Asian peoples, for example, exhibit the entire range of cultural complexity,

497

from the band-organized hunters and gatherers of the Malay Peninsula to the horticultural villagers of Vietnam, to the feudalities of the Kachin hills in Burma, to the peasants of Thailand, to the pastoralists of Mongolia, to the communes of China, to the industrial capitalists of Hong Kong and Japan. If humanity consisted entirely of Asian races, 99 percent of the total known variety of customs and institutions would still be present on earth.

The existence of genetic control over differences and similarities in the world cultural inventory is also wholly contradicted by established facts concerning the processes by which culture is propagated across generations and transmitted from one population to another. Human infants reared apart from their parents in another breeding population invariably acquire the cultural repertory of the people among whom they are reared. Children of English-speaking whites reared by Chinese parents grow up speaking perfect Chinese. They handle their chopsticks with flawless precision and experience no sudden inexplicable urge to eat Yorkshire pudding. Children of Chinese reared in white U.S. households speak the standard English dialect of their foster parents, are inept at using chopsticks, and experience no uncontrollable yearning for bird's nest soup or Peking duck. (I am told that the 1970 Yorkshire pudding cooking contest was won by a Chinese.)

Social groups and individuals drawn from a vast variety of populations have repeatedly demonstrated their ability to acquire every conceivable aspect of the world cultural inventory. American Indians brought up in Brazil incorporate complex African rhythms into their religious performances; American blacks who attend the proper conservatories readily acquire the distinctly non-African requisites for a career in classical European opera. Jews brought up in Germany acquire a preference for German cooking; Jews brought up in Yemen prefer Middle Eastern dishes. Under the influence of fundamentalist Christian missionaries, the sexually uninhibited peoples of Polynesia began to dress their women in dowdy "Mother Hubbards" and to follow rules of strict premarital chastity. Australian aborigines reared in Sydney show no inclination to hunt kangaroo, create circulating connubia, or mutilate their genitals; they do not experience uncontrollable urges to sing about witchetty grubs and the Emu ancestors. The Mohawk Indians of New York State specialize in construction trades, and help to erect the steel frames of skyscrapers. Walking across narrow beams eighty stories above street level, they are not troubled by an urge to build wigwams rather than office buildings. The evidence of acculturation on every continent and among every major race and micro breeding population proves beyond dispute that the

Figure 22-3. THROUGH OTHER EYES. What a white man looked like to a Tlingit wood carver. (Museum of the American Indian, Heye Foundation)

overwhelming bulk of the response repertory of any human population can be acquired by any other human population through learning processes and without the slightest exchange or mutation of their genes.

The New Scientific Racism

During the twentieth century the old doctrines of scientific racism have been steadily eroded by the cumulative evidence bearing upon the ability of members of all races to acquire knowledge and skills in the most advanced and complex branches of science and technology. As a result, the question of whether there are biologically "superior" and "inferior" peoples has come to rest upon the measurement of increasingly more subtle differences in cultural performance. Thus it is readily conceded by the modern-day counterparts of Thomas H. Huxley that the distribution of the alleged genetic capacities for cultural performance is such as to produce overlapping curves that place the majority of the members of *all* races within a common panhuman "normal" distribution. At the present time the main source of disagreement concerns the extent to which the *variance*—the deviation from the average—can be accounted for by hereditary as opposed to cultural and other environmental factors.

The dispute between the racial determinists and the cultural and environmental determinists is being focused increasingly on the measurement of intellectual abilities. The reason for this focus is not self-evident and deserves additional comment.

In the nineteenth century the assumed absolute racial superiority of Euro-Americans was said to consist of a generalized aptitude for "civilization." In the United States, slavery was rationalized as a system of paternalistic tutelage that was necessary in order to protect the biologically "childlike" and "primitive" black from the harmful effects of competition with more civilized races. Dire predictions were made concerning the fate-worse-than-slavery that awaited the freed slave. Indeed some racists became abolitionists in the hope that free Afro-Americans would prove so incapable of managing their own affairs that they would soon die out. These predictions, to say the least, have proved unfounded. Nonetheless the position of Afro-Americans within the class hierarchy has remained markedly different from that of whites. In the U.S., blacks earn only 60 percent of what whites earn on the average; disproportionately few blacks enjoy upper-middle-class status; and still fewer have penetrated into the ruling class (U.S. Bureau of the Census 1969; U.S. Economic Council 1974; Bryce 1974).

As it became evident that Afro-Americans had the capacity for working-class "civilization," attention shifted to the question of whether they had the capacity for achieving upward mobility in a complex competitive social hierarchy. The scientific racists now dropped the notion of a generalized, racially determined "aptitude for civilization" and concentrated instead on finding genetic reasons for the failure of the blacks to achieve economic parity with white workers.

Since upward mobility in the United States is closely linked with years of schooling, the cause of the discrepancy between white socioeconomic achievement and black socioeconomic achievement is widely attributed to differential success in getting an education. Among the new group of scientific racists, the relatively poor educational performance of the blacks is linked in turn to an alleged genetic inability to acquire skills in reading, mathematics, and logic, the mastery of which is, for many whites, the key to better jobs and higher incomes. "Intelligence" is the name psychologists give to the innate biological factor assumed responsible for the mastery of these verbal, mathematical, and logical skills.

Race and Intelligence

Under the influence of preconceived notions concerning the origin of social inequality, intelligence was at first regarded as a completely fixed essence or trait that could not be affected by an individual's life experience and culture. Karl Pearson, one of the most influential figures in the application of statistical measures to biological variation, wrote in 1924:

".. . the mind of man is for the most part a congenital product, and the factors which determine it are racial and familial; we are not dealing with a mutable characteristic capable of being moulded by the doctor, the teacher, the parent or the home environment." [quoted in Hirsch 1970:92]

Various tests were devised to measure this fixed ingredient. Most of them, including the widely used Stanford-Binet I.Q. test, present in varying combinations tasks involving word meanings, verbal relationships, arithmetical reasoning, form classification, spatial relationships, and other abstract symbolic material (Thorndike 1968:424). Since these tasks are similar to the kinds of tasks by which general academic achievement is assessed, it is not surprising that intelligence tests are good predictors of academic success.

Early in this century it was shown that black schoolchildren scored considerably below white schoolchildren on intelligence tests. Hence

500

it was concluded that blacks were innately less intelligent than whites. Race, then, was the reason they did not perform as well or continue as long in school as whites. If their distribution in the class hierarchy was skewed in the direction of the lowest incomes it was because they were biologically inferior to whites. If they were poor, it was their own fault.

Early Intelligence Testing

The era of large-scale intelligence testing began when the United States entered World War I. To determine their military assignments, thousands of draftees were given so-called Alpha and Beta tests. After the war, psychologists arranged the results according to race, found the expected correlations between blacks and lower scores, and concluded that the innate intellectual inferiority of the blacks had been scientifically proved (Yerkes 1921).

The army tests were scored by grades lettered A to E. The percent distribution for 93,073 whites and 18,891 blacks on, above, and below, the middle grade of C was as follows:

	Below C	C	Above C
Whites	24	64	12
Blacks	79	20	1

These results were seized upon to justify the maintenance of inferior social status for blacks in and out of the army. Subsequent analysis, however, showed that the scores were useless as measurements of the genetic factors governing intelligence (Bagley 1924). They were useless because the tests had not distinguished between the assumed hereditary effects and the equally plausible effects of cultural and other environmental factors. The strength of the environmental factors became apparent when the scores of blacks from five Northern states were compared with the scores of blacks from four Southern states:

	Below C	C	Above C
Northern Blacks	46	51	3
Southern Blacks	86	14	0

The most plausible explanation for the superiority in the performance of Northern blacks over Southern blacks is that the Northerners had

501

been exposed to environmental conditions favorable to achieving higher test scores. Among such conditions would be quality and amount of schooling, experience with test situations, diet, and conditions of life in home and neighborhood. Further attempts to interpret the test results in terms of possible environmental effects showed that the differences between the races disappeared when the comparison was restricted to literate New York blacks and literate Alabama whites:

	Below C	C	Above C
Alabama Whites	19	72	9
New York Blacks	21	72	7

When illiterate Alabama whites were compared with illiterate New York blacks, the relationship of "superiority" and "inferiority" was reversed:

	Below C	C	Above C
New York Blacks	72	28	0
Alabama Whites	80	20	0

In order to account for the failure of mass testing to prove the white's innate intellectual superiority, the scientific racists advanced an ingenious hypothesis. The discrepancy between the Northern and Southern scores was attributed to the selective migration of the innately more intelligent blacks. The most intelligent blacks had left the South and had congregated in the Northern cities. Thus the Northern black was a self-selected genotype who represented the upper limit of Afro-American intelligence.

Studies were now carried out that showed that northward- and city-bound blacks did indeed score higher on intelligence tests than those who were content to live in rural Southern towns and villages. But a plausible alternative explanation of this correlation is that the decision to emigrate was a result of a better education and other environmental factors that simultaneously tend to raise performance.

To test the selection-through-migration theory Otto Klineberg (1935; 1944), an anthropologically trained social psychologist, studied the relationship between the length of time that Southern black migrants had lived in the North and their I.Q.'s. Klineberg found that the scores of twelve-year-old Southern-born black girls improved proportionately to the number of years that had elapsed since they left the South:

502

Years in New York City	Average I.Q.
1–2	72
3–4	76
5–6	84
7–9	92
born in New York	92

Although this study seemed at the time to provide definitive proof of the importance of environmental factors in intelligence scores, racial determinists have been indefatigably imaginative in coming up with additional objections. Dwight Ingle (1968:114), for example, has recently suggested some reasons why the World War I Northern blacks performed better than Southern whites: (1) the standards for admitting blacks to the army were higher than for whites; and (2) in the Southern states the whites with the highest intelligence were more readily promoted to officer status and thus did not take the test.

Recent Intelligence Testing

As Klineberg's data indicated, the change in residence brought the I.Q.'s of Southern black girls up to the level of Northern blacks in seven to nine years. Instead of concluding that I.Q. tests were measuring something other than a fixed, innate characteristic, the racial determinists concentrated on building a new line of defense against their environmentalist critics. For the first time it now was freely admitted by all concerned that I.Q. scores could be influenced by life experience. Obviously the gap between black and white I.Q. scores could be narrowed, but could the gap ever be closed? The I.Q.'s of Southern migrants merely rose to the limit of the average black Northerner's score, but that score remained some 10 points below the average of the Northern white I.Q. This difference between the Northern black and Northern white I.Q. persists to the present moment. If black and white I.Q.'s are compared on a national basis, the difference is still greater, amounting to about 15 points (Shuey 1966).

The still numerous and influential racial determinists in the field of psychology and genetics no longer propose that the entire 15-point I.Q. difference between white and blacks is due to innate, hereditary factors. It is now generally recognized that environmental influences are capable of raising or lowering a group's average. Various attempts have been made, therefore, to restrict comparisons between the races to samples matched for environmental conditions. The most common

503

type of control involves matching socioeconomic status as indicated by occupation and income. On the basis of such attempts at controlled comparison, 5 of the 15 points at issue are generally conceded by the racial determinists to environmental effects, and 10 points are attributed to racial heredity (Shuey 1966: Jensen 1969). That is, when middle-class blacks are compared only with middle-class whites and working-class blacks are compared only with working-class whites, an average discrepancy of some 10 points remains.

Can Psychologists Control for Bigotry and Exploitation?

There is no reason to assume that environmental influences can be evened out simply by matching white and black job categories and income levels. The environmentally imposed disadvantages that blacks bring to the I.Q. testing situation are the result of historical processes begun during slavery and perpetuated into the twentieth century. Due to the exigencies of cotton production and of police-military control under slavery, the mass of U.S. blacks were trained to become docile, unskilled field hands. The whites tried to keep the blacks illiterate and to instill in them the belief that they were intellectually inferior. Whites deliberately sought to destroy the blacks' self-respect and communal pride (Haller 1971; Blauner 1973; Montagu 1974).

Within the contemporary black household, regardless of class, the direct and indirect effects of the trauma of slavery and the era of white supremacy continue to make themselves felt. Most black children are still educated in poor schools by ill-trained personnel. In integrated situations they have been the victims of prejudiced teachers who are convinced that blacks lack the capacity to learn and who frequently believe out of fear and prejudice that black children should be discouraged from attempting to learn.

The curricula that black students must master are still being designed primarily by white educators on behalf of the educational needs of white students whose enculturation experience is not affected by the trauma of racial prejudice and discrimination. These curricula automatically confer advantages upon white children and automatically penalize blacks. The content of every course, be it arithmetic, spelling, English, history, or social studies, assumes a type and degree of preschool and out-of-school preparation more characteristic of white than of black children (Rosenfeld 1972).

504

Intelligence tests, in other words, predict the ability of black children to compete with white children in a white school system. They are designed by whites to test children who have been prepared for the test-taking situation by patterns of thought and behavior common to white enculturation but not to black enculturation (Talbert 1973). Black and white children do not have the same training and practice in word meanings, verbal relationships, arithmetical reasoning, form classification, spatial relations, and other abstract symbolic problems that in one version or another constitute the substance of the Stanford-Binet and similar intelligence tests (Cohen 1969; Kozol 1972).

Children do not have the same motivational basis for taking tests in school and for striving to compete and excel in test performances. They have different expectations concerning the probable outcome of testing based upon previous experiences of success or failure, and these expectations also enhance or hinder the test performances. The entire life-experience of blacks in community and region is everywhere warped and strained by prejudice and discrimination. As long as these patterns of superordination and subordination persist, the environment of neither the middle- nor lower-class whites can be equated with the grossly defined class analogues among the blacks (cf. Cole et al. 1971; Wax et al. 1971; Scribner and Cole 1973; Montagu 1974).

Intelligence and Heritability

It should be made clear that black children from families in upper-income brackets have an average I.Q. that is higher than the average for whites in general. In a practical sense, therefore, the question of whether blacks are innately more or less intelligent than whites now rests upon the issue of whether it is possible to bring the I.Q.'s of lower-income black children up to the present white average. In anthropological perspective the closing of a 15-point I.Q. differential through cultural change is eminently feasible. But widespread interest remains in any research that tends to confirm the politically and morally more convenient belief that the I.Q. gap is not the result of exploitation, discrimination, and prejudice but rather of innate and unmodifiable racial deficiencies for which whites are not responsible.

Recently the racial determinist position has received support from the work of the psychologist Arthur Jensen. According to Jensen (1969) about 80 percent of the gap between average black and white I.Q.'s may be unmodifiable through environmental manipulation. Jensen's conclusion is based upon the calculation of the *heritability* of intelligence. Heritability expresses the amount of variance (statistical

505

dispersal above and below the average) that is theoretically attributable to genetic factors. Hence 80 percent heritability of I.Q. means that in the observed distribution of I.Q. scores, 80 percent of the spread above and below I.Q. 100 is due to heredity. The best calculations of I.Q. heritability depend upon the comparison of the scores of identical twins (same sperm, same ovum) with nonidentical twins and other relatives.

It should be emphasized that the value of 80 percent for I.Q. heritability employed by Jensen is based largely upon the study of white twins (ibid.: 43). Thus, to begin with, there is the question of whether the heritability of I.Q. is the same for blacks as for whites. According to Scarr-Salapatek (1971b), conceivably I.Q. could be highly heritable among whites but not among blacks. The transfer of the 80 percent heritability of intelligence among white twins to blacks in general is thus methodologically inadmissable.

A more important point to bear in mind is that even if I.Q. heritability were equally high among whites and blacks, unknowably large changes in I.Q. scores could still be produced by altering the environment of black children. For "whatever the heritability of I.Q. (or, it should be added, of any characteristic), large phenotypic changes may be produced by creating appropriate, radically different environments never before encountered by [the] genotype" (Scarr-Salapatek 1971a:1224). This can best be seen by brief reference to the relationship between heritability and changed environment in the classic case of human stature. Identical twins tend to be very similar in height; hence there is a high index of heritability for stature—90 percent. But this high value of heritability for stature completely obscures the fact that the enrichment of diet, especially in proteins and vitamins, has produced large increases in the average height of twins (and of everyone else) in the past few generations (Tanner 1968). As Lee J. Cronback (1969:342) has pointed out, although the term "heritability" is standard in genetics, it "is mischievous in public discussion, for it suggests to the unwary that it describes the limit to which environmental change *can be* influential." In the words of behavior geneticist Jerry Hirsch (1970:101): "High or low heritability tells us absolutely nothing about how a given individual might have developed under conditions different from those in which he actually did develop."

By far the most devastating critique of the racial determinists' position, however, involves a recalculation of the value of heritability based on twin studies. Gross errors in methodology and analysis have been demonstrated in the various studies relied on by Jensen. These studies failed to take into consideration the fact that identical twins reared in the same household receive similar treatment more frequently than nonidentical twins reared in the same households. (One reason for this is that identical twins are always of the same sex but nonidentical twins may be of opposite sex!) They also failed to take into account the fact that orphaned identical twins tend to be placed with foster parents of similar socioeconomic backgrounds more frequently than nonidentical twins (Kamin 1974).

Identical twins are of the same sex, are frequently dressed alike, given the same toys and mistaken for one another. Thus large differences in correlation of identical and fraternal [nonidentical] twins do not necessarily mean high heritability, or any heritability.
. . .

We conclude that the evidence used to support high heritability of I.Q. performance actually yields low estimates of heritability consistent with zero and not larger than the upper limit of [15 percent].   [Schwartz and Schwartz 1974: 248–249]

This means that if blacks have the same heritability for I.Q. as whites, only 15 percent at most, and possibly zero percent, of the 15-point difference in I.Q. can be accounted for by genetic factors.

Changing I.Q.'s

Available evidence contradicts the view that the gap between white and black I.Q. scores cannot be eliminated by environmental modification. I.Q. scores are far from being rigidly fixed attributes that individuals carry through life like eye color or the whorls on their finger tips. Normal home-reared middle-class children change their I.Q.'s by substantial amounts while growing up. Between the ages of two-and-a-half and seventeen the I.Q.'s of home-reared middle-class children change on the average 28.5 points. According to one source: ". . . one of every three children displayed a progressive change of more than 30 points, and one in seven shifted more than 40 points" (McCall et al. 1973:70). Removal of various environmentally imposed handicaps is known to produce upward modifications of 15, 20, and even 30 points in average I.Q. scores.

Part of the handicap suffered by black children consists of the I.Q. examination setting itself. Black children are often unfamiliar with test situations, intimidated by an examiner of another race, and lack motivation and interest in the test procedure (Katz et al. 1968). It has been found that many of the extremely low (60 or less) scores occur when children fail to understand the nature of the task set before them. Children may require as much as seven hours of rapport sessions with the examiner before they fully understand what they are supposed to do and are relaxed enough to work at an optimal level (Kagan 1969:276). Jensen himself attributes a large portion of the differences in I.Q. scores to the test situation. Retesting children who had learned to be "completely at home" in his laboratory "rarely failed" to produce an 8-to-10 point gain (1969:100). Jensen states that he "would put very little confidence in a single test score, especially if it is the child's first test and more especially if the child is from a poor background and of a different race from the examiner" (ibid.). Yet the reported 15-point I.Q. deficit is based on testing situations that do not conform to Jensen's criteria of "accurate I.Q. testing under . . . optimal conditions."

Much larger gains in I.Q. are reported when children reared in severely deprived environments are transferred to more "normal" situations. Children in orphanages provide the classic example. It has been known for some time that a 35-point increase can be produced if orphanage children are placed in good foster homes before they are three years of age. Those who are not removed from the orphanage tend to be placed eventually in state institutions for the mentally retarded (Hunt 1969:290).

Studies of identical twins, far from confirming Jensen's view, clearly show that the range of environments now available could readily account for the entire 15-point spread between black and white averages. The average interpair differences in 38 pairs of identical twins reared apart in Great Britain was 14 points on the verbal I.Q. At least 25 percent of twins reared apart in this study had within-pair I.Q. differences in excess of 16 points (Gottesman 1968:32).

Direct experimental refutation of the misleading use to which Jensen has put the concept of heritability is provided by a mounting number of preschool enrichment programs. Bereiter and Engelmann (1966) worked with fifteen black preschool children from low-income families in which older siblings were encountering problems in school. The children, whose median age was four years, six months, were given intensive instruction in basic language skills, reading, and arithmetic. In order to eliminate the "irrelevant" 6-to-8 point gain in I.Q. expected merely when children become adjusted to schooling, I.Q. testing was not initiated until the second month. The average at this time was 93. Five months later, on retesting, the average was slightly over 100. Greater gains—16.9 points—are reported from similar types of programs after one year (Karnes 1968). A control group—children not exposed to intensive training—lost 2.8 points during the same period! After four years of tutoring, a group of

508

Milwaukee infants whose mothers had I.Q.'s of less than 70 attained a mean of I.Q. 127 as compared with a mean of I.Q. 90 in an untutored control group (Heber 1969). These experiments prove that even if high estimates of heritability are correct, massive changes in the pattern of I.Q. performance would result from placing children of low I.Q. parents with high I.Q. parents (Scarr-Salapatek 1971b; Layzer 1974).

The evidence indicates that I.Q.'s can be changed. No one knows by how much. The new racial determinists' attempt to prove that the change cannot be as large as 15 points will never be convincing if an effort has not been made to bridge the gap by equalizing every environmental variable that is known to have some influence upon the test scores. What this would amount to, of course, is nothing less than the elimination of black subordination down to the last trace of bigotry and discrimination. In the words of psychologist Robyn Dawes:

> The assertion that the discrepancy between the average white and average black I.Q. in the United States is due in some part to genetic differences is equivalent to the assertion that if there were no differences in the environments of whites and blacks there would still be a difference in their average intelligence. It may not be productive to examine this assertion with correlational studies of samples drawn from United States society as it exists. Perhaps a better method would be to attempt experimental evaluation of how I.Q. differences would change if in fact the environments of blacks and whites were equivalent. In other words, the best way to settle this controversy might be to eliminate racism. [1972:230]

I.Q. and Class

As I remarked earlier, the nineteenth-century elites looked down upon peasants and the urban working class as a species apart. The convenience of being able to blame poverty and exploitation upon the victims of poverty and exploitation is so great that genetic explanations of stratification phenomena will probably always find ready acceptance as long as stratification persists. Just as I.Q. differences correlate with race, so too do I.Q. differences correlate with class. "The upper class scores about thirty I.Q. points above the lower class," wrote Richard Herrnstein (1971) in a widely publicized article. "A typical member of the upper class gets a score that certifies him as intellectually 'superior,' while a typical member of the lower class is a shade below average." Using Jensen's estimates of an I.Q. heritability of 80 percent, Herrnstein concluded that present-day class membership was primarily determined by genetic factors. The

United States already is a *meritocracy*—that is, those who earn the most money on the average have the highest I.Q.'s. To the extent that educational opportunities are offered more equitably to all children, the meritocracy will become more rigid, and heredity will eventually account for 80 percent of the pattern of membership in the stratification hierarchy. Or so says Herrnstein.

If the revised estimates of I.Q. heritability are sustained, this view need not be taken seriously. However, even if I.Q. heritability is as high as .80, certain aspects of Herrnstein's argument should be placed in an appropriate anthropological context. It should be made clear that poverty and class exploitation are products of the evolution of culture, not of the evolution of I.Q.'s. Although hereditary I.Q. differences have always existed, and although such differences have always been important in social life, poverty and class exploitation have *not* always existed. If a culture fails to eliminate poverty and exploitation, it cannot be a *meritocracy.* No human beings *merit* that kind of treatment. Furthermore Herrnstein's emphasis upon hereditary I.Q. differences as the key to merited positions in a stratification hierarchy ignores the role of technology in cultural evolution. Individuals who have myopia do not merit starvation because they cannot find their way to the supermarket—technology provides them with corrective lenses. Similarly people who cannot extract the square root of a 10-digit number in their head need not resign themselves to washing dishes for the rest of their lives. Cheap computers have already corrected for such hereditary "defects" just as effectively as cheap glasses have made hereditary differences in eyesight entirely irrelevant in modern life. There is no reason to suppose that other aspects of "intelligence" are not equally susceptible to technological or other forms of cultural modification. Finally it should be noted that the curve of the distribution of wealth and power in the United States bears no resemblance to the curve of the distribution of I.Q. scores. Ninety-nine percent of all I.Q.'s fall between 80 and 140. How can such a distribution explain the fact that the wealthiest 4.5 percent of adults possess an average of $200,000 of wealth while half of the population possesses an average of less than $3,000 per person (see p. 406)? Clearly the extraordinarily lopsided distribution of income is more a matter of the inheritance of wealth than the inheritance of genes. I for one refuse to admit that a typical member of the top .1 percent of wealthy adults is four thousand times smarter than I am.

510

I.Q. and Culture

In anthropological perspective I.Q. heritability is a trivial if not meaningless measure. "Intelligence tests are . . . at most tests of achieved ability" (Bodmer and Cavalli-Sforza 1970:19). Intelligence as measured by the Stanford-Binet I.Q. test measures how much a child has learned that is relevant to success in Euro-American schools compared with other children of the same age, sex, socioeconomic status, and cultural system.

Use of the heritability concept by testers of intelligence ignores the subordination of genetic adaptation to cultural adaptation during the past 3 million years of hominid biological and cultural evolution. The greater the amount of cultural difference between populations, the more trivial and futile the heritability measurements. For this reason the highest recorded I.Q. gains in controlled studies are reported from populations with the greatest cultural contrasts. In Israel, for example, Jewish immigrants from Arab countries show a 20-point gain in one year (Bereiter and Engelmann 1966:55–56).

When psychologists first began to recognize that the Stanford-Binet I.Q. test was "culture-bound," they attempted to develop substitutes that would be "culture-free" or "culture-fair." None of these tests are or ever will be "culture-free" or "culture-fair." It is a contradiction in terms to suppose that any enculturated human being can be approached in such a way as to overcome or cancel out the effects of enculturation. In the words of Paul Bohannan:

There is no possibility of any "intelligence" test *not* being culturally biased. The content of an intelligence test must have something to do with the ideas or with the muscle habits or with habitual modes of perception and action of the people who take the test. All these things are culturally mediated or influenced in human beings. . . . This is not a dictum or a definition—it is a recognition of the way in which cultural experience permeates everything human beings perceive and do. [1973:115]

A major portion of many intelligence tests consists of vocabulary lists that obviously depend on a child's enculturation experience especially as regards the number and kinds of books read and adults listened to. Other questions depend on degree of compliance to moral or aesthetic standards. A question asked of seven-year-olds on the Stanford-Binet test is: "What's the thing for you to do when you have broken something that belongs to someone else?" "Feel sorry" and "Tell 'em I did it" are wrong answers. "Pay for it" and "Tell them I'm sorry" are correct. To the anthropologists more is being said here about the culture of the examiners than about the intelligence of the test-takers.

511

Kpelle Logic

Certain basic cognitive capacities are shared by all human groups regardless of culture. "All cultural groups thus far studied have demonstrated the capacity to remember, to generalize, form concepts, operate with abstractions, and reason logically" (Scribner and Cole 1973:553). However, there are marked differences in the way these capacities are used in the solution of particular problems in different cultures. Certain apparently illogical conclusions, for example, may actually be perfectly consistent with unstated premises shared by a culture's participants but not by foreign observers. Consider the following syllogism:

> Flumo and Yakpalo always drink cane juice (rum) together. Flumo is drinking cane juice. Is Yakpalo drinking cane juice?

Western logic obliges one to conclude that Yakpalo must be drinking cane juice because Flumo and Yakpalo always drink cane juice at the same time. Among the Kpelle of Liberia the answer is different:

KPELLE MAN: Flumo and Yakpalo drink cane juice together, but the time Flumo was drinking the first one Yakpalo was not there on that day.

EXPERIMENTER: But I told you that Flumo and Yakpalo always drink cane juice together. One day Flumo was drinking cane juice. Was Yakpalo drinking cane juice that day?

KPELLE MAN: The day Flumo was drinking the cane juice Yakpalo was not there that day.

EXPERIMENTER: What is the reason?

KPELLE MAN: The reason is that Yakpalo went on his farm on that day and Flumo remained in town on that day.   [Cole et al. 1971: 187–188]

The hidden premise in this answer is that it is absurd to believe that two people would always drink rum together. Learning to think the absurd (see p. 392) requires a great deal of training.

One of the most interesting of the supposedly "culture-free" tests is known as the *Draw-a-Man Test* (F. Goodenough 1926). This test purports to test intelligence cross-culturally by scoring children for the completeness with which they depict the parts of the human figure. Hopi children of ages six and seven averaged 124 on these tests, the same as U.S. upper-middle-class suburban children. At the lower end of the distribution of Draw-a-Man I-Q.'s are the Bedouin Arab children of Syria with an average of 52:

The most obvious correlate of this variation in mean I.Q. is amount of contact with the pictorial art. Among Moslem Arab children, whose religion prohibits representative art as graven images, the range in mean Draw-A-Man I.Q. is from 52 to 94.   [Hunt 1969:29]

There is no reason to suppose that Bedouin children reared by U.S.

suburban or Hopi foster parents would not experience a Draw-a-Man "improvement" of 72 points.

Jensen and other racial determinists regard it as "ridiculous" to suppose that the entire U.S. I.Q. can be shifted upward by more than a few points. Yet there is nothing about the Stanford-Binet I.Q. level suggesting that it cannot be improved by an amount equal to that which is obviously feasible on the Draw-a-Man Test. The belief that many I.Q. testers have about the fixity of racial potentials is merely a derivative of their belief in the fixity of culture. A 70-point gain in I.Q. obviously cannot be expected given the present system of education, social stratification, domestic organization, and ideology. But culture has in no sense reached its final form. Knowledge of the upper limits of human intelligence cannot be derived from the test scores of U.S. schoolchildren.

Psychologists and geneticists who persist in putting forward genetic explanations of poverty and exploitation cannot be regarded merely as disinterested scientific observers. The poor and exploited would be scientifically in error were they to conclude that such scientists were not their political enemies. Continuation of the nature-nurture debate within societies that have conspicuously failed to provide adequate nurturing for so many millions of children is at best a luxury that those children cannot afford. Charles and Betty Lou Valentine have put it this way:

Despite widespread recognition that intergroup environment-heredity questions cannot be settled within the existing social system, no one acts on the two most obvious conclusions. One, the absolute prerequisite to solid answers to these questions is dismantling the present order of society. Two, in the absence of radical equalization throughout the system, such nature-nurture issues are merely diversionary questions. Likewise, all the agonizing appraisals of whether and how intergroup inequality might be reduced neatly circumvent a pair of obvious answers. First, effective parity among human groups cannot be expected without radically restructuring the entire hierarchical system of intergroup relations. Second, such a restructuring will require revolutionary change in all major aspects of society, from control over productive resources to ideology and value patterns. As long as considerations of this order continue to be evaded by all or most discussants, future controversies are hardly likely to be more insightful or productive than the present equality debate. [1975]

VARIETIES OF RELIGIOUS
EXPERIENCE

Most of the cultures of the world encourage or compel people to acquire beliefs in the existence of beings and forces analogous to what is meant in Western traditions by the term "supernatural." These beliefs, together with certain activities and institutions with which they are associated, constitute the realm of religion, myth, and magic. In this and the following chapter I shall identify the principal varieties of supernatural beliefs with the end in view of explaining why they have come into existence and how they contribute to the integration and disintegration of cultural systems.

Animism

The earliest anthropological attempt to define religion was that of E. B. Tylor. For Tylor the essence of religious belief was the idea of "god." Most Western peoples would probably still find such a belief an essential ingredient in their own conception of what constitutes religion. The Victorian Age in which Tylor lived, however, tended to regard religion in even narrower terms, often restricting the concept to Christianity, and relegating other people's gods to the realm of "superstition" and "paganism." Tylor's principal contribution was to show that the Judeo-Christian concept of God was essentially similar to supernatural concepts found the world over.

Tylor attempted, with considerable success, to show that the idea of god was an elaboration of an even more general concept of "soul." In his book *Primitive Culture,* Tylor demonstrated that "the doctrine of souls" occurs to some extent and in one form or another in every society. He gave the name *animism* to such beliefs. The common denominator of animism is the belief that inside the ordinary visible tangible body there is a normally invisible, normally intangible being. Throughout the world souls are believed to play a role in dreaming, possession (see below), drug-induced visions, shadows, reflections, fainting, loss of consciousness, and birth and death. Tylor reasoned that the basic idea of soul must have been invented in order to explain all these phenomena. Once established, the basic idea was embroidered upon, ultimately giving rise to an enormous pantheon of animistic entities, including the souls of humans, animals, plants, and material objects; gods, demons, sprites, devils, ghosts, saints, angels, and all similar beings.

Tylor has been criticized by twentieth-century anthropologists for his suggestion that animism arose as a result of the attempt to understand human and natural phenomena. I certainly agree that religion is much more than an attempt to explain puzzling phenomena. But there is no reason to ignore the intellectual convenience of the soul idea.

It should be stressed that each culture has its own animistic pantheon and its own specific elaboration of the soul concept. Some cultures insist that people have two or more souls; and some cultures believe that certain individuals have more souls than others. Among the Jívaro of Eastern Ecuador, for example, three kinds of souls are recognized: an ordinary, or "true," soul, an *arutam* soul, and a *muisak* soul (Harner 1972b).

Figure 23-1. BUSHMAN CURING. Shaman in trance. (DeVore/Anthro-Photo)

The Three Souls of the Jívaro

The true soul is present from birth inside every living Jívaro, male and female. Upon a person's death this soul leaves the body and goes through a series of transformations. During the first phase of its afterlife the true soul returns to its body's birthplace and recapitulates its former life in an invisible form. The major difference between the two existences is that after death the true soul cannot eat real food and thus remains perpetually hungry. Needless to say the Jívaro do not look forward to this experience. Finally, when the true soul has repeated the entire life history of its deceased owner, it changes into a demon that roams the forest, solitary, hungry, and lonely. This is the second phase, and it lasts for the equivalent of another lifetime. The true soul then dies again and changes into a *wampang,* a species of giant moth that is occasionally seen flitting about. The living try to feed it because it too is perpetually hungry.

After a length of time about which the Jıvaro are uncertain, the *wampang* finally has its wings damaged by raindrops as it flutters through a rainstorm, and falls to die on the ground. The true soul then changes into water vapor amidst the falling rain. All fogs and clouds are believed to be the last form taken by true souls. The true soul undergoes no more transformations and persists eternally in the form of mist. [Harner 1972b:151]

No one is born with the second Jívaro soul—the *arutam.* It must be acquired. All men and some women seek to acquire one because the possessor of an arutam feels great power and cannot be killed. To obtain an arutam, the Jívaro fast, bathe in a sacred waterfall, and drink tobacco water or the juice of a plant containing the hallucinogenic substance *datura.* The arutam appears in the depths of the forest in the form of a pair of giant jaguars or a pair of huge snakes, rolling over and over toward the soul-seeker. When the apparition gets close, the Jívaro, despite their terror, must run forward and touch it. Later, when the soul-seekers are sleeping, the arutam soul will enter their body and lodge in their chest. People who possess an arutam soul speak and act with great confidence, and they feel an irresistible craving to kill their enemies. Warriors and other exceptionally powerful individuals may possess more than one arutam soul at a time. Unfortunately an arutam soul cannot be a permanent possession. Just before the soul-possessor engages in a killing, his arutam soul leaves him. Eventually, wandering in the forest, it will be captured by another soul-seeker.

The third Jívaro soul is the *muisak*—the avenging soul. The muisak comes into existence only when people who formerly possessed an arutam are killed by their enemies. Unless precautions are taken, the

516

muisak will leave the victim's body and attack its killers. To thwart the avenging soul, the Jivaro believe that it is best to cut off the victim's head and "shrink" it to trophy form. Properly handled in ritual dances, the head forces the avenging soul to confer powers upon the possessors of the trophy. Later, when the avenging soul has been used to the killer's advantage, a ritual is performed to send it back to the village from which it came. The women sing:

> Now, now, go back to your house where you lived.
> Your wife is there calling from your house.
> You have come here to make us happy.
> Finally we have finished.
> So return.   [ibid.:146]

Animatism

Tylor's identification of religion with animism is entirely too narrow and ethnocentric. As Robert Marett (1914) pointed out, the attribution of lifelike properties to rocks, pots, storms, and volcanoes does not necessarily mean that souls are the cause of the lifelike behavior. To distinguish the concept of a life-force from that of soul, Marett introduced the term *animatism*. Marett was especially impressed with instances of concentrated animatistic force that gave certain objects, animals, and people extraordinary powers independent of the power derived from souls and gods. To label this concentrated form of power, he used the Melanesian term *mana*. Thus an adze that makes intricate carvings, a fishhook that catches large fish, a club that kills many enemies, or a rabbit's foot that brings "good luck" have large amounts of mana. People, too, may be spoken of as having more or less mana. A woodcarver whose work is especially intricate and beautiful possesses mana, whereas a warrior captured by the enemy has obviously lost his mana.

In its broadest range of meaning, mana simply indicates belief in a powerful force. Many vernacular relationships not normally recognized as religious beliefs in Western cultures can be regarded as mana. For example, vitamin pills are consumed by many millions of people in expectation that they will exert a powerful effect on health and well-being. Soaps and detergents are said to clean because of "cleaning power"; gasolines provide engines with "starting power" or "go-power"; salespeople are prized for their "selling power"; and politicians are said to have *charisma* or "vote-getting power." Some people fervently believe that they are "lucky" or "unlucky"—which could easily be translated as a belief in control over varying quantities of mana.

517

Once mana is accepted as a religious category almost all folk beliefs can be seen as quasi-religious in nature. You might even want to consider popular attitudes toward the forces known as electricity, gravity, and atomic energy as manifestations of a belief in mana.

Natural and Supernatural

One way to restrict the definition of religion is to distinguish between natural and supernatural beliefs. It must be emphasized, however, that few cultures neatly and conveniently divide their beliefs into natural and supernatural categories. In cultures where people believe that ghosts are always present, it is not necessarily either a natural or a supernatural rite to provide dead ancestors with food and drink. It is simply what one does in order to fulfill a duty and to stay well. Similarly when a shaman blows smoke over a patient and triumphantly removes a sliver of bone allegedly inserted by the patient's enemy, the question of whether the performance is natural or supernatural is probably best regarded as having no cognitive relevance.

Writing of the Gururumba of the highlands of Western New Guinea, Philip Newman notes that they "have a series of beliefs postulating the existence of entities and forces we would call supernatural." Yet the contrast between natural and supernatural is not cognitively relevant to the Gururumba themselves:

It should be mentioned . . . that our use of the notion "Supernatural" does not correspond to any Gururumba concept: they do not divide the world into natural and supernatural parts. Certain entities, forces, and processes must be controlled partially through *lusu*, a term denoting rituals relating to growth, curing, or the stimulation of strength, while others need only rarely be controlled in this way. Entities falling within this realm of control are here included in our "supernatural." However, *lusu* does not contrast with any term denoting a realm of control where the nature of the controls differ from *lusu*. Consequently *lusu* is simply part of all control techniques and what it controls is simply part of all things requiring human control. [1965:83]

Sacred and Profane

Recognizing the ethnocentric bias in supposing that all cultures maintain a sharp cognitive distinction between natural and supernatural beliefs, some anthropologists have suggested that the true hallmark of a religious belief or religious practice is the emotional state of the participant. Robert R. Marett, Alexander Goldenweiser,

518

Figure 23-2. GURURUMBA MEDICINE. This man is inducing vomiting by swallowing a three-foot length of cane. After he has pushed it all the way into his stomach he will work it up and down until he vomits. It is thought to be necessary to do this to rid the individual of contaminating influences gotten through contact with females. (American Museum of Natural History)

and Robert Lowie were among those who sought the essence of religion in the "religious experience." Lowie characterized this experience as consisting of "amazement and awe," a feeling that one is in the presence of something extraordinary, weird, sacred, holy, divine, (1948:339). Lowie was even willing to rule that beliefs about gods and souls were not religious beliefs if the existence of these beings was taken for granted and if, in contemplating them, the individual did not experience awe or amazement.

The theoretician who made the greatest contribution to this way of looking at religion was Emile Durkheim. Like many others, Durkheim proposed that the essence of religious belief was that it evoked a mysterious feeling of communion with a sacred realm. Every society has its *sacred* beliefs, symbols, and rituals, which stand opposed to ordinary or *profane* events. Durkheim's distinctive contribution was to relate the realm of the sacred to the control exercised by society and culture over each individual's consciousness. When people feel that they are in communion with occult and mysterious forces and supernatural beings, what they are really experiencing is the force of social life. Humanity exists only because we are born into and sustained by

519

Sacred and Profane

Figure 23-3. SACRED AND PROFANE. Shoes are left outside the Mosque, symbolizing the transition from ordinary, mundane affairs to the realm of the holy and extraordinary. (UPI Photo)

society and culture. And in our awe of the sacred, we express our dependence on society in symbolic form. Thus, according to Durkheim, the idea of "god" is but one form of the worship of society.

This approach to the definition of religion presumes a knowledge of the fluctuating, variable, internal emotional state of the individual members of a society. Such knowledge is difficult to achieve. To the extent that such knowledge is feasible, it is clear that variations in the degree of amazement and awe associated with belief is a matter of considerable significance in its own right. Moreover most anthropologists have lost interest in trying to understand the origin of the sacred in general. A more pertinent question is why some cultures invest certain phenomena with awe and wonder while others regard the same phenomena as profane. Why, for example, are pigs in Melanesia the focus of elaborate rituals while elsewhere they are regarded as merely good to eat (see p. 566)? In his surmise that sacred ideas had social origins Durkheim pointed the way toward the answers to such questions.

Magic and Religion

Sir James Frazer attempted to define religion in his famous book *The Golden Bough*. For Frazer the question of whether a particular belief was religious or not centered on the extent to which the participants felt that they could make an entity or force do their bidding. If the attitude of the participants was one of uncertainty, if they felt humble and were inclined to supplicate and request favors and dispensations, then their beliefs and actions were essentially religious. If they thought they were in control of the entities and forces governing events, felt no uncertainty about the outcome, and experienced no need for supplication, then their beliefs and practices were examples of magic rather than of religion.

Frazer regarded prayer as the essence of religious ritual. But even awesome spirits and gods are not always approached in a mood of supplication. For example, prayers among the Navajo must be letter-perfect to be effective. But this does not mean that the Navajo expect that letter-perfect prayers will always get results. The line between such prayers and "magical spells" is hard to draw. Certainly supplication cannot be taken as characteristic of verbal communication between people and their gods. As Ruth Benedict pointed out, "cajolery and bribery and false pretense are common means of influencing the supernatural" (1938:640). Thus the Kai of New Guinea swindle their ancestral ghosts as they swindle each other; some cultures try to outwit the spirits by lying to them. The Tsimshian of the Canadian Pacific Coast stamp their feet and shake their fists at the heavens and call their gods "slaves" as a term of reproach. The Manus of the Bismarck Archipelago keep the skulls of their ancestors in a corner of the house and try their best to please "Sir Ghost." If a person falls ill the Manus may angrily threaten to throw Sir Ghost out of the house:

Then you will be made to understand . . . This man dies and you rest in no house. You will but wander about the edges of the island (used for excretory purposes).   [Fortune 1965:216]

Figure 23-4. PRAYER. Worshippers at a mosque in Lahore, Pakistan. (United Nations)

521

An additional important part of Frazer's scheme was his attempt to distinguish magic from science. The magician's attitude, he claimed, was precisely that of the scientist. Both magician and scientist believe that if A is done under the proper set of conditions, then B will follow regardless of who the practitioner is or what the attitude toward the outcome may be. A piece of an intended victim's fingernail tossed into the river or pins stuck into an effigy doll are believed to accomplish their results with the automatic certainty characteristic of the release of an arrow from a bow or the generation of heat from fire. Frazer recognized that if this was going to be the essence of the distinction between magic and religion, then magic differed little from science. Indeed he called magic "false science" and postulated a universal evolutionary sequence in which magic with its concern about cause and effect relationships gave birth to science, whereas religion evolved along completely independent lines.

Frazer's scheme has not withstood the test of field work. The attitudes with which fearful Dobuan magicians dispose of fingernails and confident Zuñi priests whip up yucca suds to bring rain do not conform to Frazer's neat compartments. Human behavior unfolds as a complex montage in which awe and wonder, boredom and routine, power and impotence are all present at the same time.

The degree of anxiety and supplication associated with any sequence of behavior is probably regulated more by the importance of the outcome to the participants than by their philosophy of cause and effect. It must be admitted, however, that not enough is known about the inner psychological state of priests, magicians, shamans, and scientists to make any firm pronouncements in this field.

The Organization of Religious Beliefs and Practices

Religious beliefs and rituals seem to involve an infinite variety of thoughts, feelings, and practices. Yet in this domain as in all others there are orderly processes. A good way to begin to understand the diversity of religious phenomena is to inquire if there are beliefs and practices associated with particular kinds and levels of social structure.

A fourfold classification of religious phenomena from this viewpoint has been offered by the anthropologist Anthony F. C. Wallace (1966). Wallace identifies: (1) *individualistic cults*, (2) *shamanistic cults*, (3) *communal cults*, and (4) *ecclesiastical cults*.

522

1. The most basic pattern of religious life involves individualistic beliefs and rituals. Each person is a specialist; each individual enters into a relationship with animistic and animatistic forces as each personally experiences the need for control and protection.

2. As Wallace points out, no culture known to anthropology has a religion that is completely individualistic, although the Eskimo and other hunters and food-gatherers lean heavily in this direction. Every known society also exhibits at least the *shamanistic* level of religious specialization. The term *shaman* derives from the word used by the Tungus-speaking peoples of Siberia to designate the part-time religious specialist consulted in times of stress and anxiety. In cross-cultural applications, however, the term *shaman* may refer to individuals who act as diviners, curers, spirit mediums, and magicians for other people in return for gifts, fees, and prestige.

3. At a more complex level of social structure, *communal* forms of beliefs and practices become more elaborate. Groups of nonspecialists organized in terms of age grades, men's societies, clans, or lineages assume responsibility for regular or occasional performances of rituals deemed essential for their own welfare or for the survival of the society. While communal rituals may employ specialists such as shamans, orators, and highly skilled dancers and musicians, once the ritual performance is concluded, the participants revert to a common daily routine.

4. The *ecclesiastical* level of religious organization involves a full-time professional clergy or priesthood. These professionals form a bureaucracy that monopolizes the performance of certain rites on behalf of individuals, groups, and the whole society. Ecclesiastical bureaucracies are usually closely associated with state-level political forms. In most instances the leaders of the ecclesiastical hierarchy are members of the ruling class and, in some instances, a state's political and ecclesiastical hierarchies are indistinguishable.

As Wallace points out, the individualistic, shamanistic, communal, and ecclesiastical varieties of beliefs and rituals form a *scale.* That is, each of the more complex levels contains the beliefs and practices of all the less complex levels. Consequently among societies with ecclesiastical forms there are also communal types of organizations, shamanistic performances, and strictly individualistic beliefs and rituals.

Individualistic Beliefs and Rituals: The Eskimo

The individualism of much of Eskimo belief and ritual parallels the individualism of Eskimo productive activity. Hunters alone or in small groups constantly match their wits against the cunning and strength of animal prey and confront the dangers of travel over the ice and the threat of storms and month-long nights. The Eskimo hunter was equipped with an ingenious array of technological devices that alone made life possible in the Arctic. But the outcome of the daily struggle remained in doubt. From the Eskimo's point of view, it was not enough to be well-equipped with snow goggles, fur parkas, spring-bone traps, detachable, barbed harpoon points, and powerful compound bows. One also had to be equipped to handle unseen spirits and forces that lurked in all parts of nature and that, if offended or not properly warded off, could reduce the greatest hunter to a starving wretch. Vigilant individual effort was needed to deal with an extensive pantheon of human souls, animal souls, place spirits, Sedna (the Keeper of the Sea Animals), the Sun, the Moon, and the Spirit of the Air (Wallace 1966:89). Part of each hunter's equipment was his hunting song—a combination of chant, prayer, and magic formula— which he inherited from his father or father's brothers or purchased from some famous hunter or shaman. This he would sing under his breath as he prepared himself for the day's activities. Around his neck he wore a little bag filled with tiny animal carvings, bits of claws and fur, pebbles, insects, and other items, each corresponding to some Spirit Helper with whom he maintained a special relationship. In return for protection and hunting success given by his Spirit Helpers, the hunter would observe certain taboos, refrain from hunting or eating certain species, or avoid trespassing in a particular locale. Numerous additional taboos were obeyed in order to avoid hardships for individuals and for the group. For example, a hunter should never sleep out on the ice-edge. Every evening he must return either to land or to the old firm ice that lies some distance back from the open sea because the Sea Spirit does not like her creatures to smell human beings while they are not hunting (Rasmussen 1929:76). Care must also be taken not to cook land and sea mammals in the same pot; fresh water must be placed in the mouth of recently killed sea mammals, and fat must be placed in the mouth of slain land mammals (Wallace 1966:90). Some of these "superstitions" may have alleviated psychological stress or have had a positive-functioned relationship to hunting or some other aspect of Eskimo life. For example, not sleeping out on the ice obviously merits consideration as a safety precaution.

524

Individualistic Beliefs and Rituals: Vision Quests

Although it often appears to individuals that their beliefs are a product of a unique psychic experience, it is apparent in cross-cultural perspective that religious beliefs and practices always exhibit cultural patterning. This is true even under the influence of drugs, during trance states, and in dreams and visions, in highly individualized contexts. (Some drugs, however, do produce specific sensations that are quite uniform cross-culturally [Naranjo 1967; Harner 1972a].)

A form of individualistic religion that is especially common in North and South America involves the acquisition of a personal guardian spirit or supernatural protector. Typically this spirit protector is acquired by means of a visionary experience induced by fasting, mortification of the flesh, or ingestion of hallucinogenic substances. The Jívaro youth's search for an arutam soul described above is one variant of this widespread complex. Each arutam vision is slightly different from the next, yet all who have arutams are protected against death.

For many North American Indian men the central fact of life was also an hallucinatory vision. Young men aspired to this hallucinatory

Figure 23-5. SIOUX VISION. Section of pictographic biography done by Rain In The Face. In a dream, (left), the lightning tells him that, unless he gives a buffalo feast, the lightning will kill him. He gives the feast, one part of which consists of filling a kettle with red hot buffalo tongues, of which he eats in order to save his life. He dreams (right) of buffalo again; while dancing, he is shot by an arrow which enters the feathers. In removing it, he soon vomits and grabbing a handful of earth, rubs it into the wound, healing it rapidly. (Museum of the American Indian, Heye Foundation)

experience as a necessary prelude to success in love, warfare, horse-stealing, trading, and all other important endeavors. In keeping with their code of personal bravery and endurance, they sought these visions primarily through the mortification of the flesh.

The young Crow Indian, for example, craving the visionary experience of his elders, went alone into the mountains, stripped off his clothes, and abstained from food and drink. If this was not sufficient he chopped off part of the fourth finger of his left hand. Coached from childhood to expect that a vision would come, most of the Crow vision-seekers were successful. A buffalo, snake, chicken-hawk, thunderbird, dwarf, or mysterious stranger would appear; miraculous events would unfold; and then these strange beings would "adopt" the vision-seeker and disappear. Scratches-face, one of Robert Lowie's informants, prayed to the morning star:

Old woman's grandson, I give you this (finger-joint). Give me something good in exchange . . . a good horse . . . a good-natured woman . . . a tent of my own to live in.

Lowie reports that after cutting off his finger, Scratches-face saw six men riding horses. One of them said, "You have been poor, so I'll give you what you want." Suddenly the trees around them turned into enemy warriors who began to shoot at the six horsemen. The horsemen rode away but returned unscathed. The spokesman then said to Scratches-face, "If you want to fight all the people on the earth, do as I do, and you will be able to fight for three days or four days and yet not be shot." The enemy attacked again, but Scratches-face's benefactor knocked them down with a spear. Lowie observes, "In consequence of his blessing Scratches-face struck and killed an enemy without ever getting wounded. He also obtained horses and married a good-tempered and industrious woman" (1948:6).

Although each Crow's vision had some unique elements, they were all usually similar in the following regards: (1) Some relevation of future success in warfare, horse-raiding, or other acts of bravery was involved. (2) The visions usually occurred at the end of the fourth day—four being the sacred number of the North American Indians. (3) Practically every vision was accompanied by the acquisition of a sacred song. (4) The friendly spirits in the vision adopted the suppliant as their child. (5) Trees or rocks often turned into enemies who vainly shot at the invulnerable spirit beings. Lowie concludes:

He sees and hears not merely what any faster, say in British Columbia or South Africa, would see and hear under like conditions of physiological exhaustion and under the urge of generally human desires, but what the social tradition of the Crow tribe imperatively suggests.   [ibid.:14]

526

Shamanistic Cults

Shamans are people who are socially recognized as having special abilities for entering into contact with spirit beings and for controlling supernatural forces. The full shamanic complex includes some form of trance experience during which the shaman's powers are augmented. *Possession,* the invasion of the human body by a god or spirit, is the most common form of shamanic trance. The shaman goes into a trance by smoking tobacco, taking drugs, beating on a drum, dancing monotonously, or simply by closing the eyes and concentrating. The trance begins with rigidity of the body, sweating, and heavy breathing. While in the trance the shaman may act as a *medium,* transmitting messages from the ancestors. With the help of friendly spirits shamans predict future events, locate lost objects, identify the cause of illness, prescribe cures, and give advice on how clients can protect themselves against the evil intentions of enemies.

There is a close relationship between shamanic cults and individualistic vision-quests. Shamans are usually personalities who are psychologically predisposed toward hallucinatory experiences. In cultures that use hallucinogenic substances freely in order to penetrate the mysteries of the other world, many people may claim shamanic status. Among the Jívaro, one out of every four men is a shaman, since the use of hallucinogenic vines makes it possible for almost anyone to achieve the trance states essential for the practice of shamanism (Harner 1972b:154). Elsewhere becoming a shaman may

Figure 23-6. ACHUARA SHAMAN. Preparing a potion from pieces of a hallucinogenic vine. (Eric and Jane Ross)

527

be restricted to people who have what Western medicine regards as a mental disease, schizophrenia, which is characterized by auditory and visual hallucinations.

An important part of shamanic performance in many parts of the world consists of simple tricks of ventriloquism, prestidgitation, and illusion. The Siberian shamans, for example, signaled the arrival of the possessing spirit by surreptitiously shaking the walls of a darkened tent. Throughout South America the standard shamanic curing ceremony involves the removal of slivers of bone, pebbles, bugs, and other foreign objects from the patient's body. The practice of these tricks should not be regarded as evidence that the shaman has a cynical or disbelieving attitude toward the rest of the performance. The human mind is fully capable of blocking out and compartmentalizing contradictory or inconvenient information both through suppression into unconsciousness and through rationalization ("it's a trick but it's for their own good"; or "it's a trick but it works").

Although trance is part of the shamanic repertory in hundreds of cultures, it is not universal. Many cultures have part-time specialists who do not make use of trance but who diagnose and cure disease, find lost objects, foretell the future, and confer immunity in war and success in love. Such persons may be referred to variously as magicians, seers, sorcerers, witch doctors, medicine men, and curers. The full shanamic complex embodies all the subspecialties suggested by these terms.

Tapirapé Shamanism

The shamanic complex of the Tapirapé Indians of Brazil contains many typical elements. Tapirapé shamans derive their powers from dreams in which they encounter spirit beings who become the shaman's helpers. Dreams are caused by souls leaving the body and going on journeys. Frequent dreaming is a sign of shamanistic capability. Mature shamans, with the help of their spirit familiars, can turn into birds or launch themselves through the air in gourd "canoes," visit with ghosts and demons, or travel to distant villages and settlements forward and backward through time. Here is an account of how the shaman Ikanancowi acquired his powers:

In his dream [Ikanancowi] walked far to the shores of a large lake deep in the jungle. There he heard dogs barking and ran in the direction from which the noise came until he met several forest spirits of the breed called *munpí anká*. They were tearing a bat out of a tree for food. [The spirits] talked with Ikanancowi and invited him to return to their village, which was situated upon the lake. In the village he saw *periquitos* (Psittacidae) and many *socó*

528

(*Butorides* sp.), birds which they keep as pets. The *ančúnga* had several
plots of *kauí* [porridge] and invited Ikanancowi to eat with them. He refused
for he saw that their *kauí* was made from human blood. Ikanancowi
watched one spirit drink of the *kauí* and saw him vomit blood immediately
afterwards; the shaman saw a second spirit drink from another pot and
immediately spurt blood from his anus. He saw the *munpí anká* vomit up
their entrails and throw them upon the ground, but he soon saw that this
was only a trick; they would not die, for they had more intestines. After this
visit the *munpí anká* called Ikanancowi father and he called them his sons;
he visited them in his dreams frequently and he had *munpí anká* near him
always.   [Wagley 1943:66–67]

Tapirapé shamans are frequently called upon to cure illness. This
they do with prestidigitation and the help of their spirit familiars
while in a semitrance condition induced by gulping huge quantities of
tobacco.

Treatment of the sick is the shaman's most common duty and the use of
tobacco is always a necessary prelude and accompaniment to this. Unless
the illness is serious enough to warrant immediate treatment, shamans
always cure in the late evening. A shaman comes to his patient, and squats

529

Tapirapé Shamanism

near the patient's hammock; his first act is always to light his pipe. When the patient has a fever or has fallen unconscious from the sight of a ghost, the principal method of treatment is by massage. The shaman blows smoke over the entire body of the patient; then he blows smoke over his own hands, spits into them, and massages the patient slowly and firmly, always toward the extremities of the body. He shows that he is removing a foreign substance by a quick movement of his hands as he reaches the end of an arm or leg.

The more frequent method of curing, however, is by the extraction of a malignant object by sucking. The shaman squats alongside the hammock of his patient and begins to "eat smoke"—swallow large gulps of tobacco smoke from his pipe. He forces the smoke with great intakes of breath deep down into his stomach; soon he becomes intoxicated and nauseated; he vomits violently and smoke spews from his stomach. He groans and clears his throat in the manner of a person gagging with nausea but unable to vomit. By sucking back what he vomits he accumulates saliva in his mouth.

In the midst of this process he stops several times to suck on the body of his patient and finally, with one awful heave, he spews all the accumulated material on the ground. He then searches in this mess for the intrusive object that has been causing the illness. Never once did I see a shaman show the intrusive object to observers. At one treatment a Tapirapé [shaman] usually repeats this process of "eating smoke," sucking, and vomiting several times. Sometimes, when a man of prestige is ill, two or even three shamans will cure side by side in this manner and the noise of violent vomiting resounds throughout the village.   [ibid.:73–74]

It is interesting to note in conjunction with the widespread use of tobacco in American Indian rituals that tobacco contains hallucinogenic alkaloids and may have induced visions when consumed in large quantities.

Shamans and Witchcraft

Only a thin line separates shamans from witches. Since shamans have the power to cure they also have the power to kill. Much shamanic activity is devoted to the problem of identifying who is responsible for the sickness and death that occurs in their band or village. As I indicated in Chapter 17, shamans play an important role in the maintenance of law and order in prestate societies by blaming misfortunes on individuals who can be killed or ostracized without damaging the fabric of social unity. Under conditions of continuing stress caused by repeated defeats in warfare, floods, droughts, or epidemics, people often lose faith in their shamans, decide that the shamans are really witches, and execute them.

With the development of ecclesiastical forms of religion and bureaucratized hierarchies of priests, the exercise of shamanic powers by individuals outside the ecclesiastical structure is suppressed. All

530

Figure 23-8. SHAMANISTIC CULT. A shaman obtaining personal power at a shrine near Chichicastenango, Guatemala. (Eugene Gordon)

Figure 23-9. GUATEMALA CHURCH. Descendants of Maya Indians praying at the entrance of Catholic church in Chichicastenango. (United Nations)

531

shamans in such contexts tend to be regarded as antisocial witches and "magicians." As in band and village cultures, the established ecclesiastical and civil authorities still find it convenient to blame misfortunes on specific individuals. In fact, the urgency to find some human being upon whom rampant misery, disease, and death can be blamed is greater in stratified than in egalitarian cultures. Witch-hunting serves the function of befuddling people concerning the source of their troubles. And in stratified societies the real cause of their trouble is likely to lie at least to some extent in the fact that they are being exploited by a ruling class. Where all shamans are regarded with suspicion, the authorities try to find their witches by techniques that they themselves control. Hence the prevalence of such techniques as throwing persons accused of witchcraft into the water to see who won't sink, or giving poisons to the accused to see who won't throw up, or giving them hot irons to see who won't get burnt. Many societies that have ecclesiastical hierarchies torture people into confessing that they are witches.

Church and state in Renaissance Europe (both Catholic and Protestant) hold the record for using torture as a means of identifying witches. Making use of the belief that witches fly through the air to attend sabbats, the inquisitors insisted that each witch not only confess to being a witch but that he or she also name the other persons who were in attendance at the sabbat. Failure to confess and name names meant that the accused would be returned repeatedly to the torture chamber. Cooperative individuals were strangled before the

Figure 23-10. "THERE IS A LOT TO SUCK." European baby-eating witches depicted by Goya. (The Brooklyn Museum, A. Augustus Healy Fund and others)

torch was put to the pyre around the stake. The first people to be accused were defenseless or homeless women and children.

Initially no one named members of the clergy or nobility out of fear of being tortured until they recanted. As the people being tortured worked their way up toward naming prominent and protected individuals, however, the "witch craze" would suddenly cease, and the inquisitors would move off to the next town. Altogether about half a million people were burned to death during the two centuries when this system was at its peak.

It seems likely that few of the people who were executed had any knowledge of how to fly to sabbats. As Michael Harner (1972a) has shown, the real European flying witches made use of an ointment manufactured from nightshade, henbane, belladonna, and other plants that contain the skin-penetrating hallucinogenic substance atropine. Application of these substances to the feet and to the genitals produces a comatose condition for as much as forty-eight hours during which vivid sensations of flying are experienced. Since the real witches rubbed themselves with the ointment before flying off to a sabbat, it seems likely that they went to the sabbats in mind alone and not in body.

Communal Beliefs and Rituals

No culture is completely without communally organized religious beliefs and practices. Even the Eskimo have group rites. Frightened

Figure 23-11.
COMMUNAL RELIGION. The Hare Krishna sect is an egalitarian religious commune whose members provide for each other's material and spiritual welfare. (Eugene Gordon)

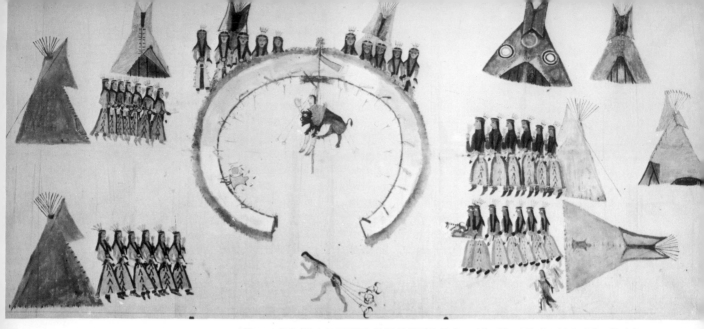

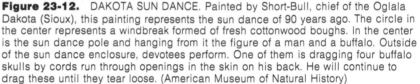

Figure 23-12. DAKOTA SUN DANCE. Painted by Short-Bull, chief of the Oglala Dakota (Sioux), this painting represents the sun dance of 90 years ago. The circle in the center represents a windbreak formed of fresh cottonwood boughs. In the center is the sun dance pole and hanging from it the figure of a man and a buffalo. Outside of the sun dance enclosure, devotees perform. One of them is dragging four buffalo skulls by cords run through openings in the skin on his back. He will continue to drag these until they tear loose. (American Museum of Natural History)

and sick Eskimo individuals under the cross-examination of shamans publicly confess violations of taboos, which have made them ill and which have endangered the rest of the community.

Among the Plains Indians there were annual public rites of self-torture and vision-quest known as the Sun Dance. Under the direction of shaman leaders, the Sun Dancers tied themselves to a pole by means of a cord passed through a raw slit in their flesh. Watched by the assembled group, they walked around the pole and tugged at the cord, until they fainted or their skin ripped apart. These public displays of endurance and bravery contributed to the maintenance of the marauding and warfare that the Plains tribes depended on for their existence.

Communal rites fall into two major categories: (1) *rites of solidarity* and (2) *rites of passage.* In the rites of solidarity, participation in dramatic public rituals enhances the sense of group identity, coordinates the actions of the individual members of the group, and prepares the group for immediate or future cooperative action. Rites of passage celebrate the social movement of individuals into and out of groups or into or out of statuses of critical importance both to the individual and to the community. Reproduction, the achievement of

534

manhood and womanhood, marriage, and death are the principal worldwide occasions for rites of passage.

Rites of Solidarity: Totemism

Rites of solidarity are widely associated with clans and other segmentary descent groups. Such groups usually have names and emblems that identify group members and set one group off from another. Animal names and emblems predominate, but insects, plants, and natural phenomena such as rain and clouds also occur. These group-identifying objects are known as *totems*. Many totems such as bear, breadfruit, or kangaroo are useful or edible species, and often there is a stipulated descent relationship between the members of the group and their totemic ancestor. Sometimes the members of the group must refrain from harming or eating their totem. There are many variations in the specific forms of totemic beliefs, however, and no single totemic complex can be said to exist. Lévi-Strauss (1963a) has suggested that the unity of the concept of totemism consists not in any specific belief or practice but in certain general logical relationships between the named groups and their names. No matter what kind of animal or thing serves as totem, it is the contrast with other totems rather than their specific properties that renders them useful for group identification.

The Arunta of Australia provide one of the classic cases of totemic ritual. Here each individual takes the totem of a sacred place near which one's mother passed shortly before becoming pregnant. These places contain the stone objects known as *churinga*, which are the

Figure 23-13. TOTEMIC SOLIDARITY. Arunta men preparing themselves for totemic ritual. (American Museum of Natural History)

535

visible manifestation of each person's spirit. The churinga are believed to have been left behind by the totemic ancestors as they traveled about the countryside at the beginning of the world. The ancestors later turned into animals, objects, and other phenomena constituting the inventory of totems. The sacred places of each totem are visited annually during rites known as *Intichiuma.*

Here is a description of the Intichiuma of the witchetty-grub men: They slip away from camp. Under the direction of their headman they retrace the trail taken by *Intwailiuka,* the dawn-time witchetty-grub leader. All along this trail, they come upon the churinga and other mementos of Intwailiuka's journey. One sacred place consists of a shallow cave inside of which is a large rock surrounded by small rounded stones. The headman identifies the large rock as the body of the witchetty-grub and the small stones as the witchetty-grub's eggs. The headman begins to sing, tapping the rocks with a wooden bough while the others join in, tapping with twigs. The song asks the witchetty-grub to lay more eggs. The headman then strikes each man in the stomach with one of the "egg stones" saying, "You have eaten much food." The party then moves on to the next sacred place underneath a large rock where Intwailiuka used to cook and eat. The men sing, tap with their twigs, and throw egg stones up the cliff, as Intwailiuka did. Then they march on to the next sacred place which is a hole four or five feet deep. The headman scrapes away the dirt at the bottom of this hole, turning up more witchetty-grub churinga. The stones are carefully cleaned, handed about, and then replaced. The party stops at a total of ten such spots before returning to camp. In preparation for their return, the men decorate themselves with strings, nose bones, rat tails, and feathers. They also paint their bodies with the sacred design of the witchetty-grub. While they have been gone one of the witchetty-grub men has constructed a brush hut in the shape of the witchetty-grub chrysalis. The men enter the hut and sing of the journey they have made. Then the headman comes shuffling and gliding out, followed by all the rest, in imitation of adult witchetty-grubs emerging from their chrysalis. This is repeated several times. During this phase of the ceremony all non-witchetty-grub spectators are kept at a distance and obliged to follow the orders of witchetty-grub men and women (Spencer and Gillin 1968).

The multifunctional nature of these rituals should be evident. Witchetty-grub people are earnestly concerned with controlling the reproduction of witchetty-grubs, which are considered a great delicacy. But the restricted nature of the ritual group also indicates that they are acting out the mythological dogma of their common ancestry. The witchetty-grub totem ceremonies reaffirm and intensify the sense

536

of common identity of the members of a regional community. The ceremonies confirm the fact that the witchetty-grub people have "stones" or, in a more familiar metaphor, "roots" in a particular land.

Rites of Passage

Rites of passage accompany changes in structural position or statuses that are of general public concern. Why are birth, puberty, marriage, and death so frequently the occasions for rites of passage? Probably because of their public implications: the individual who is born, who reaches adulthood, who takes a spouse, or who dies is not the only person implicated in these events. Many other people must adjust to these momentous changes. Being born not only defines a new life but it also brings into existence or modifies the position of parent, grandparent, sibling, heir, age-mate, and many other domestic and political relationships. The function of rites of passage is to give communal recognition to the entire complex of new or altered relationships and not merely to the changes experienced by the individuals who ostensibly are the center of attention.

Rites of passage conform to a remarkably similar pattern among widely dispersed cultures. First, the principal performers are separated from the routines associated with their earlier life. Second, decisive physical and symbolic steps are taken to extinguish the old statuses. Often these steps include the notion of killing the old personality. To promote "death and transfiguration" old clothing and ornaments are exchanged for new and the body is painted or mutilated. Finally, the participants are ceremoniously returned to normal life.

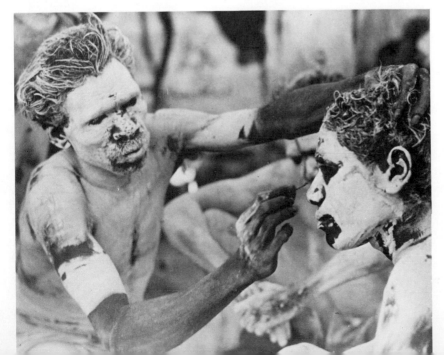

Figure 23-14. RITE OF PASSAGE. Male puberty initiate in Arnhemland, Australia, being painted with white clay. (American Museum of Natural History)

Figure 23-15. DEATH IS A FOCUS FOR RELIGION IN MOST CULTURES. Dogon funeral dancers (top right). The Crow scaffold burial (top left) shows a common means of disposing of the dead in sparsely inhabited regions; the Peruvian mummies (bottom) show another method, which is common in arid climates. (Eugene Gordon—top right; Museum of the American Indian, Heye Foundation—top left; American Museum of Natural History—bottom)

538

Circumcision

This pattern of rites of passage can be seen in the male initiation ceremonies of the Ndembu of Northern Zambia. Here, as among many African and Middle Eastern peoples, the transition from boyhood to manhood involves the rite of circumcision. Young boys are taken from their separate villages and placed in a special bush "school." They are circumcised by their own kinsmen or neighbors and after their wounds heal they are returned to normal life. Among the Ndembu the process of publicly transforming boys to men takes four months and is known as *mukanda*. Victor Turner (1967) has given a detailed account of a mukanda that he was permitted to witness in 1953. It began with the storage of food and beer. Before the actual circumcision took place, a clearing was made in the bush and a camp was established. This camp included a hearth at which the mothers of the boys undergoing circumcision cook food for them during their seclusion. There were also drums and dance grounds and a special hearth. On the day preceding the circumcision the circumcisers danced and sang songs in which they expressed antagonism to the boys' mothers and made reference to the "killing" that was about to take place. The boys and their families assembled at the campsite, fires were lit, and a night of dancing and sexual license was begun.

Suddenly the circumcisers entered in procession, carrying their apparatus. . . . All the rest of the gathering followed them as they danced crouching, holding up different items of apparatus, and chanting hoarsely. In the firelight and moonlight the dance got wilder and wilder. [1967:205]

Meanwhile the boys sat in a line attended by their mothers and fathers. During the night they were repeatedly awakened and carried about by their male relatives. The next morning they were given a "last supper" (i.e., a last breakfast) by their mothers, "each mother feeding her son by hand as though he were an infant." The boys tried not to look terrified as, after breakfast, the circumcisers, their brows and foreheads daubed with red clay, danced about brandishing their knives.

The actual circumcision took place in another clearing some distance away from the cooking camp. The boys remained in seclusion at this site, which is known as the "place of dying." They slept in a brush lodge watched over and ordered about by a group of male "guardians." After their "last breakfast" the boys were marched down the trail toward the "place of dying." The guardians came rushing out, seized them, and tore off their clothes. The mothers were chased back to the cooking camp where they began to wail as at the announcement of a death. The boys were held by the guardians while circumcisers

539

"stretch out the prepuce, make a slight nick on top and another underneath as guides, then cut through the dorsal section with a single movement and follow this by slitting the ventral section, then removing sufficient of the prepuce to leave the glans well exposed" (1967:216).

During the seclusion at the place of dying, the boys were subject to the strict discipline of their guardians. "They had to maintain a modest demeanor, only speak when spoken to, fetch and carry anything required at the double, and run errands." In former times they were sent on dangerous hunting missions and subjected to severe beating for breaking discipline or displaying cowardice. The novices were terrorized at night by the sound of the *bullroarer*—a flat disk that makes a whirring noise as it is whirled about on the end of a string. Masked dancers whom they believed to be "red grave people" appeared suddenly and beat them with sticks. These same monsters visited the cooking camp, danced before the women, and terrorized the little children. Throughout their seclusion the boys were taught the rules of manhood, how to be brave and sexually potent. They were lectured to, harrangued, and made to answer riddles rich in symbolic meanings.

For the rites of return the boys were daubed all over with white clay, signifying their new being. Then they were brought into the cooking camp and shown to their mothers.

At first the mothers wailed, then their mourning turned to songs of rejoicing as each realized that her son was safe and well. It is impossible to describe adequately the ensuing scene of complete, uninhibited jubilation. The guardians ran around in an inner circle, the mothers danced beside them . . . while other female relatives and friends made up an outer ring of joyful chanting dancers. The men stood outside the whirl, laughing with pure pleasure. Dust rose in clouds.   [1967:255]

The next morning the seclusion lodge was burned, the boys were washed in the river and given new clothes, and then each performed the dance of war, as a sign of manhood.

In many cultures girls are subject to similar rites of separation, seclusion, and return in relationship to their first menses and their eligibility for marriage. There is a widely practiced operation known as *clitoridectomy,* which among girls is the analogue of circumcision. In this operation the external tip of the clitoris is cut off. Among many Australian groups both circumcision and clitoridectomy were practiced. In addition the Australians knocked out the pubescent child's front tooth. Males were subject to the further operation of *subincision,* in which the underside of the penis was slit open to the depth of the urethra.

540

The pattern of the rites of passage characterizes many modern rituals, although the phases of separation, seclusion, and return may appear in rapid succession. At college graduation ceremonies, for example, the graduates are assembled somewhere offstage. They put on special costumes. When they march in they remain segregated from their relatives and friends. They are given advice by the equivalent of the Ndembu guardians and are handed a ceremonial document. Then they return to their joyous relatives and friends to mingle freely with them once again.

Ecclesiastical Cults

Ecclesiastical cults have in common the existence of a professional clergy or priesthood organized into a bureaucracy. This bureaucracy is usually associated with and under the control of a central temple. At secondary or provincial temple centers the clergy may exercise a considerable amount of independence. In general, the more highly centralized the political system, the more highly centralized the ecclesiastical bureaucracy.

The ecclesiastic specialists are different from both the Tapirapé shamans and the Ndembu circumcisers and guardians. They are formally designated persons who devote themselves full time to the rituals of their office. These rituals usually include a wide variety of

Figure 23-10.
ECCLESIASTICAL BUREAUCRACY. Priests of the temple of Tano, Abron, Ivory Coast. (Alexander Alland, Jr.)

541

Figure 23-17.
ECCLESIASTICAL CULT. Ordaining the Episcopalian bishop in the Cathedral of St. John the Divine. (Charles Gatewood)

techniques for influencing and controlling animistic beings and animatistic forces. The material support for these full-time specialists is usually closely related to power and privileges of taxation. As among the Inca (p. 385), the state and the priesthood may divide up the rent and tribute exacted from the peasants. Under feudal conditions the ecclesiastical hierarchy derives its earnings from its own estates and from the gifts of powerful princes and kings. High officials in feudal ecclesiastical hierarchies are almost always kin or appointees of members of the ruling class. In the case of modern ecclesiastical hierarchies, tax support may be indirect but nonetheless vital. In the United States, for example, church-owned real estate and church earnings on stocks and other investments are tax exempt and gifts to religious groups are tax deductible.

The presence of ecclesiastical organizations produces a profound split among those who participate in ritual performances. On the one hand there is an active segment, the priesthood, and on the other the passive "congregation," who are virtual spectators. The members of the priesthood must acquire intricate ritual, calendrical, and astronomical knowledge. Often they are scribes, historians, and learned persons. It must be stressed, however, that the nonspecialists do not altogether abandon their individualistic shamanistic and communal beliefs and rituals. These are all continued in local or domestic

542

contexts despite more or less energetic efforts on the part of the ecclesiastical hierarchy to stamp out what it calls idolatrous, superstitious, pagan, heathen, or heretical beliefs and performances.

The Religion of the Aztecs

Many of the principal characteristics of belief and ritual in stratified contexts can be seen in the ecclesiastical organization of the Aztecs of Mexico. The Aztecs held their priests responsible for the maintenance and renewal of the entire universe. By performing annual rituals, priests could obtain the blessing of the Aztec gods, ensure the well-being of the Aztec people, and guard the world against collapse into chaos and darkness. According to Aztec theology the world had already passed through four ages, each of which had ended in cataclysmic destruction. The first age ended when the reigning god, *Tezcatlipoca,* transformed himself into the sun and all the people of the earth were devoured by jaguars. The second age, ruled over by the feathered serpent, *Quetzalcoatl,* was destroyed by hurricanes that changed people into monkeys. The third age, ruled over by *Tlaloc,* god of rain, was brought to a close when the heavens rained fire. Then came the rule of *Chalchihuitlicue,* goddess of water, whose time ended with a universal flood, during which people turned into fish. The fifth age is in progress, ruled over by the sun god, *Tonatiuh,* and doomed to destruction sooner or later by earthquakes.

The principal function of the 5,000 priests living in the Aztec capital was to make sure the end of the world came later rather than sooner. This could be assured only by pleasing the legions of gods reputed to govern the world. The best way to please the gods was to give them

Figure 23-18. TEMPLE OF QUETZALCOATL, THE PLUMED SERPENT. (Walter R. Aguiar)

543

gifts, the most precious being fresh human hearts. The hearts of war captives were the most esteemed gifts since they were won only at great expense and risk.

Aztec ceremonial centers were dominated by large pyramidal platforms topped by temples. These structures were vast stages upon which the drama of human sacrifice was enacted at least once a day throughout the year. On especially critical days there were multiple sacrifices. The set pattern for these performances involved first the victim's ascent of the huge staircase to the top of the pyramid; then at the summit the victim was seized by four priests, one for each limb, and bent face up, spread-eagled over the sacrificial stone. A fifth priest cut the victim's chest open with an obsidian knife and wrenched out the beating heart. The heart was smeared over the statue of the god and later burned. Finally, the lifeless body was flung over the edge of the pyramid where it rolled back down the steps.

All aspects of Aztec ritual were regulated by intricate calendrical systems understood only by the priests. By means of their calendars, the priests kept track of the gods who had to be appeased and of the dangerous days, neglect of which might have occasioned the end of the world.

The Aztecs calculated the year as having 365 days. They divided this period into 18 months of 20 days each ($18 \times 20 = 360$), leaving 5 days over as an annual unlucky period. Each of the 20 days had a name, and each was numbered consecutively from 1 to 13. Every $13 \times 20 = 260$ days, the number 1 occurred at the beginning of a month. This period of 260 days was meshed with the 365-day year. Every 52 years the beginning of the 260-day and 365-day cycles coincided. The most holy days were those associated with the end of each 52-year cycle. At this time the priests struggled mightily to prevent the end of the world. The altar fires, which had burned perpetually for 52 years, were extinguished along with all the fires throughout the kingdom. The people destroyed their household furnishings, fasted, and prayed, awaiting the ultimate catastrophe. Pregnant women were hidden away and children were prevented from falling asleep. At sunset on the last day the priests ascended an extinct volcanic crater at the center of the Valley of Mexico and anxiously watched the skies for signs that the world would continue. When certain stars passed the meridian, they sacrificed a captive and kindled a new fire in the victim's breast. Runners bore torches lit from this sacred fire throughout the kingdom.

It is believed that during a 4-day dedication ceremony of the main Aztec temple in Tenochtitlán, 20,000 prisoners of war were sacrificed in the manner described above. A yearly toll of some 4,000 human

544

beings were sent to their death to placate the bloodthirsty gods who reigned over each day name and each day cycle of 13, 20, 260, and 365 days, and the five annual days of danger. Most of these victims were prisoners of war, although local youths, maidens, and children were also sacrificed from time to time (cf. Vaillant 1944; Coe 1962; Soustelle 1970).

Figure 23-19.
TENOCHTITLÁN. A reconstructed view of the Aztec capital with its numerous temple-topped pyramids. (American Museum of Natural History)

The Relativity of Religious Beliefs

It is frequently said that all religions tend to converge on the same fundamental truths about nature and human existence. This view is contrary to what is known about the great diversity of beliefs and rituals found among the peoples of the world. There is no single unifying theme underlying all religions. All religions are multifunctioned: they provide psychological comfort in times of distress; they help people to make sense out of inexplicable events; they provide common goals, rules of conduct, and a sense of communion for the members of social groups; and they provide expressive outlets for the joys and sorrows of human existence. But there is no uniformity in the way these functions are fulfilled. All religions do not, for example, ward off the threat of death with the idea that the soul is immortal, nor do all religions preach the sanctity of human life, the oneness of the universe, or the goodness of God. Religions are as diverse as the cultural systems in which they are embedded. For every distinctive form of technology, economy, and domestic and political organiza-

545

tion, there are equally distinctive forms of religious belief and ritual. And just as there has been no single direction along which all human cultures have evolved, so too there is no single direction along which all religions have tended to evolve. For example, there is no discernible universal tendency for monotheistic religions to replace polytheistic religions or for religions based on "reason" to replace those based on "faith." To understand beliefs and rituals, anthropologists have found it necessary to study the particular ecology and social structure in which particular beliefs and rituals play a functional role.

Religion and Science

Recognizing the enormous variety of beliefs and rituals that characterize the domain of the sacred and the supernatural, anthropologists have been unable to reach agreement on a definition of religion. This has resulted in a tendency to define religion in ever-more inclusive terms until, by some definitions, almost all cultural thought and behavior takes on a religious coloration. For example, a widely cited definition of religion by Clifford Geertz goes as follows:

A system of symbols which acts to establish powerful, persuasive and long-lasting moods and motivations in men by formulating conceptions of a general order of existence and clothing these conceptions with such an aura of factuality that the moods and motivations seem uniquely realistic. [1965:206]

To accept Geertz's definition is to include as religion not only the specific phenomena discussed in this chapter but the entire ideological sector of cultural systems as well. There is much to be said in favor of regarding the emic aspects of technology, reciprocity, redistribution, kinship, marriage, and other widespread cultural complexes as religion. All of these phenomena are supported by animistic and mana-like "systems of symbols which act to establish powerful, persuasive and long-lasting moods." I do not object to describing phenomena such as patriotism and capitalist or communist ideology as religious beliefs, nor do I object to describing ceremonies like saluting the flag, stockholders' meetings, and May Day parades as religious rituals. The anthropologist's task is neither helped nor hindered by including or excluding these phenomena within the definition of religion. The problem is not to find out what is and what is not religious; rather, the problem is to explain why some societies salute flags while others fondle their churingas, why some societies believe in Horatio Alger while others believe in Chairman Mao.

There is one extension of the definition of religion, however, to

546

which anthropologists must object. By Geertz's definition science in general and anthropology in particular would also have to be regarded as religions. The characterization of science as just another form of religion with its own peculiar rituals of observation and experiment and its own peculiar "aura of factuality" hinders anthropology and deflects it from its attempt to explain cultural differences and similarities in a scientific fashion. It does this by encouraging the belief that scientific facts and theories have no greater claim to credibility than any other types of facts and theories. This conception of science and of anthropology fails to emphasize the fact that science is a unique evolutionary product whose procedures for establishing its "aura of factuality" are without precedent in the history and ethnography of human thought. Science alone, among sacred or secular forms of religion that I know of, is dedicated equally to the proof and disproof of its current body of beliefs and practices. Unlike religious beliefs, whether concerned with arutam souls, the Holy Trinity, or Old Glory, scientific beliefs are held only provisionally and are or ought to be deliberately and perpetually the object of an unremitting attempt by those who hold them to prove themselves wrong. No "system of symbols" other than science has ever bestowed rewards upon those who invalidate as well as those who validate its fondest truths.

Religious and scientific beliefs may be distinguished in this sweeping fashion only if it is emphasized that neither science nor religion enjoys a monopoly on truth. Both science and religion may consist of false as well as true beliefs. The difference between them is the method underlying the establishment of any particular belief, be it true or false. In the case of scientific belief the method involves the formulation of hypotheses whose truth value is subjected to systematic, controlled predictive and retrodictive tests. Religious beliefs, on the other hand, are based upon a minimum of such tests or none at all. Moreover many religious beliefs cannot conceivably be tested for truth or falsity. Beliefs in God, soul, and afterlife, for example, rest on faith rather than on systematic observation, prediction, and empirical testing. Finally, it must be admitted that many scientific beliefs are held religiously—that is, that they have not been subjected to the rigorous attempts at disproof demanded by true science. No doubt such beliefs can be found in this book. If anthropology is encouraged to flourish and expand along scientific rather than religious lines it will sooner or later identify my religious beliefs and subject them to the appropriate tests. This is unlikely to happen, however, if one believes that science is just another religion.

547

THE ADAPTIVENESS OF
RELIGIOUS BELIEF
AND RITUAL

In general there is a close functional correspondence between religious beliefs and rituals on the one hand and ecology and social structure on the other. This is not to say that religion is a mere passive "reflex" of the other parts of the cultural system. On the contrary, religious beliefs and rituals frequently play a crucial role in organizing the impulses leading toward major restructurings of social life. But in general and in the long run the content and organization of religions are constrained and shaped by ecology and social structure. In this chapter I shall discuss the principal ways by which anthropologists attempt to understand the differences and similarities among religions. It will be shown that even beliefs and rituals that appear to be irrational, whimsical, and maladaptive often possess important positive functions and are explicable in terms of recurrent adaptive processes.

Religion and Political Economy

The contrast between individualistic and shamanistic religions and ecclesiastical religions reveals the general adaptiveness of religious phenomena. Full-time specialists, monumental temples, dramatic processions, and elaborate rites performed for spectator congregations are incompatible with the ecology and social structure of hunters and food-gatherers. The Aztec practice of sacrificing large numbers of prisoners of war rests upon the prior existence of a predatory and expansionist state apparatus. Similarly the complex astronomical and mathematical basis of Aztec ecclesiastical belief and ritual is never found among hunters and gatherers or low-energy agriculturalists.

Can this order of dependency be reversed? Can it be argued that the predatory and expansionist state apparatus rested upon the need to sacrifice prisoners in conformity with Aztec ecclesiastical belief and ritual? I think not. It is true of course that the bloodthirsty nature of the Aztec gods contributed to the intensification and spread of Aztec warfare by imparting a "holy" purpose to the state and its expansionist military campaigns. But the religious motivation for capturing and sacrificing enemies can scarcely be regarded as the cause of Aztec warfare. Virtually all state-level societies at one time or another engage in expansionist military campaigns (see p. 199). Furthermore warfare is endowed with some religious purpose among virtually all prestate societies. For example, the Jívaro, no less than the Aztecs, were motivated by sacred beliefs when they sought to ambush an enemy and capture an avenging soul. But this desire did not and could not result in massive military expeditions. Hundreds of captives awaiting sacrifice could not be kept at the small, isolated Jívaro households. Instead the Jívaro quickly skinned their victim's head and face to make a portable shrunken trophy that they could carry with them as they fled back to their home territory. In both the Jívaro and Aztec cases, religious beliefs and rituals are thus closely adapted to the kind of warfare compatible with given ecological and structural conditions.

Figure 24-1.
ADAPTIVENESS OF RELIGION. Sikh Holy Man adds goggles and bicycle chains in fulfillment of traditional requirement that he wear metal object, such as a knife. Ritual and belief may change as fast as any other part of culture. (UPI Photo)

High Gods and Stratification

The idea of a single high god who creates the universe is found among cultures at all levels of economic and political development. These high gods, however, play very different kinds of roles in running the universe after they have brought it into existence. Among hunter-gatherers and other prestate peoples the high gods tend to become inactive after their primordial task is done. It is to a host of lesser gods, demons, and souls that one must turn in order to obtain supernatural assistance. On the other hand, in stratified societies the high god bosses the lesser gods and tends to be a more active figure to whom priests and commoners address their prayers (cf. Swanson 1960).

The reason for this difference is that prestate peoples have no need for the idea of a central or supreme authority. Just as there is an absence of centralized control over strategic resources in life, so in religious belief, the denizens of the spirit world of people like the Jívaro lack decisive control over each other. They form a more or less egalitarian pantheon. On the other hand, inculcation of the belief that superordination and subordination regulate relationships among animistic beings is of considerable value in obtaining the cooperation of the commoner classes in stratified societies.

Figure 24-2. RELIGION AND STRATIFICATION. Bishops and other high prelates of the Corpus Christi Cathedral in Cuzco, Peru, are an awe-inspiring sight to an Indian peasant. (Sergio Larrain/Magnum)

	Societies	
"Supernatural" Morality"	with social classes	without social classes
Present	25	2
Absent	8	12

Source: Adapted from Swanson (1960:166).

One way to achieve conformity in stratified societies is to convince commoners that the gods demand obedience to the state. Disobedience and nonconformity result not only in retribution administered through the state's police-military apparatus but also in punishments in present or future life administered by the high gods themselves. In prestate societies, for reasons discussed in Chapter 17, law and order are rooted in common interest. Consequently there is little need for high gods to administer punishments for those who have been "bad" and rewards for those who have been "good." However, where there are strong inequalities, private property, interest, rent, or primogeniture, the gods are believed to take a lively interest in the degree to which each individual's thoughts and behavior are immoral or ethically subversive. The coalescence between morality and religion is thus a characteristic of class-structured society. This has been rather conclusively demonstrated in Guy Swanson's cross-cultural study. As can be seen from the table, where social classes are absent, religion is relatively unimportant as a means of enforcing general rules of conduct. The main exceptions relate to the control of women.

Religion and Sexual Politics

This is the point to recall that the male-supremacist complex common to war-making prestate cultures is in part sustained by appropriate religious beliefs and rituals. Women are almost universally excluded from tapping the principal sources of religious power just as they are systematically excluded from the inner circle of domestic and political power. Even where the individualistic rituals prevail, women tend to have less access to the supernatural than men. Women rarely participate in the vision-quests that give males the confidence to be aggressive and to kill with impunity. Women are seldom permitted to take the hallucinogenic substances that give males direct knowledge of the reality that lies behind worldly appearances (see p. 271).

551

As the men ritually ingest the various hallucinogens that let them journey into the hidden world, women remain bystanders, baffled and terrorized by the personality transformations and strange antics of their brothers and husbands. Among the Yanomamö, for example, the men take a substance called *ebené,* which, in addition to putting them in contact with the *hekura,* or invisible mountain demons, causes green mucus to flow out of their nostrils. They run about the village on all fours, snarl and grimace like wild animals, and brandish their clubs and spears at women and children who cross their path. The men administer the ebené by blowing it up each other's nostrils through 3-foot-long hollow tubes:

As the drug would be administered, each recipient would reel from the concussion of air, groan, and stagger off to some convenient post to vomit. Within ten minutes of taking the drug, the men would be bleary-eyed and wild, prancing around in front of their houses, stopping occasionally to vomit or to catch their breath. In each group there would be one man particularly adept at chanting to the *hekura* . . . while the others retired to the sidelines in a stupor, green slime dripping from their nostrils. [Chagnon 1968:109]

Male-supremacist beliefs and practices are also everywhere certified and given an aura of sanctity by means of origin myths. The Yanomamö say that in the beginning of the world there were only fierce men who were formed from the blood of the moon. Among these early men was Kanaborama whose legs became pregnant. From Kanaborama's left leg came women and from his right leg came feminine men—those who are reluctant to duel and who are cowards in battle. (Note that a comparable myth in the Jewish, Christian, and Moslem religions certifies the inferiority of women by having the first man's chest become pregnant.)

To the extent that shamanic cults are dominated by persons who have access to and who know how to prepare and use hallucinogens, male control over these substances imposes a severe handicap upon

Figure 24-3. RELIGION AND SEX IN BALI. Similar rules are common around the world. (Eugene Gordon)

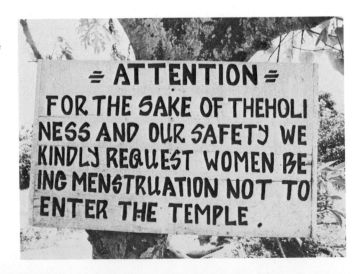

552

Figure 24-4. MOURNING AND SEXUAL POLITICS. This New Guinea widow must wear her signs of mourning for a year. Many cultures enjoin long periods of mourning for widows but not for widowers. Perhaps this represents an effort on the part of males to make sure that a wife will not derive any satisfaction from the death of her husband. (American Museum of Natural History)

women. Even where hallucinogens do not play an important role in the shamanic complex, however, males usually maintain control over the knowledge necessary for achieving visions and trances and for carrying out acts of sleight-of-hand.

Communal cults in general are also pervaded by male-supremacist beliefs and rituals. One of the most widespread of all communal complexes has as its explicit aim the retention of a male monopoly on the myths and rituals of human origins and the nature of supernatural beings. This complex in its most developed form involves secret male initiation rites; male residence in a separate men's house from which women and children are excluded; masked male dancers who impersonate the gods and other spiritual beings; the bullroarer, which is said to be the voice of the gods and which is whirled about in the bush or under cover of darkness to frighten the women and uninitiated boys; storage of the masks, bullroarer, and other sacred paraphernalia in the men's house; threat of death or actual execution of any woman who admits to knowing the secrets of the cult; and threat of death or execution of any man who reveals the secrets to women or uninitiated boys.

Finally, ecclesiastical types of religions are also characterized by a pervasive functional interconnection between male-dominated rituals and myths on the one hand and male supremacy on the other. The established high priests of Rome, Greece, Mesopotamia, Egypt, ancient Israel, and the entire Moslem and Hindu world were men.

553

Figure 24-5. CAYUGA MAN WITH MASK AND BULL ROARER. "The better to frighten you with my dear." (Museum of American Indian, Heye Foundation)

High-ranking priestesses with autonomous control over their own temples are everywhere the exception, even when the ecclesiastical cults include female deities. Today males continue to dominate the ecclesiastical organization of all the major world religions. All three major religions of Western civilization—Christianity, Judaism, and Islam—stress the priority of the male principle in the formation of the world. They identify the creator god as "He" and to the extent that they recognize female deities, as in Catholicism, assign them a secondary role in myth and ritual.

Revitalization

The relationship between religious belief and ritual on the one hand and ecological and social structural conditions on the other is dramatically evident in the process known as *revitalization*. Under severe ecological and politico-economic stress associated especially with colonial conquest and intense class or minority exploitation, beliefs and rituals tend to be concerned with achieving a drastic improvement in the immediate conditions of life and/or in the prospects for an

554

afterlife. These beliefs and rituals are sometimes referred to as *nativistic, revivalistic, millenarian,* or *messianic* movements. The term "revitalization" is intended to embrace all the specific cognitive and ritual variants implied by these terms (cf. A. Wallace 1966).

Revitalization is a process of interaction between a depressed caste, class, minority, or other subordinate social group and a superordinate group. Analysis of these movements exclusively in terms of their stated goals and motives leads to taxonomic exercises that bear little relationship to the evolving dynamic of revitalization. Some revitalization movements emphasize passive attitudes, the adoption of old rather than new cultural practices, salvation through rewards after death; others advocate more or less open resistance or aggressive political or military action. These differences are not the result of the capriciousness of revitalization leaders. Much depends on the extent to which the superordinate groups are prepared to cope with the challenge to their power and authority. Direct challenges to political authority, as, for example, in a Joan of Arc type vision, are not to be expected where there is no possibility of military action. If the revitalization is sufficiently passive, the superordinate group may find it advantageous to encourage, or at least not to inhibit, the spread of

Figure 24-6. INTERIOR OF MEN'S HOUSE, NEW GUINEA. The men use the masks to terrify the women and children. (American Museum of Natural History)

555

the revitalizing beliefs and rituals. Fundamentalist and revivalist Christian sects are politically conservative revitalizations that throw the onus of sickness, poverty, and psychological distress back onto the individual. Disciples are urged to stop smoking, drinking, lying, cheating, and fornicating in order to achieve a new identity free from sin that will entitle them to eternal life. In some cases Christian fundamentalist revitalization is explicitly linked with conservation of the political status quo through patriotic sermons and devotion to the struggle against atheism and "godless communism." Many revitalizations, however, lack an overt, unambiguous political theme, whether conservative or revolutionary. This does not mean that the political functions of revitalization can be disregarded, but rather that the particular circumstances may not be appropriate for a mature phase of political struggle.

Revitalizations that take place under conditions of massive suffering and exploitation sooner or later result in political and even military probes or confrontations even though both sides may overtly desire to avoid conflict. The black churches in the United States have a history of increasingly politicized revitalization, culminating in the Black Muslim movement. To understand the pace of this politicization one must study the larger economic and political context in which the struggle for racial equality has been taking place in the United States. In other words, none of the specific beliefs and rituals of revitalization movements can be understood apart from the matrix of the political economy.

American Indian Revitalization

Widespread revitalizations were provoked by the European invasion of the New World and the conquest and expulsion of the American Indian peoples and the destruction of their natural habitat.

As early as 1680 the Pueblo Indians of New Mexico underwent a violent politico-religious conversion led by the prophet Popé. According to Popé's visions the Christian God had died. Under his direction the Catholic missionaries were burned at the altars of their churches and all European artifacts were destroyed.

Other parts of the United States experienced armed or passive revitalization organized around visions and prophecies in synchrony with the European expansion. A common theme of these revitalizations concerned the defeat and expulsion of the white invaders. In the Great Lakes region the Indian chief Pontiac was inspired by the visions of a Delaware Indian prophet to attack the whites.

556

Later there arose the Shawnee prophet Tenskwatawa, who foresaw the expulsion of the whites if the Indians would give up alcohol and depose their peace chiefs. The prophet's twin brother, Tecumseh, formed a military alliance among tribes as far apart as Florida and the Rocky Mountains. Tenskwatawa himself was killed at Tippecanoe on the Wabash River during an attack against forces led by William Henry Harrison. This battle made Harrison famous. He and John Tyler successfully campaigned for president and vice-president under the slogan "Tippecanoe and Tyler Too" as heroes responsible for the suppression of the rebellious "savages."

As the more openly political and militaristic revitalizations were crushed by disease, starvation, and military defeat, they were replaced by more passive forms of revitalization. Thus the successor to Tenskwatawa was Kanakuk, who prophesied that if the Kickapoo would give up warfare, lying, stealing, and alcohol, they would find vast green lands to replace those stolen from them by the whites. Needless to say, Kanakuk's visions were as inaccurate as Tenskwatawa's, since the obedient Kickapoo were forced farther and farther West onto smaller and smaller reservations.

Revitalization in the Northwest Territories was led by the prophet Smohalla, known as the "Dreamer." Conversations with the Great Spirit had convinced Smohalla that the Indians must resist the white man's attempt to convert them to farmers. His visions and prophecies inspired Chief Joseph of the Nez Percé who led an unsuccessful rebellion against the whites in 1877.

The most famous of the nineteenth century Indian revitalization movements was the Ghost Dance, also known as the Messiah craze. This movement originated near the California-Nevada border and roughly coincided with the completion of the Union Pacific Railroad. The Paviotso prophet Wodziwob (or Tavibo) envisioned the return of the Indians' dead ancestors. These dead Indians were going to return from the spirit world in a great train whose arrival would be signaled by a cataclysmic explosion. Simultaneously the whites would be swept from the land, but their buildings, machines, and other possessions would be left behind. To hasten the arrival of the ancestors, there was to be ceremonial dancing accompanied by the songs revealed to Wodziwob during his visions. A second version of the Ghost Dance was begun in 1889 under the inspiration of Wovoka. A vision in which all the dead Indians had been brought back to life by the Ghost Dance was again reported. Ostensibly Wovoka's teachings lacked political content, and as the Ghost Dance spread eastward across the Rockies its overt political significance remained ambiguous. Yet for the Indians of the plains, the return of the dead meant that they would outnumber the whites.

557

Among the Sioux there was a version that included the return of all the bison and the extermination of the whites by a cataclysmic landslide. The Sioux warriors put on Ghost Dance shirts, which they believed would make them invulnerable to bullets. Clashes between the U.S. Army and the Sioux became more frequent, and the Sioux leader Sitting Bull was arrested and killed. The second Ghost Dance movement came to an end with the massacre of two hundred Sioux at

Figure 24-7. WOUNDED KNEE. In the first battle (top), 1890, two hundred Sioux Indians were killed by U.S. Army. In the second battle (bottom), 1973, militant Indians occupied the village of Wounded Knee, South Dakota, and exchanged gunfire with U.S. Marshalls. (Museum of the American Indian, Heye Foundation—top; Wide World Photos—bottom)

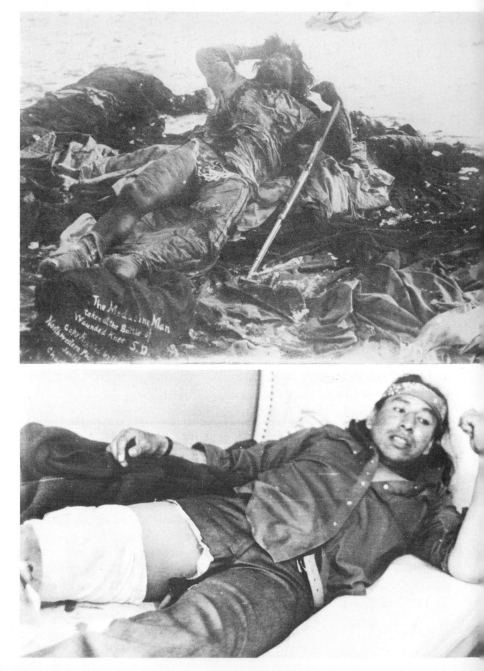

558

Figure 24-8. PEYOTE CEREMONY. Delaware Indians of Oklahoma spend the night in prayer and meditation. At right, they emerge to greet the dawn. Painting by Ernest Spybuck. (Museum of the American Indian, Heye Foundation)

Wounded Knee, South Dakota, on December 29, 1890 (Mooney 1965).

After all chance of military resistance was crushed, revitalization among the American Indians took an increasingly introverted and passive form. Visions in which all the whites are wiped out cease to be experienced, confirming once again the responsiveness of religion to political reality. The development and spread of beliefs and rituals centering upon peyote, mescal, and other hallucinogenic drugs are characteristic of many twentieth-century American Indian revitalizations. Peyote ritual involves a night of praying, singing, peyote eating, ecstatic contemplation followed by a communal breakfast. The peyote-eaters are not interested in bringing back the buffalo or making themselves invulnerable to bullets. They seek rather self-knowledge, personal moral strength, and physical health [La Barre 1938; Stewart 1948].

> The peyote religion is a syncretistic cult, incorporating ancient Indian and modern Christian elements. The Christian theology of love, charity, and forgiveness has been added to the ancient Indian ritual and aboriginal desire to acquire personal power through individual visions. Peyotism has taught a program of accommodation for over 50 years and the peyote religion has succeeded in giving Indians pride in their native culture while adjusting to the dominant civilization of the whites.   [Stewart 1968:108]

Peyotism and allied cult movements do not of course signal the end of political struggle on the part of the American Indians. On the contrary, the struggle has intensified in recent years with the emer-

559

gence of the Red Power Movement. But the Indians' attempt to hold on to and regain their stolen lands no longer depends on visions. Rather the struggle is now being carried out through the rituals of lawyers, politicians, novelists, Washington lobbyists, sit-ins, and land-ins (Deloria 1969; Walker 1972).

Cargo Cults

In New Guinea and Melanesia revitalization is associated with the concept of *cargo.* The characteristic vision of the Melanesian revitalization prophets is that of a ship bringing back the ancestors and a cargo of European goods. In recent times, airplanes and spaceships are the favorite means of delivering the cargo (cf. Worsley 1968).

In one of the earliest movements, that of 1893 at Milne Bay in New Guinea, a prophet foretold volcanic eruptions and tidal waves followed by the appearance of the ancestors' ship and a period of great abundance of pigs and fruit and all good things. In order for this to happen, however, all the available pigs and other foodstuffs had to be consumed and all European goods had to be abandoned. After the tidal wave failed to appear, the colonial officials jailed the prophet to prevent further disturbances.

In 1914 on the island of Sabai in the Torres Strait, prophets promised the arrival of the ancestors in a steamship laden with money, flour, canned goods, and other valuables. With the aid of the ancestors the British administrators would be killed or driven off the island, and there would be a period of great abundance. The leaders of the movement, inspired by Wesleyan missionaries and impressed by the enmity between the Germans and the British, called themselves *German Weslin.* The leaders took military titles such as general and captain and ordered all the men to the graveyard where prayers were addressed to the ancestors as well as to the Christian God, who was believed to be in charge of loading the cargo. The colonial administrators intervened, exiled the leaders, and prohibited further cult activity.

A similar revitalization occurred among New Guinea peoples living along the Gulf of Papua. Known as the *Vailala Madness,* it was begun by the prophet Evara, who foretold the arrival of the ancestors in a steamship filled with flour, rice, tobacco, and rifles. Wooden poles connected by strings were erected in imitation of radio transmitters so that the ancestors could be guided into port. Like Evara, many of the cult participants trembled and had visions of the future.

560   On the island of Espiritu Santo in the New Hebrides the cargo cults

have had a long and bitter history. In 1923 the prophet Ronovuro predicted that the Europeans would prevent the cargo ship from landing. The plantation laborers murdered a plantation owner in order to warn the Europeans not to interfere. Government reprisals quelled the movement, but it broke out again in 1939 (Malefijt 1968).

As a result of the abundance of goods displayed by U.S. military forces during the Pacific Island campaigns of World War II, many recent revitalizations have stressed the return of the Americans as much as the return of the ancestors. Thus in Espiritu Santo in 1944 the prophet Tsek urged his people to destroy all European goods and throw away their clothes in preparation for the return of the mysteriously departed Americans. Some of the American-oriented revitalizations have placed specific American soldiers in the role of cargo deliverers. On the island of Tana in the New Hebrides the John Frumm cult cherishes an old G.I. jacket as the relic of one John Frumm, whose identity is not otherwise known. The prophets of John Frumm build landing strips, bamboo control towers, and grass-thatched cargo sheds. In some cases beacons are kept ablaze at night and radio operators stand ready with tin-can microphones and earphones to guide the cargo planes to a safe landing.

An important theme in many of the more recent cults is that the cargo planes and ships have been successfully loaded by the ancestors at U.S. ports but the local authorities have refused to permit the cargo to be landed. In other versions the cargo planes are tricked into landing at the wrong airport. In a metaphorical sense these sentiments are applicable to the actual colonial contexts. The peoples of the South Seas have indeed often been tricked out of their lands and resources (M. Harris 1974b).

The belief system of the cargo cults vividly demonstrates why the assumption that all people distinguish between natural and supernatural categories is incorrect. Cargo prophets who have been taken to see modern Australian stores and factories in the hope that they would give up their beliefs return home more convinced than ever that they are following the best prescription for obtaining cargo. With their own eyes they have observed the fantastic abundance that the authorities refuse to let them have (Lawrence 1964).

After World War II Americans came to be regarded as no less "supernatural" than the ancestors. In 1964 the island of New Hanover became the scene of the Lyndon Johnson cult. Under the leadership of the prophet Bos Malik, cult members demanded that they be permitted to vote for Johnson in the village elections scheduled for them by the Australian administration. Airplanes passing overhead at night were said to be Johnson's planes searching for a

561

place to land. Bos Malik advised that in order to get Johnson to be their president, they would have to "buy" him. This was to be done by paying the annual head tax to Malik instead of the Australian tax collectors. When news reached New Hanover that an armed force had been dispatched to suppress the tax revolt, Malik prophesied that the liner Queen Mary would soon arrive bearing cargo and U.S. troops to liberate the islanders from their Australian oppressors. When these events failed to materialize, Malik accused the Australian officials of stealing the cargo. The tax revolt continued to spread, and by 1965 more than $82,000 had been collected to "buy" Johnson and there were 150 cultists in jail.

The confusion of the Melanesian revitalization prophets is a confusion about the workings of cultural systems. They do not understand how the productive and distributive functions of modern industrial society are organized, nor do they comprehend how law and order are maintained among state-level peoples. To them the material abundance of the industrial nations and the penury of others constitutes an irrational flaw, a massive contradiction in the structure of the world. I find it difficult not to agree with them.

Christianity and Revitalization

Revitalization also lies at the root of the fundamental myths of Western civilization. Judaism and Christianity are messianic religions born out of the struggles against poverty, colonialism, and imperialism in the ancient Middle East. The ancient Jewish state, founded by David and his son Solomon, was conquered and ruled over by a succession of powerful empires: Egyptian, Assyrian, Babylonian, Persian, Greek, and Roman in that order. Each successive conquest only strengthened the hope of the Jews themselves that they would eventually achieve an imperial status of their own. This hope was nourished by the principal post-Babylonian prophets of the Old Testament—Isaiah, Jeremiah, Zechariah, and Ezekiel—all of whom predicted that God would eventually send a divine liberator—a messiah—to establish the ultimate, one, true, just, holy, and everlasting empire. During the period of Roman rule messianic cults and messiahs were as common in Palestine as cargo prophets in the South Seas and messiahs and ghost dancers among the Indians of the Western plains. As in all revitalization movements, the colonial authorities and the cultists eventually came into direct military-political conflict. In the year that Jesus was born, two thousand messianic cultists were crucified by the Roman governor, Varus. A

562

Figure 24-9. TEMPLE OF JERUSALEM. Lower walls in this photo were part of the monumental temple built by King Herod and the scene of events recounted in the New Testament. El Aksa mosque, whose dome appears at right, was built on top of the Herodian walls, left in ruins by the Roman conquest of Jerusalem in 70 A.D. (UPI Photo)

continuous series of military-messianic uprisings preceded and followed the messianic episodes involving John the Baptist and Jesus. By A.D. 55 revolutionary cultists led by "religious frauds" ranged over the countryside "plundering the houses of the well to do, killing the occupants, and setting fire to the villages, till their raging madness penetrated every corner of Judea" (Josephus 1970). These uprisings culminated in two full-scale messianic wars, both of which came close to destroying Roman control. In the first, which lasted from A.D. 68 to A.D. 73, the Roman forces were led by Vespasian and his son Titus. These generals became emperors of Rome because of their suppression of the revolt. Among the Jewish messiahs and prophets who kept the war going, the most famous was Manahem. Josephus blamed the million deaths suffered by the Jews on Manahem and the other messiahs—"false messengers [who] beguiled the people into believing that supernatural deliverance would yet be theirs." The second and final great uprising against Rome occurred in A.D. 132–136. It was led by Bar Kochva—Son of a Star—who, because of his miraculous victories, was identified by the chief rabbi of Jerusalem as the long-awaited messiah. The people reported seeing Bar Kochva mounted on a lion. After Bar Kochva was killed in battle, the Romans leveled a thousand villages, executed a half-million cultists, and shipped thousands more abroad as slaves (W. Wallace 1943).

Christianity and Revitalization

It is clear that the spread of the peaceful Jewish messianic cult that eventually became Christianity was closely related to the unsuccessful attempts of the Jewish military messiahs to topple the Roman Empire. Although Jesus was crucified in A.D. 30 or 33, it was not until after Jerusalem was destroyed by Titus that the Gospels were written. With the generals who had conquered Israel sitting on the imperial throne, many Jews and other minorities living under Roman rule rejected the idea of a military salvation and turned instead to the dream of redemption by a messiah whose "kingdom" was not of this world. There is considerable evidence that the image of Jesus as the "Prince of Peace" may not have been formed until after the fall of Jerusalem (Brandon 1968a, b; M. Harris 1974b). One thing seems certain: regardless of Jesus' intentions, the Roman governor treated him as if he were guilty of a political crime. Crucifixion was the common fate of all convicted military-messiahs and their followers.

Revitalizations in Europe

With the conversion of the Roman Emperor Constantine, Christianity became the official religion of the Roman Empire. Like other established ecclesiastical religions it played a key role in the defense of the privileges and inequalities characteristic of the relationship between the ruling class and the peasantry during the Middle Ages. Yet these were essentially the same conditions that had nourished the original messianic impulses of the first century A.D. Christianity promised that the messiah would return and finally establish a new kingdom free of poverty and toil. This doctrine never completely lost its revolutionary potential. Starting with the tenth century, Europe was wracked by a continuous series of religious wars, crusades, peasant revolts, and messianic uprisings. The fundamental cause of these upheavals was the rise of capitalism. The development of trade, markets, and banking forced the feudal ruling class into enterprises aimed at maximizing profits. As a result the paternalistic relationships characteristic of feudal manors and castle barons were undermined. Landholdings were divided, and serfs and servants gave way to renters and sharecroppers. Peasants lost their land, and great numbers of people began to drift about looking for jobs in the towns. Pauperization and alienation increased. So too did the predictions about Christ's return.

More and more frequently people thought they saw the end of the world unfolding before their eyes. The sin and luxury of the clergy, the polarization of wealth, famines, plagues, the threat of Islam, and the

564

incessant wars between rival factions of the nobility gave rise to a continuous series of messianic revitalizations. Many of the crusades actually consisted of rag-tag armies raised by messianic prophets. In the fourteenth century the people of Thuringia sold their possessions, stopped working, and prepared for the Last Judgment by whipping themselves till the blood ran. During the fifteenth century the Taborites prepared themselves for the end of the world by abolishing private property and establishing a military commune of "free spirits" led by messianic prophets. In 1476 a shepherd named Hans Böhm had a vision in which he was told, like the cargo prophets, that the poor should stop paying taxes and that all people would soon have equal access to the woods, streams, pastures, and game. Great pilgrimages were launched from all over Germany toward Böhm's house in Niklashausen. The people marched in long columns, holding hands, singing revolutionary songs, and greeting everybody as "brother" and "sister."

The birth of Protestantism was closely linked to the European messianic movements at the beginning of the sixteenth century. Martin Luther was convinced that he too was living in the Last Days and that the return of Christ was imminent. Yet he condemned the radical communitarian peasant movements aimed at the redistribution of wealth. His disciple Thomas Müntzer turned against him and accused Luther of being in league with those responsible for the misery of the peasants. Müntzer characterized the lords and princes who supported Luther as "ungodly scoundrels," "the scoddods of usury, theft, and robbery," and "robbers who use the law to forbid others to rob." Convinced that the great peasant revolt of 1525 was the beginning of the new kingdom, Müntzer took command of the peasant army. God spoke to him and promised him victory. He told his followers that he would protect them against the enemy's artillery by catching the cannonballs in his coatsleeve. Müntzer's army was routed, and he was captured, tortured, and beheaded. Similar messianic movements continued all during the sixteenth and seventeenth centuries, of which those associated with the Anabaptists are best known.

It is clear that these communitarian revitalizations, with their basis in the Christian principles of brotherhood and sisterhood, love, charity, and the condemnation of wealth, were in turn the direct antecedents of the secular revitalizations that led to the French Revolution and to the radical egalitarian doctrines of Marx and Lenin. It is ironical therefore that Marx should have characterized religion as the "opium of the people" (1973:14). Under conditions appropriate for the development of messianic leadership, religion again and again has proved itself capable of mobilizing downtrodden and exploited masses

565

into revolutionary armies. Depending on the underlying conditions, therefore, religion may be totally conservative or totally radical and everything else between (Cohn 1962; Thrupp 1962; Lanternari 1963; Hobsbawm 1965; E. Wolf 1969).

Ecology and Religion

A number of recent studies have explored the possibility that certain widespread religious beliefs and practices may exert a conservative restraint on population in relationship to ecological carrying capacity. I have already described the importance of the beliefs and rituals which govern the Tsembaga Maring's cycle of peace and war (Ch. 13). In Rappaport's words this complex helps to maintain:

an undegraded biotic environment, limits fighting to frequencies which do not endanger the survival of the regional population, adjusts man-land ratios, facilitates trade, distributes local surpluses of pig throughout the regional population in the form of pork and assures to members of the local group rations of high quality protein.   [1971:60]

Another interesting example of the relationship between ecology and religion has been studied by Omar Khayyam Moore (1969). Many

Figure 24-10. FARMER AND HIS BULLOCKS. Animals are being taken in search of water during drought in Rajasthan. Unless these animals survive the farmer will be unable to plow when the rains come. (United Nations for FAO)

peoples of the world practice a form of divination known as *scap-ulimancy,* the prediction of future events by inspection of the cracks and spots that appear on the burnt shoulder blades of slaughtered animals. For this purpose the Labrador Naskapi prefer the shoulder blades of caribou. The bone is boiled, wiped clean, hung up to dry, and fitted with a handle. In the divination ritual the bone is held over hot coals. The heat causes spots and cracks to form on the bone. These spots and cracks are "read" according to standard rules in order to predict where game will be found on the next hunt. It is highly unlikely that there is any positive correlation between the condition of a burnt shoulder blade and the location of game. It would seem, therefore, that this is a trait whose adaptive value cannot explain its existence. Yet, as Moore suggests, there may be a hidden ecological relationship here that would confer an adaptive advantage on groups practicing scapulimancy. The value of shoulder blades as a source of information about the location of game may reside in the randomness of the spots and cracks. Moore assumes that the spots and cracks occur in random configuration but that the game are *not* randomly distributed over the land. Hunting in the area indicated by scapu-limancy, in other words, is like following a table of random numbers. The advantage of following such a procedure is that it prevents the skilled hunters from "outguessing" the game and thereby hitting the mark so often that the ecological balance is threatened. In this view

Figure 24-11. SACRED ANIMAL. This denizen of Calcutta is not wandering about aimlessly. Its owner knows where it is. (Moni Nag)

567

Ecology and Religion

scapulimancy is employed by the Naskapi and other hunters and gatherers because of its unintended effectiveness as a conservation mechanism.

Many additional instances of ecologically adaptive religious rituals and beliefs await further study.

The Sacred Cows of India

The most puzzling religious beliefs and rituals are those that seem to work against the maximization of productive capacity under conditions of severe population pressure and food shortage. Sometimes it appears as if a whole population is deliberately limiting its chances of survival in order to observe some religious custom or taboo.

A classic example is that of the Hindu treatment of cattle. Everyone agrees that the human population of India subsists on inadequate calorie and protein rations. Yet the Hindu religion bans the slaughter of cattle and taboos the eating of beef. These taboos are often held responsible for the creation of large numbers of aged, decrepit, barren, and useless cattle. Such animals are depicted as roaming aimlessly across the Indian countryside, clogging the roads, stopping the trains, stealing food from the marketplace, and blocking city streets. A closer look at some of the details of the ecosystem of the Indian subcontinent, however, suggests that the taboo in question increases rather than decreases the capacity of the present Indian system of food production to support human life.

The basis of traditional Indian agriculture is the ox-drawn plow. Each peasant farmer needs at least two oxen to plow the fields at the proper time of year. To replace these oxen a farmer also needs at least one cow. Despite the impression of surplus cattle, the central fact of Indian rural life is that there is a shortage of oxen, since one-third of the peasant households own less than the minimum pair. Obviously, therefore, the cows must be too old, decrepit, and sick to do a proper job of reproducing. At this point the ban on slaughter and beef consumption is thought to exert its deleterious effect. For rather than kill dry, barren, and aged cows, the Hindu farmer is depicted as ritually obsessed with preserving the life of each sacred beast, no matter how useless it may become. From the point of view of the farmer, however, these relatively undesirable creatures may be quite essential and useful. The farmer would prefer to have more vigorous cows, but is prevented from achieving this goal not by the taboos against slaughter but by the shortage of land and pasture.

568   Even barren cows, however, are by no means a total loss. Their dung makes an essential contribution to the energy system as fertilizer and as cooking fuel. Millions of tons of artificial fertilizer at prices beyond the reach of the small farmer would be required to make up for the loss of dung if substantial numbers of cows were sent to slaughter. Since cow dung is a major source of cooking fuel, the slaughter of substantial numbers of animals would also require the purchase of expensive dung substitutes, such as wood, coal, or kerosene. Cow dung is cheap because the cows do not eat foods that can be eaten by people. Instead they eat the stubble left in the fields and the marginal patches of grass on steep hillsides, roadside ditches, railroad embankments, and other nonarable lands. This constant scavenging gives the impression that they are roaming around aimlessly devouring everything in sight. But most cows have an owner, and in the cities, after poking about in the market refuse and nibbling on neighbors' lawns, each animal returns to its stall at the end of the day.

Figure 24-12. SACRED COWS OF INDIA. Cattle are ecologically more valuable than cars in India. (UPI Photo)

Figure 24-13. SACRED COWS OF LOS ANGELES. Unlike the sacred cows of India, these mechanical pets excrete poisons instead of fertilizer. (George Gardner)

In a study of the bioenergetic balance involved in the cattle complex of villages in West Bengal, Stewart Odend'hal (1972) found that "basically, the cattle convert items of little direct human value into products of immediate human utility." Their gross energetic efficiency in supplying useful products was several times greater than that characteristic of agro-industrial beef production. He concludes that "judging the productive value of Indian cattle based on western standards is inappropriate."

Although it might be possible to maintain or exceed the present level of production of oxen and dung with substantially fewer cows of larger and better breeds, the question arises as to how these cows would be distributed among the poor farmers. Are the farmers who have only one or two decrepit animals to be driven from the land?

Aside from the problem of whether present levels of population and productivity could be maintained with fewer cows, there is the theoretically more crucial question of whether it is the taboo on slaughter that accounts for the observed ratio of cattle to people. This seems highly unlikely. Despite the ban on slaughter, the Hindu farmers cull their herds and adjust sex ratios to crops, weather, and

570

regional conditions. The cattle are killed by various indirect means equivalent to the forms of benign and malign neglect discussed in Chapter 13 with respect to human population controls. The effectiveness of this form of control may be judged from the following fact. In the Gangetic plain, one of the most religiously orthodox regions of India, there are 213 oxen for every 100 cows (267).

Stepping away from the point of view of the individual farmer, there are a number of additional reasons for concluding that the Hindu taboos have a positive rather than negative effect upon the carrying capacity of the ecosystem. The ban on slaughter, whatever its consequences for culling the herds, discourages the development of a meat-packing industry. For reasons previously suggested (p. 250), such an industry would be ecologically disastrous in a land as densely populated as India. In this connection it should be pointed out that the protein output of the existing system is not unimportant. Although the Indian cows are very poor milkers by Western standards, they nonetheless contribute critical if small quantities of protein to the diets of millions of people. Moreover a considerable amount of beef does get eaten during the course of the year since the animals that die a natural death are consumed by carrion-eating outcastes. Finally, the critical function of the ban on slaughter during famines should be noted. When hunger stalks the Indian countryside the slaughter taboo helps the peasants to resist the temptation to eat their cattle. If this temptation were to win out over religious scruples, it would be impossible for them to plant new crops when the rains began. Thus the intense resistance among Hindu saints to the slaughter and consumption of beef takes on a new meaning in the context of the Indian ecosystem. In the words of Mahatma Gandhi:

Why the cow was selected for apotheosis is obvious to me. The cow was in India the best companion. She was the giver of plenty. Not only did she give milk but she also made agriculture possible.   [1954:3]

25

ART

Painting, sculpting, making music, singing, and dancing are activities that occur in every society. *Art,* on the other hand, is an emic category of modern Euro-American civilization. Euro-American schoolchildren are enculturated to the idea that art and nonart are cognitively contrastive categories. They learn to believe that some paintings, carvings, songs, dances, and stories are not art. The basis of the contrast cannot be stated in precise terms. No one has succeeded in formulating a definition of art that would permit an anthropologist to segregate art from nonart in all the cultures of the world. In Western civilization a particular performance is deemed artistic or not by a distinct group of authorities who make or judge art and who control the museums, conservatories, critical journals, and other organizations and institutions devoted to art as a livelihood and style of life. Most cultures lack any semblance of an art establishment. This does not mean they lack aesthetic standards. A painted design on a pot or a rock, a carved mask or club, a song or chant in a puberty ordeal, are subject to critical evaluation by both performers and spectators. All cultures distinguish between less satisfactory and more satisfactory performances in decorative, pictorial, and expressive matters as well as in the construction of a canoe or the slaughter

Figure 25-1. INDONESIAN DRAMA (facing page, left). Combines artistry and craftsmanship in many media. (Eugene Gordon)

Figure 25-2. ART AND ADORNMENT (facing page, right). Shell made into nose ornament enhances beauty and prestige of this man from Asmat, New Guinea. (Eugene Gordon)

of a pig. But these activities are usually performed and judged by part-time specialists or by a large percentage of the total community of performers, spectators, and consumers.

Art and Practicality

Basic to the modern Western idea of art and nonart is the exclusion of designs, stories, and rhythms, that have a definite use in day-to-day subsistence activities and that are produced primarily for practical purposes or for commercial sale. Carpenters are distinguished from people who make wooden sculptures, bricklayers from architects, housepainters from those who apply paint to canvas, and so forth. A similar opposition between art and practicality is seldom found in other cultures. Many works of art are produced and performed in overt harmony with utilitarian objectives. People everywhere, whether specialists or nonspecialists, derive pleasure from embellishing and

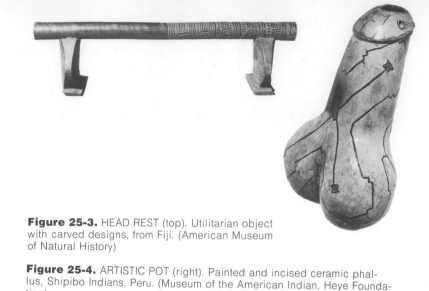

Figure 25-3. HEAD REST (top). Utilitarian object with carved designs, from Fiji. (American Museum of Natural History)

Figure 25-4. ARTISTIC POT (right). Painted and incised ceramic phallus, Shipibo Indians, Peru. (Museum of the American Indian, Heye Foundation)

Figure 25-5. CARVED CEREMONIAL ADZE (left). Many great works of art are highly elaborated versions of humble utilitarian objects. This example is from the Cook Islands. (American Museum of Natural History)

perfecting the contours and surfaces of pots, fabrics, wood, and metal products. Presumably the pleasure derived from artwork associated with utilitarian crafts arises from a biologically selected capacity for making and using tools. Art in the sense of craft virtuosity is part of human nature. All cultures, however, recognize that certain individuals are more skilled than others in making utilitarian objects and in embellishing them with pleasurable designs. Anthropologists regard the skilled woodcarver, basketmaker, potter, weaver, or sandalmaker as an artist even if the cultures in which these crafts are performed lack a distinction between art and nonart.

Art and Technology

The widespread appreciation of technical control over diverse materials and physical media—wood, stone, pigments, clays, vibrating strings, and resonating columns of air—is not simply a matter of

Figure 25-6. ART HAS MANY MEDIA (facing page). American Indian cultures produced these objects. Gold mummy mask with green stone eyes, Chimu, Peru (top left). Globular basket with coiled weave, Chumash, California (top right). Feathers of blue and yellow form design of Tapirapé mask, Brazil (center left). Painted wooden kero, or beaker, representing ocelot head, Inca, Peru (center right). Ceramic jar, Nazca, Peru (bottom left). Blanket, in blue, black, and white, with stripes and frets, Navajo (bottom right). (Museum of the American Indian, Heye Foundation)

aesthetic pleasure. Art is utilitarian not merely because it often occurs on or in association with useful objects but because art often stimulates the perfection and invention of new tools and subsistence techniques.

Throughout the Paleolithic period it is impossible to say where technology ends and art begins, or where art ends and technology begins. A Solutrean laurel leaf blade is as much an aesthetic expression as a device for cutting flesh (p. 182). The symmetry of nets, baskets, and woven fabrics is essential for their proper functioning. Even in the development of media of musical expression there are technological benefits. For example, there was probably some kind of feedback between the invention of the bow as a hunting weapon and the twanging of taut strings for musical effect. No one can say which came first, but cultures with bows and arrows invariably have musical strings. Wind instruments, blowguns, pistons, and bellows are all related. Similarly metallurgy and chemistry relate to experimentation with the ornamental shape, texture, and color of ceramic products. Thus there are adaptive advantages when craftsmen and craftswomen are encouraged to rub and polish, trim and smooth, stretch and pull, and experiment with the raw materials of their crafts. Small wonder that many cultures regard technical virtuosity as mana. Others regard it as the gift of the gods, as in the classical Greek idea of the Muses—goddesses of orators, dancers, and musicians—whose assistance was needed if worthy artistic performances were to occur.

Art and the Machine

One of the most striking peculiarities of the cognitive domain of art in contemporary Western culture is the downgrading of technical virtuosity. The modern metallic and plastic surfaces as embodied in an automobile or a dishwasher are definitely nonart. Indeed, from the point of view of the producer, standardized, machine-made objects are the exact antithesis of art. Mass production extinguishes the aesthetic pleasure that accompanies craft production. The routinization and division of labor of industrial systems alienates the workers from the creative process, and this alienation constitutes a hidden psychological cost whose ultimate consequences are as yet unknown.

Since the modern artist cannot match the technical virtuosity of a computerized die-cutter or automated lathe, there is a tendency to assert the independence of art from craft. Some members of the art establishment, and many professional artists who must earn their living from the sale of handmade products, have even come to regard

576

technical virtuosity as an antivalue. To the bewilderment of millions who derive aesthetic pleasure from an automobile's perfect painted surface and their clotheswasher's glittering chrome nobs, artists have turned to the production of items deliberately made to appear technically ingenuous, childlike, rough, and imperfect. The antithesis between industrial machine products and art reflects in part an attempt by the art establishment to prevent devaluation through mass production. This resistance accounts for the downgrading of "reproductions." No matter how faithful to the "original," copies are considered inferior and of little value by the Euroamerican art establishment.

Art and Cultural Patterning

Modern Euro-American art is unusual in another respect. Most preindustrial artwork is deliberately fashioned in the image of a preexisting pattern. It is the task of the artist to replicate the pattern by original combinations of culturally standardized elements—familiar and pleasing sounds, colors, lines, shapes, and so on. Too perfect a replication results in boredom for the artist and art appreciator; hence there is always some tolerance for innovation. But in most cultures artists never dream of producing works that are not recognizable examples of an established pattern.

Figure 25-7. NORTHWEST COAST ART STYLE. This style is noted for its representation of real and mythical animals and human beings shown with conventionalized natural features upon a carefully filled flat or 3-dimensional design field. Heads and faces are exaggerated in size, and the joints, backbones, ribs, and internal organs are often visible. From British Columbia, Canada. Top—Haida chief's frontlet mask with the hawk crest, in wood and abalone. Middle left—ladle of mountain sheep horn from the northern region, depicting two wolves, a bear, a man, and a raven. Middle right—dagger handle, representing two bears and a man, ivory with abalone inlay; origin unknown. Bottom left—Tsimshian chief's raven rattle with a hawk on the breast and a man receiving power from a frog on the back. Bottom right—shaman's charm in bone; figures represent the spirits from whom the shaman obtains his power. (de Havenon Collection)

Figure 25-8. MAORI CANOE PROW. The Maori of New Zealand are among the world's greatest wood carvers. (American Museum of Natural History)

It is the repetition of traditional and familiar elements that accounts for the major differences between the artistic products of different cultures. For example, Northwest Coast American Indian sculpture is well known for its consistent attention to animal and human motifs rendered in such a way as to indicate internal as well as external organs symmetrically arranged within bounded geometrical forms. Maori sculpture, on the other hand, requires that wooden surfaces be broken into bold but intricate filigrees and whorls. Among the Mochica of ancient Peru the sculptural medium was pottery, and the Mochica pots are famous for their representational realism in portraiture and in depictions of domestic and sexual behavior. Hundreds of other easily recognizable and distinctive art styles of different cultures can be identified. The continuity and integrity of these styles provide the basic context for a people's understanding and liking of art (cf. Fig. 25-7, 25-15, and 25-16).

Establishment art in modern Western culture is unique in its capacity to separate form and meaning from tradition. It is taken as normal that art must be interpreted and explained by experts in order to be understood and appreciated. Since the end of the nineteenth century the greatest artists for the Western art establishment are the individuals who break with tradition, introduce new culture styles, and at least for a time render their work inscrutable to a large number of people. Joined to this deemphasis upon tradition and continuity is the peculiar recent Western notion of artists as Faustian figures, people struggling in lonely isolation against limitations set by the preexisting capability of their audience to appreciate and understand true genius.

Figure 25-9. WHAT DOES IT MEAN? Fur-covered cup, saucer, and spoon by Méret Oppenheim. (The Museum of Modern Art. Cup, 4³/₈″ diameter; saucer, 9³/₈″ diameter; spoon 8″ long.)

Figure 25-10. MUD
ARCHITECTURE. Layer of
mud protects adobe bricks.
Towers are purely orna-
mental. Dogon village, Mali.
(Eugene Gordon)

Figure 25-11. ART AND
ARCHITECTURE. Brightly
painted faces on a men's
house in the Sepik River basin, New Guinea. (UPI Photo)

579

Thus modern Euro-American art is dominated by an unprecedented concern with novelty. Artists consciously strive to be the originators of new patterns. They compete with each other in a struggle to invent new elements to replace the standard elements employed by their predecessors. Modern aesthetic standards decree that originality must take precedence over intelligibility. Indeed a work of art that is transparently intelligible automatically invites condemnation by the art establishment. Many art critics more or less consciously take it for granted that novelty must result in a certain amount of obscurity. What accounts for this obsession with being original?

One important influence is the reaction to mass production. For the same reasons that mass production leads to a downgrading of technical virtuosity, it also leads to the downgrading of all artwork that closely resembles the objects or performances that others have produced. Another factor to be considered is the involvement of the modern artist in a commercial market in which supply perennially exceeds demand. Part-time band- and village-level artists are concerned with being original only to the extent that it enhances the aesthetic enjoyment of their work. Their livelihood does not depend on obtaining an artistic identity and a personal following. Still another factor to be considered is that the rate of cultural change has been so rapid in recent years, that to some extent the premium conferred upon originality merely reflects the obsolescence of all traditional values and institutions.

Art and Religion

The history and ethnography of art are inseparable from the history and ethnography of religion. Art as an aspect of supernatural belief and ritual goes back at least forty thousand years. As previously discussed, European Upper Paleolithic cave paintings undoubtedly played a role in magico-religious rituals aimed at controlling the movements, reproductive patterns, and vulnerability of the Pleistocene megafauna. The Venus statuettes also undoubtedly possessed

Figure 25-12. ART, SEX, AND RELIGION. Since sexuality is widely viewed as a gift of the gods, art in religious contexts often celebrates the beauty of the human form. This example is from a temple in Rajasthan, India. (The Brooklyn Museum, Gift of Mr. and Mrs. Richard Shields)

Figure 25-13. MASK WITHIN MASK. Wearer of this Kwakiutl mask uses strings to pull eagle apart, revealing human face. (American Museum of Natural History)

magico-religious significance. It seems likely that groups capable of paintings and sculpture also employed rituals involving music and dance. Masked figures are depicted in some of the late Magdelenian murals (see pp. 183, 184), but it is impossible to attribute any precise religious meaning to them.

Among contemporary cultures art is intimately associated with all four organizational levels of belief and ritual. For example, at the individualistic level, magical songs are often included among the revelations granted the Plains Indian vision-seekers. Even the preparation of trophy heads among the Jívaro must meet aesthetic standards, and singing and chanting are widely used during shamanic performances. On the communal level, puberty rituals provide occasions for myth- and story-telling. Body-painting is also widely practiced in communal ceremonies. Singing, dancing, and the wearing of masks are common at both puberty and funerary rituals. Much artistic effort is expended in the preparation of religiously significant funerary equipment such as graveposts and shrines. Many cultures include ceremonial artifacts like pottery and clubs, points, and other weapons among a deceased person's grave goods. Ancestors and gods are often depicted in statues and masks that are kept in men's houses

Figure 25-14. MASK WITHIN MASK WITHIN MASK. Whale conceals bird, which conceals human face, which conceals face of wearer. Another Kwakiutl masterpiece. (American Museum of Natural History)

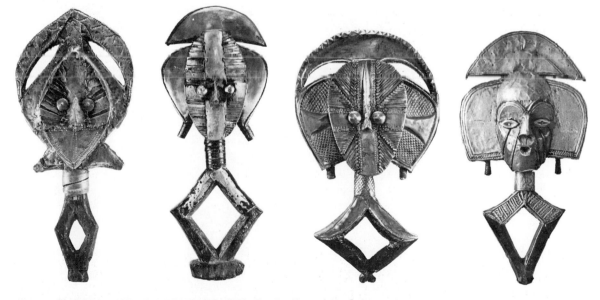

Figure 25-15. BA KOTA FUNERARY FIGURES. The Ba Kota of the Gabon Republic place the skeletal remains of dead chiefs in bark boxes or baskets surmounted by Mbulu-ngulu guardian figures of wood faced with brass or copper sheets or strips. Although each figure expresses the creative individuality of the artist, they all conform to the same stylistic pattern. (de Havenon Collection)

Art and Religion

Figure 25-16. DOGON ANCESTOR FIGURES. Found on a variety of ritual objects, they may be carved singly or in groups of two, four, or eight. One constant of the Dogon style is the repetition of pointed beard or chin and exaggerated breasts and abdomen. Other notable facets of the style include the angular opposition of flexed knees to bent elbows or to arms raised with elbows facing front in supplication. From Mali Republic, Northern region. From left to right—ritual food vessel with mounted ancestor figure; female ancestor with child; granary door with ancestor figures whose protection of the family millet supply is thus invoked; dance mask of a man's head surmounted by a kneeling female ancestor. (de Havenon Collection)

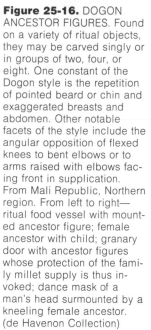

Figure 25-17. ASMAT GRAVEPOST. Around the world much talent has been lavished on commemorating the dead. But styles and media vary enormously. (Eugene Gordon)

or in shrines. Churingas (p. 535), the Arunta's most sacred objects, are artfully incised with whorls and loops depicting the route followed by the ancestors during the dream time. On the ecclesiastical level, art and religion are fused in pyramids, monumental avenues, stone statuary, monolithic calendar carvings, temples, altars, priestly garments, and a near infinite variety of artful ritual ornaments and sacred paraphernalia.

It is clear that art, religion, and magic satisfy similar psychological needs in human beings. They are media for expressing sentiments and emotions not easily expressed in ordinary life. They impart a sense of mastery over or communion with unpredictable events and mysterious unseen powers. They impose human meanings and values upon an indifferent world—a world that has no humanly intelligible meanings and values of its own. They seek to penetrate behind the façade of ordinary appearance into the true, cosmic significance of things. And they use delusions, dramatic tricks, and sleight-of-hand to get people to believe in them.

Figure 25-18. ART AND FUNERALS. Rites of passage provide the context for much artistic effort as shown in this ceremony among the Dogon of Mali. (See Fig. 23-15, and also Figs. 23-17, 23-19, and 25-21) (Eugene Gordon)

583

Art and Religion

Art and Politics

The intimate relationship between art and religion guarantees art an important role in politics. In stratified cultures, religion is a means of social control, and the skills of the artist are harnessed by the ruling class to implant religious notions of obedience and to sanctify the status quo. Contrary to the popular modern image of the artist as a free spirit disdainful of authority, most art is politically conservative. Ecclesiastical art interprets the world in conformity with prevailing myths and ideologies justifying inequities and exploitation. Art makes the gods visible as idols. Gazing upon massive stone blocks carved as if by superhuman hands, commoners comprehend the necessity for subservience. They are awed by the immense size of pyramids and fascinated and befuddled by processions, prayers, pomp, and sacrifices of priests in dramatic settings—golden altars, colonnaded temples, great vaulted roofs, huge ramps and stairways, windows through which only the light from heaven passes.

The church and state have been the greatest patrons of the arts in all but the last few hundred years of history. With the rise of capitalism, ecclesiastical and civil institutions became more decentralized, and wealthy individuals to a considerable extent replaced church and state as the patrons of the arts. Individualized sponsorship promoted greater flexibility and freedom of expression. Politically neutral, secular, and even revolutionary and sacrilegious themes became common. The arts became established as secular forms of entertainment. To protect and preserve their new found autonomy, the art establishment invented the doctrine of "art for art's sake." Free to express themselves, the artists were no longer sure

Figure 25-19. GOLD DEATH MASK OF TUT. Another example of the interrelationship of art, religion, and politics. (Metropolitan Museum of Art)

Figure 25-20. EASTER ISLAND STATUES. Carved by a prehistoric people whose identity is unknown. (Eugene Gordon)

584

Figure 25-21. ART AND
RELIGION. Notre Dame
Cathedral, Paris. No one ever
had to ask what it meant, but
how it was built remains a
mystery. (French Government
Tourist Office)

what they wanted to express. They devoted themselves more and
more to idiosyncratic and obscure symbols organized into novel and
unintelligible patterns, as discussed earlier in this chapter. And the
patrons of art, concerned less and less with content, increasingly
looked toward the acquisition and sponsorship of artwork as a prestigious commercial venture that yielded substantial profits, tax deductions, and a hedge against inflation. In contrast, art in the
communist countries has been returned to state sponsorship and is
deliberately used as a means of convincing the citizens that the
postrevolutionary status quo is equitable and inevitable.

Art for Art's Sake?

In the absence of church or state sponsorship the artist must be
prepared for a life of poverty and material insecurity. Yet the artist's
life-style is very attractive in other regards. Ideally art for art's sake is
the antithesis of work for money's sake. Artistic effort is the very
opposite of the work that degrades the industrial wage earner. It is not
routinized, has no unit value, and at times cannot be bought at any
price. Unlike the factory worker, artists control the products of their
own, unalienated labor; their work is their essence. But if the artist is

Figure 25-22. ART FOR ART'S SAKE. Claes Oldenburg's "Two Cheeseburgers, with Everything." (The Museum of Modern Art, Philip Johnson Fund. 1962. Enamel paint on plaster-covered burlap, 7″ x 14³/₄″ x 6⁵/₈″.)

indeed the model of a free and unalienated individual, what accounts for the morbid themes prevalent in the biographies of so many geniuses of Western art? Why the restlessness, bitterness, lack of personal fulfillment, and high incidence of neurotic symptoms? One interpretation is that to be truly creative is necessarily painful. Thus, according to Freud, art is the product of blocked impulses and emotions (sublimation). But there is no indication that individuals in other cultures who excel in artistic talents are afflicted with the Faustian disabilities of the contemporary artist. An alternative interpretation is that the tragic aspects of the artistic personality are related to the social isolation that modern artists must endure as long as their work primarily fulfills a personal urge to be creative, regardless of whether it is meaningful, useful, or entertaining to others.

In anthropological perspective the creative freedom of the modern artist appears illusory. The theme of "art for art's sake," the stress on breaking traditions, the search for completely new individualized styles, appear in Western history as the determined product of definite cultural conditions. Art for art's sake is associated with the rise of capitalism and its stress on individual initiative; the division of society into complex and antagonistic regions, ethnic groups, and class strata; the proliferation of ecclesiastical organizations; the decline in religious moral authority; and the accelerating pace of cultural evolution. In this context the Faustian creativity of art for art's sake signifies nothing so much as the enforced diversion of vast amounts of creative energy from the arenas of political and economic conflict. Thus even those artists who spurn traditions and deny their responsibility to anyone or anything but themselves and their genius no more escape the conditioning effects of their cultural milieu than the lone Crow warrior in quest of a vision (cf. Bunzel 1929; Boas 1955; Marian Smith 1961; Wingert 1962; Holm 1965; Fraser 1966; Lomax 1968; Berndt and Berndt 1971; Otten 1971; Lomax and Berkovitz 1972).

586

PERSONALITY, SEX, AND
THE INDIVIDUAL

Many cultural anthropologists use terms and concepts drawn from
psychology and psychiatry to study culture and the relationships
between culture and the individual. A key concept in this approach is
personality. Personality, as defined by Victor Barnouw, "is a more or
less enduring organization of forces within the individual associated
with a complex of fairly consistent attitudes, values, and modes of
perception which account, in part, for the individual's consistency of
behavior" (1973:10). Anthropologists who rely primarily upon the
concept of personality for their descriptions of a society's patterns of
behavior, thought, and feeling or who are primarily concerned with
the relationships between culture and personality are said to be
concerned with the subfield known as *culture and personality*. In
this chapter I shall discuss some of the ways in which personality
varies cross-culturally and some of the functional and causal relationships between culture and individual thought and behavior.

Culture and Personality

Culture is an abstraction that summarizes the patterned ways in
which the members of a population, think, feel, and behave. Personality is an abstraction that summarizes the patterned ways in
which a given individual thinks, feels, and behaves. Theoretically a
description of the average or typical personality patterns present in a
given population should constitute a description of the culture of that
population. In practice, however, this is not the case; the reason is

587

that the concepts that are employed in describing the thinking, feeling, and behaving of personality types are different from those that are employed in describing the thinking, feeling, and behaving of cultural types. In describing personalities, psychologists use concepts such as aggressive, passive, anxious, obsessive, hysterical, manic, depressive, introverted, extroverted, paranoid, authoritarian, schizoid, masculine, feminine, infantile, repressed, dependent, and so forth. Here is part of a more extensive list of terms appropriate for the study of personality that appeared in a recent study.

practical	composed under stress	lethargic
economical	orderly	anxious
careful	methodical	stubborn
reserved	loyal	indolent
patient	unimaginative	inert
cautious	stingy	pedantic
steadfast, tenacious	suspicious	obsessive
imperturbable	cold	possessive

Source: Erich Fromm and Michael Maccoby, *A Mexican Village: A Sociopsychoanalytic Study* (Englewood Cliffs, N.J.: Prentice-Hall, 1970), p. 79.

If these concepts are employed to describe an entire population, the resultant description will obviously not add up to a description of modes of production and reproduction, domestic and political economy, systems of war and peace, or magico-religious rites and institutions. Because of these differences in basic descriptive concepts, the question arises as to what is the relationship between the personality characteristics of a given population and the culture of that population.

Patterns and Themes

Many different proposals have been made concerning how to treat the relationship between personality and culture. One popular option acknowledges the fact that culture and personality are two different ways of looking at the propensity to think, feel, and behave characteristic of a given population and uses psychological terms to characterize institutions and whole cultural systems. For example, Ruth Benedict in her famous book, *Patterns of Culture,* characterized the institution of Kwakiutl potlatch as a megalomaniacal performance. She saw potlatch as part of a *Dionysian* pattern that was characteristic of all the institutions of Kwakiutl culture. By Dionysian she meant the desire to achieve emotional excess as in drunkenness or frenzy. Other cultures, such as the Pueblo Indians, she saw as *Apollonian—*

588

given to moderation and the "middle of the road" in all things. Benedict's *patterns* were psychological elements reputedly found throughout a culture, "comparable to the chromosomes found in most of the cells of a body" (Wallace 1970b: 149). Most anthropologists have rejected such attempts to use one or two psychological terms to describe the immense repertory of personalities and functionally distinct institutions that can be found in even the simplest cultures.

Some anthropologists attempt to identify dominant *themes* or values that express the essential or main thought and feelings of a particular culture. The "image of limited good" is one such theme whose limitations have already been discussed (p. 468). Themes and values are readily translatable into personality traits. For example, the image of limited good allegedly produces personalities who are jealous, suspicious, secretive, and fearful. The culture of poverty also has its psychological components: propensity to consume, lack of future-time orientation, sexual promiscuity. An important theme in Hindu India is the "sacredness of life," and an important theme in the United States is "keeping up with the Joneses." The problem with attempts to portray cultures in terms of a few dominant values and attitudes is that contradictory values and attitudes can usually be identified in the same cultures and even in the same individuals. Thus, although Hindu farmers believe in the sacredness of life (cf. Opler 1968), they also believe in the necessity of having more bullocks than cows (see p. 571); and although many people in the United States believe in trying to keep up with the Joneses, there are millions who believe at the same time that conspicuous consumption is foolish and sinful.

Basic Personality and National Character

A somewhat different approach to culture and personality postulates that every culture produces a basic or deep personality structure that can be found in virtually every individual member of the culture. When the populations involved are state-organized, there is a tendency to refer to basic personality as *national character.* The notion of basic personality structure has always enjoyed considerable popularity among casual travelers to foreign lands as well as among scholars. For example, how often have you heard it said that the English are "reserved," the Brazilians "carefree," the French "sexy," the Italians "uninhibited," the Japanese "orderly," the Americans "outgoing," and so forth? Gerardus Mercator, the Belgian father of cartography, wrote the following descriptions of European basic personalities in the sixteenth century:

Franks: simple, blockish, furious
Bavarians: sumptuous, gluttons, brazen-faced
Swedes: light, babblers, boasters
Saxons: dissemblers, double-hearted, opinionative
Spaniards: disdainful, cautious, greedy
Belgians: good horsemen, tender, docible, delicate

In a similar vein, Herbert Spencer, one of the founders of modern sociology and anthropology, had this to say about non-Western basic personalities:

Samoans: Not so lively as Tahitians. Good humored, social in disposition, very desirous of pleasing, and fond of amusement and traveling. Indolent, fickle, and deceitful.
Dyaks: Not very impulsive. Seldom except on festive occasions going the length of boisterous mirth. Generally mild, polite, and respectful of superiors. Sociable, amiable, sympathetic and capable of strong mutual attachments.
Andaman Islanders: Vivacious and affectionate; impulsive and frightfully passionate; revengeful, crafty, and merciless. Suspicious of strangers to an inconceivable degree. Manifest no ferocity when once subdued. [cf. M. Harris 1968:400]

Modern scholarly versions of basic personality structure make use of more sophisticated psychological concepts, most of which owe something to the influence of Sigmund Freud and psychoanalysis. Geoffry Gorer's (Gorer and Rickman 1949) characterization of Great Russian Personality is a case in point. According to Gorer, Great Russians share a personality structure typified by a kind of manic-depressive complex—an alternation between a period of extreme dependence, acceptance of discipline, and passivity followed by a period of orgiastic outbursts of rage and self-indulgence. Gorer traced this personality structure to the experience in infancy of being tightly swaddled intertwined with periods of sudden freedom during which children kick violently when the swaddling is removed. He felt that historical events such as the Bolshevik revolution and the confession of guilt at the Stalin purge trials were in some way related to the need for restraint coupled with the need for expressing one's pent-up rage that had been engendered by the swaddling experience. This interpretation of Great Russian personality has been widely criticized on the grounds that Gorer was unable to show that most of the leaders of the Bolshevik revolution were in fact swaddled as children.

The concept of a culturally determined personality type is acceptable only with recognition that the range of personalities in every

590

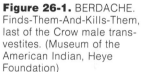

Figure 26-1. BERDACHE. Finds-Them-And-Kills-Them, last of the Crow male transvestites. (Museum of the American Indian, Heye Foundation)

society is quite large. In every society many individuals have personalities that deviate widely from the statistical mode (most frequent type), and the variances and ranges of individual personalities produce wide bands of overlap between populations. For example, it would certainly be correct to characterize the basic type of Plains Indian male personality as an aggressive, independent, and fearless person. Yet it is known from the institution called *berdache* that there were always some young men whose vision-quests were doomed to failure and who found themselves temperamentally unsuited to the warrior's calling. Donning female dress and dedicating themselves to female domestic and sexual specialties, these men found acceptance among their people.

Very little is actually known about the amount of variance of personality in different societies. It is certain, however, that complex, state-level populations consisting of millions of people contain an enormous variety of types. Moreover the more complex the criteria used to define basic personality, the more likely that the modal type of personality will be found in relatively few individuals. Anthony Wallace (1952), who used twenty-one dimensions of personality to define basic personality among the Iroquois, found that the modal type was shared by only 37 percent of the total sample.

Basic Personality and National Character

Childhood Training and Personality

The attempt to explain Russian national character as a product of infant swaddling reflects the influence of Sigmund Freud's theories of personality. According to Freud, infantile and prepubescent childhood experiences are the most important factors in the development of an individual's personality. Infant and early childhood experiences center on basic body parts, functions, and urges. Freud theorized that all intact and healthy adults must pass through a series of developmental stages. First there is concern with the mouth and food functions, then a concern with the bowels and excretory functions, and later a concern with the genitals and sexual functions. These stages are referred to as the oral, anal, and phallic stages of childhood development. Patterns of coping with the gratifications and frustrations of these stages of psychological growth stay with people throughout their lives and largely determine the organization of their adult personalities.

Anthropologists interested in culture and personality have generally accepted Freud's fundamental proposal that forgotten or repressed childhood experiences are the primary source of adult personality. But they have enlarged the scope of childhood experiences deemed relevant to adult personality formation to take account of the enormous diversity of culturally patterned relationships between infants and adults. These relationships are known as *childhood training practices.* For example, the feeding, cleaning, and handling of infants constitute culturally patterned activities that vary widely from one society to another. Gorer was certainly correct in noting that in many cultures infants are constrained by swaddling bandages or cradle boards that immobilize their limbs. Elsewhere freedom of movement is encouraged. Similarly nursing may be on demand at the first cry of

Figure 26-2. SWAZI MOTHER AND CHILD. Cultures vary greatly in the amount of body contact between mothers and infants.

Figure 26-3. JAVANESE GIRL AND BROTHER. One way to free mother for work in the fields is to turn over the care of infants to six-year-old sister. (United Nations)

hunger or at regular intervals at the convenience of the mother. Nursing at the mother's breast may last for only a few months, several years, or not at all. Supplementary foods may be taken in the first few weeks, stuffed into the baby's mouth, premasticated by the mother, played with by the baby, or omitted entirely.

Weaning may take place abruptly, as where the mother's nipples are painted with bitter substances; and it may or may not be associated with the birth of another child. In some cultures infants are kept next to their mother's skin and carried wherever the mother goes; elsewhere they may be left behind in the care of kinswomen. In some cultures infants are fondled, hugged, kissed, and fussed over by large groups of adoring children and adults. In other instances they are kept relatively isolated and are touched infrequently.

Toilet training may begin as early as six or as late as twenty-four months; mode of training may involve many different techniques, some based on intense forms of punishment, shame, and ridicule, others involving suggestion, emulation, and no punishment.

Treatment of infant sexuality also varies widely. In many cultures mothers or fathers stroke their babies' genitals to soothe them and stop them from crying; elsewhere the baby is prevented from touching its own genitals and masturbation is severely punished.

593

Childhood Training and Personality

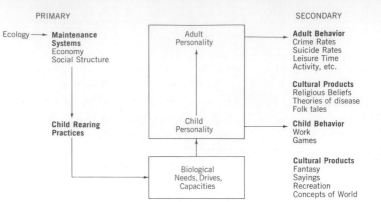

Figure 26-4. THE RELATIONSHIP OF BASIC PERSONALITY TO ECOLOGY, CHILD-REARING PRACTICES, AND SECONDARY AND PROJECTIVE INSTITUTIONS. (After Levine 1973:57)

Another series of variables relevant to personality formation consists of later childhood and adolescent experiences. Numbers of siblings; their relationships and mutual responsibilities; patterns of play; opportunities to observe adult intercourse, to engage in homosexual or heterosexual experimentation; incest restrictions; and type of threat and punishment used against culturally prohibited sexual practices all are relevant to the neo-Freudian anthropological concept of childhood training practices.

Figure 26-4 depicts one theory of how these childhood training practices may be related to personality and to other aspects of culture. The basic variables influencing child-rearing patterns are presumed to be influenced by the nature of the domestic, social, political, and economic institutions. These in turn are influenced by the ecosystem. Child-rearing practices are constrained by the necessity of satisfying certain biologically determined universal needs, drives, and capacities that all human infants share (e.g., oral, anal, and genital urges). The interaction between the child-rearing practices and these biological needs, drives, and capacities produces child personality. As in the classic Freudian model of personality, Figure 26-4 indicates that adult personality is largely the outgrowth of psychodynamic processes begun in infancy. In further concordance with Freud's theory, Figure 26-4 shows that an understanding of child and adult personality is necessary in order to understand the cultural beliefs and behaviors that are listed to the right of the personality box. Personality, in other words, is seen as mediating between one set of institutions and another—between a set of personality-forming institutions and a set of personality-projective institutions.

Alorese Basic Personality

A hypothesis concerning how personality mediates between sets of institutions has been made with respect to the people of Alor. As

594

described by Cora Du Bois (1960), the Alorese have a very low level of esteem for their ancestors. Like many other peoples the Alorese make wooden effigies of the deceased, which they use for ritual purposes. But Alorese effigies are singularly ill-fashioned and once used are immediately discarded. Unlike other Oceanian cultures the Alorese do not provide the ancestral spirits with housing nor do they worry about feeding them. According to Emil Oberholzer, the psychoanalyst who worked with the data provided by Du Bois, Alorese religion becomes more intelligible when it is viewed as a projection of basic personality. Based on his examination of Rorschach ink-blot tests administered by Du Bois, Oberholzer characterized the Alorese basic personality as follows:

They are indifferent and listless; they let things slide and get dilapidated . . . conscience and its dynamic expression is not developed. . . . Outlets offered by a capacity for long-lasting enthusiasm and self-sacrifice, for sublimation, contemplation, and creative power—all of these are ruled out. There must be emotional outbursts and tempers, anger and rage. . . . The Alorese must be lacking in individual personal contact, living beside one another but not with one another. . . . Either there are no friendships . . . or there are none that are deeply rooted.   [Quoted in Barnouw 1973:158]

Another aspect of Alorese basic personality that is relevant to their indifference toward the ancestral spirits is their failure to idealize their parents. What is responsible for this personality syndrome? Turning to the childhood training experiences, Du Bois found that Alorese infants are frustrated by inadequate and irregular nursing. About ten days after giving birth, the Alorese mother resumes work in her food gardens. Instead of taking her infant with her to the fields, as is common among many horticulturalists, the Alorese mother leaves her baby with its father, grandparents, siblings, or any other kinfolk who happen to be available. Nursing is often postponed for several hours until the mother's return. Alorese children are notable for the length and intensity of their temper trantrums. Thus as adults the Alorese are suspicious and distrustful, display slovenly workmanship, and seem to have little interest in the outside world. It has been suggested that the infant pattern of oral frustration instills hostility toward the mother, and that this in turn is responsible for the apathetic and emotionally stunted adult personality that in turn is responsible for an apathetic and uncreative conception of the ancestor spirits.

Although the analysis of the causes of Alorese basic personality seems quite plausible, not enough is known about the effect of many other possibly relevant variables to draw firm conclusions. For example, leaving the child behind each day may indicate a marked amount

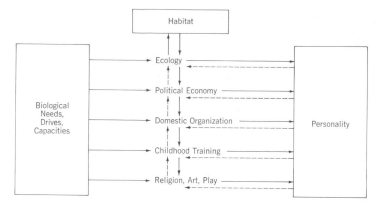

Figure 26-5. AN ALTERNATIVE SCHEMATIC OF THE RELATIONSHIP BETWEEN BASIC PERSONALITY, CULTURE, AND NATURE. Dotted arrows indicate feedback.

of hostility of Alorese mothers toward their children, and it may be their hostility rather than oral frustration per se that lies at the basis of the tantrums and later apathy (cf. Barnouw 1973). Moreover additional variables not controlled for in the psychoanalytic approach may actually be decisive. Thus nutritional factors—adequacy of calorie, vitamin, and protein ration—and the incidence of disease—dysenteries, parasitical infection, anemias—undoubtedly also account for significant personality differences.

Many observers have suggested that the apparent listlessness and fatalism so often attributed to peasant populations in the underdeveloped tropics are caused by inadequate diets. This raises the possibility that personality concepts and psychodynamic mechanisms may not be needed as mediators between the ecology-maintenance system and the secondary or projective institutions. People who are hungry and physically ill are not likely to pay much attention to the refinement of their religious artwork.

An alternate way of conceptualizing basic personality is to see it largely as the determined product of all the institutions that comprise a cultural system. This alternative is diagrammed in Figure 26-5. Note that Figure 26-5 rejects the Freudian premise that personality is fixed primarily during childhood. Also rejected is the Neo-Freudian premise that childhood experiences concerned with oral, anal, and genital training have a more decisive impact on personality than do the multitude of other influences that impinge on children during their enculturation (to be discussed below). Figure 26-5 depicts culture as mediating between nature (habitat and biological needs, drives, and capacities) and the individual (personality), whereas Figure 26-4 depicts the individual as mediating between one part of culture and another. In the latter case a theory of psychodynamic processes is required in order to explain the occurrence of many cultural traits. In the former no such theory is required.

596

Alternative Models of Male Initiation Rituals

A clearer view of these alternatives can be obtained from John Whiting's (1969) attempt to use a psychodynamic theory to explain the occurrence of severe male puberty rites. These rites are defined as severe when they involve circumcision or other forms of mutilation, prolonged seclusion, beatings, and trials of courage and stamina. Whiting has shown that statistical correlations exist between such rites and seven other factors: (1) protein scarcities, (2) nursing of children for one or more years, (3) a prohibition on sex relations between husband and wife for one or more years after the birth of their child, (4) polygyny, (5) domestic sleeping arrangements in which mother and child sleep together and father sleeps elsewhere, (6) child training by women, and (7) patrilocality.

Following our model, the following chain develops: Low protein availability and the risk of Kwashiorkor [a protein deficiency disease] were correlated with an extended postpartum sex taboo to allow the mother time to nurse the infant through the critical stage before becoming pregnant again. The postpartum sex taboo was significantly correlated with the institution of polygyny, providing alternate sexual outlets to the male. Polygyny, in turn, is associated with mother-child households, child training by women, resultant cross-sex identity, and where patrilocality is also present, with initiation rites to resolve the conflict and properly inculcate male identity. [Harrington and Whiting 1973:492]

"Cross-sex identity" refers to the psychodynamic process by which boys who are reared exclusively by their mothers and older women identify themselves with their mothers and other women. Where patrilocality is present, functional consistency demands that adult males must have strong identification with their fathers and other males. Hence there is a conflict between what the male must do and think as an adult and what he is trained to do and think as an infant. Severe male initiation ceremonies are thus required to resolve this conflict by breaking the prepubescent identity. I have attempted to diagram the functional-causal links in Whiting's model in Figure 26-6.

The most important claim of this psychodynamic model is that the occurrence of severe male initiation rites cannot be understood apart from the psychological conflict concerning sex roles. It is the need for

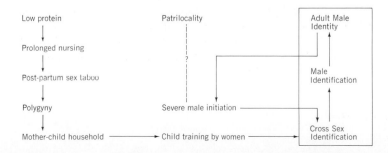

Figure 26-6. PSYCHODYNAMIC MODEL OF RELATIONSHIP BETWEEN LOW PROTEIN DIET AND SEVERE MALE INITIATION.

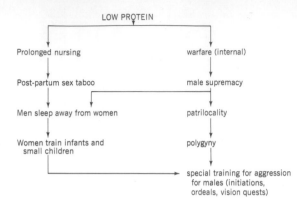

Figure 26-7. NONPSYCHO-LOGICAL MODEL OF RELA-TIONSHIP BETWEEN LOW PROTEIN DIET AND SEVERE MALE INITIATION.

adult male identity that determines the severe initiation, and it is the severe initiation that produces the adult male identity. The contribution of patrilocality to the severe male initiation is left ambiguous. And the relationship of patrilocality to the rest of the system is left unspecified. It is clear, however, that if one wishes to study the process of personality formation, this model has much to offer.

But in my opinion, if one wants to study culture as distinct from personality, this system is unnecessarily complicated. Alternative, less complex, and more comprehensive models equally consonant with the ethnographic facts can be constructed. Figure 26-7 shows one such alternative that links severe male initiation with the prestate warfare systems discussed in Chapter 13. In this model severe initiation rites for boys are viewed as consistent with the needs of fraternal interest groups involved in intensive warfare (see p. 269). No structural conflict is seen in the fact that women train infants and small children. Such a conflict would exist only if women did not treat little boys and little girls differently or if women trained boys to be more submissive than girls. The model predicts that the severity of the rites is governed by the severity of warfare involving fraternal interest groups and that if there is intensive internal warfare men will sleep away from women and children regardless of whether there is prolonged nursing or a postpartum sex taboo.

Other Influences on Personality

The Freudian theory of the psychodynamics of personality formation can be criticized in two regards: (1) personality is affected by cultural forces that are more general than the childhood training practices that have occupied the attention of neo-Freudian anthropologists; and (2) adult personality is directly affected by a wide range of cultural conditions, more or less independently of childhood experiences.

Radically different domestic organizations and political economies

598

obviously imply rather sharp personality differences. For example, reciprocal exchange patterns of the Bushmen as contrasted with redistributive exchange patterns among the Kwakiutl lead to patterns of modesty and self-deprecation on the one hand and boastfulness and self-glorification on the other (see p. 290). It is not necessary to assume that there are oral, anal, or genital childhood training practices that are especially relevant to these contrasts. Highly generalized forms of approval and disapproval from peers, parents, siblings, and strangers actively experienced or passively observed throughout an individual's life are more than adequate to account for the attitudes and behavior appropriate to reciprocal as opposed to redistributive exchange systems. Among societies that keep a portion of their population in bondage as slaves the mentality of slave and slave-owner need not be shaped primarily by different Freudian child-training practices. Obviously it is convenient to owners and masters to inculcate servile attitudes in the children of peons and slaves and other exploited groups, but this is more likely to be done through conscious, overt threats and punishments rather than through subtle toilet training or nursing schedules whose effects are not yet well understood even by psychoanalysts. Several studies (Barry, Child, and Bacon 1959; Aberle 1961a) have pointed out that wherever hunting constitutes an important subsistence technique, special emphasis is placed upon rearing self-reliant and persevering males with high frustration thresholds. Peasant populations, on the other hand, are frequently marked by submissiveness, fatalism, and anxiety. Similarly Robert Edgerton (1971) has shown that pastoralists in East Africa tend to be more open, are overtly aggressive, and show considerable independence, whereas neighboring farming peoples are passive, anxious, and covertly hostile. It is not necessary to assume that the personality attributes in question—whose existence cannot be doubted—are produced and sustained only by contrastive sets of influences impinging on childhood. Individuals reared in cultural settings where rents, landlords, taxes, jails, and police officers are unknown are surely subject to an entire life-long field of distinctive conditioning influences relevant to personality.

Too great an emphasis upon childhood training practices neglects the fact that it is adults who do the training and that the behavior and thought of these adults respond to the stresses and opportunities of adult life. Any regimen of childhood training practices probably has a wide latitude of potential effect simply by virtue of the extent to which adults are hungry or well fed, sickly or in good health, laden with debts or fears, hopeful or in despair.

Some of the most powerful influences on personality in the world

599

today emanate from the institutions of politico-economic systems that impinge simultaneously and totally upon every phase of the life-cycle, from birth to death. The political economy of communist China, for example, appears to be creating profound changes in the personality structure of its educated elites by an unremitting barrage of rewards, precepts, threats, and promises designed to eradicate individualistic, competitive, and other "bourgeois" traits deemed incompatible with the emergent communist personality. The influence of capitalism on personality is no less pervasive. Children reared in political economies dominated by the price-market-and-profit complex are enculturated to the belief that everything has its price—that air, water, and land are commodities. People have a price at which they can be induced to "sell out." They are also encouraged to compete with each other in order to increase their "net worth" calculated in dollars. And they are exposed not only in early childhood but throughout their entire lives to advertising arts that legitimize lies and deceptions as the means of accumulating personal wealth and power.

According to Freudian theory, competitive entrepreneurial personalities—hard-driving people who amass capital by saving instead of spending—are "anal" types who have been subjected to severe toilet training and derive pleasure from withholding their feces in infancy and their money in adulthood. However, no one to my knowledge has thus far been able to demonstrate that the most successful entrepreneurs are people who are most severely toilet trained nor that capitalists in general are more anal than socialists.

(2) There has always been a considerable amount of opposition among psychologists to Freud's emphasis upon childhood as the primary source of adult personality. An individual's pattern of behavior and thought is a product of the experiences of the past interacting with the constraints and opportunities of the present. Not infrequently the constraints and opportunities of the present overshadow much of what was learned in the past and radically reorganize the personalities of individuals and whole groups. Stanley Milgram (1974) has been able to show that under experimental conditions a wide range of adult personalities will accept the role of authoritarian disciplinarians and administer what they believe to be dangerous high-voltage electric shocks to human subjects in order to obtain obedience. Radical reorganizations of adult personality are also implicit in phenomena such as political brainwashing associated with detention in prisoner of war and concentration camps. Studies of inmates of Nazi death camps indicate that there was a convergent reorganization of personality in many individuals of diverse backgrounds toward a submissive, self-hating complex that has been compared with the personality

600

complex found under slavery (Cohen 1953; Elkins 1961). One of the most dramatic examples of the power of "adult training techniques" is the wartime conversion of civilians into tyrant officers and enlisted automatons skilled in the art of war. Also to be considered is the erosion of spontaneity and responsibility characteristic of an adult life spent in the service of some immense faceless bureaucracy (Merton 1940).

Several other examples of the impact of present conditions on adult personality have been dealt with in previous chapters. Cargo cults, military messianism, and other convulsive revitalization phenomena involve a sudden reorganization en masse of adult behavior patterns. Much of the discussion of the culture of poverty and of the problems of underdevelopment also indicated that adults were constrained by institutional structures to act in certain ways that could not be changed much by altering childhood training practices. Similarly the structure of relations between races and castes continually recreates and reinforces hates, fears, and tensions among adults as well as among children.

The Ephemerality of Modal Personality and Dominant Values

Culture and personality studies sometimes give the impression that modal personality, whether expressed in Freudian psychodynamic terms or in terms of dominant themes and values, is the stable, enduring core of social life. (Abram Kardiner once claimed that the basic personality structure of Western civilization had not changed in two thousand years.) But it is no less true of modal personality than of all other aspects of culture that change is the rule and stasis the exception. Ruth Benedict (1934) stressed the peaceful, noncompetitive, and even-tempered disposition of the Pueblo Indians. Yet, as I mentioned earlier (p. 556), during the sixteenth and seventeenth centuries the Pueblos of New Mexico fought a series of bloody messianic wars against the Spanish invaders. During these abortive struggles, the Spanish colonists were massacred and the bodies of priests and administrators were piled on the altars of the churches which then were burned to the ground.

Similar reversals from peaceful to warlike propensities or vice versa are quite common. The Jews in Nazi Germany failed to organize an effective resistance against Hitler's genocidal programs and were depicted as having lost their capacity for forceful struggle. In one generation, however, Jewish refugees created Israel, a militaristic

601

Figure 26-8. TOKYO DEMONSTRATION. Students face riot police during Okinawa Day demonstrations. (UPI Photo)

state whose citizen-soldiers formed themselves into one of the world's most formidable armies.

During World War II the Japanese were described as pathologically obedient. Postwar generations of Japanese college youth, however, have proved even more rebellious than their U.S. counterparts. During the 1960s every major Japanese campus was the scene of pitched battle between thousands of students and police officers. In addition, open contempt for parental authority is exhibited by large numbers of Japanese youth who have abandoned traditional Japanese clothing, etiquette, music, and family life in favor of Western models.

The shift in modal personality among American blacks should also be noted. The Afro-American male was once depicted as a psychologically damaged individual whose aggressive impulses were turned inward giving rise to feelings of worthlessness and inadequacy. In their effort to please members of the superordinate white groups, blacks were said to exaggerate their own shortcomings by accepting the self-image of a slow-witted, affable, shuffling "sambo." With the advent of the black power movement, the sambo stereotype was broken. Black leaders characterized by haughty self-confidence,

602

sharp wit, and penetrating intelligence, fought the sambo image in the courts and in the streets, as well as in the nursery (Hannerz 1970).

Weston La Barre (1966) called the Aymara of Bolivia "morose, cruel, vindictive, sullen, hateful, and treacherous" on the basis of his analysis of Aymara folktales. Every Aymara tale collected by La Barre turned out to be concerned with conflict over food, deceitfulness, chicanery, violence, busybody informers, murderers, and sorcerers. As in the case of the Chimborazo peasants of Ecuador, the temperament of the Aymara reflects a historic process of sustained deprivation and exploitation at the hands of both Indian and Spanish ruling classes.

If the Aymara, as evidenced in their folktales (and indeed throughout the rest of their culture), are apprehensive, crafty, suspicious, violent, treacherous, and hostile, one important reason for this may be that such a character structure is an understandable response to their having lived for perhaps as long as a millennium under rigidly hierarchic and absolutist economic, military, and religious controls.   [La Barre 1966:143]

Recent studies of the Aymara indicate that this picture is changing rapidly as a result of new economic, military, and political conditions in Bolivia (Heath 1966; Plummer 1966).

Oedipus and Masculinity

According to Freud a traumatic, universal, and unavoidable conflict takes place during the years preceding puberty. This conflict is called the *Oedipus conflict* and it is engendered by biologically determined sexual strivings and jealousies within the nuclear family. The awakening sexuality of young boys is directed first toward their mothers. Discovering that his mother is the sexual object of his father, a boy finds himself in competition with his father for sexual mastery of the same woman. The father, while providing protection, also provides stern discipline. He suppresses his son's attempt to express sexual love for his mother. The son is deeply frustrated and fantasizes that he is omnipotent and that he will kill his father. This seething hostility and jealousy arouses fear and guilt in the young boy: fear, because the father in fact or in fancy threatens to cut off his penis and testicles; and guilt, because the father is not only hated but also loved. To resolve this conflict successfully the young boy must redirect his sexuality toward other females and learn how to overcome his fear and how to express his hostility in constructive ways.

For the young girl Freud envisioned a parallel but fundamentally different trauma. A girl's sexuality is also initially directed toward her

603

mother. But at the phallic stage the little girl makes a fateful discovery: she lacks a penis. She blames her mother for this and redirects her sexual desires away from her mother toward her father.

Why this takes place depends upon the girl's reaction of disappointment when she discovers that a boy possesses a protruding sex organ, the penis, while she has only a cavity. Several important consequences follow from this traumatic discovery. In the first place she holds her mother responsible for her castrated condition. . . . In the second place, she transfers her love to her father because he has the valued organ which she aspires to share with him. However, her love for the father and for other men as well is mixed with a feeling of envy because they possess something she lacks. Penis envy is the female counterpart of castration anxiety in the boy. . . . To some extent, the lack of a penis is compensated for when a woman has a baby, especially if it is a boy baby.   [Hall and Lindzey 1967:28]

Further developments for the girl are also different. Although she must learn to accept the incest barriers between herself and her father, her passive role does not call forth the energetic repression that is directed toward the male's Oedipal strivings.

Starting with Bronislaw Malinowski's (1927) research on the avunculocal Trobriand family (see p. 342), anthropologists have criticized the concept of the Oedipus complex on the grounds that it fails to take into account culturally determined variations in domestic organization. In the Trobriands, for example, it is the boy's uncle, not his father, who disciplines him. Nonetheless anthropological research has not been able to disprove the widespread, if not universal, occurrence of psychodynamic patterns that resemble Oedipal strivings in the minimal sense of sexually charged hostility between older generation males and their sons or nephews (cf. Roheim 1950; Parsons 1967; Foster 1972; Barnouw 1973). However, extreme skepticism is warranted toward the view that even this aspect of the Oedipus complex is universal because of innate and inevitable instinctual urges.

The psychodynamics of the Oedipus complex take for granted or postulate as instinctual what I have been calling the masculine-male complex. A nineteenth-century Viennese variant of this complex, stressing activity, bravery, physical prowess, virility, aggressive sexuality, and the dominance of males over females provided the model for what Freud considered to be normal human behavior. One can agree with Freudians that wherever the objective of child-rearing institutions is to produce aggressive, manipulative, fearless, virile, and dominant males, some form of sexually charged hostility between the junior and senior males is inevitable. But this does not mean that the Oedipus complex is an inevitable outcome of human nature. For, as I have shown, the masculine-male complex is closely related to popula-

604

Figure 26-9. FREUD'S MILIEU. A turn-of-century middle-class father with his two sons. Stern but protective. (The Bettmann Archive)

tion control strategies and warfare, both of which are eminently subject to cultural control.

Psychoanalytically oriented scholars have long noted the correlation between warfare and intergenerational hostility among males as expressed in puberty rituals and mythic themes. In the words of Maurice Walsh and Barbara Scandalis (1975):

As an outgrowth of the psychoanalytic approach to an understanding of social motivation and behavior it is our hypothesis that primitive male initiation rites and modern organized warfare are equivalent behavior patterns . . . both must have a single unconscious motivating force in common—which is the Oedipal rivalry. . . . Psychoanalytic research demonstrates that the Oedipal rivalry alone of all possible causes furnishes adequate explanation for . . . institutionalized situations where sons become the victims of murder at the hands of an "enemy" as the result of the manipulation of the "father" generation. . . . The aggression of the sons and the father is thus unconsciously transferred to the "enemy" men and to the women and children who are raped and destroyed by the projection onto them of the repressed aggressive and sexual desires. . . .

This view corresponds to the general culture and personality model that insists that one cannot understand the causal-functional relationships among institutions without the mediation of personality concepts. A model of the Freudian view of the causes of war would look like this:

$$\text{Biological Drives} \longrightarrow \text{Oedipus Complex} \longrightarrow \begin{cases} \text{Male Initiation} \\ \text{War} \end{cases}$$

Oedipus and Masculinity

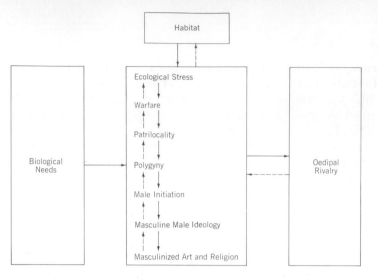

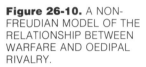

Figure 26-10. A NON-FREUDIAN MODEL OF THE RELATIONSHIP BETWEEN WARFARE AND OEDIPAL RIVALRY.

An alternative model consistent with the model on page 598 and with the explanation for warfare and the male-supremacist institutions discussed in Chapter 24 is shown in Figure 26-10. The inclusion of feedback arrows in Figure 26-10 might seem to make the difference between the two models rather trivial. But this is far from true. From the standpoint of practical significance the two models are diametrically opposed. In the first model, the prime way to prevent war is to change the Oedipus complex. In the second, the prime way to prevent war is to change the cultural factors that are responsible for ecological stress.

Oedipus and Femininity

Freud believed that little girls necessarily undergo an Oedipal development sharply distinct from that of little boys. As just shown, girls are supposed to suffer the life-long trauma of penis envy as a result of their discovery that they are anatomically "incomplete." In this fashion Freud sought to ground the psychological supremacy of males in the unalterable facts of anatomy—hence the Freudian aphorism: "Anatomy is destiny." Their lack of a penis "debases" women and dooms them to a passive and subordinate role—the role of the "second sex." For Freud the best hope that a woman has of overcoming her penis envy is to accept a passive secondary role in life, develop her charm and sexual attractiveness, marry and have male babies.

Her happiness is great if later on this wish for a baby finds fulfillment in reality, and quite especially so if the baby is a little boy who brings the longed-for penis with him.   [Freud quoted in Millet 1970:185]

606   At this point the Freudian mythos closely resembles the ideology of

the *couvade,* an institution whereby males in some societies observe prenatal taboos, confine themselves to the hammock when their wife gives birth, and remain in seclusion when she goes back to work, thereby asserting male supremacy over the birth process. Comments Millet: "Freudian logic has succeeded in converting childbirth . . . into nothing more than a hunt for a male organ. It somehow becomes the male prerogative even to give birth, as babies are but surrogate penises" (1970:185).

Ethnographic research indicates that viable social systems can perfectly well embody alternative definitions of ideal male and female temperaments. Margaret Mead's (1950) study of three New Guinea tribes—the Arapesh, Mundugumor, and Tchambuli—is the classic anthropological work on the spectrum of cultural definitions of ideal masculine and feminine personalities. Mead discovered that among the Arapesh both men and women are expected to behave in a mild, sympathetic, and cooperative manner, reminiscent of what we expect from an ideal mother. Among the Mundugumor, men and women are expected to be equally fierce and aggressive, and both sexes satisfied Mead's criteria for being masculine. Finally, among the Tchambuli, the women shave their heads, are prone to hearty laughter, show comradely solidarity, and are aggressively efficient as food-providers. Tchambuli men, on the other hand, are preoccupied with art, spend a great deal of time on their hairdos, and are always gossiping about the opposite sex. Although Mead's interpretations have been challenged as too subjective, there is no doubt that marked contrasts in sex roles do exist in different cultures and that in few parts of the world outside of nineteenth-century Vienna can one find the precise configuration that Freud believed to be universal. For example, Mervyn Meggitt (1964) has proposed a classification of New Guinea highland cultures into two groups on the basis of the extent which they act like "prudes" or "lechers."

Among the Mae Enga, who are Meggitt's archetypical "prudes," men and women sleep apart. A man never enters the sleeping room at the rear of his wife's hut, and a woman never enters the men's house. Contact with menstrual blood can cause sickness and death for a Mae Enga man. Mae Enga men believe that intercourse is debilitating, and after intercourse they undergo purification by sitting in a smokey hut to protect themselves. Mae Enga bachelors swear sexual abstinence until they are married and feel uneasy and anxious if sex is discussed, especially if women are present. In contrast, the Kuma, who are Meggitt's "lechers," share sleeping quarters, have no fear of female pollution, do not practice purification or initiation rites, and gain prestige through boasting about their conquests. Kuma girls attend

607

courting parties at which they select sexual partners from among both married and unmarried males. Intercourse is discussed openly by both sexes. Lorraine Sexton (1973) has suggested that these differences may be associated with the high population pressure being experienced by the Mae Enga and the relatively low population density of the Kuma, prudery being a mechanism that cuts back on the frequency of intercourse and thus limits fertility.

Culture and Sexuality

Very little of a reliable nature is actually known about human sexuality in relation to culture. Anthropologists are certain however that knowledge about sexuality gained from the study of people living in one culture can never be taken as representative of human sexual behavior in general. All aspects of sexual relationships from infantile experiences through courtship and marriage exhibit an immense amount of cultural variation. Many different arrangements of "lechery" and "prudery" occur. For example, among the Mangaians of Polynesia boys and girls never hold hands, and husbands and wives never embrace in public. Brothers and sisters must never even be seen together. Mothers and daughters and fathers and sons do not discuss sexual matters with one another. And yet both sexes engage in intercourse well before puberty. After puberty both sexes enjoy an intense premarital sex life. Girls receive varied nightly suitors in their parents' house, and boys compete with their rivals to see how many orgasms they can achieve. Mangaian girls are not interested in romantic protestations, extensive petting, or foreplay. Sex is not a reward for masculine affection; rather, affection is the reward for sexual fulfillment:

Sexual intimacy is *not* achieved by first demonstrating personal affection; the reverse is true. The Mangaian . . . girl takes an immediate demonstration of sexual virility and masculinity as the first test of her partner's desire for her and as the reflection of her own desirability. . . . Personal affection may or may not result from acts of sexual intimacy, but the latter are requisite to the former—exactly the reverse of the ideals of western society.   [Marshall 1971:118]

According to a consensus reached by Marshall's informants, males sought to reach orgasm at least once every night, and women expected each episode to last at least fifteen minutes. They agreed on the following table as indicative of typical male sexual activity:

608

Approximate Age	Average Number of Orgasms per Night	Average Number of Nights per Week
18	3	7
28	2	5–6
38	1	3–4
48	1	2–3

Source: Ibid.: 123.

A very different attitude toward sexual activity appears to be characteristic of Hindu India. There is a widespread belief among Hindu men that semen is a source of strength and that it should not be squandered:

> Everyone knew that semen was not easily found; it takes forty days and forty drops of blood to make one drop of semen. . . . Everyone was agreed . . . that the semen is ultimately stored in a reservoir in the head, whose capacity is twenty *tolas* (6.8 ounces). . . . Celibacy was the first requirement of true fitness, because every sexual orgasm meant the loss of a quantity of semen, laboriously formed.   [Carstairs 1967; quoted in Moni Nag 1972:235]

Contrary to popular stereotypes concerning Hindu eroticism, there is evidence that coital frequency among Hindus is considerably less than among U.S. whites in comparable age groups. Moni Nag gives the following tabular resumé of average weekly coital frequency for Hindu and white U.S. women:

Age Group	White U.S. Women	Hindu Women
10–14	—	.4
15–19	3.7	1.5
20–24	3.0	1.9
25–29	2.6	1.8
30–34	2.3	1.1
35–39	2.0	0.7
40–44	1.7	0.2
over 44	1.3	0.3

Source: Adapted from Nag (1972:235).

It is also clear, again contrary to popular impressions, that India's high level of fertility and population growth is not the result of sexual overindulgence caused by "not having anything else to do for entertainment at night."

Anatomy Is Not Destiny

Since differences in the anatomy and physiology of human males and females are so obvious it is easy to be misled into believing that sex-linked roles and statuses are primarily biological rather than cultural phenomena. Men are taller, heavier, and stronger than women; hence it is "natural" that hunting and warfare should be male specialties. Men have higher levels of testosterone; hence they are "naturally" more aggressive, sexually and otherwise, and are "naturally" dominant over women. Moreover since women menstruate, become pregnant, and lactate, they "naturally" are the ones to stay at home to care for and feed infants and children. But modern anthropology stands opposed to the view that anatomy is destiny. Males are not born with an innate tendency to be hunters or warriors or to be sexually and politically dominant over women. Nor are women born with an innate tendency to care for infants and children and to be sexually and politically subordinate. Rather it has been the case that under a broad but finite set of cultural and natural conditions certain sex-linked specialties have been selected for in a large number of cultures. As the underlying demographic, technological, economic, and ecological conditions to which these sex-linked roles are adapted change, new cultural definitions of sex-linked roles will emerge.

Despite the prevalence of male-dominated political and military institutions, enough evidence exists to document a great range of female roles and statuses in different societies. As Karen Sacks (n.d.) has argued, one cannot go from the proposition "women are subordinate as regards political authority in most societies to women are subordinate in all respects in all societies." Contrasting several African cultures, Sacks (1971) found that Mbuti and Lovedu women maintained control over their garden produce, participated in food exchanges, gave beer feasts, married wives with cattle bride-price (see p. 319), and held political office. But among the Ganda women could not dispose of land, nor of bananas for making beer, and held no political power.

Anthropological research lends strong support to the view that the particular definitions of masculinity and femininity found in many

Figure 26-11. FEMALE SHAMAN. Piegan "medicine woman." Shamans are usually males. (Museum of the American Indian, Heye Foundation)

Figure 26-12 (opposite, top). BURDEN BEARER. In many cultures women are expected to carry infants plus heavy loads. This woman is returning to her home near Agwarra, Northern Nigeria. (United Nations)

Figure 26-13 (opposite, bottom). CARRYING WATER IS USUALLY WOMAN'S WORK. Amhara woman, Ethiopia (left); Guatemalan woman (right) with water pot resting on small grass coil. (Eugene Gordon)

610

Figure 26-14 (left). WOL-OFF WOMAN. Pail is for carrying fish. (Eugene Gordon)

Figure 26-15 (right). ARUNTA MOTHER AND CHILD. All purpose carrying dish on head and digging stick in hand. (American Museum of Natural History)

contemporary societies may be unnecessarily restrictive and unrealistically demanding. The prevalent fear of sexual deviance; the male's preoccupation with sexual potency; and the female's obsession with motherhood, sexual competence, and sexual attractiveness cannot be accounted for or justified by purely biological factors. Alternate standards of masculinity and femininity more responsive to individual differences are perfectly compatible with human nature.

Sex Roles in Industrial Society

Under industrial conditions, most of the male-dominated specialties in agriculture, industry, and government cannot be said to benefit from the extra quantum of muscle power associated with the male physique. Although menstruation, pregnancy, and lactation involve disadvantages in a few situations requiring rapid mobility or continuous effort under stress, modern governments and corporations are already adjusted to high levels of absenteeism and frequent change of personnel. Moreover with the long-range trend toward decreased fertility under industrial conditions women are pregnant on the average less than 3 percent of their lives.

It is sometimes argued that menstruation interferes with the capacity of women to make rational decisions under stress and hence that

612

the exclusion of women from positions of industrial, governmental, or military leadership continues to be based upon a realistic adjustment to biological givens. However, the association between menstruation and irritability, depression and physical pain, is not necessarily a biological given. There is wide variation in the psychological states associated with menstruation among women in different cultures. An alternate hypothesis is that the folklore about menstrual disabilities is itself at least in part a product of male supremacy rather than one of its causes. Noting that the Arapesh of New Guinea do not report menstrual pains, Margaret Mead (1949:220) has suggested that the only consistent factor among women who manifest such pains is "exposure during childhood to another female who reported menstrual pain." There is no reason to doubt that the psychological impairment experienced during menstruation can be reduced by an enculturation program aimed at minimizing instead of maximizing the expectation of distress.

Menstruation cannot be considered a barrier to sexual parity in positions of leadership and control. The top leadership of the U.S. military-industrial-educational establishment, and of the equivalent groups in the Soviet Union and other contemporary great powers, consists of men who are chronologically well past their physical prime. Many of these leaders suffer from high blood pressure, diseases of the teeth and gums, poor digestion, failing eyesight, hearing losses, backaches, fallen arches, and other clinical syndromes associated with advancing age. Like menstruation these disorders also frequently produce psychological stress. Healthy, premenopausal women certainly enjoy a biological edge over the typical male "elder statesman." As for older, postmenopausal women, biological parity with men exists by definition.

It is thus difficult to see how the distribution of sex-linked roles in contemporary industrial states can be accounted for by appeal to biological imperatives or adaptive ecological processes. The political and economic subordination of women to men in industrial contexts makes sense only as a stratification phenomenon—it is adaptive primarily for the superordinate stratum.

Industrialization has set the stage for the end of the long epoch of male supremacy. Yet sexual inequality continues to be a prominent feature of both capitalist and communist industrial systems. In the United States the entrance of women into spheres of work and positions of authority previously preempted by males should not be mistaken for sexual equality. For women who have the good fortune to penetrate the top-paying professions and who acquire senior administrative and executive responsibilities and rewards, the new

613

Figure 26-16. SOVIET UNIVERSITY STUDENTS. Female students outnumber males. (Sovfoto)

feminine consciousness may indeed provide genuine personal liberation. But in the United States only a tiny fraction of males or females can hope to escape the alienating, degrading, and boring jobs that are characteristic of the present-day industrial wage-labor market. The welcoming of additional millions of semiskilled female workers to the U.S. work force may simply reflect the decreasing purchasing power of the average worker as a result of long-term inflationary trends. This prospect is especially ominous for black and other minority groups whose families already contain two wage earners. Middle-class white females enjoy an advantage over black and white lower-income females in competition for middle-class jobs. Their entrance into the job market can only retard the rate of advance of black families and increase the disparity between average family incomes among blacks and whites. As noted by the President's Council of Economic Advisors (U.S. Economic Council 1974), this danger will increase in proportion to the success that women experience in earning as much money as their husbands: "If a strong positive correlation between incomes of husbands and wives should develop, this correlation could increase relative income inequality among families." The implication of this analysis is not that women are ill-advised to seek sexual parity, but that a failure to understand the constraints and possibilities of the larger system within which the struggle for women's liberation is being waged may lead—not for the first time in history—to paradoxical and undesired results (cf. Gold 1973).

614

Women's status in the Soviet Union is a case in point. Sexual equality was and still is a fundamental aim of the Bolshevik revolution and the Soviet State. Women were to be transformed from housewives to workers to take their place alongside of men in the struggle to build the new communist society. Fifty years after the revolution women have indeed succeeded in entering every segment of the economy and administration formerly occupied by men. They are construction workers, street cleaners, engineers, doctors, ditch-diggers, scientists, polit bureau chiefs. But at the same time they are still expected to assume primary responsibility for keeping house, shopping, cooking, and caring for the children. And this double burden has prevented them from reaching the highest positions in the top fields of science, industry, and government, which still continue to be dominated by men (Rosenthal 1975).

Determinism, Science, and Culture

Regardless of the precise set of factors that ultimately account for the formation of personality, it is clear that in general personality is a product of cultural variables. These variables in turn are associated with causal processes that obey the basic uniformitarian principle of science: under similar conditions, similar causes produce similar effects.

Although anthropology has not been able to develop firm causal explanations in the domains reviewed in this book, many plausible hypotheses and theories can be advanced. There seems no reason to doubt that all the major varieties of cultural phenomena, including modal personality types, can eventually be explained by deterministic principles.

Patterning of individual personality to conform with culturally determined variables poses a major dilemma for the conscious, concerned student and citizen. If individual behavior is largely a predictable outcome of cultural conditioning, what significance does anthropology attribute to the strivings of individuals to change their personalities or to modify their cultures? Are we all automatons fated to act out our particular predestined personal and cultural configuration? Is our sense of free will merely an illusion? Can we hold ourselves and each other responsible for the choice of personal and cultural life-style that we exhibit?

It has been said that a determinist view of human history leads either to fanaticism or fatalism. Fanaticism is the belief that history is on one's side and that there is no alternative course of action that can

615

be rationally entertained. Fatalism is the belief that an outcome, whether desirable or undesirable, will occur regardless of individual striving. Neither of these attitudes is justified by the facts and theories described in this book.

Modern anthropology rejects both fanaticism and fatalism on the grounds that the determinism governing cultural phenomena is a matter of probability rather than of certainty.

Probabilistic Causality

The principle of uniformitarian relationships concerns *similar* variables under *similar* conditions *tending* to give rise to *similar* consequences. As you have seen, correlations indicative of causal processes are never fulfilled in 100 percent of the cases. Indeed, most of the generalizations discussed in this book have weak levels of predictability compared with what a chemist or a physicist would be willing to accept (although anthropology's "batting average" would be quite respectable among meterologists and geologists).* Exceptions may arise from several different sources: errors may be made in data collection and processing; the statement of the initial conditions may be inadequate; the conditions may be undergoing evolutionary change; and finally, the generalization itself may be poorly constructed. All these sources of error may be reduced to one: lack of sufficient information, or incomplete knowledge.

Whether uncertainty arises from the free will of the human actor or the lack of omniscience on the part of the anthropologist is one and the same thing from the point of view of the individual. The fact is that one cannot be certain that a particular set of cultural conditions will always produce a particular cultural or personality type. If you believe that you cannot alter your personality or your culture, and if you act or do not act accordingly, you simply render the most probable outcome more probable. On the other hand, if you believe that there is one and only one possible outcome, and act accordingly, you may

*Many readers will be familiar with the fact that even in physics no claim for 100 percent predictability is made. In the realm of microparticles Heisenberg's "principle of indeterminacy" reigns, one of whose practical consequences is the inability to predict the order in which the atoms in a radioactive substance will undergo decay. Probability rather than certainty also reigns in macrophysics. For example, it has never been shown that gravitational force is constant for all regions of space or for all phases of cosmic evolution. Thus the paradigm "one-exception-falsifies-the-law" is no more applicable to physics than it is to anthropology. True the predictability normally associated with physics is much higher than that associated with anthropology. But that is because physics eliminates all poorly controlled conditions and variables, that is, it avoids the study of actual historic events.

616

increase the probability of that outcome but you can never render it a certainty.

Thus recognition of the probabilistic nature of scientific prediction effectively solves the classical problem of how to account for free will in a universe that exhibits uniformitarian regularities.

The findings of anthropology are opposed to the view that the individual is helpless before the implacable march of history and that resignation and despair are appropriate responses for those who are discontent with present-day social conditions.

The future is never so completely predictable as to render the alternatives irrelevant or superfluous. The probabilistic nature of cultural evolution imposes nothing so certainly upon the individual as the necessity of making choices. Each decision to accept, resist, or change the current order alters the probability that a particular evolutionary outcome will occur. Men and women of deep moral conviction are never driven to despair or acquiescence by the knowledge that the way of life they seek for themselves and their children seems remote and improbable. It is perfectly rational to meet the challenge of bad odds by redoubling one's efforts.

For the activist, scientifically informed predictions about the probable trajectories of events and probable consequences of struggling for or against a particular outcome are urgent practical matters. In making an informed political decision, however, the fact that one's choice may itself be a product of deterministic conditions is *not* a matter of practical consequence. The same kind of probabilistic calculations pertain to individual decisions as to the course of history. You are not obliged by science to believe that you can act in one and only one way. While the predictions of cultural anthropology are predicated upon the subordination of the individual to the forces of enculturation, every society nonetheless exhibits a wide spectrum of individual personalities. Enculturation is a form of programming, but knowledge of the content of the program is always quite incomplete. Thus individuals never possess anything more than a probabilistic knowledge of how they will act under given contingencies.

At the same time, I hold it perniciously false to suppose that all cultural events are equally probable and that by mere force of will the inspired individual can alter the trajectory of an entire cultural system in a direction convenient to any philosophy. Convergent and parallel trajectories far outnumber divergent trajectories in cultural evolution. Most people are conformists. History repeats itself in countless acts of individual obedience to cultural rule and pattern, and individual wills seldom prevail in matters requiring radical alterations of deeply conditioned beliefs and practices. Revolutions,

617

alterations of deeply conditioned beliefs and practices. Revolutions, therefore, require great opportunities as well as great men and women.

If anthropology has any suggestion to those seeking to participate in the creation of novel varieties of personal and cultural life, it is that to change the world one should first try to understand it. The importance of this advice varies directly with the odds against the desired personal or cultural innovation. When the odds are drastically against a hoped-for outcome, avoidable ignorance of the causal factors at work amounts to moral duplicity, especially if others are called upon to risk their lives and sacrifice their well-being. In this sense disciplined knowledge of culture, people, and nature is a moral obligation of all men, women, and children who truly love each other.

BIBLIOGRAPHICAL
REFERENCES

ABEGGLEN, JAMES
1970   "The Economic Growth of Japan." *Scientific American* 222, No. 3 (March):31–37.

ABERLE, DAVID F.
1961   "Culture and Socialization." In *Psychological Anthropology: Approaches to Culture and Personality*, Francis Hsu, ed., pp. 381–399. Homewood (Ill.): Dorsey Press.

ACHESON, JAMES M.
1972   "Limited Good or Limited Goods: Response to Economic Opportunity in a Tarascan Pueblo." *American Anthropologist* 74:1152–1169.
1974   "Reply to George Foster." *American Anthropologist* 76:57–62.

ADAMS, M., AND J. V. NEIL
1967   "The Children of Incest." *Pediatrics* 40:55–62.

ADAMS, RICHARD N.
1968   "An Inquiry into the Nature of the Family." In *Selected Studies in Marriage and the Family*, R. F. Winch and L. W. Goodman, eds., pp. 45–57. New York: Holt, Rinehart and Winston.
1970   *Crucifixion by Power.* Austin: University of Texas Press.

ADAMS, ROBERT MCC.
1966   *The Evolution of Urban Society: Early Mesopotamia and Prehispanic Mexico.* Chicago: Aldine.
1972   "Patterns of Urbanization in Early Southern Mesopotamia." In *Man, Settlement, and Urbanism*, P. J. Ucko, R. Tringham, and G. W. Dimbleby, eds. Cambridge (Mass.): Schenkman.

ALLAND, ALEXANDER, JR.
1970   *Adaptation in Cultural Evolution: An Approach to Medical Anthropology.* New York: Columbia University Press.
1972   *The Human Imperative.* New York: Columbia University Press.

ALLAND, ALEXANDER, JR., AND BONNIE MCCAY
1973   "The Concept of Adaptation in Biological and Cultural Evolution." In *Handbook of Social and Cultural Anthropology*, J. Honigmann, pp. 143–178. Chicago: Rand McNally.

ARDREY, ROBERT
  1961   *African Genesis: A Personal Investigation into the Animal Origins and Nature of Man.* New York: Atheneum.

ARON, RAYMOND
  1966   "Social Class, Political Class, Ruling Class." In *Class, Status, and Power: Social Stratification in Comparative Perspective*, R. Bendix and S. M. Lipset, eds., pp. 201–210. New York: Free Press.

AZEVEDO, THALES
  1956   "Classes sociais e grupos de prestigio na Bahia." *Arquivos de Universidad de Bahia* 5.

BACH, EMMON W.
  1964   *An Introduction to Transformational Grammars.* New York: Holt, Rinehart and Winston.

BADA, JEFFREY F., R. A. SCHROEDER, AND G. F. CARTER
  1974   "New Evidence for the Antiquity of Man in North America." *Science* 184:791–793.

BAGLEY, WILLIAM C.
  1924   "The Army Tests and the Pro-Nordic Propaganda." *Educational Review* 67:179–187.

BAKER, PAUL
  1958   "Racial Differences in Heat Tolerance." *American Journal of Physical Anthropology* 16:287–305.

BAKOS, L., AND A. L. MACMILLAN
  1973   "Malignant Melanoma in East Anglia, England: An Eleven Year Survey by Type and Site." *British Journal of Dermatology* 88(6):551–556.

BAO, RUO-WANG (JEAN PASQUALINI), AND RUDOLPH CHELMINSKI
  1973   *Prisoner of Mao.* New York: Coward, McCann & Geoghegan.

BARBER, BERNARD
  1968   "Social Mobility in Hindu India." In *Social Mobility in the Caste System*, J. Silverberg, ed., pp. 18–35. The Hague: Mouton.

BARNES, J. A.
  1960   "Marriage and Residential Continuity." *American Anthropologist* 62:850–866.

BARNOUW, VICTOR
  1973   *Culture and Personality.* Homewood (Ill.): Dorsey Press.

BARRAU, JACQUES
  1967   "De l'homme cueilleur á l'homme cultivateur: L'example océanien." *Cahiers de Histoire Mondiale* 10:275–292.

BARRY, HERBERT, I. L. CHILD, AND M. K. BACON
  1959   "Relation of Child Training to Subsistence Economy." *American Anthropologist* 61:51–63.

BARTHELME, DONALD
  1970   *City Life.* New York: Farrar, Straus, and Giroux.

BAYARD, DONN T.
  1968   "Excavations at Non Nok Tha, Northeastern Thailand: An Interim Report." *Asian Perspective* 13:109–143.

BEATTIE, JOHN
  1960   *Bunyoro: An African Kingdom.* New York: Holt, Rinehart and Winston.

BEAUMONT, PETER, AND J. C. VOGEL
  1972   "On a New Radiocarbon Chronology for Africa South of the Equator." *African Studies* 31:155–182.

BECK, BENJAMIN

1973   "Cooperative Tool Use by Captive Hamadryas Baboons." *Science* 182: 594–595.

1975   "Primate Tool Behavior." In *Socio-Ecology and Psychology of Primates*, R. H. Tuttle, ed. The Hague: Mouton. [In press.]

BELL, WESLEY, R. LEKACHMAN, AND A. SCHORR

1974   *Public Policy and Income Distributions.* New York: N. Y. U. Center for Studies in Income Maintenance Policy.

BENDER, DONALD R.

1967   "A Refinement of the Concept of Household: Families, Co-residence, and Domestic Functions." *American Anthropologist* 69:493–503.

BENDIX, REINHARD, AND S. M. LIPSET, EDITORS

1966   *Class, Status, and Power: Social Stratification in Comparative Perspective.* New York: Free Press.

BENEDICT, RUTH

1934   *Patterns of Culture.* Boston: Houghton Mifflin.

1938   "Religion." In *General Anthropology*, F. Boas, ed., pp. 627–665. New York: Columbia University Press.

BENNETT, JOHN

1975   "Ecosystem Analogies in Cultural Anthropology." In *The Concepts and Dynamics of Culture*, B. Bernardi, ed. The Hague: Mouton. [In press.]

BEREITER, CARL, AND S. ENGELMANN

1966   *Teaching Disadvantaged Children in Preschool.* Englewood Cliffs: Prentice-Hall.

BERG, ALAN

1973   *The Mutation Factor: A Study Jointly by the Foundation For Child Development and the Brookings Institution.* Washington: The Brookings Institution.

BERGGREN, WILLIAM A.

1969   "Cenozoic Chronostratigraphy, Planktonic Foraminiferal Zonation, and the Radiometric Time Scale." *Nature* 224:1072–1075.

1972   "A Cenozoic Time Scale." *Lethaia* 5:195–215.

BERNDT, CATHERINE H. AND RONALD M. BERNDT

1973   *The Barbarians.* Hammondsworth (Eng.): Penguin Books.

BERREMAN, GERALD D.

1960   "Caste in India and the United States." *American Journal of Sociology* 66:120–127.

1966   "Caste in Cross-cultural Perspective." In *Japan's Invisible Race: Caste in Culture and Personality*, G. de Vos and H. Wagatsuma, eds., pp. 275–324. Berkeley: University of California Press.

1972   "Race, Caste, and Other Invidious Distinctions in Social Stratification." *Race* 13:385–414.

1974   "Social Identity and Social Interaction in Urban India." In *Ethnic Identity: Cultural Continuity and Change*, L. Romanucci-Ross and G. De Vos, eds. Palo Alto (Cal.): National Press Books. [In press.]

BEVER, T. G.

1970   "Cognition and the Development of Language." In *Cognition and Language Learning*, J. R. Hayes, ed., pp. 279–362. New York: John Wiley.

BIGELOW, ROBERT

1975   "The Role of Competition and Cooperation in Human Evolution." In *War: Its Causes and Correlates*, M. Nettleship, R. D. Givens, and A. Nettleship, eds., The Hague: Mouton: [In press.]

621

BINFORD, LEWIS
    1972   *An Archaeological Perspective*. New York: Seminar Press.
BIRCH, HERBERT
    1968   "Boldness and Judgement in Behavior Genetics." In *Science and the Concept of Race*, M. Mead and others, eds., pp. 49–58. New York: Columbia University Press.
BIRDSELL, JOSEPH B.
    1968   "Some Predictions for the Pleistocene Based on Equilibrium Systems Among Recent Hunter-Gatherers." In *Man the Hunter*, R. Lee and I. DeVore, eds., pp. 229–249. Chicago: Aldine.
    1970   "Local Group Composition Among the Australian Aborigines: A Critique of the Evidence from Fieldwork Conducted Since 1930." *Current Anthropology* 11:115–142.
    1972   *Human Evolution: An Introduction to the New Physical Anthropology*. Chicago: Rand McNally.
BIRMINGHAM, DAVID
    1966   *Trade and Conflict in Angola*. Oxford: Clarendon Press.
BISHOP, W. W.
    1973   "The Tempo of Human Evolution." *Nature* 244:405–409.
BLAU, PETER, AND O. D. DUNCAN
    1967   *The American Occupational Structure*. New York: John Wiley.
BLAUNER, ROBERT
    1973   *Racial Oppression in America*. New York: Harper and Row.
BLOCH, MARC
    1961   *Feudal Society*. Chicago: University of Chicago Press.
    1964   "Feudalism as a Type of Society." In *Sociology and History: Theory and Research*, W. J. Cahnman and A. Boskoff, eds., pp. 163–170. New York: Free Press.
BLUM, HAROLD
    1964   "Does Sunlight Cause Skin Cancer?" *University Magazine* 21:10–13.
BOAS, FRANZ
    1955   *Primitive Art*. New York: Dover.
BOCK, W. D.
    1970   "*Hyalinea baltica* and the Plio-Pleistocene Boundary in the Caribbean Sea." *Science* 170:847–849.
BODMER, W., AND L. L. CAVALLI-SFORZA
    1970   "Intelligence and Race." *Scientific American* 223, No. 4 (October):19–29.
BOHANNON, PAUL
    1973   "Rethinking Culture: A Project for Current Anthropologists." *Current Anthropology* 14:357–372.
BOKONYI, SANDOR, R. J. BRAIDWOOD, AND C. A. REED
    1973   "Earliest Animal Domestication Dated?" *Science* 182:1161.
BORDAZ, JACQUES
    1970   *Tools of the Old and New Stone Age*. Garden City: Natural History Press.
BORDES, FRANÇOIS
    1968   *The Old Stone Age*. New York: McGraw-Hill.
BOSERUP, ESTHER
    1965   *The Condition of Agricultural Growth: The Economics of Agrarian Change Under Population Pressure*. Chicago: Aldine.
BOTTOMORE, T. B.
    1966   *Classes in Modern Society*. New York: Random House, Vintage.
BOULDING, KENNETH E.
    1973   *The Economy of Love and Fear*. Belmont (Cal.): Wadsworth.

Bibliographical References

BRACE, C. LORING
    1967   *The Stages of Human Evolution: Human and Cultural Origins.* Englewood Cliffs: Prentice-Hall.

BRACE, C. LORING, H. NELSON, AND N. KORN
    1970   *The Incompleat Fossile Man: A Brief Atlas of Human Evolution.* New York: Holt, Rinehart and Winston.

BRAIDWOOD, ROBERT J.
    1969   *Prehistoric Men.* Glenview (Ill.): Scott, Foresman.

BRAIDWOOD, ROBERT J., AND G. R. WILLEY, EDITORS
    1962   *Courses Toward Urban Life: Archaeological Considerations of Some Cultural Alternates.* Chicago: Aldine.

BRAIN, C. K.
    1975   "Some Aspects of the South African Australopithecine Sites and Their Bone Accumulations." In *Early Man in Africa,* C. Jolly, ed. London: Duckworth. [In press.]

BRANDON, S. F. G.
    1968a   *Jesus and the Zealots: A Study of the Political Factor in Primitive Christianity.* New York: Scribner.
    1968b   *The Trial of Jesus of Nazareth.* London: B. T. Batsford.

BROCK, A., AND G. ISAAC
    1974   "Paleomagnetic Stratigraphy and Chronology of Hominid-Bearing Sediments East of Lake Rudolf, Kenya." *Nature* 247:344–348.

BRONOWSKI, J., AND U. BELLUGI
    1970   "Language, Name, and Concept." *Science* 168:669–673.

BRONSON, BENNET
    1972   "Farm Labor and the Evolution of Food Production." In *Population Growth: Anthropological Perspective,* B. Spooner, ed., pp. 190–218. Cambridge: M. I. T. Press.
    1975   "The Earliest Farming: Demography as a Cause and a Consequence." In *Origins of Agriculture,* C. Reed, ed. The Hague: Mouton. [In press.]

BROWN, JUDITH K.
    1970   "A Note on the Division of Labor by Sex." *American Anthropologist* 72:1073–1078.

BROWN, ROGER
    1958   *Words and Things.* Glencoe (Ill.): Free Press.
    1973   *A First Language.* Cambridge: Harvard University Press.

BROWN, ROGER, AND A. GILMAN
    1960   "The Pronouns of Power and Solidarity." In *Style in Language,* T. Sebeok, ed., pp. 253–276. Cambridge: M. I. T. Press.

BROWN, ROY E., AND J. D. WRAY
    1974   "The Starving Roots of Population Growth." *Natural History* 83, No. 1:46–53.

BRYCE, HERRINGTON J.
    1974   "Are Most Blacks in the Middle Class?" *The Black Scholar* 5, No. 5:32–36.

BUETTNER-JANUSCH, JOHN
    1973   *Physical Anthropology: A Perspective.* New York: John Wiley.

BULLARD, WILLIAM R., JR.
    1966   "Settlement Pattern and Social Structure in the Southern Maya Lowlands During the Classic Period." In *Ancient Mesoamerica,* J. A. Graham, ed., pp. 137–145. Palo Alto (Cal.): Peek Publications.

BUNZEL, RUTH
    1929   *The Pueblo Potter.* New York: Columbia University Press.

623

BURLING, ROBBINS
   1969   "Linguistics and Ethnographic Description." *American Anthropologist*
           71:817–827.
BUTZER, KARL
   1971   *Environment and Archaeology: An Ecological Approach to Prehistory.*
           Chicago: Aldine.
CAMBEL, HALET, AND R. J. BRAIDWOOD
   1970   "An Early Farming Village in Turkey." *Scientific American* 222 (March):
           50–56.
CAMPBELL, BERNARD G.
   1975   "Some Problems in Hominid Classification and Nomenclature." In *Early Man
           in Africa*, C. Jolly, ed. London: Duckworth. [In press.]
CARLISLE, RONALD, AND M. SIEGEL
   1974   "Some Problems in the Interpretation of Neanderthal Speech Capabilities: A
           Reply to Lieberman." *American Anthropologist* 76:319–322.
CARNEIRO, ROBERT
   1970   "A Theory of the Origin of the State." *Science* 169:733–738.
CARNEIRO, ROBERT, AND DAISY F. HILSE
   1966   "On Determining the Probable Rate of Population Growth During the Ne-
           olithic." *American Anthropologist* 68:177–181.
CARSTAIRS, G. M.
   1967   *The Twice-born.* Bloomington: Indiana University Press.
CARTMILL, MATT
   1974   "Rethinking Primate Origins." *Science* 184:436–443.
CASTEEL, RICHARD
   1972   "Two Static Maximum Population Density Models for Hunter-Gatherers."
           World Archaeology 4:20–40.
   1975   "The Relationship Between Population Size and Carrying Capacity in a
           Sample of North American Hunter-Gatherers." In *Prehistoric Cultural Adap-
           tations in Western North America*, D. Browman, W. Irving, and W. Powers,
           eds. The Hague: Mouton. [In press.]
CAVALLI-SFORZA, L. L.
   1972   "Origin and Differentiation of Human Races." *Proceedings of the Royal
           Anthropological Institute for 1972*, pp. 15–26.
CHAGNON, NAPOLEON
   1968   *Yanomamö: The Fierce People.* New York: Holt, Rinehart and Winston.
   1974   *Studying the Yanomamö.* New York: Holt, Rinehart and Winston.
CHANG, K. C.
   1973   "Radiocarbon Dates from China: Some Initial Interpretations." *Current An-
           thropology* 14:525–528.
CHAPLIN, RAYMOND
   1969   "The Use of Non-morphological Criteria in the Study of Animal Domestication
           from Bones Found on Archaeological Sites." In *Domestication and Exploita-
           tion of Plants and Animals*, P. J. Ucko and G. W. Dimbleby, eds., pp. 231–246.
           Chicago: Aldine.
CHARGOFF, ERWIN
   1974   "Building the Tower of Babble." *Nature* 248:776–779.
CHESNOV, IA. V.
   1975   "Domestication of Rice and the Origin of Peoples Inhabiting East and South-
           east Asia." In *Aspects of East and Southeast Asian Cultures*, W. E. Sibley, ed.
           The Hague: Mouton. [In press.]
CHEVIGNEY, PAUL
   1969   *Police Power: Police Abuses in New York City.* New York: Pantheon.

624

CHILDE, V. GORDON
1952   *New Light on the Most Ancient East.* London: Keegan Paul.

CHOMSKY, NOAM
1973   "The General Properties of Language." In *Explorations in Anthropology: Readings in Culture, Man, and Nature*, Morton Fried, ed., pp. 115–123. New York: T. Y. Crowell.

CHU'U TUNG-TSU
1964   "Chinese Class Structure and Its Ideology." In *Sociology and History: Theory and Research*, W. J. Cahnman and A. Boskoff, eds., pp. 218–235. New York: Free Press.

CLARK, GRAHAME
1967   *The Stone Age Hunters.* New York: McGraw-Hill.

CLARK, J. DESMOND
1972   "Mobility and Settlement Patterns in Sub-Saharan Africa: A Comparison of Late Prehistoric Hunter-Gatherers and Early Agricultural Occupation Units." In *Man, Settlement, and Urbanism,* P. J. Ucko, R. Tringham, and G. W. Dimbleby, eds., pp. 127–148. Cambridge (Mass.): Schenkman.
1975   "A Comparison of Late Acheulian Industries of Africa and the Middle East." In *After the Australopithecines: Stratigraphy, Ecology, and Culture Change in the Middle Pleistocene,* K. Butzer and G. Isaac, eds. The Hague: Mouton. [In press.]

CLARKE, R. J., F. C. HOWELL, AND C. K. BRAIN
1970   "More Evidence of an Advanced Hominid at Swartkrans." *Nature* 225:1219–1222.

CLIGNET, REMI
1970   *Many Wives, Many Powers: Authority and Power in Polygamous Families.* Evanston: Northwestern University Press.

CLOUD, WALLACE
1973   "After the Green Revolution." *The Sciences* 13, No. 8:6–12.

CLUTTON-BROCK, JULIET
1969   "The Origins of the Dog." In *Science in Archaeology,* D. Brothwell and E. Higgs, eds., pp. 303–309. London: Thames and Hudson.

COALE, ANSLEY
1974   "The History of the Human Population." *Scientific American* 231, No. 3 (September):41–51.

COE, MICHAEL
1962   *Mexico.* New York: Praeger.
1966   *The Maya.* New York: Praeger.
1968   *America's First Civilization: Discovering the Olmec.* New York: American Heritage.

COE, MICHAEL D., AND K. V. FLANNERY
1966   "Microenvironments and Mesoamerican Prehistory." In *Ancient Mesoamerica: Selected Readings*, J. A. Graham, ed., pp. 46–50. Palo Alto (Cal.): Peek Publications.

COHEN, ELIE
1953   *Human Behavior in the Concentration Camp.* New York: W. W. Norton.

COHEN, MARK
1975   "Population Pressure and the Origins of Agriculture: An Archaeological Example from the Coast of Peru." In *Origins of Agriculture*, C. Reed, ed. The Hague: Mouton. [In press.]

COHEN, MYRON L.
1968   "A Case Study of Chinese Family Economy and Development." *Journal of Asian and African Studies* 3:161–180.

1975   *Kinship and Contract: The Chinese Family on Taiwan.* New York: Columbia University Press. [In press.]

COHEN, ROSALIE
1969   "Conceptual Styles, Culture Conflict, and Non-verbal Tests of Intelligence." *American Anthropologist* 71:828–856.

COHN, BERNARD
1955   "Changing Status of a Depressed Caste." In *Village India: Studies in the Little Community*, M. Mariott, ed., American Anthropological Memoirs, No. 83:55–77.

COHN, NORMAN
1962   *The Pursuit of the Millennium.* New York: Harper and Row, Torchbooks.

COLE, JOHNETTA
1970   "The Power Elite: Its Influence, Its Manipulation and Control of the Lower Classes, Particularly of Blacks." Paper presented to the 69th Meeting, American Anthropological Association, San Diego, November 18–22.

COLE, M., J. GRAY, J. GLICK, AND D. SHARP
1971   *The Cultural Context of Learning and Thinking.* New York: Basic Books.

COLLINS, DESMOND
1969   "Culture Traditions and Environment of Early Man." *Current Anthropology* 10:267–316.

CONDOMINAS, GEORGE
1957   *Nous avons mangé la foret de la Pérre-Genie Goo.* Paris.
1972   "From the Rice Field to the Miir." *Social Science Information* 11:41–62.

CONSTABLE, GEORGE
1973   *The Neanderthals.* New York: Time-Life.

COOK, SHERBURNE F.
1972   *Prehistoric Demography.* Reading (Mass.): Addison-Wesley.

COON, CARLETON
1962   *The Origin of Races.* New York: A. A. Knopf.
1965   *The Living Races of Man.* New York: A. A. Knopf.

COWGILL, G. L.
1964   "The End of Classic Maya Culture: A Review of Recent Evidence." *Southwestern Journal of Anthropology* 20:145–159.

CRONBACK, LEE J.
1969   "Heredity, Environment, and Educational Policy." *Harvard Educational Review* 39:338–339.

CURTAIN, RICHARD
1975   "Labor Migration in Papua, New Guinea." In *Migration, Change, and Development: Implications for Ethnic Identity and Political Conflict*, H. I. Safa and B. Du Toit, eds. The Hague: Mouton, [In press.]

DAHL, ROBERT
1961   *Who Governs? Democracy and Power in the American City.* New Haven: Yale University Press.

DALTON, GEORGE
1965   "Primitive Money." *American Anthropologist* 67:44–65.
1969   "Theoretical Issues in Economic Anthropology." *Current Anthropology* 10:63–102.
1972   "Peasantries in Anthropology and History." *Current Anthropology* 13:385–416.

DAVIS, KINGSLEY
1967   "Population Policy: Will Current Programs Succeed?" *Science* 158:730–739.

DAWES, ROBYN
1972   "I. Q.: Methodological and Other Issues." *Science* 178:229–230.

626

DAY, M. H., AND T. I. MOLLESON
   1973   "The Trinil Femora." In *Human Evolution*, M. H. Day, ed., pp. 127–154. London: Taylor and Francis.

DEACON, H. J.
   1975   "Demography, Subsistence, and Culture During the Middle Pleistocene in Southern Africa." In *After the Australopithecines: Stratigraphy, Ecology, and Culture Change in the Middle Pleistocene*, K. Butzer and G. Isaac, eds. The Hague: Mouton. [In press.]

DE HAVENON, ANNA L.
   1970   "The Quantification and Analysis of Family Authority Structure." Mimeographed.

DE LAGUNA, FREDERICA
   1968   "Presidential Address:1967." *American Anthropologist* 70:469–476.

DELORIA, VINE
   1969   *Custer Died for Your Sins*. London: Collier-Macmillan.

DE LUMLEY, HENRY
   1975   "L'evolution culturelle en France dans son cadre paleo-ecologique pendant le Pleistocene moyen." In *After the Australopithecines: Stratigraphy, Ecology, and Culture Change in the Middle Pleistocene*, K. Butzer and G. Isaac, eds. The Hague: Mouton. [In press.]

DE LUMLEY, HENRY, AND M. A. DE LUMLEY
   1974   "Pre-Neanderthal Human Remains from Arago Cave in Southeastern France." *Yearbook of Physical Anthropology* 17: 162–168.

DENHAM, WOODROW
   1970   "Nonhuman Primate Behavior: A Note on Recent Research." *American Anthropologist* 72:365–367.

DENT, C. E., AND OTHERS
   1973   "Effect of Chapattis and Ultra-Violet Radiation on Nutritional Rickets in an Indian Immigrant." *Lancet I* (June):1282–1284.

DENTAN, ROBERT
   1968   *The Semai: A Non-Violent People of Malaya*. New York: Holt, Rinehart and Winston.

DERMAN, WILLIAM
   1975   "Co-ops in Guinea: Problems of Transformation." In *Popular Participation in Social Change: Cooperatives, Collectives, and Nationalized Industry*, J. Nash, J. Dandler, and N. Hopkins, eds. The Hague: Mouton. [In press.]

DESPRES, LEO
   1975   "Ethnicity and Resource Competition in Guayanese Society." In *Ethnicity and Resource Competition in Plural Societies*, L. Despres, ed. The Hague: Mouton. [In press.]

DEVEREUX, GEORGE
   1967   "A Typological Study of Abortion in 350 Primitive, Ancient, and Pre-Industrial Societies." In *Abortion in America*, H. Rosen, ed., pp. 95–152. Boston: Beacon Press.

DEVORE, IRVEN, AND S. L. WASHBURN
   1963   "Baboon Ecology and Human Evolution." In *African Ecology and Human Evolution*, F. C. Howell and F. Bourlière, eds., pp. 335–367. Chicago: Aldine.

DEVOS, GEORGE, AND HIROSHI WAGATSUMA, EDITORS
   1968   *Japan's Invisible Race: Caste in Culture and Personality*. Berkeley: University of California Press.

DILLINGHAM, BETH, AND B. ISAAC
   1975   "Defining Marriage Cross-culturally." In *Being Female: Reproduction, Power and Change*, D. Raphael, ed. The Hague: Mouton. [In press.]

DIVALE, WILLIAM

1972   "Systematic Population Control in the Middle and Upper Paleolithic: Inferences Based on Contemporary Hunters and Gatherers." *World Archaeology* 4:221–243.

1974   "Migration, External Warfare, and Matrilocal Residence." *Behavior Science Research* 9:75–133.

DIVALE, WILLIAM, AND MARVIN HARRIS

1975   "Population, Warfare, and Male Supremacy." Annals of the New York Academy of Sciences. [In press.]

DJILAS, MILOVAN

1957   *The New Class: An Analysis of the Communist System.* New York: Praeger.

DOBKIN DE RIOS, MARLENE

1972   *Visionary Vine: Psychedelic Healing in the Peruvian Amazon.* San Francisco: Chandler.

DOBYNS, HENRY

1966   "Estimating Aboriginal American Population: An Appraisal of Technique with a New Hemisphere Estimate." *Current Anthropology* 7:395–449.

DOLE, GERTRUDE

1966   "Anarchy without Chaos: Alternatives to Political Authority Among the Kui-Kuru." In *Political Anthropology*, M. J. Swartz, V. W. Turner, and A. Tuden, eds., pp. 73–88. Chicago: Aldine.

DOMHOFF, G. WILLIAM

1967   *Who Rules America?* Englewood Cliffs: Prentice Hall.

1970   *The Higher Circles: The Governing Class in America.* New York: Random House.

DUBOIS, CORA

1960   *The People of Alor: A Socio-Psychological Study of an East Indian Island.* Cambridge: Harvard University Press.

DUMOT, LOUIS

1970   *Homo Hierarchicus: The Caste System and Its Implications.* Translated by Mark Sainsbury. Chicago: University of Chicago Press.

DUNN, FREDERICK L.

1970   "Cultural Evolution in the Late Pleistocene and Holocene of Southeast Asia." *American Anthropologist* 72:1041–1054.

EDGERTON, ROBERT

1971   *The Individual in Cultural Adaptation: A Study of Four East African Peoples.* Berkeley: University of California Press.

EHRLICH, PAUL H., AND A. H. EHRLICH

1970   *Population Resources and Environment: Issues in Human Ecology.* San Francisco: W. H. Freeman.

EISENSTADT, S. N., EDITOR

1968   *The Protestant Ethic and Modernization: A Comparative View.* New York: Basic Books.

ELKINS, STANLEY

1961   "Slavery and Personality." In *Studying Personality Cross-Culturally*, Bert Kaplan, ed., pp. 243–267. Evanston: Row, Petersen.

ELLIS, DAVID

1975   "The Advent of Food Production in West Africa." In *West African Cultural Dynamics: Archaeological and Historical Perspectives*, B. K. Swartz, ed. The Hague: Mouton, World Anthropology. [In press.]

ELVIN, MARK

1974   *The Pattern of the Chinese Past.* Stanford: Stanford University Press.

628

EMBER, MELVIN, AND CAROL R. EMBER
1971   "The Conditions Favoring Matrilocal versus Patrilocal Residence." *American Anthropologist* 73:571–594.

EMILIANI, CESARE
1968   "The Pleistocene Epoch and the Evolution of Man." *Current Anthropology* 9:27–47.
1971   "The Last Interglacial: Paleotemperatures and Chronology." *Science* 171:571–573.

EPSTEIN, T. SCARLETT
1968   *Capitalism, Primitive and Modern: Some Aspects of Tolai Economic Growth.* East Lansing: Michigan State University Press.

EVANS-PRITCHARD, E. E.
1940   *The Nuer, A Description of the Modes of Livelihood and Political Institutions of a Nilotic People.* Oxford: Clarendon Press.

FAINSOD, MERLE
1967   *How Russia Is Ruled.* Cambridge: Harvard University Press.

FEI HSIAO-T'UNG AND CHANG CHIH-I
1947   *Earthbound China: A Study of Rural Economy in Yunnan.* Chicago: University of Chicago Press.

FELDMERSEN, ROBERT A.
1966   "Toward the Classless Society?" In *Class, Status, and Power: Social Stratification in Comparative Perspective*, R. Bendix and S. M. Lipset, eds., pp. 527–533. New York: Free Press.

FIRTH, RAYMOND
1957   *We, The Tikopia: A Sociological Study of Kinship in Primitive Polynesia.* Boston: Beacon Press.

FITTKAU, E. J., AND H. KLINGE
1973   "On Biomass and Trophic Structure of the Central Amazon Rain Forest Ecosystem." *Biotropica* 5:1–14.

FLANNERY, KENT
1969   "Origins and Ecological Effects of Early Domestication in Iran and the Near East." In *Domestication and Exploitation of Plants and Animals*, P. J. Ucko and G. W. Dimbleby, eds., pp. 73–100. Chicago: Aldine.
1972   "The Origin of the Village as a Settlement Type in Mesoamerica and the Near East: A Comparative Study." In *Man, Settlement, and Urbanism*, P. J. Ucko, R. Tringham, and G. W. Dimbleby, eds., pp. 23–53. Cambridge (Mass.): Schenkman.
1973   "The Origins of Agriculture." *Annual Review of Anthropology, Volume 2*, B. J. Siegel, A. R. Beals, and S. A. Tyler, eds., pp. 270–310. Palo Alto (Cal.): Annual Reviews Press.

FORBIS, RICHARD G.
1974   "The Paleoamericans." In *Prehispanic America*, S. Gorenstein, ed., pp. 11–28. New York: St. Martin's Press.

FORMAN, SHEPARD
1970   *The Raft Fishermen.* Bloomington: University of Indiana Press.
1975   *The Brazilian Peasantry.* New York: Columbia University Press. [In press.]

FORTES, MEYER
1969   *Kinship and the Social Order: The Legacy of Lewis Henry Morgan.* Chicago: Aldine.

FORTUNE, REO
1965   *Manus Religion.* Lincoln: University of Nebraska Press.

629

FOSTER, GEORGE M.

1967   *Tzintzuntzan: Mexican Peasants in a Changing World.* Boston: Little, Brown.

1972   "The Anatomy of Envy: A Study in Symbolic Behavior." *Current Anthropology* 13:165–202.

1974   "Limited Good or Limited Goods: Observations on Acheson." *American Anthropologist* 76:53–57.

FOUTS, ROGER

1973   "Acquisition and Testing of Gestural Signs in Four Young Chimpanzees." *Science* 180:978–980.

FRANK, ANDRÉ G.

1964   "On the Mechanisms of Imperialism: The Case of Brazil." *Monthly Review* 16:284–297.

1967   *Capitalism and Underdevelopment in Latin America: Historical Studies of Chile and Brazil.* New York: Monthly Review Press.

FRANKE, RICHARD W.

1973   *The Green Revolution in a Javanese Village.* Ph.D. dissertation, Harvard University.

1974   "Miracle Seeds and Shattered Dreams." *Natural History* 83, No. 1 (January):10 on.

FRASER, DOUGLAS

1966   *The Many Faces of Primitive Art: A Critical Anthology.* Englewood Cliffs (N.J.): Prentice-Hall.

FRIED, MORTON H.

1965   "A Four Letter Word That Hurts." *Saturday Review* 48 (October 2):21 on.

1967   *The Evolution of Political Society: An Essay in Political Anthropology.* New York: Random House.

1968   "The Need To End the Pseudoscientific Investigation of Race." In *Science and the Concept of Race,* M. Mead and others, eds., pp. 122–131. New York: Columbia University Press.

1972   *The Study of Anthropology.* New York: T. Y. Crowell.

FRISCH, JOHN E.

1968   "Individual Behavior and Intertroop Variability in Japanese Macaques." In *Primates: Studies in Adaptation and Variability,* P. C. Jay, ed., pp. 243–252. New York: Holt, Rinehart and Winston.

FRISCH, ROSE, AND JANET MACARTHUR

1974   "Menstrual Cycles: Fatness as a Determinant of Minimum Weight for Height Necessary for Their Maintenance or Onset." *Science* 185:949–951.

FRY, ROBERT

1970   "The Determinants of Settlement in Peten Maya Sites." Paper presented to the 69th Meeting of the American Anthropological Association, San Diego, November 18–22.

FURTADO, CELSO

1965   *Diagnosis of the Brazilian Crisis.* Berkeley: University of California Press.

GALBRAITH, JOHN

1958   *The Affluent Society.* New York: Houghton-Mifflin.

1967   *The New Industrial State.* New York: Houghton-Mifflin.

GANDHI, MOHANDAS K.

1954   *How To Serve the Cow: Ahmedabad.* Navajivan Publishing House.

GARDNER, B. T., AND R. A. GARDNER

1971   "Two-Way Communication with a Chimpanzee." In *Behavior of Non-Human*

Bibliographical References

Primates, A. Schrier and F. Stollnitz, eds., Volume 4:117–184. New York: Academic Press.

GEARING, FRED, AND B. A. TINDALE
1973   "Anthropological Studies of the Educational Process." In *Annual Review of Anthropology, Volume I*, B. J. Siegel, A. R. Beals, and S. A. Tyler, eds., pp. 95–105. Palo Alto: Annual Reviews.

GEERTZ, CLIFFORD
1963   *Agricultural Involution: The Process of Ecological Change in Indonesia*. Berkeley: University of California Press *for* The Association of Asian Studies.
1965   "Religion as a Cultural System." In *Reader in Comparative Religion: An Anthropological Approach*, W. A. Lessa and E. Z. Vogt, eds., pp. 204–216. New York: Harper and Row.

GILL, J. B., AND IAN MCDOUGALL
1973   "Biostratigraphic and Geological Significance of Miocene-Pliocene Volcanism in Fiji." *Nature* 241:176–180.

GIVENS, R. D.
1975   "Aggression in Nonhuman Primates: Implications for Understanding Human Behavior." In *War: Its Causes and Correlates*, M. Nettleship, R. D. Givens, and A. Nettleship, eds. The Hague: Mouton. [In press.]

GLUCKMAN, MAX
1955   *Custom and Conflict in Africa*. Oxford: Blackwell.

GOLD, SONIA
1973   "Alternative National Goals and Women's Employment." *Science* 179:565–660.

GOLDSCHMIDT, WALTER
1973   "The Brideprice of the Sebei." *Scientific American* 229, No. 1 (July):74–85.

GONZÁLEZ, NANCY L.
1970   "Towards a Definition of Matrilocality." In *Afro-American Anthropology: Contemporary Perspectives*, N. E. Whitten and J. F. Szwed, eds., pp. 231–243. New York: Free Press.

GOODENOUGH, FLORENCE L.
1926   *Measurement of Intelligence by Drawings*. Chicago: World Book.

GOODENOUGH, WARD H.
1970   *Description and Comparison in Cultural Anthropology*. Chicago: Aldine.
1971   *Culture, Language, and Society*. Reading (Mass.): Addison-Wesley.

GOODMAN, PAUL
1967   "The Universal Trap." In *Profile of the School Dropout*, D. Schreiber, ed., pp. 40–53. New York: Random House.

GORENSTEIN, SHIRLEY, EDITOR
1974   *Prehispanic America*. New York: St. Martin's Press.

GORER, GEOFFREY, AND J. RICKMAN
1949   *The People of Great Russia*. London: Cresset.

GORMAN, CHESTER F.
1969   "Hoabinhian: A Pebble-tool Complex with Early Plant Associations in Southeast Asia." *Science* 163:671–673.
1975   "*A priori* Models and Thai Prehistory: A Reconsideration of the Beginnings of Agriculture in Southeastern Asia." In *Origins of Agriculture*, C. Reed, ed. The Hague: Mouton. [In press.]

GOTTESMAN, J. J.
1968   "Biogenetics of Race and Class." In *Social Class, Race, and Psychological Development*, M. Deutsch, I. Katz, and A. R. Jensen, eds., pp. 7–51. New York: Holt, Rinehart and Winston.

631

GOUGH, E. KATHLEEN
    1959   "Criterion of Caste Ranking in South India." *Man in India* 39:115–126.
    1968   "The Nayars and the Definition of Marriage." In *Marriage, Family, and Residence*, P. Bohannan and J. Middleton, eds., pp. 49–71. Garden City: Natural History Press.

GOULD, HAROLD
    1971   "Caste and Class: A Comparative View." *Module* 11:1–24. Reading (Mass.): Addison-Wesley.

GOULD, J. E., M. HENEREY, AND M. C. MACLEOD
    1970   "Communication of Direction by the Honey Bee." *Science* 169:544–554.

GOULD, RICHARD, D. KOSTER, AND A. SONTZ
    1971   "The Lithic Assemblage of the Western Desert Aboriginese of Australia." *American Antiquity* 36:149–169.

GOULD, STEPHEN T.
    1974   "The Race Problem." *Natural History* 83, No. 3:8.

GRAHAM, EDWARD
    1975   "Yuman Warfare: An Analysis of Ecological Factors from Ethnohistorical Sources." In *War: Its Causes and Its Correlates*, M. Nettleship, R. D. Givens, and A. Nettleship, eds. The Hague: Mouton. [In press.]

GRAVES, THEODORE
    1974   "Urban Indian Personality and the Culture of Poverty." *American Ethnologist* 1:65–86.

GREGOR, THOMAS A.
    1969   "Social Relations in a Small Society: A Study of the Mehinacu Indians of Central Brazil." Ph.D. dissertation, Columbia University.

GREGSON, RONALD
    1971   "Labor Migration in Central Africa: Theory, Methodology." Mimeographed.

GROSS, DANIEL R.
    1970   "Sisal and Social Structure in Northeastern Brazil." Ph.D. dissertation, Columbia University.

GROSS, DANIEL R., AND B. UNDERWOOD
    1969   "Technological Change and Caloric Costs on Northeastern Brazilian Sisal Plantations." Paper presented to the 136th Annual Meeting, Section H, American Association for the Advancement of Science, Boston, December 26–31.

GUTGESELL, VICKI
    1970   "'Telanthropus' and the Single Species Hypothesis: A Re-examination." *American Anthropologist* 72:565–576.

HALL, CALVIN, AND G. LINDZEY
    1967   "Freud's Psychoanalytic Theory of Personality." In *Personalities and Cultures: Readings in Psychological Anthropology*, Robert Hunt, ed., pp. 3–29. Garden City: Natural History Press.

HALLER, JOHN S.
    1971   *Outcastes from Evolution*. Urbana: University of Illinois Press.

HAMBLIN, DORA JANE
    1973   *The First Cities*. New York: Time-Life.

HANCE, WILLIAM A.
    1964   *The Geography of Modern Africa*. New York: Columbia University Press.

HANKS, LUCIEN
    1972   *Rice and Man: Agricultural Ecology in Southeast Asia*. Chicago: Aldine.

HANNERZ, ULF
    1970   "What Ghetto Males Are Like: Another Look." In *Afro-American Anthropolo-*

gy: Contemporary Perspectives, N. E. Whitten and J. F. Szwed, eds., pp. 313–328. New York, Free Press

HANSEN, GARY T.
1972   "Indonesia's Green Revolution: The Abandonment of a Non-market Strategy Toward Change." *Asian Survey* 12:932–946.

HARDING, ROBERT
1975   "Meat Eating and Hunting in Baboons." In *Socio-Ecology and Psychology of Primates*. R. H. Tuttle, ed. The Hague: Mouton. [In press.]

HARLAN, JACK
1975   "Origins of Cereal Agriculture in the Old World." In *Origins of Agriculture*, C. Reed, ed. The Hague: Mouton. [In press.]

HARLAN, JACK R., AND D. ZOHARY
1966   "Distribution of Wild Wheats and Barley." *Science* 153:1074–1080.

HARNER, MICHAEL J.
1962   "Jívaro Souls." *American Anthropologist* 64:258–272.
1970   "Population Pressure and the Social Evolution of Agriculturalists." *Southwestern Journal of Anthropology* 26:67–86.
1972a   "The Role of Hallucinogenic Plants in European Witchcraft." In *Hallucinogens and Shamanism*, Michael Harner, ed., pp. 127–150. New York: Oxford University Press.
1972b   *The Jívaro: People of the Sacred Waterfalls*. Garden City: Natural History Press.

HARRINGTON, CHARLES, AND J. WHITING
1972   "Socialization Process and Personality." In *Psychological Anthropology*, Francis Hsu, ed., pp. 469–507. Cambridge (Mass.): Schenkman.

HARRIS, ANNE S.
1970   "On Women in Academe." *American Association of University Professors Bulletin* 56:283–295.

HARRIS, DAVID
1975   "The Origins of Agriculture: Alternate Pathways Toward Agriculture." In *Origins of Agriculture*, C. Reed, ed. The Hague: Mouton. [In press.]

HARRIS, MARVIN
1958   *Portugal's African "Wards": A First Hand Report on Labour and Education in Mocambique*. New York: American Committee on Africa.
1966   "The Cultural Ecology of India's Sacred Cattle." *Current Anthropology* 7:51–66.
1968   *The Rise of Anthropological Theory*. New York: T. Y. Crowell.
1970   "Referential Ambiguity in the Calculus of Brazilian Racial Identity." *Southwestern Journal of Anthropology* 26:1–14.
1972   "Portugal's Contribution to the Underdevelopment of Africa and Brazil." In *Protest and Resistance in Angola and Brazil*, Ronald Chilcote, ed., pp. 209–223. Berkeley: University of California Press.
1974a   *Patterns of Race in the Americas*. New York: W. W. Norton.
1974b   *Cows, Pigs, Wars, and Witches: The Riddle of Culture*. New York: Random House.

HARRISON, R. J., AND W. MONTAGNA
1969   *Man*. New York: Appleton-Century-Crofts.

HART, C. W. M., AND A. R. PILLING
1960   *The Tiwi of North Australia*. New York: Holt, Rinehart and Winston.

HASSAN, FERKI
1973   "On Mechanisms of Population Growth During the Neolithic." *Current Anthropology* 14:535–540.

633

HASWELL, M. R.
    1953   *Economics of Agriculture in a Savannah Village: Report on Three Years'
            Study in Genieri Village.* London: Colonial Research Studies, No. 8, H.M.S.O.

HAUGEN, EINAR
    1975   "Linguistic Relativity: Myths and Methods." In *Language and Thought:
            Anthropological Issues*, W. C. McCormack and S. A. Wurm, eds. The Hague:
            Mouton. [In press.]

HAVILAND, WILLIAM
    1970   "Tikal, Guatemala and Mesoamerican Urbanism." *World Archaeology* 2:186–
            198.

HAYDEN, BRIAN
    1972   "Population Control Among Hunter/Gatherers." *World Archaeology* 4:205–
            221.

HAYNES, VARICE
    1973   "The Calico Site: Artifacts or Geofacts?" *Science* 181:305.

HAZARD, THOMAS
    1960   "On the Nature of the Numaym and Its Counterparts Elsewhere on the
            Northwest Coast." Paper presented to the 127th Annual Meeting of the
            American Association for the Advancement of Science, Denver.

HEATH, DWIGHT
    1966   "The Aymara Indians and Bolivia's Revolution." *Inter-American Affairs*
            19:31–40.

HEBER, RICK F.
    1969   *Rehabilitation of Families at Risk for Mental Retardation.* Milwaukee:
            University of Wisconsin Rehabilitation Center.

HEIDER, KARL G.
    1969   "Visiting Trading Institutions." *American Anthropologist* 71:462–471.
    1972   *The Dani of West Irian.* Reading (Mass.): Addison-Wesley.

HEILBRONER, ROBERT L.
    1966   *The Limits of American Capitalism.* New York: Harper and Row.

HEIZER, ROBERT F.
    1960   "Agriculture and the Theocratic State in Lowland Southeastern Mexico."
            American Antiquity 26:215–222.

HELMS, MARY
    1970   Matrilocality, Social Solidarity, and Culture Contact." *Southwestern Journal
            of Anthropology* 26:197–212.

HENRY, JULES
    1963   *Culture Against Man.* New York: Random House.

HERRE, WOLF, AND M. RÖHRS
    1975   "Zoological Considerations in the Origin of Farming and Domestication." In
            Origins of Agriculture, C. Reed, ed. The Hague: Mouton. [In press.]

HERRNSTEIN, RICHARD
    1971   "I.Q." *The Atlantic Monthly* 228. No. 6 (Sept.):43–58, and (Dec.):101–10.

HERSKOVITS, MELVILLE J.
    1938   *Dahomey, An Ancient West African Kingdom.* New York: J. J. Augustin.

HERTZLER, JOYCE O.
    1965   *A Sociology of Language.* New York: Random House.

HIDE, ROBIN
    1974   Personal Communication.

HIEBERT, PAUL
    1969   "Caste and Personal Rank in an Indian Village: An Extension in Techniques."
            American Anthropologist 71:434–453.

634

HIERNAUX, JEAN
1969   *Égalité ou inégalité des races*? Paris: Hachette.

HIGGS, E. S., AND M. R. JARMAN
1972   "The Origins of Animal and Plant Husbandry." In *Papers in Economic Prehistory*, E. S. Higgs, ed., pp. 3–13. Cambridge (England): Cambridge University Press.

HILL, JANE
1972   "On the Evolutionary Foundations of Language." *American Anthropologist* 74:308–317.

HIRSCH, JERRY
1970   "Behavior-Genetic Analysis and Its Biosocial Consequences." *Seminars in Psychiatry* 2:89–105.

HOBSBAWM, E. J.
1965   *Primitive Rebels*. New York: W. W. Norton.

HOELSCHER, H. E.
1969   "Technology and Social Change." *Science* 156:68–72.

HOGBIN, H. IAN
1964   *A Guadalcanal Society: The Kaoka Speakers*. New York: Holt, Rinehart and Winston.

HOLLOWAY, RALPH L.
1967   "Tools and Teeth: Some Speculations Regarding Canine Reduction." *American Anthropologist* 69:63–67.
1970   "Australopithecine Endocast (Taung Specimen, 1924): A New Volume Determination." *Science* 168:966–968.
1972   "Endocranial Volumes of Early African Hominids, and the Role of the Brain in Human Mosaic Evolution." *Journal of Human Evolution* 2:449–459.
1973   "New Endocranial Values for the East African Early Hominids." *Nature* 243:97–99.

HOLM, BILL
1965   *Northwest Coast Indian Art: An Analysis of Form*. Seattle: University of Washington Press.

HOROWITZ, DAVID
1966   *Hemispheres North and South: Economic Disparity Among Nations*. Baltimore: Johns Hopkins Press.

HOWELL, F. CLARK
1966   "Observations on the Early Phases of the European Lower Paleolithic." In *Recent Studies in Paleoanthropology*, J. D. Clark and F. C. Howell, eds., pp. 88–201. *American Anthropologist* 68, No. 2, Part 2 [Special Publication].
1969   "Remains of Hominidae from Pliocene/Pleistocene Formation in the Lower Omo Basin, Ethiopia." *Nature* 223:1234–1239.

HOWELL, F. CLARK, AND YVES COPPENS
1974   "Inventory of Remains of Hominidae from Pliocene/Pleistocene Formation in the Lower Omo Basin, Ethiopia (1967–1972)." *American Journal of Physical Anthropology* 40:1–16.

HOWELL, F. CLARK, AND B. WOOD
1974   "Early Hominid Ulna from the Omo Basin, Ethiopia." *Nature* 249: 174–175.

HOWELLS, WILLIAM W.
1959   *Mankind in the Making: The Story of Human Evolution*. New York: Doubleday.
1973   *Evolution of the Genus Homo*. Reading (Mass.): Addison-Wesley.
1975   "Neanderthal Man: Facts and Figures." In *Paleoanthropology: Morphology and Paleoecology*, R. H. Tuttle, ed. The Hague: Mouton. [In press.]

HULSE, FREDERICK
  1973   *Human Species: An Introduction to Physical Anthropology*. [2nd edition.]
          New York: Random House.

HUNT, J. M.
  1969   "Has Compensatory Education Failed? Has It Been Attempted?" *Harvard
          Educational Review* 39:278–300.

HYMES, DELL
  1971   "Introduction." In *The Origin and Diversification of Language*, M. Swadesh,
          J. F. Sherzer, eds. Chicago: Aldine.

IANNI, F. A. J., AND E. STORY, EDITORS
  1973   *Cultural Relevance and Educational Issues: A Reader in Anthropology and
          Education*. Boston: Little Brown.

IKEGAMI, YOSHIHIKO
  1975   "*Meaning* for the Linguist and *Meaning* for the Anthropologist." In *Language
          and Thought: Anthropological Issues*, W. C. McCormack and S. A. Wurm,
          eds. The Hague: Mouton. [In press.]

INGILIS, GORDON
  1970   "Northwest American Matriliny: The Problem of Origin." *Ethnology* 9:149–
          159.

INGLE, DWIGHT J.
  1968   "The Need to Investigate Biological Differences Among Racial Groups." In
          Science and the Concept of Race, M. Mead and others, eds., pp. 113–121. New
          York: Columbia University Press.

INKELES, ALEX
  1966   "Social Stratification and Mobility in the Soviet Union." In *Class, Status, and
          Power: Social Stratification in Comparative Perspective*, R. Bendix and S.
          M. Lipset, eds., pp. 516–526. New York: Free Press.

IRVING, W., AND C. HARRINGTON
  1973   "Upper Pleistocene Radiocarbon-Dated Artifacts from the Northern Yukon."
          Science 179:335–340.

ISAAC, GLYNN
  1971   "The Diet of Early Man: Aspects of Archaeological Evidence from Lower and
          Middle Pleistocene Sites in Africa." *World Archaeology* 2:278–298.
  1975   "The Archaeological Evidence for the Activities of Early African Hominids."
          In *Early Man in Africa*, C. Jolly, ed. London: Duckworth. [In press.]

ITANI, JUN'ICHIRO
  1961   "The Society of Japanese Monkeys." *Japan Quarterly* 8:421–430.

JACOBS, NORMAN
  1958   *The Origin of Modern Capitalism and East Asia*. Hong Kong: Hong Kong
          University Press.

JANZEN, DANIEL
  1973   "Tropical Agroecosystems." *Science* 182:1212–1219.

JELINEK, JAN
  1969   "Neanderthal Man and *Homo Sapiens* in Central and Eastern Europe."
          Current Anthropology 10:475–503.

JENKINS, FARISH
  1972   "Chimpanzee Bipedalism: Cineradiographic Analysis and Implications for the
          Evolution of Gait." *Science* 178:877–879.

JENNINGS, JESSE
  1974   *Prehistory of North America*. [2nd edition.] New York: McGraw-Hill.

JENSEN, ARTHUR
  1969   "How Much Can We Boost I.Q. and Scholastic Achievement?" *Harvard
          Educational Review* 29:1–123.

636

Bibliographical References

1973   *Educability and Group Difference*. London: Methuen.

JOHNSON, ALLEN W.
1974   "The Allocation of Time in a Machiguenga Community." Mimeographed.

JOHNSON, FRANCIS
1964   "Racial Taxonomies from an Evolutionary Perspective." *American Anthropologist* 66:822–827.

JOLLY, CLIFFORD
1970   "The Seed-Eaters: A New Model of Hominid Differentiation Based on a Baboon Analogy." *Man* 5:5–26.

JORGENSEN, JOSEPH G.
1971   "Toward Ethics for Anthropologists." *Current Anthropology* 12:321–356.

JOSEPHUS, FLAVIUS
1970   *The Jewish War*. Translated by G. A. Williamson. Baltimore: Penguin. [Written First Century A.D.]

KABERRY, PHYLLIS
1970   *Aboriginal Woman, Sacred and Profane*. London: Routledge. [Initially published 1939.]

KAGAN, JEROME
1969   "Inadequate Evidence and Illogical Conclusions." *Harvard Educational Review* 39:274–277.

KAMIN, L. J.
1974   *The Science and Politics of I. Q.* Potomac (Md.): Earl Bauman and Associates.

KAPLAN, L., T. LYNCH, AND C. SMITH
1973   "Early Cultivated Beans (*Phaseolus vulgaris*) from an Intermontane Peruvian Valley." *Science* 179:76–77.

KARNES, M. B.
1968   "A Research Program to Determine the Effects of Various Pre-School Programs." Paper presented to the American Educational Research Association, Chicago.

KATZ, I., T. HEUCHY, AND H. ALLEN
1968   "Effects of Race of Tester, Approval, Disapproval, and Need on Negro Children's Learning." *Journal of Personality and Social Research* 8:38–42.

KATZ, JEROLD
1971   *The Underlying Reality of Language and Its Philosophical Import*. New York: Harper and Row, Torchbooks.

KAY, PAUL
1970   "Some Theoretical Implications of Ethnographic Semantics." *Bulletin of the American Anthropological Association*, Vol. 3, No. 3, Part 2:19–31.

KELSO, A. J.
1974   *Physical Anthropology* [Second edition]. Philadelphia: Lippincott.

KENNEDY, KENNETH
1975   "Biological Adaptation of Prehistoric South Asian Population to Different and Changing Ecological Patterns." In *Biosocial Interrelations in Population Adaptation*, F. Johnston, E. Watts, and G. Lasker, eds. The Hague: Mouton. [In press.]

KENDALL, A. C.
1972   "Rickets in the Tropics and Subtropics." *Central African Journal of Medicine* 18:47–49.

KLEIN, LEWIS, AND DOROTHY KLEIN
1975   "Social and Ecological Contrasts Among Four Taxa of Neotropical Primates." In *Socio-Ecology and Psychology of Primates*, R. H. Tuttle, ed. The Hague: Mouton. [In press.]

637

KLEIN, RICHARD
    1973   "Geological Antiquity of Rhodesian Man." *Nature* 244:311–312.
KLINEBERG, OTTO
    1935   *Negro Intelligence and Selective Migration.* New York: Columbia University Press.
    1944   *Characteristics of the American Negro.* New York: Harper.
KNIGHT, ROLF
    1965   "A Re-examination of Hunting, Trapping, and Territoriality Among the Northeastern Algonkin Indians." In *Man, Culture, and Animals: The Role of Animals in Human Ecological Adjustments.* A. Leeds and A. P. Vayda, eds., pp. 27–42. Washington: American Association for the Advancement of Science.
    1974   "Grey Owl's Return: Cultural Ecology and Canadian Indigenous Peoples." *Reviews in Anthropology* 1:349–359.
KOLATA, GINA
    1974   "!Kung Hunter-Gatherers: Feminism, Diet, and Birth Control." *Science* 185:932–934.
KOLKO, GABRIEL
    1962   *Wealth and Power in America: An Analysis of Social Class and Income Distribution.* New York: Praeger.
    1969   *The Roots of American Foreign Policy.* Boston: Beacon.
KORTLANT, A.
    1967   "Experimentation with Chimpanzees in the Wild." In *Progress in Primatology*, D. Starck, R. Schneider, and H. Kuhn, eds., pp. 185–194. Stuttgart: Gustav Fischer.
KOTTAK, CONRAD P.
    1971   "Social Groups and Kinship Calculation Among the Southern Betsileo." *American Anthropologist* 73:178–192.
KOZOL, J.
    1972   *Free Schools.* New York: Bantam.
KRIESBERG, LOUIS
    1970   *Mothers in Poverty: A Study of Fatherless Families.* Chicago: Aldine.
KROEBER, ALFRED L.
    1948   *Anthropology.* New York: Harcourt, Brace.
KUPFERER, H. J., AND A. J. RUBEL
    1973   "The Consequences of a Myth." In *To See Ourselves: Anthropology and Modern Social Issues*, T. Weaver, ed., pp. 103–107. Glenview (Ill.): Scott, Foresman.
KURTÉN, BJÖRN
    1972   *The Ice Age.* New York: G. P. Putnam.
LA BARRE, WESTON
    1938   *The Peyote Cult.* Yale University Publications in Anthropology, No. 19. New Haven: Yale University Press.
    1966   "The Aymara: History and Worldview." *Journal of American Folklore* 79:130–144.
LABOV, WILLIAM
    1972a   *Language in the Inner City.* Philadelphia: University of Pennsylvania Press.
    1972b   *Sociolinguistic Patterns.* Philadelphia: University of Pennsylvania Press.
LAKOFF, R.
    1973   "Language and Woman's Place." *Language in Society* 2:45–79.
LANCASTER, JANE
    1968   "On the Evolution of Tool-using Behavior." *American Anthropologist* 70:56–66.

LANNING, EDWARD P.
1970   "Pleistocene Man in South America." *World Archaeology* 2:90–111.
1974   "Western South America." In *Prehispanic America*, S. Gorenstein, ed., pp. 65–86. New York: St. Martin's Press.

LANTERNARI, VITTORIO
1963   *The Religion of the Oppressed.* New York: A. A. Knopf.

LASKER, GABRIEL
1973   *Physical Anthropology.* New York: Holt, Rinehart and Winston.

LATTIMORE, OWEN
1962   *Inner Asian Frontiers of China.* Boston: Beacon.

LAVE, LESTER, AND E. SESKIN
1970   "Air Pollution and Human Health." *Science* 169:723–733.

LAWRENCE, PETER
1964   *Road Belong Cargo: A Study of the Cargo Movement in the Southern Madang District, New Guinea.* Manchester: University of Manchester.

LAYZER, DAVID
1974   "Heritability Analyses of I. Q. Scores: Science or Numerology?" *Science* 183:1259–1266.

LEACH, EDMUND R., EDITOR
1960   *Aspects of Caste in South India, Ceylon, and Northwest Pakistan.* Cambridge (England): Cambridge University Press.

LEACH, EDMUND R.
1968   "Polyandry, Inheritance, and the Definition of Marriage, with Particular Reference to Sinhalese Customary Law." In *Marriage, Family, and Residence*, P. Bohannan and J. Middleton, eds., pp. 73–83. Garden City: Natural History Press.

LEACOCK, ELEANOR B.
1954   *The Montagnais "Hunting Territory" and the Fur Trade.* Memoir 78, American Anthropological Association.
1969   *Teaching and Learning in City Schools: A Comparative Study.* New York: Basic Books.
1973   "The Montagnais-Naskapi Band." In *Cultural Ecology: Readings on the Canadian Indians and Eskimos*, B. Cox, ed., pp. 81–100. Toronto: McClelland and Stewart.
1975   "Class, Community, and the Status of Women." In *Women Cross-Culturally: Change and Challenge*, R. Leavitt, ed. The Hague: Mouton. [In press.]

LEAKEY, LOUIS S. B., AND V. M. GOODALL
1969   *Unveiling Man's Origins.* Cambridge, Mass.: Schenkman.

LEAKEY, MARY
1975   "Cultural Patterns in the Olduvai Sequence." In *After the Australopithecines: Stratigraphy, Ecology, and Culture Change in the Middle Pleistocene*, K. Butzer and G. Isaac, eds. The Hague: Mouton. [In press.]

LEAKEY, RICHARD
1970   "New Hominid Remains and Early Artifacts from Northern Kenya." *Nature* 226:223–230.
1973a   "Further Evidence of Lower Pleistocene Hominids from East Rudolf, North Kenya, 1972." *Nature* 242:170–173.
1973b   "Evidence for the Advanced Plio-Pleistocene Hominid from East Rudolf, Kenya." *Nature* 242:447–450.

LEE, RICHARD B.
1968   "What Hunters Do for a Living, or How to Make Out on Scarce Resources." In *Man the Hunter*, R. B. Lee and I. DeVore, eds., pp. 30–43. Chicago: Aldine.

1969a   "Eating Christmas in the Kalahari." *Natural History Magazine*, Vol. 78, No. 10 (Dec.):14 ff.

1969b   "!Kung Bushman Subsistence: An Input-Output Analysis." In *Environment and Cultural Behavior: Ecological Studies in Cultural Anthropology*, A. P. Vayda, ed., pp. 47–79. Garden City: Natural History Press.

1972a   "The Intensification of Social Life Among the !Kung Bushmen." In *Population Growth: Anthropological Perspectives*, Brian Spooner, ed., pp. 343–350. Cambridge: M. I. T. Press.

1972b   "The !Kung Bushmen of Botswana." In *Hunters and Gatherers Today*, M. G. Bichiere, ed., pp. 327–367. New York: Holt, Rinehart and Winston.

1973a   "Mongongo: The Ethnography of a Major Wild Food Resource." *Ecology of Food and Nutrition* 1:1–15.

1974   "Male-Female Residence Arrangements and Political Power in Human Hunter-Gatherers." *Archives of Sexual Behavior* 3:167–173.

LEE, RICHARD B., AND I. DEVORE, EDITORS

1968   *Man the Hunter*. Chicago: Aldine.

LEEDS, ANTHONY

1970   "The Culture of Poverty: Conceptual, Logical, and Empirical Problems, with Perspectives from Brazil and Peru." In *The Culture of Poverty: A Critique*, E. Leacock, ed., pp. 47–49. New York: Simon and Schuster.

LEES, SUSAN, AND D. BATES

1974   "The Origins of Specialized Nomadic Pastoralism: A Systemic Model." *American Antiquity* 39:187–193.

LENNENBERG, ERIC H.

1967   *Biological Foundations of Language*. New York: John Wiley.

LENSKI, GERHARD

1970   *Human Societies*. New York: McGraw-Hill.

LEONE, MARK, EDITOR

1972   *Contemporary Archaeology: A Guide to Theory and Contribution*. Carbondale: Southern Illinois University Press.

LEROI-GOURHAN, ANDRÉ

1968   "The Evolution of Paleolithic Art." *Scientific American*, 218, 2 (February):58–70.

LESSER, ALEXANDER

1968   "War and the State." In *War: The Anthropology of Armed Conflict and Aggression*, M. Fried, M. Harris, and R. Murphy, eds., pp. 92–96. Garden City: Natural History Press.

LÉVI-STRAUSS, CLAUDE

1963a   *Totemism*. Boston: Beacon Press.

1963b   *Tristes Tropiques*. New York: Atheneum.

LEWIS, OSCAR

1961   *The Children of Sanchez: Autobiography of a Mexican Family*. New York: Random House.

1966   *La Vida: A Puerto Rican Family in the Culture of Poverty—San Juan and New York*. New York: Random House.

1968   "The Culture of Poverty." In *Poverty in America*, L. A. Ferman, J. Kornbluh, and A. Haber, eds., pp. 405–415. Ann Arbor: University of Michigan Press.

LICHTHEIM, GEORGE

1961   *Marxism: An Historical and Critical Study*. New York: Praeger.

LIEBERMAN, PHILIP, AND E. S. CRELIN

1974   "Speech in Neanderthal Man: A Reply to Carlisle and Siegel." *American Anthropologist* 76:323–325.

LIEBERMAN, PHILIP, E. S. CRELIN, AND D. H. KLATT

1972 "Phonetic Ability and Related Anatomy of the Newborn, the Adult Human, Neanderthal Man, and the Chimpanzee." *American Anthropologist* 74:287–307.

LIEBOW, ELLIOT

1967 *Tally's Corner: A Study of Negro Street-Corner Men*. Boston: Little, Brown.

LINTON, RALPH

1949 "The Natural History of the Family." In *The Family: Its Function and Destiny*, R. N. Anshen, ed., pp. 18–38. New York: Harper.

LIVINGSTONE, FRANK B.

1959 "A Formal Analysis of Pre-scriptive Marriage Systems Among the Australian Aborigines." *Southwestern Journal of Anthropology* 15:361–372.

1968 "The Effects of Warfare on the Biology of the Human Species." In *War: The Anthropology of Armed Conflict and Aggression*, in M. Fried, M. Harris, and R. Murphy, eds., pp. 3–15. New York: Doubleday.

1969 "Genetics, Ecology, and the Origins of Incest and Exogamy." *Current Anthropology* 10:45–62.

LIZOT, JACQUES

1971 "Aspects economique et sociaux du changement cultural chez les Yanomamis." *L'Homme* 11:2–51.

LOMAX, ALAN, EDITOR

1968 *Folksong Style and Culture*. Washington: American Association for the Advancement of Science.

LOMAX, ALAN, AND NORMAN BERKOWITZ

1972 "The Evolutionary Taxonomy of Culture." *Science* 177:228–239.

LORENZ, KONRAD Z.

1966 *On Aggression*. New York: Harcourt, Brace and World.

LOVEJOY, C. OWEN

1974 "The Gait of Australopithecines." *Yearbook of Physical Anthropology* 17:147–161.

1975 "Biochemical Perspectives on the Lower Limbs of Early Hominids." In *Primate Functional Morphology and Evolution*, R. H. Tuttle, ed. The Hague: Mouton. [In press.]

LOVEJOY, C. O., K. G. HEIPLE, AND A. BURSTEIN

1973 "The Gait of Australopithecus." *American Journal of Physical Anthropology* 38:757–780.

LOWIE, ROBERT H.

1948 *Primitive Religion*. New York: Liveright. [Initially published 1924]

LUNDBERG, FERDINAND

1968 *The Rich and the Super Rich*. New York: Lyle Stuart.

LYNCH, OWEN

1973 "Man and Theory in the Sociology of Louis Dumont: An Empiricist's Reply." Paper presented to the IXth International Congress of Anthropological and Ethnological Sciences, Chicago.

MCCALL, R. B., M. I. APPLEBAUM, AND P. S. HOGARTY

1973 *Developmental Changes in Mental Performance*. Monographs, Vol. 38, No. 3, Society for Research in Child Development.

MCGREW, W. C., AND C. E. G. TUTIN

1973 "Chimpanzee Tool Use in Dental Grooming." *Nature* 241:477–478.

MCHENRY, HENRY

1974 "How Large Were the Australopithecines?" *American Journal of Physical Anthropology* 40:329–340.

641

MACLEISH, KENNETH
    1972   "The Tasadays: The Stone Age Cavemen of Mindanao." *National Geographic* 142:219–248.

MACNEISH, RICHARD
    1964   "Ancient Mesoamerican Civilization." *Science* 143:531–537.
    1968   "Early Man in the Andes." *Scientific American* 224, No. 4 (April):34–46.
    1972   "The Evolution of Community Patterns in the Tehuacán Valley of Mexico, and Speculation about the Cultural Processes." In *Man, Settlement, and Urbanism*, P. J. Ucko, R. Tringham, and G. W. Dimbleby, eds., pp. 67–93. Cambridge (Mass.): Schenkman.

MAGUBANE, B.
    1971   "A Critical Look at Indices Used in the Study of Social Change in Colonial Africa." *Current Anthropology* 12:419–466.
    1975   "The Native Reserves (Bantustans) and the Role of the Migrant Labor System in the Political Economy of South Africa." In *Migration, Change, and Development: Implications for Ethnic Identity and Political Conflict*, H. I. Safa and B. Du Toit, eds. The Hague: Mouton. [In press.]

MALEFIJT, ANNEMARIE
    1968   *Religion and Culture: An Introduction to the Anthropology of Religion.* New York: Macmillan.

MALINOWSKI, BRONISLAW
    1927   *Sex and Repression in Savage Society.* London: Routledge and Kegan Paul.

MAMDANI, MAHMOOD
    1973   *The Myth of Population Control: Family, Caste, and Class in an Indian Village.* New York: Monthly Review Press.

MANGLESDORF, PAUL
    1974   *Corn: Its Origin, Evolution, and Improvement.* Cambridge: Harvard University Press.

MANN, ALAN, AND E. TRINKAUS
    1974   "Neandertal and Neandertal-like Fossils from the Upper Pleistocene." *Yearbook of Physical Anthropology* 17:169–193.

MARLER, PETER, AND M. TAMURA
    1964   "Culturally Transmitted Patterns of Vocal Behavior in Sparrows." *Science,* 146:1483–1486.

MARETT, R. R.
    1914   *The Threshold of Religion.* London: Methuen. [Initial publication 1909.]

MARSHACK, ALEXANDER
    1972a   "Upper Paleolithic Notation and Symbol." *Science* 178:817–828.
    1972b   *The Roots of Civilization.* New York: McGraw-Hill.

MARSHALL, DONALD
    1971   "Sexual Behavior on Mangaia." In *Human Sexual Behavior*, D. Marshall and R. Suggs, eds., pp. 103–162. Englewood Cliffs: Prentice Hall.

MARTIN, JOHN
    1973   "On the Estimation of Sizes of Local Groups in a Hunting-Gathering Environment." *American Anthropologist* 75:1448–1468.

MARTIN, PAUL S.
    1973   "The Discovery of America." *Science* 179:969–975.

MARTIN, PAUL S., AND H. E. WRIGHT, EDITORS
    1967   *Pleistocene Extinctions: The Search for a Cause.* New Haven: Yale University Press.

MARTIN, R. D.
    1967   "Toward a Definition of Primates." *Man* 2:377–401.

642

MARX, KARL
    1973   *On Society and Social Change*, Neil Smelser, ed. Chicago: University of Chicago Press.

MARX, KARL, AND F. ENGELS
    1948   *The Communist Manifesto.* New York: International. [Initially Published 1848]

MASON, CAROL
    1964   "Natchez Class Structure." *Ethnohistory* 11:120–133.

MASON, J. ALDEN
    1957   *The Ancient Civilizations of Peru.* Harmondsworth (England): Penguin.

MEAD, MARGARET
    1949   *Male and Female.* New York: Morrow.
    1950   *Sex and Temperament in Three Primitive Societies.* New York: Mentor.
    1970   *Culture and Commitment.* Garden City: Natural History Press.

MEGGERS, BETTY
    1971   *Amazonia: Man and Culture in a Counterfeit Paradise.* Chicago: Aldine.

MEGGITT, MERVYN J.
    1964   "Male-Female Relationships in the Highlands of Australian New Guinea." *American Anthropologist* 66:204–224.
    1965   *The Lineage System of the Mae Enga of New Guinea.* London: Oliver and Boyd.

MELLAART, JAMES
    1967   *Çatal Hüyük: A Neolithic Town in Anatolia.* New York: McGraw-Hill.

MENCHER, JOAN
    1965   "The Nayars of South Malabar." In *Comparative Family Systems*, M. F. Nimkoff, ed., pp. 163–189. Boston: Houghton Mifflin.
    1975   "The Caste System Upside Down: Or, the Not So Mysterious East." *Current Anthropology* 16. [In press.]

MENGE-KALMAN, WENDY
    1974   "Private Property and Social Behavior in the Monogamous Stage of the History of the Family." Mimeographed.

MERRICK, H. V., J. DE HEINZELIN, P. HAESAERTS, AND F. C. HOWELL
    1973   "Archaeological Occurrences of Early Pleistocene Age from the Shungura Formation, Lower Omo Valley, Ethiopia." *Nature* 242:572–575.

MERTON, ROBERT
    1940   "Bureaucratic Structure and Personality." *Social Forces* 18:560–568.

MICHAEL, R. P., AND E. B. KEVERNE
    1968   "Pheromones in the Communication of Sexual Status in Primates." *Nature* 218:746–749.

MILGRAM, STANLEY
    1974   *Obedience to Authority: An Experimental Overview.* New York: Harper and Row.

MILLER, HERMAN P.
    1971   *Rich Man, Poor Man.* New York: T. Y. Crowell.

MILLER, S. M., F. RIESSMAN, AND A. A. SEAGULL
    1968   "Poverty and Self-Indulgence: A Critique of the Non-deferred Gratification Pattern." In *Poverty in America: A Book of Readings*, L. A. Ferman, J. L. Kornbluh, and A. Haber, eds., pp. 416–432. Ann Arbor: University of Michigan Press.

MILLER, WALTER B.
    1968   "Focal Concerns of Lower Class Culture." In *Poverty in America*, L. A. Ferman, J. A. Kornbluh, and A. Haber, eds., pp. 396–405. Ann Arbor: University of Michigan Press.

643

MILLET, KATE
    1970   *Sexual Politics*. New York: Doubleday.
MILLON, RENÉ
    1970   "Teotihuacan: Completion of the Map of the Giant Ancient City in the Valley of Mexico." *Science* 170:1077–1082.
    1973   *The Teotihuacan Map*. Austin: University of Texas Press.
MINTURN, LEIGH, AND JOHN T. HITCHCOCK
    1963   "The Rajputs of Khalapur, India." In *Six Cultures, Studies of Child Rearing*, B. B. Whiting, ed., pp. 203–361. New York: John Wiley.
MITCHELL, WILLIAM
    1973   "The Hydraulic Hypothesis: A Re-appraisal." *Current Anthropology* 14:532–535.
MIYADI, D.
    1967   "Differences in Social Behavior Among Japanese Macaque Troops." In *Progress in Primatology*, D. Starck, R. Schneider, and H. Kuhn, eds. Stuttgart: Gustav Fischer.
MONDLANE, EDUARDO
    1969   *The Struggle for Mozambique*. Baltimore: Penguin.
MONTAGU, ASHLEY M. F.
    1968   *Man and Aggression*. (Editor.) New York: Oxford University Press.
    1971   "Foreword." To *A Dissertation on the Poor Laws*, by Joseph Townsend. Berkeley: University of California Press.
    1974   *Man's Most Dangerous Myth: The Fallacy of Race*. (5th edition.) New York: Oxford University Press.
MOONEY, JAMES
    1965   *The Ghost Dance Religion*. Chicago: University of Chicago Press. [Initially published 1896.]
MOORE, OMAR K.
    1969   "Divination—A New Perspective." In *Environment and Cultural Behavior: Ecological Studies in Cultural Anthropology*, A. P. Vayda, ed., pp. 121–129. Garden City: Natural History Press.
MORRELL, W. P.
    1968   *The Gold Rushes*. London: Black.
MORREN, GEORGE
    1973   "Woman the Hunter." Paper presented to the 72nd Annual Meeting of the American Anthropological Association, New Orleans, November 28–December 2.
MORREY, ROBERT, AND JOHN MARWITT
    1975   "Ecology, Economy, and Warfare in Lowland South America." In *War: Its Causes and Correlates*, M. Nettleship, R. D. Givens, and A. Nettleship, eds. The Hague: Mouton [In press.]
MOSKOS, CHARLES
    1969   "Why Men Fight." Transaction 7, November: 13–23.
MOYNIHAN, DANIEL P.
    1965   *The Negro Family, the Case for National Action*. Washington: U. S. Dept. of Labor.
MUNSON, PATRICK
    1972   "Archaeological Data on the Origins of Cultivation in the Southwestern Sahara and Their Implications for West Africa." Paper presented to the Burg Wartenstein Symposium, No. 52, Wenner-Gren Foundation for Anthropological Research, New York City.
MURDOCK, GEORGE P.
    1967   *Ethnographic Atlas*. Pittsburgh: University of Pittsburgh Press.

644

MURDOCK, GEORGE P., C. S. FORD, A. E. HUDSON, AND OTHERS
1961   *Outline of Cultural Materials.* New Haven: Human Relations Area Files.

MURPHY, ROBERT
1956   "Matrilocality and Patrilineality in Mundurucu Society." *American Anthropologist* 58:414–434.

MURRAY, JACQUELINE
1970   *The First European Agriculture.* Chicago: Aldine.

MYRDAL, GUNNAR
1957   *Rich Lands and Poor: The Road to World Prosperity.* New York: Harper and Row.

1970   *The Challenge of World Poverty: A World Anti-Poverty Program in Outline.* New York: Pantheon.

NAG, MONI
1972   "Sex, Culture, and Human Fertility: India and the United States." *Current Anthropology* 13:231–238.

NAPIER, JOHN
1970   *The Roots of Mankind.* Washington: Smithsonian Institution.

NARANJO, CLAUDIO
1967   "Psychotropic Properties of the Harmala Alkaloids." In *The Ethnopharmacologic Search for Psychoactive Drugs*, D. Effron, editor. Washington: National Institute of Health.

NATIONAL RESEARCH COUNCIL
1969   *Report of the Committee on Persistent Pesticides.* From the Division of Biology and Agriculture, to the U.S. Department of Agriculture. Washington: National Academy of Sciences.

NEEDHAM, JOSEPH
1970   *Clerks and Craftsmen in China and the West.* Cambridge (England): Cambridge University Press.

NEEDHAM, JOSEPH, AND W. LING
1959   *Science and Civilization in China,* Volume III. Cambridge (England): Cambridge University Press.

NETTING, ROBERT
1969   "Ecosystems in Process: A Comparative Study of Change in Two West African Societies." In *Contributions to Anthropology: Ecological Essays*, D. Damas, ed., National Museum of Canada Bulletin 230:102–112. Ottawa: National Museum of Canada.

NEWMAN, PHILIP L.
1965   *Knowing the Gururumba.* New York: Holt, Rinehart and Winston.

NEWMAN, RUSSELL
1970   "Why Man Is Such a Sweaty and Thirsty Naked Animal: A Speculative Review." *Human Biology* 42:12–27.

NEWMEYER, FREDERICK
1975   "Linguistic Theory and Linguistic Practice: The Class Nature of Hypocrisy." In *Approaches to Language: Anthropological Issues*, W. C. McCormack and S. A. Wurm, eds. The Hague: Mouton, [In press.]

NURGE, ETHEL
1975   "Unwanted Births and Abortions in Cross-cultural Perspective." In *Being Female: Reproduction, Power, and Change*, D. Raphael, ed. The Hague: Mouton, [In press.]

OAKLEY, KENNETH
1966   *Frameworks for Dating Fossil Man.* Chicago: Aldine.

645

ODEND'HAL, STEWART
1972   "Energetics of Indian Cattle in Their Environment." *Journal of Human Ecology* 1:3–22.

ODUM, EUGENE P.
1969   "The Strategy of Ecosystem Development." *Science* 164:262–270.

OPLER, MORRIS
1968   "The Themal Approach in Cultural Anthropology and Its Application to North Indian Data." *Southwestern Journal of Anthropology* 24:215–227.

ORANS, MARTIN
1968   "Maximizing in Jajmaniland: A Model of Caste Relations." *American Anthropologist* 70:875–897.

OTTEN, CHARLOTTE M., EDITOR
1971   *Anthropology and Art: Readings in Cross-Cultural Aesthetics.* Garden City (N. Y.): Natural History Press.

OTTERBEIN, KEITH
1970   *The Evolution of War: A Cross-Cultural Study.* New Haven: Human Relations Area Files.
1972   "The Anthropology of War." In *The Handbook of Social and Cultural Anthropology*, J. Honigman, ed., pp. 923–958. Chicago: Rand McNally.

PADDOCK, WILLIAM, AND E. PADDOCK
1973   *We Don't Know How: An Independent Audit of What They Call Success in Foreign Assistance.* Ames: Iowa State University Press.

PARKER, RICHARD
1972   *The Myth of the Middle Class.* New York: Harper and Row, Colophon Books.

PARKER, SEYMOUR, AND R. KLEINER
1970   "The Culture of Poverty: An Adjustive Dimension." *American Anthropologist* 72:516–527.

PARSONS, ANNE
1967   "Is the Oedipus Complex Universal?" In *Personalities and Cultures: Readings in Psychological Anthropology*, Robert Hunt, ed., pp. 352–399. Garden City: Natural History Press.

PARSONS, LEE, AND BARBARA PRICE
1971   "Mesoamerican Trade and Its Role in the Emergence of Civilization in Mesoamerica." In *Observations on the Emergence of Civilization in Mesoamerica*, R. F. Heizer and J. A. Graham, eds. Berkeley: Archaeological Research Facility, University of California.

PARTRIDGE, T. C.
1973   "Geomorphological Dating of Cave Openings at Makapansgat, Sterkfontein, Swartkrans, and Taung." *Nature* 246:75–79.

PATTERSON, THOMAS
1973   *America's Past: A New World Archaeology.* Glenview: Scott, Foresman.

PECKMAN, JOSEPH, AND B. OKNER
1974   *Who Bears the Tax Burden?* Washington: Brookings Institution.

PELTO, PERTTIE
1970   *Anthropological Research: The Structure of Inquiry.* New York: Harper and Row.

PELTO, PERTTIE, AND GRETL PELTO
1973   "Ethnography: The Fieldwork Enterprise." In *Handbook of Social and Cultural Anthropology*, J. Honigman, ed., pp. 241–248. Chicago: Rand McNally.

PERKINS, DEXTER
1964   "Prehistoric Fauna from Shanidar, Iraq." *Science* 144:1565–1566.

646

PIDDOCK, STEWART
1965 "The Potlatch System of the Southern Kwakiutl: A New Perspective." *Southwestern Journal of Anthropology* 21:244–264.

PIKE, KENNETH L.
1967 *Language in Relation to a Unified Theory of the Structure of Human Behavior* [2nd edition]. The Hague: Mouton.

PILBEAM, DAVID
1975 "Hypothesis Testing in Paleonthropology." In *Paleoanthropology: Morphology and Paleoecology,* R. H. Tuttle, ed. The Hague: Mouton, [In press.]

PIMENTEL, DAVID, L. E. HURD, A. C. BELLOTTI, AND OTHERS
1973 "Food Production and the Energy Crisis." *Science* 182:443–449.

PING-TI HO
1975 "The Indigenous Origins of Chinese Agriculture." In *Origins of Agriculture,* C. Reed, ed. The Hague: Mouton. [In press.]

PIVEN, FRANCES, AND R. W. CLOWARD
1971 *Regulating the Poor: The Function of Public Welfare.* New York: Random House, Vintage Books.

PLOG, FRED T.
1974 *The Study of Prehistoric Change.* New York: Academic Press.

PLUMMER, JOHN
1966 "Another Look at Aymara Personality." Behavior Science Notes, *HRAF Quarterly Bulletin* 1:55–78.

POLGAR, STEVEN
1972 "Population History and Population Policies from an Anthropological Perspective." *Current Anthropology* 203–215.

POSPISIL, LEOPOLD
1963 *The Kapauku Papuans of West New Guinea.* New York: Holt, Rinehart and Winston.
1968 "Law and Order." In *Introduction to Cultural Anthropology,* J. Clifton, ed., pp. 200–224. Boston: Houghton Mifflin.

PREMACK, DAVID
1970 "A Functional Analysis of Language." *Journal of the Experimental Analysis of Behaviour* 14:107–1255.
1971 "On the Assessment of Language Competence in the Chimpanzee." In *The Behavior of Nonhuman Primates,* A. M. Schrier and F. Stollnitz, eds., vol. 4, pp. 185–228. New York: Academic Press.

PRONKO, N. H.
1969 *Panorama of Psychology.* Belmont: Brooks Cole.

PROTSCH, REINER, AND R. BERGER
1973 "Earliest Radiocarbon Dates for Domesticated Animals." *Scientific American* 79.

PULESTON, D. E., AND O. S. PULESTON
1971 "An Ecological Approach to the Origin of Maya Civilization." *Archaeology* 24:330–337.

RADCLIFFE BROWN, A. R.
1952 *Structure and Function in Primitive Society: Essays and Addresses.* London: Cohen and West.

RAPPAPORT, ROY A.
1967 "Ritual Regulation of Environmental Relations among a New Guinea People." *Ethnology* 6:17–30.

647

1968   *Pigs for the Ancestors: Ritual in the Ecology of a New Guinea People.* New Haven: Yale University Press.

1971   "Ritual, Sanctity, and Cybernetics." *American Anthropologist* 73:59–76.

RASMUSSEN, KNUD

1929   *The Intellectual Culture of the Iglulik Eskimos.* Report of the 5th Thule Expedition, 1921–24, Volume VII, Number 1. Translated by W. Worster. Copenhagen: Gyldendal.

RENFREW, COLLIN

1973   *Before Civilization: The Radiocarbon Revolution and Prehistoric Europe.* New York: Knopf.

RICHARDS, PAUL

1973   "The Tropical Rain Forest." *Scientific American* 229 (December): 58–68.

RIEGELHAUPT, J. F., AND S. FORMAN

1970   "Bodo was Never Brazilian: Economic Integration and Rural Development Among a Contemporary Peasantry." *Journal of Economic History* 30:100–116.

ROACH, JACK L., L. GROSS, AND O. R. GURSSLIN, EDITORS

1969   *Social Stratification in the United States.* Englewood Cliffs: Prentice-Hall.

ROBERTS, PAUL

1964   *English Syntax.* New York: Harcourt Brace.

ROBINSON, JOHN T.

1973   *Early Hominid Posture and Locomotion.* Chicago: University of Chicago Press.

ROHEIM, GÉZA

1950   *Psychoanalysis and Anthropology.* New York: International University Press.

ROHNER, RONALD

1969   *The Ethnography of Franz Boas.* Chicago: University of Chicago Press.

ROPER, MARILYN K.

1969   "A Survey of the Evidence for Intrahuman Killing in the Pleistocene." *Current Anthropology* 10:427–459.

1975   "Evidence of Warfare in the Near East from 10,000 to 4,000 B. C." In *War: Its Causes and Correlates*, W. Nettleship, R. D. Givens, and A. Nettleship, eds. The Hague: Mouton. [In press.]

ROSALDO, MICHELLE, AND LOUISE LAMPHERE, EDITORS

1974   *Woman, Culture, and Society.* Stanford: Stanford University Press.

ROSENFELD, G.

1972   *"Shut Those Thick Lips": A Study of Slum and School Failure.* New York: Holt, Rinehart and Winston.

ROSENTHAL, BERNICE

1975   "The Role and Status of Women in the Soviet Union." In *Being Female: Reproduction, Power, and Change*, D. Raphael, ed. The Hague: Mouton, [In press.]

ROSS, ERIC, AND JANE ROSS

n. d.   Personal communication

ROTHBERG, ABRAHAM

1972   *The Heirs of Stalin: Dissidence and the Soviet Regime, 1953–1970.* Ithaca: Cornell University Press.

RUNBAUGH, DUANE M., T. V. GILL, AND E. C. VON GLASSERFELD
1973   "Reading and Sentence Completion by a Chimpanzee (Pan)." *Science*
        182:731–733.

RUSCHE, GEORG, AND O. KIRCHEIMER
1939   *Punishment and Social Structure.* New York: Columbia University Press.

RUYLE, EUGENE E.
1971   *The Political Economy of the Japanese Ghetto.* Ph. D. dissertation, Columbia
        University.
1973a   "Genetic and Cultural Pools: Some Suggestions for a Unified Theory of
        Biocultural Evolution." *Human Ecology* 1:201–215.
1973b   "Slavery, Surplus, and Stratification on the Northwest Coast: The Ethnoener-
        getics of an Incipient Stratification System. *Current Anthropology* 14:603–
        631.
1975   "Energy and Culture." In *The Concepts and Dynamics of Culture,* B.
        Bernardi, ed. The Hague: Mouton. [In press.]

SACKS, KAREN B.
n. d.   "Comparative Notes on the Position of Women." Mimeographed.
1971   "Economic Bases of Sexual Equality: A Comparative Study of Four African
        Societies." Ph. D. dissertation, University of Michigan.

SAFA, HELEN I.
1967   *An Analysis of Upward Mobility in Lower Income Families: A Comparison
        of Family and Community Life among American Negro and Puerto Rican
        Poor.* Syracuse: Youth Development Center.
1968   "The Case for Negro Separatism: The Crisis of Identity in the Black Communi-
        ty." *Urban Affairs Quarterly* 4:45–63.

SAHLINS, MARSHALL D.
1958   *Social Stratification in Polynesia.* Seattle: University of Washington Press.
1961   "The Segmentary Lineage: An Organization of Predatory Expansion." *Ameri-
        can Anthropologist* 63:322–345.
1968   *Tribesmen.* Englewood Cliffs: Prentice-Hall
1971   "Poor Man, Rich Man, Big Man, Chief." In *Conformity and Conflict: Read-
        ings in Cultural Anthropology,* J. Spradley and D. McCurdy, eds., pp.
        318–332. Boston: Little, Brown.

SAHLINS, MARSHALL D., AND ELMAN SERVICE, EDITORS
1960   *Evolution and Culture.* Ann Arbor: University of Michigan Press.

SALZMAN, PHILIP, EDITOR
1971   "Comparative Studies of Nomadism and Pastoralism." *Anthropological
        Quarterly* 44, No. 3:104–210.

SAMULSSON, KURT
1964   *Religion and Economic Action: A Critique of Max Weber.* New York: Harper
        and Row, Torchbooks.

SANDAY, PEGGY
1968   "The 'Psychological Reality' of American-English Kinship Terms: An Informa-
        tion-Processing Approach." *American Anthropologist* 70:508–523.
1973   "Toward a Theory of the Status of Women." *American Anthropologist*
        75:1682–1700.

SANDERS, WILLIAM T.
1972   "Population, Agricultural History, and Societal Evolution in Mesoamerica." In
        Population Growth: Anthropological Perspective, B. Spooner, ed. Cam-
        bridge: M. I. T. Press.

SANDERS, WILLIAM T., AND B. PRICE
1968   *Mesoamerica: The Evolution of a Civilization.* New York: Random House.

649

SANJEK, ROGER
    1972   "Ghanaian Networks: An Analysis of Interethnic Relations in Urban Situations." Ph.D. dissertation, Columbia University.
SAPIR, EDWARD
    1921   *Language.* New York: Harcourt Brace.
SARAYDAR, S., AND I. SHIMADA
    1971   "A Quantitative Comparison of Efficiency Between a Stone Axe and a Steel Axe." *American Antiquity* 36:216–217.
SARTONO, S.
    1975   "Implications Arising from Pithecanthropus VIII." In *Paleoanthropology: Morphology and Paleoecology*, R. H. Tuttle, ed. The Hague: Mouton, [In press.]
SCARR-SALAPATEK, S.
    1971a   "Unknowns in the I. Q. Equation." *Science* 174:1223–1228.
    1971b   "Race, Social Class, and I.Q." *Science* 174:1285–1295.
SCHALLER, GEORGE B.
    1963   *The Mountain Gorilla.* Chicago: University of Chicago Press.
    1965   "The Behavior of the Mountain Gorilla." In *Primate Behavior: Field Studies of Monkeys and Apes*, I. DeVore, ed., pp. 324–367. New York: Holt, Rinehart and Winston.
    1972   *The Serengeti Lion.* Chicago: University of Chicago Press.
SCHALLER, GEORGE B., AND GORDON LOWTHER
    1969   "The Relevance of Carnivore Behavior to the Study of Early Hominids." *Southwestern Journal of Anthropology* 25:307–341.
SCHEFFLER, HAROLD
    1973   "Kinship, Descent, and Alliance." In *Handbook of Social and Cultural Anthropology*, J. Honigman, ed., pp. 747–793. Chicago: Rand McNally.
SCHLEGEL, ALICE
    1972   *Male Dominance and Female Autonomy.* New Haven: Human Relations Area Files Press.
SCHUMAN, HOWARD
    1969   "Sociological Racism." *Transaction* 7, No. 2: 44–48.
SCHURMANN, H. FRANZ
    1966   *Ideology and Organization in Communist China.* Berkeley: University of California Press.
SCHURMANN, H. FRANZ, AND O. SCHELL, EDITORS
    1967   *The China Reader.* New York: Random House.
SCHWARTZ, M., AND J. SCHWARTZ
    1974   "Evidence Against a Genetical Component to Performance on I. Q. Tests." *Nature* 248:84–85.
SCRIBNER, S., AND M. COLE
    1973   "Cognitive Consequences of Formal and Informal Education." *Science* 182:553–559.
SEBEOK, THOMAS
    1972   *Perspectives in Zoosemiotics.* The Hague: Mouton.
SENGEL, RANDAL
    1973   "On Mechanism of Population Growth During the Neolithic." *Current Anthropology* 14:540–542.
SEXTON, LORRAINE
    1973   "Sexual Interaction and Population Pressure in Highland New Guinea." Paper presented to the 72nd Annual Meeting of the American Anthropological Association, New Orleans, Nov. 29–30.

650

SHUEY, AUDREY M.
  1966   *The Testing of Negro Intelligence*. New York: Social Science Press.

SILVERSTEIN, MICHAEL
  1972   "Linguistic Theory: Syntax, Semantics, Pragmatics." In *Annual Review of Anthropology*, B. Siegal and A. Beals, eds., pp. 349–382. Stanford: Stanford University Press.

SIMONS, ELWYN L.
  1968   "A Source for Dental Comparison of Ramapithecus with Australopithecus and Homo." *South African Journal of Science* 64:92–112.
  1969   "The Origin and Radiation of the Primates." *Annals of the New York Academy of Sciences* 167:319–331.
  1975   "Diversity Among the Early Hominids: A Vertebrate Paleontologist's Point of View." In *Early Man in Africa*, C. Jolly, ed. London: Duckworth. [In press.]

SIMONS, ELWYN L., AND P. ETTEL
  1970   "Gigantopithecus." *Scientific American* 222 (January): 77–85.

SIMPSON, DAVID
  1968   "The Dimensions of World Poverty." *Scientific American* 219 (November):27–35.

SIMPSON, GEORGE G.
  1949   *The Meaning of Evolution: A Study of the History of Life and of Its Significance for Man*. New Haven: Yale University Press.

SIPES, RICHARD
  1973   "War, Sports, and Aggression: An Empirical Test of Two Rival Theories." *American Anthropologist* 75:64–86.
  1975   "War, Combative Sports, and Aggression: A Preliminary Causal Mode of Cultural Patterning." In *War: Its Causes and Correlates*, M. Nettleship, R. D. Givens, and A. Nettleship, eds. The Hague: Mouton. [In press.]

SLOBIN, DANIEL
  1973   *Studies in Child Language Development*. New York: Holt, Rinehart and Winston.

SMITH, C. T.
  1970   "Depopulation of the Central Andes in the 16th Century." *Current Anthropology* 11:453–460.

SMITH, JAMES D.
  1973   *The Concentration of Personal Wealth in America*. Washington: The Urban Institute.

SMITH, J., S. FRANKLIN, AND D. WION
  1973   *The Distribution of Financial Assets*. Washington: The Urban Institute.

SMITH, M. G.
  1968   "Secondary Marriage among Kadera and Kagoro." In *Marriage, Family, and Residence*, P. Bohannan and J. Middleton, eds., pp. 109–130. Garden City: Natural History Press.

SMITH, MARIAN, EDITOR
  1961   *The Artist in Tribal Society*. New York: Free Press.

SMITH, PHILIP
  1972a   *The Consequences of Food Production*. Reading (Mass.): Addison-Wesley.
  1972b   "Land Use, Settlement Patterns, and Subsistence Agriculture." In *Man, Settlement, and Urbanism*, P. J. Ucko, R. Tringham, and G. W. Dimbleby, eds., pp. 409–425. Cambridge (Mass.): Schenkman.

SMITH, PHILIP, AND C. YOUNG, JR.
  1972   "The Evolution of Early Agriculture and Culture in Greater Mesopotamia: A Trial Model." In *Population Growth: Anthropological Implications*, Brian Spooner, ed., pp. 5–19. Cambridge: M. I. T. Press.

651

SOLECKI, RALPH
1955   "Shanidar Cave Paleolithic Site in Northern Iraq." In *Smithsonian Institution Report for 1954*, pp. 389–425. Washington: Smithsonian Institution.
1971   *Shanidar: The First Flower People.* New York: A. A. Knopf.

SOLECKI, ROSE
1964   "Zawi Chemi Shanidar, a Post-Pleistocene Site in Northern Iraq." In *Report of the VIth International Quarternary*, pp. 405–412. Warsaw, 1961.

SOLHEIM, WILLIAM
1967   "Southeast Asia and the West." *Science* 157:896–902.
1970   "Relics from Two Diggings Indicate the Thais Were the First Agrarians." *New York Times*, Jan. 12.

SOLZHENITSYN, ALEXANDER
1974   *Gulag Archipelago.* New York: Harper and Row.

SORENSON, RICHARD
1972   "Socio-Ecological Change Among the Fore of New Guinea." *Current Anthropology* 13:349–383.

SORENSON, RICHARD, AND P. E. KENMORE
1974   "Proto-Agricultural Movement in the Eastern Highlands of New Guinea." *Current Anthropology* 15:67–72.

SOUSTELLE, JACQUES
1970   *Daily Life of the Aztecs.* Stanford: Stanford University Press.

SOUTHWORTH, FRANKLIN
n. d.   "Linguistic Masks for Power: Some Relationships Between Semantic and Social Change." (Published in Anthropological Linguistics May 1974)
1969   " 'Standard' Language and Social Structure." Paper presented to the 68th Annual Meeting of the American Anthropological Association, New Orleans, Nov. 20–23.

SPECK, FRANK G.
1915   "The Family Hunting Band as the Basis of the Algonkian Social Organization." *American Anthropologist* 17: 289–305.

SPENCER, BALDWIN, AND F. J. GILLEN
1968   *The Native Tribes of Central Australia.* New York: Dover.

SPENGLER, JOSEPH J.
1969   "Population Problem: In Search of Solution." *Science* 166:1234–1238.

SRINIVAS, M. N.
1955   "The Social System of a Mysore Village." In *Village India: Studies in the Little Community*, M. Marriott, ed., pp. 1–35. Memoir 83, American Anthropological Association.

STACK, CAROL
1974   *All Our Kin: Strategies for Survival In a Black Community.* New York: Harper and Row.

STEINHART, JOHN, AND CAROL STEINHART
1974   "Energy Use in the U. S. Food System." *Science* 184:307–317.

STEWARD, JULIAN H.
1955   *Theory of Culture Change: The Methodology of Multilinear Evolution.* Urbana: University of Illinois Press.
1968   "Causal Factors and Processes in the Evolution of Pre-Farming Societies." In *Man the Hunter*, R. B. Lee and I. DeVore, eds., pp. 321–334. Chicago: Aldine.

STEWART, OMER C.
1948   *Ute Peyotyism.* University of Colorado Studies, Series in Anthropology, No. 1. Boulder: University of Colorado Press.
1968   "Lorenz/Margolin on the Ute." In *Man and Aggression*, M. F. Ashley Montagu, ed., pp. 103–110. New York: Oxford University Press.

Bibliographical References

STURTEVANT, EDGAR H.
1964   *An Introduction to Linguistic Science.* New Haven: Yale University Press.

SUGIYAMA, YUKIMARU
1969   "Social Behavior of Chimpanzees in the Budongo Forest, Uganda." *Primates* 10:197–225.

SUSSMAN, ROBERT
1972   "Child Transport, Family Size, and Increase in Population During the Neolithic." *Current Anthropology* 13:258–259.

SUTTLES, WAYNE
1960   "Affinal Ties, Subsistence, and Prestige among the Coast Salish." *American Anthropologist* 62:296–305.

SUZUKI, AKIRA
1975   "The Origin of Hominid Hunting: A Primatological Perspective." In *Paleoanthropology: Morphology and Paleoecology*, R. H. Tuttle, ed. The Hague: Mouton. [In press.]

SUZUKI, H., AND F. TAKAI, EDITORS
1970   *The Amud Man and His Cave Site.* Tokyo: University of Tokyo Press.

SWADESH, MORRIS
1971   *The Origin and Diversification of Language*, Joel F. Sherzer, ed. Chicago: Aldine.

SWANSON, GUY E.
1960   *The Birth of the Gods: The Origin of Primitive Beliefs.* Ann Arbor: University of Michigan Press.

TALBERT, CAROL
1973   "Studying Education in the Ghetto." In *To See Ourselves*, T. Weaver, ed., pp. 310–314. Glenview (Ill.): Scott, Foresman.

TANNER, J. M.
1968   "Earlier Maturation in Man." *Scientific American* 218, No. 1 (January): 21–27.

1973   "Regulation of Vitamin D Metabolism." *Nature* 245:180–182.

TEFFT, STANTON
1975   "Warfare Regulation: A Cross-Cultural Test of Hypotheses." In *War: Its Causes and Correlates*, M. Nettleship, R. D. Givens, and A. Nettleship, eds. The Hague: Mouton. [In press.]

TELEKI, GEZA
1973   "The Omniverous Chimpanzee." *Scientific American,* 288 (January): 32–42.

THOMAS, DAVID
1974a   "An Archaeological Perspective on Shoshonean Bands." *American Anthropologist* 76:11–23.
1974b   *Predicting the Past.* New York: Holt, Rinehart and Winston.

THORNDIKE, R. L.
1968   "Intelligence and Intelligence Testing." *International Encyclopedia of the Social Sciences* 7:421–429.

THRUPP, SYLVIA, EDITOR
1962   *Millennial Dreams in Action.* The Hague: Mouton.

TOBIAS, PHILIP V.
1965   "New Discoveries in Tanganyika: Their Bearing on Hominid Evolution." *Current Anthropology* 6:391–411.
1973   "Implications of the New Age Estimates of the Early South African Hominids." *Nature* 246:79–83.

TRIMINGHAM, R.
1959   *Islam in West Africa.* Oxford (England): Clarendon Press.

653

TURNER, VICTOR W.
1967   *The Forest of Symbols: Aspects of Ndembu Ritual.* Ithaca: Cornell University Press.

TUTTLE, RUSSELL H.
1969   "Knuckle-Walking and the Problem of Human Origins." *Science* 166:953–961.
1975   "Knuckle-Walking and Knuckle-Walkers: A Commentary on Some Recent Perspectives on Hominid Evolution." In *Primate Functional Morphology and Evolution*, R. H. Tuttle, ed. The Hague: Mouton. [In press.]

TYLOR, EDWARD B.
1871   *Primitive Culture.* London: J. Murray.

UBEROI, J. P. SINGH
1962   *Politics of the Kula Ring: An Analysis of the Findings of Bronislaw Malinowski.* Manchester: Manchester University Press.

UCKO, PETER J., AND A. ROSENFELD
1967   *Paleolithic Cave Art.* London: Weidenfeld and Nicolson.

UNITED NATIONS
1973   *Implementation of the Industrial Development Strategy* (E/5267/ST/ECA/ 178).
1974a   *Study of the Problems of Raw Materials and Development: Evolution of Basic Commodity Prices Since 1950* (A/9544).
1974b   *Problems of Raw Materials and Development.* Note by the Secretary-General of UNCTAD (UNCTAD/OSG/52).

U. S., AGENCY FOR INTERNATIONAL DEVELOPMENT
1971   *Rice in the Philippines.* Country Crop Papers. Washington: East Asia Technical Advisory Office.

U.S., BUREAU OF CENSUS
1969   *Trends in Social and Economic Conditions in Metropolitan Areas.* Washington: USGPO.

U.S., ECONOMIC COUNCIL
1974   *Economic Report to the President, Transmitted to Congress.* Washington: USGPO.

UPTON. LETITIA, AND N. LYONS
1972   *Basic Lack: Distribution of Personal Income and Wealth in the United States.* Cambridge (Mass.): Cambridge Institute.

VAILLANT, GEORGE C.
1966   *The Aztecs of Mexico.* Baltimore: Penguin. [Initially published 1941]

VALENTINE, CHARLES A.
1969   "Culture and Poverty: Critique and Counter." *Current Anthropology* 10:181– 201. [With comments.]
1972   *Black Studies and Anthropology: Scholarly and Political Interests in Afro-American Culture.* Reading (Mass.): Addison-Wesley.

VALENTINE, CHARLES A., AND B. L. VALENTINE
1970   "Making the Scene, Digging the Action, and Telling It Like It Is: Anthropologists at Work in a Dark Ghetto." In *Afro-American Anthropology: Contemporary Perspectives*, N. E. Whitten and J. F. Szwed, eds., pp. 403–418. New York: Free Press.
1975   "Brain Damage and the Intellectual Defense of Inequality." *Current Anthropology* 16:[In press.]

VAN DEN BERGHE, PIERRE
1972   "Sex Differentiation and Infant Care: A Rejoinder to Sharlotte Neely Williams." *American Anthropologist* 74:770–771.

654

VAN GINNEKEN, J. K.
1974 "Prolonged Breastfeeding as a Birth Spacing Method." *Studies in Family Planning* 5:201–208.

VAN LAWICK-GOODALL, JANE
1964 "Tool-Using and Aimed Throwing in a Community of Free-Living Chimpanzees." *Nature* 201:1264–1266.

1965 "Chimpanzees on the Gombe Stream Reserve." In *Primate Behavior*, I. DeVore, ed., pp. 425–473. New York: Holt, Rinehart and Winston.

1968 "Tool-Using Bird: The Egyptian Vulture." *National Geographic* 133:630–641.

1972 "Expressive Movements and Communication in Chimpanzees." In *Primate Patterns*, P. Dolhinow, ed., pp. 25–84. New York: Holt, Rinehart and Winston.

VAYDA, ANDREW P.
1961 "Expansion and Warfare among Swidden Agriculturalists." *American Anthropologist* 63:346–358.

1968 "Hypotheses about the Function of War." In *The Anthropology of Armed Conflict and Aggression*, M. Fried, M. Harris, and R. Murphy, eds., pp. 85–91. Garden City: Natural History Press.

1970 "Maoris and Muskets in New Zealand: Disruption of a War System." *Political Science Quarterly* 85:560–584.

1971 "Phases of the Process of War and Peace Among the Marings of New Guinea." *Oceania* 42:1–24.

VISHNU-MITTRE
1975 "The Archaeobotanical and Palynological Evidences for the Early Origin of Agriculture in South and Southeast Asia." In *Gastronomy: The Anthropology of Food and Food Habits*, M. Arnott, ed. The Hague: Mouton. [In press.]

VOGEL, CHRISTIAN T.
1975 "Remarks on the Reconstruction of the Dental Arcade of Ramapithecus." In *Paleoanthropology: Morphology and Paleoecology*, R. H. Tuttle, ed. The Hague: Mouton. [In press.]

VOGT, EVON Z.
1969 *Zinacantan.* Cambridge: Harvard University Press.

VOGT, EVON Z., AND F. CANCIAN
1970 "Social Integration and the Classic Maya: Some Problems in Haviland's Argument." *American Antiquity* 35:101–102.

VON FRISCH, KARL
1950 *Bees: Their Vision, Chemical Senses, and Language.* Ithaca: Cornell University Press.

VON KOENIGSWALD, G. H. R.
1975 "Java Early Man: Catalogue and Problems." In *Paleoanthropology: Morphology and Paleoecology*, R. H. Tuttle, ed. The Hague: Mouton. [In press.]

VON KOENIGSWALD, G. H. R., AND P. TOBIAS
1964 "A Comparison Between the Olduvai Hominids and Those of Java and Some Implications for Hominid Phylogeny." *Nature* 204:515–518.

WADE, NICHOLAS
1973 "The World Food Situation: Pessimism Comes Back Into Vogue." *Science* 181:634–638.

WADEL, CATO
1973 *Now, Who's Fault Is That?: The Struggle for Self-Esteem in the Face of Chronic Unemployment.* Institute of Social and Economic Research, Memorial University of Newfoundland.

WAGAR, J. A.
1970 "Growth versus the Quality of Life." *Science* 168:1179–1184.

WAGLEY, CHARLES

    1943   "Tapirapé Shamanism." Boletim Do Museu Nacional (Rio de Janiero) *Antropología* 3:1–94.

    1969   "Cultural Influences on Population: A Comparison of Two Tupi Tribes." In *Environment and Cultural Behavior: Ecological Studies in Cultural Anthropology*, A. P. Vayda, ed., pp. 268–279. Garden City: Natural History Press.

WAGLEY, CHARLES, AND M. HARRIS.

    1958   *Minorities in the New World*. New York: Columbia University Press.

WALKER, ALLAN, AND PETER ANDREWS

    1973   "Reconstruction of the Dental Arcades of *Ramapithecus wickeri*." *Nature* 244:313–314.

WALKER, DEWARD

    1972   *The Emergent Native Americans*. Boston: Little, Brown.

WALLACE, ANTHONY F. C.

    1952   *The Modal Personality Structure of the Tuscarora Indians, as Revealed by the Rorschach Test*. Bulletin 150, Bureau of American Ethnology. Washington: USGPO.

    1966   *Religion: An Anthropological View*. New York: Random House.

    1970a   "A Rational Analysis of American Kinship Terminology." *American Anthropologist* 72:841–845.

    1970b   *Culture and Personality*. 2nd ed. New York: Random House.

WALLACE, ANTHONY F. C., AND J. ATKINS

    1960   "The Meaning of Kinship Terms." *American Anthropologist* 62: 52–80.

WALLACE, JOHN

    1973   "Tooth Chipping in the Australopithecines." *Nature* 244:117–118.

    1975   "Dietary Adaptations of Australopithecus and Early Homo." In *Paleoanthropology: Morphology and Paleoecology*, R. H. Tuttle, ed. The Hague: Mouton. [In press.]

WALLACE, WILSON

    1943   *Messiahs: Their Role in Civilization*. Washington: American Council on Public Affairs.

WALSH, MAURICE, AND B. SCANDALIS

    1975   "Institutionalized Forms of Intergenerational Male Aggression." In *War: Its Causes and Correlates*, M. Nettleship, R. D. Givens, and A. Nettleship, eds. The Hague: Mouton. [In press.]

WARNER, W. LLOYD, EDITOR

    1963   *Yankee City*. New Haven: Yale University Press.

WARNER, W. LLOYD, M. MEEKER, AND K. EELLS

    1949   *Social Class in America: A Manual for the Measurement of Social Status*. Chicago: Chicago Research Association.

WASHBURN, SHERWOOD, AND C. S. LANCASTER

    1967   "The Evolution of Hunting." In *Human Evolution: Readings in Physical Anthropology*. N. Korn and F. W. Thompson, eds., pp. 67–83. New York: Holt, Rinehart and Winston.

WAX, MURRAY, S. DIAMOND, AND F. O. GEARING

    1971   *Anthropological Perspectives on Education*. New York: Basic Books.

WEBER, MAX

    1952   *The Protestant Ethic and the Spirit of Capitalism*. New York: Charles Scribner.

WEAVER, MURIEL PORTER

    1972   *The Aztecs, Maya, and Their Predecessors*. New York: Seminar Press.

656

WEINER, J. S.
1973   *The Tropical Origins of Man*. Reading (Mass.): Addison-Wesley.
WEISS, GERALD
1973   "A Scientific Concept of Culture." *American Anthropologist* 75:1366–1413.
WELLS, PATRICK, AND A. WENNER
1973   "Do Honey Bees Have a Language?" *Nature* 241:171–175.
WENDORF, F., AND R. SCHILD
1975   "The Use of Ground Grain During the Late Paleolithic of the Lower Nile Valley, Egypt." In *The Origin of African Plant Domesticates*, F. Wendorf and R. Schild, eds. The Hague: Mouton.
WENDORF, F., R. SCHILD, AND S. RUSHDI
1970   "Egyptian Prehistory: Some New Concepts." *Science* 169:1161–1171.
WERNER, OSWALD, AND J. FENTON
1973   "Method and Theory in Ethnoscience or Ethnoepistemology." In *A Handbook of Method in Cultural Anthropology*, R. Naroll and R. Cohen, eds., pp. 537–578. New York: Columbia University Press.
WEST, JAMES
1945   *Plainville, U. S. A.* New York: Columbia University Press.
WHEATLEY, PAUL
1970   *The Pivot of the Four Corners: A Preliminary Inquiry into the Origins and Character of the Chinese City*. Chicago: Aldine.
WHITE, BENJAMIN
1973   "Demand for Labor and Population Growth in Colonial Java." *Human Ecology* 1:217–236.
1974   "Reply to Geertz and van der Walle." *Human Ecology* 2:63–65.
1975   "The Economic Importance of Children in a Javanese Village." In *Population and Social Organization*, Moni Nag. ed. The Hague: Mouton. [In press.]
WHITING, JOHN M.
1969   "Effects of Climate on Certain Cultural Practices." In *Environment and Cultural Behavior: Ecological Studies in Cultural Anthropology*, A. P. Vayda, ed., pp. 416–455. Garden City: Natural History Press.
WHORF, BENJAMIN
1956   *Language, Thought, and Reality*. New York: Wiley.
WILBERT, JOHANNES
1972   *Survivors of Eldorado*. New York: Praeger.
WILLIAMS, SHARLOTTE N.
1971   "The Limitations of Male/Female Activity Distinction among Primates." *American Anthropologist* 73:805–806.
1973   "The Argument Against the Physiological Determination of Female Roles." *American Anthropologist* 75:1725–1728.
WILLS, CHRISTOPHER
1970   "Genetic Load." *Scientific American* 222, No. 3 (March): 98–107.
WILSON, MONICA
1963   *Good Company: A Study of Nyakyusa Age-Villages*. Boston: Little, Brown.
WINGERT, PAUL
1962   *Primitive Art: Its Traditions and Styles*. New York: Oxford University Press.
WITTFOGEL, KARL A.
1957   *Oriental Despotism: A Comparative Study of Total Power*. New Haven: Yale University Press.
1960   "A Stronger Oriental Despotism." *China Quarterly* 1–6.

657

WOLBERG, DONALD
    1970   "The Hypothesized Osteodontokeratic Culture of the Australopithecinae: A Look at the Evidence and the Opinions." *Current Anthropology* 11:23–37.

WOLF, ARTHUR P.
    1966   "Childhood Association, Sexual Attraction, and the Incest Taboo: A Chinese Case." *American Anthropologist* 68:883–898.
    1968   "Adopt a Daughter-In-Law, Marry a Sister: A Chinese Solution to the Problem of the Incest Taboo." *American Anthropologist* 70:864–874.

WOLF, ERIC R.
    1959   *Sons of the Shaking Earth*. Chicago: University of Chicago Press.
    1966   *Peasants*. Englewood Cliffs: Prentice-Hall.
    1969   *Peasant Wars of the Twentieth Century*. New York: Harper and Row.
    1972   Comment on Dalton's "Peasantries and Anthropology in History." *Current Anthropology* 14:410–411.

WOLF, ERIC R., AND SIDNEY MINTZ
    1957   "Haciendas and Plantations in Middle America and the Antilles." *Social and Economic Studies* 6:380–412. Kingston, Jamaica: University College of the West Indies.

WOLPOFF, MILFORD H.
    1968   "'Telanthropus' and the Single Species Hypothesis." *American Anthropologist* 70:477–493.
    1970   "The Evidence for Multiple Hominid Taxa at Swartkrans." *American Anthropologist* 72:576–607.
    1971   "Competitive Exclusion Among Lower Pleistocene Hominids: The Single Species Hypothesis." *Man* 6:601–614.
    1974   "The Evidence for Two Australopithecine Lineages in South Africa." *Yearbook of Physical Anthropology* 17:113–139.
    1975a   "Sexual Dimorphism in the Australopithecines." In *Paleoanthropology: Morphology and Paleoecology*, R. Tuttle, ed. The Hague: Mouton. [In press.]
    1975b   "Analogies and Interpretation in Paleoanthropology." In *Early Man in Africa*, C. Jolly, ed. London: Duckworth. [In press.]

WORSLEY, PETER
    1968   *The Trumpet Shall Sound: A Study of "Cargo" Cults In Melanesia*. New York: Schocken.

YERKES, ROBERT
    1921   *Psychological Examining in the United States Army*. National Academy of Science Memoirs No. 15. Washington: National Academy of Science.

ZERRIES, O.
    1968   "Some Aspects of Waica Culture." *Proceedings of the 31st International Congress of Americanists, Saõ Paulo*, pp. 73–88.

ZOHARY, DANIEL, AND M. HOPF
    1973   "Domestication of Pulses in the Old World." *Science* 182:887–894.

658

GLOSSARY

adaptation: the process by which organisms, or cultural elements, undergo change in form or function in relation to their environment in order to succeed.

affinal: a relationship based on marriage.

age grades: in some societies, formally institutionalized segmentation of the population, by sex and chronological age, with **rites of passage** announcing the transition from one status to the next.

agriculture: generally, the cultivation of domesticated crops; specifically, involving plants and animals jointly, and with the use of the plow.

alleles: variants of **genes** which occupy the same location on corresponding **chromosomes,** and may effect trait differences.

animatism: the attribution of humanlike consciousness and powers to inanimate objects, natural phenomena, plants, and animals.

animism: belief in personalized yet disembodied beings, such as souls, ghosts, spirits, and gods. Compare **animatism.**

artifacts: material objects made by human hands, and having specifiable uses and **functions.**

ascribed status: the attributes of an individual's position in **society,** which are involuntary and often inevitable, such as sex, age, and inheritance.

assimilation: disappearance of a group—usually a **minority**—through the loss of biological and/or cultural distinctiveness.

avunculocal residence: relocation of a couple after marriage with or near the groom's mother's brother.

band, local: a small, loosely organized group of hunter-gatherer families, occupying a specifiable territory, and tending toward self-sufficiency.

basic personality: certain culturally defined traits expected to characterize generally members of a societal group.

659

Bergmann's Rule: that warm-blooded species tend to develop larger, heavier bodies in the colder limits of their range.

biface tools: flintlike nodules worked by percussion on both surfaces to yield well formed cutting and scraping edges.

bilateral descent: rule by which ego traces **kinship** equally through antecedents and offspring of both sexes.

blade tools: long, thin flakes with relatively parallel edges, struck from a core.

blood feud: vengeful confrontation between opposing groups of kin, set off by real or alleged homicide or other crimes, and involving continuing alternative retaliation in kind.

blood groups: populations which are characterized genetically by a high frequency of a specific blood type.

blood types: the several types of blood cells, which are hereditary traits, not externally apparent.

brachiation: locomotion, usually through trees, by swinging by the forelimbs held overhead. Gibbons are especially noted for this.

breeding population: a segment of a population, usually delimited on geographical or cultural lines, characterized by a high level of interbreeding, in which one or more distinctive genes occurs with particular frequency. See also **gene pool**.

bride-price: goods or valuables transferred by the groom's kin to recompense the bride's relatives for her absence.

caloric cost: the food-energy efficiency of an economic system measured as work hours expended to produce the average daily food ration.

cargo cult: a revitalization movement native to Melanesia based on the expectation of the imminent return of ancestors in ships, planes, and trains bringing treasures of European manufactured goods.

carrying capacity: the population of a species which a particular area or ecosystem can support without suffering deterioration.

caste: widely applied as a term to a self-enclosed **class** or subclass; often a stratified, endogamous descent group with its cultural characteristics, limited status, mobility, and access to economic resources.

choppers: stone implements made from water-worn stream pebbles, in the tradition of the earliest known hominid **artifacts**.

chromosomes: threadlike structures within the cell nucleus, composed of **DNA**, which transmit information that determines heredity.

clans: kin groups whose members assume—but need not demonstrate—descent from a common ancestor.

class, social: one of the stratified groupings within a society, characterized by specific attitudes and behavior, and by differential access to power, and to basic resources.

clines: the gradual changes in traits and gene frequencies displayed by members of a species along the lines of an environmental transition.

cognatic lineage: a group whose members trace their descent genealogically from a common ancestor.

collaterals: persons who are **consanguineal kin**, sharing a common ancestor, but in different lines of descent, such as cousins.

communal rites: ceremonies, largely religious, carried out by the social group for its reinforcement, usually by nonprofessional specialists and celebrants.

consanguineal: relationship between persons based on biological ties, in contrast with the **affinal** tie of marriage.

core tools: stone implements made by shaping a large lump or core, such as the hand axe.

corvée: a forced labor draft imposed by a government for public road and building construction, often in lieu of taxes.

couvade: customary restrictions on the activities of a man often associated with his wife's lying-in and birth of their child.

cranium: the part of the skull that encloses the brain.

cross cousins: persons of either sex whose parents are siblings of the opposite sex; as offspring of a father's sister and mother's brother. Compare **parallel cousins.**

cultural relativism: the principle that all cultural systems are inherently equal in value, and that the traits characteristic of each need to be assessed and explained within the context of the system in which they occur.

culture: the patterns of behavior and thought learned and shared as characteristic of a societal group.

culture area: a geographical region characterized by a certain complex of trait elements, occurring as shared by several cultural groups, due to common ecological adaptation and/or history.

dental formula: a coding of the numbers of incisor, canine, premolar, and molar teeth, in sequence, in one quadrant of the lower and upper jaws. Used as a trait in anthropoid classification.

descent reckoning: the rule for ascertaining an individual's kinship affiliation from among the range of actual or presumed connections provided by birth to a particular father and/or mother.

determinism: the assumption that in cultural phenomena, as in physico-chemical and biological spheres, the processes of growth, change, and evolution are subject to similar principles of causality.

diffusion: refers to the way in which cultural traits, ways, complexes, and institutions become transferred from one cultural group to another.

dimorphism, sexual: the occurrence of differentiation as in color, structure, size, and other traits between male and female members of the same species.

divination: arrival at an expectation or judgment of future events through the interpretation of omens construed as evidence.

DNA (deoxyribonucleic acid): the long-stranded molecule which makes up the principle component of **chromosomes.** Varied arrangements of DNA determine the genetic code which influences biological heredity.

domesticant: a domesticated plant or animal.

double descent: customary reckoning of affiliation of an individual in **kin groups** of both parents.

ecology: the structuring of adaptations to the environment, as comprised of relationships among the natural habitat and its plant, animal, and human populations.

economy: the management of the production, distribution, and consumption of the natural resources, labor, and other forms of wealth available to a cultural system.

ecosystem: the community of plants and animals—including humans—within a habitat, and their relations to one another.

egalitarian: type of societal group at the cultural level lacking formalized differentiation in access to, and power over, basic resources among its members.

emics: descriptions or judgments concerning behavior, customs, beliefs, values, and so on, held by members of a societal group as culturally appropriate and valid. See **etics**.

enculturation: the process by which individuals—usually as children—acquire behavioral patterns and other aspects of their culture from others, through observation, instruction, and adaptation.

endogamy: the principle that requires persons to take their spouses from a prescribed local, kin, or status grouping with which they are already affiliated.

ethnocentrism: the tendency to view the traits, ways, ideas, and values observed in other cultural groups as invariably inferior and less natural or logical than those of one's own group.

etics: the techniques and results of making generalizations about cultural events, behavior patterns, artifacts, thought, and ideology that aim to be verifiable objectively and valid cross-culturally. See **emics**.

evolution, general: the observation that in cultural systems as well as in living organisms there has been a directional emergence of progressively more complex levels of organization, integration, adaptation, and efficiency.

exogamy: the rule that forbids an individual from taking a spouse from within a prescribed local, kin, status, or other group with which they are both affiliated.

extended family: a domiciliary aggregate of two or more **nuclear families**, comprised of siblings and their spouses and children, and often including their parents and married children.

family, linguistic: a group of related languages historically derived from a common antecedent language.

family, societal: a domiciliary and/or kin grouping, variously constituted of married and related persons and their offspring, residing together for economic and reproductive purposes. See also **nuclear family**; **extended family**.

family, taxonomic: a category employed in the phylogenetic classification of plants and animals, just above the level of genus.

feudal system: a type of historical socioeconomic organization involving a network of obligations, in which the **peasants** are structured inferiors to their lord, and are bound to provide certain payments and services in exchange for apparent privileges.

fossils: remains or traces of plants or animals, preserved—usually by mineralization—from the geological past.

functions: the purposes served by artifacts, patterns of behavior, and ideas, and the ways in which they contribute toward maintenance, efficiency, and adaptation in the cultural system.

gene flow: the movement of genetic material from one **gene pool** to another as a consequence of interbreeding.

gene pool: the sum and range of variety contained in the genes present within a given **breeding population**.

genes: the chemical units of heredity, arranged in the **chromosomes**.

genetic code: the arrangement of chemical components in the DNA molecules and on chromosomes, carrying information concerning the inheritance of traits.

genotype: the total gene complement received by an individual organism from its parents; as distinguished from the external appearance manifest in the **phenotype**.

geographic race: a **breeding population**, usually of considerable spatial extent, which can be expressed in terms of the frequencies of specifiable, characterizing genetic traits.

ghost dance: a **revitalization movement** which appeared on the North American Plains during the 19th century, hailing the departure of the whites, and the restoration of Indian traditional ways.

headman: in an **egalitarian** group, the titular head who may lead those who will follow, but is usually unable to impose **sanctions** to enforce his decisions or requests, or deprive others of equal access to basic resources.

heritability: in biology, the extent to which the manifestation of a particular trait can be attributed to transmission by genetic inheritance.

hominids (*Hominidae*): the taxonomic family including all living and extinct types and races of humans and protohumans. See **hominoids**.

hominoids (*Hominoidea*). the taxonomic superfamily of anthropoids, including all extinct and contemporary varieties of apes and humans, and excluding the monkeys and prosimians. See **hominids**.

ideology: the rational and emotional factors which function to establish and maintain communication among the technoeconomic, sociopolitical and other aspects of the cultural system.

incest: socially prohibited mating and/or marriage, as within certain specified limits of real or putative **kinship**.

industrialization: an advanced stage of technoeconomic development observed particularly in modern states and colonizing powers, characterized by centralized control of tools, labor input, the techniques and organization of production, the marketing of goods, and cash wages.

irrigation civilization: an advanced type of preindustrial society associated with the control of extensive, man-made facilities for crop irrigation and land drainage. Also usually characterized by social stratification, urban nucleation, and sophisticated, centralized political institutions.

kin group: a social aggregate of individuals related by either **consanguineal** ties of descent or **affinal** ties of marriage.

kinship: the network of culturally recognized interpersonal relations through which individuals are related to one another, by ties of descent or marriage.

663

kinship terminology: the set of terms by which members of a kin group customarily address or refer to one another, denoting their relationship.

levirate: custom favoring the remarriage of a widow with her deceased husband's brother or surrogate close male relative.

Liebig's Law: points out that in biological evolution assuredly, the processes of adaptation and selection respond to the given minimal potentialities of the environment.

lineage: a kin group whose members can actually trace their relationship through specific, known genealogical links along the recognized line of descent, as either **matrilineal** or **patrilineal**.

magic: the practice of certain rituals which are presumed to coerce desired practical effects in the material world, or in persons.

mana: term for the impersonal pervasive power expected in certain objects and roles. See **animatism**.

matrifocal family: a domiciliary group comprised of one or more adult women, and their offspring, within which husband-fathers are not permanent residents.

matrilineal descent groups: persons who reckon their kin group affiliation through females exclusively.

matrilocal residence: after marriage, location of a couple in or near the wife's mother's domicile.

messianic movement: a movement offering **revitalization** or salvation through following the spiritual or activist leadership of a prophetic individual or messiah; often against vested authority.

microliths: quite small, trapezoidal-shaped flakes of flinty stone; usually set in rows in wooden or bone hafts.

modal personality: the type of **basic personality** perceived to be characteristic of a cultural system, or of one of its strata or subgroups.

morpheme: the basic linguistic form which combines one or more units of sound (**phonemes**) with at least a minimal meaning.

mutation: innovative change in gene structure, transmitted to the offspring.

neolocal residence: after marriage, relocation of a couple without reference to the parental domicile of either spouse.

nuclear family: basic social grouping comprised of male and female parents and their offspring.

parallel cousins: persons whose parents are siblings of the same sex, as the son and the daughter of two sisters.

parallel cultural evolution: represented by instances in which significant aspects, patternings, or institutions in two or more cultural systems undergo similar adaptations and transformations; presumably in response to the operation of similar causal and dynamic factors.

patrilineal groups: persons whose descent reckoning is through males exclusively.

patrilocal residence: after marriage, location of a couple with or near the husband's father's domicile.

peasants: food-producing farm workers who form the lower economic stratum in preindustrial and underdeveloped societies, subject to exploitive obligations in the form of rent, taxes, tribute, forced labor service (**corvée**), and the like.

personality: the structuring of the inherent constitutional, emotional, and intellectual factors that determine how a person feels, thinks, and behaves in relation to the patterning of his cultural context.

phenotype: the characteristics of an individual organism that are the external, apparent manifestations of its hereditary genetic composition. See **genotype**.

phoneme: a single vocal sound (*phone*), or the several variants of such a sound (*allophones*), which a listener recognizes as having a certain linguistic function.

phonetic laws: statements about the shifts in the sound values of certain vowel and consonant phonemes, which have occurred regularly in time within languages, and reveal past historic relations between languages.

pluralism: where a national or regional population is composed of several cultural minorities with incompatible institutions, and in open contention for power.

political economy: treating the role of political authority and power in production, distribution, and consumption of goods and services.

polyandry: marriage of one woman with two or more males simultaneously.

polygamy: marriage involving more than one spouse of either sex.

polygyny: marriage of one male with two or more women simultaneously.

race: a population in which one or more genetic traits—externally apparent—have predominating frequencies.

reciprocity: the principle of exchanging goods and/or valuables without overt reckoning of economic worth or overt reckoning that a balance need be reached, to establish or reinforce ties between persons.

racism: the attitude that certain psychological and/or behavioral traits may be inherent in the genetic composition of a **race**.

revitalization movement: reaction by a minority group to coercion and disruption, often under **messianic** leadership, aiming to reclaim lost **status**, identity, and well being.

rites of passage: communally celebrated rituals that mark the transition of an individual from one institutionalized **status** to another.

roles: patterns of behavior related to specific situations.

sanctions: means employed by a social group to coerce a conformity with expected or desired behavior, by means of rewards or punishments.

semantic universality: potentiality of all languages for generating utterances capable of conveying information relevant to all aspects of experience and thought, without limits as to time or veritability.

shaman: a practitioner of magico-religious rites for **divination**, possession, illusion, curing, and the like, mainly in **egalitarian**-level societies.

sororate: custom by which a deceased wife is replaced by a sister or other surrogate female kin.

status: position or standing, socially recognized, ascribed to or achieved by an individual or group. Compare **role**.

taxons: the names applied to label specific taxonomic classifications, and the organisms which fall within such a classification.

totems: plants, animals, phenomena, or objects symbolically associated with particular descent groups as identifying insignia.

universal pattern: a set of categories comprehensive enough to afford logical and classificatory organization for the range of artifacts, traits, ways, and institutions to be observed in any or all cultural systems.

uxorilocal residence: when husband relocates to live in wife's home.

virilocal residence: when wife relocates to live in husband's home.

warfare: formalized armed combat between groups of people who represent rival territories or political communities.

Glossary

INDEX

Numbers in italic indicate pages with illustrations

behavior, 360; social orderliness, 355

Barber, Bernard, on study of castes, 425

Bar Kochva, Judean leader, 563

Barnouw, Victor, on personality, quoted, 587

Barotse (Zambia), marital devotion in, 318

basic personality structure, 589–91 (*see also* modal personality; personality); Alorese, 594–96; and sociocultural system, *594, 596*

basic resources, access to, 352–59; by local bands, 358; and political power, 366; by social classes, 396, 401; in stratified societies, 374, 386

Bat Cave (New Mexico), 222

Bathonga (Mozambique), extended family of, 316–17

battle casualties (*see also* sex ratios; warfare): among hunter-gatherers, 262–3; and population growth, 264–5; of sedentary villages, 263–4; and sex ratios, 262, 264

behavior patterns: actual vs. presumed, 163; communication of, 161; culture and, 144; descriptions of, 159; emics and etics of, 162–3; enculturation of, 145–6; *see* tool using

behavior types, and sexuality, 607–8

beliefs (*see also* religious beliefs; thought control): individualistic, 525–6; in natural and supernatural, 518

Benedict, Ruth: on cajoling the supernatural, 521; on Kwakiutl potlatch, 290–1; on Pueblo personality, 601

berdache (Plains Indian), 591

Bergman's rule, 112

Beringia (Bering Straits), 209

Bering Straits migration, 209

betrothal, infant (Kadar), 322

biface tools, *81,* 82, *83, 84* (*see also* stone tools)

big man (Oceania), 375

bilateral descent, 335–9 (*see also* cognatic groups; kindred; lineages); neolocality and, 340; reckoning, 333; technoeconomic aspects, 339; terminology, 351

bilocal residence, 339–42

Binford, Lewis, on hand axes, 173

biological adaptation, 17; bipedalism, 32; competitive exclusion in, 53; forelimbs of primates, 24–5; genetic, 111–13; hominoid dentition, 36; human hairlessness, 39; natural selection and, 17, 23; primate, 23–5; primate offspring per birth, 25; racial traits, 112; skin color, 112–4; terrestrial hominids, 32

biological classification, 19–20

biological evolution, 7, 17, 111; and cultural evolution, 164, 170 (*see also* cultural evolution); genetics of, 15–6; process, 111; time sequence, 43–4

biological factors, in personality formation, 594, 596

biological heredity, 58

biological reproduction, cultural diffusion versus, 168

bipedalism: of australopithecines, 46, *47;* hominid trait, 32; human trait, 84; human sexuality and, 38–9; in language evolution, 42

birth control (*see* population control)

birth rate, 456

birth spacing, 312

black churches, U.S., 556

black ghetto culture, 475

Black Muslim movement, 556

blacks (*see also* Afro-Americans): education, 504; as genetic hybrids, 104; intelligence testing, 501–4; job opportunities, 480; matrifocality of, 485–7; modal personality shift, 602; racial stratification, U.S., 499–500; social classification, 104; speech behavior, 132; in U.S., 415; B. T. Washington on, 419–20

blade tools, stone, 172, 180, *180, 181* (*see also* stone implements)

blood feud, 370–2

blood relationship, descent as, 332

blood types: distribution of, *106, 107–8, 108;* as races, 107

Boas, Franz: on grammatical equivalency, 129; potlatch studies of, 292

boasting, economic exchange and, 290–1

body adornments (New Guinea), *162*

Bohannan, Paul, on I.Q. test bias, quoted, 511

Böhm, Hans, mentioned, 565

bone implements, Aurignacian, *182*

Borlaug, Norman, mentioned, 450

Brace, C. Loring, on sweating as adaptive, 39

braceros (migratory labor), 471

brachiation, 29, 31

Brahmans (Hindu caste), 422–3

brain case volume: australopithecine, 46–7; comparison of, *78;* of *H. erectus, 78,* 80; of *H. sapiens, 78; Pithecanthropus* expansion, 79; *Sinanthropus,* 79

brain enlargement: as human trait, 85; in primates, 26; and tool use, 58

Brazil: Japanese migrants to, 418; legitimacy in, 320; race classification in, 104; sisal cultivation, 471–4, *474*

breeding population, 98

bride-price, 324; cattle as, 295–6; 371; in Dahomey, 319; 321; dowry and, 326; feud compensation, 371; legitimacy and, 325; marriage reciprocation and, 329; service as, 326; technoeconomic aspects, 324, 326; and wife replacement, 330

bride-service, 326

Bunyoro (Uganda): feudalism, 382; political organization, 380

bureaucracy: Chinese, 435, 437; ecclesiastical, 541–3; flood control irrigation and, 374; Inca, 384; preindustrial, 302; and production control, 435–6; in state systems (*see* statehood)

burials, ritual, 179–80, 260 (*see also* Middle Paleolithic)

Bushman (South Africa): band size, 262; economic system, 282–3; food-energy production 234–5; headmanship, 366; personality formation, 599; settlement pattern, 237; social orderliness, 355; social organi-

28; of Old World monkeys, 28; of *Parapithecidae,* 44

Dentan, Robert: on reciprocal exchange, 290; on Semai headmanship, 366

dentition: of carnivorous mammals, 67–8; and dietary factors in australopithecines, 47–8; hominid, 36–7, 62; hominid and pongid compared, 36–7; of monkeys, *28*

deoxyribonucleic acid (DNA), 7–10

descent, rules of, 333–6 (*see also* kin groups; kinship terminology, *and specific types by name*)

description, anthropological, 159, 161, 163 (*see also* emics, etics)

Despres, Leo, on minority identities, 419

determinism: concept and role, 5; in culture history, 615–6; diffusion and, 167–8; of education *vs.* intelligence, 500–4; of intelligence, 500–4; racial, 494; in cultural evolution, 228

developing countries, growth of, 430–1

development aid technicians (CREFAL), 469–71

development, socioeconomic, 427

Devonian period, 43

dharma (path of duty), 423 dialects (*see* language, linguistic behavior)

diet (*see* nutrition)

diffusion: cultural (*see* cultural diffusion); of New World plant cultivation, 212–3

digits, primate opposable, 24

Dinka (Sudan), 370

Dionysian culture pattern, 588

displacement, linguistic, 117

Divale, William: on sex ratios, 262–3; on warfare, 260

divination, 363 (*see also* shamanism); conflict resolution by, 364

division of labor (*see* labor; sexual division of labor)

divorce, 324–5, 344

Djetis bed (Java), *Pithecanthropus* find, 79

DNA (deoxyribonucleic acid), 7–10

Dobuans (Melanesia): kula trade, 287–8; magic of, 522

dogs, domestication and symbiosis of, 187, 188, 194

Dole, Gertrude, on Kuikuru shamanism, 363–4

domestication of animals (*see* animal domestication)

domestic groups (*see also* family; households): activities, 310; conflict resolution in, 331; matrilocal, 343; personality formation and, 598

dominance hierarchies, primate and hominid, 64

dominance, male (*see* male dominance)

double cousins, 337

double descent reckoning, 335

dowry, 326 (*see also* bride-price)

Draw a Man Test, 512–3

dreams, and shamanism, 528–9 (*see also* vision quest)

drift, genetic, 15

drift, phonological, 141

drugs (*see* hallucinogens)

Dryopithecinae, ape fossils, *45, 46*

Du Bois, Cora, on Alorese personality, 595

Dubois, Eugene, fossil find, 79

Durkheim, Emile, on sacred force in society, 519–20

Dutch: colonialism in Java, 342–3, 458; trade in Japan, 445–6

dynastic incest (*see* sibling marriage)

Eastern Woodlands Complex (U.S.), 223

East India Company, 443

East India, 442 (*see also* Indonesia, Java)

East Rudolf (Kenya), habiline finds, 78

eating, techniques of, *146*

ecclesiatical level (*see* religious organization)

ecological adaptation, 156–7; analysis of, 239; economy and, 281; evolutionary, 54; and industrialization, 232, 428; of maintenance systems and personality, 596; Mesolithic, 187; in plant domestication, 190; religious, 548; in rivalrous redistribution, 292–4; in sub-

sistence technology, 230–1; warfare as, 279–80

ecology (*see* ecological adaptation; ecosystems)

economic development (*see also* economic organization; industrialization; underdevelopment): CREFAL projects, Mexico, 469–71; national rates, 429–30; peasant resistance to, 461–3; racism of, 492; and religion, 438–9; sisal project, Brazil, 472–4; skepticism of, 480; in Tzintzuntzan, Mexico, 469–71

economic exchange, 157, 282–4, 290–1 (*see also* kula; potlatch; redistributive exchange; trade)

economic exploitation, conditions for, 402–3

economic organization (*see also* economic development; economic exchange; economy): under capitalism, 305; of castes, 426; characterization, 281; coercive, 289, 297, 402–3; communistic type, 282; egalitarian, 281–2; evolution of, 288–9; exploitation, 402–3; kula, 287–8; of minorities, 426; *see* potlatch; preindustrial, 253, 281–6; reciprocal and redistributive, 288–94 (*see also* redistributive exchange); of states, 199–200, 297–9, 302, 307–9

economy (*see also* energy; productivity; *and particular periods and systems*): definition of, 281; and social structure, 157

ecosystems: competitive exclusion in, 54; demography and, 233; dynamics of, 233; and economy, 281; Mesoamerican versus Middle Eastern, 228

Ecuador, 461–4 (*see also* Aymara; Chimborazo valley; Jívaro

Edgerton, Robert, on personality, East Africa, 599

education (*see also* enculturation; intelligence testing; personality formation): of blacks, 500, 504; class differences, 409–10; controversial subjects, 389–91; and intelligence, 500–4; measurement of, 500–1; and upward mobility, U.S., 500

efficiency (*see* energy; productivity; technoeconomic factors)

egalitarian groups (*see also* band level organization): aggression in, 370; capitalist elements, 305; conflict in, 361; economic aspects, 282; economic redistribution, 274–6, 289–90 (*see also* redistributive exchange); headmanship, 365–6, 374–6; homicide control in, 370–1; political organization, 368; population limits, 368–9; religious organization, 523; transformation of, 374; warfare, 368; women in, 345

Eisenhower, Dwight D.: on consumption, 478; on military-industrial complex, 408

elite, political, 412 (*see also* ruling class)

Elvin, Mark, on Chinese bureaucracy, 437

emics: defined, 169–71 (*see also* etics); in description and explanation, 162–4

empires (*see* statehood *and specific instances*)

enclaves (*see* castes; minorities; *also specific instances*)

encomiendas, 302, 462

enculturation (*see also* child rearing; education; personality formation): of children, 314–5; concept of, 145–6, 150–2; disruption of, 150; English, 315; and ethnocentrism, 146; Euro-American, 314; as explanatory, 152; generation gap in, 150; for I.Q. tests, 504–5, 507, 511; intercultural, 498; limitations, 150; linguistic, 119, Masai, 314; matrifocal, 485–7; outside home, 314; polygynous, 313; and poverty, 476–7; in primates, 26–7; process, 164; as programming, 151–2

endogamy, 326; in castes, 413, 421–3, 426; ethnic, 417; evolution of, 338–9; genetics of, 307–8; Hindu caste, 423; matrilocal village, 345; in minority groups, 417; of social classes, 413

energy: agro-chemical inputs, 451; class control, 397; food production expenditures, 234–7; Green Revolution input, 450–4; hunting-gathering group, 234–5; metabolic sources, 233; preindustrial flow, 233–4, 428; socioeconomic system levels, 427–8; systemic flow of, 233

England, 394–5 (*see also under specific topics*)

English language: and German compared, 140; grammar, 129; historic change, 139–41; phonemics, 120; phonological changes, 139; thought patterning, 133

entertainment, thought control as, 388–9

environment (*see also* ecological adaptation; technoenvironmental analysis): in cultural similarity, 168; degrading of, 249–50; destruction of, 232; and food-energy systems, 239; in food production intensification, 249–50; influences of, 231; Liebig's Law of the Minimum, 239; in pastoral nomadism, 246–7; in slash-burn farming, 241–2; and socioeconomic development, 429; and subsistence, 230–3, 241–2; technological role, 231–2

epicanthic fold, 98; Bushman-Hottentot, 102; incidence distribution, 103

Eskimo (Circum-Polar): beliefs and rituals, 524; conflict resolution, 362; kin groups, 339; kinship terminology, 350–1; law and order, 361–2; leadership, 366; procreation beliefs, 333; protein intake, 428; social orderliness, 355; song contest, 362

Espiritu Santo I., cargo cults, 560–1

estrous cycle, 37–8

Eta (Japan), 416–7

ethnic differences: and class levels, 416–7; dialects in, 132; of jati subcastes, 426; of minorities, 415–26

ethnocentrism: in animism, 515; and enculturation, 146–7; of the middle class, 475

Ethnographic Atlas (Murdock), 350, 351, 352, 497

ethnography, 1; and archaeological reconstruction, 261

etics, 159–61 (*see also* emics); of class status, 425; of communication, 161–2; of exploitation, 403; of warfare, 275–6

Euro-Americans: art tradition of, 572–3; bilateral family of, 338; kin group organization of, 339; kinship terminology of, 335; neolocality of, 340

Europe: Africa's penetration by, 497; agriculture of, 435; capitalist expansion, 436–7; China contacts, 433–4; China domination, 435; cultural development in, 492, 494–5; feudalism in, 300–1, 382–3; industrial revolution in, 437; interracial variation, 99; Japan entry, 442, 445; Neolithic economy of, 204; political economy, 435–6; post-feudal development, 437–8; preindustrial, 433–6; technological development, 432

Eutheria, humans as, 23

Evans-Pritchard, E. E., on Nuer political organization, 369

evolutionary descent, human, 43–54

evolution: biological (*see* biological evolution); cultural (*see* cultural evolution); general, 18; process of, 5–18

exchange, economic (*see* economic exchange)

exogamy (*see also* endogamy): band strategy of, 328; biological role of, 328–9; corporate groups and, 329; definition, 326; evolutionary position, 338; technoeconomic aspects, 328–9; in unilineal groups, 338; warfare and, 329

explanation, sociocultural, 163

exploitation: by classes, 402; of communist peasants, 305; definition of, 402–3; and feudalism, 301; inquiry into, 5; and national wealth, 459–60; and population growth, 457; racial classification for, 104; religious revitalization and, 554–6

extended family, 316–8, 324–5; Bathonga, 316–7; child rearing, 325; Chinese, 317–8; kinship terms, 351–2; male dominance in, 324; polygynous, 316; Rajput, 318

facial features: hominid and pongid compared, 35–6; racial traits in, 98
family (*see also* extended family; nuclear family): bride-price and, 326; corporate interests, 316–7, 326; landownership in bands, 356; matrifocal, 485–6
family planning, 454–5 (*see also* population control)
farming societies (*see* horticultural villages)
fatherhood: biological vs. cultural, 331–3; in matrilineal groups, 345–6; of Nayar, 316–9; of Trobrianders, 333
Fayum (Egypt), fossil find, 44–5
feasting, redistributive (*see also* redistributive exchange): food display and, 375–6; on pigs, Tsembaga, 244; rivalrous, 375
feeding adaptations, in pongids and hominids, 36
feeding, and human sexuality, 39
Fell's Cave (Patagonia), Paleolithic artifacts, 211
female deities, 554
female father-husband (Dahomey), 319, 321
female infanticide (*see* infanticide)
female sexuality: cross-cultural comparison of, 608–9; human traits, 39; Oedipal complex and, 606–7; population growth and, 265
femoral angle, diagram of, *47*
Fergusson, Adam, on changing institutional forms, 142
fertility figurines, 181–3, *183*
feudalism, 300–1, 382–3; African and European compared, 383; of African kingdoms, 495–7; Bunyoro, 382; English pre-Norman, 382; exploitation under, 301; fealty in, 382; Japanese, 442, 446; in Java, 442; lords' obligations, 300; peasants under, 300–1; productivity in, 383; ruling class in, 383; transformation of, Japan, 446

feudal peasants, 300–1
fire, early hominid use of, 84, 86, 177
Firth, Raymond, on Tikopia chiefs, 379
flake tools, 172 (*see also* stone implements): Acheulian, 173; Solutrean, 182
Flannery, Kent, on sedentary seed gatherers, 193
Folsom: projectile points, *210*; stone tools, 210
food production (*see also* agriculture; animal keeping *and under other specific types and groups*): of ancestral hominids, 66–9; Bushman, 234–9; cash crop, 469–74; Chinese village, 245–6; Eastern Woodlands, 223; efficiency in, 234; energy expenditures in, 234–7; environment and, 239; evolution of, 67; exploitation of, 377; exportable surplus, 246; *see* hoe cultivation; *see* hunter-gatherers; *see* industrialized farming; intensification and degradation of, 248–50; by irrigation, 244–6; labor productivity of basic technologies, diagram, *230*; and labor expended, 253; landownership and, 299; Mesoamerican, 213–4; Mesolithic, 187; Natufian, 192; Neolithic, 189–90; New World plant, 212–4; Pacific North America, 223; Paleolithic, 171, 185–6; of pastoral nomads, 246–7; peasantry and, 300–5; pig-keeping as, 243–4; *see* plant cultivation as; political control of, 373–4; and population, 248–50, 272–3; preindustrial, 251; *see* seed gathering as; *see* slash and burn gardening; social control over, 373–4, 377; state formation and, 280; state organization of, 299; and stratification, 377; system efficiency in, 248–9; technological changes in, 230–1; and wage labor, 465; and warfare, 259–60
food sharing, hominid, 63–4
foot structure, hominid, 32
forced labor, 466–8 (see also, corvée)

Ford Foundation, 450
Fortes, Meyer, on descent, 331*n*
Foster, George: on CREFAL projects, 468–71; on peasant conservatism, 471; theory of limited good, 468–71
Franke, Richard, on Green Revolution, Java, 451–3
Frazer, James: on magic and religion, 520–2; on science *vs.* magic, 522
freeloader, problem of the, 284
French Revolution, and messianic revitalization, 565
Freud, Sigmund (*see also* Freudian approach): on anatomy as destiny, 606; on artistic creativity, 586; on child development, 592; influence of, 590, 592; on male dominance, 604; on Oedipal conflict, 603–6
Freudian approach: model of personality formation, 594; psychodynamics of personality change, 598, 600; to warfare, 608
Freudian psychodynamics questioned, 598, 600
Fried, Morton, on band ownership, 356–7
functional unity, of sociocultural systems, 153–4
function, in cultural replication, 150–2
Fur (Sudan): households, 315; bachelor house, 315–6
fur trade, and family landownership, 356

Galbraith, John Kenneth, on political power of U.S., 405
Ganda (Africa), women's status in, 610
Gandhi, Mohandas K., on the sacred cows, 571
Garcilaso de la Vega, chronicles of, 385–6
Geertz, Clifford: on colonialism, 441; on economic development, 447; religion defined by, 546
gene flow, 15 (*see also* gene frequencies; genes; genetics; races); in clinal variances, 103–4; interracial, 99–104; as societal boundary, 145
gene frequencies: clinal distribu-

tion of, 104; nonconforming, 104–9

genealogical linkage, 337 (*see also* cognatic groups; heredity)

gene pools, 96–9

generation gap, 150

genes (*see also* genetics): alleles, 13–15, 97; chromosomes and, 7–11; definition of, 10; deleterious, 327–8; dominant, 13–4; flow of (*see* gene flow); frequencies of (*see* gene frequencies); geographical distribution, 99–109; heterozygous, 13; homozygous, 13; recessive, 13–4, 327–8

genetic code, 7–16, 118 (*see also* heredity; heritability)

genetic drift, 15

genetic replication, 164

genetics (*see also* biological evolution; gene flow; heritability): chromosomes, 7–15; DNA code 7–16; of heterogeneous populations, 327; of inbreeding, 327–8; of inequality, 491; of stable populations, 327

genetrix, defined, 332

Genieri (Gambia): food energy system, 236–7; population and efficiency, 249; technoeconomic efficiency, 239, 249

genitor, defined, 332

genotype(s), 13–6, 97, 99

geographic races, 99, 102, 107, 110 (*see also under* races)

geological time, evolutionary count of, 43–4

German language, 139–41

German Weslin (cargo cult), 560

gestation, in primates, 25–6

Ghana (Africa), medieval, 383, 495–7

Ghost Dance, 557–9

gibbons, 28–9, 32; communication among, 117

gift giving (*see also* redistributive exchange): economic exchange and, 284; in industrialized societies, 285; kula exchange, as 287–8; nuclear family and 284–5; in trade partnerships, 287–8

glacial periods, 186

Gluckman, Max, on Barotse marriage, 318

God, 545, 547 (*see also* gods); and Jewish messianism, 562;

Judeo-Christian concept, 514

gods, 550 (*see also* animism); Aztec, 543; concepts of, 514–5; high gods and stratification, 550–1

Golden Bough, The (Frazer), 520

Goldenweiser, Alexander, on religious experience, 518–9

gold mining, forced labor, South Africa, 466–8

Gombe National Park (Tanzania), 56–9, 67

Gorer, Geoffrey, on Great Russian personality, 590, 592

gorilla, *30*, 31; cranial cavity compared, *78*

Gough, E. Kathleen: on caste hierarchies, 426; on Nayar marriage, 318

Gould, Shane, swimming record, 269

graciles (*Australopithecus*): characteristics, 47–50; distribution, 51–2

grammar (*see also* language; linguistic behavior): analogy systems in, 125; categories and thought, 136–7; efficiency of, 128–30; equivalencies of, 128–30; in language, 123–6; linguistic development and, 128–9; and society, 13–2, 137; and status, 137; structures, deep, of, 124–5, 129, 160; and thought, 133–6

Graves, Thomas, on personality and poverty, 483, 485

Gravettian: hunting, 182; industry, 181

Great Russian personality, 590, 592

Greece, cultural development of, 494–5

Greenberg, Joseph, on semantic universality, 116

Green Revolution, 449–54

Gregor, Thomas, on Mehinacu headman, 367–8

grooming, in primates, 26

groom price, 326

Gross, Daniel, on sisal farming, Brazil, 472

Grotte du Vallonet (France), stone tools at, 80

group prejudices, of minorities, 420

group solidarity, and segregation, 419

growth, biological, 7

Guayana, minorities in, 419

Gururumba (New Guinea), beliefs of, 518

Gusii (Kenya), bachelor residence of, 314

habilines (*see also* australopithecines; graciles; protohumans; *Robustus*): anatomical traits, 51; australopithecine differences, 54; cultural adaptations of, 85; dentition, 68; disappearance, 81; emergence, 51–2; East Rudolf find, 51, *51*; human character, 84; mandible find, *51;* as predators, 67; as tool makers, 54; tool use by, 55, 58

habitat: impacted, 379; Paleolithic, 379

habitations: adobe brick, 198; Gravettian, 182; Mogollon, 222; prefarming villages, 193; Pueblo Bonito, 223

hacienda, 462

Haida (Pacific Northwest), matrilineal tendencies, 347–8

hair: as mammalian trait, 21; as racial trait, 98; wavy, incidence of, 103

hairlessness, human, as adaptive, 39–40

hallucinogens, use of: by Jívaro, 527; by shamans, 362–3, 527, 552–3; women and, 551–2; by Yanomamö, 552

hand axes (*see also* stone implements): Acheulian, *81*, 82, 172; Acheulian absences, 84, 173; China absences, 84; European absence, 173; Mousterian, *178*; at Olduvai Gorge, 82

hand, hominid dexterity, 32–3

Hardy-Weinberg equilibrium, 14–16

Harlan, Jack, on wild wheat gathering, 193

Harner, Michael: on descent and inheritance, 263; on farming kin groups, 341; on Jívaro souls, 514; on witch sabbat flights, 533

harpoons, Magdalenian, *182*

Harrison, William Henry, mentioned, 557

Hart, C. W., on Tiwi warfare, 261–2

human nature: consciousness and, 143; language competence and, 85, 116

Human Relations Area Files, 156

human sacrifice, Aztec, 388, 544–9

human traits, 84–5

hunter-gatherer societies: band organization of, 260 (*see also* band level organization); battle casualties of, 262; bilocal residence, 341; carrying capacity, 202; cultural variation of, 238; ecological variation, 237–9; economic reciprocity, 282; food and energy in, 234–5; high gods of, 550; kin groups, 341; labor productivity, 230, 234–6, 249; population limiting practices, 201; present-day status, 172; productive efficiency, 201, 253; religious systems, 548–50; sex ratios in, 262–3; subsistence insecurity, 186, 234–9, 248; trade among, 285–7; warfare among, 260–3

hunting activities (*see also* hunter-gatherer societies): of Acheulians, 83, 86; of ancestral hominids, 67–8; and animal domestication, 194, 196; cultural consequences of, 85–7; dogs in, 187; by Gravettians, 182; of *H. erectus*, 84–7; and human nature, 66–74; by protohumans, 71; Magdalenian, 182–3; Mesolithic, 187; Mesoamerica, 214; New World Paleolithic, 210–1; *see* Pleistocene megafauna; and social organization, 86; of women, 87; Yanomamö, 276–7

husband's mother, role of, 317–318

husbands, role in matrilocal groups, 344

Huxley, Thomas H., on race differences, 492

hybrids, genetic: clinal distributions as, 103; intraracial variants and, 99

hydraulic civilization, in China, 435 (*see also* irrigation civilization)

iconographic symbols, 119

ideology (*see also* thought control; values and attitudes): capitalistic, 438–9; definition of, 156, 157–8; economic exploitation and, 403; Hindu social, 422–3; institutions for control of, 385–96 (*see also* law and order); in kinship, 331, 339; in paternal solidarity, 343; Protestant ethic as, 439; religion as, 536; social functions of, 157–8; Soviet, 403–4; of unilineal descent groups, 341

image of limited good, 468–71, 589

impacted habitat, 379

implements (*see also* stone implements): bone, *182*, 208; early New World, 208; Upper Paleolithic, *182*

inbreeding, in small populations, 327

Inca (Andean South America): afterlife, 386; brother-sister marriage, 327; empire dating, 225; energy levels, 428; food production, 384; plow, 227; political organization, 384–6

incest (*see also* endogamy; inbreeding): Chinese avoidance, 317–8; fear of, 326–8; Oedipal aspects of, 603–4

incisors, "shovel shaped," 98–9

India (*see also* Hindu India): caste system in, 421–6; Green Revolution in, 450; population control, 455

Indo-European language family, 140

Indonesia (*see also* Java): colonialism in, 441–5; Green Revolution in, 450–3

industrialization (*see also* industrialized societies; postindustrial development): conditions of, 307–8; criteria of, 428; ecological hazards of, 232; evolution of, 432–3; and impoverishment, 459–60; of Japan, 445–7; labor intensification under, 253; and oriental despotism, 435–6; productivity maximization in, 252; wage labor and, 307–8; warfare and, 260

industrialized farming, 250–2, 451 (*see also* agro-industrial system)

industrialized societies: access to basic resources in, 358; bilateral descent in, 339; domestic arrangements in, 314; economic reciprocity in, 283–4; emergence of, 190; enculturation breakdown in, 150; energy resources of, 233; environment factor in, 231; food production in, 251; gift giving in, 285; kinship in, 339; nuclear family in, 339–40; sex-linked roles in, 612–3; technoeconomic aspects of, 428; thought control in, 387–95; and underdeveloped nations, 427; warfare and population pressure in, 280

industrial revolution: causes of, 432–3; in England, 394–5; European, 394–5, 437

infancy, in primate adaptation, 25, 27

infant betrothals, Kadar, 322

infanticide, female, 201, 266; under colonialism, 459; eugenic effects of, 112, 328; and male dominance, 267, 272; methods of, 266–7 (*see also* abortion; population control); and population control, 459; sex ratio and, 267; in underdeveloped countries, 429

infant mortality rates, in developing countries, 431

infant sexuality, 533

infant training (*see* child rearing)

inflective languages, 129

information processing, by humans, 54–5

infrahuman communication, 126–8

initiation rites, male (*see* male initiation rites)

intelligence (*see also* intelligence testing: I.Q. scores): and culture, 511; definition of, 500; and education, 500–4; genetic factors in, 500; heritability of, 505–7; and migration, 502–3; race and, 500; testing of, 500–1

intelligence quotient scores (*see* I.Q. scores)

intelligence testing (*see also* intelligence; I.Q. scores): enculturation for, 505; environmental factors and, 501–4; motivational factors in, 504–5; racial aspects of, 501–2, 505; racism and, 505–6; validity of, 501

tics, 485–7; occurrence, 486; and welfare, 486–7

matrilineal descent (*see also* kin groups): avunculocal residence and, 346; contradictions in, 345–7; Crow type terms and, 353–4; diagram of *335;* of Iroquois, 348; male dominance and, 345–6; of Natchez, 414–5; of Navajo, 347; in patrilocal societies, 349; reckoning of, 272, 334, 338; reversion of, 345; technoeconomic aspects, 344; tendencies toward, 347–8; in virilocal groups, 349; and warfare, 348

matrilocal groups (*see also* matrifocal family): avunculocal residence and, 346; brother's role in, 344–5; divorce in, 344; domestic units, 343–4; hostility suppression in, 348; in-marrying males in, 344; of Mundurucu, 348; residence in, 342; technoeconomic factors favoring, 347; warfare and, 348

matrisib, 338

Mauer (Germany), *Homo erectus* fragments at, 80

maximal lineages, 338; Nuer, 369

Maya (Yucatan): calendar, 228; culture, 218–20; labor supply, 219; language and sociopolitical development, 134; lowland civilization collapse, 219–20

Mbuti (Zaire), women's status among, 610

Mead, Margaret: on female and male personalities, 607; on intergenerational relations, 150; on menstrual pain, 613

Meganthropus, 78, *79*

Meggitt, Mervyn, on New Guinea sexuality types, 607–8

Mehinacu (Brazil), headmanship of, 367–8

Melanesia: cargo cults, 560–2; pig feasts, 154; redistributive feasts, 289; trade in, 282, 286, 287

melanin skin pigment, 113

Mencher, Joan, on Hindu caste system, 423–4

Mendel, Gregor, on heredity, 13–4

men's houses, 314–6

menstrual cycle, 37–8

menstrual pain, 613

mental capabilities, of primates, 27

Mercator, Gerardus, on basic personality types, 589–90

meritocracy, 510

Mesolithic period, 171, 187, 190

Mesoamerica (*see also* Aztec; Maya; Mexico; Olmec): agricultural production, 228; animal domestication, 216; calendrical reckoning, 228; civilizations of, 216–8; cultural evolution of, 213–5; hieroglyphic writing, 228; highland civilizations, 220–1; impacted habitat of, 380; incipient agriculture, 215; lowland civilizations, 216–8; maize domestication, 213; Olmec culture, 217; Paleolithic subsistence, 213; technology, 227; Teotihuacán, 220–2; wheel principle in, 227

Mesozoic era, 44

messianic movement(s), 555 (*see also* cargo cults; revitalization movements); Anabaptists, 565; crusades as, 565; Christianity and, 564; European political aspects, 564–5; factors producing, 562; of Hans Böhm, 565; of Jesus of Nazareth, 562–4; in Judea, 562–4; in medieval Europe, 564–5; and radical politicization, 565–6; of Taborites, 565 (*see also* peasant revolts)

metabolic resources, 233

metallurgy: Chinese *493;* developmental logic of, 229; historical development, 494; New World development, 227

Metatheria, 23

Mexico (*see also* Mesoamerica): European penetration, 212, 222, 497; Green Revolution in, 450, 453–4; impacted habitat of, 380

microliths, 188

middle class subculture, 41, 475

Middle East: incipient agriculture of, 215; Mesolithic culture, 191; Neolithic, 216

Middle Paleolithic period: burial rites, 179–80; chronology, 179; developments, 178–80; technology, 172

migration: Bering Straits route, 209–10; of displaced peasants,

465–6; of minorities, 417–8; of New World hunters, 211; of peasants to cities, 483–5; selective by intelligence, 502–3

migratory farm labor, 471

migratory wage labor, 465–6

Milgram, Stanley, on authority, 600

millenarian movements, 555 (*see also* messianic movements; revitalization movements)

Miller, Herman, on individual wealth, U.S., 406

Miller, Walter, on poverty, 475

Millet, Kate, on Freudian logic, 607

minifundia (land holding), 303

minimal lineages, 338; Nuer, 369

mining gold, by forced labor conscription, 466–8

minorities: adaptive capacity of, 417–8; assimilation of, 417; class stratification of, 415; discrimination against, 425–6; endogamy of, 417; ethnic character of, 415–26; group consciousness in, 420–1; Hindu castes as, 425–6; pluralism of, 417–8; racial character of, 415–7, 420–1; segregation of, 419, 425; solidarity of, 418, 419; types of, 415–6

Miocene epoch, 44–5, 98–9

Mississippian complex (U.S.), 223

mixtos (racial minority), 415

Mnong-Gar (Vietnam), slash and burn economy, 241

modal personality, 589–91, 601–3

modes of production (*see under* production)

Mogollon (U.S. Southwest), settlement pattern, 222

money (*see also* wealth): as bride-price, 324–5, 371; as capital, 436; characteristics of, 295–6; as currency, 295–6, 297; in egalitarian redistributions, 295–6; Kapauku, 306; prestige valuables as, 295–6, 326; shell and bead, 287; shells as, 295; valuables as, 295–6, 324

monkeys: adaptive radiation of, 53; characterization of, 38–9; tool use by, 55–6

monogamy, 312 (*see also* nuclear family); child rearing in, 325; psychological aspects of, 313

monumental construction: Andean, 224–5; Aztec, 221, 544; Cholula, 221; esthetic aspects, 583; Hohokam, 223; Mayan, 218; Mesoamerican, 216–22; Mississippian, 223; New World, 217–25; Olmec, 216–7; pyramidal, 216, 223; religious, 388; stone idols, 216–7, *217;* Tenochtitlán, 221; Teotihuacán, 220–1; Tihuanaco, *224;* Tula, 221

Moore, Omar Khayyam, on ecology and scapulimancy, 566–7

Morgan, Lewis Henry: on descent, 338; on evolution, 338–9; on kinship terms, 349–50

morphemes, 122–3

Morren, George, on women in subsistence, 271

mother's brother, 344–5 (*see also* avunculocal residence)

mother-child relations, as primate trait, 26–7

motherhood: and male initiation rites, 597; rights of, 312, 313, 317, 319, 321

mother-in-law (husband's mother), 317–8

Mt. Carmel (Palestine), burials, 179

Mousterian industry, 178, *178, 179;* distribution, 185, flake technique, 181

Moynihan, Daniel P., on matrifocal family, 485

mukama (Bunyoro ruler), 380

mukanda (Ndembu circumcision), 539–40

Mundugumor (New Guinea), sex and temperament, 607

Mundurucu (Amazon), warfare, 348

Müntzer, Thomas, peasant leader, 565

murder (*see* homicide)

Murdock, George Peter (*see also* *Ethnographic Atlas*): on nuclear family, 310–1; on residence, 343; universal patterns of, 156

Murngin (Australia): battle casualties, 262; procreation beliefs, 333

muisak soul (Jívaro), 515–7

mutations, genetic, 15

Nambikwara (Brazil), chiefs of, 366–7

names, totemic, 535

Naskapi (Labrador), scapulimancy and hunting, 567–8

Natchez (Mississippi Valley), marriage classes, 414–5

national character, 589–90

native reserves, 466

nativistic movements, 555 (*see also* cargo cults; revitalization movements)

Natufians (Palestine), subsistence pattern, 192

natural habitat: in anthropological inquiry, 4; as communal property, 356; spoken reference to, 131

natural resources (*see* basic resources, access to; environment)

natural selection, 15–6; adaptation and, 17; character of, 164; cultural *vs.* biological models of, 165; of marsupials, *22, 23;* and warfare, 259–60

natural *vs.* supernatural, belief in, 518

Navajo (U.S. Southwest): matrilocal organization of, 347; poverty behavior, 483–5; prayer concept, 521

Nayar (Kerala, India): family (*taravad*) organization, 318, 345–6; marital arrangements, 318–9; matrilocal pattern of, 345–6; sex relationships of, 319; soldier caste, 348

Ndembu (Zambia), circumcision rites, 539–40

neandertaloid type humans, 87–93, 179

Near East, Neolithic transformation of, 190–1

neck structure, of hominids and pongids, 34

Needham, Joseph, on Chinese inventiveness, 434

neo-Freudian concepts, of personality formation, 596

Neolithic period: in Africa, 207, 495; Asiatic spread, 205–7; carrying capacity, 202–3; characterization of, 189–90; in China, 205; European spread of, 204; farming complex adaptation, 222; Middle Eastern spread, 190–1, 197; in New World, 212–6; into North

America, 222; nutritional aspects of, 201; population growth and, 203; settlement patterns, 172; societies characterized, 171–2; in Southeast Asia, 206–7; spread of the, 204–5; technoeconomic aspects, 197–8, 428; technological development, 199, 432–3; warfare during the, 261

neolocal residence, 339–40, 342 (*see also* postmarital residence)

Newman, Philip L., on Gururumba beliefs, 518

New World (*see also* Andean region; Mesoamerica *and other specific groups and localities*): agriculture, 212–6; arrival of people in, 208–9; big-game hunter migrations, 210–1; civilization of, 216–221, 223–8; human fossils, 208; metallurgy, 227; Neolithic developments, 212–6; *see under* New World monkeys; population, 209; state formation, 216; stone tool techniques, 210–1; technological development, 226

New World monkeys (*Ceboidea*): characteristics, 38; Fayum Oligocene fossils of, 45

Nez Percé (Idaho), war of 1877, 557

Nigeria, population growth in 455

noble savage, myth of, 355

nomadism, pastoral, 246–7

nonmetabolic energy resources, 233

Non Nok Tha (Thailand), Neolithic developments at, 207

nonverbal communication, 159–163

Northwest Pacific Indians, 290–291; technoeconomic factors among, 239

nuclear conflict, and Oedipal conflict, 603, 604–5

nuclear family (*see also* households; kin groups; matrifocal family): American contemporary, 311, 315; band level, 356; characteristics of, 310–2, 318–9; child rearing in, 325; consumption by, 340; Euro-American, 339; functions of, 311, 314–15; inbreeding and,

327; industrialized society and, 339–40; kinship terms in, 351, 352; limitations of, 311–2; *see under* Nayar type; polygamy and, 312–3; psychological aspects of, 313; reciprocal exchange in, 285; urban poor and, 485–90

Nuer (Sudan), 369–72

numaym (Kwakiutl cognatic lineage), 341

nursing: by Alorese, 595; and male initiation rites, 597

nutrition: animal protein needs, 242–3; and australopithecine dentition, 47–8; kwashiokor disease, 597; male initiation rites and, 597; in Mesoamerica, 213–4; and national development, diagram, *429;* Neolithic, 201, 428; New World animal protein, 215; Paleolithic, 185, 201; per capita supply, *430;* personality differences and, 596; protein supply by nations, *430*

Nyakusa (Tanzania), bachelor houses, 314

Oberholzer, Emil, on Alorese personality, 595

Oceania (*see also* Polynesia): big man chief, 375; racial variation in, 103; redistribution systems in, 377; rivalrous feasts in, 375

Odend'hal, Stewart, on cattle of India, 570

Oedipus complex: in girls, 603–4; feminine manifestations, 606–7; Malinowski's exception to, 604; masculine manifestations of, 603–4; nuclear conflict and, 603; penis envy and, 604; warfare and, 604–5

Oldowan complex, 81–2 (*see also* Olduvai Gorge); tools, 81–2, 172, 433

Old Stone Age (*see* Paleolithic period)

Olduvai Gorge (*see also* Oldowan complex): cultural succession at, 81–2; fossil finds, 50–2, 78, 80; habiline finds, 50, 78; *Homo erectus* at, 80; mandible find, *51;* photo, *82;* tool finds at, 52, 172

Old World monkeys (*Cercopithe-*

coidea), 28, 45

Oligocene epoch, 44–5

Oligopithecus, 44, *45*

Omaha kinship terms, 353

Olmec (Mesoamerica), 216–8; massive stone head, *217*

Omo (Ethiopia): industry, 172; tool finds at, 52

oral frustration, Alorese, 595

oral passage, diagram, *121*

orangutans, 30–2

oriental despotism: in China, 434–5; in communist states, 393; and industrialization, 435–6; technoeconomic aspects of, 437

origin myths (*see* creation myths)

orthognathism, 35–6

paganism, 514

Pajitanian culture (Java), 83

Pakistan, Green Revolution in, 450

Paleolithic period (*see also* Lower Paleolithic; Middle Paleolithic; Upper Paleolithic): Andean manifestations, 210; art and technology, 576; characteristics, 171–2; climate, 186; economic depletion, 186; extent, 171; industries, 185, 204; New World artifacts, 208, 210; population growth, 259; stages, 172; technological developments, 432; warfare, 261

Paleozoic era fossils, 43

parallel-cousin marriage, 328 (*see also* cross-cousin marriage; parallel-cousin terminology)

parallel-cousin terminology, *335,* 353 (*see also* cross-cousin terminology)

parallel cultural developments: characterized, 163, 212; in complex societies, 216; in Mesoamerica and the Middle East, 228

paramount chiefs, 378, 380 (*see also* chieftains)

Parapithecidae, 44, *45*

parentage (*see also* descent): biological *vs.* cultural, 331

parents, reciprocal exchange with children, 285

parliamentary democracy, 435

passage, rites of, 534, 537–8, 541

(*see also* communal rites; male initiation rites; rituals)

pastoralists: nomadic, 246–7; personality structure, 599

patriclans, 338, 369 (*see also* clans)

patrilineages, 335, 338 (*see also* lineages)

patrilineal descent (*see also* kin groups; patrilineal kin groups; patrilocal residence): diagram of, *335;* evolutionary position of, 328; prevalence of, 272, 343; reckoning, 334, 336, 338; of village horticulturalists, 343

patrilineal kin groups (*see also* patrilineal descent): technoeconomic aspects of, 343; wives in, 344

patrilocal residence (*see also* patrilineal descent; postmarital residence): characteristics of, 342–3; disruption of, 347; and male initiation rites, 597–8; in matrilineal societies, 349; warfare and, 348

patronymics, 336

Patterns of Culture (Benedict), 291, 292, 588

Paviotso (Nevada), revitalization movement, 557

Pearson, Karl, on intelligence, 500

peasant revolts (*see also* peasants): Anabaptists in, 565; factors producing, 562–4; messianic background, 564; and Protestantism, 565

peasants, 299–305; access to natural resources by, 357; adaptability of, 461–4; capitalist type, 302–3; cash obligations of, 452; characteristics of, 300; Chinese, present day, 305; communist type, 305; conservatism of, 461–3, 471, 476; debt peonage, 463; development aid and, 463; displacement by sheep enclosures, 394–5; economic development and, 461–3; expropriation of, 465–6; feudal type, 300–1; forced labor, 466; in the Green Revolution, 451–3; in Java, 445; landownership by, 303, 462; in Mexico, 468–471; Neolithic, 428; penny capitalism of, 303; personality structure,

in, 365–6; lowland Maya, 219; Nuer, 369–370; politico-military exploitation in, 459–60; power in, 299; punitive force and, 366; of the Soviet Union, 403–4; in state level societies, 299, 365–6; in the United States, 404–5

polyandry, 312, 319, 360 (*see also* Nayar; polygamy; polygyny; wife lending)

polygamy (*see also under* polyandry): household activities under, 313; occurrence of, 312; sexual arrangements in, 312–3

polygyny (*see also under* polyandry): in band level groups, 360; in extended families, 316; occurrence, 312; male initiation rite correlation of, 597; royal, Bunyoro, 382; Yanomamö, 265

Polynesia (*see also* Oceania): redistribution systems in, 376–7; stratification in, 376–7

Pongidae (*see* pongids)

pongids (*see also* chimpanzees; gibbons; gorilla; orangutans): ancestral indications of, 45; canine teeth of, 62–3; cultural equipment of, 40–1; dental formula of, 29; family, 32; and hominids compared, 32–7; sexual behavior among, 62–3; terrestrial quadrupedalism of, 31

population (*see also* population control; population growth; population pressure; races): in biological groups, 96–99; density of, 248–50, 264–5; and ecosystems, 233; *see* genetics; New World aboriginal, 209; and productivity, 430; and subsistence, 248–50; and warfare, 264–5

population control (*see also* abortion; infanticide; population; population growth): family planning as, 454–5; by hunter-gatherers, 201; in preindustrial societies, 201, 203, 258–9, 266–7; and sex ratios, 266–7; by sexual abstinence, 266–7; pig keeping and, 275; and warfare, 265, 279

population growth (*see also* population; population control; population pressure): and

battle casualties, 264–5; *see* carrying capacity; and crop dispersals, 213; and cultural innovation, 165; and economic resources, 272–3; in egalitarian systems, 368–9; explosive recent, 455–8; in India, 455; in Java, 457–8; and living standards, 454, 456; and medical advances, 456; in migratory societies, 238; in Mississippian phase, 223; Neolithic rate of, 203; in Nigeria, 455; on Peruvian coast, 224; prehistoric, 171; preindustrial, 257; stabilization of, 266–7; and technoeconomic developments, 259–60, 454–5; tendencies toward, 258; at Teotihuacán, 220; Upper Paleolithic, 201–2; and wage labor, 465; and warfare, 264–5; Yanomamö, 278

population pressure (*see also* carrying capacity; population growth): in hunter-gatherer groups, 203; in seed-gathering groups, 203; and warfare, 260, 276

Portuguese colonialism, 441–2, 466–8, 498

Portuguese day names, 136

Pospisil, Leopold: on Kapauku headmen, 368; on Kapauku "primitive capitalism," 305–6

possession, animistic, 515, 527

postindustrial development, 428 (*see also* industrialization; industrialized societies)

postmarital residence (*see also specific types indicated*): ambilocal, 340, 342; amitalocal, 342; avunculocal, 342–3, 346–8; bilocal, 339–42; Euro-American, 339; male centered, 343; *see* matrilocal groups; neolocal, 339, 340–42; nuclear, 312–3, 339; *see* patrilocal residence; transformations of, 349; types of, 342–6; *see* unilineal descent groups; uxorilocal, 342 (*see also* avunculocal); virilocal, 342, 343, 349 (*see also* patrilocal residence)

potlatch, 290–4, 588 (*see also* redistributive exchange)

poverty: anthropology of, 5; of blacks, 415, 475, 479, 480–2; causes of, 475–7; continuity of,

488; and crime, 394–5; as cultural adaptation, 461, 474–7, 483–5, 589; function of, 490; and gratification, 477–9; heritability and, 491; of Kapauku, 306; as labor reserve, 489; matrifocal family and, 485–7; and peasant conservatism, 476; personality effects of, 483–4; in preindustrial societies, 306; and race discrimination, 479; self-perpetuation of, 475; statehood and, 307; subcultural characteristics of, 476, 479; technoeconomic bases of, 481–3; as technological unemployment, 482–3; and thought control, 395; and unemployment, 482–3; of urban poor, 476; values and attitudes of, 483–5; *see* welfare; and work, 479, 488–9

power (*see under* basic resources; law and order; political organization; statehood): of business corporations, U.S., 406–7; economic exploitation and, 402; social classes and, 396–8, 402, 408; and wealth, 405–6

prayer, 521

preagricultural villages, 192–193, 197 (*see also* seed gathering)

prebends, 301–2, 462

prehensile limbs, primate, 24

prehensile tail, anthropoid, 29

prehistoric periods, 171–97 (*see specific periods*)

preindustrial societies (*see also under* band level organization; egalitarian groups; feudalism): age hierarchies in, 399; communism in, 288, 305, 359–60; economic organization in, 281–97; energy flow in, 233–4; energy levels in, 428; population control in, 201, 203, 258–9, 266–7; population growth in, 257, 259; poverty in, 306; productivity in, 253; protein intake in, 428; sex hierarchies in, 399; thought control in, 387–8; trade patterns in, 285–6; warfare in, 264

Premack, David, on communication with chimpanzees, 126

prestige, economics of, 292–3, 309 (*see also* redistributive exchange)

priesthood (*see also* religious organization; shamans): ecclesiastical, 523, 530, 541–543; male dominance in, 553–554; political role of, 387–8

Primate Research Institute, Kyoto, 59–60

primates, order of (*see also* anthropoids; baboons; hominids; hominoids; *Homo;* human beings; monkeys; protohumans): aggressive behavior in, 64–6; arboreal adaptation, 23–5; characteristics of, 23–6; emergence dated, 44; evolution of, 23–4; food sharing of, 63–4; offspring per birth, 25; social behavior, 26; tool use by, 55–8; visual acuity, 25

primitive capitalism, Kapauku, 305–7

primitive communism, 282, 305, 359–60

Primitive Culture (Tylor), 514

primitive societies (*see* preindustrial societies)

procreation, folk beliefs about, 332–3

productivity (*see also* energy; food production; technoeconomic factors): burcaucratic control of, 435–6; Bushman, 234–5, 239, 249; and capitalism, 308–9; class patterns of, 397; environment and, 231–2; feudal control of, 383–4; food-energy efficiency in, 234–7; the headman and, 374–5; in hoe cultivation, 236–7; of hunter-gatherers, 201, 234–5; of industrial farming, 250–2; Neolithic mode of, 201; of preindustrial Europe, 435–6; in slash and burn cultivation, 239–41; of slavery, 441; state surplus, 384; and technology, 229–30; of Tsembaga Maring, 239–44

prognathism, 35, 98

projectile points (*see* stone implements)

propaganda, 388–90 (*see* thought control)

property (*see also* landownership; wealth): male control of, 271–2; politics of, 299; uni-lineal descent group rights to, 341

prophecy: in cargo cults, 560–2; in revitalization movements, 556–61

Propliopithecus, 45, *45*

prosimians, 27

protein (*see* nutrition)

Protestant ethic, capitalism and, 438–9 (*see also* work ethic)

Protestanism: and economic development, 438; rise of, 565

protohumans (*see* australopithecines; hominids; *Homo; Homo erectus*): hunting activities of, 66–74; meat eating by, 67, 70–1; transitional chronology of, 75; tool use by, 58, 60–1, 69

Proto-Indo-European languages, 140

Proto-West Germanic language, 140, 144

Prototheria, 21

psychoanalysis, 590 (*see also* Freud; psychodynamics)

psychodynamics, of personality formation (*see also* basic personality structure; Freud; Freudian approach; personality; personality formation): concept of, 596; ecology-maintenance systems in, 596–8; in male initiation rites, 597–8; of Ocdipal patterns, 603–7; of warfare, 604–5; Whiting's application of, 597

public opinion: in conflict resolution, 361; in egalitarian contexts, 369; and shamanism, 364

Pueblo (New Mexico): Apollonian pattern, 588–9; prehistory of, 223; revitalization movement of, 556; personality shift, 601; uprising, 601

puberty rites, male, 597 (*see also* male initiation rites)

Pueblo Bonita (Arizona), 223

Punnett Square (formula), 13–4

Pygmalion (Shaw), 415

pygmies (Ituri Forest) 286

pyramids (*see* monumental construction)

quadrupedal posture: in hominoids, 28–9; terrestrial, in pongids, 31

races (*see also* racial classification; racial differences; racial traits; raciation; racism): archetypes, 98–9, 111; breeding populations as, 98; clinal variations in, 102–104; concept of, 96, 98, 111; determinism of, 494; ephemerality of, 110–1; ethnic differences and, 416; genetic differences and, 97–8; geographical, 99, 102, 107, 110; minorities as, 415–7; number of, 98; scientific ideas of, 104, 491–2; stereotypes of, 102, 104; validity of concept, 99

racial classification (*see also* races; racial traits): by blood type, 107–8; Brazilian, 104; of Carleton Coon, 110; distribution of, 101; exploitation by, 104; past approaches to, 110; problems in, 102; traits for (*see* racial traits); in the U.S., 104; variants of, 99–104

racial differences (*see also* races; racial traits): contemporary, 96; and cultural differences, 498; in enculturation for testing, 504–5; and ethnography, 497–8; geographical, 99, 102, 107, 110; in Hindu castes, 426; in historical-evolutionary perspective, 492; intelligence and, 500; and intelligence testing, 501–2, 505; and poverty, 479; social stratification by, 499

racial differentiation (*see* raciation)

racial trait(s), 98–9 (*see also* racial classification; racial differences); adaptive significance of, 112; of American Indians, 209; blood types as, 107–8; color blindness as, 107; clinal variations of, 102–4; East Asian, 209; of fossil hominids, 110; prognathism as, 98

raciation, 111 (*see also* races; racial differences; speciation): agriculture and, 114–5; biological significance of, 96; cultural selection and, 112; process of, 99; social significance of, 40, 97; and speciation, 110–1

racism: and cultural influences, 498; intelligence and, 500, 504, 513; new scientific approach to, 499–500; scientific basis of, 491–2; selective migration hypothesis, 502; technoeconomic aspects of, 492; testing intelligence and, 505–6

Rajput (India), extended family, 318

ramage, 337 (*see also* cognatic groups; lineages)

Ramapithecus, 46, *46,* 78

Rappaport, Roy: on ecology of warfare, 556; on Tsembaga efficiency, 239–40; on Tsembaga pig feasting, 274

reciprocal exchange, 282–3, 290 (*see also* gift giving; redistributive exchange); in bands, 360; economics of, 157, 282–4; freeloaders and, 284; generosity in, 290–1, 376; gift giving in, 284–5; in industrialized societies, 283–4; kula as, 287–8; marriage and, 329; in nuclear families, 284–5; *vs.* redistributive exchange, 290–2; sexual, in bands, 360; trade as, 285–6

redistributive exchange, 288–9 (*see also* reciprocal exchange); boasting in, 290–1; of Bunyoro, 380; capitalistic traits in, 305; by chieftains, 379–80; in egalitarian groups, 374–6; feasting as, 244, 289, 375–6; by headmen, 367–8; of Kapauku, 307; marriage and, 326; in Oceania, 377; and personality, 599; in Polynesia, 376–7; potlatch as, 290–4; as prestige mechanism, 292–3; *vs.* reciprocal exchange, 290–2; and stratification, 376–7; as tax source, 377, 380; by Tikopia, 379

reduction division, *11*

religion, 387–8, 514 (*see also* religious beliefs; religious organization; rituals); authority and, 550–1; Aztec, 388, 543–5; capitalism and, 438; definition of, 546; economic development and, 438; Eskimo, 524; functional aspects, 545–6; individualistic level, 522–6 (*see also under* religious organization); monumental construction and, 388; political aspects, 548–54; radical political force of, 565–6; revitalization and, 555–66; and science, 546–7; sexual politics and, 551–4; shamanistic, 527–8; and social structure, 522–3; sociological concept of,

519–20; Tylor's approach to, 514; women and, 551–4

religious beliefs (*see also* religion; rituals): animatism, 517; animism, 514–5, 517; definition of, 521; ecological implications of, 566–71; emotional aspects of, 518–9; in god(s), 514–5; individualistic, 525–6; Lowie's concept of, 519; magic and, 520–2; *mana,* 517–8; relativism of, 545–6; sacred *vs.* profane, 519

religious organization (*see also* religion): communal level, 523, 533–5; ecclesiastical level, 523, 530, 532, 541–3; individualistic level, 522–6; levels of, 522–3; and political organization, 548–54 (*see also* thought control); shamanistic level, 523, 527–8 (*see also* shamanism)

religious practices (*see* rituals)

rent, 299; of capitalistic peasants, 302; of communist peasants, 305; as coercion, 357–8; and landownership, 299: *see* taxes

replication: biological *vs.* cultural, 168; cultural process of, 164

reproduction, human (*see also* genetics; heredity; marriage; population; procreation; sex): biological, 7–10, 168; by cell division, 7–10; family and, 311, 314–5, 322–3; success in, 16

residence, postmarital (*see* postmarital residence)

revenge, dynamics of, 370–2

revitalization movements (*see also* messianic movements; peasant revolts): ancestor return in, 557, 560; black church as, 556; cargo cults as, 560–2; Christianity as, 556, 562–4; definition of, 554; among Delawares, 556; European, 562–6; Ghost Dance as, 557; in Judaism, 562–4; Kickapoo, 557; Messiah craze, 557; New World penetration and, 556–60; peyote ritual as, 559; political economy of, 554–6; Pueblo Indian, 556; revivalism as, 555; Shawnee, 557; Sioux, 557–8

revivalistic movements (*see* revitalization movements)

Rhesus monkey, *26*

rhinarium, 28

rickets, 113–4

rites of passage (*see under* rituals)

rituals (*see also* burials; male initiation rites; religion; shamanism): Arunta, 535–6; tec, 543–5, 548–9; circumcision, 539–40; communal, 533–41; death, *538;* ecclesiastical, 541–5; human sacrifice as, 388, 543–5, 548–9; in hunting economies, 186; as natural *vs.* supernatural practices, 518–9; Ndembu, 539–40; prayer as, 521; *see* redistributive exchange as; rites of passage, 534–41; Tapirapé, 528–30; totemic, 535–6; in Upper Paleolithic cave art, 183–4; Venus figurines and, 181–2; witchetty grub, 536

Robinson, John T.: on australopithecine diet, 47; on *Telanthropus,* 80

"robust" type, australopithecines, 46–50, *46, 49* 78

Robustus (*see* "robust" type)

Rockefeller Foundation, 450

roles, sex linkage of, 610

Roman empire: cultural development, 494–5; energy levels in, 27–8; rule over Judea, 562–4; socioeconomic development, 427–8

Rorschach tests, 595

Rossel I., money of, 297, 305

Rousseau, Jean Jacques, on primitive nobility, 355

ruling class: as caste, 413; characteristics of, 401; class mobility and, 414; control of production by, 373; feudal, 383–4; Inca, 384; protective institutions, 386; in religious organizations, 523; self-effacement of, 412; of Soviet Union, 403–5; state formation and, 393; in U.S., 403–5, 408, 413

Sacks, Karen, on women's status, 610

sacred, concept of, 519–20

sacred cows, India, 568–71

Sacsahuaman, *384,* 385

Safa, Helen Icken, on housing and cooperation, 475

Sahlins, Marshall D., on consumption of goods, 309; on stratification in Polynesia, 376–7

Saibai I. (Torres Str.), cargo cult, 560

sanctions: against freeloaders, 284; against incest, 326–8; and political power, 366; against unwed mothers, 321–2

Sandia projectile point, *210*

Sapir, Edward, on grammatical equivalence, 129–30

scapulimancy, 567

Scarr-Salapatek, S., on I.Q. methodology, 506

schizophrenia, shamans and, 528

science: in anthropology, 147; education for, 389; magic *vs.*, 522; religion and, 546–7

scientific racism, 491–2, 495

sedentary villages, preagricultural (*see also* settlement patterns): Mesoamerican and Middle Eastern compared, 216; Middle Eastern sites, 192–3; Nile Valley site, 197; nomad pastoralist domination of, 247; at Shanidar, 192; Southwestern U.S., 222; technoeconomic aspects of, 193–4; warfare among, 261, 263–4

seed-gathering subsistence: in Mesoamerica, 214; Natufian, 192; Nile Valley complex, 197; in present-day groups, 172; technoeconomic aspects of, 190–1; wild grain technology, 193–4

segments, lineal (*see* lineages)

Semai (Malaya): headmanship of, 366; reciprocal exchange of, 290

semantic productivity, 131

semantic universality, 116, 119–20; and consciousness, 143; ideological functions of, 157–8; infrahuman communication and, 127; and inter-speech translation, 133; scientific description complicated by, 159

sept, 337 (*see also* lineages)

serfs, 300–1, 383 (*see also* peasants)

settlement patterns (*see also*

cities; sedentary villages; territoriality; urban centers): Anasazi, 223; Bushman, 237; environmental factors in, 231; lowland Mayan, 218; Mesoamerican, 216–8; Mesolithic, 188; Natufian, 192; Neolithic, 172; Paleolithic, 171; permanent type, 191, 192–4; plow cultivation and, 198–9; *see* seed gathering villages; slash and burn cultivation and, 218; in southwestern U.S., 222; Tehuacán Valley developments, 215; at Teotihuacán, 220; at Tikal, 218; of walled towns, 198; and warfare, 261

sex (*see* female sexuality; male dominance; sex differences; sex ratios; sexual behavior; sexuality; women)

sex differences (*see also* sex ratios; sexual behavior): in athletic performance, 268–9; canine-tooth reduction and, 62; and descent reckoning, 271–2; among early hominids, 86–7; hierarchies of, 398–9; in *Homo erectus*, 87; and industrialization, 269, 612–3; in prestate societies, 399; in roles of hunting peoples, 86–7; in social class roles, 398–9; in sociocultural roles, 610; in warfare roles, 268–9

sex ratios: among hunter-gatherers, 262–3; in infanticide, 267; of junior age persons, 265–7; male dominance and, 272; population control and, 266–7; technoeconomic aspects of, 267–8; and warfare, 264, 268

sex relations (*see under* sexual behavior)

Sexton, Lorraine, on sexual behavior and population pressure, 608

sexual behavior (*see also* female sexuality; male dominance; sex differences; women): in band level groups, 360; communism in 360; cooperation among humans in, 63; and culture, 608–12; and group conflict, 360; in Hindu India, 609; and initiation rites, 597; of Mangaians, 698–9; marriage

and, 311–21; of Nayar, 318–9; *see* Oedipus complex; in personality formation, 596–8; premarital, 322; and temperament, 607–8

sexual communism, 360

sexuality (*see also* sex differences; sexual behavior): cultural limitations of, 266; hairless bodies and, 39; human, 37–9; infant, 593; intersex differences, 271; receptivity in, 37–9

sexual politics (*see also* male dominance; women): and religion, 551–5

shamanism (*see also* witchcraft): conflict resolution and, 363, 364; cults of, 527–8; definition of, 527; divination in, 363; ecclesiastical suppression of, 530, 532; Eskimo, 524; hallucinogen use in, 362–3, 527, 552–3; level of religious organization, 523, 530–2; possession in, 515, 527; public opinion and, 364; rites and practices of, 363, 518, 524, 527–8; social controls and, 363; souls in, 516; Tapirapé, 527–9; techniques of, 363–4, 527–8

Shanidar (Iraq): ritual burials in caves, 179–80; seed gathering technology, 192

share cropping, Ecuador, 462

Shawnee (Tennessee), revitalization, 557

sheep enclosures, farmers displaced by, 394–5

shell money, 295

Shudras (Hindu caste), 423

siamang, 29, 32

sibling marriages, 327, 376, 386 (*see also* incest)

sickle cell anemia, 109, 111

silent trade, 286

Simpson, George Gaylord, on survival, 460

Sinanthropus pekinensis, 79, 84

Sinhalese (Sri Lanka), trade of, 286

Sioux (So. Dakota): polygynous family of, *313;* revitalization, 558–9

sisal farming, 472–4

sister exchange, 326, 348

sister marriage (*see* sibling marriages)

Skhūl cave burials, 179

skin color (*see also* geographic races): as adaptations, 112–4; differences explained, 114–5; rickets and, 113–4; subsistence and, 114

slash and burn cultivation (*see also* agriculture; plant cultivation): environment and 241; food-energy system in, 239–42; labor efficiency of, 249; and Mayan decline, 242; in Mesoamerica, 217; patrilineality and, 343; Philippine fields, *249;* production intensification in, 248; productivity of, 239–41, 253; reforestation and, 241, 244; of Tsembaga Maring, 239–41, 273–4; and urbanization, 218; of Yanomamö, 276

slavery: aftereffects of, 504; and colonialism, 440–1; development in Africa, 497; economic disadvantages of, 441; and peasantry, 302; personality formation and, 599, 601; trauma of, 504

Smith, M. G., on premarital chastity, 322

social anthropology, 1, 145

social behavior, learned: aggression in hominids as, 64; and brain enlargement, 26–7; homicide as, 66; and mental capabilities, 27; in prehominids, 40; in the primate order, 26

social controls (*see also* conflict resolution; law and order; thought control): by education, 389–90; ideological, 386–95; by physical coercion, 392–5; shamanism and, 363; in the Soviet Union, 403–4; in stratified societies, 386

social evolution, 2 (*see also* cultural evolution)

social heredity, 58–60

social organization (*see* family; kin groups; marriage; political organization; religious organization; social structure)

social phenomena, and culture, 144–5

social practice, and language, 135

social status, and language, 131, 137

social stratification (*see* stratification, social)

social structure, 145, 156–7

society: concept of, 145; sacred force in, 519–20

sociocultural systems (*see also* social organization; society; *under* technoeconomic factors): characterization of, 152–6; cultural affects in, 150–2; describing and analyzing, 159; development of, 163; disruption of, 154–6; ecosystems and, 233; functional unity of, 153–4; and personality, 596; religion and, 546; and reproductive success, 153; technology in, 229; the universal pattern in, 156–8

socioeconomic development, 427–31 (*see also* colonialism; industrialization; industrialized societies; underdevelopment)

solidarity, rites of, 534–7 (*see also* kinship behavior; male initiation rites; redistributive exchange; rituals)

Solutrean industry, 182–3

song contest, Eskimo, 361–2

Songhay (Songai) (Mali), 383, 495–7

sorcery, 364 (*see also* shamanism; witchcraft)

sororate, 330

soul(s): concept of, 514–5; Jívaro, 515–7

sound change, phonetic laws of, 139–41

sound formation, 120–1

South Africa, Union of, gold mining in, 466–8

Southern California, fossil hominid find, 208

Southwestern U.S., early sedentary villages, 222

Soviet Union: Communist Party role in, 403; despotism in, 393; education in, 389; political organization of, 403; ruling class in, 394, 403–5; women's status in, 615

Spanish colonial penetration: of America, 212; of Japan, 442; of Mexico, 222; Pueblo resistance to, 601

speciation (*see also* raciation): biological uniqueness of, 168; criterion of, 97; and human variation, 110–1; process of, 96

species, biological, 96–7

speech, and social differences, 131–2, 137, 409, 415 (*see also* language; linguistic behavior; sound change; sound formation)

Spencer, Herbert, on basic personalities, 590

spider monkey, 53

Spirit Cave (Thailand), plant cultivation indicated, 206

spirit helper, Eskimo, 524

spirits (*see* animism; supernaturals)

Squid Cove, Newfoundland, poverty in, 482

Stack, Carol, on black poverty and welfare, 487

Stanford-Binet Test, 500, 511, 513

Starr Carr (England), Neolithic site at, 187

states (statehood) (*see also* political development; political organization): African indigenous, 495–7; Andean region, 223–6; Aztec, 221; class differences in, 414 (*see also* stratification); communistic, 305, 393, 403–4; conflict control in, 370; in developing nations, 428; economic aspects of, 297–8; expansion of, 380; formation of, 190, 219, 373–4, 379–80; in Hawaii, indigenous, 376; impacted habitat and, 379–80; Inca, 384; labor service under, 302; landownership and, 298–300; law and order in, 255–6; and marketing, 287; Marx on, 393; Mayan, 218–9; money and, 295–6; Neolithic emergence of, 199; New World development, 216; peasants under, 302; political evolution of, 373–4, 379–80; political power and, 365–6; poverty and, 307; prebendal grants under, 300–2; religious organization and, 523, 530, 541–3; 550–1; *see* stratification; subsistence productivity and, 280; taxation and, 299; technoeconomic aspects of, 199–200, 219; in underdeveloped societies, 427; and warfare, 261, 280

stature, as racial trait, 98–9

status, values and attitudes of, 461

stinkards class (Natchez), 414

stone idols (*see under* monumental construction)

stone implements (*see also* tool making; tools and tool-using): Acheulian, *81,* 82–3, 173, 176; Asian Lower Paleolithic, 177; Aurignacian, 181, *182;* axes, efficiency of, 240; bifaces, *81, 82, 83, 84;* blades, 172, 180, *180,* 181; choppers, 81–2, *81, 84,* 433; at Choukoutien, *84;* at Clacton, 83, 173; cores, 83, 172; flake points, 172; flakes, 83, 172–3, 182; Folsom, *210;* Gravettian, 181; at Grotte du Vallonet, 80; Lower Paleolithic, 172; Middle Paleolithic, 172; Mousterian, 178, *178, 179,* 181, 185; New World Paleolithic, 208–12, *210;* Oldowan, 81–2, *81,* 172, 433; Olduvai Gorge find, 52, 172; at Omo, 52, 172; pebble tradition, *55,* 172–3; Perigordian, 181, *182;* polyhedrals, 173; prehistoric periods and, 171; Solutrean, 182–3; *vs.* steel, efficiency compared, 240; Upper Paleolithic, *180,* 180–3; at Vértesszöllös, 172

stratification, social (*see also* castes; classes, social; states): in Africa, 380; age factor in, 314–5, 399; of blacks, U.S., 419–20; Christianity and, 426; class distinctions and, 400–1; conditions promoting, 379–80, 402; consciousness of, 402; development of, 373–4, 377–80; economic redistribution and, 288–9, 376–7; economic specialization and, 424, 426; education and, 389, 409–10, 500; ethnic differences in, 416–7, 420–1, 426; exploitation and, 402; *see* feudalism; food production and, 373–4, 377; genetic rationale of, 509; high gods and, 550–1; in Hindu India, 422–4; ideological support for, 388; and I.Q. scores, 508–10; *see* law and order; life-style and, 408–9; *see* minorities; mobility in, 414; in Oceania, 376–7; of peasants, 300–5; personality and, 599; political controls and, 365–6, 386; in Polynesia, 376–7; and poverty, 475–7; and race, 420–1, 497–

500; and redistribution, 376–7; and religious revitalization, 555; ritualized, in castes, 425; *see* ruling class; and speech, 131–2, 137, 409, 415; and statehood, 302, 373–4, 379–86, 396–7; in Tahiti, 376; in Tikopia, 378–9; in Trobriand Is., 378; in United States, 395, 400, 403–5, 413, 415–6, 425–6; warfare and, 280; of women, 399

streetcorner men, 480–2

subcastes *(jatis),* Hindu, 423, 425–6

subclans, 338, 378 (*see also* clans)

subcultures: classes as, 409; of poverty, 475

subincision, 540

sublineages (Kapauku), land-ownership of, 306

subordinate groups, exploitation of, 402–3

subsistence activities (*see* food production)

Sudanese kinship terminology, 350

Sumerians, cultural development, 494

Sun Dance (Plains Indians), 534

sun god, 388

sun king: Inca, 385; pharonic Egypt, 387–8

supernaturals: beliefs in (*see* religious beliefs); concepts of, 514, 518; manipulation of, 521; *vs.* natural forces, 518; politicoeconomic status of, 548–50

superordinate class, 402, 413 (*see also* ruling class)

superstition, 514

superstructure, sociocultural, 156

surplus productivity, 246, 299, 384

survivals, functional utility of, 153

survival, struggle for, 16

suspensory feeding, by hominoids, 31

Swanson, Guy, on morality and stratification, 551

Swartkrans (So. Africa), fossil finds at, 48, 80

sweating, human, adaptive role of, 39

swidden cultivation (*see* slash

and burn cultivation)

symbols: iconographic, 119; for kinship diagrams, 333; linguistic, 119

taboos: couvade, 607; Eskimo hunting, 524; Hindu caste, 423; marital, 327

Taborite movement, 565

Tahiti, stratification in, 376

tailored clothing, 182–3

Taiwan, extended family in, 317

Tally's Corner (Liebow), 480

Tamil (Malabar, India), procreation beliefs, 333

Tapirapé (Brazil): extinction of, 154; shamanism, 528–9

Tarascans (Mexico), peasant economy, 468–71

taravad (Nayar household), 345–6

Taung (So. Africa), skull find, 50

Tax, Sol, on "penny capitalism," 303

taxation: feudal, 384; food production as, 377; Inca, 384–5; peasants and, 300, 465–6; population stimulus, 457–8; and redistribution, 382; rents as, 299

taxons: biological criteria for, 85; defined, 19; in human phylogeny, 20

Tchambuli (New Guinea), sex and temperament among, 607

technoeconomic factors (*see also* ecological adaptation; economic organization; energy; environment; technoenvironmental analysis): in animal domestication, 196; in bride-price, 324, 326; in cattle raising, 198–9; in hunting-gathering society, 238–9; in irrigation farming, China, 245–6; in Mayan collapse, 220; in Mayan development, 218–9; in Mesoamerican developments, 215–7; in the Middle Eastern Neolithic, 216; in the Neolithic, 189–90; in Oriental despotism, 437; in Peruvian coastal developments, 224–5; in sex ratios, 267–8; in statehood, 199–200, 216, 218–22; in stratification, 373–4; in underdevelopment, 449–45

technoenvironmental analysis (*see also* ecological adaptation;

Tylor, Edward Burnett: on culture, 144; on religious beliefs, 514–5, 517
Tzintzuntzan (Mexico), economic development aid, 468–71

ultraviolet radiation, skin color adaptation to, 113
underdevelopment, in nations (*see also* colonialism; industrialization; industrialized societies): and colonialism past, 429, 439–40; and consumption, 427; definition of, 427–8; emergence from, 430–1; ethical aspects of, 439; genetic aspects, 491; infant mortality and, 429; political economy of, 230, 427–8, 449; politico-military threat in, 459–60
unemployment, conditions effecting, 482–3
unilineal descent groups (*see also* kin groups): characteristics of, 338, 341; *vs.* cognatic groups, 341–2; descent reckoning in, 333–5; in horticultural villages, 342; ideology of, 341; kinship terminology in, 352–3; *see* matrilineal descent; *see* patrilineal descent; postmarital residence in, 342–3; technoeconomic aspects of, 342; territoriality of, 341
United East India Company, 442
United States: Army intelligence tests, 501–4; black revitalization, 556; business corporations, 407; class differences in, 400, 413; corporate shareholders in, 406; a cultural theme, 589; economic development, 440; economic inequality, 395; elections in 404–5; individual wealth, 406; intelligence tests, 500–4; as meritocracy, 510; military and Pacific cargo cults, 561–2; minorities in, 415; physical repression, 395; races in, 104, 415–6; ruling class, 403–8; sex discrimination, 399; *see under* stratification; upward mobility, 500; wealth concentration, 405; women workers, 614
universal patterns, 156–8
Upper Paleolothic (*see also* stone implements; technology): blade

technique, 180–1, *181;* cave painting, 183–4, 187; New World migration, 209; population growth, 201–2; regional achievements, 492; termination of, 186–7
upward mobility, social, 426, 500
urban centers (*see also* settlement patterns): in China, 206; law and order in, 358; in Mesoamerica, 220; Middle East emergence, 119; Mississippian, 223; peasants displaced to, 465–6; poverty in, 476; proletariat in, 465; technoeconomic aspects of, 199–200; at Teotihuacán, 220; at Tikal, 218; in walled towns, 198; and warfare, 261
Utes (Utah), 134
uxorilocality, residence in, 342

Vailala Madness, cargo cult, 560
Vaishyas (Hindu caste), 423
Valentine, Charles, on black ghetto culture, 475
Valentine, Charles and Betty, on heredity and environment, 513
values and attitudes (*see also* ideology; thought control) class differences, 475; image of limited good, 468–71; of impoverished classes, 474; of peasant conservatism, 461–3, of peasants toward wage labor, 465–6; on poverty, 478–80; of subordinate groups, 461
Van Lawick-Goodall, Jane, on chimpanzee tool use, 56–7
variables, explanations for, 152
varnas (Hindu grades), 422–3
vaygu'a, kula trade ornaments, 287
Vedda (Sri Lanka), trade of, 286
Venus statues, 181–2, *183,* 580
verbal activities, 161 (*see also* emics, etics)
vertebral column, in hominids, 33–4
Vertebrata: characteristics of, 21; geology of, 43
Vértesszöllös (Hungary): fossil fragments at, 80; stone tool finds, 172–3
virilocality, 342–3; with matrilineal descent, 349
vision, acuity in primates, 25

vision quest, 525–7; failure of, 591
Vitamin D selectivity theory, 114
vocabulary, and culture, 130–1
vocal tract, 121, *121*

Wadel, Cato, on unemployment, 482–3
wage labor (*see also* forced labor; labor; wages): characteristics of, 308–9; colonialism and, 465; consumption by, 309; peasant farmer conversion to, 473; peasant reluctance toward, 466; plantation, 303; and poverty reserves, 488–9; and subsistence farming, 465
wages (*see also* wage labor), 464–6
Wagley, Charles: on Tapirapé extinction, 154; on Tapirapé shamanism, 529–30
Wallace, Alfred, on bioevolution, 17
Wallace, Anthony F. C., on Iroquois personality, 591; on religious organization, 522–3
walled towns, 198
warfare: absence of, 260; Andean, 225; casualties of, 262–3; causes of, 275; complementary opposition and, 369; and cultural innovation, 165; culture and personality models for, 605–6; definition of, 260; disputes over women in, 272; ecology and, 279; in egalitarian societies, 368; and food supply, 259; functional aspects, 143; of horticultural villages, 341; of hunter-gatherers, 260; male dominance and, 267–72; male initiation rites and, 605; male personality and, 598; matrilocal residence and, 348; Mesoamerican, 221; and natural selection 259; Neolithic, 198, 261; Nuer, 369; and Oedipal conflict, 605; Paleolithic, 261; of pastoral nomads, 247; of patrilocal groups, 348; personality transformation for, 601; *vs.* personal retribution, 261; population control and, 279; population growth and, 259, 264–5; and polygyny, 265; preindustrial, 260; prevention models, 605–6; psychological

explanation of, 275–6; and religion, 548–9; of sedentary groups, 261–4; sex ratio and 264, 268; sex roles and, 268–9; sister exchange and, 348; and states, 261, 374; subsistence resources and, 273–5; territory and, 261; of Tiwi bands, 261–2; of Tsembaga Maring, 273; woman shortage and, 272; 360; women's capabilities for, 269

Warner, Lloyd: on Murngin casualties, 262; on U.S. class criteria, 400

Washington, Booker T., on behavior for blacks, 419–20

WASPS, as U.S. caste, 425

Watusi (Rwanda, Africa), as genetic type, 99

wealth (*see also* money; redistributive exchange); bride-price and, 295–6, 324; of business, U.S., 408; class affiliation and, 412; in class mobility, 413; distribution of, U.S. 405–8; and exploitation, 459–60; *vs* income, 406; and intelligence, 510; prestige, 295–7, 324; of workers, U.S., 413

weaning, childhood, 593

Weber, Max, on Protestant ethic, 438

welfare: Aid to Families with Dependent Children, 486–90; and matrifocal families, 485–7; practices in, 479; values and attitudes toward, 482–3

West African states, 495–7

White, Benjamin, on child labor in Java, 457–8

Whiting, John, on male puberty rites, 597

Whorf, Benjamin, on thought elements in language, 133–4

wild grain techniques, 193–4

Wilson, Woodrow, on U.S. political control, 408

Wissler, Clark, universal pattern of, 156

witchcraft: crime and, 363; detection of, 364–5; freeloader and, 284; functional aspects, 153–4; sabbat flying and, 533; shamanism and, 363–4, 528–32; social disruption by, 365; suppression of, 532

witchetty-grub totem rites, 536

Wittfogel, Karl: on Chinese hydraulic civilization, 435; on oriental despotism, 392

wives (*see also* women): band sharing, 360; Eskimo stealing, 362; in patrilineal groups, 344

Wolpoff, Milford, on australopithecine diet, 47

women (*see also* female sexuality; motherhood; sexual behavior; wives): athletic abilities of, 46, 268–9; anatomy and roles of, 610; attitudes toward, 267, 269–71; *see* bride-price; in Catholicism, 554; class exploitation of, 399; conflict over, 348; economic role, 271, 282; in egalitarian groups, 345; in extended families, 324; Freud's view of, 606–7; hallucinogens denied, 551–3; hunting by, 87; in industrial society, 612–4; in matrifocal groups, 486; in matrilocal groups, 344; military potentials of, 269; in patrilineal groups, 344; and religious powers, 251–4; sexuality of, 609; shortage of, 272,

360; stratification of, 399; workers, U.S., 614

work (*see* work ethic): futility of, 480–2; in polygamous households, 313

work ethic: of peasants, 466; and poverty, 479, 489; Protestant concept, 438–9; rejection of, 481; in Tzintzuntzan, 571; and underdevelopment, 439; and welfare, 482–3, 489

writing: Chinese early, 205; Mesoamerican, 228

Xavier, Francis, 442, 445

yams, redistribution and feasting, Trobriand, 378

Yankee City, social stratification, 400

Yankee kinship terminology, 351

Yanomamö (Brazil-Venezuela): battle casualties, 263–5; creation myth, 552; hallucinogen use by, 552; population growth, 265; sexual behavior, 360; sex tyranny, 399; subsistence productivity, 276–8; women's role among, 282

Yaqui (Mexico), 453

Yerkish (chimpanzee language), 129

Yucatan (*see also* Maya), impacted habitat of, 380

Yukon, fossil bone tool find, 208

Zawi Chemi Shanidar (Iraq), *196*

zero principle, in Mesoamerica, 228

Zinjanthropus, fossil find, 52

Zuni (New Mexico) (*see also* Pueblo): magic of, 522

zygote, 11